The Manuscripts of Rye and Hereford Corporations

Great Britain. Royal Commission on Historical Manuscripts

Gr. Brit.—HISTORICAL MANUSCRIPTS COMMISSION.

THIRTEENTH REPORT, APPENDIX, PART IV.

THE MANUSCRIPTS

OF

RYE AND HEREFORD CORPORATIONS; CAPT. LODER-SYMONDS, MR. E. R. WODEHOUSE, M.P., AND OTHERS.

Presented to both Houses of Parliament by Command of Her Majesty.

LONDON:
PRINTED FOR HER MAJESTY'S STATIONERY OFFICE,
BY EYRE AND SPOTTISWOODE,
PRINTERS TO THE QUEEN'S MOST EXCELLENT MAJESTY.

And to be purchased, either directly or through any Bookseller, from
EYRE AND SPOTTISWOODE, EAST HARDING STREET, FLEET STREET, E.C., and
32, ABINGDON STREET, WESTMINSTER, S.W.; or
JOHN MENZIES & Co., 12, HANOVER STREET, EDINBURGH, and
90, WEST NILE STREET, GLASGOW; or
HODGES, FIGGIS, & Co., LIMITED, 104, GRAFTON STREET, DUBLIN.

1892.

[C.—6810.] *Price 2s. 4d.*

CONTENTS.

o 64161.

THE MANUSCRIPTS OF THE CORPORATION OF RYE.

1568, October 3.—Will of Thomas Fletcher of Rye, directing that his body be buried in the church of Rye. He appoints his wife Bridget, his executrix, and leaves legacies to the children of Robert Browne and Joan his wife, to Robert Carpenter and Joan his wife, to "Marye Wallis of Romnye, my nevey," to Ursula Marden and to Clement Marden's child. *Copy.*

1568[-9], March 19.—Order by the Mayor and Jurats of Rye that a door be made into the churchyard out of the south chancel, for making and laying the ordnance there.

1569, March 28.—Indenture between Ambrose, Earl of Warwick, master of the ordnance, and the Mayor and Jurats of Rye; witnessing the receipt by the latter of certain ordnance and stores. *Printed in Holloway's History of Rye, p.* 309.

1569, April 15.—John Pilfort, Frenchman, ordered to be punished by standing in the pillory and to have one of his ears nailed thereto, because he presumed to come into the town since his banishment.

1569, April 29.—Francis Macquery fined 3*li.* 6*s.* 8*d.* for that contrary to the order given to him he did lie at his mother-in-law's house. His mother Mercy Poskyns also fined for keeping Frenchmen, drinking and banquetting, in her house.

1569, August 6.—Nicholas Demoye of Morles [Morlaix] in Brittany, merchant, and Nowell de Bloath of Rascoo fined for bringing into the town certain "idoletorius idoleces."

James Fryes of Harlenden [Harlingen] in West Friesland, glasier, John Johnson *alias* Huson of Flushing, mariner, and —— Cowper warned to depart the town with their wives and children "for theyr mysbeleyves contrarie to christian relegian."

1570, May 8.—Obligation by Pierre Bois, Frenchman, merchant, dwelling at Rye, to pay a certain sum of money to Jehan le Balleur, burgess and merchant of Dieppe now at Rye. Witnesses, Nicolas Parque and Allain Henry, merchants of Rye.

1570, June 16.—[The Mayor and Jurats of Rye to the Lord Warden.]

"It may please your good Lordshippe that Comissary hath taken a shippe of Deape [Dieppe] with oyles, which he hath sold unto the merchante for 300*li.*, and this morninge hath brought in his shippe of warre in suche sort as that doinge will cause greate troble towards the Inglishmen that are at Deape and Rone [Rouen]; which doeinge of Comissary we utterly dislyke that he shuld so bowldly presume to come into our towne, after he had committed a piracy as beforesaid, without your honor's leave, to the greate slaunder of our towne, as those have brought us in by that fact. We have therefore accordinge to our dewties thought good to certefy your honor thereof, as we may from your good Lordship receave order what wee shall do heerein as may best answer your content and our safegard." *Draft.*

1571, September 6.—The Mayor and Jurats of Sandwich to the Mayor and Jurats of Rye.

Proposing to make Mr. Manwood a gift of seven pounds in consideration of his services to the Ports. *Copy.*

1571, September 9.—The Mayor and Jurats of Rye to the Mayor and Jurats of Sandwich.

Approving of the gift of seven pounds to Mr. Manwood. *Copy.*

1571, September 10. Sandwich.—The Mayors of Sandwich and Rye to [Lord Cobham, the Lord Warden].

By the advice of their counsel, Mr. Serjeant Manwood, they request his Lordship to appoint a meeting to settle all controversies between themselves and his Lordship.

1571, September 13.—Lord Cobham to the Mayor of Rye.

Whereas it is thought that the trouble of Captain Graymont, now detained prisoner in Rye for "whasshing" of money, is come rather of private malice than of just cause, it is thought meet by Lord Burghley that he be not proceeded against as yet, but be sent to his Lordship under safe guard. Has sent up the money washed. *Seal of arms.*

1571, September 15.—[The Mayor of Rye] to Sir William Cecil, Lord Burghley.

According unto my Lord Warden's letters "I have sent unto your honor Capytaine Graymont, late taken at Ry uppon suspicion of washinge and diminyshinge the Quenis Majesties quoyne, together with his examynacion herin closed." *Draft.*

> *Enclosure.*—The examination of Francis Boysant *alias* Captain Grammont, taken on August 2. He states that he arrived at Bristol from Rochelle about two months past. From thence he went to various places till he came to Rye. He brought with him three melting pots which he purchased in London and has melted money for the past half year. In an inventory of his goods there is mention of a purse containing "2 dubill duccattes, 1 Batenbrugh angell, 2 crownes French, 1 Philipps doller of silver, 1 Philipps 12*d.* pec., 2 seugt peics."

1571, September 20.—In "le Pallaice Haule of the Bushope of Canturbury" before Master Manwod, Serjeant-at-law, William Crispe "Lortenen" of Dover Castle and others.

Questions "to be demanded and determined uppon with reformacon of greiffs."

The first four questions relate to the jurisdiction and procedure of the Chancery Court at St. James' Dover and the Admiralty Court. The fifth, to the enjoyment of wrecks and "findals." The sixth and seventh, to the goods and "findals" of pirates and the imprisonment of pirates. And the eighth, to the sending of copies to the Ports of special letters of the Ports service remaining with the Lord Warden.

1571, September 22.—Recognizance by Nicholas Fowler, "appointed and licenced to keep a victualinge house within the towne of Ry for this yere to come, for the releiff of his poore neighbours and other good, honest, wayfaringe and travailinge persons." The conditions of the said recognizance are that "the said Nicholas Fowler do at all tymes hereafter, duringe this said yere to come, kepe and mayntaine his house with convenient victuals, and not mayntaining beds nor sufferinge in his house at any tyme or tymes any unlawfull games, nether sell ne utter any victuals within or without his house in tyme of Devine service to be celebrated in the Parishe Church of Rye uppon the Sondaies and holy daies, nor in the night after convenient tymes, that is to saie, after the houres of nyne of the clocke at afternone of every day in the sommer and eight of the clocke at afternone in the tyme of winter, except in case of necessitie, nether after the same houres receive any suspecte person or persones (other then suche as he will answer for) into his house, to enter drinke or lodge, without the speciall commandment of Mr. Maior or of some one of the jurats, nor at any tyme or tymes do suffer to remayne in his house any idle persons longe to sit singinge, drinkinge, or idly to the mayntenance of idlenes and of idle persons. And also the said Nicholas Fowler do, duringe all the said tyme of his victualinge, sell his drinke, as well out of doores to his neighbours as within, and the same by the measure of the hoopid poote commonly called a thirdindeale and half thirdendeale, and also uppon the ordinary and accustomed fishe daies do victuall his said house with fishe uppon the tables accordinge unto the lawes and statutes of this realme, not kepinge any common or pety tapesters, and payinge such duties as he is appointed for his victualinge, and kepinge all other honest lawfull and decent orders as perteyneth to an honest victualer within the said towne of Ry." *Draft.*

1571, September 28, Dover Castle.—Lord Cobham, "Constable of the Castle of Dover, Lord Warden of the Five Ports" etc., to the Mayor and Jurats of Sandwich and Dover, the Bailiffs and Jurats of Hythe, the Mayor and Jurats of Romney, and of the ancient towns of Rye and Winchelsea, and the Bailiff and Jurats of Hastings.

"I charge and commande you and every of you that within the precinct of your severall liberties, every of you immediately by vertue heref, doe geve ordre that no manner of victuell from hensforth shall passe to be carried to the sea for the victualinge or relife of the flete nowe serving the Prince of Orenge." *Copy.*

[1571, September.]—Certificate by the Mayor and Jurats of Rye that they have chosen Henry Mynge and Robert Carpenter, Jurats, to appear and be at the City of Canterbury on Thursday, September 20, at the Bishop's Palace Hall there, before Serjeant Manwod and others appointed by the Lord Warden, to hear what is to be alleged for and concerning such controversies as at this present are between the said Lord Warden and the Five Ports and their members.

1571, October 4. The Court.—Lord Cobham to Mr. William Crispe, Lieutenant of Dover Castle.

"Where divers complaintes are daily brought unto the Quenis Majestie of greate and heynous spoilles committed upon the seis by certaine captains, who, namying themselves to be in the Prince of Orenge's service, suffer no man to passe by them untakin or unspoiled, and namely have of late (as it is informid) in very violent sorte taken divers shippes laden with riche marchandizes belonging as well to the Company of the Marchantes of the Stillyard as to sondry other honest marchantes of Italy and other places, whiche prises they have brought uppon this Hir Majesties coaste and thare utterid the wares and marchandizes by them spoiled, being also relevid frome thence with victuals, munition and other provisions to the great slaunder of the realme and impechment of the haunt and traffique of marchandize. Leike as the

Quenis Majestie cannot but fynd this disorder very strange, and must nedes for justice sake se the same reformid with convenient spede, so hath hir Highnes willid me to require you, in hir Majesties name, to cause dilligent and substanciall order to be forthwith taken thorough out all the portes and crekes within my rule, not only that the said Captaines or others, beinge men of warr, that shall haunt that coast uppon any manner of pretence, be not in anywise sufferid to resort into any of the same portes, or to be relevid with victuals, or any other necessaries, or to utter or sell any of the goods by them taken unto any of hir Majesties subjectes, but also to give exprese commandment unto the officers of the Portes that they faile not to cause the said men of warr, capitains and others, against whom any complainte shalbe made, to be apprehended with their shipes and company, and the goodes that they shall have taken in whos handes soever the same shalbe founde, to be steyid and commytted by inventory unto sure custody to be answered unto suche as by order of justice shalbe founde to have right therunto. Which order hir Majestie muche marvaileth hath not ben heretofore better observid consideringe howe often warninge hath ben at severall tymes gevin therof, as well by hir Highnes proclamations heretofore sett fortho in that behalf, as by my letters wrytten by hir Majesties commandement for that purpose. Whereunto hir Majestie requireth you and them hensforth to have speciall regarde." *Copy.*

1571, October 28. Greenwich.—The Lords of the Council to the Mayor, Customer, Comptroller and Searcher of the town of Rye.

"Forasmuch as it is perceavid that uppon a gracious and merciful disposition in the Quenes most excellent Majestie in granting favor to suche strangers as of late time have been compellid for the avoyding of the calamities and trobles that were in sondrey countryes beyonde the seas, besides a great multitude of good, honeste and devoute poore and afflicted people, there are allso another nombre of evill disposed people under color of religion and pietie lately entred at sondry portes and crekes into the realme, whereby the naturall good subjectes are like not only to be corrupted with the evil conditions of them which are nawght, but allso by the excesse nombre of bothe sortes shall sustaine divers wayes suche lackes as is not mete to be born withall, besydes other inconveniences justly to be feared by practises of the lewder sorte. For remeady herof her Majestie hath willid us presently and without delay to take order for redresse herof and therewith allso to cause such moderation to be used as in no city or towne there should be any greater nombre of strangers, thowghe they be of honest conversation, suffered to resorte and abyde otherwise then may stand charitably with the weale, or at least without damage of the naturall subjectes and inhabitants of the same places. Whereuppon as we have directid order to other counties, cities, and townes so do we at this present to you, willing and commanding you forthwith to take order, that beginning the 10th day of the next moneth, at which time a like inquisition shall be begoun through other the maritime counties of the realm, you do by all good meanes that in you do lye, cause a good and certen serche to be made howe manie straingers of every nation are within that towne and, distinctly aparte, howe manie are come into that towne since the 25th of Marche laste, and by what quallitie and meanes they do lyve and sustayne themselves, and howe they doe inhabite, and in what sorte they doe resorte orderly to any churches and places of prayer to heare and use devyn services and sacramentes, as by the ecclesiasticall lawes of this realm they ought to do, or otherwise wheare any straingers are tolleratid withall by the Busshop of the diocese to use devyne services in theire owne mother tunges, and hereof to make to us certificat. And further you shall circumspectly and charitably consider amongste yourselves being publique officers there, usinge conference therin with the Busshop of the diocese, if he be nere unto you, or with the ordinary parson or curat of the place, whether the whole numbre of straingers now residing in that towne, being of honest conversation, may, without damage to the naturall good subjectes of the same, continew in as greate a nombre as they now are. And if the nombre shall seme to you to greate, to consider howe many may be suffred to remayne and in what sorte and to what other places convenient for their relief the excessé may be sent to have habitation, so as order may be given for that purpose; wherein we do not meane that any regard shall be had but only to suche straingers as are knowen to be honest in conversation and well disposed to the obedience of the Quenes Majestie and the realm, for it is ment and so wee will you that all other straingers of contrary sorte that shall not shew a good and open testymony to be obedient, as above is said, shall be charged as unprofitable persons to departe by a reasonable time. And therin you shall use all carefulnes and circumspection to cause them indeede to departe the realm. Besydes this you shall cause a due serche to be made what armour or offensive weapons anie strangers have in theire houses, and, if causse so shall seme requisite, to comit the same into the custody of some mete parsons of that towne that maye be answearable for the same to the owners. And of all thes the premisses we chardge yow with all speade to make to us answeare by wrighting with your opinions in anie thing concerning the same. When you have considered of the persones whome you thinke meete to be sent away out of the realme, we wolde that you shoulde advertise us of the nombre, quallities and conditions of their trade, and maner of lyving of the same persones so mete to be sent oute of the realme, before they be sent away." *Signed and Seal of arms, broken.*

1571, October 28.—A certificate by the Mayor and Jurats of Rye that about 10 years past "one mother Margery," who then dwelt in the Almshouse of Rye, was for certain notorious offences "such as any Christian harte wold abhore to here spoken of much less to be used," driven out of the said town. She being suspected of witchcraft, the then Mayor caused the said almshouse to be searched, and there was found amongst other things "a good quantitie of rawe beff" to the intent that as that beef decayed so the bodies of divers persons against whom she bore malice should also decay. Which things were proved, for one among her victims "being by her wytchcraft most cruelly tormented in his body at last hanged himself." Since her banishment the town had not been troubled with the like.

1571, November 3. Canterbury.—Richard [Rogers, Suffragan of] Dover, Thomas Godwyn [Dean of Canterbury] and Thomas Lawse [Prebendary of Canterbury] to the Mayor of Rye or his Deputy.

"Where it hathe byn complayned unto us on the parte of Joane Wilkinson, sometyme dwelling in your towne of Rye, that one Peter Greeneway of Hythe in the diocese of Canterbury hath not only contracted hymseálf in matrimony with the same Joane but also verie ungodlie hath mysused hir bodie and therby gotten hir with child. Upon which complaynt the said Peter, being convented before us, and the matter objected unto him, denyed the same. Wheruppon the said

Joane being present alleaged that there were divers credible witnesses resiant within the towne of Rye or nere theraboutes that can depose of the same contract. Wherfor in consideration of justice and pitie herin wee desire you, that, upon notice gyven by the said Joane, you wold call before you, with as convenient sped as you may, such persones as she pretendeth to be hir wytnesses in this behalf, and them examyne concerning the said pretended contract." *Signed.*

1571, November 13.—The Mayor and Jurats of Rye, the Customer, Comptroller and Searcher thereof to [the Lords of the Council].

"According to your lettres datid the 28th day of October 1571 we have with our minister Mr. Philpot (for that the Lord Bushope was not nere unto us) made serch and inquirye thorough our Towne of such strangers as are resiant within the same, according to the tenor of the same letters. The true certificate whereof we send your honors herein closid. And as yet [we] se no cause but the same persons may have continuance (if it so stand with your honors' pleasures). As towchinge their armore it is but small and shall from tyme to tyme be looked unto and considerid of, as apperteyneth." *Draft.*

Enclosure.—1571, November 10.—The names of the members of the French Church in Rye.

Those who have dwelt long before March last in Rye and "are of very honest behaviour."

CHRISTOPHER FALLOYSE, his wife and servant, with two or three children; Ambrose Demoye and his wife; Cornelize Soyer, his wife and servant; John Mercer, a widower, and his servant; all Walloons and merchants; Bonaventure Dusseville and his wife, a bookbinder.

Frenchmen "of honest conversation inhabiting before March last."

GUILLAMME BOUCHERET, merchant, his wife and servant; Alain Henri, merchant; Claude de Hue and his wife; Piere Sommellier, clockmaker, and his wife; Jan de Torchy, merchant; Nicholas le Tellier, minister, his wife and servant; Jan le Febure and his wife; Jan de le Croix, merchant, and his wife.

Those who remain in Rye and have lived there before March last, "but of no churche that is knowen all of good and honest conversation so far as is yet understandid."

JOHN FROTTIER, locksmith, and his wife; John Swayne, cooper,* and his wife; Peter Blocket, Frenchman, and his wife; Frauncis Cauchie, his wife and mother; Jaques Oucktell and his wife; John Matue, a Flemynge, his wife and certaine children; Robert Castell, his wife and four children.

[With the foregoing are several rough slips of paper containing information, in some cases apparently returned by the strangers themselves, from which the foregoing seems to have been compiled. A few examples follow showing the peculiarity of spelling, &c.]

JOHN FROTTIR, a dosen of onfonst gons and 2 fornise and a pistol, a woerd dagger and a holbard.

Pitter Somli his wief an 2 childeren and hi haet ben in abbeting hir 2 jaer hi haet 2 fornis gons and 2 onfornist and a sowerd.

---

* Described on another slip of paper as "Docheman which hathe byn hare three years, and hys wyf came over at Bartholemew last past."

Bonnawentur Aswil, a sowerd, his wif and 2 childeren.
Willem Bocceret hat a wif 3 childere and hat inabbitted hir 3 jaer.
Pitter Blocket, his wif, a son inhabbeting 2 jaer.
Alen Harri, his wyf, a doghter, hat inabbitte hir 6 jaer; a gon morman, a sowerd an degger.
Glowe Defew and Jane hys wyf, Pettar hys son, Rechell, Josewa.
Franses Mesar, Cornelles Sawyer and Marre hys wyfe, and Jhon Mersar a boye, Fleppar, a mayd.
Robart Castell and his wyffe and 4 chelderen.
Franses Cossewe and Merse hys wyffe and Maryane Cosseu hys mother.
Jakes Autell and Mary hys wyf.
Jhon Mattes and Margat hys wyf, 4 chelderen.

1571, December 3.—Certificate by the Mayor and Jurats of Rye, that whereas it seems by relation of Ambrose Demoye of Rye, merchant, that Hector Joly, Pierre Brisse and Jehan Prevost, merchants of Rouen, lately had some wines taken by freebooters, and that Francis Delobell of Rouen, merchant factor, authorised by the aforesaid merchants of Rouen, had written his letters to the said Ambrose Demoy authorising him to deal with the freebooters for the wine; the said Ambrose has brought before the said Mayor and Jurats honest and discreet merchants, that is to say, Gillam Ackman, Lewis Sohire, Johan Dewilliam, and Hance Hanson all merchants commorant in Rye, who have sworn that the said letters sent to the said Ambrose are the true handwriting of Francis Delobell.

1571, December 22. London.—Roger Manwod to the Mayor and Jurats of Rye.

"Forasmuche as Robert Goodwyn, an Englishman borne, and naturallyzed a denizen in France ys stayd with yow for some evydent injury by hym don agynst Mr. James Morlye of Ledes, in goodes laden by John Boothe, servant to the said Mr. Morley, in the porthes beyond the sea to the value of a thousand fyve hundryth poundes. And bycause thyre ys a maryne cause growing in foreyn porthes beyond the sea by reason wherof yow cannot do justyce to the porthes in your common court, but of necessyty justyce ys to be done in the Court of Admyralty. Therefor for due admynistering of justyce you must without delaye uppon attachment of the said Goodwyn by an offycer of the Castel of Dovor, delyver hym to be conveyed thyther ther to remayn tyll the cause shall be so answeryd and determined of thereby. For your instruction, that this by law and justyce ought to be don and no prejudyce to your fraunchyze or liberty."

1571[-2], January 24. Westminster.—The Lords of the Council to all Mayors, Jurates and others to whom it appertain.

"Wheras in the absence of the Lord Warden of the Cinque Portes commission is given to Sir Henry Crispe, Sir Thomas Scott, knightes, William Crispe, Lieutenant of the Castle of Dover and to Edward Bois, esquire, or to any two of them for the repressinge and ponisshinge of pyrates, rovers and such as dysorderedlie go to the seas, their aiders, receptors and mainteyners; and also for the better maintenaunce of justice and the ponishment of wrong-doers, as the cases shall require, uppon the coast, from tyme to tyme, as in their commission and instructions to the same more lardglie apereth. For so much as occasion shall oughten tymes require your aide and assistances for the better apprehension of offenders and otherwise to the execution of justice with more expedition; we have thought mete to require you that when motion shall be made unto you in such cases by them, that you further them and their directions in that parte to the best of your powers. Wherin as our meaninge is not to infrindge any liberties or privileges, so we doubt not but that you and all good subjectes do thinke yt convenient that every man should geve the best helpe he maie to the furtheraunce of justice, which beinge so much required at your handes, we doubte not of your conformitie therin accordinglie." *Copy.*

1571[-2], January 25.—The Mayor and Jurats of Rye to [the Mayor and Jurats of Romney ?].

Enclosing letters from Serjeant Manwood which had been received from Hastings without any advice either from there or Winchelsea "which we suppose was for that they would first understand the myndes of the rest of the Portes or els for that they so playnely understod not the lettres, being Mr. Manhode's oune hand,* with which all are not acquaynted." *Draft.*

1571[-2], February 12.—William Cryspe to the Bailiffs, Jurates and all officers of the Five Ports.

"Wheras for the spedie reformation of theis great disorders and unchristian depredations daylie frequented uppon this her Majestys coastes, there hathe bene of late a commission grauntid from her Highnes unto Benjamin Gonson and William Holstocke, Esquires, with certaine instructions signed and delivered unto them by the Lordes of her honorable Councell, the copies wherof I send unto you by this bearer, hereunto annexed, for the better testimonie of the same; and also the copies of the Lords of her Counsells letters addressed unto Sir Henry Crispe and others for the further procedinge in the same, togethers with certaine instructions by them geven unto you to be followed and observed, with letters also addressed unto you frome theire honors for theire assistaunce in the same, thes are therefore in her Majesty's name requiringe you and by the authoritie of your Lord Warden's office commandingo you and every of you, to whome on this case it shall apperteyne, (perusing the said severall commissions and takinge notice of the same) to take copies of the said severall instructions and letters addressed unto you, and to proced therin and in every pointe therof accordinge to the true meaninge of the same." *Copy.*

Enclosure I.—1571, October 21.—The Lords of the Council to [Sir Henry Crispe, Mr. William Crispe, Sir Thomas Scotte and Edward Boyes].

"Wheras the Quenes Majesty, upon sundry grevous complaintes exhibited by divarse marchantes, as well strangers traffiqueinge into this Realme as by her owne naturall subjectes, of the great and continuall piracies and spoiles committed uppon their shippes and merchandizes by pirattes and rovers on the seas, caused first straight order and commandment to be given and published as well by her Highnes severall proclamations as by letters addressed frome us to all her Majesty's officers and ministers to whome it mought in anywise belong, not only to forbearo to ayde, assiste or releave any of the sayd pyratts or rovers with any manner of victualls, munition or other necessaries, but also to geve ordre and expresse charge that neyther any the sayd

* Sergeant Manwood wrote a most obscure hand.

pyrattes, rovers, or men of warre, or any of their companye shold be admitted to come into any of her Majesty's portes, nor yet any of her Majesty's subjects permitted to bargaine or batter with them or buy anie of their goodes or wares that shold be by any of them taken or spoiled. And sithens that tyme, nowe of late uppon further complainte made, her Majestie fyndinge that notwithstandinge the former orders and proclamations, the said pyrattes and rovers wher dailie received into sondry portes of this realm, and speciallye within some of the Fyve Portes within the Countie of Kent, and releaved with all necessaries, ye and lodged openlie in the houses of some officers that ought to have bene rather the punishers of them, moost graciously regardinge the due execution of justice for spedie and exact reformation to be had in the premisses, did addresse speciall commission unto Benjamyne Gunstone, esquire, Treasurer of the Admiraltie and to William Holdstocke, esquire, Comptroller of her Majesty's Navi, to repaire unto the sea coastes of the realme in that county of Kent, and there, accordinge to certaine instructions deliverid unto them for that purpose, to apprehende and committe to safe custodie as well the persons of as many the said pyrattes and rovers as mought anywise be founde in any port of this realme as their shippes with their goodes wares and merchaundizes that should be found in any of them. And in leike manner to commit to safe warde all such of her Majesty's subjectes of what degree or condition soever they were, either officers or others, that shold be founde either to have bought or trafiqued with any of the sayd pyrates or anywaies to have releaved or assisted them contrary to her Majesty's former proclamation and orders in that behalf, as by the said commission and instructions dated the third of October last (the true coppie wherof we understand some of you have had delivered unto you) more plainely maye appere. For so much as uppon the reporte of the said commissioners declaringe their proceedinges in the premisses we find great towardnes of reformation of the enormities aforesaid, if the tenor and purpose of the said commission and instructions may be continued and dailie put in execution, we have thought mete, seeinge the Lord Cobham beinge the Lorde Warden of the Five Portes is nowe here so stayed by her Majesty's commandment, as he is not presentlie to be imploied in this service, to require you Sir Henry Crips as your age and helth may suffer and you Mr. William Crips that are Lieutenant under my Lord Cobham at Dover, and you Sir Thomas Scotte and you Edward Boyes as persons of whome we have very good opinion, usinge herein, as cause shall seme requisite, the service of the Mayors of Dover and Sandwich that you fouer three or two of you takinge notice of the said commission and instructions apointed to Mr. Gunstone and Mr. Holdstocke do use your uttermost indevors in all places within the Fyve Portes to put all the necessary pointes of the same spedilie in due execution frome tyme to tyme as occasion serveth and shall inquire, in as ample manner as they themselves mought have done by vertue of the same, and so we do in her Majesty's name fully aucthorize you by theis our letters. And further that you take order that all shippes and goodes belonginge to anye the said pirattes or rovers that shall come into any the Quenes Majesty's havens may be stayed and inventories therof to be made and the merchandizes to remayne in safe kepinge by your apointment in the handes of suche persons as may be answerable for the same. And if any claime shalbe made to any parte therof within reasonable tyme by the subjectes of the Frenche Kinge, the Esterlinges, the Grave of Embden or eny others with whome her Majesty hath amitie and libertie of entercorse, and do spedelye without delaye prove their right therunto lawfull by the due course of the lawes in such cases used, that you do then take order that they and every such maye have restitution accordinglye, and that which shall not be in reasonable tyme challenged as above is said, ye may leve to them that brought the same into the havens with order that they departe awaye with the same assone as they maye. And whereas the said Gunstone and Holdstocke, by vertue of their commission, have committed to prison in Dover fyftie fyve persons, and in Sandwich fowerskore the same remayninge at great charges, we have thought convenient that by your discretions a choise shold be made of tenne out of them of Dover and 15 of them at Sandwich of the best that you shall thinke mete to be kept, and the rest by your good skille to be sent out of the realme as they may accompt themselves discharged by favor, and not suffered to retorne. And even as in this service ther is a speciall choise made of you for the greate regarde that her Highness hath to the execution of justice and to the repressinge of theis evills that have so long continued to her Majesty's great discontentation, so is there no one point that you ought to be more carefull of nor to thinke yourselfes more charged with, than that you diligently foresee by provident order that no persons may victuall any of the frebutters nor buy anythinge of them, but the offenders in such cases without respect of persons may be apprehended and imprisoned without baile or mayne prise till you shall have precise commandment frome us to the contrary. And whereas we send you herewith coppy of an inventory taken by the said Commissioners of suche goodes as uppon serche made was founde at Dover, supposed to be had frome the freebutters, amongest which there was in Courtnei's shipe of Dover and now laden into a hoye called the *Whit Cocke* of Dover 22 lastes of tarr, three dryefittes of tallowe, thre packes with flax and one hundred of lose flax in bondelles, reported to be kept to the use of Thomas Cobham and Francis Barties, for as much as both they, for offence against her Majesty, are at this present imprisoned, it is meit that of those parcelles specially you do make staye of, to her Majesty's use. And we shall very well like also that you make perticuler inquiry of all the doinges of Thomas Cobham in these his dealinges with the freebutters or eny others of their conditions, specially touchinge the raunsominge of a Flemyng that to escape the frebutters did swime frome a shipe in Dover Rode to the towne, and what you shall finde in that behalf donne by him to advertice us with as good spede as you maye. And without respect of faviour towardes him of whome we heare so many complaintes for his misbehavior as we cannot passe the same over without this manner of inquisition. And lastly beinge willing with this our desier of redress to understand in whose part slackness hath bene used in this case, contrary to her Majesty's good intention, we do require you to advertise us what hath bene donne in the Commission that was latelie sent downe this sommer under her Majesty's great seale for the enquirye of theis causes, and to enforme us to whos handes it came and wher it presently remayneth." *Copy.*

Enclosure II.—1571[-2], February 12.—" Instructions geven to all Maiors, Balives, and Jurates of the Five Portes and their members by Sir Henrie Crispe and Sir Thomas Scott, knyghtes, William Crispe and Edward Boyce, Esquiers, as followeth."

" First, that you the said Maiors, Balives, and Jurates shall, upon the sight herof, presentlie see delivered out of this realme all such prisoners of the freebutters as wer committed unto your safe custodies (if any such there be) by verteu of the former Commission directed unto Mr. Gonson and Mr. Holstocke, not to retorne.

Item, that you shall foresee, as much as in you lyeth, that no person or persons of your townes or liberties do buy, sell or batter with any of the said frebutters, pyrates, rovers or men of warre, nor shall in anywise suffer them to have any kinde of victuall frome your said towne or liberties.

Item, if it shall happen by fowle wether or otherwise that any of the shippes or botes of the said frebutters, rovers or men of warre do come within your havens or harboroughes, that then you shall staye the said shippes and botes with the goodes they shall have aborde and their men untill such tyme as you shall make us, the said Sir Henry Crispe, Sir Thomas Scotte, William Crispe and Edward Boyce or two of us acquainted therewith.

Item, if it shall happen anie within your said townes and liberties do buye, sell, batter or victuall anie of the said frebutters or men of warre, that then you shall committ them so offending to prison, there to remaine without baile or maine prise untill you have certified us the said Commissioners or two of us.

Item, that no man within the said townes or liberties shall go aborde the said freebutters, rovers or men of warre without a speciall licence or ticket from you the said Maior, Balives or Jurates or two of you.

Item, that wheras the former Commission directed to Mr. Gonson and Mr. Holstocke and the instructions for the same hath not hetherto bene executed within your liberties, you, the said Maiors, Bailives and Jurates takinge copies of that instructions, shall make enquire therof accordinge to the tenor of the same.

Item, of your procedinges in these instructions as also in the instructions geven unto Mr. Gonson and Mr. Holstocke (wherin we are aucthorized by vertue of the Counsels letters to us directid), you shall certifie us, the said Commissioners, or two of us, frome tyme to tyme as ofte as occasion shall serve therunto.

Item, what you or any of you of yourselves know or by the reporte of others justly to be proved to be donne (contrary to theis our orders and instructions geven unto you) within your townes or liberties sence the first daie of the date of our Commission directed unto us, you shall indelayedlye certifie us of the same." *Copy.*

1571[-2], February 16.—The Mayor and Jurats of Rye to William Cryspe, Lieutenant of Dover Castle.

"Theis are to signifie unto you that the 15th of this instant moneth of Februarye, we received from you under the seale of office from Dover Castle the coppies of the commission with the instructions to the same [annexed] graunted from the Quenis Majestie to Mr. Gonson and Mr. Holstocke, esquires, and also the coppies of the Lords of the Councel's letters addressed unto Sir Henry Crispe and others with certaine instructions of new unto us made, and the Councel's letters concerning the same; all towchinge to the reformation of the abuses donne upon the seies by pyrates, rovers and suche as dysorderedly go to the seis, and also to make staie of suche frebutters, rovers and men of warre with their shipes and boates as shall happen to come within our liberties, as the same commission, letters and instructions more plainely do declare. By verteu wherof, sithens the receipt of the premisses, that is to saie this present daye and date hereof, we have within our liberties at Ry made staye of one Hendrike Thomas, his levetenant, his boate and company, being to the nomber of six persons in the whole, and also have stayed one Capitaine Davy and his company which are aland, being foure persons, whos boate with the rest rydeth at anker in the Puddle within the liberties of Winchelsey and have thought good to advertise your worshipes of the same, sending you hereinclosed the aucthoritie that the said Hendrike Thomas goeth to the sey withall, prayinge to be certified backe againe what we shall farther do herein. And that we may understand who shall be said disorderedly to goo to the seies and who not, and whom we may lett passe and who nott. As for goods and marchandize they have none nether have made sale of any within our liberties, to our knowledges." *Draft.*

1571[-2], February 17. London.—David Lewes and others to the Mayor of Rye.

By virtue of Her Majesty's commission to us directed, we will and require you to certify us in writing, within ten days, what goods, wares, merchandises, ready money, ships or other vessels belonging to any subjects of the King of Spain have been arrested or stayed in your port since the third day of January, 4 Elizabeth, how the same have been disposed, and also to let us know of such as you know or vehemently suspect to have concealed such goods. *Signed.*

1571[-2], February 19. Dover Castle.—William Cryspe to [the Mayor and Jurats of Rye].

"I have received your letter perceiving therbie that you have made stay of two flie botes the one apperteininge to one Henrike Thomas, the other to Capteine Davie, whom (for that they brought in no prizes with them nor yet other goodes, and beinge forced to com in for safe garde of lyfe, not havinge comitted anie facte wherwith thei are to be charged) you may suffer to departe without any further staye for they themselves are not to be deteined, but suche prises or goodes which thay shall bringe into your harboroughes untyll profe shalbe made to whome it shall apperteine, and yf it do not apperteine unto anie with whome the Quenes Majestie hath amitie and free libertie of entercorse, then it is to be delivered to them ageine and they presentlie to departe with it and not to make sale within your port or liberties, onlesse they have anoyed anie of her frendes, alies and subjectes; of whome specially you ought to make staye and to certifie us that restitution made accordinge to her Highnes pleasure." *Signed.*

1571[-2], February 21. The Palace at Westminster.—Queen Elizabeth to William Crispe, Esquire, Lieutenant of Dover Castle and to the Mayor of the town of Dover.

"We are frome time to time informid of the great disordres and spoiles made by a certen flote of shippes pretendinge to serve the Prince of Orrange in those our narrow seas and specially uppon the coste of Kent, and the spoiles and prices are brought comonly into that our Porte of Dovor and there solde derectly against our commaundementes expressed by severall proclamacions and to the slander of that towne. Besides this we also perceive that the Conty de la Marq, who also pretendith to have aucthority over that flote, doth lodge in that our towne of Dover, to whome alsoe a multytude of them which serve in that flote doe resort otherwise then in any former tyme hath bene used in that towne beinge a principall porte and as an eie of our realme. All which considered we will and charge you forthwith to geve knowledge to the said County de la Marque that allthough at his beinge with us, uppon his request, we were content to graunt unto him our pasport to passe out of our realme with certeyne armour belonginge to himselfe, yet we never ment that he should contynew in that towne and principall porte to make the same a place of assemblie for all his companie to resorte to him; nether have we herd frome the Prince of Orrange of anie speciall requeste made for that purpose, but contrarywise of late we have bene advertised by our Ambassador out of Fraunce frome the County Ledovick, brother to the said Prince, that the meaninge of the said Prince is not that either the said County de la Marque, or anie other pretendinge to serve the said Prince, should, in such sorte as they doe, haunte our narrow seas or lye in any of our portes to the offence of any our subjects or the subjects of any our friends. Wherefore ye shall commaund him to geve order that the flote may departe frome our sea coast, and that both himselfe and his traine doe departe oute out of that towne and porte of Dovor. And if he shall refuse so to doe, you shall first use some perswasions in respect of the generall complaintes made of all merchants havinge cause to passe and repasse the seas by that coast, and specially for that yt was never seane nor suffered that any straungers of any nation hath bene suffred to continue in that towne but for passage only. And if such reasons shall not move him for to yeald to departe, you shall then lette him understand that you may not suffer him nor any of his to remain there. And to that ende we would have yow consider how yow maye, if he will persist wilfully to continue, remove him thence by barring him victuells or otherwise as yourselves shall thinke best, usinge therin all directe meanes rather then force untill yow may here further frome us or our Counsell.

We will you, the Liuetenant of the Castell of Dovor, to send to the Mayor of Sandwich and all other officers of the Portes to use the same order for excludinge thes manner of people. And suerly if they shall not, you may well assure them without respect to their liberties they clayme, we will inquire of thes contemptes and negligences in usinge our commaundements and sease our liberties into our hands." *Copy.*

1571[-2], March 2. London.—The Commissioners appointed for the receipt of Certificates of such goods as have been stayed pertaining to subjects of the King of Spain to the Mayor of Rye.

"Where it hath pleased the Quenes Majestie to addresse her Highnes commission to us and others to examyn what goodes, debts shippes, money, or other thinges were, and are nowe, arrested in anie of the King of Spaynes domynions belongiug, to anie of her Highnes subjects to the end that satisfaction maye be made to them of suche goodes, wares, marchaundises, money, debtes, and other thinges belonging to anie of the said King of Spayn's subjects as have bin arested in any her Highnes domynions. We have therefore thought good to signifie the same to you and withall to requiere you to geve notice thereof to all suche dwelling within your libertie as shall have any juste cause to make demaunde for any goodes, wares, or marchaundises staied, as is aforesaid, and that they doe make theire repaire to us, the said commissioners, with all conveynyent spede at the Guildhall in London where we mynde to sitt everie Saterdaie and Mondaie for that purpose." *Signed.*

1571[-2], March 9.—The Mayor and Jurats of Rye to the Lords of the Council.

"Whereas this present daye the date hereof we have received from the Livetenaunte of Dover Castle the Quenis Majesties letters for the avoydinge from the Portes the flete of shipes of thos which pretend to serve the Prince of Orrenge on the Narrowe Seies, it may please your honours to be advertised that we have callid suche persons before us, which wee thought to be of that fleete remayninge in our Towne, very late thether dryven by impietosatie (*sic*) of wether, their ships lyinge in the Camber, and have used towardes them for their departure accordinge to the foresaid letters, who very humbly have desired us fyrst to signifie unto your honours their licences which they have (as they saie) absolutely frome the Prince of Orenge, before their departure. And forasmuch as the Quenis Majesties said letters do concerne suche as pretend the service of the Prince of Orenge to this offence of hir Graces subjectes or subjects of eny other hir Highnes friendes and theis persones, alledginge their lawfull aucthoritie as they terme it, we thought good with as muche convenient speede as might be, fyrst to signifie unto your honours their licences by this messenger and so to staie as concerninge thos persons till your farther pleasures be therin knowen. As touchinge the Conty de la Marque and thos knowen of his company we meane in nowise towardes them other then hir Majesties letters do require and the leike to thes persons had ben donne if their said humble petition had not benne." *Draft.*

1571[-2], March 10.—A declaration by John Philpot, Preacher of the word of God, that on the nineth of the said month of March going to supper with one Anthony Coxe in Rye, it happened that "one George Sere of the same towne called him into his house where one Thomas Wilkin, a mariner of Lie in Essex, tooke him, the said John Philpot, aside into a wyndow and signified that he had matter of importance which he would make relation of, which was that beinge of late with his barke at St. Mallowes in Brytanie to loade certaine goodes hee did perfaitly understand that a certaine nobleman of Scotland named the Lord Flemynge did ly and staie in the said towne of St. Mallows for aide of certaine shipes to be passed into Schotland by the meane of the Guyes; and affermid moreover that being in the company of a Scotishe man in the said towne of St. Mallowes, who was of the retynew of the said Lord Flemynge, that the Scotishe man uttered very presumptuously many trayterous wordes against the state of this realme of England, affirminge that it was pity that the Duke did not bring to passe that hee had taken in hand. And that even [if] yt were longe, the quarrell of the Duke should be avenged, and that it shuld never be well till the boy of Scotland shuld hold both the Realmes of England and Scotland.

1571[-2], March 14.—The Mayor and Jurats of Rye to the Bailiff and Constable of Havant.

"Whereas by this berrer, Edmond Gest, we understand that one William Simpson of Yorkshire is steyed with you upon some suspeckte, and remayneth till advertisement of his honesty and behavior, theis are to signifie unto you for trothe that the same William Simpson of late departid from Ry about the fyveth of this moneth with some suche person as perswaded him of some gainfull bargaine, now fallen out to his trouble, he beinge taken emongest his acquaintance at Ry to be a very honest man and of substance, as well the same doth appeare for that at his departure he left his waires, beinge clothe, in divers honest men's hands in Ry, who are debtors unto him for it till his retorne; and while he was here at Ry lodged in the house of one Thomas Simpson, an honest housholder, where he also lefte certaine of his clothe being northen dosens." *Draft.*

1571[-2], March 16.—The Mayors, Bailiffs and Jurates of the Five Ports to Dr. Lewes and others, the Commissioners appointed for the receipt of certificates of such goods, as have been stayed, pertaining to the subjects of the King of Spain.

We have received your letters. "The effecte of which your letters as with all our hartes we are redy and willing to accomplish if they came orderly. So are we to request your worshipes to be advertised that without breach of our liberties we may not make retorne of the same, excepte they were fyrst directed to our Lord Warden, and so frome his honours office unto us by letters of attendance. For as by our charters we are not to appere afore eny Commissioners out of our liberties, so are we not to make certificate or retorne of eny matter comyng from eny Comyssioner without the same be by order sent to our Lord Warden, and so frome him to us, as is aforesaid." *Draft.*

[There is a long correspondence amongst the various Ports, on this matter, of which the above letter is the result.]

1571[-2], March 19.—The Mayors, Bailiffs and Jurats of the Five Ports and their members to Lord Cobham.

"We have received lettres addressed unto us from certain Commyssioners appointed concerning the staye of certen shipps, wares, goodes and merchandizes which were stayed here by the restreynt ever sythence the thirde daye of January in the eleaventh yeare of her Majesties reigne, whereof they will us to make certyfficate. The which, for that they come not orderly by lettre of attendaunce (according to auncient custome), we thought yt our dutie, before answer made, to signefie the same unto your Lordship, for that we do take yt to be bothe prejudyciall unto your Lordshipps office, as also infringement to our lyberties and charters, wherein we crave your Lordshippes favorable assistance and furtherance in answeringe the same. For bycause we were very lothe to certefie anythinge either hurtful to your Lordshipps office or imparement of our liberties, what we have don herein pleaseth your honor to have conference with the bringers hereof, they can more fully certefie your Lordship." *Draft.*

1571[-2], March 20.—Depositions of Gerdte Gormers of Haunborugh [Hamburg], master of the hulk called the *Fortune of Hamborugh*. The deponent says that being at Burwaye in France he took into the said hulk 75 packs of white paper. As this deponent was passing through the seas he met with an English ship called the *Hull* the master of which ordered him "in the Quenes Majesties name of

England" to lower his sails which he did. The men of the *Hull* then came aboard this deponent's ship and took away his best anchor, cut his cables asunder and took also ten whole packs of the said paper, spoiled two other packs and then departed.

1572, April 4.—Depositions taken before George Raynoldes, Deputy, John Donnynge, Mayor of Rye, John Sharpe, Clement Cobbe, Henry Geymer, Robert Fowler, William Davy and William Tolkin.

"Leonard Dirrickson de Swartawale by the Brille was taken by the frebutters with a fisherboate, the 29th of Marche laste, being in his fyshing boate with fyve or six men right against the Maese [Meuse], and kepte him to ransom his boate and his men at 100 crownes, and his boate and his men be sent home for that monye, for which the capitaine of the said frebutters hath a bond of the said Dirrickson to paie at Dover."

Clause Lyneson of Ciricksey [Zirikzee] in Zealand "saieth that on Tuesdaye, the 25th of Marche laste, a certain hoye being bound with marchandize frome Emden to London, came aborde the fyshing boate of the said Clause before the Mase beinge afyshinge, in which hoye were a company of passengers beinge frebutters to the nomber of 30 persons, sodenly lepte into his boate and then the hoye departed to London. When theis frebutters had taken this said Clauses boate they afterwardes tooke another fysher boate of Ciricksey, which is the boate that nowe is come into Rye, and sent the said Clauses boate and his men home, savinge himself and one of his men, which they kepte. The master's name of the boate nowe come into Rye is Cornelis Jobson of Ciricksey with his foure men."

1572, April 5.—The Mayor and Jurats of Rye to the Lords of the Council.

"On Thursday laste beinge the third of this instant in thafter none, there came into Rye Creke a fysher boate of the burden of 20 tonnes or theraboutes, in which were eight fyshermen in their fyshing apparell and thirtie other persones termed frebutters. Wheruppon we caused the boate to be serchid and founde nothinge but only suche weapons as they had for their owne defence, for uppon examynation of the fyshermen it apperid that the said frebutters (or passengers as they tooke them) came in a hoye frome Emden which was bownd to London with marchandize and by the waye againste the Mase [Meuse], the 25th of Marche laste, bordid a little fysher boate and came all into that boate, and then the hoye departid on hir voyage; the next daye followinge they bordid another fysher boate nere the same place and tooke out the master and one man of the first boate, and sent the same boate and the resideu of the men home. The 29th of Marche they bordid another fysher boate and tooke out the master and sent the boate and the rest of the men home, and in all this tyme did not hurte or ill intreate any of them as the fyshermen themselves declare. The boate and fyshermen are of Ciricksey in Zeland, beinge of sondry companies of whome we have sufferid some to departe home beinge only servantes and the resideu with their boate we reteyne, till your honors pleasures be herin knowen.

The frebutters say that they are licencid by the Prince of Orenge whos licences we send herinclosed and the captaine remaynith at Rye being sicke and weke with six or sevin of his company, for at their arrivall they had nether bredd nor drinke nor had eny in seven or eight daies before. The rest to avoid charges are departid. It is the first time that they have ben in England as they saie and knewe nothinge of the orders late taken towchinge suche persones." *Draft*

1572, April 10, Ashford.—A certificate made by Thomas Pett and others touching the "mysdemanor of the two abusers of the Divyne gefte of God in Medicene, callinge themselves by the name of Tomlens the elder and the younger, the father and the sonne."

"The 15 day of December laste paste the elder Tomlyn came to Asheforde, and toke his yn at the bayliffes house and their spreede his banners and sett up his billes with declarations that he cowlde do wonders, and allurede many people, beinge market day. But when the market was done Master Pett, vicar of Asheforde, and Thomas Quydler had hym in examination and founde hym farre unable and unmete to practise physicke and chirurgery or any parte or parcell thereof; notwithstandinge he had so many billes and testimonyes of other places, and especially a licens geven by the ordenary to practise his arte of cuttinge, in the Dioces of Canterbury, wherby we, so abused for that tyme, lett him goo quyetly untill we had some prove of hym and his doinge by the detryment of dyvers of our neighbors, but first we reproved hym aud forbade hym the admynystration of a certayne purgation wherwith his sonne dangerede many. Notwithstandinge our charge to the contrarye, the 3rd day of Marche laste, the said Alexander Tomlyn gave two purgations, the one to Mary Lawrance which was servant to William Padnall, bailiffe, the other to one Edward Ponett, and purged them both that they dyede shortelye after. And, to be shorte, for the most parte all they that he mynystrede unto in eny case are likewise dangerede of liffe. Also betwen thes two they had a woman suspected of whordome and laide in the stocks by the constable."

1572, April 27. London.—G. Winter and John Hawkins [commissioners for the reformation of disorders of the freebooters to Anthony Godderd].

"Where wee are credibly informed that one Robert Jacson of Ry hath of late offendid and transgressed contrary to the Quenis Majesties orders and proclamations of late sett forth in all her townes and portes uppon the sea costes of Kent, Sussex, Hampshire and the west parts of her Hignes coasts of England, for victualinge or making eny kynde of traffique with the frebutters or rovers. For the ponishing and reformynge of all such offenders hir Majestie haith aucthorised us George Wynter and John Hawkins, Esquires, by hir Highness commission under hir Great Seale of England. Wherfore we require you Anthony Godderd to apprehend the said Robert Jacson and him salfly to convey and bringe to London before us and if he shall make eny resistance, or shall refuse to obey your arrest, then you shall require thassistance of the Maior of Ry or of eny other the Quenis Majesties officers in Ry or elswhere within hir Highnes realme whersoever, and so to commit him to the next gaole or prison." *Copy.*

1572, April 28.—The Mayor's deputy at Rye and the Jurats there to Mr. George Wynter and Mr. John Hawkins, commissioners for reformation of disorders of the freebooters.

"Although the Commission sent from you by Anthony Godderd, this bearer, were mistaken and your precepte or mandation to him directed, for thapprehending of Robert Jacson comith unorderly, for that none of our freemen or inhabitantes for eny cause is by writ, precept or mandation frome eny Commissioners to be apprehended or attached, but that fyrst the same to be directed to our Lord Warden or his Deputie, and so to us by letter of attendance frome Dover Castle, yet we have takin this order that the same Robert Jacson shalbe with your Worships at London, or elswhere, on Fryday next, and as towchinge the word mensioned in your instructions gevin to the said Anthony Godderd wee will (nowe knowing the same) do our indevors for the staie thereof if it may come to our view about which this said berer staied at the writinge hereof, and can uppon his retorne informe you further therein by word of mouthe." *Draft.*

1572, May 3.—A request made by all the fishermen of the town of Rye unto Clement Cobbe and Henry Geymer, jurats and Barons to the Parliament for the town of Rye.

"In primis, that it wold please them, this parliament, to have conference with the residewe of the barons of the portes and also with the burgeseis of Yermouth and Knights of the Shires where are fysher townes, and for the drawinge of a bill to be exhibited this Parliament for the mayntenance of the fishermen of this realme, and avoydinge of strangers fyshermen and also for the avoydinge of the fyshe brought into this realme by the Quenis subjects beinge caught on the seies by strangers.

Item, Ry hath had thirty-four boats to Scarborouge for codd and lyngge within theis fifteen yeris, and nowe the last yere ther was not above thre.

Item, the reason therof is for that the strangers, viz.: Scotland, Flaunders, Fraunce, do bring in so much of that fishe, that ther is no utterance for our fishermen when they have taken ther fyshe.

Item, when our merchants goo to Hamborough and Emden they beynge there ladinge with fishe, a hundred tounes, six skore tonnes and upwardes, which is no small quantitie, the utterance whereof is the decay of the utterance of our fyshermens fishe all alongest the sea coaste.

Item, they of Flanders do send their fishe into Fraunce where our English marchantes doe buy it and soe bringe it into the Realme.

Item, the merchants of Scotland do the leike with their Scottishe fyshe which is also a great hindrance to the whole fyshinge of the Realme.

Item, the leike order do all theis strangers kepe with herringe when herringe time is.

So that the Quenis subjectes furnishinge themselves with Flemish fyshe, Scottishe fyshe, and Frenche fyshe, the fishermen of England are fayne to lay up their boats and seke other trades, wheras if this strange fyshe were abolished, they shuld be able in small tyme to trade the seis as in tymes past they have donne, and aswell to furnish the Quenis subjects as the stranger, and as good peneworthes; besides the byrnninge upe of a greate nomber of mariners which now are utterly decayed.

Fresh fishe.

Item, divers of our Englishe men with their crones and ketches, generally and contynually do trade the coast of Flaunders and Callice, where, with their redy mony they not only buy of the ketches of that partes, strangers playce, coddes and all such kinde of fresh fyshe as thoes strange ketches take, and so bringe it into the Realme to the utter decaye of our fyshermen which bringe upe yougth to plye the takinge of fish themselves, beinge fourteene, fifteene or sixteene men and a boye or two in a boate beinge noe small nomber in our lyttle towne as Ry is, when they had utterance for their fishe, but also they the said Englishe ketches frome tyme to tyme convey awaye a number of redy monye with the buyinge of fyshe of thoes strangers ketches."

1572, May 4.—[The Mayor and Jurats of Rye] to Sir William Fleetwood, Recorder, and Mr. John Branch, Sheriff of London.

"This 4th of May we received your lettres of the first of the same, perceyving therby that the murtherer is apprehendid which murderid Arthur Halle. Wheruppon we have clerly released the messenger beinge at some libertie before, but not fully dischargid. Longe before the receypte of your said lettres, viz: the last day of Aprill last past we caused 12 men to be sworne *super visum corporis, &c.*, who thoroughly viewing the body of the murdered person have presented thus in effecte: That John Julians of Ry, in the County of Sussex, mariner, brought a dry pipe frome London in which, the 29th of Aprill the 14th yere of the raigne of our Soveraigne Lady Quene Elizabeth, about tenne of the clocke in the night, a deade body of a man, unto them unknowen, was founde, but by the testymony of the messenger sent by John Branch the Shireff of London, the body of one Arthure Hall of London, marchant. Which said body of the said man, to them unknowen, had these woundes following, viz: on the head three woundes of little depthe but rather brused, his throte cutt, and thrust into the lefte side with a dager or gret kniff: the wound so depe that they felt no bottom therof, his lefte legge cut asonder by the kne underneth and honge by the skynne. The murderer they knowe not but by reporte, one Martin Bullock. Which view so taken the body was, the Fryday the second of May in the forenone, being put in a coffin, buried in one of the chauncels of the church of Ry. Thus have we procedid herin as we thought meete." *Draft.*

1572, May 20.—St. James'.—The Lords of the Council [to the Lord Warden].

"Beinge informed that some captaines in the Cittie of London, or neare aboute the same, have lately mustered soldiers and putt them in armore uppon entent, as it is reportid, to transport them over the seas. Forsomuch as the Quenes Majestie doth utterly mislike that any captaines or soldiers should in such sorte goo over without her speciall licence, theis are to require you, and straightly to charge you, that if any such matter be attemptid neare about you or under your rule that you use all meanes and dilligence that you cann, not only to staie all such entreprises to proceade in any muster, but also that you suffer none to pass in such sorte over at any porte under your charge. And if you shall find any person being the Quenes Majesty's subjecte that shall attempt the one or the other you shall make staie of all such untill you have enformed us and shall theruppon receyve further direction in that behalf." *Copy.*

1572, May.—Proceedings in a suit in the Queen's Court held at Rye, as to the descent of certain property of John Jervis of Rye. Pedigree of John Jervis.

1572, June 17.—The Mayor and Jurats of New Romney [to the Mayor and Jurats of Rye].

"By auncient usage and custome tyme out of mynd contynued two browhulds or brotherrelds generall, by the wisdome and pollicie of our predecessors, barons of the five portes, were provided and ordaynid yerely to be holden at the Towne and Porte of Newe Romney, wherof one the Twesday next after the Feast [of] St. Margaret for the presentation of our Bailles chosen to be at the Towne of Great Yermouth in the tyme of the faier there. Which brotherild at this tyme apperteynith to us to areare. Wherfore we pray you all Maiors and Baillies of the Five Portes and members that every of you, with two or thre of your discreat combarons, to be at the said Towne and Porte of Newe Romney the said daie above named at eight of the clocke of the said daie in the forenonne, electid, aucthorizet and returnid under your common seales there and then to here and to have relation of the good sped and governaunce of our Baillies aforesaid, and further of all other matters and causes nedfull and profitable for the universall wealth of our franchieses, usages, and customes."

1572, June.—Proclamation by John Donynge Mayor of Rye, and the Jurats and Commonalty of the same Town that "whereas emongest other the auncient customes of the sayd town of Ry it is conteynid that in case any man or woman dy within the sayd fraunches of Ry, and their heirs be within age, then the Maior shall have the viewe of the child and all his landes, rentes, and tenements and of all his movable goodes and by the Maior and Jurats the child shalbe put unto warde to the next kinsman, that the child hathe of his blood, unto whome the sayd inheritaunce may not discend, and all his goods and cattals shalbe deliverid unto the said gardian by Indenture made betwene the said Maior and the said gardian until the tyme the child be of full age; and the one parte of the said Indenture shall remayn in the comon Treasory. And in case there be none of the childs' blodd, then the Maior shall take and deliver the said goodes and cattals unto some sufficient man of the fraunchies, in kepinge, until the tyme that the child be come to his full age at which tyme the child shall have them deliverid unto his use. And wheras Augustynne Swetinge, late of Ry aforesaid, inholder, havinge foure children, that is to saie, Thomas, Harry, Susan and Brydget all within age, unto whome he gave by his last Will and Testament the some of threskore poundes of lawfull money of England, that is to saie, unto Thomas, 20*l*., unto Harry, 20*l*., unto Susan, 10*l*., and unto Brydget 10*l*., and made Margaret his wiff executrix of his said last Will and Testament, and so died, who takinge upon her the charge of the same by hir last Will and Testament did geve unto the said Thomas, Harry and Brydget also hir children the some of Thirty poundes, thre christeninge shetes and a Turky ringe, that is to say, unto Thomas 10*l*. and a christeninge shete, unto Harry 10*l*. and a christeninge shete, and to Brydget 10*l*. and a christeninge shete and a Turky ringe, to the foreseid Susan a bedsted, a fetherbed, a single coverlet of dornex, a blanket and a bolster. And of the same hir last Will and Testament ordaynid and made William Fawconer hir executor, and so died. After whoes death the said William Fawconer took uppon him the execution of the said last Will and Testament of the said Margaret, all the foresaid children being within age. Know ye, that we the said Mayor and Jurats, for that the said children and every of them at this present are within age, aswell by vertue of the foresaid auncient custome as also accordinge to our auncient usages tyme out of mynd in the like cases used, have taken into our handes and the daie and date hereof have received of the foresaid William Fawconer of all foresaid legaces of mony and goodes to the use of the children aforesaid the same to use, order and dispose accordinge to our said auncient custome and usages, and of the same mony and goodes by theis presents do clerly acquite and discharge the said William Fawconer, his executors and administrators."

1572, July 5.—Inquisition taken before John Baily, deputy of John Donninge, Mayor of the town of Rye and Coroner of the Lady the Queen within the same town. The jury say that William Johnson feloniously killed and murdered John Crosbowe outside the east gate of the said town, in the Queen's highway there. *Latin. Seals attached.*

1572, August 9.—Order by the Mayor and Jurats of Rye for public prayer and fast.

In consideration of this unseasonable weather, a token of God's great displeasure, threatening no small miseries and calamities to fall upon us, and that for our loose life and neglecting to do our duties as we ought to serve God, that on Monday next and every Monday till it please God to stay this unseasonable weather, the people and inhabitants of this town of all ages and sorts diligently repair to the Church both to call upon God by prayer and also for hearing his word both forenoon and afternoon, at such time as the bell shall be tolled.

And for the better continuance of the people in godly fervency and prayer it is ordered that a general holy and solemn fast be kept by all sorts from sixteen to sixty years (sick folk and labourers in the harvest being excepted) who are wished only to content themselves that day with bread and drink, that they may be the more apt to prayer.

1572, August.—Correspondence as to a special Gestlinge of the Western Ports and dispute whether it shall be held at Winchelsea or Hastings.

1572, September 21.—The Lords of the Council to the Commissioners for the Five Ports, in the absence of the Lord Warden.

"For as much as it is apparent that many have since the universall murders violently committed in Paris and other partes of France, fledd unto this realme and do yet continue to save their lives as the verie law of God and nature doth require, of whome alsoe common and christian charitie ought to move us to have compassion, yet we thinke also verie convenient to have certaine knowledge frome tyme to tyme what numbers and what sortes of persones they are that do come unto the realme uppon this occasion, and to foresee that under pretence thereof no other sorte of daungerous persons do transporte themselves. And therefore we require you to give some present order to all the portes and landinge places within that County that good regarde be hadd and speciall observation kept and regester made what persons do arrive and their names, there qualities and there occasions as they shall alledge of their comming, and to what places they do determyne to repaire further into the realme, and frome tyme to tyme, that is, every foretene daies or oftener if the numbers do encrease, advertisement to be sent to us and therof we earnestly requier you to take some care and to signifie to us your opinions of their arrivall if you find any cause to doubte thereof." *Copy.*

Enclosure

"The names of such persons as be chosen and aucthorised to take charge for the serch of all suche as shall passe in or out at any of the Portes and Crekes underwrytten."

At Dovor.
Thomas Andrewes.
William Hartflett.

At Sandwiche.
Henrie Butlers.
Alexander Cobbe.

At the Downes.
Peter Hamond.
At Folkeston.
Robert Holidaye, Maior. }
Richard Reade.
At Hithe.
Roger Starre. }
Giles Elingworth.
At Lydd.
John Stengghill, Junior. }
John Hublethwaite.
At Margate in the Isle of Tennet.
John Blowfeld. }
Henrie Petitt.
At Ramsgate.
John Johnson. }
Roberte Speiklin.
At Broidstare.
Michaell Webbe. }
John Culmere.
At Faversham.
Robert Jagge. }
Thomas Inche.
At Milton.
John Thorneton. }
Thomas Spicike.
At Queneborourogh.
Elias Grafte. }
—— Burlacie.

1572[-3], March.—Bond by which Francis Maquery, together with Marten Cauchie, his wife, stands to keep an award of Francis Mercher, Ambrose de Moye, Robert de la Place and William Butcher, merchants of Rye, touching a suit pending between the said Francis Maquery and Francis Cauchie and Massela le Creux, his wife.

1573, August 3.—Order for a present to the Queen.

It is agreed by this assembly that there shall be given to the Queen's Majesty at her coming to Rye for a present, a hundred angels in a purse.

1573, August 18-22.—The Mayor and Jurats of Dover to the Mayor and Jurats of Rye.

Approving of the selection Mr. John Donning, Jurat, to execute the Office of Bailiff to Yarmouth. [Similar letters from the Mayor and Jurats &c. of Winchelsea, Hythe and Romney.]

1573, August 21.—"One hundred Calivers to guard the Queen at Dover."

The Lord Warden having written to the Mayor and Jurats of Rye to have a hundred "Caliverers" at Dover to be in garrison during her Majesty's abode. It is granted that there shall go a hundred calivers, besides "the ensigns drume, phife and vj holberds."

1573, September 8.—Safe conduct granted by the Mayor of Rye to Vincent Henry, Frenchman, who had been at Rye for six months "a cause des troubles de France," to go with his ship, pinnace, and crew to Holland, and from thence to Rochelle.

1573, September 17.—"A decree concerning the two hundred pounds."

It is ordered that Mr. Gaymer, Mr. Cobbe, Mr. Tolken, William Ratcliff, John Jacson and John Fagge, chamberlain, shall ride to the Lord Warden and carry the 200*li.* with them which was received of the merchant of France; and what these persons shall do and consent to therein, the Mayor, Jurats and Commons will hold themselves content therewith.

[1573, September 18.—The Mayor and Jurats of Rye to the Lord Warden.]

"Yesterday at our Court hall we assembled our commons to have their consents for an order betwene your Lordship and us to be had concerning the 200*li.* we received of the marchante's gifte; the case being suche as without the commons consentes we might not deale. Whereuppon three of our Jurates were chosen to resort forthwith unto your Honor as well for and concerninge that money as also for discharge of the men of warre here staied by your Lordship's commandment, for that by an order taken in the towne all suche persons are to departe within a certaine tyme which draweth to ende, diverse being alredy departid, and a grete manye staying uppon theis men to goo with them to Rochell. After which our assemblie, lettres came to our handes, very late in the evening, from the Lordes of her Majesties Councill willinge us to receive all suche somes of mony of Henry Gaymer as were by him receyvid of the Frenche marchant as it were by way of ransome and the same forthwith to send to Her Majestys principall Secretary. So this morninge we have again called together our commoners and again imparted unto them the effect of the same lettres, who suerly are much grevid at the same considering the great charge they have of late benne at frankely and of mere goodwill and now to be subjecte to an extreame cease as well for the levyinge of the said 200*li.* being alredy by the consent of the Maior, Jurates and Commons had frome the said Henry Gaymer and dispersid emongest a nombre of poore men for their labors about the townes business, saving 30*li.* as also to have forthwith almost the leike some for to be bestowed about the water workes of the towne, which not beinge donne our Landgate will shortly awaye and not to be made againe for 1000*li.*; also havinge lost by reason of callinge our men frome their worke to prepare for her Majesty's comynge, a stone wall by force of the sea which was made for defence of the same gate that stood us in seven score poundes and yet more must out of hand be bestowed to defend it this winter, which wilbe no small charge, besides our keeis and wharffes which may not be forflowen. Theis thinges wilbe very burdenous to our commons which we wold to God your Lordship did as well knowe as we doe, and are leike to feele. And nowe to departe frome that mony beinge so frely geven doth kill the hartes of them clene. In consideration whereof we most humblie beseche your Honor to stand our good Lorde and that with your favor and good will we may enjoye that mony without eny further troble; and if your Lordship will nedes have it then must we crave of your Honor some staie for levyinge it by way of cease, as we are determined, havinge of purpose sent theis berres [bearers] to have conference with your Lordship about the same for in you it lieth to staie all." *Draft.*

[1573], September 23.—Certificate by Mayor of Rye (John Donninge) to the "Bayley of the town of Diep and others assistaunte to

RYE MSS.

hym in justice" that "wheras our neighbours William Ferrall and Thomas Ferrall of Rye are by you staied and kept in prison, and chieflie as we understand on the reporte of some of your towne to you that shold affirme and saie these our neighbors to be rovers, pyrattes and maynteyners of theves. And forasmuch as it is not only the parte of every good christian to testifye the truthe of his knowledge in matters doubtfull being therunto required, but also a charitable dede, and for that yt is necessary that eche person be reported of as his deserts doth justly require. Know ye that we, the said Maior and Jurattes together with the consent of all other our neighbours whos names be here undersubscribed, at the requests of our honest neighbours Alice Ferrall and Johan Ferrall the wyves of those our neighbours William Ferrall and Thomas [Ferrall] do signyfie and declare to you for truth, that the said William Ferrall and Thomas Ferrall hath dwelled in our said town of Ry by the space of 30 years togethers during all which tyme they or either of them have bene of good name, fame and honest conversation, not knowne, reputed or taken for eny suche kinde of notorious cryme or lewde demeanour as aforesaid is surmised or alleged against them or either of them."

[1573, September.—The Mayor and Jurats of Rye to the Lords of the Council.]

"Whereas we have received your Honor's letters of the 13th of this instant by which your Honor's requier us forthwith uppon the receipte thereof to send up by some assured persone suche some and somes of money as Henry Gaymer, our late Maior, received of a merchaunt of Diep as yt were for his raunsome, the same to remaine in deposit and sequestracion in the handes of her Majesty's Principall Secretary. It may please your good Lordships to be advertised that the said merchaunt did frankely and freely of his mere goodwill give unto our towne the some of 200*li.* for and in consideration of the curtezie he found at our handes in ayding hym to save hys goodes which Comyssary and Corba had taken from hym and not for his raunsome, which said merchaunt paied the same unto the sayd Henry Gaymer, then Maior, unto the use of the towne, who sithens the election of the newe Maior, which was within sixe dayes after the receate thereof, according to our orders hath delyvered it over unto us to the use of the sayd towne ; and which sayd 200*li.* is disbursed emongest dyvers persons to whome the towne was indebit and not to be had according to your Honors requests without assesse to be made emongest us, which will be grevious unto our inhabitantes considering their late charges they have bene at and yet are lyke to be about certen workes spedily to be done for defence of the sea from our towne, having alredy lost one pece of worke when her Majestie was at Rye which cost us 140*li.* and yet must be made againe. In consideration whereof we most humblie beseche your Honors to stand our Lords, that with your favors and good wills we may enjoye that pece of money which the said merchant so frely hath given unto us." *Draft.*

1573, October 2.—Indenture between Richard Bushop of Rye, master and owner of the ship *Mary Thomas* of the burden of 70 tons, and Robert Farley and Cornellis Sohier of Rye, merchants, concerning voyages of the said ship to Rochelle and elsewhere. *Draft.*

1573, October 16.—Bond by Nicholas Boniface of Rye, minstrel, and Anthony Boniface of Rye, mercer, for the appearance of Anne Boniface before the Mayor and Jurats.

1573, October.—[———] to the Lord Warden.

"May it please your Honor that one Cornelys Sohier offereth to passe at Ry, by vertu of this licence which I send your Honor herein closed, one hundrethe barrells of candells and hathe bought uppe here at Rye all the candells within the towne that were to be had; and further causeth Frenchmen to make candells for him in covert places of the towne wherby he doth cause great want of candells. So yt is right honorable that I have caused the candells to be stayed in the shoppes wher they now bee untill your Honors pleasure be therin knowen and have sent this messenger of purpose and the rather for that the hole towne doth take offence by the sayd Cornelys, doon against them for the sayd candells as knowith God."

[1573], November 11. London.—Roger Manwood to the Mayor and Jurats of Rye.

"Whereas certen goodes late belonginge to myne old frend Mr. Thomas Byrchett, decessyd, a jurat of your town, and after hys death belonginge to his wydow and sonne Thomas, executors of hys testament, and by hyr death belonginge to Thomas Byrchett the son, the survyving executor, now for her quyet and contentation permytted to . . . . . . with hyr, and sythens hyr death (for good concorde to be had bytwen the three sonnes) wherin I travayled, were lefte in sauff custody within the late dwellinghouse of the sayd Byrchett's wydowe and ellswher, in right now belonging to Thomas Byrchett the survyving executor. And wheras Peter Byrchett, the myddell son, for hys just desert and offence ys atteynted of felony and murder, least by pretence therof, he (notwithstanding the truthe of the case) shuld perchance intermeddyll with any of the sayd goodes as belongs to hym, wheras in truthe they dyd not belong to hym. Therfore to prevent injury to be attemptyd, I have adreysed the said Thomas Byrchett, the survyving executor, to come down to you and shewe the testament of hys sayd father; and that in your presence an inventory shalbe made of the goodes ther within your town remayning, wherin the two younger sonnes have had any entermedlyng. And after inventory taken the same to remayn in sauffe custody where they be, without removing of any part therof or of any evydences or wrytyngs. And hereafter when you, or any of your counsyll, will take tyme to examyne and shew what ryght to any parte of the sayd goodes can be claymed . . . . . that shallbe don, whiche by your own counsyll, shallbe allowyd of, in right and equyty. Thus advysing you herin to use a diskrete order consonant to right and quyet according to justyce I doe take my leave."

[1573], November 26. Serjeants Inn.—William Lovelace to the Mayors, Bailiffs and Jurats of the Cinque Ports.

"Wheras there hath bene some stryffe betwene your Lord Warden and you, which matters as I heare are drawne to some articles or pointes. Wheruppon ther may, uppon good consideration, some resolution of paccyfycation, growe, which cannot well be without suche conference together of yourselves in assembly at a gestlinge as in the like you have used, and althought I neyther knowe the greffes nor yet of any side have byn procurid or insyniated (*sic*) in this matter more then some frome Hithe delivered unto me, yet I thought it convenient as one that for your yerelie fee ought to respect your doeinges to wishe you to assemble together and theruppon to consulte, that seeinge all thinges must have an end, the sonner yt is in hand the sonner you shall rypp your owne quitnes with hym that is your hedd and maie stand you in all your sutes and doeinges, havinge his favor, in gret stedd, otherwise such poore sutes as some of your townes have or anie of yourselves maie have, cannot well by any sute to his Lordship be urgid to be furthered. Thus leving the consideration thereof to yourselves as one that both doth honor hym and well wisheth unto you all, I trust you will take this my wrytinge in good parte."

1573, November 26. Rye.—The Mayor and Jurats of Rye to Sir Thomas Palmer, knight, at Goodwood.

"Our neighbour Robert Jacson the 24th daie of this instant month of November and not before, hath received into his howse for his provicion towardes the victulinge of this towne, out of a bot of Chichester callid the *Elizabeth of Chichester*, wherof Richard Laurens is master, 54 quarters of wheat and twenty quarters of malt which he ladid at Chichester; by virtue of license from the Right Honorable the Lord High Treasurer of England unto you only, in that behalf he standeth bounden unto yow [and we] for the returning of our certificates in that behalf accordingly." *Draft.*

1573, November 26.—The Mayor and Jurats of Rye to the Mayor and Jurats of Sandwich.

"We have received your lettres makinge mension of a coppy of a booke come to your handes beinge sett downe by Mr. Justice Manwood as it is thought, the which your lettres by us considered of, we cannot but well leike of your motion therin conteyned, havinge also received, as we take it, the leike coppie. And as there are divers thinges in that coppie not wholly to be misleiked of, for that they tend to a Godly purpose which is for a quietnes to be had betwene our Lord Warden and us, so are there divers thinges not fully to be leiked of, as they are pennid for that they are partly against our charters and customes and the statutes of the realme, as we yet conceyve of them, wherefore we thinke it not amys that a gestlinge be had at Romney in tyme convenient so as it be after Christmas if so longe it maye staye, otherwise at your discretions for appointment of the daye backe againe by your lettres by this bearer; at which tyme for our partes we will, God willing, be redy to attend." *Draft.*

1573, November 29. London.—Lord Cobham to the Mayor and Jurats of Rye.

"Where my servant Robert Jacson is arested in yower Cowert of Estrangers or comonley cawled a Cowrt of Pyepowders att the sewt of Mr. Sheperd, his landlord, for the rent supposed by his lease to be dewe emonge other thinges of and for the marshes lately surrownded wyche, by her Majesties specyall commandement and by the lettres of the Lordes of her Highnes Pryvey Counsell, owght so to remayne, I am for some causes me movinge to requyer you thatt the sayd sewte maye stey and lykewyse thatt he may have lawfull favor in other his causes wyche ys no other requyred then may stand with the rules of justyce wyche as itt is reasonable, so have I thereof no misdowght." *Signed. Seal of arms.*

1573, December 9.—The Bailiff and Jurats of Tenterden to the Mayor and Jurats of Rye.

"Whereas by your letter of late, by us from yow receyvid you request certeyne of us to be at the Gestlinge holden at Romney the Tuesday the 15th of this instant moneth of December and to come aucthorised under common seale, we intend, God willinge, to be then there accordingly. And the boke which we receyvid from you concerninge the articles drawen by Mr. Justice Maniwood you shall receyve agayne by this bearer." RYE MSS.

1573, December 10.—The Mayor and Jurats of Rye [to the Lord Warden].

Concerning his Lordships letter touching a suit between his servant Robert Jacson and Mr. Sheperde they think that Jacson has little cause of complaint.

The facts of the case are as follows:—Shepherde brought his action of debt against Jacson to recover a year's rent of *50li.* for a "brewehouse, a wind mille and certaine mershelande in St. Mary mershe"—*30li.* from the brewhouse and mill and *20li* for the marsh. Sheperde "required a Court for Strangers" which they could not deny for their custom is that if one be a stranger and the other a freeman or indweller, the Court shall be kept from day to day forenoon and afternoon, yet they granted Jacson three delays, though the like was never done before, so that Jacson has no just cause to think amiss of any person herein. They hope therefore the Lord Warden will see that he has no cause of complaint. They add that Jane Bennet an impotent widow has an action against Jacson for *15li.* for rent. Another person had recovered upwards of *19li.* against him by the verdict of a jury; these and other matters they have staid for the present hoping it will pleasure him and he in the mean while [will] take some reasonable order. *Draft.*

1573, December 28.—Certificate by [the Deputy of the Mayor, and the Jurats of Rye] that "whereas a certaine hoye of Hollond, whereof is master John Johnson of Targo in Hollond aforesaid, laden at Roterdam with 25 laste [of] herringes to be transported unto Roan in Normandy and by the waye had taken out of the said hoye at Floshinge fyve laste of the said herringes, and afterwardes by tempest of weather was dryven on land at Shoreham with twenty last of the said herringes. Theis are to signifie unto you that the daie and yere underwritten came before us, the said Depute and Juratts, Elizabeth Wolters of Rye, widowe, Anne Martin, the wiff of Bawdewin Martin, and Catherine Cornelison, the wiff of Allin Cornelison of Ry, marchantes, who accordinge to the order emongest them used, have procurations to deale in their husbandes affaires in their absences, which said Elizabeth, Anne and Catherine beinge sworne uppon the Holy Evangests do severally affirme for truthe, that the said herringes in the foresaid hoye cast on land at Shoreham or thereabouts is the proper goods of Hance Hanson of Ry marchant and of the said Elizabeth Wolters, widow, and of the foresaid Bawdwin Martin and Allin Cornelison foure parteners, and not perteyninge nor belonginge to eny other person. And farther the said Elizabeth Wolters for herself and the said Anne and Catherin do by vertue of the procurations which they have frome their said husbands for and in the behalf of their said husbands, in the presence of us the said Maior and Jurates, geve their full power aucthoritie to the foresaid Hance Hanson, the said herringes, and every parcell of them, as well to the use of them the said Elizabeth Wolter, widowe, Bawdwin Martin and Allin Cornelison as to his owne use beinge one of the parteners, to sell, lade againe, merchandize and proffit of them to make, as to his discretion shall seme good, promisinge to hold as fyrme, and thereof to allow all and whatsoever the said Hance Hanson shall do or procure to be donne about the said herringes."

[1573.]—The Mayor and Jurats of Rye to "Mounsieur Sigone, Capten of Deape."

"We have received your lettres wherin you write to understand the cause of the imprysonment with us at Rye of a boye who is the sonne of one Mary, the husband (*sic*) of one Nicholas Duplis. Know you that we likewise desire to be certefied from your Honor the cause wherfore William Verroll and Thomas Verroll breatheren (men of honest behaviour and life) are deteyned so long tyme, for none or very small cause, prisoners with you at Deape then shall we accordinglie answer your requeste. In the meantime we pray you to do good intreatment unto our neighbors abovesaid. And as for the boy or eny other, you shall command us to doo that justice requireth." *Draft.*

[1573.]—[The Mayor and Jurats of Rye to "the Honorable Monsieur Sigoniey, Mayor of Dieppe.]

"Whereas we have dyvers and sondry tymes writen unto you for our poore neighbour William Ferrall who is deteynid in prison and maie not be releassed without payment of 60 crowns having already spent all that he hath. We well perceive that the more we write the lesse our letters be regardid and the poor man more cruellie handled. Theis are therefore to advertise you that accordinglie as our said neighbour is delt withall, we meane to deale with the boie which is here in pryson and forthwith to send hym to our castell; for more hurt then is don to our neighbour cannot well be, excepte you take his lyfe from hym. Wherefore deale as therein you please, for we meane to write no more in the cause." *Draft.*

[1573.]—Petition by William Fyrrall of Rye, mariner, addressed to the Lord Warden, setting out that "in the moneth of August last past, duringe the tyme of hir Majesties beinge at Ry, your said servant had his barke taken and freighted for the Lord Ambassador of England to transporte his gelding frome Ry aforesaid unto Deipe and had in his barke as a passenger one Thomas Grene of Winchilsey, marchante, who by the waye uppon the sea entreated your Honor's said servant to borde a certaine vessel there beinge, which was a frebutter or suche leike person to your said servant then unknown, of whome the said Thomas Grene bought or otherwise compounded for fyve barrels of whit herringes and them ladid into the barke of your Honor's said servant, affyrming that which he did was lawfull and honest, for which he your Honor's said servant shuld incurr no danger, who beinge a simple plaine man gave credit unto the sainges of the said Thomas Grene. So it is, right honorable, that presently after the arrivinge of your Lordship's said servant with his barke at Deipe, the owner of the said herringes seinge his marke upon the barrels made challenge unto them, and caused the barke of your said servant to be ceased and himself comittid unto prison, layinge unto his charge that he had pyratically robbed him of his ship laden with herringes to the valewe of foure hundred poundes sterlinge and upwardes; wheruppon the said Thomas Grene conveyed himselfe away and came over into England and your said poore servant was kept in streight prison somtyme in the dongeon and somtyme more at large laden with irons by the space of sixtene weeks before eny end or agreement could be had with the owner of the said herringes; duringe which tyme your said servant was dryven to such extreme charge that or he could be fully discharged, it cost him foure hundred crownes of the somme besydes the losse of his tyme the greiff of his poore wiff and family, havinge had hetherto no recompence of the said Thomas Grene for the same, he beinge the only cause of all his trouble and charge to the utter undoinge of your Honor's said poore servant, his said poore wiff and family if some remedy by your Lordships meanes be not had. In consideration whereof, may it please your Honor for God-sake and in waye of equitie, to wryte your favorable letters unto the Maior and Jurats of Ry that whensoever the said Thomas Grene shall happen to come within their liberties, that they will cause him to be attached and by their order cause him to make recompence unto your said poore servant for his damage and losse which he hath susteyned." *Draft.*

[1573.—The Mayor and Jurats of Rye to Roger Manwood.]

Asking his opinion on the pleadings in suit between Francis Maquery and Francis Cauchy and apologizing for not before remitting the yearly fee due to him which however, God willing, shall be duly paid. *Draft.*

1573[-4], January 9.—"At St. Stevins my house neere Caunterbury." Opinion by Roger Manwood concerning a dispute between the Town of Rye and the children of Peter Byrchett, as to the goods of the said Peter claimed by the town as *catalla felonum* by reason of attainder. The document concludes :—"Thus moche for the satysfyinge of the towne concerninge theyr right. That nothinge maye be unlaufullye attempted nor to move dyscorde, unquyett or unkyndenes to be betwene the Towne and the twoo survyvinge sonnes; bycause theyr father and mother were my ould assured freendes whyles they lyved and the Towne also my freendes." *Signed.*

1573[-4], January 16. An order that Philipe Fairefeld and Angell Shawe, for their pains taken this summer with the "drome and phife" when the Queen's Majesty was here, shall have 40*s.*, a livery a piece, and from henceforth 40*s.* a year, besides the benevolences of the Commons for their going abroad in the winter nights with their drum and fife for the watches.

1573-4, February 1. Rye.—Sir Thomas Guldeford to Sir Thomas Palmer, Dr. Worley (?) and Henry Marvin.

"Being at Ry, I find the want of corne to be no lesse than was reported unto us at Wyston, and daily the lacke encreasith by reason that no releife comyth. If they perishe for famyne it cannot be answered, the nombre of people of this towne is greate, the hole realme is relived with fish from hence; it is a part of the County of Sussex scituate barenly for corne and hath alwaies had their provision out of your rape and seking nowher els have barganid for it there. The victalers have alredy laid out their stock of money uppon yt and have no newe to supplie to bye yt elswhere, I pray you most hartelie to have consideration of them. It is a towne of defense, bordering uppon the sea; the people are generally forwardes in all good services, and greate pytie it were to suffer them to wante. And ye may assure yourselves that their is a very precise order kept by Mr. Maior and the Juratts that no corne which is brought hyther ys caried to any other place, but all ys spent here without any conveyeinge. I wryte this unto you of my owne knowledge and therefore doe eftstones most hartelie desire you to license them to transporte it."

[1573-4, after February 28.]—Certificate by John Doninge, Mayor of Rye, that "forasmuche as it is a charitable thinge to testyfie the truth in matters doubtfull, and that eche parte be knowne according as he justlie deservith, and wheras Richard Crofte of Brenfort in the County of Middlesex, bocher, is suspected to have lead his life lewdlie, by reason it is to many unknown wher he late inhabited. Theis are therefore to certifie you for truth that the said Richard Crofte came to Ry aforesaid to the house of Nicholas Purvage of the same towne, inholder, with whome he is acquainted, without any company, the 18th daie of October last past where he inhabited and dwellt untill the last daie of February then next foloweing, during all which tyme he remaynid within the towne and used himself honestlie and uprightlie, so far as ever we could perceive or knowe."

1573[–4], February.—Order by the Mayor, Jurats and Commons of Rye "that wheras the common passengers before this daie hath contrary to the commandement gevin unto them generally, that they nor any of them shuld bringe or cause to be brought any manner of person or persons whosoever, onles they be marchantes, gents, common postes, or messengers and suche leike, of any the Frenche or Flemishe nation, which commandment so gevin the said common passengers have lyttle regarded or sett by, but have brought over great nombres of the Frenche, being very poore people, both men, wemen and children to the great crye and greiff of the inhabitantes of Ry and other places about the same. In consideration whereof, to the end the same may be restrayned from comynge hether, it is ordered that from henceforth no common passenger of the town or fisherman which shall fortune to come from Diepe or any of the parts from beyond the seas, as well out of the partes of France or Flaunders as any other place, shall bringe nor suffer to be put on land any of the Frenche or Flemishe nation here (except merchants and the others before excepted) to contynue or dwell upon pain of 40*s*."

1573[–4], March 10.—Memorandum of the weight of bread taken. Commencing "James Welles, his ij *d.* loffe contains—xxvij oz., his whit loffe contains—viij oz. di."

1573[–4], March 23.—Safe conduct for Harmon Tyse (?) master of a ship called *Lesperans* of Rye with 11 mariners and 2 boys, to pass with a cargo of salt belonging to Baldwin Martin, of Rye, merchant, to "Dannske [Dantzic] in Polland" and to return to Rye.

[1573–4, March.]—Certificate by John Doninge, Mayor of Rye, that Thomas Carr of Rye aforesaid, tailor—"who is suspected to have killed a deer in the Lord Montagues park at Battell on the 19th of the instant moneth of Marche"—is confined to his house by illness. *Draft.*

1574, April 10.—Safe conduct granted by the Mayor and Jurats of Rye to Lawrence Langlois, mariner, master of a ship of Rye called the *Hound* of which Thomas Bennard of Rye is owner "together with nineteen maryners in the said ship, all of the religion and French church, at this instant within the towne of Ry, beinge of good name, fame and honest conversation," to sail from Rye to "Noarwage" and from thence to Rochelle with merchandize and so to return again. Also similar safe conduct to the same persons in the same ship, with the same crew to sail from Rye to "Dannske [Dantzic] in Poland" and to return again.

1574, April 22.—Certificate by the Mayor and Jurats of Rye "that about the 24th daie of the moneth of Marche laste paste, arivid here in the harbor called the Puddle nere unto the said towne of Ry, from a place called the Porte [Oporto] in Portugale a certaine barke of the burden of 40 tonnes or theirabountes called the *Seigneur de Porte* laden with orringes and mannid with six men and two boyes, the master named Gonsal Alvus, the pylat Autan Pyz, Antonyo Maio and Alvare Aves, two of the auncient mariners. Which said barke of Portugale lyinge theire in open roode, a certain man of warre of Floshinge, came and roode at anker harde unto hir, wherof the Portugales stoode in doubte as of their ennemye, which being well perceivid of the inhabitantes of Ry, certaine of them went abord the said Portuigall barke to helpe fetche her into the creke of Ry, being a dry harbor, for hir farther saftie being very faier wether, which said barke so brought into the said creke and ground, the common place of ladinge and unladinge, she was so weake that hir sides and seames did open in suche sorte as they were constreynid by the space of two daies and two nightes to kepe the pompes, but all prevailed not, for at the laste the said barke sonke and the orringes in hir laden for the moost parte wet with salt water and swimmith in the bottom of the said barke loose, and thoes which were saved dry beinge about the nombre of fiftie thousand besides a fewe that were sold were laden out of the said Portuigall barke into another small vessell to be transported to London, and by the way was taken on the sea by men of Floshinge and so carried into Flaunders. So as in the ende the said Portuigalls lost not only all their ladinge of orringes (excepte a few which they have sold here at Ry for their victualls) but also theire barke in such weake state as she is not able to go eny more to the sea, nether is of any valewe otherwise then to be pulled in pieces."

[1574, April ?].—Presentments by a jury relative to eating meat at prohibited seasons.

"Item, we founde the 3rd day of Marche in Lenaes howse motten being kerude (cured) withe salte.

Item, more we fownde that same daye in Rychard Ketes howse motten and lame.

Item, we fowne at Neechell Rorsells a denur withe fleshe being the 6th day of Marche.

Item, that Harry Sharpe dyd saye to us that he hathe killed three motens.

Item, we have found that Byam hathe killed motten and lame and mete drest in his howse."

1574, May 10.—Certificate by the Mayor and Jurats of Rye that they had committed the ship called the *Seigneur de Porte* (as her master and company had left her "myndyng not to deale or meddle with the same") to the keeping of Thomas Edolf one of "our combarons" of Rye who ("for that the said barke lay wholy uppon spoile, beinge of no valewe other then to pull a sonder to the fyer,") by sowndes of drum according to the custom of the town, sold her. The bare hull and masts realised 3*l*. 16*s*. sterling, and her boat with the oars, 15*s*. sterling. The sum realised by the tackle with "a mayne saile, a foresaile, a myssen saile and one topsaile, two ankers, one cable of hempe and two other of basse, together with 44 hundred of brassell and other small implements" is not given. The money so realised is to be handed over by Thomas Edolf to the person or persons who can show proper title thereto. *Draft.*

1574, May 11.—Order by the Mayor and Jurats of Rye that none of the inhabitants of Rye neither young nor old shall in the morning any day assay out of the town, with drums, flags or otherwise, into the

RYE MSS.

woods of any man to gather or cut down any "bowes" without licence of the owners.

1574, May 17.—[The Mayor and Jurats of Rye to ——.]

Relative to a sum of *50li.* bequeathed by Mr. Wells to the poor of Rye for ever, payable out of his lands in the town and his marsh without the walls. *Draft.*

1574, May 17.—Safe conduct granted by Henry Gaymer, Deputy of the Mayor of Rye, to "Jaques Piochean, master and owner of a shipe called *Lesperance* apperteyninge to the towne of Olderon [Oleron] in the County of Poytu, within the realme of Fraunce, of the burden of three score tonnes or theraboutes with sixtene marryners and twenty passengers, Frenchmen, in the same shipe," to sail from Rye aforesaid directly unto the town of Rochell within the said realme of France.

1574, May 18.—Safe conduct granted by Henry Gaymer, Deputy to the Mayor of Rye, to Marten Havard, master and owner of the *Goesoftlie* of Rye of the burden of 12 tons, with "foure marryners and twelve passingers, Frenchmen, in the said boate" to sail from Rye to "Saint Mallowes within the realme of Fraunce ther to sett on land his said passingers." *Draft.*

1574, May 21.—Safe conduct granted by Henry Gaymer, deputy of John Donning Mayor of Rye, to Robert Commissary, mariner of Rye, master of the ship *Bonaventure*, to convey twenty-five passengers Frenchmen to the "Bay of Hog [la Hogue] within the realme of Fraunce" and then return to Rye. *Draft.*

1574, June 2nd.—"Want of munition within the towne of Ry wherof they desire supplie as followeth :—

Inprimis, cariages for the ordinaunce in Gonne Gardin accordinge to the note taken by the worshipfull Master William Crispe, Livetenante of Dover Castle, and Mr. —— Partridge Esquires, Commissioners appointid for view of the same.

Item, pikes - - - - -	100
Item, calivers furnished - - - -	50
Item, serpentine powder - - - -	2 laste
Item, corne powder - - - - -	2 barres."

1574, June 3.—Mr. Lame, the French physician, fined for allowing his chimney to fire and Fraunces Maquery fined for going on board the freebooters without license.

1574, June 7.—The Mayor and Jurats of Rye to the Mayor and Jurats of Winchelsea and the Bailiff and Jurats of Hastings.

"Yester eveninge being the 6th of this present monythe a certen person, to us unbeknowne, delyverid unto the handes of one of the Jurats of Rye a subpena directed oute of the Kinges Benche unto me, John Dunninge, Mayor of Rye, and three other of the Jurates named in the same wryte, personally to appere in the Kinges Benche on Frydaye next to answer to suche thinges as then and there shalbe objected agaynst us. And the lyke wrytes were also delivered to other of the Jurates for there lyke appearance. In which severall wrytes are included the Mayor and all the Jurates. The messenger assone as he had delyvered the wrytes departed and could not be found to be talked withall. And forasmuche as this kynde of dealinge is not only very strange but also contrary to our lybertes and charters, we have thoughte it good to imparte the same unto your Worshipps, requyring herein your brotherly councells and advyce and allso your ayde and helpe if nede requyer. For yf we should appere, yt were contrary to our lybertes, and yf we no not appere we shall . . . . in contempte. Wherfore your councelles and ayde herin, together with your severall answers we requyre to be sent by this bearer."

1574, June 8.—The Mayor and Jurats of Winchelsea to the Mayor and Jurats of Rye.

"We have receaved and perused your lettres of the 7th of June. And as the matter seameth strange to you so doth it to us. And whereas you wryte for our councell herin, surely we thincke that it shalbe best to be well advysed howe you do apeare, and whereto; and that you have good councell and lerned herein least the same shold torne to the infringing of our liberties; and for that we are fullye resolved that you will deale circumspectly herein as it is nedefull, we for our partes will not only be ayding to you wherein we may, but also be contrybutory to suche charges as you shall chaunce to expende in the defence of our liberties according to charter and our auncyent customs."

1574, June 15.—Roger Manwood to the Mayor of Rye.

"In that for the matter betwene your neighbours Mercer of Ry and Tench of Sandwich by my medyation endid, I ment that eche prysoner (being at equall pryces for raunsome) shold by eche party be sett at liberty. And nowe fynding that there is much difference betwene the charges of the one and the charges of the other, I have therefore thought good thus farr to explaine myne order that I will see the true and reasonable proportion of the charges of your Ry prisoner and the like of the Sandwich prysoner, and then to make such an equall dyvident as in reason and equity shall be mete and consonant to my true intent and meaning."

1574, June 18. Paris.—Letter from "Valentine Dale, Doctor of Lawe and Ambassador resident for the Queenes Majestie with the Frenche Kinge" addressed "to all Maiors, Sheriffs, Baylifes, Constables and all other the Quenes Majesties Officers" granting a safe conduct to "Francesco Giuliano, Francini Florentine and Imperia his wyfe, Thomas de Nicolao Florentine, Vincentio Siciliano, Francesco Brandini, Giacomo Gatamomole (?) and his wyfe, Barnardino Cherubini of Cremona, Donato da Lece Marcantonia of Ancona and Golpino da Talliccio and his servaunt with their pistolles and haquebuses to the nomber of 9" in order that they may repair to the Court about their private affairs.

1574, June 19.—Safe conduct granted by Henry Gaymer, deputy to John Donning, Mayor of Rye, for William Machon, owner of the bark *Lesperance* with 20 mariners and 20 passengers to pass from Rye to Rochelle to land her passengers and return to Rye.

1574, June 29.—Certificate by Henry Gaymer, deputy of John Donninge Mayor of Rye, that on the above date "there came before him John Shoven, of Diepe marriner, master of a ship called the *Will of God* of Diep of the burden of 60 tons or thereaboutes, and stated on oath that on the 6th of May last he sailed from St Lucas in Spaine freightid with oyles and olives belonging to Robert Colman of Amyas in Fraunce, and Oliver Fisher, citizen and ironmonger of

RYE MSS.

London; and that on the 6th of June, nere St. Vallereis upon the coast of France" he was taken "by a French barke called the *Bonaventure*, whereof one John Mesenguet was master, and of which barke Nicholas Degraung and Robert Comissary are owners. Which said ship of the said John Shovan and the said goodes and merchandize so by the said John Mesenguet and his company taken, were by them brought nere to the town of Ry aforesaid where the said shipe with the said goodes and merchandize laie at an anker in the sea by the space of 6 daies gretlie to the spoile of the said merchandize. And further the said John Shovan saith that in the tyme of their lieng at anker as aforesaid, by a composition and agreement by hym made, in the name of the said Robert Colman with the said John Mesenguet, the said shipe, goodes and merchandize, was released and were brought into the harbour of Ry, where not only the said ship, but also the goodes and merchandize as aforesaid in the same, had been without great help cast awaie." *Draft.*

1574, July 8.—Depositions concerning a dispute as to the payment by Thomas Grene for certain barrells of herrings taken by some "free-butters" of Rye from a "droger."

1574, July 17.—At the "Redd Lyon" in Rye. Memorandum of agreement touching "the controversie betwene the hundred of Gestlynge and Gostrore concernynge the watche at Farelyght beacones in the said hundred of Gestlynge, by the frendlye medyation of Master Sheperde, and soe thus yt was agreed, *videlicet;* that the said hundred of Gostrowe shall, from St. Jeames Day nexte, alwayes, towardes the watche of the said beacones, whensoever eny watche there shalbe commaunded and kept, yeld and paye to the hundred of Gestlynge every third night 10*d.* and so after that rate duringe all and singuler tymes of watchinge there. For the testymonye of the which agreement the seales of eche hundred interchangeably shalbe fixed unto a wryttynge indented thereof to be made before Mychelmas next comynge. Provyded alwayes, that the payment of the said 10*d.* every third nyght and so after the same rate, shall cease and be voide whensoever any severall and distinct beacones and beacon watche or beacone watches shalbe commanded by warrant from the Lord Levetenant, Hight Commissioners or Justices of Peace of the said shire, commanded to be kept within eche and every of the said hundreds. Provyded also, that the said hundred of Gestlyng shall not require nor have any further contribution or ayde towardes the said watchinge at the said beacones at Farelyght out of the said hundred of Gostrowe, notwithstandinge that any tyme hereafter there shalbe watchinge at the see syde or at any other place within the said hundred of Gestlynge."

1574, July 28.—Depositions of George Sandon that "about St. James was twelvemonth" the deponent being taken a prisoner at Dieppe, at which time there were some Englishmen put into the dungeon there and being desirous to know who those prisoners were, and the cause of their straight imprisonment, he requested the keeper that he might go and see them or else they might be brought up to him; the keeper at length consented if the deponent would pay his "foye" according to the custom of the said prison, to which he agreed, and so the three prisoners were brought to this deponent and they all made merry at dinner in the said prison, and the said three prisoners said in the presence of William Verrall of Rye also a prisoner that one Greane of Winchelsea bought five barrells of herrings out of a pirate for which herrings they were now put in prison, and the said Verrall requested him to take note of their words.

1574, August 22.—Safe conduct to Nicholas de Graunge, owner of the bark *Lesperance*, whereof Cautin Parrys is master together with Nicholas Gollet, John Busher, Michael Raymes, Ezechiell Emery, John Vincent, Arkus Bawdwyn and Anthony Churling, mariners in the said bark, all of the French church within the town of Rye, to sail to Daniske [Dantzic] and Kingsbury [Konigsberg] in casual trade of merchandise and return to Rye.

1574, September 13.—Depositions of John Torsey and Nicholas Chantereau, merchants, taken before William Davy, Mayor of Rye and others. They say that "wheras Robin de Gardeine of St. Valeries was indebted to Monsieur Richard Merret in the some of 50*li.* sterling or theraboutes and was in the custody of the said Torsey and not to departe from his company, yt happenid on a tyme that he was absent an houre and a half, wheruppon the said Torsey misleiked of him that he wold departe. And the said Torsey came to the said Merret and gave hym warnyng of the said Robin de Gardin to loke unto hym. Wheruppon the said Merret was mynded to put the said de Gardin in prison, wheruppon Jacques de Vymew de Abvile entreated the said Merret that he wold not put the said Robin Degardin in prison and he wold be bound for hym both his body, his shipe and goodes that the said Robin de Gardin shuld not goe awaie; but if he did go awaie he wold answere for hym by his body, shipe and goodes. Hereuppon the said Merrett did permitt the said de Gardin to goe at large."

1574, October 6.—The Mayor of Rye [to the Lord Warden]. As to actions in a court for strangers, between Richard Mere and Jaques de Vimew; and between Jaques Beliart and Jaques Vimew. [A certificate in the same suits, in which the parties are described as of the French Church.] *Draft.*

1574, October 20.—The Bailiffs and Burgesses of Great Yarmouth to the Mayors, Bailiffs, Jurats and Commonalty of the Towns and Ports of Hastings, Winchelsea, Rye, Romney, Hithe, Dover and Sandwich.

"And where ther hath bene both of long tyme and of late certain controversies and unquiet questions betwene your combarons and baylifes, deputed for you on the one parte, and us and our predecessors, governors of this towne of the other parte, for and concerning our and your jurisdiction and aucthoritye here in Great Yermouth duringe the tyme of the fre faier; and although (God be thanked) there hath not of late growne any great unquietnes hereof, yet to the intent that the Quens Majesties service on both our partes in this behalfe maie be the better performed, and that this litle sparke of unquietnes betwene us maie be utterly extinguyshid and quenched and that firme and unfayned amytie maie be in place hereof established and confirmid amongest us, we the Baylifes of this towne for the tyme being with the consent of our brethren and assistance therein doth both and instantlie and hartelie beseche your Worship that at the nexte Easter terme it wold like you, by your absolute and irrevocable commission, to geve aucthority to such persones as you shall pleas, and we for our parte will make the like commission, that both our commissioners, then metinge maie either emongest themselves or els by indifferent namynge of compotent arbitrators then make a resolute discussing and ende of all controversies and questions betwene your jurisdiction and ours towching the said free faier."

1574, October.—Correspondence between the Mayor and Jurats of Rye and William Crispe, Lieutenant of Dover Castle, and others as to the enforcement of the orders set out by royal proclamation against the transportation of horses, mares or geldings.

1574, November 24.—The Mayor and Jurats of Rye [to the Lord Warden].

"May it pleas your good Lordship to be advertised that not only we but also the contry rounde aboute us is in great want of salt, and, except some foresight be therein had, in tyme it will be farre worse. And for that divers tymes vessels of salt is brought to the Nesse and thereaboutes which we dare not meddle with by reason of the late commandment to the contrary, and from tyme to tyme is bargayned for and had to other places; we thought good not only to signifie the same unto your Honor but therewithall to desire your Lordship's favor that when any such thinge shall happen to come that bargayninge for the same and entringe to paye her Majesty's custome, if eny complaint shall happen to be made to your Lordship therof you will stand our frend therin." *Draft.*

[1573–1574. The Mayor of Rye to ——.]—Relative to obligations by which the town's combaron Daniel Mynge is bound to M. Pottell and Madam Helayne, both of Dieppe. Refers to Mynge's wife, Anne Rybaulte, and to payments made by the said Mynge to one M. Duboys, surety for Pottell and Helayne, of, amongst other sums, "a rose noble," and "a Frenche croune."

[1573–1574.]—Proclamation concerning disorderly conduct within the town of Rye.

"That where certaine lewd and malicious persons, voyde of all feare of God, only sporting and delighting themselves in ungraciousnes, have practised of late within this towne, not only by knocking at mennes dores under pretence to speak with them to beraye with filthe and oeduer suche as come unto the dore, but alsoe accustome to affixe upon diverse men's dores certeine infamous libells and skrolls containing dishonest reproche of the persons upon whose dores they are affixed, to the great offence of Almightie God and to the great disturbance and disquietnes of the quiet state and peace of this towne; Mr. Maior therfore and his brethern having a carefull regard to avoyd cause of suche ill sequels as might enssue without reformation of the premisses, doo therefore straightlie charge and command in hir Majesties name all manner of persons whatsoever inhabiting within this towne or otherwise, to abstain henceforth from such lewde malicious and ungracious disorder upon paine that every freeman duelie condemned of the same to be disfraunchised for ever of the liberties of the said towne, without hope of the recoverie of the same, and every one not being free to be streightlie and severelie punished to the exxample of others according to the discrecion of Mr. Maior and his brethern." *Draft.*

[1574.] — Declaration by Pierre Rogers stating that "wheras Nicholas Russell, Capitaine of a shipe called *Lesperance*, aucthorised under the County Mongomery, to make warre for the cause of religion, aboute the 22nd daye of Maye laste paste did release unto the foresaid Peire Rogers, a barke of Newhaven in Fraunce called the *Nicholas* laden with 12 last 8 barrels and a half of codefishe, which he the foresaid Captaine had taken uppon the seies and compounded with the said Peire Rogers for the releacement of the same, Know ye that I, the said Peire Rogers, for divers considerations me movinge have bargayned and sold and by theis presents do fully and clerly bargaine sell and releace unto William Didsbury of the auncient towne of Ry, marchant, the foresaid barke with hir furniture, taccle and apparrell whatsoever to the same barke apperteyninge, frely and clerly, in consideration of the price of the fish together with the foresaid 12 last 8 barrels and a halfe of coddfishe at the price of twenty and sevin shillinges lawfull mony of England for every barrell for the which I acknowledge myself fully satysfyed, contented and paid by theis presents. To have and to hold all the aforesaid barke, taccle, apparrell and furniture together with the foresaid 12 last 8 barrels and a half of codefishe to the said William Didsbury, his executors and assigns, to the proper use and behoof of the same William Didsbury, his executors and assignes for ever."

[1574.]—Certificate by Henry Gaymer, Deputy of John Donning, Mayor of Rye, that "about the 30th daie of Maie last past before the the date hereof" Michell Maignen and John Constantin, fishermen, "masters of two severall botes of Pollett in Fraunce using the trade of fishinge" were taken prisoners by John Sinaii of Rochell "captaine of a barke aperteyninge to the said towne;" Nicholas Lameshin in Constantin's boat was taken "as pledge and prisoner for all the hole company of the said two botes" until 60 crownes were paid to the said John Sinaii for the ransome of Lameshin and the "residewe of the company of the said two botes."

The certificate goes on to say that the said Michell Maignen had come to Rye "to inquire out the said John Sinaii for to paye him the said 60 crownes for the raunsome of the said two botes company and redemying home the said Nicholas Lameshin" but that he could find neither Sinaii nor Lameshin; and so, "being redy to paie the said 60 crownes for raunsome as aforesaid to the said John Sinaii," required this certificate. *Draft.*

[1574.]—Letter of the Mayor and Jurats of Rye praying the Queen's Commissioner in the county of Sussex to permit Thomas Harmon and Anthony Toppey (?) "two of our honest neighbours" to transport corn from Chichester to Rye.

[1574.—The Mayor and Jurates of Rye] to Sir Thomas Palmer, Sir Thomas Guildford, Sir Thomas Sharley, Mr. Hoyning and Doctor Wurley.

"There are in our towne with us inhabitinge a great nomber of pooer people of the French church, as is not all togethers to your worships unknowne. So it is right worshipful that one Haunce Haunson, of the same towne, merchaunt, an honest neighbour and one of the said French church, hath bought of Simone Skypper, Maior of Arundell, the nomber of 100 quarters of wheat, onelie for the provision of the pooer French people, which will not onlie be a comfort unto them but also a great comodyty unto us. Theis are therefore to pray you to permitt the said Haunce Haunson to transport the same 100 quarters of wheat from Arundell aforesaid unto the said town of Ry, being for provision as abovesaid, under such orders as your Worships have taken and appointed and as to you shall seme good; wherein ye shall not only pleasure the said pooer French people of the same towne, who shall be bound daylie to pray for your Worshippes, for whome in this case he hath onlie traveled but also we for our parts beholding to you for your curteyies as knowith the Almighty." *Draft.*

[1574.]—Same to same.

"Whereas there is one letter written unto you in the recommendation of Hawcce Haunson to make provisyon of 100 quarters of wheate for the French churche, theis are in most humble wise to desier you Worshippes nott to suffer the said Hawnce Hawnson to make suche provision for that we are, since the writinge thereof, crediblie enformed the said Hawnce to be a subtle and lose man and suche a one as hath byn a conveyor of corne, although his friends have made great recommendation of his dealinge in honestye, as wold have simply used himself in that trust committed unto him for the provision of the pooer French churche. We, moved in pyttye for their releafe, supposed him mete for their supply, did make bold to recommend hym to your Worships for that provision, but now knowing him to be a conveyor directlye againste honestye and truthe, disallow him as one not worthy of that trust." *Draft.*

[1574.]—Safe conduct for Robert Comyssary of Rye, mariner, in the *Bonaventure*, "having aborde hym the nombre of forty persons being all of the Religion" to sail from Rye aforesaid "unto the Isle of Capdevert and from thence to Serlion uppon the Coast of Gynney about their lawfull and honest affaires, traficque and busynes to be done" and then return to Rye. *Draft.*

[1574.—The Mayor of Rye to the Lord Warden.]

"In the moneth of January last past the bearers hereof Jacques Nealle and Vincent . . . ., merchants resident within the towne of Ry, and of the French church, had certen goodes and merchandize laden at Diep in France in a vessel of Diep, whereof one Nicholas Verron, marryner, was master, to be transported from the said town of Diep unto Ry, which goods were uppon the sea nere unto Hasting, taken awaie by certen Englishmen to the utter undoeing of the said poer men; and understanding by them that your Worship hathe made staie of those goodes, theis are therefore, on the behalf of the pooer men, in justice to beseche you to stand theire good frend in ayding them to have their goods again, paieing such dueties and charges as aperteyneth, wherin the pooer men and their famyle shall not only be bound to pray for you but also we for our partes redy to pleasur you in eny thing we maie as knowith the Almighty."

1574[-5], January 20.—Certificate by the Mayor of Rye upon the depositions of Guillaume Disbery, merchant, Rephe Serlle, his servant, Gilles Henrison, Corneille Soyer, and Vincent Lailler, residing in Rye, as to a claim by the said Disbery for supplying board and lodging to "Mr Jacques le Breton appelle Mons. le Seneschal" who, with his wife and children, lodged in the house of the said Disbery from 15 November 1572 till January 1573 and then left for London. *French.*

1574[-5], February 26. London.—William, Lord Cobham, and William Lovelace to the Mayors, Bailiffs and Jurats of the Five Ports and two ancient towns and their members.

"Whereas many and divers metinges have ben betwene your Commissioners of the Ports and the City of London for matters of withernam and in the ende growne towardes some likelihood of agrement. And for that it is a matter of great waight and requirith good foresight, it is thought mete that a gestlinge be holden at Dovour the Wednesdaie in Easter weeke nexte, against which tyme ye are to seke out in every place of your Portes and members, what recordes ye have to defend and countervaill suche matter as the Cittie hath shewid for their sending of proces unto you."

Postscript.—" Ye shall do well also to bring with you at that tyme all such proces and wrytynges concerninge withernam beyond the seas and especially to the Lowe Countries." *Copy.*

1574[-5], February 28.—Order by the Mayor and Jurats of Rye that all such persons called passengers with their barques and crayres within the town of Rye, between the said town and Dieppe in France, shall orderly take their turns without encroaching one upon the other and each one shall stay until his turn comes.

1574[-5], February 28.—Order by the Mayor and Jurats that the Chancel on the south side of the church shall be closed up and planked for laying in of the town's ordnance and munition, and that a hole shall be made through the stone wall of the church out of the chancel into churchyard, at the charge of the Town.

1574[-5], March 2.—From " my house in London." Lord Cobham to [the Mayor and Jurats of Rye].

" Complainte comes daylie to her Majesties Councell of daily spoilles committed on the seas by sondry pyratts uppon our coast . . . . . . And where at this tyme it is thought that sondry pyrattes be now uppon the coast I praie you learn what they be and what spoiles hath ben latelie comitted by them." *Copy.*

1574[-5], March 10.—The Mayor and Jurats of Dover to the Mayors, Bailiffs and Jurats of Hastings, Winchelsea, Rye, Romney, Hythe and Sandwich.

Summoning them to a special gestling, assembly or meeting to be held at Dover, on the sixth of April, to deliberate upon divers urgent and weighty causes touching the Liberties of all the Ports. The summoning to such gestling by custom pertaining to the Mayor and Jurats of Dover *Copy.*

1574[-5], March 10.—Certificate by William Davy, Mayor of Rye, that certain fine yarn was spun by Vincent Gloria and Jane, his wife, and their servants, French people who had inhabited the town of Rye for the space of one year.

1574[-5], March 17.—The Mayor and Jurats of Rye to William Crispe, Lieutenant of Dover Castle.

" Accordinge to the transcripte of our Lord Warden's letter annexed to a letter of attendance concerninge frebutters, we have made dilligent inquirie towchinge the same and cannot fynde eny thinge to be advertised, other then on Monday last there were at the sea fure or fyve miles from Ry about fyve or six vessels of the frebutters but what spoiles hath ben by them lately committed we know not, for within our towne or liberties none of them come nether any are there that deale with them." *Draft.*

1574[-5], March 18.—The Mayor and Jurats of Rye to the Lord Bishop of Chichester.

" Wheras the ordnaunce and munition perteyning to our towne and wherwith frome her Majestie we are chargid, is from tyme to tyme to great charge unto us in repayring the carriage and necessaries therto belonginge, by reason of want of a necessary storehouse nere unto the place where the same is to be occupied, for the better saefgarde therof, the buildinge wold be so burdenus unto us, consideryngе the infinite charge we are at in waterworks and suche lecke as our abilitie not able to reach therunto. Therfore by consent of our commons at a generall assemblie for that purpose, we have thought a certain ile on the south parte of the chancell of our churche, which servith to small purpose otherwise, fytt and necessary to that use, beinge decently closid in frome open seight. And for that we wold not attempte eny suche matter before we had made your Lordship privie therunto, for that your consent is therin to be hadd, we thought good to advertise your Honour of the premises besechinge your good Lordship to graunte us your good will herein, myndinge so to use the same as shall be well thought of in all respectes for the better furtheringe of hir Majesties service as occasion shalbe." *Draft.*

1574[-5], March.—Correspondence, articles and depositions concerning a dispute between the Mayor and Jurats of Rye and the Company of Fishmongers of London as to the supply of fish for London by the fishermen of Rye.

[1575, March.]—"Wheras sondry good lawes are ordaynid for the abstinence frome fleshe, aswell uppon the accustomed fish daies as in the tyme of Lent, the which, thorough libertie, are smally observid within this town to the evill example of all persons thether resortinge especially beinge a fysher towne. And to the end that the inhabitants within the said towne shuld not bo ignorant howe severely thoes lawes are pretendid to be put in execution, nether that eny excuse of ignorance shall prevaille, Mr. Maior and his brethern the jurates do gove warning herby unto all inholders, victulers and other inhabitantes, within the said towne and liberties of the same, that they make no provision of fleshe or other such victuall prohibited against the tyme of Lent or for other accustomed fyshe daies, or suffer eny to be spent in their houses contrary unto the lawes ordaynid for the same (excepte suche persons as by thoes lawes are to be permitted) having licence of Mr. Maior and the minister of the churche. Assuringe all persons that shall be knowen to offend herein that the lawe shalbe put in execution for the same without favor."

1575, April 21.—Certificate by the Mayor and Jurats of Rye to the Mayor and Aldermen of the City of Bristol.

"That forasmuche as we are creadably informid that certaine persons of the Frenche, one namid Thomas Benarde, another Michell Russell and the third Nicholas du Cheyne who about the sixt of this instant came into the Roade of Bristowe in a certain shipe laden with brasell from Rochell, and at this instant staied in the said citie of Bristowe as persons of mislyvinge, usinge spoile and roberies on the seies; and for that it is requested of us to testifie the truth of our knowledges towchinge thoes persons, their lyvinge and demeanor, we cannot but for charitie sake testifie the truthe in suche cases beinge a parte of true Christianitie. And therfore theis are to signifie unto you for undoubtid trothe that the sayd thre persons have ben here abyding in the town of Ry by the space of theis thre yeres, fled frome their contrey with their wyves and children for their saftie, and during all this tyme hetherto have used and behaved themselves very honestly and towardes the sustentation of themselves their wyves, children and family have followed the trade of marchandize as tyme hath required, without committing any spoile, robbery or pyracy on the seies so farr as we could ever learn or understand. Nether hath eny complaine of the ill dealinge of them or any of them come unto us at any time. And as towchinge the said Thomas Benarde, marchant of the said brasell, and

Michill Russell owner of the said shipe, their two wyves and household at this instant is abydinge in Rye aforesaid; and Nicholas du Cheyne abyding with his father here in Ry, a very honest old man. Wherfore we pray you to extend your lawfull favors towardes them that they be not farther trobled, molested or staied." (*Draft.*)

1575, April 27.—Letters of consent by the Mayors and Jurats of the Cinque Ports to the nomination of Mr. Justice Manwod and Mr. Serjeant Lovelace to be of the quorum in a general commission appointed to debate certain controversies of withernam, between the City of London and the Cinque Ports.

1575, May 20.—Articles of Agreement between the City of London and the Ports.

It is agreed that Mr. Serjeant Lovelace and Mr. Recorder proceed to end the matter of private "doleances" of citizens by arbitrament, such as by Letters missive out of any of the Five Ports, which causes to be by them ended before the first day of Michaelmas term; and if they cannot agree by that term then the parties are to abide the order of the Lord Chief Justice, the same order to be made before the last day of Michaelmas term. The corporations of the Ports, from whence such processes shall come, shall before the last day of August, be bound to George Eaton, Chamberlain of the City of London, to stand to the said arbitrament and umpirage.

As to the residue of the matters of strife between the City of London and the Ports for their liberties and customs, further conference is to be had by persons commissioned to compound the same matters, before the fourth of November. *Draft.*

[Bond, in accordance with the above terms, dated 26 August 1575.]

1575, May.—Depositions of Guillaume Roussel and Alexandre Constance, that being in a barque of Rochelle with one Michel le Clerc, they were boarded by pirates and in the fray the said Michael was killed. Depositions made at the request of Michel Regnoult(?), brother-in-law (*frere en loy*) of Catheryne, widow of Michel le Clerc. *French.*

Similar depositions dated 2 June, 1575 by Robert Commissere, Pierre Janderme, John Mesenget and Louis Darque.

[1575], June 8.—From Cobham. Lord Cobham to the Mayors, Bailiffs and Jurats of the Five Ports.

"I send you here inclosed the copie of the Quene's Majestie's lettres directed unto me towcheng the exspellinge of certen persons out of this realme, whom the King of Spaine hathe by his lettres unto her Highnes signified to be rebells unto hym. And like as I am by her Majesty commaundid to see the contentes thereof duly executed within the jurisdiction of the Fyve Portes, so do I require you, and in her Majestie's name, straightlie charge and command you and every of you, that you have unto the same suche care and regarde as is by her Highness required." *Copy.*

Enclosure.—Letter from Queen Elizabeth to Lord Cobham, Lord Warden of the Cinque Ports dated St. James', 16 April, 1575.

"Whereas our very good brother, frynd and alley, the Kynge Catholique of Spayne hath at our request, accordinge to the treatyes of the auncient amytie now of very longe tyme made and contayned, betwixt his noble ancestors and ours, banished out of the Lowe Contries suche notorious rebels and traytors as we by our letters have namid, requiringe the leike and reciproke shew of amitie on our parte againste his rebels, of the which the said Kinge hath namid to us by his letters, bearinge date the 25th of November last past, which came not to our handes but in this moneth of Aprill, as the Prince of Orange the principall, and as ayders, helpers and abettors of the conspiration against the said Kinge, the Earles of Coulemberge, Vandenberges, the Lordes of Lunoy, Esquerdes, Lombres, Bernaud de Merode, Lorde of Rumes, Philipp de Marnix, Lorde of St. Aldegonde, Charles Boisot, Doctor Junina, Arnold Vandendrop, Lorde of Mansarte, the Lorde of Haultain, Vandenleple, of Lovain, of Blioul, of Breda, the Lord of Neufville, Anthoney de Lannoy, Lorde of Baylbouel, Lorde of Noyelles, Mr. Reyndr of Eudrscryn, Pietre Wasteel, Philipp Vanderta, John Rubens, Philipp Doublei, Adolphe Vanderta, Floris Botselldre, Philipp de Renes, Christopher de Iselsteyne, Anthony de Broukhorst, John de Holtzwille, Claude Goetgebuer, Jacques of Windgarder de Hugo, Gwillauma de Erelon Matteuessey, William of Nivelt, Thomas Rollema, Doctor Heluncke, Spitloff of Swollis; by whos menes, as the said Kinge hathe advertised us, divers townes bothe in Holland, Zelonde and Gerderlande are revoltid frome the obedience of the said Kinge. Wherefore the said Kinge doth require of us that all theis rebells and all that do adhere unto them shoulde be put forthe of our realme and that neither theye nor none of their shippes, goodes or marchaundize shoulde be admitted into our realme or any traffiquie to be had with them. For the first parte of our said brothers' request to our knowledge, nor cannot understand that any one of the persons so to us namid are within any part of our realme at this present; but yf any be or shalbe founde hereafter to remaine in any parte of your jurisdiction, we straightlye charge and command you to cause them immediatly to avoyde our realme uppon their uttermost perill. And though you shall not understand of any them (*sic*) to be presently within your jurisdiction, yet shall you geve straight charge and commandment in our name to all officers in our Fyve Portes that none of them be hereafter sufferid, either to come into any the said Portes at any tyme or to have any ayde succor or releiff of men, armor or victuall out of any part of your jurisdictions. And that our subjectes have no traffique with them, untill such tyme as they be reducid to the obedience of theire naturall Lorde and Prince. And this fayle you not to do as you tender our pleasure." *Copy.*

1575, June 17.—The Mayor and Jurats of Rye to Lord Cobham, Lord Warden of the Five Ports, etc.

"And wheras heretofore your Lordship wrote your lettres to us for the French to avoide the towne by midsomer next, we accordingly gave notice to the Elders of their church and at this instant have put them in mynde thereof, who answerith that they know not what to say therin, and home they are loth to go. And for that the tyme draweth ny, we thought good to send our towneclerke to your Lordship with a booke deliverid us from those seid Elders, conteyninge the whole nomber of them nowe in the towne and to understand your Lordships further pleasure therein. And though we could very well spare them, yet what your Honor shall thinke well of concerninge their departure or abode we shall for our partes leike well of also." *Draft.*

1575, June 18.—Certificate by the Mayors, Bailiffs, Jurats and Commonalty of Hastings, Winchelsea, Rye and Tenterden that they consent to the appointment of William Lovelace, Esquire, Serjeant at law, Robert Carpenter of Rye, Jurat, Stephen Dowle, Common Clerk of the said town of Hastings and William Appleton Common Clerk of the town of Rye to deal between the said towns and the City of London concerning the matter of withernam.

1575, June 25.—Certificate by the Mayor and Jurats of Rye that "the 22nd daie of June last past arryvid in the harbour of Rye aforesaid a boat of Weymouth called the *Marling*, wherof Robert White of Weymouth aforesaid is master, with the nomber of four thousand biskettes of Michell Russell's of Ry aforesaid, Frenchman, is now mindid with his said boat and marriners togethers with 30 persons of the Frenche to make his repaire frome Ry aforesaid to Weymouth aforesaid. Which said persons of the French are marriners aperteyning to a shipe of Nicholas Russell of Ry aforesaid, Frenchman, being at Waymouth aforesaid. Theis are to desire you to permit and suffer quietlie the said Robert Whit with his said marriners and passengers to passe by you to Waymouth aforesaid, without any your lettes or hindraunces using them honestly as they ought to do, and so as they offend not in any of our Quenes Majesties lawes."

1575, July 6.—Safe conduct from the Mayor and Jurats of Rye to Michael Russell, mariner, master and owner of a ship called *Lesperaunce*, together with forty mariners, all being of the French Church, to sail from Ry to "thizles of Surreis" [Azores ?] in lawful trade of merchandise.

1575, July 30.—Memorandum signed by R. Bakere that "one John of Rye dwelling at Newenden, Thomas Rofe of Rye and Thomas Wood of Rye, Robert Collyer of Tenterden and Roger Morris dwelling in Sussex upon Thursday was sennight, being the 21th daye of this moneth, assembled themselves together, as I am enformed, in the Parishe of Stone in the Ile of Oxney, and there the said John of Rye was named by the others to be their Capitayne, and the said Thomas Rofe his Sargent, and the others to be his soldyers and the said John of Rye requyred dyvers of the inhabitants within the said Ile to be sworne to hym to be his soldiers and suche as refused to doo, he abused with threatninge woordes and otherwise."

1575, August 16.—[The Mayor and Jurats of Rye] to Lord Cobham.

"Wheras in April last we wryt our lettres unto your Honor on the behalf of John Engram and John Convas, thereby requestinge your favorable letters unto Monsr de la Mailleray, Vice-Admirall at Kilbeff, desyringe his ayde for restitution of a boate and hir furniture, to the value of 24*l*., pertayninge to the said Engram, stollen out of our creke and there sold; and also for 5*l*. 10*s*. due unto the said Convers so as we should have no cause to make staye of any of those parties till restitution were made accordingly. Wheruppon your Honor (we thanke you) did directe your letters to the said Vice-Admirall to that effecte but as we understand, nothinge donne in the cause. And nowe there is one of that partes (and as we thinke) of Kilbeff itself which by force of wether is come into the Camber and dryven upe to a place called Wayneweye. Wherfore we beseche your Honor in the behalf of our said poore neighbours, to direct your Lordshipps letters unto your servant Ratliff therby willinge him, by vertue of your Honors office of

Admiraltie, to make staye of him and his boate for that he is within your Lordships jurisdiction of Admiralte, uppon which staie he maye be suter unto your Lordship for the end of the cause betwene our neighbors and him as unto your Honor shall seme good. And as towchinge your letters sent to the Bayliff of Deipe, on the parte of the said Convers againste Nicholas Jorden, the messenger saith he did deliver the same to the Bayliff, but at his comynge awaye the Bailly was not in place to answer him, but Jorden said he had your Lordships letters and answer should be made the next passage, which yet is not done though the passage longe sithens come." *Draft.*

1575, August 17.—The Mayor and Jurats of Rye to Mons. Sygrine, Captain of Dieppe.

"Wheras one Malherbe of Deipe sent over to Ry this berrer John Burten for recovery of his shallope which was staied at the Nesse, we with our letters to our Lorde Warden aydid him in sort, as his Honor was content the said John Burten should have the shallope agaire. Sithens which tyme a new staie was made of hir by reason of a notable pyracie she had done on certaine fishermen of Brighelmeston in mackerell season last, takinge away their mackerels, throwinge their men overborde, robbing them of their monye, hanginge them upe at the yarde and cuttinge of some of their eares, a matter very lamentable and not sufferable. Nevertheless for that we were given to understand the said piracy was committed before the said Malherbe had to deale with the said shallope, we were (of goodwill which we have unto your towne) content to wryte againe to our Lord Warden for releacement of the said shallope, which his Honor grantid also and is deliverid to the said Burten this beirer. It may please you to be advertised that notwithstanding our good willes and courtesy shewed to the said Malherbe in helpinge him againe to his shallope, he the said Malherbe very much misusith us in his speche sayinge that we are the maynteyners of theves, searovers and pirates and such ill persons, castinge it in our passengers tethe so as they cannot be in quiet for him, wherin we thinke ourselves very much misusid and trust that you will not suffer eny of your people so to abuse us for our good willes. And although the said John Burten wich the said Malherbe sent over for his shallope, hath ben sithens his commynge arovinge at the sea and tooke 30*s.* sterling of a French captaine to go arovinge for him and was arovinge till the Quenis shipes tooke him, and as Thomas Swynet and his company can shewe you sent him awaye, yet for that he is one of your towne we have not ponishid him but referrid the same to your discretion without eny such contumelious wordes as the said Malherbe usith against us." *Draft.*

[1575, August ?—The Lord Warden to the Lieutenant of Dover Castle.]

"Wheras of late the Maior, Jurates and Commonaltie of Ry at their general assemblie in Ry, did for the better government of that towne devise a certaine decre and order for a common councell of 24 of the auncient and discretest commoners to joyne with the Maior and Jurates in the publique affaires of the towne, a thing very godly and necessarye, commonly used in moost good cities and townes; which decre and order was exhibited unto me to be perusid and recordid in my office at Dovor Castle and which I deliverid to Robert Vincent, my clerke, to that ende, and my seale of office to be set thereunto for the better confirmation of the same. Sithens which time, as I am advertised, some evill disposed persons have impougnid the same decre and order with a greate abuse therin not tollerable. Wherfore theis are to will you to make out a commission from my said office to Mr. William Lovelace, Esquire, Sergeant at the lawe, yourself, my Lyvetenant, William Davy, Maior of Ry, Robert Sheperd and John Sharpe of Northiam, Esquires, and Richarde Fletcher, minister of the worde of God within the towne of Ry, to this effect—that yow six, fyve, foure or thre of yow shall have full power and aucthoritie as well to examyn the said decre and order of the Common Councell, howe mete and necessary the same is for the government of the said towne, as also by all waies and meaus to examyn suche persons as are vehemently suspectid for abusinge the same and the persons refusinge to be sworne, and to be examined to bynde over to appere before me at suche daies and tymes as to your wisdomes shall seme good; and of your doinges herein to advertise me." *Copy.*

1575, September 1.—Commission from the Lord Warden to the Mayor of Rye and others to examine witnesses upon certain interrogatories.—The interrogatories attached are as to the breaking of the windows of the chambers of George Syere, jurat, and Robert Daniel, on the 6th or 7th of January last past; as to sewing on twenty-four "knaves of cardes" upon an old piece of "linsey wolsey cloth"; as to the writing of certain words on the "backsyde of the Quene of Clobbes" fastened to the same cloth; as to the writing of the letters R D C P upon the knave of clubs, being the foremost card fastened to the same cloth; as to the interpretation of the said letters and as to who hung up the said cloth with those cards above the stairs at the Court hall.

1575, September 12.—Petition of the Bakers of Rye to the Mayor Jurats and Common Council of Rye.

"Whereas as well in auncient tyme as nowe of late daies, good and holsome lawes have bene by the state of this realme devised, ordeynid and enacted for the better maintenance of the subjectes of the same; emongest which said lawes yt is ordeynid how eche sort of people, being handycraftesmen or of occupation, shold use the trade and lyvinge wherein they have bene laufully traynid upe and servid for the same as the said lawes do apointe. Nevertheles it maye please your Worshipes, dyvers persons do seke unto themselves by sinister waies and contrary to those good lawes certaine trades to live by, and not only to lyve by but ynordinatlie to gaine, to the utter overthrow of their neighbours which have laufully used thoes occupations and servid for the same accordinge to the said lawes. Emongest which sort of people certaine of the brewers of this towne use the trade and occupation of bakers, not having bene apprentices to the same nor so lawfully servid in the same trade as they therby maie justlie challenge to use the said occupation of bakinge, to the utter ympoverishment of the bakers of the said towne, ther wyves, children and familye, and contrary to all lawe, equitye and good conscience; wherby we whos names are underwriten shall be constraynid to geve over, and for ourselves to seke some other meanes to live, and to leve our wyves and children, yf in tyme remedy be not by your Worshipes provided for the same." *Signed by* James Welles, John Mylles, Edward Turner, Phylep Candy and Wylyame Golde.

1575, September 20.—The Mayor and Jurats of Rye to the Bishop of Chichester.

"Wheras we havinge, under hir Highness, the government of this towne of Ry and endevoringe ourselves (as dutie byndeth) to the uttermost of our powers to bringe the people inhabitinge within the same to suche a civill and vertuous order of lyvinge as the worde of God dayly taught unto us doth require, do fynde that for want of ayde by your Lordship we cannot so thoroughly procede therin as willingly we wolde and as with all our hartes we dutifully do wish; for in divers crymes and offences not sufferable emongest the professors of Christian religion we dare not so farr deale as many tymes the present facte requireth, and when cause of correction is ministered, lest it shuld be laid to our charge we ponishe suche crymes as merely dothe apperteyne unto the spirituall jurisdiction, a matter often allegid, wherby vice escapith unponished. The courses wherin we want your Lordships ayde we leve unto the relation of this berer Mr. Fletcher, our precher and minister, which by him to your Lordship being declarid we humbly crave your Lordship's favor and consent, as by you and him shalbe thought mete and in sorte as we maye the more stronglier subdue vice and advaunce vertue, not cravinge anythinge that shall seme hinderfull to your Lordship's officers in thoes causes by diminishinge eny fees or duties, but rather to augment the same in doinge of justice." *Draft.*

1575, September 26. Chichester.—Richard [Curteys], Bishop of Chichester, to the Mayor and Jurats of Rye.

"Whereas in your letter which I receyved of Mr. Fletcher, minister of your towne of Ry, you made request unto me that the ecclesiasticall jurisdiction might be exercysed within your Porte of Rye. Mr. Fletcher, whom I have acquayntid with my mynd in that behalf, shall certyfye you of my whole resolution therein.

"I am also to desyre your fryndshypp and favor towardes your sayd mynyster Mr. Fletcher, whome nowe I have receyved to be Chapleyne, that you woulde setto your helpynge hande so to sett forwarde the matter as that he maye as well have the lyvynge and vycaridge as he have the troble and charge of your towne. And I will so joine with you as my furderance in no respect shalbe wantynge." *Signed.*

1575, October 6.—The Mayor and Jurats of Rye to Monsieur Sigoine.

"The boate of this berers husbande with such goodes as was in hir, late taken by men of warre at the seas was by our Lord Warden's meanes rescuid and by his Lordshipe, at our humble sute and request, to hir redeliverid, not doubtinge but that we shall fynde the leike courtesie at your handes in causes leike, though hetherto we have not so founde of them of Deipe, notwithstandinge the frendships we have shewed them and dayly do shew unto them; for not only we, divers and sondry tymes, but also our said Lorde Warden, have wrytten unto the Bayliff and other officers of Deipe in a cause dependinge betwene a poore neighbor of ours named John Convers and one of their towne named Nicholas Jorden and can have no redresse but answers howe they have cald him and examined him and can fynde no suche matter as we wryte for; they, more creditinge his deniall beinge in his owne defence then our ofte wrytinge of the truthe, beinge a thinge manifestly knowen unto us and so true as we cannot for justice sake but avouche the trothe therof and that the said Jorden dothe manifest wronge and injurye to the said Convers what culler soever he laye on the cause to hide the truth therof." *Draft.*

1575, October 8.—Depositions taken before William Davy, Mayor of Rye. Mathew Tarp of Haukhurst in the County of Kent says that about a month past being at Rye he delivered to the servant of Edward

Bryan glover and "ostler of the George," one clock to keep safely and re-deliver to the said Matthew which he hath not done.

1575, October 8.—Depositions taken before the Mayor of Rye concerning the payment of a sum of money borrowed by Nicholas Duailly from "Maistre Richart Mire, advocat en la court de parllement de Rouan, age de xl ans ou environ, resident en ceste ville de la Rie pour raison des troubles de France" for ransoming a merchant ship captured by a privateer of the Prince of Condé. Depositions by Vincent Dugart, merchant of Dieppe, aged 36, resident in Rye by reason of the troubles in France, Mathieu Chauvin of Dieppe, resident in Rye for the same reason, aged 60, and Gilles Lubiais, merchant of Dieppe, resident in Rye for the same reason, aged 45. *Signed. French.*

1575, October 10. Castle of Dover.—Sir William Broke, Lord Cobham, Lord Warden, Chancellor and Admiral of the Cinque Ports, to the Mayors, Bailiffs and Jurats of the said ports, towns and members.

"Wher as latly we have receyved lettres of advertysement from her Majestie that the Spanisshe Flete was seen in the cost of Devonsheire abowt the beginninge of this monethe of October; the generall of the which flete hath opteyned her Majestyes lycence for their sawffcondiuct in any her Majestyes harboroughes and roades. Whereuppon, one the behalf of her sayd Majestye and by vertewe and aucthoryte of our office aforesayd, wee commande and strictly charge you that yf the sayd flete shall com within her Maiestyes roades or harboroughes within your libertyes, that they be used in favourable sorte and that with all curtysye for so ys yt her Majestys pleasure. And furthermore we charge and command you and every of you that uppon the very fyrst discoverye of the sayd flete by any of your enhabitantes or by any of your selfes, uppon any of your coastes and townes, that you fourthwith with all hast and diligence doo advertise us therof so as wee may bee advertised from tyme to tyme howe they passe and lye at road." *Seal broken.*

1575, October 14.—Record of the attachment of the goods of John Baptista Barnasalia for a debt of thirty-five pounds owing to the Queen for custom.

[1575], October 16.—The Mayor and Jurats of Rye to the Bishop of Chichester.

"We have by the relation of our minister Mr. Fletcher understoode your Lordship's favour and goodwill towardes us concerninge the exercisinge of the ecclesiastical jurisdiction within our towne, for which we not only yelde your good Lordshippe most harty thankes, but have also under our common seal acknowlidgid the same to procede only frome your Lordship and not frome any right we challenge eny way And as touchinge our friendshipe towardes Mr. Fletcher concerninge the havinge of the vicaridge, what in us is to be donne he shall not want, so as we myght fyrst understande your Lordshipes pleasure which waye to begyn the matter for his furtherance, which we wolde wishe to be in suche sorte as none have cause of greiffe eny waye, and our helpe shall no waye want to our powers." *Draft.*

1575, October 16.—The Mayor and Jurats of Rye to Lord Cobham.

"Uppon the lamentable complaine of our poore neighbors the bakers, we did with good and longe deliberation consider of their cause and fyndinge that there decaye is suche as without spedy reformation they shall not have wherewith to mayntaine their wyves, children and family which are not fewe in nomber, a thinge in conscience to be lamentid, and we for remisenes in dutie to be gretly blamid. And sith the overthrow of theis poore men is happenid by reason of the brewers (who oughte by the lawes of this realme not to be bakers also) have by our sufferance (but the rather for that Robert Jacson is towardes your Lordship) used bothe to bake and brewe of longe tyme, wherby Robert Jacson (God be thankid) is growen to good welthe and the whole company of the bakers therby utterly impoverished. And fyndinge that by no reasonable perswasion frome us, nether with the lamentable complaine of the bakers, thoes brewers wold leve bakynge, we were dryven by justice and conscience to provide for their releiff the spedier. Wheruppon we did with consent of Maior, Jurates and Common Councell make a certaine decre, lawfull as we thinke for the better mayntenaunce of them their wyves, children and family, a matter in civill government worthy lokinge into when the state of a common weale is preferred before the pryvate gayne of a fewe, which decree we required Mr. Gaymer to acquaynte your Honor with, at his last beinge with you, who uppon his retorne advertysed us that your Lordship had the viewe thereof, and also of your Honor's well lykinge of the same, humbly besechinge your good Lordship's ayde and contynuance therin, wherof we have no doubte, being a matter that doth concerne (and that accordinge to the lawes of the realme) the releiff of those who are brought to the brinke of decay." *Draft.*

1575, October 20.—Marriage Settlement of John Paplin of Rye, fisherman, and Margaret Almon widow of William Almon, late of Rye, fisherman, deceased.

1575, October 26.—Dieppe.—Mons: Sigongnes to the Mayor of Rye.

Complaining that two fishing boats of Dieppe were boarded by a ship of war from Rye, the captain of which was one George Beuse and the crew partly French and partly Flemings. *French. Signed.*

1575, October 30.—The Court.—Lord Cobham to the Mayors, Bailiffs and Jurats of the Cinque Ports.

"Of late I receyved a lettre from Mr. Secretarie Walsingham whereby I understand that my very good Lord, the Lord Admirall, did to his great costes and charges sett to the seas two shipps, havinge in them very nighe 200 men, for the defence of the fishermen as well of the coasts of Norfolk and Suffolk as also the Portes; towardes which charges his Lordship thinketh that those which received benefitt therby shuld be contributors for the same. Theis are therefore to requier you and every of you to deale with the fishermen dwelling within the Portes in such sort that my Lord Admirall be so used by them towardes the defraying of his said charges by way of contribution (every man according to his rate)." *Copy.*

1575, October.—William, Lord Cobham to the Mayor and Jurats of Rye.

"Accordinge to your requests I ame right well contente thatt the boote of Deape be delyvered, and so to that ende I have taken order wythe Ratclyffe. Seinge the French (specyaeley those of Deape) fyndes us here so reddy to doo them justyce you shall do well by your letters to signeffey unto them thatt you loke for the like att there handes, wyche yf they doo nott perfforme it maye be occasion for us to stey in pleasuringe of them as we have donne." *Seal of arms.*

1575, November 3.—The Mayor, Jurats and Preacher of Rye to "the Reverend Father" and the rest of his colleagues Commissioners for causes ecclesiastical.

"May yt please you to understand that according to your lettres of the 7 of June last past we have caused all that be of yeres of discretion of the Frenche and other straungers abyding within our towne to cum before us and subscribe those articles which within your letters were inclosed. Among whome we found none that semed in any point to impung or dissent in judgment from any part of the same, but redely subscribed and signed them with ther owne handes and signes, as appereth by an instrument thereof herewith sent to your Honours." *Draft.*

1575, November 5.—The Mayor and Jurats of Rye to the Mayors and Jurats of Hythe, Dover and Sandwich.

"There is come unto us Mr. Barnes with letters from our Lord Warden, and demandith from our fishermen, 16*d.* for every share of their Yermouth voyage, towardes the charges the Lord Admirall hath bene at for his shipps, for wastinge this yere. And for that it semeth to us the same shippes were sett forth by his Honour at the sute of thoes of Norfolk and Suffolke and we, no warninge thereof eny waye and understandinge Mr. Barnes came alongest the coast from you, thought good to write theis our letters prayinge you to advertise us what you have don therin, and whether you have graunted to eny suche matter or not, or what ye meane to do about the same for that we wolde be lothe to graunt to enythinge that shuld in tyme to come be a president or hurtfull unto or against our people." *Draft.*

1575, November 24.—The Mayor, Jurats and Commonalty of Maidstone to the Mayor and Jurats of Rye.

"Whereas some discordes have lately happened betwen yowe of the towne and port of Rye and us of Maideston tochyng directly none of ower materiall rightes or titles but rather framed upon poynts of unkindness, that the same may therfor cease, ende and determyne and olde frendship and entrecourse betwene yowe and us spryng agayn and renue, to that intent we are mutually resolved that all causes of our contravercies shalbe herd decyded and finally ended by the indifferent consideration and judgement of Mr. Appleton, your town clerk, and Henry Fyssher, ower towne clerk, to be herd and debated at Maidston aforesaid before Hillarye terme next. And that in the meanetyme the inhabitantes of Maideston aforsaid withowt any impechement or vexation, by withername or otherwise, shall and may resorte unto your towne and port of Rye and elswher within the Fyve Portes and the liberties and members of the same, ther to merchandice and otherwise deale accordinge [to] ther accustomed manner, under your letters sealed with your common seale to be sent unto us imediatly testifieng and affirmyng the same. For whiche shewes of peace and concorde wee gyve unto God our hartie prayses and shall and will under His lovying kindnes bend owerselfes and wee hope so will you to suche intentes and purposes."

1575, December 5.—Order by the Mayor and Jurats of Rye, that the constables in every ward shall each night go through their wards to see lanthorne and candle hung out by such as are of ability to maintain the same; and the Mayor and Jurats in their several wards to see the same executed, and those that make default to send some one person of the house to ward there to remain until it be the pleasure of the Mayor to release him.

1575, December 10.—The Mayor and Jurats of Rye to Monsieur de Sigongnes.

"Long sithens we receyved your lettres requesting us to do what we might to gett at libertie certaine of Diepe staied by Captaine Banse at the seas the which to our powers we did accomplish havinge the said Banse his wiff here at Ry, we founde the meanes that she shuld send to hir husbande to releace his prysoners who saide she wolde, and therfore we wold gladly understand what became of them and whether they were releacid accordinglie or not." *Draft.*

[1574–1575.]—Lease of the office of the "Waterbayliweke" of the town of Rye by John Yonge to William Didsbury, for the term of four score years.

[1574–1575.]—Petition of John Hamond, carpenter, to the Mayor and Jurats of Rye for payment of his bill of thirteen pounds for a certain piece of work done in the church.

[1574–1575.]—A list of ships belonging to Rye with the names of their owners and masters.

[1574–1575.]—Certificate by the Mayor and Jurats of Rye that John Preston *alias* Dabredin, the younger, arrived at Rye from France on 28 August 1572 and has used the occupation of surgery and behaved himself very honestly.

[1574–1575.]—Indenture of apprenticeship by which William Appleton of Rye places his daughter, Anne Appleton, to serve eight years as maidservant to Thomas James of Pleyden. Usual clause as to supplying meat, drink and apparel. *Draft.*

[1575.]—William Davy, Mayor of Rye, and the Jurats of the same town to John Convers, serjeant at the virge within the town of Rye.

Commanding the said serjeant to take in withernam, of the goods and chattels of the commonalty of the City of London being to be found within the town of Rye or liberties of the same, the sum of 33*li.* 12*s.* 8*d.* for the damages of William Appleton, one of the combarons of Rye, which the said William had received by process of withernam, in the nature of an action of trespass, sent to the Lord Mayor and Aldermen of the City of London, against their resiant Eusebius Wodd, and to the said William adjudged in the Court of our Sovereign Lady the Queen held before the Mayor and Jurats of Rye. And if the said serjeant can find no goods nor chattels of the said commonalty of the City of London within the said town of Rye, that he take in withernam the body of some one of the said commonalty if he be to be found within the said town or liberties, and him safely in prison to keep, until such time as he shall have satisfied the said William of the said sum, according to the ancient usages and customs of the town of Rye in such cases provided. *Draft.*

[1575.]—Complaint addressed to the Lord Warden by Gabriel de Bures, Esquire, Roger Helboult, Jehan le Dentu, Perre Bourdinvill and Nicholas Ruault, merchants of Dieppe, that in February 1575 (French style) they sailed from Dieppe, and were boarded by French and English pirates, amongst whom was Robert Clement of Rye. *French.*

1575[–6], January 27.—Depositions of John Barrow of Rochell, mariner, of the age of 22 years, taken before William Davy, Mayor of

Rye. He says that "about the moneth of September last past, this deponent being at Newport in thizle of Wight where one Captain Charles de la Mason was also, which captaine bought a certen boate of the burden of 5 tonnes or thereaboutes, which boate the said Charles de la Mason did furnish forth of Newport aforesaid to warr against the Papistes their enemies, with victualles and other thinges necessary. Of which said boate one Lewes Lunell of Newhaven in Fraunce was captaine and master, and this deponent one of the company. With which said boate, furniture and victualles the said Captaine Lewes Lunell with his companye did take uppon the seas a certein boate of Kilbeif now at theis portes within the harbour of Rye aforesaid. Which donne the said Captaine Lewes with his company entered into this said boate in the harbour and sent awaie the boate apertaining to the said Captaine de la Mason unto Newport againe with three of his companye." *Signed.*

1576, January 31.—Power of Attorney by Adrienne Jourdain, widow of Jacques Cousture, the younger, living at Rye in consequence of the troubles in France, to Nicollas Jourdain her father and Guillielme Collent, lawyer, for the disposition of the property of the late Jacques Couster her husband, who died at sea, and which property comes to her by the custom of Normandy. *Signed. French.*

1575[-6], February 10.—Depositions taken before the Mayor and Jurats of Rye.

Nicholas Goullette of "Pollett" in France, mariner, master of a ship of Rochell, saith that "the said Charles and Birtot about 15 monethes past went a warfare together and did take iiij ships of Portingale laden with salt, wherof iij of them were caried to Rochell and the iiijth the said Charles was put in." He further deposes that the said Charles had eleven shares for himself and one for his boy every share amounting to five francs for which he should have for every share ten livres.

1575[-6], February.—Correspondence between the Mayor and Jurats of Maidstone and the Mayor and Jurats of Rye as to a question of withernam.

1575[-6], March 6.—From the Court, Lord Cobham [to the lieutenant of Dover Castle].

"The Quenes Majestie beinge lately informid by the greveous complaintes of sondry hir merchantes and good subjectes, of the great wronges, spoilles and losses that they have receyvid at the seies by them of the towne of Floshinge besides other insolences committed againste all suche generally as passe the narrowe seas, a matter in nowise convenient to be suffered within hir Highness owne stremes; hir Majesties plesure therfore is, that, uppon this notice gevin unto you by theis my lettres, you shall forthwith geve order throughout all the Fyve Portes to make staye of all suche shippes barkes and other vessels belonginge to any of them of the town of Floshinge where any of them shall aryve, and leikewise to put in saff kepinge all the captaines, masters and mariners and all goodes and marchandizes that shalbe founde in the saide shippes, untill uppon advertisement to be made unto me, by my order further direction shalbe gevin. It is meant that the arrest shall extende to all them of Zealand as to thoes of the partes of Floshinge; and what you shall do herin to advertise me with expedition. Lett the captains of the Downes have also knowledge

RYE MSS.

of theis lettres as well as all the Maiors and Bayllifes of the Cinque Portes." *Copy.*

1575[-6], March 24.—"From my house at the Tower hill." Lord Cobham to Mr. William Crispe, Lieutenant of Dover Castle.

"The Quenes Majestie being given to understand that dyvers captaines and souldiers, her Majesties subjectes, do prepare themselves to passe the seas to the service of some forren prince or governors, a matter heretofore forbidden, that is much to her Majesties discontentation; her pleasure therefore is and so I am commanded to signifie unto you that you geve present order thoroughout all the lymits of the Fyve Portes that none of her Majesty's subjectes be suffered for that purpose and in suche sorte, to passe without her Majesties lycence." *Copy.*

1576, May 3.—Certificate by the Mayor and Jurats of Rye to the Bishop of Chichester that Richard Fletcher, M.A., and late fellow and president of Corpus Christi College, Cambridge, being called hither of such as have the dealing in that behalf, to preach in the church of Rye, hath administered the sacraments as becomes a good minister of Jesus Christ and no less in the other life amongst us visiting our sick with diligence and doing his duty to the good example of the people.

1576, May 3.—Examination of John Bennet.

"Jhon Bennet being called before Mr. Maior and Mr. Fletcher, who hath the ordinary jurisdiction, upon May-day last in the church of Rye to answer to his beinge in a tabern house in tyme of Divine service and preching upon Ester Munday in the forenone, which day is appointed by law to cum together to hear the word of God and to pray, used these or such like quareling wordes, when according to his fact he was apoynted to pay 12*d.* to the use of the poore, that it was extorted from him and never would prosper with the poor and that yt was done only of malice and spite agaynst him. Which and other contumclious wordes Mr. Fletcher, precher, having by commission jurisdiction in causes of correction, hering, reproved, with whom he furthwith made comparison that he was as good, as honest and well born as he, that he the said Mr. Fletcher did eat and drink him; to which quareling when Mr. Fletcher answered that he never cost him since his coming to town a cup of could water, he answered—nor never shuld, dwelt he never so long there—in the presence of Mr. William Davy Maior, Mr. Dunning, Mr. Harris, Mr. Mercer, jurats and others. Farther he said at the bench upon the market place that he was as good a man and well born as Mr. Fletcher, for his father was a butcher and Mr. Fletcher's father a wever, with other reproches. His brother Robert also departing within the church sayd openly that he would call the churchwarden, knave of yt."

1576, May 16.—Depositions taken before the Mayor of Rye touching certain vessels sailing under the authority of the Prince de Condé. *French.* 8 *pp*

1576, May 31.—Articles of agreement between the Barons of the Cinque Ports and the Bailiffs of Yarmouth touching the jurisdiction at Great Yarmouth during the Fair. *Copy.*

1576, June 30.—The Mayor and Jurats of Rye to the "Borroughmasters of Donkerke."

"Havinge great workes in hande aboute our harbor and nedinge the advice of men of experience, and understandinge that with you are certaine persons well seane in suche affayres, we thought good to address theis our lettres unto you therby to desier your good willes for the furtheringe of this berer James Milles, whome we send as a speciall messenger to bringe frome Donkerke suche a man as is well seane and conynge in suche workes, that the rather by your helpe the person mete for our purpose may come with this said messenger who we hope shall safly aryve here and his paines and travell well recompencid." *Draft.*

1576, July 25. Westminster.—The Lords of the Council to all Vice Admirals, Justices of the Peace, Mayors, Sheriffs, Bailiffs, Constables and all owners of ships, shipmasters and others.

"We do signifie unto you hir Majesties pleasure that upon the seight of theis our letters to be brought unto you by Robert Heythar, the berrer hereof, you shall geve order that if there be any shippes belonginge to hir Majesties subjectes or laden with the goodes of any hir said subjectes presently within any haven or creke of that county or shall arryve thether at any time, that they departe not from thence untill further order shalbe gevin by us in that behalf. And further if the said berrer shall have occasion uppon such instructions as he hath recyvid from us, to send to the seas any small boate, pynase or barque you shall in that behalf see him provided as well of suche a vessell as shalbe nedeful, as of men, mariners and victualls and of all other furnitures and necessaries requisite for the purpose at reasonable and convenient prices. And of this you may not fayle, as ye tender the furtherance of her Majesties intendid service to the benefytt of hir subjectes, and will answer to the contrary at your perilles." *Copy.*

1576, September 4.—Report of the three Dutchmen, namely, Mihill de Browne of Dunkirk, Aumon Duport of Newport and Anthony Morreau of Dunkirk, carpenter.

They have viewed and seen the harbour of the Camber and see no likelihood of bringing it to the first estate, because the sea has carried away the head thereof, yet the next "brack" that is joining to it might with great charges be made a head with a great depth and length within the said Camber. And in consequence of the great charges and the small assurance they see in the continuance of it, they "mean not to council you to go about it."

They recommend another scheme for carrying three waters into one channel, building out the jetty, etc.

Aumon Duport and Anthony Morreau promised to come again when sent for.

1576, September 24.—[The Mayor and Jurats of Rye] to the Bishop of Chichester or his Judge appointed at Lewes about the late order taken for the bringing in of Wills and Administrations.

"Upon publique citinge in our church of all suche . . executors and administrators sithens the begynninge of the yere 1570 to bringe in all their Wills, Administrations . . . . Inventories to Lewes before the fyrst of October next, our people are very doubtfull what the cause shulde be, and think themselves gretly burdenid to travell so farr, and thereuppon have made complaint unto us, divers beinge at Yermouth on fyshinge, some beyond the seaes, some are women and covert baron and their husbands frome home, some are impotent persons and not able to travaill, some povertie will not permit; and over that the nomber are not fewe that shuld appere which semith strange that suche a sudden apparence shuld be of so gret a nomber uppon so short a warninge the fyrst publishinge therof beinge but on Fryday laste. For all which causes, and to avoid the greiffe and charge of our people herin, and also willing to shewe ourselves obedient, we have thought good to wryte unto your Honor by this messenger moost humblie desyringe that it will plese your good Lordship to signifie unto us what the cause is of bringinge in their Willes, Administrations and Inventories and also that it wold please you for the ease of our people to appointe some person mete, and as to your Honor shall seme good, to sitt here at Rye to have the viewe and orderinge of such Willes, Administrations and Inventories as now are called for." *Draft.*

1576, October 18. Hampton Court.—The Lords of the Council to [the Mayor and Jurats of Dover].

Forasmuch as complaints have been made to us that upon pretence of writs of withernam, you have arrested divers subjects of her Majesty's allies for small sums which is likely to cause inconveniency to her Majesty's subjects trafficking abroad, we have thought fit to require you forthwith to send to us some person of your town sufficiently instructed as well of your said right claimed by Charter as also of the particulars of the arrest of some men of Dunkirk in Flanders and one Andrew Muller, a skipper of Hamburg. *Copy.*

1576, November 12.—[The Mayor and Jurats of Rye] to Mr. Serjeant Haynes and Mr. William Haynes.

There is a young man named Richard Clarke with whom we have been divers times troubled for small "pykers," and we suppose that if he were straightly kept and under correction, he would amend his folly. We therefore request your aid to help his friends to place him in Bridewell. *Draft.*

[1576], November 14. Serjeants Inn.—B. Lovelace to the Mayor and Jurats of Rye.

Requesting that search may be made for such records as are in the town of Rye, touching the custom of process, whereupon withernam doth lie. *Signed.*

1576, December 11.—[The Mayor and Jurats of Rye] to the Bishop of Chichester.

"In November laste certaine of our neighbors accordinge to ther yerly order laide ther monies together to make their provision of wheat for their housboldes; somme a quarter, somme two quarters according to their abilities, and with a small boate of 10 tonnes went to Sidlesham in Sussex hoping to have furnished themselves as in tymes past, and repayred to your Honor for lycence, who, as they said, wold graunt them none, uppon which annswer they retorned home without brynginge any grayne at all savinge bread made of two bushels of meale; sithens which tyme, as it is said, one Kybe, miller of Sidlesham, and others have ben called before your Lordship for the same supposinge they were such persons as were not to be victualed." *Draft.*

[1575–1576].—Complaint of Robert Wyman of Hawkhurst to the Mayor and Jurats of Rye that whereas by the last will and testament of Johan Welles of Rye, late deceased, widow, a certain legacy of 50*l.* was given for the purpose of purchasing lands within two years after the decease of the said Johan, the issues whereof to go towards the relief of the poor of Rye. The said Robert Wyman being the next heir of the said Johan calls the attention of the Mayor and Jurats of Rye to the fact that the money has been misappropriated, and begs them to inquire into the matter. *Extract of the Will of Joan Wells attached.*

[1575–1576.]—Certificate by William Davy, Mayor, and the Jurats of Rye that whereas by complaint of the honest persons of the occupation of "cordiners or shomakers" within Rye that their living in their trade decreases to the apparent impoverishment of their families, apprentices and covenant servants by reason of foreign incomers as also by reason of the French and other foreign strangers flying to the said town for succour, and there use the same occupation whereby the honest householders of the said occupation are not able to live. It is therefore granted to the said householders and their successors that they shall be one company and fellowship and shall elect yearly one master and two wardens of the said company and fellowship with power to make ordinances, etc. *Endorsed* "A like copie of the Mercers grant made to the Cordiners."

1576.—Robert Paynter, servant unto the Queen's Majesty and deputy for the Earl of Warwick, master of her Highness' ordnance and William Pelham, Esquire, lieutenant of the same, to the Queen's lieutenant of her ancient town of Rye or his deputy.

"This shallbe in the Quen's Majesty's name be vertye of har hitnes kommycon unto me doreted straytlye to charge and kommand you, all ackuses layd a parte, and a pone the resete her of that you do in quer withe in your harber, of anye bote or vesell that is redye to go to London and to staye him untell the later end of the holydayes to kary salt peter to the toner for the Quen's use."

1576[–7], February 3. Hampton Court.—The Lords of the Council to Lord Cobham.

"Wheras we are creadably informid that divers masters of ships and passengers, specially of the towne of Dover, returninge from Calice, Dunkerk and other places of beyond the seas for lucre and gaine contrary to their duties and good orders of auncient tyme observid, have of late used to land some of their passengers in the Downes and other crekes frome whence they have passed without any searche or knowledge of hir Majesty's officers who have charge to looke unto suche matters. Forasmuche as we are gevin certenly to understande that by this meanes divers fugitives and other disordered subjectes which heretofore had retyred themselves into thoes partes, are returned into the realme, wherof some remayninge yet unknowen, secretly workinge and procuringe great mischief emongest other her Highnes well disposed subjectes, we have thought good to require your Lordship to geve order that it may be duly examined, what masters of shippes and passengers of the said towne of Dover or other places under your jurisdiction, have within the space of three moneths last past brought over out of Flanders, frome Callies or any other place of the realme of Fraunce, any person whom for rewarde or other cause they landid in any other place then in any ordinary porte, what he was, and whether he myndid to repaier, together with suche other particularities and circumstances fytt to be understood therin wherof we shall desier your Lordshipp to certefie us as sone as ye conveniently maye. And to the intent the leike inconveniences happen not hereafter, hir Majestie's plesure and commaundement is, that your Lordship shuld straightly charge and commaunde all and every masters of ships and passengers, ether at Dover or in any other place under your jurisdiction, usinge to repaire unto the places of beyond the seas, not to land any passengers comynge into this realme but in the ordinary and accustomed portes where her Majesties officers be resident, unlesse it shall be by necessary cause and constrainte of tempest and fowle wether and in that case also bringe the persons, if it conveniently may be, or at least the names of the passengers so landed to the next officers of the port or portes adjoyninge." *Copy.*

1576[-7], February 10.—The Bailiff and Jurats of Hastings to the Mayor and Jurats of Rye.

"We are given to understand that presently in the Parishe of Westfield nere unto Brede there is a forge to be erectyd, the which yf it take effecte wylbe to the undoyng of these towneshipes. And forasmuch, worshipful syrs, as before this tyme we have travaylyd in and about the like matter and by meanes of our sute, staye therof made, as you do know, we have thought it good to make you prevye thereof praying of you to consider of it among yow and that we by your letters may knowe what you do mynde to do therein either to lett it pass or ells to joyne togethers in sute to the Lordes of the Councell for the staye of the same, as heretofore we have done and by their Honors order stayed."

1576[-7], February 12.—[The Mayor and Jurats of Rye] to the Mayor and Jurats of Hastings.

"We have received your letters makinge mention of a iron furnes leike to be erected at Westfyld, but ye geve no present note by whome, or who be the aucters and cheiff doers therin, which is the principall matter to frame our sute uppon, for such persons may have the delinge therwith as good advise must be had before we begyn; but assure yourselves that we for our partes will not be remise in that sute, wishing for that you be nerest that place that by some meanes ye travell to understand the whole and present truth of thoes procedinge by what persons and in what forme, and then frame a letter to all the whole portes and their members, declaringe that excepte ye have their ayde ye shall not be able to resist it, and put them in mynde howe that not only you but Ry, Winchilsey, Lidd, Hide, Dover, Sandwich, the whole Isle of Thanet and divers other places alongest the seacoast shall feele the smarte therof not only for want of fuell, but specially for tymber, as well for buildinge of shipes, crayres, botes and other vessels, as also for buyldinge of houses, tymber and piles for water workes which nowe is had, and hereafter will not if this worke take place. And so beyond you as farr as Brightelmeston is leikewise served frome thes partes. Your letter framed to this effect with present knowledge given of the proceedinge therin shall cause these partes alongest the [coast] rather to joyne with you and to make frendes accordingly." *Draft.*

1576[-7], February 16. Westminster.—The Lords of the Council to all Mayors, bailiffs and head officers of Cities and others which have or shall have the appointments of searchers and sealers of leather.

"Where dyvers tanners in sundrye partes have often tymes made earnest and humble complayntes to us that they weare not able to performe certeyne braunches of the statute made in the fifte year of the Quene's Majestie's reigne, and have therefore of late procured our well beloved frende Edward Dier, Esquier, to be a suter to her Majestie to moderate the extremytie of the statute. Whereuppon her Majestie of her gracious disposition, havinge regarde to the benefytt of her subjectes, graunted power by her Highenes letters patents to the said Edward Dier, in her Highenes name, to dispence with certeyne suche braunches of the said statute in which the inconvenience and ymposs-sybylytie by the tanners was alledged. By the which graunt not only the said tannors but also all lordes of lyberties and others havinge the appointment of searchers and sealers of lether, are most graciously releved and provided for; for the more true and perfect dealinge towardes her subjectes her Highenes pleasure and commaundement is, that you and every of you from heusforthe shall make choice of sufficient and convenient searchers and sealers of leather according to the braunche of the said statute in that case provided, and that upon request unto you or any of you to be made by the said Edward Dier, his Deputye or Deputies, you shall presently and from thensforth yearly appointe, sware and bynde the said searchers and sealers to be appoynted in good somes of money to her Majestie's use with condition that they nor any of them shall not allowe or seale in their offices of searchinge or sealinge any lether but suche as shalbe well wrought, sufficiently tanned, and allowing by the wrytinge indented of the said Edward Dier, or his Deputie or Deputies, accordinge to her Majesties letters patents to hym graunted." *Copy.*

1576[-7], February 20. London.—Lord Buckhurst to the Mayors, Bailiffs and Jurats of Hastings, Winchelsea and Rye.

I have received your writing concerning my woods and ironworks at Oer and in answer, I thank you for your neighbourly manner of proceeding. It is manifest that the abundance of woods within three miles of every of your towns is so great that it would be impossible for twenty such towns as yours to use them as fuel. Besides this it seems strange that you of Rye should seek fuel out of my woods being for the most part eight miles distant, and I cannot tell what to imagine, knowing that heretofore and all likelihood for ever hereafter, you must be wholly provided from "Beckly, Northyham, Udymer and Iden," and insomuch as you in respect of your great store and abundance, both have been and daily are the transporters of no small quantity of the same woods, even to parts beyond the seas; and within the last two years you have sold and transported not so little as 1,000 tons of timber. As to you of Hastings and Winchelsea the one being distant from my woods five miles and the other very near two there are plenty of woods lying nearer to you and of better sort than mine, and the proportion of fuel you yearly spend being very small I cannot see what reason you can imagine that the use of my fuel for ironworks can bring any damage to you.

1577, April 1.—Certificate by the Mayor and Jurats of Rye, that there of late dwelt at Rye one John Davison, who afterwards dwelt at Winchelsea where he died. He had three sons of whom one named John, the eldest, is now an ironmonger dwelling in London. And that John Davison the father was brother to Thomas Davison who sometimes dwelt at Rye and married the widow of one Hearne.

1577, April 24.—Lord Cobham to the Mayor and Jurats of Rye.

"I had procured letters from my Lords of her Majesty's Councell to the Justyces and Commissioners of those musters, nott to deale with the portes and there members, whereuppon you shall not nede to obey their warrants butt curteously to lett them to understand thatt yow are discharged from there proceadinge wyth yow, wyche shalbe shorteley signeffyed unto them. You are notwithstandinge to understand that you are to be charged wythe the furnisshinge and trayninge of certeyne herquebussers as shalbe delivered and appoynted unto you by my order." *Signed. Seal of arms.*

1577, April 24.—[The Mayor and Jurats of Rye] to Lord Cobham.

"At midnight last we recyvid a precepte frome the Lord of Aburgaveney for the apprehension of one Thomas Worsley, who presently we apprehended and have him in salf custody and have answered his Honor that we may not deliver him without order frome the Lordes of her Majesty's most honorable Privy Councell to our Lorde Warden, and how that with spede we have advertised your Lordship. The precepte we herwith send your Honor and certaine letters which the said Worsley had in his tronke. The cause of his apprehencion, as we are informed, is, that on Monday last ther was found at Tonbridge uppon the bedd where the said Worsley laye, and two of his frendes that came down with him to Rye, a coppie of a bull made against her Majestie and the state of the realme wheruppon the other two returninge backe by Tunbridge were staied by the Lord of Abergaveney and caried with him to his place at Comfort. We thought it not good to sende the said Worsley as he required but first to acquaint your Honor therof and to have him sente as heretofore hath ben accustomed in such cases as well in consideration of your Honors privileges as our liberties."

[Postscript] "John Mewes / William Button } The two gentlemen afore spoken of."

Draft.

1577, May 21.—The Mayor and Jurats of Rye to M. Mihill de Browne of Dunkirk, Aumon Duport of Newport and Anthony Mordau of Dunkirk.

Whereas in September last you came to Rye to view our harbour and give your advice for the amendment thereof (for which we thank you) and you, Aumon Duport and Anthony Mordau, promised to come whensoever we should send for you; we now having fully determined to proceed with the works, desire you upon the receipt hereof to come to us with as much speed as may be. And we desire you Mr. Mihill de Browne to forward your two neighbours to us according to your promise. *Draft.*

1577, May 22.—[The Mayor and Jurats of Rye] to the Lieutenant of Dover Castle.

"Accordinge to your late letters concerninge the musters for which we yeld yow harty thankes, we have procedid and we and our member of Tenterden met at Winchelsey, with Hastinges and their members, for the selectinge of thos 40 persons which by the portes and their members in Sussex is to be found towardes the nomber of 300 in Sussex, where we agreid that we and our member shuld fynde 20 of thoes 40 which was well liked of. Hastinges with his members would find 16 and Winchelsey wold be charged but with thre, so as some difference is betwene them for one man; not doubtinge but they will agree frendly therin. For our parts our men shall be ordered and trayned as apperteynith. And whensoever your Worshippe please to come to take the musters ye shalbe hartely welcome, and we redy to geve our attendance as dutie requirith." *Draft.*

1577, May 25.—Safe conduct from John Lucas, Mayor of Dover, and the Jurats of the same place, for William Edwardes, Captain and late "servitor" in Flanders, who arrived at Dover May 22 with four score soldiers of his retinue, and remained there to hear if her Majesty pleased to entertain them, and having received answer was minded to repair to Rye with thirty of the same retinue. *Seal of arms.*

1577, May 26.—Certificate by the Mayor and Jurats of Rye that on May 25 1577 Fraunces Meicher, Cornelis Sohier and Michell Falloys, merchants of Rye, made declaration that Frances de Tresegnys abiding within the town of Rye did marry in the said town one Anne de la Porte of "Valencine" [Valenciennes ?] and had issue a daughter named Anne who survived her mother for three months and was buried here at Rye.

1577, May 30. Dover Castle.—Richard Barrey to the Mayors and Bailiffs of Dover, Folkstone, Hythe, Romney, Lydd, Rye, Winchelsea, Hastings and Faversham.

Letter of summons to be at St. James' Church, Dover, on Tuesday June 4 to confer upon certain letters of commission and instructions from the Queen. *Copy.*

1577, June 4.—Safe conduct from the Mayor and Jurats of Rye for William Edwardes *alias* Captain Edwardes late "servitor" in Flanders who lately came from Dover with thirty of his retinue, and is now minded to go to Hastings, and so along the coast to the City of Chichester and from thence to Portsmouth there to pass over to the Isle of Wight to Captain Horsey. The said Captain and the "said xxx[ty] persons have contynued emongest us not idely but occupied in tryninge our people to the caliver shoot wherein him self and others of his said retynue have showed them selves (to our judgmentes) worthy and good soldiors." *Draft.*

1577, June 20.—The Mayor and Jurats of Rye to the Burgomaster of Dunkirk and others his assistants in Justice there.

We thank you for showing us the courtesy to permit these bearers Mathewe Rickward and Cornelis Rickeward, his son, to come to us when we sent for them and request you will show us that friendship as to suffer them or one of them (if both may not be spared) to return to us within ten or twelve days to finish that piece of work which they have begun, otherwise our common people will report that they have taken the thing in hand which they are not able to end. *Draft.*

1577, June 23. The Court.—William, Lord Cobham, to the Mayor and Jurats of Rye and the Bailiff of Hastings.

Requesting particulars of piracies committed by Frenchmen upon her Majesty's subjects upon the English Coast. *Copy.*

1577, July 1. Greenwich.—The Lords of the Council to all Mayors, Sheriffs and other officers of her Majesty's ports.

Order that Nippevile *alias* Etemer or Stevin Debruese, a Frenchman, escaped from the custody of the Serjeant of the Admiralty, be not permitted to cross the seas. *Copy.*

1577, July 1.—Petition of the Company and Fellowship of Drapers and Tailors within the town of Rye that whereas by grant under the common seal there were granted to the said Company divers articles and orders by them to be executed, and especially that none should occupy the mystery or occupation either of woollen draper or tailor within the said town, other than such as had either been apprenticed with one of the said Company or being freeborn should first make agreement with the said Company, upon a certain pain for every day occupied. That divers persons occupy the said trades, contrary to the said grant for which the said Company beg redress. *Copy. Note on back.* Answered, to have redress according to the true intent and meaning of the grant.

1577, August 2.—Lord Cobham to Mr. Richard Barrey, Lieutenant of Dover Castle.

Her Majesty having of late heard that sundry spoils and depredations have been committed upon the seas by certain disordered persons suspected to be Englishmen, and having their repair to and fro into sundry ports and havens within the Five Ports for the redress whereof, and preservation of good peace between her Majesty and other foreign Princes, her Majesty has commanded that you give order in all ports and havens and other places under my charge, that from henceforth no ship or other vessel be suffered to depart to the seas until the owner, lader and master thereof do put in bonds and sufficient sureties to the value of the ship and furniture to her Majesty's use, not to damage any of the subjects of any foreign Prince with whom her Majesty is in amity and specially the subjects of the realm of Scotland. But it is not meant that fishermen or coastmen or known merchants going only to their trade without any warlike furniture shall be subject to this order, unless there be some apparent cause of suspicion. *Copy. Enclosure:—Form of bond.*

1578, November 15.—Inquisition taken at Rye before John Fagge, the Mayor, and others by virtue of a commission directed to them. The jurors say that Captain Stewarde, Captain Stepany, Captain Comissary, Captain Demure, Martin Haward, Lewis Sohier, Robert Castell, Nicholas Dugrange, Morrys du Boys, Captain Depome, Bates of Saltash, Relf of Ower, Sander Harrold, Captain Vallery, Captain Clarse, George Bankes, Captain Bouse, Captain Lumbynion and Danyell Mynge, do not dwell within the liberties of the town of Rye nor have they lands or goods there, that there are two of the name of John Bennet, one a sailor and one a tailor, that John Mylles is not worth anything, that Fraunces Maquery is worth 10*li.*, that Nicholas Purvage is worth 5*li.*, that Manuell Allon is worth 20*s.*, that Robert Farley is worth 10*li.*, that Captain Braband is worth 5*li.* and Mihill Russell is worth 20*li.*

1578, November 21.—The Mayor and Jurats of Rye to the Mayor of Rochell.

Letter of process touching a debt owing by Charles de la Mason of Rochell to John Donnynge of Rye.

1578, November 30, Richmond.—The Lords of the Council to [the Lord Warden].

As to fines for piracy to be levied upon the following persons at the following ports, viz.:—Hastings, Michael Dallery; Winchelsea, Robert Perse and Francis Bolten; Rye, Michell Russell, Fraunces Maquery, Nicholas Purvaye and Captain Braband; Lydd, Robert Lawles, Robert Barget, John Priduaux, William Seabrand and John Michell; Romney, Robert Symons, James Gardener and William Gaurard; Hythe, George Michell; Folkestone, Richard Goddyn. *Copy.*

1578, December 3.—The Mayor and Jurats of Rye to the Bishop of London and others the Commissioners for Causes Ecclesiastical.

Your messenger delivered to us your commission concerning the apprehension of William Scott, gentleman, and others and with all diligence we helped him with such aid as was most meet in so weighty a business, in which dealing our minister and preacher here Richard Flecher, and Mr. Edolf, one of our Jurats, took such pains and diligent care as no doubt worthy of great commendation, after the apprehension of the said Scott with one who is thought to be a priest; "and beinge brought to towne, the people very desirous to se him and his maskynge apparrell for contentation of their myndes, and to the ende they might behold the vanitie therof, we were so bold to apparrel him accordingly, and passinge the streats was beheld both of yonge and olde to no small nomber whose acclamations and disleikinge of suche vanyties we refer to the report of the messenger." *Draft.*

1578–1579.—Instructions to the Constables of Rye upon the late proclamation against the common use of "dagges, handgunes, harquebuts, calivers and coats of defence."

"Ye are to make serche within your warde frome tyme to tyme as ye shall se cause, and that with dilligence, for small dagges called pocket dagges, aswell in any man's house to be suspected for the same as in the shoppes and houses of artificers as do make the same, and all them shall cease and take, and them deliver to Mr. Maior or to one of the jurates of your warde.

Ye are to have a dilligent care to suche as ye shall see to carry any dagges, pistolles, harquebusies, calivers and suche leike in the stretes or other places within the liberties (excepte at the days of common musters and to the places of exercise for the shot) and if ye fynde eny to carry eny such peces to staie them and to cease the said peces, and them to present to Mr. Maior or one of the jurates of your ward.

Ye shall make staie of suche as ye shall fynde to ware pryvie coates and doblets of defence, and them to bring unto Mr. Maior or one of the jurates of your warde.

Theis thinges to execute with due dilligence ye may not faill as ye will answer the contrary at your uttermoost perill, and to make certificate to Mr. Maior and his brethern, the Jurats, from tyme to tyme of your doinges herin when ye shalbe therunto called or as tyme may geve present occasion."

1578[-9], January 8.—The Lord Warden to the Mayor and Jurats of Rye.

Whereas the Lords of the Council have fined Mihill Russell, Fraunces Maquery, Nicholas Purvage and Captain Braband of your town of Rye, for causes of piracy, I charge and command you to levy the said fines upon the said persons.

1578[-9], January 12.—Certificate by the Mayor and Jurats of Rye of the good behaviour of Andrew Ramsey, Scotchman, a mariner, who had dwelt at Rye nineteen years. *Draft.*

1578[-9], January 13.—The Mayor and Jurats of Rye to Richard Barry, Lieutenant of Dover Castle.

The persons presented in our town are from home and not at this instant in Rye; Mihill Russell hath but his wife here with her friends and his substance is his ship, Captain Braband has departed to the seas notwithstanding his wife hath promised to pay the money, Francis Maquery is in France and Nicholas Purvage we think will not be long absent. *Draft.*

1578[-9], February 13.—Certificate of the Mayor and Jurats of Rye, at the request of Vincent Dugard of Dieppe, procurator of the worshipful James Miffant, that there came before them the following honest and credible persons viz.:—John Dallet, Francis le Mercier, Cornelis Soier, Guillam Bucheret, Patrick Harvy, Allen Harry and Anthony Coque, merchants, dwelling in Rye, who being sworne deposed that the said James Miffant, with his wife Francis Soyer, did continually dwell within the realm of England from the feast of St. Bartholomew 1572 until 1578 and there lived for the cause of religion during all that time, not any way intruding themselves into the causes of war nor having any dealings that way, but very quietly behaving themselves like honest and good people.

1578[-9], February 13. London.—Sir Francis Walsingham to the Mayor and Jurats of Rye.

"This bearer my servaunt John Dowce is both honest and trustye to do her Majestie service. Theis are to desier you that when ye shall have occasion to send ether to the Courte for her Heighnes affaires or beyond the seas or ellswhere by her commaundement and direction, you will be mindfull to use his service therin." *Signed and Seal.*

1578[-9], March 7.—Certificate by the Mayor and Jurats of Rye that Nicholas Dugrange, late of Rye, now of the Isle of Guernsey, whose ship was stayed at Poole for a supposed robbery on a Portuguese ship about 25 August 1577, that the said Nicholas had a passport from the Lords of the Council and from the Lord Warden to permit him to pass his ship to Rochell. And that Fraunces le Mercier, William Bucher, Cornelis Sohier, of Rye, merchants and of great credit, who come before the said Mayor and say that the ship of the said Nicholas came into the creek of Rye in the latter end of July and did not leave till the end of September following.

1578[-9], March 14.—Certificate by the Mayor and Jurats of Rye that William Hendy "one of our combarons," late master of a barque called the *Heline* of Rye, came before them and deposed that "uppon the 12th daie of September in the yere of our Lord God 1577 as he came frome Lysborne he was chased and sett uppon in the Baye of Portingale by two barkes of Faccombe in Normandy, and layinge him aborde tooke out of his barke 8 tonnes of brassell called Farnam bucke; also they tooke frome him his maynesaile, his myssen saile, foure bases, and unrigged all the roppes of his barke and tooke awaye his boate with all his victuals and stripped him and his company of all their apparell, and wrestid one of the company with a rope aboute his hed and very much tormentid him to confess what money he had. Moreover they tooke out of his barke a Frencheman which before was put aborde the same barke by a man of warr, and the same Piere Tollin declarid to this Deponent that, as he supposed, one of the captaines of one of the said barkes of Faccombe was named Captayne Terrie; which said Piere Follin was by the said barkes of Faccombe carryed to Faccombe where he was laide in prison, beinge of kynne to Vincent Gloria of Deipe."

1578[-9], March 24.—Depositions taken before the Mayor of Rye in the suit of John Smyth, citizen and glasier of London, against Sebastian Orlanden of Venice.

Stephen Duvall, of London, Frenchman, deposed that the said Sebastian Orlanden ought to have a third part with Godfraye Delahay for making "bugles" at Beckley and that the said Godfray had sold to John Smith all the wares, stuffs and instruments which were at Beckley.

John Okes, of Beckley, glassmaker, said that he, being a workman in the glass-house at Beckley knew what glasses "amells" [enamels ?] and other things were made there, and he knew there were made there two great baskets of glass, two "paniers of canvass amell" and ten cases of "ameld" canvas.

"Sondaye Exanta" of Loraine, glassworker, said that the said Godfray did sell to the said John Smyth on 18 January last past, all the goods of the said Godfray remaining in the glass-house at Beckley with all and singular stuff to make "amells and glasse in collers" with a bundle of tools, etc.

1579, March 27.—Certificate by the Mayor and Jurats of Rye that "William Bucher, Anthony Quoc and Andro Harry, marchants, and Matthew Flory, surgeon, have ben of long contynuance within the said towne of Rye, aliens borne and now denisons, men of very grave, honest and good conversation, persons allwaies well thought of emongest us and of the cheiff of the Frenche churche, suche as very well understande the Englishe tonge, not spottid with any notorious cryme or infamy to our knowledges. As concerning Francis Tresdemer and John Elson, they are straungers borne and have not ben of leike contynuance with us and therfore not so well knowen unto us as the others aforenamed, but for that tyme they have remaynid emongest us we have not knowen them to be but of honest conversation followinge their vocations in good and Godly order to our knowledges."

[1579], April 6. Southwark.— ——— Fowle to the Mayor of Rye.

The occasion of my writing is, that whereas I am informed by Edward Fowle, my son, that one Mathewe was "abowt a boke to exibite for your toune" to the Queen's Majesty for the amending of your harbour or creek, and as I understand that this Mathewe is deceased and I am advertised that the town of Rye will give 200*li*. to him who would obtain your request of the Queen; if this be so, if you will agree thereto and your demand be not over much I will travel therein.

1579, April 10. Dover Castle.—Richard Barrey to the Mayors and Bailiffs of the Cinque Ports.

Whereas her Majesty has heretofore given order to have levied and trained in every shire a certain number of men and appointed that there should be levied within the Cinque Ports 140 men able to be furnished with calivers and shot and to be trained and kept in rediness, I require you to cause the persons so selected and appointed as aforesaid to be mustered and trained within every of your towns by your captains and leaders in Easter-week and Whitsun-week next coming, for the space of four days. *Copy.*

1579, April 30.—Proclamation touching the buying and selling of wool.

1579, May 8.—The Mayor, Jurats and Commons of Rye to Mr. Wyllerd.

"Being of late assembled together abowt causes towching the state of our towne, emongest others twas moved that consideration might be had for redresse of the destruction of woddes nere unto the towne by iron workes, leste very shortlye we shulde be clene spoyled of tymber and fuell to the utter ruen of the publique state of the place, in sort as it were too longe in theis our lettres to explaine. Mr. Carpenter openid unto us your late speches with him in that matter, and therewithall declared what frendly offer you made, not only for yourself but also in the behalf of others which we cannot but well leike of." *Draft.*

1579, May 11.—Certificate of the Mayor and Jurats of Rye that "consideringe the continual decaye of the harbor of Rye to the utter ruen and overthrowe of the said towne and having to the uttermoost of our powers bestowed great somes of mony uppon the same, wherby ther is great liklyhodd of amendment if farther help might be had, which of ourselves we are not able to supply, and so thorough want, all like to be lost which alredy is imployed upon the same. Knowe ye that we the said Mayor and Jurats and Commonalty with one assent and consent have nominated, elected and chosen Henry Gaymer and Robert Carpenter, two of the Jurats of the said towne, for us and in our names to be soliciters and suters to our Qenis Majestie or her Highnes moost honorable Pryvie Councell for some relieff and succor to be had towardes the furtheringe of the workes by us allreddy begonne for the helpinge and contynuinge of the said harbor."

1579, May 12.—The Mayor, Jurats and Commons of Rye to the Lord Warden.

"The decaye of our harbour doth so dayly growe and therby the state of the towne runnethe to suche sudden ruine as without some present releife and amendment wee shall receave a perpetual overthrow. And for that we hold your good Lordship our only refuge, do lay open the same to the vew of your honorable consideration and have made speciall choice of your Lordship's servants Henry Gaymer and Robert Carpenter to attend upon your Honor as they may by your good Lordship's directyon run such a course (to the Lords of her Majesties Counsell) for some succor therin to be had to our decayed porte, as her Majesties towne may thereby be preserved. The substance of our request which they will imparte unto you—the devise for restoringe of the haven." *Draft.*

1579, May 19. "Blackfriers in London."—Lord Cobham to the Mayor of Rye and others.

"By letters from Mr. Tresaurer and Mr. Comptroller of her Majesties household I am given to understand of divers desorders doen of late by the fishermen of your towne against her Majesties purvior and taker for sea fishe, contrarie to the articles heretofore made in that behalf between her Majestie and them, a matter somewhat strainge unto me that suche as they be shold show themselfes so contemptuous in the service of her Highnes especially in that thinge which they themselves have agreed unto and thought verie reasonable. For the quieting whereof I will and require you from time to time to have some dilligent care to see the same disorders dulie refourmede." *Signed and seal of arms.*

1579, May 19. "Blackfriers in London."—Lord Cobham to the Mayor and Jurats of Rye.

"I am sorie to understand of the decaie of your harborowe. I will be readie to pleasure your town in any cause that maie be to your preferment and make for your good therin. I finde that if you proceede to the Commission for Sewers yt will not hinder anie suite you shall undertake heareafter and therefore doe advise yow to putt the same in execution this somer." *Signed and seal of arms.*

1579, August 7.—Writ from the Lord Warden to the Mayors, Bailiffs and Jurats of the Cinque Ports.

Whereas her Majesty has directed her commission to me and others to examine, try and inquire of misdemeanours and offences done and perpetrated by pirates, their abettors and maintainers within the liberties of the Cinque Ports and their members, and that we should appoint a convenient number of honest, discreet and trusty persons dwelling there, as contained in a certain schedule annexed hereto, to be our deputies in the execution of her Majesty's said service. And whereas we the said Commissioners have received letters from the Lords of the Council accompanied with new orders to be observed for the better execution of the said Commission, we command you that you cause the persons named in the said schedule to appear before me or my Lieutenant and others the Commissioners aforesaid, at the Church of St. James the Apostle in Dover on the 12th of this instant month of August to receive further order for the execution of their said offices. *Schedule attached.*

1579, August 19.—Certificate by the Mayor and Jurats of Rye that there came before them John Osborne, Nicholas Lynge, Edward Smith, of London, merchants, Thomas Philpot with Thos Rucke of Cranbroke in Kent, merchants, and John le Roye, a post, having her Majestys packet, who declare that on the 18th of this inst. between twelve and two in the afternoon a certain flyboat manned with 30 or 40 persons all Englishmen as they appeared, near the Ness by Rye, boarded the "passage" wherein the said merchants and post came from Dieppe and spoiled them of their apparel and goods.

1579, September 11.—The Mayor and Jurats of New Romney to the Mayor and Jurates of Rye.

We have received certain letters from Sandwich the copy whereof we enclose.

Enclosure.—A letter from the Mayor and Jurats of Sandwich to the Mayor and Jurats of New Romney, undated, stating that, "we have forborne to send unto you for your resolution touching the repair of our Bailiff to Great Yarmouth. Since the beginning of this letter we have received very credible information from Mr. Cottie that they die 10 or 12 in a day at Yermouthe, and that he nor his wife wilbe there if it stay not. And, from Mr. Love, Mr. Rawe is also advertised, that such as come from the sea die within 24 houres. The aire by that meanes shoulde seeme to be infected and so the perill and dainger of such as should goe, great and very present. Yf you with the reste of the Portes will joyne with us, we will sue unto her Majesty and the Lordes of the Counsell for a dispensation for this yeare. Mr. Cotties house notwithstandinge is clere and dailie ayred. We must have present answer by the bearer hereof or else we must procede on our jornie. Yf you have the resolution of the other portes then we shall nede no further travell."

1579, September 22.—Lord Cobham to the Mayors, Bailiffs and Jurats of the Cinque Ports.

Commanding their presence at the Church of St. James the Apostle at Dover on Friday, 2 October, to receive order and direction for the executing the Queen's Commission directed to Lord Cobham and others for the suppressing of pirates, their abbettors, and maintainers. *Copy.*

1579, September 23.—Order for the preservation of the town of Rye from the plague.

"Inprimis, that Margaret Pacienc, the wiff of Robert Pacienc, and Elizabeth Grene, of Ry aforesaid, shall presently upon the decease of eny person within the saide towne, have the viewe of the body deceased whether the same were infectid with the plague or not, wherunto they are sworne.

Item, after the viewe taken they shall geve true certificate unto Mr. Maior and Mr. Flecher or one of them, what they fynde in that cause.

Item, it is ordered that thoes two persons appoynted to take the viewe shall not be chargid or compelled to stripe the persons so viewed or eny more to come in eny the said houses infectid, after advertisement gevin as aforesaid.

Item, that the house where eny suche person shall dy of the plague after certificat therof made as aforesaid, shalbe presently shette uppe and if it be a tiplinge house, the signe to be taken downe, and not beinge of abilitie to be considered of by common contribution accordinge to her Majesty's order."

Additional orders, entered in the Hundred Book. All dogs to be kept in and all curs to be killed out of hand, and whoever shall find any dogs in the streets to kill them.

Mathewe Flory "surgion, the French poticary" to prepare medicines for the sick from time to time and to be allowed out of the common contribution.

1579, November 24.—Royal Proclamation touching the price of wines. *Printed by Christopher Burker.*

1579, December 14.—Order by the Mayor and Jurats of Rye that no person whosoever that die within the parish of Rye, under the degree of the Mayor, Jurats and Common Council or any of their wives, "shall be chested or coffenid for their buriall and so incoffenid to be buried."

1579, December 15.—Royal Proclamation touching concealed lands. *Printed by Christopher Barker.*

1579, December 16.—Certificate of the Mayor and Jurats of Rye, that Guillam Blocke, a horsekeeper, hath dwelt at Rye for 30 years and hath behaved himself as becometh an honest poor man.

1579, December 20.—Royal Proclamation touching the price of French wines. *Printed by Christopher Barker.*

1579, December 25.—The Mayor and Jurats of Rye to the Mayor and Jurats of Dover.

"We have receyved your letters concerning your proces of withernam to Hamburgh, and as heretofore in the same cause we have answered so we do nowe, that we have no presidentes of antiquitie concerninge the forren partes. Winchelsey, as we take it, have very good and auncient in the tyme of Edward the third and so followinge, in the whiche the towne clerke there is experte. There remaynith in the custody of Mr. Boys a booke in parchment conteyninge the customes of eche towne of the Portes wrytten in the Latten and French tonge in the tyme of the same Kynge wherin is sett forth in eche of the customals the order to send proces to the partes beyond the seas, where the Kynge of England hath leage or amytie, we toke it that the shewinge of so auncient a booke cannot be hurtfull with Winchelsey's presidentes agreable in usage." *Draft.*

1579, December 31.—The Mayor and Jurats of Dover to the Mayor and Jurats of Rye.

"It may please you to be advertized that this day John Mercer, of your towne, deliverid to us a letter from our very good Lord Warden to us and the rest of the portes (you exceptid) directid, with the oppinion of his Counsell uppon the unlawfullnes of his disfranchizinge, requiring therby us to consider of our doinges therin and to satisfye the said Mercer that we have not wrongyd hym. And, consideration had, we with our Livetenant of Dovor Castell have satisfied him as apperteynethe, what cause enduced his disfranchisement and what suche a member as he was, ys to be thought of. Neverthelesse for that yt apperethe to us by his outward apparance that he meanethe not to acquaint the rest of the Portes with the same letters." *Seal of arms.*

1579[-80], January 8.—The Mayor and Jurats of Rye to the Bishop of London and his Colleagues of her Majesty's High Commission for Causes Ecclesiastical.

"Whereas our towne of Rye scituat uppon the coast and peopled to the nombre of 1800 or 1900 communicantes and for that cause requiringe a lernid and sufficient mynister and preacher; the vicaridge therof hath longe tyme ben entangled to one John Rolf by leace, who, reapinge the fruite of the same yerely to a greater value then the rent yeldid, hath therout made small allowaunce to our minister and preacher, and also in very dissolute sort paid the same, wherethroughe we have ben constreynid to contribute out of our common treasureye a yerely stipend for the better mainetaynance of our mynistrye. The which John Rolf, beinge a very lewd disposed person and a common disturber of the quiet and christian peace in our towne, by makinge himself an instruement of contention betwene party and partie, an enemye to our preacher and one that dispendith the frutes of our vicaredge in actions of common quarrell to the detriment and offence of many of the place, and allso hath incurred forfeyture of his leace as to us semith, for that it is demised to another, which, notwithstandinge Rolf doth still by sute prosequut, wherthroughe our people are wonderfullye drawen unto doubte and dainger of payenge or repayenge the common duties troblesome to the people, not beinge in tymes past so delt with, and allso our great care (not without our singuler detriment) leike to be utterly lefte destitute of so sufficient a man as hath these five yeres and more labored painefully amonge us. In regarde of the premisses we most humbly and hartely beseche your good Lordshipp with the rest to graunt unto one Robert Jacson, one of the Jurates of our towne, who hath the leace in reversion, the sequestration of our vicaredge fruites till suche tyme as the sute, now dependinge betwene Rolf the lesye and one Mr. Wigmore the leasor, be determynid. So that therby both our precher and mynister maye duely receave for his travaill, and allso our people maye knowe unto whome they maie without daunger paie ther accustomed duties." *Draft.*

1579[-80], January 25.—Order by the Mayor of Rye that a gathering or tax should be made towards the sustentation of the sick, and that Cowper, Widow, be appointed to go to the houses of the sick to ask what they want, and shall deliver such necessaries to them at their doors.

1579–[80], January 31.—The Mayor and Jurats of Rye to Lord Burghley.

"Whereas the town of Rye at this instant is not the best provided of corne, especially of wheate, and to prevent the sudden want that might insue we have by our frend this berer, namyd Robert Ludgater, made provision of two hundred and fyftie quarters of wheat in Norfolk to be laden at Kynges Lynne about the which he now travelith. Theis are to desire your Honor to stande somuche our good Lorde, as to graunt unto the same Robert Ludgater your favorable lettres unto the officers there for the quiet transportation of the same to Rye aforesaid ; wherein your Lorshipp shall do a great good to the poore of the same towne and we bound to you for the same." *Draft.*

1579[–80], February 25.—[The Mayor of Rye] to Lord Cobham.

"In the hulk that lately was cast awaye within the barr of the haven of Rye ther were certaine harquebusies and such leike peces, not of any grete valewe for that they are all unfurnished, in the custody of some of the towne, as Mr. Ratlyff your Honors servant well knowith, which we claime to have to the use of the towne, accordinge to our priviledges, and as is ordaynid in the booke betwene your Honor and the Portes, in the 13th article, wherein it is to be senne that forasmuche as the spoyle happenid within the haven the same apperteynith to the towne. Notwithstandinge we thought good to signifie soe much unto your Honor and therwithall to crave your lawfull favor for the enjoyinge of thoes peces before we wold take them into our handes." *Draft.*

1579[–80], March 1.—[The Mayor of Rye] to the Mayor of Rochester.

"Whereas in November laste by the pursute of Richarde Daniell of Rye, a yonge man namyd William (his surname to the said Richaude is forgotten) was at your cittie attached uppon suspicion of fellony for thinges by him imbeaselid out of the house of the said Richarde Danyell in Ry aforesaid, and the same William, so being attached as I am informid, was commytted to her Majesties gaole within the said Citie and the said Richard bownde before yow (as he saieth) by recognizance in 20*li.* to appere at the next Assises to be holden in Kent ther to geve evydence against the said prisoner. It may please yow to be advertised that it hath pleasid God of late to visit our towne with sickness, yet God be thanked somewhat stayed, notwithstanding for that the same Richard at this instant hath one sicke in his house but whereof is not yet knowen, it is thought to be dangerous that he shuld appere at the Assises amongest so great a company and himself very lothe to presume so to do lest it might be hurtful to others, consideringe the sickness is somwhat contagious, and therby himself offensive to many, whereof he wold be sory. The premises considerid, he hath desired me to signifie unto you howe it standith with us at this instant and therwithall to praye you to shewe him your lawfull favor, that for his non-apparance to geve evidence, as the case standith, he may not be dampnified by his recognizance which he saieth restith only in your courtesey." *Draft.*

1579[–80], March 6.—Order signed by John Wylson for the apprehending of Jarret Derelova *alias* Carpenter wheresoever he may be found.

1579[–80], March 23. Dover Castle.—Richard Barry to the Mayors, Bailiffs and Jurats of the Cinque Ports.

"Whereas in 1577 the Quene gave order for the training of a certain number of men within the Cinque Ports, all furnished with calivers and to be trained and kept in readiness.

"Nowe for that the tyme of mustringe draweth nere I have thought good to put you in remembraunce, and allso in her Majesties name to require yow and every of yow, that yow do cause the selected shott, within every of your severall jurisdictions, to be mustred and trained by the space of four daies in Easter weeke next, beginninge on the Mondaye; and in the like sorte in the Whitson weeke next cominge accordinge as it is appointed in the said instructions."

1580, April 7.—[The Mayor of Rye?] to Lord Cobham.

"Where as longe sithens I and others had your Lordship's consent for the attachinge of John Rolfe to be bownde to his good abaringe, and by your letter to Dovor Castle had a warrant frome thence to that effecte, untill Easter Monday last, the said Rolf could by no meanes be mett withall (havinge knowledge therof as it semid) uppon which daie he came to churche and being callid before me and commanded to warde untill he founde suerties for that cause, he delivered unto me a wryt of *supersedeas* out of the Kinge's Benche for discharge of the peace and good abaringe, a thinge never senne before within the Portes and, as it is supposed, lyeth not no more then other her Majesties wryttes in other causes. And for that I was not resolvid whether his wrytt wold serve him or not I commyttid him to warde untill I were advised." *Draft.*

1580, April 7.—John Fagge, Mayor of Rye, to Sir Francis Walsingham.

"It may please your Honor to be advertised that on Twesdaye the 29th of Marche last the passage from Deipe beinge serched, there was one Stevin Taillor, (as he saieth) servant to the Erle of Shrewsbury, staied for that ther were certaine lyttle books called the Jesus Psalter to the nomber of two dosen founde aboute him by the sercher's depute, who sent one of them to your Honour by a messenger, and in the meanetime the said Taillor kept in salf custody untill your plesure wer therin knowen. And for that betherto I have not harde enythinge therof, uppon ernist request and good bonde for his apparance before you, I have sent him with this beirer namyd Mr. Cornishe, a gentleman which is here wel knowen and often hath passed this waye, to be presented unto you with one of the said bookes herin closed, with him to deale as to your Honour shall seem good." *Draft.*

1580, April 16.—Certificate by the Mayor and Jurats of Rye, "that on Fryday morninge being the viijth daie of this instant moneth of Aprill there arryvid here, within the havon of Rye aforesaid, a certaine smalle vessel of Allaredo in Spaigne, laden with orrenges and lemondes, of the burden of 18 tonnes or theraboutes, namid the *St. John*, whereof is master under God, Peter Leucres, and sett on lande one Mr. Grafton of London, marchant, who (as himself reportid) was presently bownde to the Courte with her Majesties packet frome thoes contries. The said vessell as the master saieth, bownde for London or Andwerpe, as they shulde se occasion, with their ladinge. The which said vessel, master and mariners, on Wednisdaie the 13th of this said instant moneth of Aprill, was staied under arrest by the officers of towne of Winchelsey, nere unto the said towne of Rye, but for what cause we knowe not, but that only is the cause of the said master's here abydinge so longe, so farr as we understand."

1580, May 16.—The Mayor and Jurats of Rye to Mr. Salter, dwelling upon London Bridge.

We thank you "for your courtesey offerid to us and the people of our towne as by relation of Mr. Appleton, our towne clerke, and William Coxson, our neighbor, we have conceyved, uppon which your freindly offer and the credit we have in them we have had conference, and thought mete hereby to request you that forthwith you will make your repaire unto us with your apothecary, havinge (as we take it) a surgion sufficient that shall geve his attendance uppon you and be at your commandment. And for that we are fully perswadid by the foresaid persons that after your comynge ye will so do your endevor as we shall not nede your presence much above 6 daies, we mynde not to request eny more at your hande (excepte of your own good will ye will longer remaine) and for that tyme and for your travell and paine, the towne shall geve you 10 *li.*, which we will se truly paid unto you, besides your availes at their handes which are of abylite, the which our offer we desire you to accepte in good parte, and therwithall to accomplishe our request, not doubtinge but that God will give you good success with increase of your fame and credit." *Draft.*

1580, May 31.—Certificate by the Mayor and Jurats of Rye that John Dowce, a freeman of Rye, hatter and capper, trades in the making of white felts and keeps servants in the same town occupied in the same trade. Which felts he used to send up to London "to be orderid and died in such cullers as he plesith to have them, and so returned downe to Rye againe." Which same felts ought to have free passage to and from London.

1580, June 24.—Certificate of the sale by Peter Desmares and Gabriell Sourville, Frenchmen, at Rye, to John Tembricke of Rye, goldsmith, of two horses.

1580, July 15.—Royal Proclamation against Traitors. *Printed by Christopher Barker.*

1580, September 17. Dover Castle.—Richard Barry to the Mayors, Bailiffs and Jurats of the Cinque Ports.

Commanding the said Mayors Bailiffs and Jurats in consequence of the piracies committed upon the coast to enter into bonds not to permit any ship to be rigged, victualled or pass to the seas out of their ports except it were by some known merchant and upon trade of merchandise. *Copy.*

1580, September 26.—Depositions by Nicholas Jene of Dieppe, that being in a boat, riding at anchor in the Downs, come from London to Rye, there came a ship of war of the burden of 80 tons whereof one Martyn was Captain and one John Sohier one of the company, who boarded the boat of Dieppe aforesaid, and by force of arms took from this examinant his goods and apparel.

1580, September 27. Richmond.—Sir Francis Walsingham to the Mayor and Jurats of Rye.

"I ame given to understand that you have arrested of late certaine Frenchemen of the company of Captain Bawdry, whom you refuse to release without bondes for your indemnitye, in case any charge should be layde to their charge hereafter. Forasmuch as I am informed that there can be nothinge brought agaynst them whereby they maye be justely charged, these are to praye yowe, unlesse there maye appeare some juste cause of deteyninge them, uppon your receipte hereof to sette them at libertye withe theire bagge and baggage."

1580, October 3.—A Proclamation against the Sectaries of the Family of love. *Printed by Christopher Barker.*

1580, October 26.—Bond of Patrick Tornoye of Edinburgh to deliver up a ship with her furniture to Nicholas Corbewe at Rye which the said Patrick, being upon the Narrow Seas in warlike affairs under the licence of the Prince of Condé, had taken

1580, October 28.—Certificate by the Mayor and Jurats of Rye that on Sunday after Bartholomew day last past, the Jurats and freemen of Rye to the number of fourscore persons being assembled at the accustomed place in the church-yard, after some consultation, did chose and elect by the voice of threescore persons as Mayor, Robert Jacson. The whole number of the freeman of Rye being not many above a hundred persons, of whom, by reason of the sickness, some came not, therefore those that say that the Mayor, in the absence of the most part of the town, was by great labour chosen Mayor have most untruly uttered the same.

1580, October 31. Dover Castle.—Richard Barry to the Mayors, Bailiffs and Jurats of the Cinque Ports.

Ordering them to send in certificates of the ships and other boats with their names, burdens, owners, and likewise what masters, mariners, fishermen, or seamen be in their ports. *Copy.*

Certificates for Rye attached. 20 trading vessels ranging from 65 tons to 20 tons, employing 120 men besides boys; 31 fishing boats ranging from 22 to 10 tons, employing 200 men besides boys.

1580, November 3. A Proclamation for the prices of wines. *Printed by Christopher Barker.*

1580, November 10.—The Mayor and Jurats of Rye to "Mr. Doctor Beacon," Chancellor of Chichester.

Requesting favour on behalf of William Berewith, excommunicated for incontinent living. *Draft.*

1580, November 12. London.—James Knell to Mr. Jackson, Mayor of Rye.

"I have had conference with Mr. Mills touchinge the Star Chamber matter, and he sayeth that the reporte you heard of is utterly untrue for the cause is in such sorte dismyssed that neyther in part or all it can by any meanes be revived, and therfore wold have you free of care in that behalf. Whilest by the favorable countenance of the Lord Chefe Baron, your greate frend, by the good advyse of your Counsell and by the mosion of your Serjeant, I went about to entrench the cause of errors, and by the bulwarkes aforesaid to have made it free from the enymye and in safty, ye and beynge persuaded to have had peace, consideringe our ernest endevour on the one side and the carelesnes on the other syde, and uppon this persuasion sessed not to delve to fynyshe the trenche, and behold uppon a sodayne (as many times it chanceth in sutch affayers) the adversary, even as a lyones robbed of her whelpes, cometh with myght and mayne and maketh a merveylous forcyble and freshe assault in sutche sorte, that by my trenchinge tooles I hardly could withstand hym, for my implementes and furnytures of warre, I meane the bookes, were forgotten and lefte behynd at Caunterbury, so that yf God had not helped, it had ben harde with spades and mattockes to have made defence agaynst hot shott and longe pykes. But thus it happened that the sonne did come about and gave forth his chereful brightnes, and Mercer, the generall at this bussines, havinge impedimentes in his ies in sutch sorte that he could by no meanes abyde the dayelyght, the assault began to wexe more cold and the generall not able to abyde the saver of our mase which for the comfort of our stomaches we did use, was fayne to hyde hymself, he was so farre spent. But yet nowe with a gallant and brave shewe comes his lieutenant one Mr. Cyssy and he supployes a freshe assault. Wherfore I beseche you that yf you can send me ayde from your towne of warr, suche bookes as you have concernynge your lybertyes (which I will terme calyver shott) and from Dover Castle sutche bookes as concerne the hole Portes, the Court of Shipwaye, and Writes of Errors there brought, which I will terme bases, culveringes, dymyes cannons and . . . . . the very sight wherof maye dant the hart of the adversary."

1580, December 16.—Petition of Josephe Okeman and Mathew Fleury to the Mayor of Rye.

"This is to beseche you in most lamentable wyse to thinke upon us and our myserable estates which we have sygnyfyed unto you by wryghtinge allredy more then once, which pytyfull complaintes of ours we ar well assured that yf the same had ben exhibeted unto the Lordes of the Quene's Majestie's Prevey Counsayll, ther Honners would have vouchsafed to shewe both pyty and compassyon towardes us; but we cannott understand that you dooe so much even as think upon us which lye her at your pleaser in this your howsse which should be a place of correction but is more liker a place of tormentes, which we to truly fynd, for we ar glad to take the clothes from our owen bakes to stoppe the wyndowes and broken places, to kepe out the force of such wether as God at this present hath sent, and yet it is so lyttel purpose, wherfor we ar lyke to perysh by means therof, and therfor doe the rather give you to understand for that you maye be inexcusable when as our bloud shall, as we knowe it wyll, cail and crye unto the magesty of our ryghteous judge for vengance agaynste you, for although he, for whome we undertoke, be a wicked and perverste man not havinge the fear of God before his face nor the love of his nyghbour in his harte, yet you are in Godes place to mynester justic wyth mercy. You know, God wylleth not the death of a syner, but you kepe us her wher we be in danger of our lyfes by meanes of the wether and opennes of your howse and allso would have us to put into your hands all that lyttel thinge which we be worth and so we should com to greater myssery if it pleas God to lengthen this wretched lyfe of ours, which we knowe would be no pleasuer to any of you. Thus hopinge that if ther be any bowells of mercy wythin you we shall not remayne longe in this myssery, which we pray God to bringe to passe, unto whose tewition we commytt you."

1580, December 26. Whitehall.—The Lords of the Council to Lord Cobham.

Whereas we understand there hath been resort of pirates to divers ports within the jurisdiction of the Cinque Ports, where they are daily received and harboured by the inhabitants of the said places, making open sale of their spoils without interruption. These are therefore to pray you to take order for the staying and apprehending of such pirates. *Copy.*

[1579-1580].—Certificate by the Mayor and Jurats of Rye that one George White of Rye, turner, is the son of John White, late of Sandwich, baker, deceased, and was born at Calais. The said George is minded to set out for the town of "Blanelwall" in Wales where his kindred live and there to make claim to certain lands.

[1580].—An order signed by Lord Cobham, as to the election of the Mayor of Rye.

"Imprimis, by the auctoritie of auncient charters and priviledges heeretofore to you and your predecessors graunted, for the better tranquillitie of your towne at your next comen assembly to sett downe, ennacte, ordaine and establishe, that yearely for ever hereafter, the Maior of the towne of Rye, for the tyme beinge, and the jurates there, or the more parte of them (not havinge any leafull cause or necessarie impediment to excuse their absence in his behalfe) on the usual day of the election of your Maior, betweene the hours of 8 and 9 of the clocke in the forenoone of the same daie, shall assemble themselves together at the common hall of the said towne, and before 10 of the clocke in the same forenoone, the said Maior and Jurates, or the most parte of them, by their towne clerck, for the time being, to sett downe in writtinge under their handes or signes, or the handes or signes of the major part of them, the names and surnames of three honest and discreete personnes of the said Jurates, to the ende the commons may freely electe and chuse one of those three to be Maior there for the yeare following and soe quietly to departe untill the hour of their commen ellection of the Maior.

Item, that when their accustomed assemblie is made to the intent and purpose aforesaid, and at the usual place for the same election, the Maior and Jurates of the said towne or the more parte of them then presente, and in the presence of the Commons of the said towne, to deliver to their town clerck aforesaid the schedule, wherin the said names of the three Jurates shalbe written, to make present publication of them to the Commons aforesaid; and with an audible voice in their presence to will and require them in her Majesties name in quiet and freindly manner to proceede to the nomination and election of one of those three soe named in the said schedule or bill, to be Maior of their towne for that yeare following, withowte any disturbance or secrete practises to be used or procured by anie of the same competitors or by anie other for them or in their behalf, upon the paine of forfeictinge of some goode and round some of money, to be imposed and infliged upon the offendors in that behalf, by the discretion of the olde Maior and the consentes of the Jurates of the said towne or the most parte of them, to be distributed towardes the releiff of the poore people of your towne.

Item, that whomsoever of the said three, the said Commons by their most voices shall freely elect and give consent to be Maior of the said towne, the olde Maior for the yeare past presentely to give a corporall othe, as heretofore it hath ben accustomably used to be doen, to the newe Maior of the said towne soe elected for the yeare following which order and maner of election of the said Maior, the said Maior, Jurates and Commons to ennacte, ordeyne and decree to be kept and observed for ever, upon paine that whosoever attemptith or goeth about to violate or infringe the same, to forfeicte everie tyme he shall soe offende the some of 40*li.*, leaful money of England, the one half wherof to be to the use of your towne and the other halfe to the use of him or them that will sue for the same by bill of complainte, comprehendinge the effecte of this order and decree with the maner of the parties offence contrarie to the tenure hereof, to be exhibited and prosecuted in the Chauncelrie Court for the Portes usually holden and kept in the church of St. James at Dovor. And further the said partie or parties soe offending in anie of the said orders, for everie suche offence to be punished by waie of ymprisonment withowte baile or maine price for the space of three monethes next after the time of his conviction for anie of the said offences soe committed or doen.

Item, for the more suere performaunce herof in time to come to furder ordeyne and decree that all person and personnes hereafter to be chosen Maior or Maiors, Jurate or Jurates of your said towne, at the severall times of their elections, to be sworne in like maner well and truly to observe, fulfil, keepe, defend, and mainteyne to all intents and purposes, soe farr as in them shall lie, this order and everie thinge therin contained accordingly which othe yf anie refuse to take then he or they soe refusing the same not to be admitted to the office or degree of Maior or Jurate of the said towne but therof and of all benefittes that maie rise and growe unto him therebie to be for ever hereafter debarred and disallowed, anie lawe, priviledge or custome used or not used hertofore within the said towne, to the contrarie, in aniewise notwithstanding.

Item, more to establishe and ordeyne emongest you that from henceforth from time to time, as ocasion shall require, suche nomber of men as shall want of the Commen Councell of the said towne to be chosen, appointed, and named by the Maior and Jurates there for the time being or the most parte of them, beinge present at a commen assembly which Commen Councell with the said Maior and Jurates or the most parte [of] them, at all times hereafter at a commen assembly, shall elect and appoint owt of the said Jurates, the Burgesses to the Parliament for their said towne, and the bearers of the Canabie for Royall service and all other officers of the said towne, as often as neede shall require, except always all suche officers as heretofore of good right have been nominated and chosen by the Maior of the towne for the time being to be and remaine still at the said Maior's election and appoinctment as before it hath been usually accustomed and doen.

Item, to conclude, lett it be decreed that the Maior and Jurates or the more parte of them being presente at a commen assembly for ever hereafter as often as anie juratshipp by death or otherwise shall happen to be voyed and wanting, shall make choise and election of suche sufficient and hable person or personnes, owte of the commen councell of the said towne, as to them or the most parte of them shalbe thought most meete and convenient for that degree, to be Jurate or Jurates in his or their places, anie lawe, prescription, usage, or matter within the said towne to the contrarie herof notwithstandinge."

1580.—Various documents in connection with a suit by John Mercer against the Mayor and Jurats of Rye touching the privileges of the Cinque Ports.

1580.—Petition by the Churchwardens and Sidesmen of Rye to the Mayor and his bretheren. Whereas they have presented divers persons for drunkenness, and considering their estate were not able to bear the charge of presentment in the Spiritual Court, they pray that no taverns or victualling houses shall suffer any of those persons to drink either in or at the doors of their houses under a penalty, which they think will do a good service to God.

1580[-1], January 2.—[The Mayor and Jurates of Rye] to Mr. Holstocke, Controller of the Navy.

"This bearer Nicholas Cheston, our friend and honest neighbor, hath related unto us, that thorough the untrue reporte of one of the company that saylled in his barke, he was staied in the Sergeantes office of the Admiraltie by a certaine space for conveyinge awaye or councellinge of one Thomas Walker, another of his company, to absent himself, beinge before prest into her Majesties service, (the which ponishment he well deservid, if he had so farre offendid). And that afterwardes your Worshipe shewed him that courtesey as to lett him att liberty uppon his bond to brynge forthe the said Walker within foure monethes, for the which your frendshipe towardes him we yeld you harty thankes, and are further to crave your frendshipe towardes him that ye wold stand so good unto him to release him of his said bonde, beinge at this instant on a voyage and knoweth not when he shall retorne againe, and by that meanes may forfait his bond to his gret troble, if you be not good unto him. We are the bolder to request this much of you for that the said Cheston before us takith God to wytnes that he was not privie of the said Walker's departure in such order nether gave eny suche councell to him, and for our partes we beleve it to be true, the rather for that he is so honest a yonge man emongest us, as is obedient to all thinges as to him apperteynith, and the said Walker is not yet come unto Rye." *Draft.*

1580[-1.], January 10.—"A Proclamation for revocation of sundrie her Majesties subjectes remayning beyond the seas, under colour of studie and yet living contrarie to the Lawes of God and of the Realm. And also against the retayning of Jesuites and massing priestes, sowers of sedition, and other treasonable attempts." *Printed by Christopher Barker.*

1580[-1.], January 20.—The Mayor and Jurats of Rye to the Mayors, Bailiffs and Jurats of Hastings, Winchelsea, Romney, Hythe, Dover, and Sandwich.

"Whereas by sundry iron workes and glasse houses already erected and of some continuance, the woddes growinge nere unto the three townes of Hastinges, Winchelsey and Rye, are marvaylously wasted and decayed; and by reason of the same workes and others to be newly erectid, if spedy remedy be not had, the said woodes will in short tyme be utterly consumed in sorte as there will not eny timber be had for shippynge, waterworkes, housebuylding, nor wood for fuell, not only to the utter decaye of thoes thre townes, but also a want to your people inhabytinge farther of, as experience already teachith. And therfore we have gevin instructions to Mr. Gaymer and Mr. Carpenter, barons to the Parliament for our towne, for a bill to be drawen to the Parliament house therby to have a statut to passe for the preservation of the woddes growinge within certaine parishes lyinge nere and aboute the said thre townes." *Draft.*

[1580-1, January ?.]—Instructions to Mr. Henry Gaymer and Mr. Robert Carpenter, Barons to the Parliament for the town of Rye, for a bill to be drawn for the passing of a statute for the preservation of the woods in the several parishes following, viz.:—"Westfylde, Brede, Gestlinge, Nordiham, Beckley, the Isle of Oxney, Iden, and Woodchurch.

The causes of the destruction of these woods.

There is an iron forge in the Parish of Brede distant five miles from Rye and one mile from Brede Bridge, at which place the woods are laden with lighters and so brought down to Winchelsea and Rye. The said iron forge is nearer to Winchelsea than Hastings.

There is an iron hammer in the Parish of Westfylde, which hammer is very hurtful to the haven, for by cutting a gate the water is turned from its accustomed course to the channel and so runs to the mill of the said iron hammer.

There was of late a glass house in the parish of Beckley, which destroyed a number of woods, and now there is another in the parish of Nordiham which has already spoiled a great store of woods. Those glass houses are very hurtful for as the woods about them decay so the glass houses remove and follow the woods with small charge which the iron works cannot so easily do.

The causes why those woods in the said parishes are to be preserved.

First, for the building of ships, fishboats &c. which are the maintenance of those towns.

Secondly, the want of timber to maintain piers, harbours, groynes, jetties, capstans to wind up shipping, provisions for sluices and gutters, ship board, barrel board for barrels to preserve fish, timber for gun stocks, wheels for ordnance, planks for platforms, ash trees for "fyters and makers."

Thirdly, the want of timber for re-edifying of decayed houses in the said towns, and for new buildings.

Fourthly, the scarcity of firewood and fuel that all degrees of people there inhabiting hath, and especially the poor fishermen who go to the sea early and late, and in the cold winter and stormy weather must have fire to comfort them at their return. The decay of the fishermen will not only be the utter decay of those towns, but a loss to the maintenance of the navy, for that they are the first that train youth tothe seas, and also the lack of fish will be found in her Majesty's house, the City of London and the country adjoining and also far off.

Fifthly, if the woods be so wasted that there should be want of fuel, the situation of the said towns is so cold, unsheltered, open to the air, on the flat face of the sea, and freighted with poverty hardly able to abide the after winters force—the people will be forced to seek habitation elsewhere and those towns left unemployed and open to the enemy.

Sixthly, The following towns, situate along the sea-coast, are relieved from the woods aforesaid with fuel and with timber for building, and come to have their barques and fisherboats built at Hastings, Winchelsea, and Rye with timber out of the said woods:—Brighthelmston, Michinge, Borne, Hastings, Wynchelsea, Rye, in the County of Sussex; Lydd, Romney, Hythe, Folkstone, Dover, the Downs, Sandwich, and the Isle of Thanet in the county of Kent.

It may please you to make the Barons and Burgesses of such towns on the sea coasts as you shall think best, acquainted herewith and to ground the matter upon the glass houses with some conclusion that the said woods may be preserved to sustain the aforesaid wants and not to any other use.

A proviso that such billets called by the name of Winchelsea billets for Calais, may be made for those towns as formerly so that they keep the ancient size for that kind of billet is the fittest for those towns and for shipping and carrying along the Ports to the aforesaid towns.

Another proviso that not keeping the size of those billets a forfeiture be made and that the said towns of Hastings, Winchelsea, and Rye take the benefit thereot towards the maintenance of their harbours.

1580[-1], February 4.—Order by the Mayor and Jurats of Rye.

"Forasmuch as it falleth out apparently that George Thorpe of Rye, fisherman, tooke certaine nettes and other goodes at the seas unorderly from a man of Treaporte by reason wherof the nettes of the said Anthony Mary and his company were allso taken awaye by thoes of Treaporte, and allso findinge that restitution is not to be had on eny partie of the said goodes and nettes, for finall ende to be had in the cause and without any farther demande to be had eny waye by the said Anthony or his companey for theire nettes, It is ordered by the Maior and Jurattes of Rye aforesaid that the said George Thorpe, his executors, administrators, or assignes, shall well and truly satisfye content and paye or cause to be contentid and paied unto the said Anthonye Mary to the use of him and his company in full satisfaction and contentation of the goodes and nettes taken from them by the men of Treaporte, the some of twenty poundes of good and lawfull money of England."

1581, May 6.—Certificate by the Mayor and Jurats of Rye that there came before them "Helen Frotier, the wife of John Frotier of the said town of Rye, lockyer, and complained of the injuries wronges and rigorous usage of hir said husband of longe tyme and at this instant, towardes her the said Helen, in sorte, as she is not only lamyd in hir lymes but allso standith in continuall danger of hir lyff, and therefore ment to departe frome him unto Roan in Normandy, prayinge us to signifie the truth of our knowledges, as well concerning her demeanour towardes the said John Frotier hir said husband as also his mysdemeaner towardes his said wiff. Wherfore theis are to signifie unto you for truth that the said Helen, ever sithens we have known her, hath behavid herself well and honestly towardes the said John Frotier, hir husband, in every respecte as hath becomyd a dutefull wiff, and lekewise towardes all other persones to our knowledges. And that the said John Frotier hir husband is a very drunken and beastly person and hath from tyme to tyme contynually beaten and marvaillous evelly entreated the said Helen, his wiff, wherof she hath often complaynid and we often tymes have ponished him for his lewdnes and yet no amendment followeth, but rather the poor woman in danger of her liff then otherwise."

1581, May 19.—The Mayor and Jurats of Rye to Sir James Croft, the Controller of her Majesty's household.

"Whereas uppon the pitifull complainte of the poore fishermen of Ry order was taken by you and the rest of hir Majesty's officers of hir Highnes' Grencloth upon the 18th of Aprill laste paste, that payement shuld be made unto them of the arrerages behinde for fishe purveyed by the purvyor or his deputie, untill the first of that moneth, and that clere payment for fishe to be purveyed afterwardes, shuld be made every fyftene daies. Nowe the said fishermen have newly complayned unto us that they are not paide the said arrerages nor yet for the fishe purveyed sithens, so as they are almost fyve moneths behinde of their mony which bringeth them in so lowe state as they are not able longer to contynue their trade to the seas (as they informe us) besides the missery their wyves, children, and family are presently in. Whereuppon they meane to sue unto their Honors for some present redresse. But we callinge to remembrance your Honor's late travels taken for them and supposinge their nonpayment contrary to your said late orders is wholy unknowen unto you, have thought it moost metest first to acquaint your Honor with the same and therefore are humble petitioners unto you that the defecte may be examined." *Draft.*

1581, May 19.—A Proclamation for the continuance of a certain Act against usury. *Printed by Christopher Barker.*

1581, July 17.—Safe conduct by the Mayor and Jurats of Rye to Charles Baudrye, who, with his wife and mother, has dwelt peaceably and quietly in the town of Rye for the space of nine years, to depart, with his wife and mother and all their household to Boulogne in his ship called the *Gift of God* manned with ten men.

1581, September 6.—Depositions taken before the Mayor of Rye, at the request of Nicholas Jeue, procurator, for Barthelmewe Arnold, and James Asselin in right of their wives, Loys le Dreu in right of his mother, Catherin Biancoussin, and Jeane, her daughter, resident in Rye, as to whether Loys Biancoussin, late the husband of Mary Vassage, took and enjoyed a cellar full of coals at Dieppe, the property of Nicholas Biancoussin, his brother, deceased. Catherin Biancoussin aged about seventy years deposes that the said Nicholas Biancoussin died about 18 or 19 years past at Dieppe. Jeane, daughter of the said Catherin, aged about thirty-four years, deposes to the like effect.

1581, September 21.—"A Proclamation for adjournment of parte of Michaelmas Terme 1581." *Printed by Christopher Barker.*

1581, September 26.—[The Mayor and Jurats of Rye to Lord Cobham.]

"Ther is a piratt, wherof is Capten one Peerse, that hath made dyverse spoyles and robberyes uppon such merchauntes and passengers as traffique the passages and other places, which contynually for the space of this moueth hathe remayned against the towne of Rie and doth barr the harborough, as none can goe forth or come in, butt he doth with his force apprehend and spoile, too the great losse of the merchauntes and impovrishment of our towne. His spoyles have been dyverse and amount unto greate somes which he hath taken from passengers commynge into our towne. First he did take one of Rye that was bound to Deape, laden with packes too the valew of 700 *li.*, cruelly entreatinge our neighbours and sent the barke empty in. Then he did take a Burton's [Breton's] shippe which now the pyratt dothe use for his more force and hath sent all the maryners into Rye in most poore sort and hath fired the man of war wherin he did first robb in. Upon Sunday last past he robbed another passenger which came from Deape unto Rie and detayned them untill Monday morninge and spoyled him of all the goodes he had, where one of Canterbury lost one hundreth and fyfty poundes. Also he robbed another passenger of Rie and tooke from an Irishman three score powndes in money and all goodes ells in the same that sarved his turne. Neyther doth hee cease butt as one that pretendeth too bar all men from us. He yet remayneth in sight of the towne redy to impeach all that shall come in or goo owt, to the overthrow of her Majesty's towne and spoile of her Majesty's lovinge subjectes. And for that, right Honorable, so greate a mischefe is too bee suppressed and such a caterpiller apprehended wherunto wee have most ready hartes if wee were warranted therunto, we do therfore implore unto your good Lordship and in most humble sort beseache your Honor to have consideration of this cawse as by your Lordship's good meanes ther may bee such order taken for the apprehension of this piratt as hee may bee chastysed."

[Postscript.]—"The piratt is stronge and those that are willinge to venter their lives wold gladly be entertayned with some consideration beefore they venter forth and the charges for the shippe and munytions will not bee litle, which is also too bee considered of by your Lordship." *Draft.*

1581, September 27. Cobham.—Lord Cobham to the Mayor and Jurats of Rye.

Concerning the pirate, your instructions are not so fully laid down to me as that I am able to inform my Lords of what burden, what number of men, or how well appointed he is, wherof you shall do well to certify me at large. *Signed, and seal of arms.*

1581, September 30.—[The Mayor and Jurats of Rye] to Lord Cobham.

"Concerninge the piraie which annoyeth our town we have made further inquiry of him and of what force he is. And the Brytains whoes shepe he hath taken, which were tenn daies aborд him, do certefy us for truth that his barke is of the burden of 35 tonnes or theraboutes mannyd with 26 or 27 persons in the whole, two fawkenets and 6 small bases with certaine calivers and all other munitions for the warr; and, as they suppose, hath in consort another lyttle vessell of the burden of 18 tonnes but the perfait truth therof is not known." *Draft.*

1581, October 10.—The Mayor and Jurats of Rye to Lord Cobham.

Whereas the messenger we lately sent to your Lordship has related to us that your pleasure is we should articulate under our seal the substance of our request; we have considered thereof, and, if it stand with your Lordship's good pleasure, do think that the same is not the meetest way for divers respects, but that it would please your Honour to procure a commission for the setting forth out of the Ports such competent aid as shall from time to time be needful for the apprehension of such a pirate. *Draft.*

1581, October 16.—Order by the Mayor and Jurats of Rye "that service in the Church upon the working days shall begin, at six o'clock in the morning for morning prayers, and at five o'clock in the evening for evening prayers; and the sexton to toll to service upon those days half an hour before the hour of prayer. And also from All Saints next the great bell to be rung at four o'clock in the morning and so continue every morning until the Annunciation next."

1581, October 25. Richmond.—Lord Cobham to the Mayor, Bailiffs and Jurats of Rye Winchelsea and Hastings.

I have here inclosed sent unto you the copy of the letter the Lords of her Majesty's Privy Council, directed unto me, wherein I pray you with all diligence and expedition to take order accordingly.

Enclosure.—Letter from the Lords of the Council to Lord Cobham, dated 22 October 1581, setting out that "Wheras there hath bene here of late, out of sundry portes and creekes of the realm, divers shipps armed fourth unto the sea under coulor and pretence of newe discoveries and voiages into forreyn and unknowen partes, which beinge at the seas have and doe dayly commit piracies and spoiles as well upon the subjects of this realm, as of other princes hir Majesty's neighbours and allies in league and amytie with her Highnes, to the great discreadit of the whole realm and dishonor unto her Majestie: for the preventing of which disorder, she haveinge oftentimes heretofore, by the advice of us of her Privye Councell, sent into the maritime counties of the realme severall commissions and directions to have ben put in execution against such as shold in warleike manner arme and sett forth shipps unto the seas, wherof ther hath followed no redresse, but rather the disorder increased; hir Majestie therfore, findinge that hir former commandments herein have not ben observed as apperteyned, has willed us in hir name expressely to charge and command you that presently, uppon the receipt hereof, you cause dilligent enquiry to be made in all the portes, creekes and roades within the circuite of your jurisdiction, what shippes are at this present in rigginge and preparinge for leike voiages to the seas, and to certefie unto us the burden of the shipps, to whome they do apperteyne, and by whome they are to be armed and sett forth, and for what places their voiages are intended, and not onely [not] to suffer them or any of them to departe to the seas, but also from this time forth not to permitt any shipp to be rigged and prepared within any of the portes, creekes or roads under your charge, for any voyage to the seas (other then the shippes of knowen merchantes goeinge in ordenary trade of merchandize) unless they shall shew unto you some speciall licence therunto, either from her Majestie or from us of her Privy Councell."

1581, November 11.—A Proclamation for the prices of wine. *Printed by Christopher Barker.*

1581, November 21.—Lord Buckhurst to the Mayor and Jurats of Rye.

"I am sorie that I shold have this occasion to conceave so just a caus of your hard deling, being alwaies heretofore so desirous to have bene a favorer and fartherer of ye and your causes to my power, and not a misliker as now ye do infors me. I had thought that the private letters of meself shold have bene sufficient to have moved ye in a far greter matter then for the acceptation of my servaunt, Thomas Edolf, into your feloship again, being as ye yourselfes well know both worthy therof and injustly put from the same. But sins it pleased my Lord Cobham to ad his authoryty to my request, methinkes ye shold have had a better respect than so lightly to have regarded both the one and the other, wherin his Lordship and I having conferred together and marveling not a litell that you shold offer any such deling unto us, have yet determined ons again to write unto ye and even so to requier you that if ye can allege no just caus why you shold in this sort kepe out my said servant Edolf as you have doon from out the feloship of a Jurate in your town, that then without farther delay you will readmit him, which if you shall refuse to doe you shal geve just caus unto my Lord Warden especially, and unto me also so far furth as my power may extend, to call in question your injurious delinges therin and to seke suche reformation as to justice and equitie appertaineth."

1581, November 24.—The Mayor and Jurats of Rye to Lord Cobham.

We have received your letters directed to the Mayors, Bailiffs and Jurats of Rye, Winchelsea, and Hastings bearing date the 25th October last together with a letter from the Lords of the Council. Since the receipt of the same letters there hath not been, nor yet are, any ships or barks armed forth to any foreign parts out of this town, but only well known merchants going in ordinary trade and not taking any great voyages but only into France "Burdees or Biscay" for wines oranges or such like merchandise. *Draft.*

[1580–1581.]—Richard Porth to the Mayor and Jurats of Rye.

"Whereas I, by the most assent and consent of the good parishioners of this towne about 5 yeares past, was electid and appointid your parish clarke and therewith to have all suche wages, duties and commodities perteyning to the same office. And for that Mr. Flecher had appointed Mr. Ruck to serve under him in his absence, a greate parte of that stipent, appertayning to my foresaid fees and wages, was abridged and taken awaye, in so muche as it was scant sufficient to mayntayn me and my poor wif. And the rathor by reason of God's longe visitation amongest us, by reason wherof I could not instruct and teach children in kepeing of scole, as in tyme before I have don, which was a greate parte of my lyvinge, and the want therof gretly to my impoverishment. In tender consideration whereof, and in so much as at this instant Mr. Flecher is departid from our towne, and that (as I ame informid) Mr. Ruck hath that stipend appointid to him which Mr. Flecher had, whilest he was minister here, and further for that I know that it lieth most part in your Worshipes handes to restore those duties pertayning to my said office to me agayne, I most humbly beseche your Worshippes to extend your favourable goodwylles towardes me."

1581[-2], January 28.—Petition of the Fishermen and Mariners of Rye for a charter of incorporation.

[1581-2, January.]—The inconveniences which would grow if the fishermen of Rye should obtain an incorporation from her Majesty.

1581[-2], February 4. Dover.—Nichol Barrey to the Mayor of Rye.

"I send yow here ynclosed a letter from Mr. Secretarye Wallsyngham for 6 of your best barkes of your town to mack theyr repayr to Dover for the transportyng of musters and other for her Magystys esspesyall servys. I understand that her Magysty yn person wyll be at Dovor on Tuesday next at the ferthest. Wherefore I praye you all the hast possybell may be made of the sayed barkes to be at Dover, and that you returne aunswer by this berer how many barkes you send and of what burthen." *Seal of arms.*

1581[-2], February 4.—The Mayor and Jurats of Rye to Sir Francis Walsingham.

"This present Sonday afternone we receyved your lettres and with that dilligence that might be, have appointed fyve barkes the best and all that are at this present to be had in our towne, for that some are beneaped and the rest are dispersed on voyages to sondry places; which said fyve barkes are of the burden, mannyd and victualed as in the note herein closed apperith, and in suche good sorte as so short tyme wolde permit and, God willinge, shall departe from our towne tomorrow morning; being very sory that suche barkes were not at home as we wishe in hart for hir Majesty's service." *Draft.*

1582, April 1.—A Proclamation to denounce Jesuits traitors. *Printed by Christopher Barker.*

1582, May 29.—Certificate by the Mayor and Jurats of Rye that Doctor Fletcher, chancellor of this diocese, since the time of his coming to the office of Chancellorship had dealt very justly and uprightly in the execution thereof and therefore as he hath deserved great love among us, so we heartily desire he may long time abide and continue in this diocese, to the glory of God and the benefit of this country. *Draft.*

1582, June 25.—The Mayor and Jurats of Rye to the Bishop of Chichester.

The year past this bearer Mr. Grenewood, now our preacher, was by the then farmer of the vicarage of Rye retained to be our preacher. He having left his licences with his father in the north country we pray you not to doubt but that he hath those licences and they were shewed unto the Mayor of Rye who was the last year.

1582, October 8.—"A Proclamation for keeping the Terme at Hertford Castell and for adjournement of the same from *mense Michaelis* until *Crastino Animarum*" *Printed by Christopher Barker.*

1582, November 5.—The Mayor and Jurats of Rye to Sir Francis Walsingham.

"There is remayninge in our prison one John Hadmon *alias* Carter, a papist, which was here staied as he was passinge over sea and hath contynued by the space of 14 wekes past, of whome your Honor hath byn certefyed and of whome we thought good to put you now in rememberance, for that as yet we have noe order frome your Honor for him, he lyinge in prison miserably without mony or succor otherwise then of the cheritie of the people of our towne to whome he is a charge and they waxinge wery therof." *Draft.*

1582, November 16., Windsor.—Sir Francis Walsingham to the Mayor and Jurats of Rye.

As regards your letter of the fifth of the present touching John Hamon, now prisoner in your town, the enclosed supplication has been exhibited to me from the said party but as he has not subscribed his name to it, I have thought good to send the same to you, requiring you to cause him to subscribe it with his own hand and that you administer the oath of supremacy to him, both which if he be contented to do, you may set him at liberty.

Signed, and Seal of Arms.

Enclosure. Petition of John Hamon alias Carter, late servant of Sir Thomas Copley, resident in parts beyond the sea, in which he renounces the Romish religion and prays he may be released.

1582. November 16.—The Bailiffs and Jurats of Hastings to the Mayo and Jurats of Rye.

"Forasmuch as at this presente tyme the Citie of London ys greveously infected with the plague (a disease very contagious and infectious) by reason wheareof, thorough the great concourse of people thither resortinge, and buyinge of wares amongest those as were infected weth the same disease, many townes and places hereaboute in the countrey (the more is the pyttie) by theire owne follie are infected with the same. And we—fearinge that the lyke may happen amongest us (which God forbydd) thoroughe the resort of some unrulie people owt from some infectious place about us to our fayre that is to be holden with us one St Clementes day nexte, the 23rd of this instant moneth of November—have thought it good that the same fayre for this tyme, to eschew the same daunger, shall not be kepte."

1582, November 26.—The Mayor and Jurats of Rye to the Bishop of Dover.

Whereas there were delivered to us by one Evernden of Byddenden in Kent a precept directed from you and others, her Majesty's Commissioners in Causes Ecclesiastical, for the apprehending of certain persons abiding in the foreign as also some inhabiting in our Town, to have them forth before you at Canterbury, these are to advertise you we are willing and ready to execute your precept for the apprehending of malefactors, so also are we careful that nothing be done which may be prejudicial to our liberties, which we are sworn to maintain. For such as are within our Liberties we will see they shall be forthcoming to appear before you within any the Cinque Ports, which we desire you to take in good part until we may be advised whether the men of the Ports ought to appear before Commissioners out of their Liberties. *Draft.*

1582[-3], January 10, Canterbury.—Richard, Bishop of Dover, W. Redman and Nicholas Sentleger to the Mayor of Rye.

Whereas upon special causes us moving, we directed forth process in her Majesty's name to you, Mr. Mayor of Rye, for the apprehension of certain disordered persons, namely, Stephen Harryson and Richard Danyel, commorant within the town of Rye, which process coming to your hands took no effect, but was as we are informed contemptuously rejected, both to the derogation of Her Majesty's authority and the encouragement of those lewd persons in their wickedness. These are therefore to signify unto you that unless you send those two persons to us at our next sitting within the Cathedral Church of Christ in Canterbury, we are determined to proceed against you for your contempt and to impose a fine on you to her Majesty's use. *Signed.*

1582[-3], February 5.—The Mayor and Jurats of Rye to Richard, Bishop of Dover, and others, the Commissioners for Causes Ecclesiastical.

"The precepts you sent to the Mayor are not executed but by consent of him and his brethren the Jurates, and therfore we thinke ourselves muche abused by those who soe informed you of the contemptuous rejectment of your former proces, for in truth we receyvid the same in that dutifull sorte as became us and wrote our letters unto you touchinge the same which we sent to Mr. Everenden to be conveyed unto you, the which we suppose are not come to your handes, for if they had we doubt not but you would have accepted them in suche good parte as we shuld not have byn thought or accompted contemptuous of her Majesty's aucthoritie; for we are no such persons, and so we trust your Lordship and the rest will think us, whatsoever the informers have informed, whome only we take to be in fault in this case. Theis berers Stevin Harrison and Richard Daniell are appoynted by us to repayre unto you to answer and do as their duties apperteyneth we hoppe they have not so delt as meritith the name of lewde and wicked persons, but we thinke matter more urged against them by the complaynantes than deservith." *Draft.*

1583, April 18.—The Mayor and Jurats of Rye to the Burgomaster of Dunkirk.

"Wheras heretofore some sute and controversey hath byn dependinge betwene our combaron James Milles of the auncient towne of Rye within the liberties of the Cinque Portes of England, merchant, and divers of your burgeseis and townesmen in sorte as the honest inhabitantes and marchantes of your said towne have withdrawen themselves frome their frendly and accustomid trafiqueinge with the inhabitantes and marchantes of our towne of Rye and other of the Fyve Portes as well to the loose and hindrance of your people as of ours, theis are therefore not only to certefye you for truthe that all such sutes and controversies as the said James Milles had or might have against your said burgeseis and townesmen for any cause whatsoever is wholy fynished and endid, but also that your inhabitantes and marchantes maye frely repaire unto our towne of Rye or unto eny other of the Cinque Portes or their members in their accustomed trade, without any lett or staye of the said James Milles or of eny other for him or in his name, promisinge you by theis our letters that you and all other your burgeseis and townesmen shalbe moost lovingly and friendly welcome as in tymes past ye have byn and shall fynde us redy to shewe you eny frendshipe that in us lieth." *Draft.*

1583, April 19.—Proclamation against Retainers. *Printed by Christopher Barker.*

1583, December 2.—Presentments before the Mayor and Jurats of Rye of various offences. Common absenters from the church, occupiers of sciences and occupations contrary to the laws of the realm, victuallers for keeping idle and poor people in their houses to drink and play unlawful games, pots and other measures not lawful, several persons fined for selling sack at 8*d.* the quart and "Gasken wine" at 6*d.* the quart, forestallers, regrators, and ingrossers, common annoyances, wearing of hats (a large number of persons presented for wearing hats instead of English caps in going to church) butchers for killing of sheep called barren ewes, quarrellings and frays, fines for having wooden chimneys and chimneys that had been on fire, &c.

1583 [-4], January 7.—The Mayor and Jurats of Rye to Lord Burleigh.

"Whereas longe sithens a licence was grauntid to the right honorable the Lord Montague for transportation of his woddes convertid into billets, called billets for Callice, a kynde of fuell of longe tyme usid here and alongest the coaste, which licence staieth for that so much of his wodes as were so made into billets is alredy transported and none of his woodes cutt downe to that use for this yere. It may please your Honour to be advertised that notwithstandinge suche as have dealinge in that licence do still transporte the leike billetes in suche sorte as ther are not eny to be had to releyve the want of the pouer sorte of our towne and the coast alongest, which hath them by the peneworth and so forth accordinge to there small abilities a matter to be piteid if it were to your Honor so well knowen as it is to us, whereuppon we have here at Rye made a restraine, not sufferinge eny frome thence to be transported; and nowe the dealers therin go upe with their vessels to Winchelsey and there lade and that no small nomber so as there is not eny of that fuell to be had with us this winter tyme, and restraine ther ladinge there we cannot of ourselves, nether doth our entreaty prevaile beinge out of our liberties and yet the place such as her Majesties enemies may easely from thoes partes be conveied over sea especially under culler of transportation of billets as Docter Marten was in a vessell laden with billets and himself conveyed into a rome made in the midst of them." *Draft.*

1584.—The Mayor and Jurats of Rye to Lord Burleigh.

Whereas in January 1583 we "were humble petitioners unto your Honor for staye to be made of the transportation of billetes frome Winchelsey beside Rye for divers considerations then to your Honor shewed, beinge before a restraint for the leike at Rye, by meanes wherof they obteynid from your Honor lettres directid to the Mayor and Jurats of Winchelsea and officers of the Custome there prohibitinge them to suffer any bylletes to be transportid frome thence. Yet nowe (your Honors lettres notwithstandinge) for that they either be old in date or els not to be sene, the officers of Winchelsey do daylye suffer all vessels comynge thither to lade and transporte billets frome thence, in sorte as the people of Rye, especiallye the poor can have none for their money, beinge besides a grete nomber of the Frenche who spend much more fuell then was wonte, and lyttel or none to be had but that which comith downe out of the contry by Winchelsey water, which is out of the liberties of Rye and out of your Honors supplyantes aucthoritie to make staye or restrainte therof, by reason of which said ladinge and transportation frome Winchelsey and troble of the informers agaynst the makers of bylletes as lately was complayned to your Honor, the people generally as well Frenche as Englishe, riche and poore of the said towne of Rye are at this instant in a hard case for fuell; and other townes of the portes which were wont to bringe commodityes to Rye wherof the towne had nede, as wheate, malte and such leike and to furnish themselves thare with byllets and other fuell for their provision, refrayne their trafique for that they cannot have the commoditie they were wonte." *Draft.*

1585, April 26.—Orders by the Mayor and Jurats of Rye that the town be viewed to find out the most meet places for fortifications. That the chancel on the south side of the Church called St. Clere's chancel or chapel shall be used for the powder house.

That one thousand weight of corn powder be bought for the great ordnance.

1586, August 15.—Order by the Mayor and Jurats that the new work done by John Prowze at Gungarden shall be filled up seven feet to make a foundation, that the higher ground sink not.

1587, July 22.—Order by the Mayor and Jurats of Rye that neither Gillam Vatmer of Rye, Frenchman, nor any of the French nation inhabiting within the liberties of Rye, do retail any canvas, linen, cloth, haberdashery-ware, mercery-ware or grocery upon forfeiture of ten French crowns.

1587, September 6.—Order for Mr. Thomas Edolphe, Mayor, Mr. Henry Gaymer, Mr. Robert Carpenter, and William Appleton "common clerk" to go to Dover to consult with the Lord Warden touching the service to be done on the Narrow Seas with a request "that the same may be don so frankely and frely towards hir Majestie as is possible whereby they may shewe their bownden duties to hir Highnes &c."

1587, September 17.—Report of Thomas Edolphe, Mayor of Rye, Robert Carpenter, and William Appleton, clerk, to the Lord Warden.

"Accordinge to the late communication had with the right worshipfull Mr. Richard Barrey, esquire, your Lord Lyvetenaunte, who certefied us from your Honor, her Majesties pleasure concerninge the service hir Highnes required of the Ports and their members upon the Narrowe Seas with twelve shippes of warr, thoroughly furnished, we have, with the commons of our Towne, deliberately considered therof and fynde that our Towne is so greately impoverished by the ruyn and decaye of the Camber, Puddle and Creeke there, with the decaye of the fishinge, that our people are not able to deal so liberally in this action as their willing and dutifull myndes are redy unto, having spent their goods to helpe the harbor which hathe taken small effecte for want of ayde, yet nevertheles redy in dutifull sorte to performe thuttermoost they can as be comith good and lovinge subjectes. We, and they by us, answer and certefy to your Honor that we will fynde and prepare in a redynes whensoever hir Majestie shall please to command the same, one shippe well armed and appoynted with all thinges necessary for that service although we have no helpe therunto but only one member named Tenterden, hopinge that hir Majestie, towardes that greate charge, will permit us to enjoye the benefit of that which in tharticles underwrytten is mensioned."

The articles of our request.

(1.) That we may have "the placard" of Holland and Zealand in as ample manner as his Excellency granted the same.

(2.) That we may have such ships and goods as we shall take of the enemy and such ships and goods as we may rescue or replevy from the enemy.

(3.) That we may take and enjoy all such prohibited goods as shall be shipped to transport over the seas contrary to the laws of the realm.

(4.) That we may make lawful sale within the Liberties of the Ports of such goods or ships.

(5.) That if it happen by weather or otherwise any of our ships with their prizes come into any harbour or place out of the jurisdiction of the Ports that we may be permitted quietly to pass away into the Liberties of the Ports there to make sale without let or contradiction of the Lord High Admiral of England.

(6.) That if any question happen to arise for any of the said ships or goods so taken or rescued, that the trial may be had at the Admiralty Court held for the Cinque Ports at St. James' Church in Dover.

The furniture of the said ship to be:—Her burden to be 80 tons, and to be manned with 70 men. "For ordnance to have 3 sacres, 4 mynions, 3 fawcons, 4 fowlers, 20 muskets, 20 calyvers, 4 crossbowes to shote boltes of fyrework, 5 dozen shorte pykes, 1 dozen longe pykes, 4 roulaces of proff and 6 curates of proff."

1587, September 24.—Sale by Peter Keling of his ship and her furniture, except the cock boat, to the Corporation of Rye for 200 *li.* with an agreement that the same Peter shall have his ship again with her furniture, except the ordnance the Town shall put into her, when she has finished serving in the wars "better cheape by xx *li.* then wilbe gevin for hir."

1587, October 7, to 1588, May 10.—Money paid by Mr. Edolphe, mayor, towards the building of the pinnace. *A book giving the weekly accounts in detail under the headings of shipwrights, timber, pitch, oakum, sailcloth, etc. The sum total is* 53 *li.* 13*s.* 9*d.*

1587, November 6.—Order by the Mayor and Jurats of Rye that the watch be continued by the number of eight persons nightly to watch in form following:—at the Landgate two, at the Strandgate two, at the Gungarden two, and the other two to walk and to continue from eight o'clock at night till five in the morning, upon pain of grievous punishment, and not to depart in the morning until they have called at the Mayor's house. Also that the search shall be nightly maintained as it hath been heretofore or should have been by the Mayor and Jurats and those of the common council and to continue the same from half tide to half tide, and whosoever shall make default to forfeit for every time 6*s.* 8*d.* and to be imprisoned during the pleasure of Mr. Mayor and the Jurats. (Here follow the names of the Mayor, Jurats and common council appointed to search.)

1587[-8], January 22.—Order by the Mayor and Jurats of Rye that the fourth bell, which is cracked and broken, shall be taken down and sent to London to be sold to the greatest advantage and the money thereof coming to be employed for the buying of powder, match and other provision (in defence of the enemy) for the town of Rye. "And so conveniently as the Town shall be able, there shall be another bell bought at the general charge of the Town and to be hanged up in her room."

1587[-8], January 22.—Order that during the time of these troubles Mr. Mayor and his brethern the Jurats and all other officers of the Town shall be contributors and pay the watch of the Town as other commoners and inhabitants of the same do.

1587[-8], January 29.—Order for the town's ship to be sold to the best profit.

1588, April 8.—At an assembly of the Mayor, Jurats and Common Council, the Lords of the Council's letters to the Ports, dated the first of April, were read whereby the service of five ships is required from the Ports, and also the letters directed from the East Ports for a meeting at Dover were also read; whereupon Mr. Gaymer and Mr. Carpenter were authorised to go to Dover to the said conference.

1588, April 15.—At an assembly of the Mayor, Jurats and Common Council, Mr. Gaymer and Mr. Carpenter made relation of their proceedings at Dover about the service to be done with the five ships and a pinnace. The end whereof was that Hastings and Winchelsea with their members should find one ship of 60 tons, Rye and Tenterden one ship of 60 tons, Romney and Lydd one ship of 60 tons, Hythe to find the pinnace not under 25 tons, Sandwich and his members one ship of six score tons, Dover and his members one ship of 100 tons. These ships to be furnished by the 25th of this month of April for two months.

1588, April 15.—Certain of the Corporation of Rye appointed to deal with Captain Russell for the hiring of his ship to serve for the town in the service required by her Majesty. And upon composition had and made for the ship they are to proceed to the setting forth of the ship in all points meet for the said service.

1588, April 15.—Pier Connyoche, Frenchman, fined for firing his chimney.

1588, April 22.—The Town Council on this day chose Mr. Carpenter, Mr. Beale and Peter Kelinge to join with three of the French which Captain Russell shall appoint to apprize the ship and furniture appertaining to the said Russell, appointed to serve for the Town and to attend upon her Majesty's ships; which persons are to take an inventory and to see all things fitted as appertaineth and to have money from the Chamberlain for the same. The inventory runs as follows:—2 pieces of brass, 2 fowlers, 5 cwt. of powder, 1 cwt. of match, 15 muskets,

RYE MSS.

15 calivers, 2,500 biscuits, 14 tuns of beer, 300 nail of beef, 100 saltfish, 2 cwt. of bacon, 1 "scave" of pease, 1 cwt. of butter, 1 cwt. of cheese.

Officers of the said ship:—Mr. William Coxson chosen Captain, Mr. Edward Beale chosen Master and Josephe Okeman chosen purser.

1588, May 6.—Order by the Mayor and Jurats of Rye that the ship which is appointed to serve for the Town shall go forth on her voyage with all the expedition she may, and to be manned with 50 men and 5 boys.

1588, August 7.—Order by the Mayor, Jurats and Common Council of Rye that an inventory be taken of the pinnace and her furniture which appertaineth to the Town, and the same to be apprized and to be sold at that price, and if she cannot so be sold to be ventured to the sea by the Town by such as will venture in her at their own charges.

1588, August 7.—Account of the freight of the town ship which was taken by those that had authority to let the same ship forth to freight, and there remained due to the town clear 33*li.* 19*s.* 0*d.*

1588, October 13.—Mr. Awdeley Dannet and Mr. Robert Carpenter, jurat, chosen barons to the parliament and Mr. Carpenter to be allowed by the town for his parliament wages 4*s.* a day.

1588, October 13.—The Mayor, Jurats and Commons of Rye choose Mr. Coxon, jurat, to ride to Canterbury to meet Mr. Lieutenant there with the town certificate concerning the two ships and pinnace to be set out from the town. And his charges with a guide to be borne by the town.

1589, January 27.—Declarations before the Mayor of Rye by Pierre Destyn, Seigneur de Villeotz, living and a refugee, at Rye, damoyselle Marthe Vannissein also a refugee at Rye, wife of Maistre Jehan Lyein, minister of the Holy Gospel living at Sedan, as to the conveyance of land at Dieppe. Witnesses Jean le Forstier and Debault. *French.*

1588[-9], January 30th.—Account of money received and disbursed by Mr. Carpenter in setting forth the ship for the service of her Majesty in her fleet in the Narrow Seas. His receipts come to 181*li.* 9*s.* 0*d.* his payments to 191*li.* 3*s.* 4*d.*

1589, August 5.—Recognizance made before the Mayor of Rye by Pierre Destin, Sr. de Fivilldoetz, Marie de St Delys, widow of Charles de Nominant(?) Sr. de Sancourt and Marthe de Vannissein, wife of Jehan Lyenim, Sr. de Beaulieu. Mention also of Marye Calletot, widow of Richard Mayeu of Rouen, and her sons Danyel and Michael Mayew. Witness Jehan Wiard "advocat." *Signed. French.*

1589, September 13, Maidstone.—Thomas Randolph, Master and Controler of her Majesty's Posts, to Henry Gaymer, Mayor of Rye.

"Her Majesties pleasure is that for better expedition of such lettres as come to her Majestie's self or her Hignes Councell out of France, post horses should be layde from your towne to London in places most convenient, and to that effecte hathe given me expresse commaundement to see performed with all speede. Wherfore I praie you, Mr. Maior of Rye, to make choice in your towne of the most sufficient man that either keapeth an inne or comonlie servethe suche of horses as ordinarilie arrive out of Fraunce, and in her Majesty's name to require him to furnishe himself of thre sufficient and hable post horses at the leste to carry her Majesty's lettres or such as come from her Councell, so ofte as ether her Majestie herself or either of them please to send. And for that they shall knowe that this their service shall not be unconsidered, her Hyghnes is content to allow unto eyther of them 20*d*. per diem from the daye of their placeinge, duringe that service to be receaved quarterlie at my handes or so sone as I can have warrant for the same without faill. And to the intent they shall be the better hable to do her Majesty's service, they shall be allowed of everie man that rideth in poste 2*d*. the mile for eche horse that he rideth with, and 4*d*. for the guyde." *Signed. Seal of Arms.*

1589, November 12.—Agreement, made before the Mayor of Rye, between Pierre de Stin, Lord of Villerez, dwelling in the Parish of Villerez "Viconte de Dandely" at present residing at Rye by permission of the King of France, and Marye Calletot, widow of the late Richard Mayeu, burgess of Rouen, as guardian of Daniel Mayeu, her son, at present dwelling at Rye; concerning certain sums of money. Witnesses Jacques de la Haize on behalf of Pierre Figue "Viconte de Monstiervillier" and Jean le Forestier on behalf of "Morguy Bailliage de Gisors." *Signed. French.*

1589, November 12.—Licence from Henry Gaymer, Mayor of Rye, to John Allen to carry twenty or thirty thousand billets by the next convenient "passenger" to Dieppe for provision of himself and others of the Reformed Church there, who are greatly in need of them.

1589, November 13.—"A Proclamation against vagarant souldiers and others." *Printed by Christopher Barker.*

1589, November 16.—Agreement, made before the Mayor of Rye, between Nicolas du Val, burgess of the town of Harfleur, at present residing at Rye by permission of the King of France, and Marye Calletot widow of the late Richard Mayeu, burgess of Rouen, as guardian of Daniel Mayeu, her son, at present dwelling at Rye concerning certain sums of money. Witnesses Marye Poullain, widow of the late Master Pierre de Freueuse, councillor of the king at the Palace of Rouen at present having fled to the town of Rye, Jacques de la Haize on behalf of Pierre Figue "Viconte de Monstiervilier" and Jehan Regnard of Harfleur. *Signed. French.*

1589, November 21, London.—Henry Gaymer, Mayor of Rye, to William Tolken, deputy of the Mayor of Rye, and the Jurats there.

Mr. Knatchbull is a great suitor to the Lords of the Council to "inde" certain marshes lying above Bromhill. I told their Honours that it was so well known to me that the inning of marshes has overthrown the famous harbour of the Camber and also her Majesty's town of Rye, and therefore for my own part I thought that his intent could bring no improvement to the town of Rye or the harbour by the inning of the marshes.

Tenderden is taking a new charter, how far we may be prejudiced therein I pray you think upon, and send me your minds.

1589, November 28, Rye [London ?].—Henry Gaymer Mayor of Rye to Mr. Tolken and the Jurats of Rye.

My Lord Cobham is of mind that inning of Bromhill destroyed the Camber, and that generally inning of marshes mar good havens. He told me that her Majesty was minded to grant supply to Rye but doth stay the same for a time, and therefore he willed me to attend for her resolution. I told his Honour that it was thought at home that I trifle out the time and in the end there will nothing come.

Her Majesty having built divers new ships is minded to take from us all the ordnance that was in the *Grayhound* to put in the same ships. *Seal of arms broken.*

1589, December 1.—Obligation by Jacques Franquen of Rye, merchant. *Flemish.*

1589, December 2.—View of the salts pertaining to Guildford, Chayne Court and Christchurch, by John Stoneham and others.

"That thoes saltes of the Weanewaye and the Camber hed have many greate creekes issuing frome the mayne creeke called Weneway unto thoes saltes. And also many small creekes issuing and spreadinge abroade from thoes great creekes. And that every monethe water dothe cover the said saltes 12 tydes at the least the depthe of thre foote in some place uppon the very plaine grounde, and uppon some place more and uppon some place lesse, accordinge as the grounde dothe heithen or fall. And that the hedd of the Stoune nowe is, which some tyme was the hed of the Camber, is only mayntayned by thoes waters of the Weanewaye and wold with some small helpe, in respecte, become a very good Camber agayne in shorte tyme which otherwise by strayghteninge of thoes waters will utterly decaye, and the barr at the enterance of the Havon of Rye spedely increase, to the utter ruyn and decaye of the towne."

1589, December 18.—"A Proclamation for the prices of Wines." *Printed by Christopher Barker.*

1589, December 30, Blackfriars.—Lord Cobham to Thomas Fane.

"I have nowe by Williams receyved from you the certificate of the musters of the Portes in which I find their defaultes mensioned in this schedule inclosed, prayinge you with spede to lett every particular captayne understand of his wantes, and to give order unto them that the said wantes may be presently supplyed but especially to have their nomber of muskettes and stoore of powder increased. And the same to be certefied unto me with expedition for that I meane not to give in any certificate to my Lords till it be accordingly performed." *Copy.*

[1589.] Appointment of Nicholas Fowler to be pilot to the town of Rye during the term of his life, it being necessary to appoint such an officer in consequence of the decay of the harbour called the Camber, and the Puddle and Creek of Rye.

1589[-90], January 13.—Order by the Mayor, Jurats and Commonalty of Rye that all ships of the country and nation of France trading or coming into the Town of Rye as merchants and all men of war of the same country or realm (except those of Calais and Boulogne) being of the burden of 40 tons and upwards shall pay 6*s.* to the use of the poor of the same town, and every vessel or man of war under the burden of 40 tons to the burden of 30 tons shall pay 3*s.*

1589[-90], January 13.—"A Proclamation for the calling in and frustrating all commissions for the making of salt peter granted forth before that to George Evelin and others the 28 of January 1587, whereby many of her Majesties subjects were greatly abused as also that all peter made by the said latter commissions doe bring the same unto her Majesties store, etc." *Printed by Christopher Barker.*

1589[-90], January 20.—The Mayor and Jurats of Rye to Thomas Fane, Esquire, Lieutenant of Dover Castle.

"We meane to augment the nomber of musketes in lieu of calivers which we must do by courteous perswacions for that we have, with somwhat ado, alredy augmented them to the nomber of 29 and to increase them farther will require some tyme. But as towchinge our provision of powder which is omitted out of our roll of the selected bande; theis are farther to certefye and to that roll to be augmented, that the store of powder for our towne is one last and a half over and besides every private persons provision for the furnishing of their muskets and calivers." *Draft.*

1589[-90], January 25. The Court.—Sir Francis Walsingham to the Mayor of Rye.

"I have receaved your lettre conteyning your request that the Counties of Kent and Sussex might be directed to contribute towardes your charge in relieving the sick souldiers lately come out of Fraunce, and having made my Lordes acquainted therewithall I find them willing to take some course therein for your good, yet not resolved in what sorte untill they bee more particularly advertised frome you both of the certaine nomber of the said sicke souldiers with a catalogue of their names, the shires out of which they were imprested, the captains under whom they served, and with what pasport dismissed as also what pay they have receaved and what further they challenge to be due unto them. This done you shall receave their Lordships' further direction." *Signed, and Seal of arms.*

1589[-90], January 26. The Court.—John Wylgest (?) and John Colepeper to the Mayor and Jurats of Rye.

"We have recevid comaundment from the right Honorable the Lord Buckhurst for the bestowinge of the soldiers which were sent out of this countre into Fraunce and now ready to returne to their former places of abode so sonne as they shalbe landed. And also to see their armor and weapons saflie bestowed for the owners and that we should emparte his Lordships pleasuer herin to the Maiors of Rye, Winchelse, and Hastinge for their aide in the execution of the premises when any of the soldiers shall there lande. These are therfore to pray you yf any of the said souldiers do lande in your said towne that you would geve straight commaundement unto them presentlie to repayer to the place of their severall abodes upon payne of ymprisonment yf they be founde wanderinge without a passporte. And therefore it shalbe very well yf it would please you to make them a pasporte to pase directlie to the place of their abode and yf you think not so good to geve them comaundement to goe to the next justice in their waie to make them a pasport; but as we understand the proclamation, it appertayneth unto you to make them a pasport for that you are the next justice to the place of their arryvall yf they land in your towne, which matter we refer to your consideration. As tuchinge their armor and weapon yf they bringe anye we praie that you will make staie thereof and cause it to be laide upe for the owners, taking a note of the soldiers, of the names of the said owners and of their dwellinge places, and causeng some note to be made or marke of the armors and weapon so as the owners maie knowe them when they shall send for them" *Signed.*

1589[-90], February 2.—Order that 15*li.* of the money belonging to Francys Macquerye's children being 60*li.* and remaining in the Mayor's

RYE MSS.

hands to the town's use and by the town to be answered to those children, shall be disbursed towards the sustentation of the poor soldiers.

1589[-90], February 5.—The Mayor and Jurats of Rye to [Sir Francis Walsingham].

"We tooke a viewe of the sicke and diseased soldiers in Rye and found eighty and odd that rested uppon the townes charge eight daies in moost miserable sorte, full of infirmities in their bodies, wonderfull sicke and weake some wounded, some their toes and fette rottinge of, some lame, the skyn and fleshe of their feete torne away with contynuall marchinge, all of them without money, without apparell to cover their nakydnes, all of them full of vermyn, which no doubte wold have devoured them in very short tyme if we had not gevin them moost spedy supply, whereby we were constrayned to washe their bodies in swete waters, to take from them all their clothes and strippe them into new apparrell, both shirtes, peticootes, jerkyns, breches, and hoose made of purpose for them. Then we appoynted them severall houses for ther dyet and kepers to watche and attend them, and also chirurgions to cure their woundes and rottennes and by theys meanes we saved some 48 of them which wilbe able to do hir Majestie good service, which otherwise had perished as the other did before we could provide the leike remedy to them all, and this hath byn to the town of Rye so great a burden as we are not able to beare. And that nowe happenith amongest us is much to our greiff (God of his mercy staye it in his good tyme) for the persons in whoes houses they were lodged and dyeted and the wemen that did attend and watche them are for the moost part fallen very sicke and every day ther dieth 4 or 5 of them with the infection that they had from thoes soldiors. In consideration wherof we are humble petitioners unto your Honor and unto the Lordes of hir Majesties moost honorable Privie Councell that the burden of this great charge which we have in chearitie and dutie performed towardes God and her Majestie, be not imposed uppon us, but that we may have releiff as to your Honors shall seme moost meetest to unburden us of so great a charge. The charges appere by a cataloge of the names in the booke which herewith we send your Honour which amounteth to the some of 55*li.* 11*s.* 3*d.* besides the contynuall charge of the soldiors, that remayne in Rye at this tyme which wilbe above 40*s.* every day." *Draft. Enclosure.*—List of sick soldiers shipped at Dieppe and arrived at Rye without passports.

1589[-90], February 12.—A writ from Queen Elizabeth to the Captains or Constables "of our castles, portes, and blockhouses or their deputies" and to all other officers to whom it may appertain.

Whereas for our special service we have appointed sundry brass ordnance with their "mountures" and shot to be removed from certain of our forts, castles, and blockhouses for the furnishing therewith of sundry new royal ships, which otherwise cannot in convenient time be supplied, as the necessity of the service requireth, and that we mean to furnish all the said forts with sufficient iron ordnance of the like kind with their "mountures" and shot without delay; and therefore our will and pleasure is that you shall deliver out of your charge, to such person as the Admiral of England and our General Master of our Ordnance or to such person as shall by the Lord Warden and the Master of our Ordnance or the Lieutenant assigned or deputed, all such brass ordnance, as shall be specified in a schedule, to be conveyed by sea to the Tower of London. And whereas in the 27th year of our reign a supply of ordnance, powder, shot, munition and other habilments of war were sent to our forts, castles and blockhouses, our further will and pleasure is that a general survey be taken of all such ordnance, powder, shot, munition and other habilments of war.

In the schedule attached is given the number of "culverings demi-culverings, cannons and demi-cannons and curtal cannons" to be taken from various castles and towns all along the south coast of England. At Dover are to be taken 17 "brasse ordinance in one capten Sampson's handes that brought them from Portugall vyoge." At Corf Castle "to bring away all the brass ordinaunce that was sent in the . . . . Spanish shippe." At the end is an order that whereas divers brass ordnance of sundry kind brought into the realm "of the . . . . Portugall vyoage" and other like voyages which of right belong to her Majesty, that inquiry be made in any of the places westward of the river of . . . . of any such ordnance and the same so found to take to the Queen's use giving to the parties that make any lawful claim a note of hand acknowledging the receipt to her Majesty's use. *Copy.*

1589[-90], February 24. London.—Lord Cobham to Thomas Fane.

"Whereas last yere certeine orders were sent unto you for restraint of kyllinge and eating of flesh in the tyme of Lent, which, although for lack of due execution, wrought not that good effect which was required, yet her Majesty upon hope of better care to be had hereafter hath streightly charged and commaunded me to see the same orders to be now likewise put in execution in all the cheyfe townes and places in my Levetenancy and that I shold geve specyall order and dyrection unto you to have an extraordynary care and regard to see the said orders, which herewith I send you, more duly and diligently observed within their severall lymyttes and jurisdictions then it hath bene heretofore: which I do very ernestly recommend unto you, that with all diligence you will see them most carefully to be kepte and executed within all the Portes and their members according to the trust reposed in you. And to the ende her Majesty's gracyous purpose herein may not be defrauded by cullor of fayned sycknes or other excuse, it is thought meete that no lycence shalbe geven to any bocher or other victualler to kyll and sell fleshe, in tyme prohybyted, to any person whatsoever without speciall lycence from me the Lieutenant and that to suche only as upon good cause of sicknes and greater necessyty shalbe thought requisyt, that the prejudice dayly growing to the realme by dysordered eating of flesh in contempt of the lawes may be prohybyted." *Copy.*

1589[-90], March 9.—Certain persons appointed to deal for the vicarage of Rye to deal also for a lease of the parsonage of Rye, from Lord Buckhurst.

1589[-90], March 13. London.—Lord Cobham to Thomas Fane, Lieutenant of Dover Castle.

"I am to lett you understand that in respect of these troblesome tymes my Lordes of her Majesties most honorable Privy Counsell do think yt good that with as convenient speede as you maye, ye wold cause all the masters, subofficers, maryners and gooners, both in the Cinque Portes and members of the same, to be presentlie mustered and the names of all to bee taken from 16 to 60, chardginge them upon payne of deathe not to bee out of the way uppon any warninge; as also that yee wold cause the names to bee taken of suche as bee forthe in voyages and are shortlie too returne home, that uppon their arryvall the like commandement be also layed upon them, that uppon any sodden occasion they may be in a redynes. Which doon I hartely praie you to send me the rolles of the said musters that I may enforme my Lordes the names and number of the men and their severall habytations wher they dwell, and this to bee doon with all expedition."

1589[-90], March 19.—The Mayor and Jurats of Rye to [Lord Buckhurst].

"Whereas your Honor hath made a composition with Thomas Hebletwhaite for the vycaredge of Rye to our use, we humblye thancke your Honor therefore and for sondry other honorable curtesyes bestowed upon us. And do further herebye signyfye unto you that we will, with all honestye and care, observe suche covenauntes and conditions as your Honor hath made with Hebletwhayte." *Draft.*

1590, April 1.—Order signed by Sir John Hawkins, Sir Henry Palmer, W. Borough and B. Gonson that "whereas there have bene of late and nowe are in hande certayne newe shippes builded for her Majestie at Debtford and Woolewich, the makinge of which have bene comitted of trust to her Highenes master shipwrightes, for which woorkes they have used comissions under her Majesties great seale for takeing upp of timber, planke and other provisions and for the cariage of the same, as allso for takeing upp woorkemen for fellinge, squareinge and saweinge of timber and otherwise, in sondry shires of the realme, for which provisions, cariages and woorkemanship, to the ende the countrey in every place where such provisions have bene taken maye be fullye satisfied and payde for so much as is yet owinge and unpaide by the said shipwrightes or otherwise for the use of the Navye, the Lord Admirall and the officers of her Majesties Marine Cawses have thoughte good to cause proclamations to be made in such townes of every such shyre as may beste give knowledge to the inhabitantes of the same shyre, that they and everie of them maye bringe in notes to the Mayor, Bayliff or cheif officer of everie suche towne, within such convenient tyme as shalbe lymited, of such particular debtes as ys oweing within the same shyre for such provisions, cariages, woorkemanship, &c. and to whom and wherefore the same is dewe." *Signed.*

1590, April 6.—Order by the Mayor, Jurats and Commonalty of Rye that the Town ship be forthwith trimmed and furnished with all necessaries to make a voyage at the charge of the Corporation.

1590, April 25.—Order by the Mayor and Jurats of Rye that the Town ship being now ready to go on such voyage as she is hired for, and yet the restraint is not open, that the said ship shall presently by the grace of God go forward on her voyage and if any trouble grow by the passing of the ships and mariners without licence, the Corporation shall bear the charges thereof. And further it is agreed that the said ship shall have "an yron fawcon" which is in the possession of Edward Harris and that she shall have one of the Town's "sacres" of brass for the better furnishing of her and powder and shot from the Town store.

1590, May 8. London.—Henry Gaymer, Mayor of Rye, to Mr. Tolken and the Jurats of Rye.

The vicarage house has run to great decay and the reparation of the same will fall upon us if we provide not for the mischief before Heblethwaite seal his lease; I pray you therefore let the house be discretely viewed, for I mean to inform my Lord Buckhurst of the state of the house that Heblethwaite may be compelled at his own charge to leave the house to us well repaired, for so I am sure we must do at the end of our lease. The chancel also is much decayed that belongeth to the parsonage, of that also I pray you let a view be taken. *Seal.*

1590, May 12.—The jurats and commons of Rye to Henry Gaymer, Mayor of Rye, now being in London.

"According to your direction we have with good advice taken view as well of the vicaredge howse as of the chauncell and finde them to be greatly at reparations. The vicaredge howse wanteth three newe selles one in the hall, another in the entry and the third in the kytchen, and a newe grate and two newe postes. All which carpenter's work will cost 3*li.* at the least besides the mason worke for the repayringe of the walles and other leike worke will cost at the leike 30*s.* For the roofe of the said howse we cannot estemet the reparations for that the chambers are seeled. Also the chauncel belonginge to the parsonage, the most part of the roofe thereof is to be repaired with newe shingle the which will amounte unto 16 m.' of shingle at the least. So the reparations therof with the glase windowes will cost 15*li.* or 16*li.*" *Draft.*

1590, May 13. London.—Henry Gaymer, Mayor of Rye, to Mr. Tolken and the Jurats of Rye.

My Lord Cobham told me this morning that he had moved her Majesty of our suit which she liketh, and my Lord doubts not but she will shortly grant it after she has talked with my Lord Treasurer. I would to God it were granted "for I feare yt will have yet now some groovinges of an agew" for suits at the Court go forward by fits.

The money that we relieved the soldiers is not paid to Sir Thomas Fludd. He giveth me very good words when it shall be received. I perceive he looketh for remembrance, you may if you please bestow a dish of fish upon him. *Seal of arms broken.*

1590, June 3. The Counter in Woodstreet.—Thomas Hebylthwayte farmer of the vicarage of Rye to the Mayor of Rye.

Touching the vicarage of Rye.

1590, August 12. Dover Castle.—Thomas Fane to the Mayors, Bailiffs and Jurats of the Cinque Ports.

The Lords of the Council have thought it convenient that the forces under the Lord Warden's jurisdiction should be put in a present readiness, and my Lord Cobham has required me with all convenient speed to signify to the Captains of the trained and untrained bands within the Cinque Ports, that, by the end of harvest now ensuing, their bands may be mustered. And by rolls of the musters in 1589 it appeareth that divers of the bands have but a small number of muskets (which her Majesty greatly disliketh) for the increasing thereof my Lord Cobham requireth that the jurats of every port town and member shall each furnish one musket or more at the least, as their several abilities will serve. *Copy.*

1590, December 1.—Order by the Mayor and Jurats of Rye that all the records of this Town except the books of entry, the Hundred books, books of the Chamberlain's accounts, other files of the last year shall remain in the chest in the Court hall, those books before excepted to be in the custody of the Town Clerk.

1590[–1], January 16. Dover Castle.—Thomas Fane to [the Mayor and Jurats of Rye].

"I have receved lettres from the right honorable Lord Warden requyringe me to certefye and geve notyce unto all the Portes and their members and especially to the Commissioners there for the restraint of passengers, that they the said Commissioners do at all tymes hereafter keepe the originall pasport of all passengers departinge from their porte, or at the least a trewe copye therof, under the handes of some Commissioners as also the hande or marke of the passenger himselfe." *Copy.*

1590[–91], February 16. Greenwich.—Lord Cobham to the Mayor and Jurats of Rye.

"According to the petition delivered to my Lords of her Majesties most honorable Previe Councell, I have moved my good Lord, the Lord Admirall, for a pynace of her Majesties to keepe up and downe uppon that coaste, which he is contented to graunt; the shipp furnished with ordnance, so that yow paye the wages of the master, mariners and all other officers, and allowe for the victuellinge of her and also for the powder and shott duringe the tyme of her service for you." *Seal of arms.*

1590[–1], February 21.—[The Mayor and Jurats of Rye] to Lord Cobham.

"We have received your letters of the 16th of this present February concerneinge her Majesties pynace to be sent downe to keepe up and downe uppon the sea-coast, haveinge had conference with the Commonaltie of our towne touchinge such charges for wages, victualinge and other thinges, as is required to be allowed, we most humbly thank your Honor for your great paynes taken in the behalfe of our poore towne. The charges that is required to be borne for the settinge forth of the pynace is so greate and our towne so poore, as we are not able to accomplish the same, yet notwithstandinge (and please your Honor) we wold be very willinge emongest ourselves to sett out a shippe or twayne, without charginge of her Highnes pynace, for to keape the Leagers in awe, so we might have lycence to take suche as our shippes shall overcome and enjoye the benefytt of such pryzes as they shall lawfully take from the enemy." *Draft.*

1590[–1], March 1. The Court at Greenwich.—Lord Cobham to the Mayor and Jurats of Rye.

"I perceave that in respect of the charges and your unhabilitie you do not accept of her Majesties shippe but do offer to appoint in warlike manner two of your owne barckes to execute that service, so that you might have leave, and enjoy the benefitt of such prizes as they shall lawfullie take, which ys verie likelie I shall obteyne." *Signed. Seal of arms.*

1590[–1], March 8.—The Mayor and Jurats of Rye to the Lord Warden.

"We have decreed and concluded amonge ourselves to set forthe in warlyke manner against the Leagers of Fraunce, a shippe and a barke. The name of the shippe is the *Blessing of God*, of Rye, of the burthen of 80 tonns, who shall beare of ordynance, eight cast peces and two foulers and shall have in her 60 men. The barke is called the *Grace of God*, of Rye, of the burthen of 40 tonns, who shall beare foure cast peeces and shall have in her thirty men. So that yt wyll please their Honors to geve us leave as well to make prise and spoyle of such Leagers and their goodes as we shall happen to take, as to surprise all such pouder, shott, ordynance, and other habylymentes of warre, and victuall as we shall take goinge towerdes the said Leagers to releve and strengthen them, without paying any pension or portion of such goodes, so by us to be taken to any person in respect of the great spoyle and losse which we have alreddy susteined by them, as in respect of this our great charge in levying armes and force against them." *Draft.*

1591, March 29.—The Mayor and Jurats of Rye to Lord Cobham.

"The contynuall and dayly enormytyes and great losses which we susteine by the Leagers of Fraunce do enforce us to troble your Honor by these our often sutes for some redresse therein to be had, for so it is, if it please your Honor, that the last weke a passenger of this towne, beinge worth in merchaunies goodes of London and of goodes belonginge to this towne, six thousand crownes, was taken by those of that Leage. Wherefore we have sent the berer hereof, being the master of our owne shippe, to attende upon your Honor to knowe your honorable pleasure whether yt wyll please her Majesty to permytt us to make warre against those Leagers." *Draft.*

1591, April 1.—Order by Thomas Fane, Lieutenant of Dover Castle, to all Mayors, Bailiffs, and Jurats of the Cinque Ports to have a general view and muster of all weapons, armours and furnitures, as well of horse as foot, and to amend all defects and send in a certificate of the same.

1591, April 15.—Thomas Fane to [the Mayor of Rye].

Whereas her Majesty's ship called the *Hope* is unfurnished of the number of one hundred sufficient mariners, being in Dover Roads under the charge of Sir Henry Palmer, Admiral of her Majesty's fleet in the Narrow Seas. These are to desire you to provide twenty able men to serve in the said ship. *Copy.*

1591. April 15.—The Mayor and Jurats of Rye to the Lord Admiral.

"We understand that one shippe belonginge to this corporation is by your honorable order stayed for her Majesties service, we humbly crave of your Honor that she may be released, to the ende we may ymploye her against the Leagers of Fraunce, by whome our barkes and fysherbotes are dayly anoyed to the great ruyn of this poore towne, wherein we shalbe greatly bound to your Honor." *Draft.*

1591, April 17.—Depositions of William Bagge and Anthony Marye.

Being on board the *Jhesus* of Rye and sailing across the seas in the night they were taken prisoners to "Crottey in the Some" by Leaguers and all the goods in their ship were sold.

1591, May 8, Dover Castle.—Thomas Fane to the Mayors, Bailiffs and Jurats of the Cinque Portes, and others.

"Forasmuch as I ame advertised by letters from the right honorable our Lord Warden, that he hath receved expresse comaundement from her Majestie to cause the forces as well of the trayned as of the untreined bandes presentlye to be put in a redines, as well within the saide

Cinque Portes as within the Sheere, and also to cause the beacons along the sea costes to be watched and warded, whereupon his Honor hath (by his Lordship's letters dated the 24th of this instant monnth) geven me an especiall comaundement to requier you and in her Majesty's name streightlye to charge you and every of you, that for your partes there be noe parte of your duty neglected in that behalfe as ye and every of you will answer for the contrarye but that yee and every of you should be verye carefull in the supplies of your bandes and to stand upon your garde. These are therefore on the behalfe of our said soveraigne Lady the Queene's Majestye to will and requier you and everye of you within your severall jurisdictions to be verye carefull in the accompleshinge of the premises, in such sorte as that their be no parte of your dutyes neglected in that behalf." *Copy.*

1591, May 23.—The Mayor and Jurats of Rye to Thomas Fane.

"We have receaved of late a precept from your Worship for the takeing up of 20 maryners to be sent aborde her Majesty's shippe under the charge of Sir Henry Palmer wherein we have thought it not amys to advertyse you that the execution of this your precept is dyrectlie against our chartres and liberties, for neither our shippes nor people are compellable to any other service then the service of the Cinque Portes by the which we hold our liberties; albeit of late by her Majesties prerogative and by her Highnes' commission under her great seale of England, maryners have bene taken up within the Portes for her Highnes service, but at no tyme heretofore any such precepte hath bene awarded upon the request of any the capteines of her Majesty's Navy, except upon that present necessyty which happend when the Spanyardes were upon the coste, yet in hope that the lyke warrant in tymo to come shall not be sent unto us and presumyng also that this president shall not be prejudycyall to our liberties we have taken upe— men and sent them aborde the said shippe albeit we have not receaved any presse or conduct monny to beare their charges untyll they come aborde." *Draft.*

1591, May 23.—Robert Carpenter, Mayor of Rye, to Sir Henry Palmer.

According to the request of Mr. Lieutenant of Dover Castle, I have taken up——mariners and sent them aboard her Majesty's ship under your charge. Albeit I have received neither press nor conduct money to bear the charge of such mariners but have disbursed the same myself of curtesy for the repayment whereof I doubt not you will take present order. *Draft.*

1591, July 4.—Depositions concerning the heirs of Thomas Veryer. Elizabeth Mylls deposes that Thomas Veryer died about forty years past, and that he had issue Alice Ferryer, who married John Nicholas, and the said John has two sisters Richardine and Gyllyan, and the said John and Alice had issue John, Nicholas and Tabbetta, but what became of them she does not know.

1591, July 31.—Men termed Puritans, being accused by public fame to hold some erroneous opinions, were called before the Mayor and Jurats of Rye and examined upon the same. First, Mr. Radcliff and Nicholas Larder accused George Martin for that he, within these twelve days, said and affirmed that Mr. Grenewood, preacher of the word of God in Rye, was a malicious man, for which the said George was committed to prison till Friday next.

Thomas Hubberd of Rye, cooper, accuseth William Gyll and John Baylye for that they have reported that the right reverend father in God the Archbishop of Canterbury is John of Canterbury and the Pope of England.

Robert Redo of Rye, joiner, answered Francis Godfrey of Rye, joiner, for reporting the words last above recited and for maintaining of divers heresies and errors which are comprehended in writing under his (Rede's) hand. He also accuseth Tate, who is already in prison for striking Mr. Grenewood.

[1591, July].—The Mayor and Jurats of Rye to the Lord Admiral.

"Whereas this towne of Rye by many yeres past hath bene very populous by reason of the trade betwene England and France, and by reason of fyshinge wherewith, God hath blessed yt, and yet the most part of the people of that towne have bene altogether unlerned, being maryners and fyshermen, whereby yt hath bene thought most necessarye to have a suffycient pastor or precher whereby the ignorant might be enformed of the will and pleasure of God and the better sort reformed in lyves and conversation. For which purpose we have of long tyme ymployed Mr. Richard Grenewood, one of your Honor's chapleynes, a man very suffycient, and by reason of his experyence most meete for this congregation. But so yt is, if it please your Honor, that now of late a smale secte of purytanes, more holy in shewe then in dede, is sprong up among us who seke by all possyble meanes to remove your said chapleyne from us by reason he hath a small cure within fyve myles of Rye where he maynteineth a suffycient curat for such a flocke; and for that purpose, being thereunto procured by certeine mutynous fellowes of this towne who professe to be more pure then others and be indede much worse then in show, have procured one Browne, an informer, to preferre an information againste Mr. Grenwood for non-resydence by vertue of a penall statute. So that your Honors said chapleine is very lykely to be taken from us and to beare the penalty of the lawe." *Draft.*

[1591, July].—Robert Rede to [the Mayor of Rye?]

"I have hard Francis Godfry say that my Lord of Canterbury is but the Pope of Inglande, and call him John of Cantorburye, and that the Booke of Comon Prayer whiche he alowethe to be sayde in the Chourch is but masse translated and dumdogs to reade it, for thos ministers that do not preache they call them dumdogs, and non oft not to pray exsept they have the gifte of prayer, and that it is not lafull for them to joyne prayer withe the wickeed, and when they have bin to sermon and be com hom, will thay say on to another 'Have you bin at chourche?' 'Yea,' sayth the other. 'Then you have harde mingle mangle compair, as Latemor sayd in his sermon as they call hogs to trof in his cuntry.' 'Yea,' cothe the other, 'I harde what a good peace of worke he made like a proude felo.' Also they say that it is unpossible for an innosent to be saved from damnation because he hathe not the gift of prayer.' Upon a tyme Fraunsis Godfrye did see Mr. Walet passe in the strete he sayd to me 'Ther is a dumdog he dothe starve at Gilford and they call the Booke of Common Prayer the starving booke."

1591, August 2.—The Mayor and Jurats of Rye to the Lord Warden and Lord Buckhurst.

"Of late an Italian called Gedevilo Gienily hath bene in these partes by the procurement of sondry gentlemen about certeine water workes,

RYE MSS.

by him to be made, for the makeinge drye of diverse surrounded groundes; and amonge other his affayres he hath taken view of our decayed harbor and haven with all waters, streams, banckes, and sea markes nere aboute us; whereupon he assureth us that he both can and wyll, with a reasonable charge for so great a worke, reduce our harbor to a better perfection for securytie of barkes and shippes of great burthen then ever yt was within any memory; but the meanes howe to bringe to passe he wyll shewe to none but to your Honor and to right honorable Lord Thresurer and Lord Buckhurst." *Draft.*

1591, August 7.—Robert Rede committed to prison by Mr. Mayor and the Jurats for reporting falsely of Francis Godfrey, in saying that he maintained that there was no visible church in England, where in truth he maintained no such opinion, but only said the Brownist's hold that opinion.

1591, August 25.—"The Italian's Plot for the amendment of Rye Haven:—

The pattern hereunto joined is the figure of the Port of Rye, made according to the sight which I have had thereof. I esteem that in the space of four or five years the said port may be brought to such perfection as was never done before, except only the parcel called the Chamber at the east to the benefit of the rivers, creeks, or waters which enter into the said port as of the moors or marshes thereunto joined. The cost will be 4000 *li.* to wit—2000 *li.* ready money for the first year and 2000 *li.* "for to continewe yf it shalbe fynished all, to wete 500 *li.* every year." The conditions for the work are that there should be paid to me my wages and charges in such manner as the Privy Council suggested when I tended on her Majesty's service.

When the said port shall be deeper by three feet than it is at present, there shall be paid unto me for the half of my recompense a certain sum of ready money.

When the work shall be finished with success the said Lordes, for the complement of my recompense shall ordain unto me a pension for 25 . . . . years whereby I may have means to employ me with my industrie to maintain the said work." *Plan of Rye Harbour attached.*

1591, September 1. Dover Castle.—Thomas Fane to [the Mayor and Jurats of Rye].

"The Lords of her Majestie's most honorable Privye Councell have geven in commandement, for that their Honors are given to understand that divers of the soldiers under the conducte of suche captens as serve under the Earle of Essex, her Majesty's Generall in Fraunce, do daylye arrive frome Deipe within the Five Portes and their members; there should be staye made by the hed officer of every porte, or place of their landinge to cause the said persons so arryvinge to be presentlye apprehended and imprisoned at the place of their landinge and that such as come with pasport, the same should forthwith be sent to his Honor with their name or names and to remayne so imprisoned till you shall receve his Lordshipp's directions touchinge prosedinges againste the parties so imprisoned." *Copy.*

1591, September 6. Cobham.—Lord Cobham to the Mayor, Jurats, and Commons of Rye.

"I understand ther hath bin an Italian with you to take a vewe of your haven who pretendeth in few yeares not onlie to amend yt but to bringe yt to better passe, then ever yt was, for the cominge in of such vessels as shall repaire to that towne yf he maie be ymployed therin. Uppon which his reporte, I thought yt good to praie him to sett downe some breife discourse in Englishe unto me, both to what perfection he would undertake to bringe your porte unto, at what charge, and in what tyme: which he having don I do send the same hereinclosed unto you to consider uppon as you shall thinck good." *Signed.*

1591, October 9.—The Mayor and Jurats of Rye to Lord Buckhurst.

That it may please you to grant to John Bruster, one of our jurats, licence to transport from Chichester 200 quarters of wheat, for that "this towne of Rye standeth in an ilande or corner of the lande nere to the sea and far from any corne contrye, as for that at this tyme there is here great passage and recourse of souldyers and others into and out of Fraunce, by meanes whereof some good quantitye of corne is spent." *Draft.*

1591, October 20.—The Mayor, Jurats, and Commons of Rye to [Lord Cobham].

"We have receaved your lettres concernynge the report made to your Honor by an Italyan, for the amendment of this decayed haven and harbor of Rye and as we cannot but lyke very well of his offer, so are bound to praye to God that his presence may take good effect, and that your Honor may have all honorable happyness with long lyffe for your favor offred to us therein and for diverse other curtesyes shewed to us heretofore, and speciallye in our late sute to her Majesty for transportation of certeine graine and beare, which sayd sute we hope is eyther fynished or nere at an end by your Honors good meanes. And as the amendment of that our harbor will be a publique benefytt to many, so specyally the same will greatly pleasure us, the poore inhabitantes in this towne of Rye, for the furtheringe and advancement whereof yt shall well appeare that we wyll strayne ourselves to the uttermost, consydering our great charge lately expended about the amendment of our said harbor and our chargeable sutes for some releyffe to be had for the bettering thereof. Nothing doubtinge of her Highness furtherance towardes this worke, tending to so universall a benefytt to her subjectes and necessarye provision of fyshe for her own household." *Draft.*

1591, November 5.—Richmond.—The Lords of the Council to all Justices, Mayors, Bailiffs, etc.

Whereas of the number of men lately sent over into Normandy to the aid of the French King, divers of them are appointed to return home. These are to require you, in case there shall happen to land within any your several jurisdictions any soldier, having the passport of the Lord General or any special officer under him, that you deliver to him five shillings conduct money which shall be repaid to you. *Copy.*

1591, December 11.—The Mayor and Jurats of Rye to the Lords of the Council.

"The bearer hereof an Italyan, now of late haveng perused our haven and harbor of Rye and all the indraftes, sea markes and water springes nere unto the same, he hathe faithfullye promysed that, within fewe yeres, he will make the said haven and harbor of Rye (the Camber only excepted) more servyceable then yt hath bene at any tyme these forty yeres heretofore; which worke he wold be content to begynne in the springe of this next yere yf the same maye stand with your honorable good pleasures." *Draft.*

1591[-2], January 30.—Whitehall.—The Lords of the Council to [the Lord Warden].

"It is nott unknowne unto yow what streight order and chardge hath allmost every yere byn gyven by expresse comaundement from her Majestie for restraigninge the use of fleshe in the tyme of Lent and other dayes prohibyted, especiall in these late yeres wherein by reason of mortalytye of cattle and unseasonableness of the wether all kyndes of fleshe meate are growne to excessive prices. Nevertheless notwithstandinge these streight inhibitions and such orders as have byn sett downe for remedye of this inconvenience, there hath, to the great and just dyspleasure of her Majestie, so lytle care byn had in seinge those hollsome and necessarye orders putt in execution by all sortes of officers which ought to have care of the same, as yt ys hard to saye whether the offendors or those which should have looked to see better order kept doe deserve more blame. And in that tyme, wherein younge cattle should most be spared for increase, a greater quantitye and store is kylled then in anye other season. For these respectes we are commaunded by her Majestye to lett you understand how her Majestie doth note this slackness and remiseness in you and those that have byn appoynted and authorized in that countye to have care and regard thereof and to send unto you the orders which have byn revewed by us, wyllynge and requiringe you in her Majesties name to cause the justices of the peace and head officers of everye towne to see the same duelye putt in execution within that countye, under your lieutenancy, and to gyve your straight chardge unto all officers to looke to the same as they wyll aunswere to the contrarye." *Copy.*

1591[-2], March 16.—Whitehall.—The Lords of the Council to the Justices of the Peace for the County of Sussex and the Mayor of Rye.

Whereas we are informed that divers of the soldiers that were levied in Sussex and were delivered over to their captains, by indenture, lying at Rye to be there embarked, have fled away with their armour and furniture, whereof two of them only were by the means of Captain Power apprehended and committed to prison. Forasmuch as it is thought meet some exemplary punishment should be shewed them to warn others from committing the like offence, we are informed that by various acts it is reckoned that a soldier having received his press that his departure is felony, we have thought fit to require that the two men seeking to run away from their colours may receive such punishment as the laws provide. *Copy.*

1591[-2], March 19.—Confession by Thomas Cort and others that they have killed meat during Lent for their better living.

1592, April 11.—The Mayor and Jurats of Rye to Sir Francis Knowles and the officers of the Green Cloth.

Whereas divers poor neighbours are complained upon before you for buying of fish, not being thereunto appointed by the Fishmongers of London, for we take it that when her Majesty is fully served with fish that then it is lawful for all manner of people as well "ryppyers" as other householders to buy fish in the fish market of Rye, otherwise if the market shall be restrained to the ordinances of the Fishmongers of London for their private gain, the same would tend to the enriching of that Company of Fishmongers only and their agents, and to the impoverishment of all the fishermen of Rye. *Draft.*

1592, July 1, London.—Lord Buckhurst to the Mayor and Jurats of Rye.

"Whereas you have sondrye tymes heretofore complayned unto me of the insufficiencye of the late vicar, whearof I, havinge consideration, have procured the sayd vicar to resigne to a verye honest and sufficient man very well allowed and recomended, of whome as I understande not so good care is had as he deserveth; some of his duties (as I am enformed) being kepte from him to his hinderaunce, and prejudice of the right of his vicaredge, the gyfte of which appertayneth to me, by meanes whereof he is dryven to neglecte his studdy, by the which he might be the better hable to instructe you, and forced to consume his tyme in lawe for recoverye of suche duties as to him belonge, wherof I praye you have care for that I have byn myndefull to satisfye your desyres and to supplie the want you complayned of. The which being don and not respected by you maye geve me occasion to thincke that you do not requite my good will therein towardes you as yt deserveth." *Signed.*

1592, October 20, Hampton Court.—The Lords of the Council to the Lord Admiral and Lord Buckhurst.

"Where of late her Majesty directed her speciall lettres unto you for the levying, armyng, and furnishinge of 50 hable men to be sent out of the Countye to the Port of Rye, there to be imbarked and transported by the way of Jersey into Bryttanie for her service in those partes, her Majesty findeing now some cause not to use so great a nomber as was purposed, hath aucthorysed us by her lettres to signyfye to your Lordshipps her pleasure to spare for this present the levying of the said nomber which you shall by virtue hereof dyscharg untyll her further pleasure may be therin knowen." *Copy.*

1592, November 17.—The Mayor and Jurats of Rye to Lord Buckhurst.

By law and the custom of the parish of Rye the tithe of all kind of corn and grain belongs to the parson, and the tithe of all fruits to the vicar. One of the inhabitants of Rye grows beans, to whom does the tithe thereof belong? *Draft.*

1592[-3], February 20, Somerset House.—The Lords of Council to [The Mayors, Bailiffs, and Reeves of the Cinque Ports].

"Whereas her Majesty of late tyme to her exceeding great charge hath bene often occasioned to send over into Normandy and Bryttenie diverse troupes of souldyers to the ayde of the French Kinge and there enterteyned in her paye under Sir John Norryce and Sir Roger Wyllyams, with purpose to be imployed at occasions for the best advancement of those services. Forsomuch as by daylye experyence yt falleth out that many of those souldyers so sent over do yndyrectly withdraw themselves from those services in great nombers wherby in tyme of nede the nombers supposed to be in paye are very defectyve and weake, and consequently the services much hyndered to her Majesty's great dyshonor and touch of reputation to this natyon in generall. For so much as for the preventing hereof no better meanes can be thought for this present then to take order in this behalf with the offycers of the portes where usually they aryve from Normandy or Bryttenie or any parte of Fraunce, we have thought good to require and charge you, as well the offycers of the Admyraltye as of the Custome Houses, as you the mayors, baylyffes, portreeves, or other officers there, in her Majesty's name, ymedyatly upon receypt hereof as soone as you shall understand of any shippe or vessel to aryve in that place out of Fraunce or out of any partes from beyond the seas, that may be suspected in this behalf, that dyligent serch be made after all such persons as shall so indyrectly withdraw themselves from those services. And if you shall finde any souldyer or other person worthy of suspicion to be examyned whatsoever, knowen merchants only excepted, come out of Bryttenie or Normandy or any other parte beyond the seas without suffycyent pasport from Sir John Norryce or Sir Roger Willyams, whyle they shall be Generall, under their handes and seales, to cause them forthwith to be stayed and comytted to prison untyll further dyreccion from us in that behalf." *Copy.*

1592[-3], March 5.—The Mayor of Rye to Edmond Pelham.

"Upon examination had before me of some roges and sturdye beggers, I have found that one William Randall, clarke, now serving at Uddymer is a comen forger of passportes, whereof I have one to shewe. He is a very daungerous fellowe and wryteth many handes wherefore you shall do well to sende your warrant for his apprehencion." *Draft.*

1592[-3], March 7.—Depositions concerning George Berdesworth.

John Chambers of Norwich saith that being in the company of George Berdesworth, trumpeter, at Newhaven in Sussex, the said George was requested to sound his trumpet to which he answered he would not sound before he came before the Governor of Caen, and that the Queen could not command his sounds in Caen. When it was said to him that when the Governor of Caen heard the name of the Queen of England he bowed his head the said George made light thereof and said, Tush!

1592[-3], March 7.—The Mayor and Jurats of Rye to Mr. Carpenter, at London.

We have received advertisement from Winchelsea which they have heard from their Barons that the liberties of the Cinque Ports are likely to be impeached. Whereupon we have thought good to write unto you to understand whether it be meant that the general liberties of the Cinque Ports shall be dissolved or whether any special part thereof be impugned? *Draft.*

1592[-3], March 10. London.—Robert Carpenter to the Mayor and Jurats of Rye.

"Our generall liberties have byn by the Lord Admyrall and others of the Lordes of the Upper House called in questyon, and by them the controversye thereaboutes made so greate as we stoode all in noe smalle feare of the losse and overthrowe of them. But, thankes be to God, our greatest cares be now past for them and the onlye braunche they stand upon at this instant is the proviso for us in the byll of which they cannot as yett be drawen to allowe, bycause of the manye coullors the Portes have heretofore used in defence of straungers, to defraude the Queene, butt our hope is that by the endeavour of good frendes, whome wee have in both houses, they will be wonne to graunte the same thoughe not withoutt some addityon agaynst such forrainers as have of late and shall hereafter creepe in amongest us. Your presidents which you offer to sende wyll stande us in lyke steede for havinge here the generall charter wee deame yt agaynste the controversye being generall." *Signed and Seal.*

1592[-3], March 19.—The Mayor of Rye to the Lords of the Council.

According to your Honours letters, having found in a passenger out of France certain soldiers who are come from thence without their general's passport, I have examined them by what warrant they are departed from her Majesty's service, and they all affirm that their captains left them to the discretion of Otwell Smith at Dieppe, who together with the vice-treasurer shipped them to England. *Draft.*

1593, March 27.—Conference with Fredericke Jenabell an Italian touching the amendment of the harbour.

1593, April 7. Blackfriars.—Lord Cobham to Mr. Fane, Lieutenant of Dover Castle.

"Her Majesty beinge geven tunderstande by reason of the Kinge of Spaynes dyschargynge of many Englysh and Iryshe and Scottyshe fugytyves and rebells of pensions geven by him to them (upon what occasion yt is not certeinely knowen) many of the said partyes so discharged are lykely to come into this realme in covert and secret manner, whome her Majesty wold have safely apprehended and dyscovered by all meanes possyble. I therefore praye you to sende the copy of this my letter to every port and member within the Cinque Portes, with dyrection to the offycers thereof to make diligent serch and enquyrye upon the aryveall of any shippinge whether any such persons as aforesaid shall be transported in any such vessell and to cause all suspycyous persons to be stayed and examyned untyll their condycions may be known, with the cause of their comynge into the realme." *Copy.*

1593, May 21.—The Mayor and Jurats of Rye to the Lord Warden. Whereas we have received letters from the Lords of the Council concerning the staying and imprisoning of soldiers, arriving from part beyond the sea without sufficient passports, now two gentlemen have arrived from Britany without passport from Sir John Norryce. *Draft.*

1593, May 21.—Depositions of Tempest Shefeld and Christopher Mathew, two gentlemen lately serving under Captain Haye in Britany, who came from Dieppe without passports.

1593, May 23.—Depositions of Tempest Sheffeld that he was born at Heth near Wakefield in Yorkshire, that he served voluntarily as a petronel on horseback, that he received no pay as he served voluntarily, that his father and mother live at Wylsden in Yorkshire. Depositions of Christopher Mathew that he was born at Blechinglegh in Surrey and at his first coming into France he trailed a pike and afterwards became a carboneer, that he received no pay as he served voluntarily, that he hath a brother, Henry Mathew, Bailiff of Reygate in Surrey.

1593, June 1. Cobham Hall.—Lord Cobham to the Mayor and Jurats of Rye.

Giving order that Shefield and Mathewes be sent up to the keeper of the Marshalsea and that especial care be taken that they do not confer with one another. *Signed and Seal of Arms.*

1593, June 9.—The Mayor and Jurats of Rye to Lord Cobham.

According to your directions we have sent Sheffelde and Mathewe towards the Marshalsea. *Draft.*

1593, July 4. Cobham Hall.—Lord Cobham to the Mayor and Jurats of Rye.

Requesting a draft to be made for the Lords of the Council of the privilege Genebelli doth require for the amendment of Rye Haven. *Signed.*

1593, July 12.—Depositions of George Burton, Richard Allyn, and James Askue, soldiers lately serving in France, who had returned to England on account of sickness with incorrect passports.

1593, August 8.—Order that from henceforth that two persons every day throughout the Town do ward at the Landgate, from the departing of the watch till the watch be set, to see that none be suffered to enter the Town who may be suspected to bring infection into the Town.

1593, August 20.—The Mayor and Jurats of Rye to the Lord Warden.

Whereas three maimed soldiers, lately serving her Majesty in France, are arrived here without their general's passport having the passport of the Duke of Mountpensier, we dare not let them pass by reason of the letters of the Privy Council. We herewith send you their examinations together with a printed book containing the articles of that unhappy truce lately taken in France. *Draft.*

Enclosure.—The examinations of John Chamberleyne, late serving under Captain Masterson in France, was hurt at Drewze, has a wife dwelling in Huntingdon. Henry Harrys, late serving under Captain Masterson, was born in Devonshire, he was hurt at Drewze. George Holt, late serving under Captain de Boys, was born in Tenbery, Worcestershire, was hurt at Drewze.

1593, September 20.—[The Mayor and Jurats of Rye to the Lord Warden].

"Whereas this bearer, our neighbour Moyses Cocke, beinge by profession a merchaunt, dyd traveyle with diverse merchaundyse into that realme of Fraunce wherewith her Majesty then was and yet is in good league and amyty; yet that notwithstandinge, certeine men of Aulst in Fraunce dyd trecherously sell this said berer into the handes of Leaguers who made prise of him and put him to raunsom, contrary to all right and good reason, and to the great impoverishing of the younge man. Our humble sute unto your Honor is therefore that it will please your good Lordship to graunt to this said bearer your lawfull favor that he may compleine of this intollerable injury by way of proces tendinge to withernam, that thereby he may be releaved of his damadge herein susteined." *Draft.*

1593, September 24.—A proclamation for the adjournment of Michaelmas term and for the Courts to be held at St. Albans instead of at Westminster on account of the plague in the Cities of London and Westminster.—*Printed by Christopher Barker.*

1593, October 29.—[The Mayor and Jurats of Rye] to the Lord Warden.

"After the departure of your Honors messenger, a passenger came from Deipe to Hastinge and so the passengers came hether, among whome was Peter Browne, the post, who had her Majesty's packet and other letters to your Honor which are aborde the shippe and which he could not come by untill the barke may recover the harbour of Rye, but so sone as those letters come ashore they shall be sent to your Honor. In the meanetyme may it please your Honor to be advertised that the King of France, and his sister, and Duke de Bullion are at Deipe where Duke Longedevill is shortly expected, and it is reported that the Kinge meanes to remayne there some long tyme. Here is a page arrived which belongeth to a gentleman attendant upon the Queene's sister who alleageth that he is flead for feare of punishement for loss of his masters apparrell and he would go to a Spaniard, which serveth her Majesty, but because I suspect his arrivall to be for some other cause I have thought it good to send him to your Honor by another messenger because this messenger shall not stay." *Draft.*

1593, November 13.—The Mayor and Jurats of Rye to the Bishop of Worcester.

"Whereas by all tyme of our memory we have used to chose our Parish clarke by the voyces of the inhabitantes of this our towneshippe, tyll now of late at our last election Mr. Prescott, our vycar, hath aganeseyd our said election affirming that the same only belongeth to him by the canon lawe, and thereupon hath expelled Mr. Richard Porth, whome our towneshippe hath chosen to that office, and hath placed John Roberts thereinto." *Draft.*

1593, November 29.—The Mayor of Rye to the Lord Warden.

By reason that one John Mussey, one of her Majesty's messengers for France, at his last arrival here gave intelligence to some officers here that one Rowland Parry had spoken divers disloyal and opprobrious speeches of her Majesty in France, which same Parry being arrived here I thought it my duty to send him to your Honour. Albeit it is supposed that he hath been employed in her Majesty's affairs in France. *Draft.*

1593, December 3. Chelsea.—The Bishop of Worcester to the Mayor and Jurats of Rye.

Praying that there may be an end to the differences between Mr. Greenewood, his chaplain, and Mr. Edolph. *Signed and Seal of Arms.*

1593.—Accounts of Charges for the Town Ship on various voyages.

1593. ——— The Mayor and Jurats of Rye to the Bishop of Worcester.

"Whereas we are geven to understand that some malycyous people of the parish of Iden have gone about of late to vex and disturbe our honest neighbor Richard Fowtrell, and for that purpose have presented his wyffe of incontynency before the Chauncelor of this Dyocese, which presentment for divers causes our said neighbor hath removed before the Deane of the Arches, to the intent he wold see yf by due corse of lawe this suggestion of his enemyes may be proved trewe. And for that our neighbour feareth least there shall be some synyster practyse to reduce the said sute into the contrye, where he dowteth the matter shall not have such orderly proseding as in the place where nowe it dependeth, our humble sute therefore unto your good Lordship is in his behalf that it will please you to wryte to Doctor Cosen that this his said cause may not be remaunded but may be heard and determyned before him according to lawe and justyce and not otherwyse, without any manner of unlawfull favor to be shewed either for our sakes or his owne." *Draft.*

RYE MSS.

1593[-4], January 13.—Hampton Court.—The Lords of the Council to Sir Thomas Wilford, Sir Henry Palmer, and others.

"Wheras the inhabitants of the town of Rye have been humble sutors unto us for the repairing and amending of their decayed harbroughe and have recommended unto us for the performance of that worke Frederick Genebelly who hath shewed unto us a platte of the towne and haven and other devises of ingens for the mending of the same, whose intention is (as we perceave) to reduce the harbroughe to his former state and goodness by a newe cutte to be made throughe the salte marshes and other freshe marshes of some two myles in lengthe and three hundred paces broade to lead the waters into his wonted course alonge by the Castle, which will cost as he affirmeth some three thousand pounds, but before the same be undertaken we are desirous to understand with what probabilytie he shall be hable to performe the worke, and have thought good to require you, whose experiences and judgementes in suche causes are to us well knowen, that in some convenient tyme you or any fower of you of whome you Sir Thomas Wilford, William Borrowes and Pawle Ivye to be alwayes two, to repaire to Rye to vewe the said place and harbroughe and to conferre with Genebelly about the same, and by your good endevers to informe yourselves of every particulare that maie concerne the said worke, with the likelyhoode of the performance therof." *Signed.*

1593[-4], January 15.—Conference between the Corporation and Mr. Jenabell concerning the latter's good success in the suit to their Honours for the amendment of the harbour of Rye, who having shewed that his intent is to make an entrance into this harbour near to Dinsdale Bridge byside Winchelsea, which plan of his is generally disliked by the Corporation as a thing likely to profit others of other places and very prejudicial to them.

1593[-4], January 18.—Depositions of Elizabeth Drynkwater, widow.

"She sayeth that she supposeinge her childe to be bewytched by reason the same was very weake, she went to Hastinge to one Zacharias, who lodgeth within Goodman Combes, whome she had hard to be a connynge man, to know of him what her child lacked, who told to this examynat that one Mother Rogers had bewytched her child and gave her councell to fetch blodd of her in takeinge a knyffe and to thrust it in her buttocke, but she tooke another corse for she prycked her in the hande and thereupon presently her child tooke rest and 2 great gerles dyd heare when the said Zachary gave her that councell."

1593[-4], February 5.—Depositions of Richard Clark of Stonehouse near Plymouth that about Whitsuntide was twelve month a ship called the *Gabryell*, of Bristol, went from London "on warefare" and that Robert Stretfeld one of the company was drowned while going ashore.

1593[-4], February 15.—Order by the Mayor and Jurats of Rye that by reason that Frederick Jenebill hath most treacherously abused this township by his false illusions in promising to amend the harbour of Rye, it is agreed that henceforth they will no further intermeddle with the said Jenebill nor with any of his devices.

1594, March 28. Blackfriars.—Lord Cobham to the Mayor Jurats and Commonalty of Rye.

I have lately been acquainted with a letter you wrote in May last to Mr. John Layton, who it should seem hath by Letters Patent a grant in fee farm of all the improvements within the Town and Liberties of

Rye, made by the inhabitants of the same Town upon the waste whereof, he supposeth her Majesty to be chief lord. And as it appeared by your letter he then offered you the same Letters Patent by way of composition, if your learned counsel find the said Letters Patent of validity it were good for you to embrace his offer lest such should do it as would not be so conformable as this gentleman. *Signed and Seal of Arms.*

1594, March 31.—The Mayor and Jurats of Rye to Lord Cobham.

The infection of the plague in London and the holding of the terms in distant places from Westminster have restrained us from satisfying Mr. Clayton's (*sic*) expectation. *Draft.*

[1594, April 8.—The Mayor and Jurats of Rye] to Lord Cobham.

"Of late at the sute of Mr. John Prescott, the Vycare of Rye, we reteined Mr. Edward Danner to be preacher within this our towenshipp to whome at his request also we graunted a reasonable yerely pencyon. So it is right honorable, that on Sunday being the 7th day of this present Aprill the said Mr. Danner, beinge ascended the pulpytt at evenynge prayer to preach, the said Mr. Prescott publiquely and before the hole congregation requyred Mr. Mayor of Rye to assyst him to expell the said Mr. Danner out of the pulpytt, for that he was a mutynous fellowe, a sower of sedycion, an enemye to the State and one that contempned her Majesty's proceedings; whereupon Mr. Mayor thought it not convenient to dysturbe the preacher during his sermon, but the same being ended we have taken bonde with good suertyes of the said Mr. Danner to be forthcoming to aunswere to those thinges whereof he is by Mr. Prescott accused."

1594, April 13.—The Mayor and Jurats of Rye to Mr. Layton.

Having taken counsel we find no cause to make any composition with you for any better estate. If you suppose you can recover anything by due course of law, we will lawfully defend it as we may. *Draft.*

1594, May 4.—The Mayor and Jurats of Rye to the Lord Warden.

On Wednesday last there came into our town one Paule Formosus, apparelled in such sort as we sent him unto you, a very suspicious person and one who greatly abused the Lord Hounsden. We send you certain notes found about him. *Draft.*

1594, May 26, Greenwich.—Sir Francis Knollys and others to the Mayor of Rye.

Forasmuch as her Majesty hath of late years been very badly served with sea fish from your town and at expensive and unreasonable prices, by occasion as we are informed of the evil and indirect dealings of your fishermen, in that they keep not markets in convenient time after their boats return from the sea, but hide and sell away their fish in secret. And by means of disordered buyers, which do privately buy for London and other places in shops before her Majesty be served. These are therefore, in her Majesty's name, to request you to take present order in your town that all the fishermen do from henceforth keep their market within one hour after their boats shall return from sea, and that then they bring all their fish into the market and not to hide or keep it secretly back, as they have used to do. And further that you take order that no buyer of fish for London or other places, be suffered to buy any until such time as the bearer hereof William Angell yeoman purveyor to her Majesty, or his lawful deputy appointed thereunto, have bought so much as shall be needful for her Highness' service and none to be suffered to buy in any shops secretly. *Signed and Seal of Arms.*

1594, June 15. Dover Castle.—Sir Thomas Fane to Mr. Betts, Mayor of Rye.

"I have received lettres from our right honorable Lord Warden wherby I am given to understand that upon my humble suit unto his Lordship in the behalf of the Portes, it hath pleased his good Lordship (by earnest motion to the Lords of Her Majesty's most honorable Privie Councell) to procure their enlargement to passe alonge the coast with their boates and shippinge to Newcastle for coales, or els to crosse the seas for Bulloigne or Diepe, so as order be taken that at all tymes there be in a readiness within every porte and his member suche nombre of serviceable marinors to be employed upon 24 hours warninge as in this schedule is conteyned."

Rye to provide 20 able mariners.

Signed. Seal of Arms.

1594, June 29.—The Mayor and Jurats of Rye to [Sir Thomas Fane].

"Accordinge to the purport of your lettres which of late we receaved we will provyde to have 20 suffycyent maryners at all tymes in a reddynes, upon very smale warnyng, to serve her Majesty but we humbly beseche that we may receave such warrant by her Majesty's commission for the same service to be donne by them as in lyke cases hath bene used." *Draft.*

1594, July 1.—Order by the Mayor and Corporation of Rye that the town ship shall go on her pretended voyage towards Rochelle. God send her good return.

1594, July 4.—The Mayor and Jurats of Rye to John Phillips.

"Whereas diverse of thenhabitantes of this towneshippe have built a new shippe of the burthen of 150 tuns called the *Hercules*, whereof John Davyes is parte owner and master, we judg that sixtene tonns of such ordynance as the said master of the said shippe shall thinck meete, will be sufficient and no more then necessary for the use and defence of the said shippe, whereof we thought good to advertyse you." *Draft.*

[1594], July 9.—Sir Thomas Wilford to Sir Henry Palmer and William Borrowes.

If we must answer what probability we see that a good haven may be made in the place to us shewn, I, for my part, say none at all, the charges I suppose infintie, and if there were, the continuance very uncertain.

1594, August 24.—Order by the Mayor and Jurats of Rye that the *5li. 10s.* for the use of Francis Maquerie's children's stock shall be paid before Michaelmas.

1594[-5], January 13.—Order by the Mayor and Jurats of Rye that the town ship be sold and she is sold to William French for *100li. 0s. 8d.*

1594[-5], February 15.—Order by the Mayor and Jurats of Rye that Sir Thomas Wylford, Sir Henry Palmer, and Mr. Lieutenant do determine concerning the unjust demands of Fredericke Jenebilly against the Corporation of Rye for *82li. 9s. 0d.*

1595, August 2.—Order by the Mayor and Jurats that by reason some invasion of the enemy is suspected, it is thought good that the watch be strengthened by appointing some of good credit to search the watch.

1595, August 26.—Mr. Gaymer elected by the Mayor and Jurats of Rye to repair to Dover to understand her Majesty's pleasure concerning the setting forth of five ships to the seas, for her Majesty's service, out of the Ports and their members.

1595, December 18.—Articles of agreement between the Barons of the Cinque Ports and Marck Packman, by which the said Packman undertakes to plead the general Charter of the Cinque Ports in the Exchequer as speedily as he can, for the sum of 20*li.*

1596, August 27, Greenwich.—Lord Cobham to [the Mayor and Jurats of Rye.]

"Now that the shippe of Rye is retorned, with the rest of her Majesty's fleete, from the cost of Spayne, I have thought it good to praye and require you to see the capten and companye of her paide such severall somes of mony as are behinde and unpaid both to them and every of them, as also for the hyer of the shippe, according to your composytion betwene you and the owners, which you may not fayle to do with as much expedytion as may be, which I hope shall be so performed as that I shall heare no more of yt." *Copy.*

1596, September 9.—The Mayor and Jurats of Rye to the Governor of Dieppe.

The wife of one George Fremlyn complains unto us that her husband is unjustly sued and arrested at Dieppe for a matter of justice executed upon one Mychaell Voquelyn here in Rye, according to the laws of England, while he was a fugitive from his native country, wherefore we have searched our records and find that about two years ago a certain single woman confessed she was with child by the said Mychaell, and finding that he was a very base, lewd, and incontinent fellow, he was censured and fined, and to avoid public scandal the said Mychaell paid ten pounds to the poor of this town, for which said money he now unjustly vexeth the said Fremlyn. We hope that our neighbour shall receive before you indifferent justice as your people resorting hither shall receive here. *Draft.*

1596, [before September 12]. The humble offer and petition of the Barons of the Cinque Ports and their members to her sacred Majesty.

The said Barons offer their service of six ships and one pinnace, maintained in warlike sort to do their best endeavours to suppress all her Majestys enemies.

Note by the Lord Treasurer. The tonnage to be expressed.

The said Barons beseech her Majesty to grant them a Privy Seal for the allowance of 500 *li.* at every fifteenth as they have had since the reign of Henry the seventh.

Note. This is to be considered.

The said Barons humbly request all such ordnance as the said ships and pinnace shall want, upon bond for their redelivery, and to have necessary shot and powder.

Note. Number and quantity to be specified.

The said Barons pray that her Majesty will grant her absolute commission for the setting forth of ships in the said service and for the taking and making prize of all manner of shipping and goods, without special licence or aid, within any place, ports, havens, or creeks not in amity or league with her Majesty and the men and ships so employed to be under no rule but that of the Barons.

To grant to the Barons all such ships, goods, and persons by them taken, going to or coming from the enemy.

Note. The takers to answer her Majesty of 3 or 4 parts.

If it happen that any prize taken by the Barons be forced by foul weather to go into other ports out of the Cinque Ports within the realm of England, they may be at liberty to depart at their pleasure.

That they may make prize of any ship and goods that shall be taken in chase or be found within two leagues of the shore near to any enemy's coast.

That the said Barons will be willing to enter into bond, in the Court of Admiralty for the Cinque Ports, not to take or detain wittingly or willingly any ship or goods of persons who shall be at amity or league with her Majesty or any her subjects that shall not offend or by fight resist.

Note. The bond must be taken to his Majesty's use.

1596, September 12.—Lord Cobham [to the Barons of the Cinque Ports].

I have considered your petition and articles concerning your offer of shipping to the seas to suppress Her Majesty's enemies that there spoil her subjects, which my honourable Lord, the Lord Treasurer, hath perused and by reason of the uncertainty of your own articles can make no direct answer unto them, but hath set down upon the head of every of them his opinion, for the present, of the which you are to have due regard. *Copy.*

1596, October 31. Richmond.—The Lords of the Council [to the Lord Warden].

"Wheras her Majestie havinge byn certefied of great and spedie preparations made in Spaine with intention of some special attempte and enterprise against the realme, thinketh it nedeful that sufficient store of good and serviceable shippinge and maryners be kept in redines in the severall portes, to joyne with her Majesty's Navie on the seas as occasion shall require, for the defence of the realme. It pleaseth her Majestie therefore to commande that for this present time a generall restrainte shall be made throughout all the realme of all shipinge, so as no shippe, exceptinge of such sorte as are hereafter mentioned in this placarde, shall be suffered, after notice hereof given, to goe unto the seas untill her Majesty's pleasure be further knowen in this behalfe, for the delivery and makinge knowen of this her Majesty's commandement. These shall be to will and command you in her Majesty's name, by virtue hereof, to make your spedie and undelayed repaire unto all the porte townes alongest the sea coastes in the counties of Kent and Sussex and to give straight charge and commandment unto all and every the Vice Admiralls and other officers in the townes and portes in the said counties, that upon sight of this our warrant (the copy whereof you shall leave with them) they forthwith cause staie to be made of all such shippes and maryners within their havons and liberties as shall be either found there at this present tyme or shall hereafter repaire thether, lycencinge onely such to departe as shall be certenly knowen either to goe onley alongest the coast of this realme, from porte to porte and not to have any intention to crosse the seas into any forreine partes, or to be ordinarie passengers into the Lowe Contries or to the coast townes of France opposite unto our coaste, or to serve for the transportation of her Majesty's forces or victualles or any other such ordinarie passages into Ireland, or lastly such as shall have lycence from me the Lord Admirall uppon speciall occasion. And to the intent we may be thoroughlie informed of the performance of this service, these shall be likewise to charge and command you to bringe with you at your spedie retorne which you shall make with all dilligence, a particuler and perfecte noate under the handes of the officers of the portes of this charge and her Majesty's commandement delivered by you and of the time when you delivered the same, as also of the nomber of the vessels and maryners so founde and stayed in the severall portes uppon this commandement." *Copy.*

In the same bundle of letters is a copy of the particular for Rye required as above to be made. The largest ship is the *Hercules* of 150 tons, next the *Blessinge* of 100 tons. There are 8 crayers and 25 fishing boats and 150 mariners at home in Rye.

1596, October. Dover Castle.—Sir Thomas Fane [to the Mayors, Bailiffs, and Jurats of the Cinque Ports].

"I received a letter late from our Right Honourable Lord Lieutenant advertyseinge that one Jaques, Sir William Stanlye's lieutenant, is come to Callys and there intendeth to prepare boates to infest our sea cost, for which cause yt is his Lordship's pleasure that there should be very good watch and warde kept in every place along the sea cost where nede shall require, and that the beacons there sholde be very dulye and carefully watched."

Postscript.—"I thought it good also at this tyme to signyfye unto you that the right honorable our Lord Warden being advertysed of your great and superfluous expences commonly used at your generall assemblyes doth much myslyke thereof and wysheth you would spare the same for better uses." *Signed.*

1596[-7], January 9. Ashford.—James Martyn and others on behalf of the inhabitants of Ashford to the Mayor and Jurats of Rye.

"Wheras of late yt hath pleased God (for some cause to hym best knowen) to vysytt your towne with one of his greate roddes or scowrges wherwith he often afflicted man for synn, wherof not long sythence wee of our towne of Asheford have had manyfold experience, and as yt pleased hym of hys greate mercye then to rayse us up many frendes to have a fellowe feeling of our myseryes and to contrybute towardes the necessytye of our poore (blessed be his name therfore), so yt hath now pleased hym to move our hartes to contrybute something (according to our small abylytyes) towardes the releaving of the poore sayntes of God amongest you, the some wherof is fyve poundes, the which by this bearer wee have sent unto you, desiring you accordyng to your wisdomes and good discretions to distribute the same amongest them in such sorte and at such tyme as you shall thinke most fytt and convenyent. And thus desiring God (for his Christe's sake) to loke downe mercifully upon you and in his good tyme to withdrawe his heavye hand of correction from you and to make both you and us truly thankfull for all his mercyes and loving kyndenesses towardes us (the which are innumerable) and to give us all grace and wisdome to make use aright of these his loveing corrections upon us." *Signed.*

1596[-7], March 7. Whitehall.—**Lord Burghley to the Mayors, Bailiffs, and others of the Cinque Ports.**

"Whereas the right honourable the Lord Cobham late Lord Chamberlain and Lord Warden of the Cinque Portes, for the better government of the said Portes dyd from tyme to tyme as any just occasion was mynystered, conceave and establish divers good and necessary orders, which he delivered unto you to be dulie and carefully putt in execution by you, which in his lyffe tyme under his aucthorytie you dyd see accordinglie performed in the severall Portes as I have bene credybly enformed. Forasmuch as by reason of his Lordship's death you may make some doubt and scruple touching your warrant and aucthority to execute the sayde orders, therefore these are to notyfy unto you and to every one of you as it may concerne, that her Majesty's pleasure and comaundement is that every of you in your severall places and according to your severall officeis do contynue the execution of the said orders with lyke care and diligence and in lyke sorte and manner as you dyd in his Lordshipp's lyffe tyme." *Copy.*

1597, April 18.—The Mayor and Jurats of Rye to the Lord Treasurer.

"By reason of the universall scarsytye of corne and graine we cannot be permytted to exporte from the corne contryes of England provisyon of graine to susteine our poore people, by meanes whereof we are enforced at this time to make staye of a small barke, laden with 20 quarters of barlye, imbarked for one Mr. Bowier of London out of the west partes of this county of Sussex, where the outrage of the meaner sorte of the inhabitants is such as they will not permytt any provisyon of corne to be shipped hether, except the same shold be offered to be done by force, to the dangerous breach of her Majesty's peace. Wherefore we most humbly desyre your honorable protection and warrant that the said barly may be sold here at any reasonable price to be converted into bread for the releefe of our poore distressed inhabytantes." *Draft.*

1597, April 18.—The Mayor and Jurats of Rye to Robert Bowyer of London.

"Where a bark laden with twenty quarters of barlye consyned unto you is happened into this harbor where the scarcytye of corne and graine is over greate, we most hartelye praye you to content yourself that your smale portion of barly may be here distrybuted to a greate nomber of poore distressed people at the highest price that barly is sold or hath bene sold in these partes, to make breade to supplye the present want here, whereby you shall not only be well paide for your comodytye to the comfort of many but you shall command us in anythinge wherein we may stande you in steade." *Draft.*

1597, April 21. Whitehall. The Lords of the Council to all Vice-Admirals, Mayors, Sheriffs, and others of the Ports.

"Whereas yt is thought necessarye in respect of the great preparations that are reported to be made in forreine partes that her Majesty shold have suffycyent store of good and servyceable shippes and maryners to joyne with her Majesty's navye on the seas as occasyon shall require, for the better defence of the realme, or such other necessarye service as shall be thought fytt to be undertaken, her Majesty therefore hath thought it necessarye that a generall restraint shold be made throughout all the portes, havens, and creekes alonge the sea cost, and that no shippe, hulke or other vessel of what burthen soever shall be suffered to departe out of the severall portes where they are untyll there shall be further notyce geven of her Majesty's pleasure in that behalf unles it be from one port to another or suche vessels as doe passe betwixte England and France." *Copy.*

1597[-8], February 8. "The Queen's Majesties Proclamation, declaring her Princely intention to inhibite her subjects upon most extreme paynes from offending on the seas any persons in their ships or goods, being the subjectes of any Prince, Potentate or State, in amitie with her Majestie." *Printed by Christopher Barker.*

1597[-8]. March 17. Richmond.—The Lord of the Council to [the Lord Admiral].

Setting out that the Queen is purposed "to sett some of her shipps unto the seas" for the better manning of which "there shalbe occasion to take up some nomber of maryners and pylattes," and for that reason requiring him to repair to Dover and along the sea coast to all the several ports, creeks, and harbours to the port of Rye and so to Southampton and to command all Vice-Admirals, Mayors, and Officers to detain ships and mariners leaving for "forreine partes"; excepting such as have received his licence, and those trading from port to port or to the Low Countries, Picardy, and Normandy. *Copy.*

1598, April 16. "From the Court."—Lord Buckhurst to the Justices of the Peace in the county of Sussex.

"Whereas it pleased my Lordes of the Counsell to write their favorable lettres heretofore unto you on the behaulfe of the townesmen of Rye for some benevolent contribution to be collected in that countie towardes their great chardges and workes nowe in hand for the amendment of their decaied haven. And for as much as I am crediblie informed that their is great probalitie and assuraunce of good successe to ensue upon the said workes, and that the state of the haven hath bine alreadie viewed by men of great skyll who have confidentlie delivered their opinyons of great hope and probalitie of good successe, and that some of yourselves have bine previe and actors in the same, wherby there is not onlie great benefitt like to arryse unto the said towne, but also great proffitt and comoditie unto the whole countrey by the meanes thereof. I have therefore thought good (these thinges being so) as well in regard of their Lordshipes said lettres as chieflie in respect of the publick good that will redownde to the whole comonwealth therby, to recommend to your charitable considerations by this my privatt, the great necessitie and convenience to helpe and furder the said workes, and therewithall doe verie hartelie pray you to deale and perswade with the countie by all the best meanes you maie, to yelde to such voluntarie benevolent and commendable contribution for the reliefe and effectinge of the said workes, as to their severall good myndes and discressions shall be thought most fitt and convenient." *Signed, and Seal of arms broken.*

1598, July 4. London.—Robert Sackeville to Adrian Stoughton.

Though it may seem vain on his part to add anything to what the Council has already written to all the Justices [of Sussex] on behalf of the suit of the town of Rye, yet he gives his own testimonies to the value of the work begun upon the haven at Rye and urges "a benevolent contrybution amongest your westerne rapes towards fynishinge of the same." It is a work "profitable for the common wealth in generall and particulerly for this county of Sussex." The town of Rye has already expended much upon the work and it is a pity it should now

RYE MSS.

"miscarry for a lyttle." The town might take it "very unkyndely if their owne countrymen should fayle them."

[Followed by another letter from the same to "Edward Carril Esquire," in almost identical words.]

1598, August 23. "A proclamation for the restreining and punishment of Forestallers and Ingrossers of Corne and Graine, and for the prohibition of making of any maner of starch within her Majesties realme and dominions."

1598, September 19. Nonsuch.—The Earl of Nottingham to the Mayor and Jurats of Rye.

"As I have bene formerlie beholdenge unto you, so lett me nowe alsoe intreat your favors in helpinge me to twoe dorsers of your beste fishe and especiallie of some good conger, which I pray you to cause to be sent unto my house att Halinge on Frydaie next, and I will not onelie see the same paied for and the messenger rewarded, but I will requyte your kindenesses herein with any good favor I maie." *Signed, and Seal of arms.*

1598, September 22.—The Corporation of Tenterden to the Mayor and Jurats of Rye.

Controversies have lately arisen with their new Bailiff, Mr. Hailes which by him are referred to the Lord Warden for determination. They urge the Mayor and Jurats of Rye to write to the Lord Warden—"for so muche as we weare incorporate in the ayde and helpe of your towne of Rye"—on their behalf that by his means they may enjoy their ancient, usages, liberties, and customs." Signed "Herbert Witefeild, Edward Shortt, John Tylden, Edward Jervise, George Phillipes, William Curtis, John Funnell, George Shortt, Thomas Curtis, Thomas Tilden, Robert Tygg."

1598, [September, The Mayor and Jurats of Rye to the Lord Warden.]

Letter written in accordance with the foregoing request of the Corporation of Tenderden. *Draft.*

1598 [-9], March 13.—Blackfriars.—Lord Cobham to Sir Thomas Fane, Lieutenant of Dover Castle.

"Where compleynt hath byn made that divers badd and evill affected persons, of late going over and comyng from beyond the seas, have passed without examynation taken of them by the Commysioners for restraynt of passengers, the faulte whereof is supposed to be partlye for that suche owners and masters of shippes and boates, inkepers, victuelers, and others as have byn bound in this case have not soe duly regarded the performance of their bondes and dutyes therein as they ought, and partlye for that there are at this tyme dyvers persons that are owners and masters of shippes and boates and also dyvers inkepers, victuelers, and others that are growen upp, and admytted sythence the taking of the last bondes, that never were nor yet are bound, who in respect that they stand unbownd make no reckonynge to suffer any bad persons to passe without presenting them to the Commissioners, for redresse whereof, and for that I wold have a due and strict course observed within and throughout my jurisdiction to prevent the great daungers that otherwise might happen to the state of this her Majesty's realme, I have thought good to have newe bonds taken for that purpose throughout the Cinque Portes and their members as well of those that have byn formerly in my Lord my father's tyme, as of all others that now stand unbowned. For which purpose pray command my servant Marck Packnam, Clerk of the office, to goe alongst the Cinque Portes and their members to take such bonds and to bring them into the office. And so praying you to advertise the Portes as much by your letters, when Packnam shall goe aboute yt.

P.S. And for that I understand that by reason of sundry abuses comytted by hackenymen in this case they have byn formerly bownd, pray let them also be nowe in like manner bownd." *Copy.*

1599, March 31.—" The Queenes Majesties Proclamation declaring her princely resolution in sending over of her Army into the realme of Ireland." *Printed by Christopher Barker.*

1599, June 24. " The Courte at Grenwich."—Henry Cocke, James Quintes, and Richard Broun, to the Mayor and Jurats of Rye.

" We have perused certaine orders and articles indented agreed upon and signed by divers of the fyshermen of your towne of Rye, and Mr. Angell, her Majesty's cheife purveyor of sea fyshe, of the which we doe very well like, and have caused the same to be recorded in the comptinge house; whereof we thought it good to advertisse you, requiringe you and the sayed fishermen from tyme to tyme to see the same to be duely and truely performed, whereby her Majesty may be hereafter bothe better served and the fyshe allso maie be brought in more convenient tyme to the Courte then of late yt hath usually ben; wherein you Mr. Maior and the Jurats of your towne have ben very much to blame. Heretofore, for her Majesty's better service of sea fyshe, there have ben many good orders sett downe but by your remysse and slacke dealinge they have ben utterly neglected, but hereafter we hope that you will be more carefull of yt, for as from and under her Majesty you doe enjoye many good and profitable previlidges, so, for your better contynuance of them, it is expected by a carefull performance of your duetyes in thes services, you doe expresse your thankefull and lovinge myndes towardes her Highenes. And whereas we are informed that one Swayne of your towne, att Mr. Angell's last beinge with youe, very obstinately refused to sett to his hande to the sayed articles indented, we therefore require you Mr. Maior forthewith to call him before you and eyther procure him to sett his hande unto them or ells to take good bonde of him for his present aparance before us at her Majesty's comptinge howse, and there we doubte not but by his example other such froward and disordered persons shall be taught hereafter more obedyently to performe there duetyes, as well towardes her Highnes as allso unto you and others, which under her have authorytie over them. Of all the contentes of these our letters we will and require you to imparte them unto the whole companey of fyshermen and others allso of your towne whom yt maye eny waye concerne, whereby hereafter no man may excuse himselfe by ignorance." *Signed, and Seal of arms.*

1599, June 30. Confession of Harry Davys.—He was found as a vagrant within the town. " He is a Welshman born at Acham within two myles of Shrewsbury and that he saith that at Michelmas last was twelve monethes he was pressed at Winsor by my Lord Russell to serve in Ireland and ymediately was sent with other soldiers to Westchester, and so tooke shippinge for Ireland and landed at Waterford where he hath remayned a soldier untill Thursday last was three weekes, and then tooke shippinge at Diveling and came back againe to

Westchester, having a passport from the Lord Russell to passe to Westchester, where as he saith he left his passport with on Mr. Greene, the mayor of the towne, and so hath travelled without pasport to London and so unto Rye. And for newes he reporteth that about sixe or seven dayes in May last past the Erle of Essex travelinge from Waterford to Dumdarricke in a wood was mett withall by the wild Irishe and sett upon where he lost fifty thousand men and the Erle himselfe was wounded in the ryght arme with a muskett in such sort as he was leike to losse his arme."

1599, July 10. London.—Richard Lyffe and George Bynge to the Mayors, Bailiffs and Jurats of the Cinque Ports and two ancient towns.

"According to your commission to us given we have earnestly and painefully a longe tyme as we thinke travelled, wherin we have shewed our good will and best skill for the longe looked and hoped desire which God be praysed her Sacred Majesty this Mondaye being the 9th of July hath graunted our request to my Lord Threasurer whome we have fownde in the ende our very good Lord. And our Lord Warden hath with might and mayne dealt most honorable. We have found Mr. Attorney Generall in the knittinge up, a speciall favorer of our sutes. Our lerned Counsell we have both much trobled and hindered. Our owne paines and indevors we desire to be thought as we have deserved. The booke shall be perfected and all thinges finished as sone as her Majesty retorneth from prograce. My Lord Threasurer this Tewsdaye and our Lord Warden hath willed us to departe and goe home and my Lord Warden will send word when all is reddy to be finished. My Lord Thresurer himself told us that he and my Lord Warden wold see it be done accordinge to our desire as sone as her Majesty doth retorne. We do sende you word the rather because it were fitt you come furnished with mony that is to be defrayed for such charges as we hope you and all shall thinke well bestowed, which you must thinke is for charges past and to come for the full accomplishinge of all." *Copy.*

1599, August 3. Blackfriers.—Lord Cobham to the Mayor of Rye.

"Even now I have received letters from the Lordes, who in their providence and contynewance of care of the state hath recommended unto mee this especially, that if this rumor contynewe trewe, that so many gallies be assembled at the Groyne, their designe will be for the River of Thames and to keepe themselves from any discovery they will keepe as near the French coast as they can; their Lordships have therefore commanded mee to give straight dyrection and commandiment to you, that upon the sight heereof you sett fourth your fishermen to ply over to the French coast that by them I may trewlie bee advertised of their coming, and that by post for life this with all speede is to bee done and doubt not but you will have that care as the importance of the cause requiers, which I chardge you in her Majesty's name, as you will answer to the contrarie, see it presentlie perfourmed." *Signed, and Seal of Arms.*

1599, August 7.—The Mayor and Jurats of Rye to the Lord Warden.

"We receaved your Lordships letters of the third of this present August the fourth of the same, and according to your direction on Sonday last past, we sent out of our harbor of Rye two fisher boates of our towne well manned with 13 men apeece besides the masters, and thoroughly furnished with victualls, muskettes, powder, shott, and other munition meete for that purpose, to sayle and ply over to the French coast for advertisement to be given of the comeing of the Spaniards. And this present Tewsdaye by reason of fowle weather they were constreyned to retorne backe againe and came into the harbor of Rye. And for newes they doe certefye unto us that yesterday, being Monday, the two boates of Rye did make chase to twoe Skotishemen upon the coast of Fraunce and inquired of them what newes they could tell of the Spaniardes and one of them, beinge the bygger barke, came from Rochell and the master tolde them for certeyne trewthe that the reporte was at Rochell that there was lyinge at Groyne, abowte a fortnight past, one hundred and fifty sayle of Spaniers whereof there were 40 gallies and that they were prepared for Callyse and Flanders. And the lesser barke came from Newhaven on Saturday last past, and the master of the said barke reporteth for treweth that there is a Spanishe shippe come unto Newhaven laden with Threasure, and that the Governor of Deipe is com thether to make staye thereof. Also they saide unto our fyshermen that theire is lyinge reddy at Bryst 2 Spanishe gallies, which is all the newes they cold lerne. And thus much we thought it our duties to certefie unto your Honor and that the boates, if God send faire wether, are reddy to goe oute againe the next tyde so we here not to the contrary. We hope by your honorable good meanes the great charges in settinge oute of theese boates shall be borne by her Highness in respecte of the poore estate of our poore towne." *Draft.*

1599, August 27.—Lord Howard and Sir Walter Raleigh to Sir Thomas Fane, Lieutenant of Dover Castle.

"Wee have receyved lettres from my Lordes of the Councell which were sent unto them from the Governor of Brest, to lett their Honors know that seaven gallies belonginge to the Spanish Fleete were putt into the harborough, and that 200 sayle of shipps were seene a seaboord standing for our channel. Ther came also a pincke from the Governor of Callice this present Monday which wrote unto us confyrming the same intelligences. Wee doe therefore pray you and hartylie requyre you, as you tender her Majesty's services, to cause a couple of small barques of Dover to stand over into the sea, as farre to the westward as they can, to give us notices yf they see any fleet comyng this way, that wee may have some tyme to be lose from our anchors and that you will wryte to the Porte of Rye to doe the lyke, and satysfaction for the charge shall be made here by the Threasorer ot her Majesty's Navie, Reare Admyrall of the Fleete. And we doe further pray you to cause the Mayor of Dover to send a boat hither to the Downes with 50 tonnes of ballast." *Copy.*

1599, December 2. Dover Castle.—Sir Thomas Fane, Knight, Lieutenant of Dover Castle, to the Mayors, Bailiffs, and Jurats of the Cinque Ports and their members.

"Forasmuche as by letters from owr right honorable Lord Warden of the 30th of November last directed unto me his Lordship hathe sygnyfied that the Lordes of the Cownsell being lought to charge or trubell the contrye with any unnecessarie borthen, are content to dysemyse the beeken wache and wachies along the see cost untyell further nesytie shall requier, and hathe wylied me to discharg the same accordingly. Thes ar therfor to wyell and requier you, in har Majesty's name to charg and comand you and evrie of you, that emediatly uppon the resett or syght herof you case all the saied wachies within ether of your townes, members, and lyberties to be therwith dismysed and dyschargod untyell a new warnyng." *Signed.*

[1599.]—Letters of Attorney by the Mayor, Jurats, and Commonalty of Rye, appointing their "Combaron," Thomas Hamon, then Mayor of Rye, to become "humble sutor" to the Queen and the Council "for some releefe to be had towerds the amendment of this decayed haven of Rye." *Draft.*

[1599.—The Mayor and Jurats of Rye to the Lord Warden ?]

"Whereas about Mychaelmas last (beinge our accustomed tyme for that purpose) we chose this bearer Roberte Gyllam to be our Parish clark, with the consent of Mr. Smyth, our vycaire, yet of late (for what cause we know not) the said Mr. Smyth seketh to molest him and by compleintes made to your Worship against him to convent him before you, and also offereth at his pleasure to displace him and to place another at his owne wille, contrary to all use and custome tyme out of mynde here used in such causes. Our humble sute therefore unto you is that the injunctyons in ecclesiastycal cases and our customes, that point may be kept invyolable, that there be no emulation betwene Mr. Smyth and us nor dyscord for matters of usadge which by any and all lawful meanes we shall support and mayntein to our power. And if Mr. Smyth will seke indyrectly to usurpe upon us we shall be sory for his follye, that he, succedeing so many grave and lerned men, shold intrude himself into unnaturall sutes with us which his predecessors wold never attempt to do." *Draft.*

1599[–1600], January 13. Blackfriars.—The Lord Warden to Sir Thomas Fane.

"Where there is one Espinola, a Spaniard, a young man aboute the age of 22 yeres, of stature tall and slender, with a longe spare face, of complexion sallowe, and black heared, having very lyttle on his face, is this night broken out of prison, purposeing no doubt to convey himself over. These are therefore very hartelye to praye you to cause diligent and carefull serch to be made for him in all shippinge and other vessels comyng from hence, and to cause him to be apprehended yf he may be found, and commytted to sure and saffe custody untyll I may upon advertysement from you geve you other dyrection. I praye you wryte your letters to Sandwich, Rye, and the rest of the portes that they may take order to do the lyke there." *Copy.*

1599[–1600], March 6. Blackfriars.—The Lord Warden to the Mayor and Jurats of Rye.

"I have receaved your letter of the thirde of this instante concerninge the complainte made by the vicare of your towne againste Brooke, for certeine speeches by him delivered againste the supremacie, wherof for that the speaker of those woordes mentioned in your letter (as I do conceave) seemes to be scarsely well advised, I wish you to take good consideration and to examyne thoroughlie by the course of his other actions whether he be a man sownde in his senses or not, and whether there hath beene no former grudge or controversie betwyxte the vicar and him, and to advertise me therof, with such other circumstances as are in such a case necessarie to be weighed and considered, and what you judge to be the cause that transported him into this furye or passion of hard speeche, and upon your aunswere I will send you myne opinion what I thinke fitt to be done." *Signed, and Seal of Arms.*

1599 [—1600], March 15.—The Mayor and Jurats of Rye to [the Lord Warden].

"Accordinge to your honorable directyons we have called Brooke before us in the presence of Mr. Vycaire and have strictlye examyned him what hath moved him to denye her Majesty's supremacye; who answered us that he dyd the same with no intent to deprive her Highnes of any her regall dignyties upon earth, but that he dyd conceave that none cold be supreme but God only and next under God he acknowledged her Majesty to be the princypall governor in all causes over all her domynions. And beinge demaunded whether he dyd attribute any supremacye to any other upon earth then only to her Majesty within her government? He said no. Then we shewed him the othe of the supremacye and demaunded of him whether he wold willinglie take the same or no. And when he had deliberatly read the same he aunswered that he wold most willingly take the same and so dyd, and said further that he held him no good subject of her Majesty that wold refuse the same. Then (our good Lord) we very well knowinge of our owne knowledges that Brooke is rather over precyse in religion, haveinge read more than he understandeth then any waye affected to any papacye, and we further well knowinge that Brooke haveinge often found fault with Mr. Vycar his kinde of teachinge, wherein is small or no instruction (which opynion in Brooke we condempe not), Mr. Vycare doth greatlye envye the poore man and wold willingly accuse him unto us yet further for recusancy, upon which pointe we also examyned Brooke who answereth that he refuseth not to come to the church but doth very often repayre thether and yet syth he receaveth no instructions in the church for the good of his soule he doth sometymes absent himself from church and imployeth himself to reade the Scriptures of God at home, wherein he can better enforme himseL then Mr. Vycarre can. Now yf it please your Honor we have thought it convenient to dyscrybe unto you the qualytye and estate of this Brooke. He is by profession a tayler and of late cold not reade but by his industry, haveinge obteined knowledge to reade English, he hath waded therein farther than his capacytye can reach unto, whereby he hath over gonne his senses and consumed himself by followinge the letter of the Scriptures contrary to the intent and meaning thereof, to the detriment of himself onlye. And so haveing delt herein so farre as our knowledges will permytt us, the imperfections whereof we doubt not but your Honor will pardon." *Draft.*

1600, June 2.—"A Proclamation conteyning her Majesties pleasure how those shalbe dealt withall, which have falsly slandered her Majesties proceedings and her Ministers, by spreading vile and odious libels and brutes to stirre discontentment among her people: containing also a sharpe commandement to all Justices of Peace and other principall persons in the Countreys, to see Ingrossers of Corne and Graine duely punished." *Printed by Robert Barker.*

1600, August 13.—The Mayor and Jurats of Rye to the Lord Warden.

"On Satterday last there came to the handes of me, the Mayor of Rye, certeine lettres wrytten by Mrs. Smyth, our vycar's wyffe, or rather by Mr. Smyth, our vycar, in his wyff's name, and dyrected to their father-in-lawe in London, and in those letters was inclosed a

RYE MSS.

crucyfix of silver which herein I sende *to* your honor. Whereupon I sent for Mr. Smyth and enquired of him where he had that crucyfix, who aunswered that his wyffe had had the same a long tyme, as of the gyfte of her mother, and that now shee sent the same for a token to a child of hers in London to weare about the neck of it. Which aunswere I, the said Maior, at that tyme receaved *de bene esse* untyll I might further understand of the truth of the cause. And afterwards he was convented before me, the said Maior, and others the Jurates of Rye, and againe demanded how he came by that crucyfix. He made such aunswere as before. And because we wold not enterprise to charge or dyscharge him concernyng this matter untyll your Honor's dyrection were had therein, he was offered to use his libertye upon bond to be forthcomyng yf your Honor shold call for him, which he consented then unto. Now this day, being our Court day, we sente for him to enter into the said bonde, he refused so to do and in most unreverent and savadge manner reviled me, the said Mayor, willing me to do what I durst, and affyrmed that I dyd injustyce to offer to take such bonde of him with farre more reproachfull wordes then is meete to be repeated. For which his said abuse and to have him forthcoming untyll your Honor's pleasure be knowen, we have comytted him to prison, most humbly desiring your Honor's will and dyrection herein." *Copy*.

1600, November 27. Lambeth.—The Archbishop of Canterbury to the Mayor and Jurats of Rye.

About August last I wrote to you touching the bearer Mr. Smith, your Curate of Rye, whereby I did require you to take bond of him for his personal appearance before me. Since which time I have received no answer from you, whereat I do greatly marvel forasmuch as Mr. Smith hath been here with me and offered to make answer to such things as are objected against him; you will therefore with convenient speed send unto me what you can charge him withal. *Signed, and Seal of Arms*.

1600, December 1.—The Mayor and Jurats of Rye to the Archbishop of Canterbury.

It may please your Grace to be advertised that we never received your letters of August last touching Mr. Smith, notwithstanding we took bond of him to appear before the Privy Council. The matters that Mr. Smith is charged withal are contained in a letter to Lord Cobham. *Draft*.

1600, December 21.—Proclamation prohibiting the "use and carriage of Dagges, Birding pieces and other Gunnes contrary to the Law."

1600.—Small sheet of paper on which is written.

"Grene leaves grene
Agrene leaves greane
My harte in howlde
Thre hundred fowlde
And greene leves betwene."

1600[-1], January 2.—Order signed by Lord Howard for the arrest of John Tokens, Thomas Goldnier, Thomas Medcalfe, William Harford, and Richard Storme, late of Hamble in the County of Southampton for piracy committed upon the high seas in a ship called the *Hawk*, of Rye.

1600[-1], March 9. Dover Castle.—Sir Thomas Fane to the Mayors, Bailiffs and Jurats of the Cinque Ports.

"Where there is a writ sent out of her Majesty's Cort of Exchequer at Westminster with a scedule thereunto annexed against the late Earle of Essex and other of his company, which I send to you and every of you by this bearer, with a lettre of attendance, for you to take coppy of and to execute. Nowe forasmuch as it appeareth by the said writ that the same is to be executed and retorned with all celeritie and speede that maye be, I praye you therefore fayle not to execute and retorne the same hether with all expedition that you can, not respectinge the begyninge of the tearme wherby I may accordingly see the same retorned into her Majesty's said Cort of Exchequer, according to the tenor of the said writ." *Copy.*

Enclosure. Writ to inquire if the Earls of Essex, Rutland, and Southampton, and many others set out in a schedule attached, held lands in the Cinque Ports. Inquisition taken on 13 March in which the Jury say that the said persons had no lands or goods within the Cinque Ports.

1600[-1], March 20.—The Mayor and Jurats of Rye to the Lord Warden.

"We have had conference with this bearer, Ralphe Dester, about the recovering and amending of our decayed haven, after hee had thoroughly veiwed and perused the same. And we finde him in our judgmentes, a man very well experienced and hath delivered unto us such sufficient matter as we doubt not but our haven may be restored to his former estate, and that at a more reasonabler chargo than we imaged it wold be. We have referred the reporte thereof to be delivered unto your Honor by the said Mr. Dester, most humbly thanking your Lordship for your continuall favor towardes this poore towne." *Draft.*

1601, April 30.—Richard Lyfe to the Mayors, Bailiffs and Jurats of the Cinque Ports.

I have received letters from Mr. Norris, my Lord's Solicitor, and from Mr. Rogers, his Lordship's Secretary, both touching the sending up of twenty pounds for Dr. Seafor for the last term when your book was under the great seal. My Lord did speak to me that Dr. Seafor should have some consideration and it pleased my Lord to ask what I thought fit for him. I told him ten pounds, but it was thought he deserved twenty. I pray you not to fail but send up to Mr. Angell's house in Old Fish Street, with as much speed as you may, that twenty pounds, lest my Lord should be offended. Until my Lords have the twenty pounds for Dr. Seafor I dare not demand the book. There is also Mr. Rogers must have four pounds, he took great pains in soliciting our cause to my Lords and did always carry our books in his bosom to the Court with my Lords until her Majesty had signed it. And to Mr. More and Lewes I promised twenty shillings, they are of my Lords' Chamber. *Copy.*

1601, June 6. Dover Castle.—Sir Thomas Fane to the Mayors and Bailiffs of the Cinque Ports.

Order for the mustering of the trained bands.

1601, June 16.—The Mayor and Jurats of Hythe to the Mayors, Bailiffs, and Jurats of the Cinque Ports.

"Wheras by a decree lately made at the towne of Newe Romeney, it was enacted that from thenceforth yearly a Gestlinge should be somoned by that towne which sholde sommon the brodhull to be holden at Newe Romeney aforesaide, to begyne ymediatly after the brotherhood is ended, to which Gestlinge there shold be no more returned of every towne and member but the hed officer, two jurates, the towne clerke, and chamberlen; the somoning of which Gestlinge for this present yere apperteyneth nowe unto us. These are therefore to praye and require yow to be and appeare at a Gestlinge to be holden at Newe Romeney aforesaid the Tewsday next after the feast of St. Margaret, beinge the 21st daye of July next comeinge, imediately after the brodhull is ended, by such persons and so many of your discreetest combarons as by the said decree is required."

1601, September 10.—The Mayor and Jurats of Rye to Sir John Brokett, knight.

"Wheras the bearer hereof, Thomas Berigge, a soldier serving under your comande, hath of late byne with us in our towne of Rye and hath taken veiwe of our decayed harbor, and also hathe shewed unto us divers instrumentes of his owne makinge, intendinge, as he saith, to putt in practize to the uttermost of his power and connynge to amende our said harbor and withall assureth himself by God's helpe to effecte the same yf he may obteyne your Worship's favor and lycence to come into England, whereby he may be imployed in the same worke. And for that we very well know the man, beinge brought up in these partes, to be well experienced and stand in good hope that he maye doe us good yf he may proceed in the said worke, we most hartely desire your Worship that it may stand to your good leikeing to graunt hym lycence to come into England to take in hand the said worke, which yf it take good effecte will be not only a greate benefytt unto this poore towne but also to the state of this land." *Copy.*

1602, August 9.—Acknowledgment by William Maquery (signed Gilame Maquere), of Dieppe in Normandy, mariner, son and heir of Frauncys Maquery, late of Rye in the county of Sussex, merchant, deceased, for the sum of five pounds ten shillings received from the Chamberlain of Rye for the "rent" of three score pounds for one whole year, which sum was lent to the Corporation of Rye by Frauncys Couchy, late of Dieppe, deceased, uncle of the said William Maquery.

1602, August 17.—Order of Sir Thomas Fane and George Newman concerning the fishermen of Rye and Hastings.

"The fishermen of Rye and Hasting being presented and convicted to have offended in fyshing with netts insufficient, and of unlawfull scale, and at prohibited tymes and seasons, especially contrary to the lawes, in the night season, whereby the fysh disquieted and wanting naturall rest doe become both leane unserviceable and not so well bayted as in former tymes, are by order of this Court fyned, viz.: every boat in Rye and Hastinge shall pay for ther former default only, ten shillings, and to be further straightly charged that they offend no more as they and every of them will answer the contrary at ther uttermost perills. The rest of the forfiture are by his Lordship remitted, the fees of the offices to be payed by the offenders, only excepted."

1602, August 25.—Passport to Anne Heynes, Anne Symnpson, and Elizabeth Brown (wives of certain men, who, to the number of twenty, travelled contrary to Her Majesty's Lawes, some of whom were committed to prison and executed at Bury St. Edmunds and others sent to her Majesty's service in the Low countries) to pass to Rye and thence to Chichester.

1602, September 3.—Henry Jenens, Mayor of Portsmouth, to all Justices of the Peace mayors, sheriffs, bailiffs, constables, and others.

"Wheras the bearer hereof is sent with letters to the right worshipful Sir Robert Mansfeilde, knight, Admirall of her Majesties shippes servinge in the Narrowe Seas, and to the right worshipful Sir Thomas Fane, knight, Governer of her Majesty's Castle of Dovor, to the ende to sende six shippes which are appointed to come from Holland to be imployed in Her Majesties service to the porte of Portesmouth, where they shall meete the other seven Holland shippes which come from the coast of Spaine and are to joyne with them in the said service. These are to desire you and everie of you that if it shall happen any of the said six shippes doe stopp or putt into any harbor or place aboute you, before they shall come unto the said harbor of Portsmouth, that you will not only geve them spedie advertisement to repaire hether with the said shippes for the purpose aforesaid (for so is her Majesties pleasure) but also that it will please you to be aydinge and assistinge unto this bearer in what you maye, for the better and more spedie performance and execution of his charge and business."

1602, September 11.—Certificate by the Mayor and Jurats of Rye that Anthony Bryant, of Rye, sailor, a Frenchman born, hath dwelt in Rye forty years and hath served an apprentice in the said Town and divers times has been pressed and served in her Majesty's ships. He has been married to two English women and had children by each. All which time he has behaved himself well.

1602, October 25.—The Mayor and Jurats of Rye to Doctor Newman.

Concerning the confession of Robert Fosters' wife that Richard Dethicke, a minister, lately in prison at Rye, married her sister.

1602[-3], January 13. Blackfriars.—Lord Cobham to the Mayors, Bailiffs, and Jurats of Hastings, Rye, Hythe, and Folkestone.

"I understand there hath been of late a practice by some of the fishmongers of London to draw a combination with some fishermen of the Ports tending to the restrayning of her Majesty's prerogative Royal for the provision of sea fish for her own house, to certain particular places and for a lesser proportion than heretofore hath been accustomed, by suggesting divers corruptions and abuses of her Majesty's present officers appointed for the purveying of that kind of provisions whereof an information being exhibited in the Star Chamber, her Majesty has ordered the same to be heard before the Lords and others, her Majesty's Commissioners for her household causes, where the same was fully heard and found to have proceeded rather out of spleen to the said officers rather than any just cause of offence given, and the offenders sentenced to punishment. I have thought good to require you to have regard that all such orders heretofore established as well for the furtherance of her Majesty's service for those provisions, as for the maintenance and governance of the markets be effectually put in execution." *Copy.*

1602[-3], January 23. Dover Castle.—Sir Thomas Fane to the Mayors and Bailiffs of the Cinque Ports.

"Whereas the Lordes of her Majesties most honourable Privie Councell have addressed theire letters to his Lordship that he cause a generall muster to be taken of all the marriners and seafearinge men

RYE MSS.

fitt for service within his Lordship's wardenry and livetenannces, from the age of 16 to three score, out of which there shal be choise made and impresed to the nomber of one hundred of the most hable and sufficient men; to which ende theie are to be sent to Chetham with charge upon payne of deathe to present themselves before the officers of her Majesties Navie by the last daye of the present January there to be disposed of as shal be thought fittest, bringinge with them conveuyent apparell, and sword and dagger. And such as shall nott have meanes to furnishe themselves, that then their parentes, masters, or frindes shall furnishe them with sorde and dagger and with necessary aparell. Now forasmuch as our right honorable Lord Warden hath addressed his letters unto me willinge and requiringe me to see the tennor thereof put in execution accordinglie, these are therfore to will and requier you and in his Lordship's name streightly to charge and commande you, that you indelaydlie uppon the sight heereof cause a generall muster to bee made in every your severall portes and lymmes, of all such marryners and saylers as you have, and that theie be in redynes uppon payne of deathe at an ower's warninge to be imprested by his Lordship's officer who shall make all convenyent speed unto you for that service." *Copy.*

1603, March 26. Dover Castle.—Sir Thomas Fane to the Mayors, Bailiffs, and Jurats of the Cinque Ports.

"Having received thenclosed proclamation from our right honorable the Lord Warden this day for the proclayming of King James the sixth, Kinge of Scottes, King of England, France and Ireland, I held it fitt to send the same, that upon sight hereof you cause the same to be performed accordinglie; and for the better demonstration of our joy that we take therein, you are to discharge all such ordinance as you have in every your severall Portes so sone as the proclamation shall be reade, as also to make such bonfyers and such other ceremonies as in the leike cause hath byne accustomed at the proclaymeing of any prince."

1603, March 30.—The information of John Arkinstall of Ringy in the Parish of Bowden in the County of Chester, trumpeter, taken before the Constables of the Town of Lewes.

The said John Arkinstall saith "that uppon Sonday being the 25th of March this examinant and one Richard Archer, Barker, and Anthony Word, his fellowes (being all fower common players of interludes and shewing forth a licence to aucthorize them) were at Hastinge in Sussex at an inne there where this examinate and his fellowes lodged, and one Holland, a scholemaster at Rye, who serveth a cure under Doctor Joy at Brightlinge, comeinge into the company of this examinate and his fellowes, the said 25th of March, uttered these wordes following, viz.:—that the Kinge of Scottes was proclaymed King of England at London, and after the said Kinge was proclamed, then my Lord Beachampe was proclaymed also by one who was then at libertie, and being demanded by this examinate by whome the said Lord Beauchampe was so proclaymed, the said Holland said by the Erle of Southampton and that he the said Holland had a great horse and wold have a saddle and spend his bloode in the Lord Beauchampe's behalf."

1603, May 26. Blackfriars.—Lord Cobham to the Mayor and Jurats of Rye.

I expect you should yield me the nomination of one of your burgesses for this next Parliament. "In your choise of those of your towne that are to carry the canapy at his Majesty's coronation I wish you to be careful that the same be such, as, both for their person and the rest, may be fit for the service, as it will ymport you much." *Signed and Seal of arms.*

1603, July 7. Blackfriars.—Lord Cobham to the Mayors, Bailiffs, Jurats, and Commons of the Cinque Ports and two ancient towns.

I have this day received a letter from the Lord High Steward and others of the Lords Commissioners concerning the Coronation, which is out of the ancient course of the Summons in this kind, and ought to have been by the King's Writ; for observation of which custom I have already written and doubt not, if a precedent be found, the same shall within a few days be obtained. I send you a copy of the said letter that you may take notice of the day of Coronation and proceed with the election of persons fit for the performance of the service. In which choice "I wyshe you to be verie cautious and wary that they may be men of the meetest and comliest personage amongest you and of the best sufficiencie otherwise, as I have already goven direction in that behalf."

1603, July 9.—Petition of the Mayor and Jurats of Rye to Sir John Stanhope, one of his Majesty's Privy Council.

Whereas in times past the packets have usually been thought fit to be sent to this town as the nearest place of recourse for the service of the State, both by sea and land, until of late years the packets being sent by other ways the continuance thereof hath drawn with it from this poore town the postage and recourse of merchants and others travelling to the sea coast, the occasion whereof we can find to be and to have so long continued, by no other means but by the abuse of the rippiers, who, finding the authority which the packet requires to be drawn other ways, have for their own particular gain so exhausted upon all passengers that none at all have desired to come this way. Therefore for reformation thereof we pray that it would please you to erect a postage here and recommend unto you the bearer hereof, Jeames Apleton, to be the postmaster.

1603, July 11. London.—Edward Kelk [to the Mayors, Bailiffs and Jurats of the Cinque Ports].

As to the settlement of the claims for service at the Coronation there are six Commissioners appointed by the King, viz.:—the Earl of Shrewsbury, Lord Lumley, Lord Henry Howard, Lord Zouch, the two Lord Chief Justices, Popham and Anderson. We of Sandwich found in record that at the coronation of Queen Elizabeth, a Writ of Summons was sent to the Ports to call them to do their said service which writ I cannot find in any of the offices here. I found in the Red Book of the Exchequer a judgment and a recovery in Edward the Sixth's time for the said service on the behalf of the Ports, the matter being between the Marches of Wales and the Ports. I will search whether you are to have any allowance from the King for scarlet.

1603, July 11.—E[dward] Kelk [to the Mayors, Bailiffs, and Jurats of the Cinque Ports].

I have sought all the records in the Chancery, the Rolls, the Crown Office and the Tower for a Writ of Summons to call the Barons to do their service at the King's coronation, but can find none. The records at Dover are to be searched. His Lordship sent the Lords' letters to Sir Thomas Fane which will be all the summons the Ports shall have unless they can send me a precedent. I could have got one drawn by a clerk but the Lord Keeper will not put the seal to it, unless he sees a precedent for it. I cannot learn when the Commissioners will hold their Court to receive all claims for any service due to any persons. The Lord Steward will give sentence upon them when he holds his Court, which will be two days before the Coronation. I pray you to let Mr. Mayor, Mr. Peake and the rest of his brethren know the King will not come through the City of London. I fear your service will be to carry the canopy in the church and not from Whitehall, for he will be crowned as privately as may be, neither will he dine publicly. It is reported that the Queene shall not be crowned at this time but in the winter and then the shows and solemnities shall be. The Ports should therefore agree who shall do the service to the King and who to the Queen.

1603, July 12. London.—Francis Raworth to [the Mayor and Jurats of Rye ?]

"It is saide heere the Queene will not be crowned till wynter. His Majestie intendeth (as it is said) to be at St. James Howse two or three dayes before the daye appointed for his Coronation and from thence privatlie to Whithall and there to take his bardge and to be landed at the Parliament stayers, and from thence to be attended by the nobilitie, and no others, to the church, and the canapye to be borne by the Barons of the Portes. And yet I did enquire at the Warderope and cannot lerne that direction is geven to provide a canopie. I meane, God willinge, tomorrow in the morninge, to ride with Mr. Kelk to the Courte and theire I hope to learne whether the Queen shalbe crowned nowe or not. My Lord Steward hath not yet holden his Court or sate aboute the receavinge of the demandes of those that owe suit at his Highnes Coronation, neither is it any daye sett downe as I cane lerne."

1603, July 13.—The Mayor and Jurats of Sandwich to the Mayor and Jurats of Hastings, Winchelsea, Rye, Romney, Hythe, and Dover.

Before the receipt of the letters of Mr. Kelk, our town clerk, concerning the services of the Barons at the Coronation, we proceeded to the election of those Barons and chose only three, whereas if the Queen should now be crowned we should have chosen six. Upon sight of those letters we are much confirmed in our proceeding in that we have elected as yet no more.

1603, July 15.—Francis Raworth to the Mayors and Jurats of Hythe, Romney, Hastings, Rye, and Winchelsea.

I attended our Lord Warden on Tuesday last but he could give me no information as to whether the Queen would be crowned at his Majesty's coronation. His Honor was much offended that Mr. Edwardes was chosen one of the Solicitors about the Charters, alleging that the inhabitants of Faversham ever opposed themselves against the general Charter of the Ports and against his Lordship's jurisdiction of the Chancery Court of Dover. On Wednesday and Thursday last Mr. Kelk and myself attended at the Court, Windsor and Otelands, on my Lord High Steward who informed us that both the King and Queen would be crowned on the 25th of this month, and that two canopies were in making, yet the coronation would be private and their Majesties would take barge at Whitehall stairs and thence be landed at the Parliament house stairs, where the canopies should be ready to receive them, and from thence to go under the same into the Church of Westminster, and that the dinner, shows, and solemnities would be deferred until some further time. There are to be 32 Barons chosen out of the Ports for this service. I am secretly informed by a friend of mine that the Barons of the Ports ought to have scarlet for their gowns. I searched at the Wardrobe but was referred to the book of liveries which were given at the coronation of Henry VIII. and his Queene which is now in the custody of the Lord Chamberlain and which Mr. Kelk will endeavour to obtain. Scarlet is valued at 3*li.* 10*s.* the yard at least and crimson satin at 15*s.* the yard. The sickness is much more increased this week and is dispersed in all places about the city and therefore it will be fit that those who will be chosen to do this service should be provident where they lodge. The King and Queen and the Prince are yet at Otelands; to-morrow the King removeth to Hampton Court and the Queen and Prince will remain at Otelands till the day before the coronation.

1603, July 15.—Lord Cobham to Sir Thomas Fane, Knight, Lieutenant of Dover Castle.

These are to pray you to give order that the Ports send in to the office at Dover certificate of those chosen for service at the Coronation, that the clerk may make his return to the Lord Steward. *Copy.*

1603, July 19.—Mandate by the Mayor of Rye.

"Whereas one Avery Care (as she nameth herself to be) aboute some moneth past came unto this towne of [Rye] in base attire and in rogishe manner, yet protestinge that she came of noble parrents and was daughter and heire unto Sir Robert Care, knight, and so of longe tyme hath travelled aboute the countrie, deludinge the King's Majesty's subjectes in cosoninge manner. And whereas the said Sir Robert Care hath directed his letters to the Maior of the Towne of Rye aforesaid, as well to have her severely ponished for her abuse offered here as also to have her safely conveyed unto him to London that he may take such order with her that hereafter she may be abbridged from running so lewdly abrod, which ponishement she hath here accordingly receaved. These are therefore in the King's Majesty's name to require all constables and other officers to whome these presents shall come, to be ayding and assisting unto the bearrer hereof (whome we have sent of purpose to convey her to the saido Sir Thomas Care) for the more better and surrer passinge of her from place to place untill she may be brought unto him to receave such ponishement as to such a vagrant person apperteyneth."

1603, July 21. Hampton Court.—The Lords of the Council to the Lieutenant of Dover Castle.

"Wheras we writ unto you of late in his Majesties name to geve streight order unto the Cinque Portes for restreynt and staye of any passage for the space of 10 dayes which was intended especially for the apprehencion of Sir Griffin Markham and his bretheren, and one Watson, a preeste. Althoughe the same care and dilligence be still to be continued for the aprehension of the same persons untill they may be taken, nevertheless you shall understand that his Majesties pleasure is that for any letters or messenger that is despatched from the French Ambassador or from the Count Airenburg, the Archduke's Ambasador or from any other Prince's Embassador that is heere, the person or persons beinge certeynelie knowen to be none of those trayterous persons to be aprehended, the passage from the said portes shalbe free and open. And thereof we do pray and requier you to geve notice unto the officers of the said portes, charging them withall that they take verie great heede and be watchfull as much as is possible for them for the aprehencion of the persons above mencioned." *Copy.*

1603, August 10.—The Mayor and Jurats of Rye to Captain Cushine, Deputy to the Governor of Dieppe.

"We are informed that our passage sent from this Town of Rye to Deipe is restreyned from landinge either passengers, goodes, or merchandize there by reason that it is reported that the plague, is in this towne and nere hereaboutes, and for that we wold resolve your Worshipp faithfullye and trewly concerninge all doubtes or scruple that maye growe concerninge suche goodes, wares, or merchandize as shall passe or be transported from this place to be clere from the infection. These are therefore to signifie unto you for treweth that not only thys towne of Rye but also all the towns, villages and places nere unto this towne adjoyninge by the space of twenty miles and upwardes, the Lordes name be praysed therefore, are clere from the said infection of the plague. And for our better securitie we will not permit any goodes wares or merchandize to be brought to our towne from London or any other place suspected to be visited with the said sicknes. And therefore we desire you that such passengers, wares, goodes, or merchandize which shall from this towne be transported unto Deipe, may be, by your good meanes and tolleration, permitted to be landed and taken on shore at Deipe aforesaid." *Draft.*

[1603.]—Proclamation for the discovery and apprehension of William Ruthen and Patricke Ruthen, brethren to the late Earle of Gowrie.

1604, September 11.—Acknowledgement by William Maquery of Dieppe, mariner, of the receipt of eleven pounds from George Emery, one of the Chamberlains for the town of Rye, being due for two years rent or hire of three score pounds lent to the Corporation of Rye by one Frauncys Couchy, late of Dieppe, deceased, uncle of the said William.

1604, November.—The Earl of Northampton and others (officers of the Greencloth ?) to the Mayor and Jurats of Rye.

"Wheras upon complainte made of the scarcitie, badnes, and dearnes of sea fish in the service of his Majesty's house wee sent our letters unto you in June last by Richard Merredeth, clarke of his Majesty's Accatorye, and William Angell, his Majesty's fishmonger, to enquire and examine the reasons and causes therof and to certefie the abuses (yf any were) to the end wee might prevent by due punishment any which should goe about to hinder the good of his Majesty's service therin, wee find uppon their certifficate that by reason of a great nomber of buyers who doe buye fishe for the Fishmongers of London, and contrarie to all good order doe secretlye combyne with the fishermen to keepe back in their houses and shoppes their best fish to be convayed and carred to London, leaving the markett in a manner altogether unfurnished of good fish wherby his Majesty's Oaste is inforced many times to send to the Court unserviceable fish, being the refuse and leavings of theise menn, and also payeing unreasonable and deare prices for the same, to the great dishonor of his Majesty's service. For reformation wherof the Wardens of the Fishmongers of London, accordinge to an auncient order in their Companie, for prevention of such inconveniences have lately by our good liking appointed and nominated a certayne nomber, such as are knowne to yourselves to be honest and sufficient men, to be Oastes to buye fish for their Companie after his Majesty's Oaste hath bought his proportion of sea fish, and yf any hereafter shall presume to be an Oast or to buye fish for any privat fishmonger but such as are especially appointed by consent of the whole Companie aforesaid, or any so nominated shali presume to buye at any time any sea fish untill his Majesty bee first served, then wee will and require you to comitt the same person or persons, so offending, to prison, and presentlie to certefie his or their names to the officers of the Greenecloth that further order may be taken for punishment according to the qualetie of the offence." *Signed. Seal.*

1604, December 4, Whitehall.—The Lords of the Council to Sir Francis Fane, Sir Nicholas Parker and others, Commissioners for Sewers for the town or haven of Rye.

"Whereas we are informed that a Commissyon of Sewers being heretofore graunted for the preservation of the Haven of Rye, the proceedinges wherein have ben directly impugned and disobayed (as it is alleaged) by one Alexander Sheppard and others that have of late undertaken to inne certaine salte mershes adjoyning to that haven, who having ben dealte withall to make staye of the said woorckes in respect that the same are founde to be of great inconvenyence and annoyance to the haven, the said persons doe (as is enformed) refuze to yeeld therunto, and notwithstanding goe forward with their said woorke, to the great prejudice and hurte of that towne and others, in case tymely order be not taken for redresse of the said inconvenyence. Forasmuch as it doth importe to preferre the care of the publique good before any privat interestes, and in that respect speciall care is to be taken of that towne, wee have ben moved to requier yow to examen carefully the matter of this complaint, whether the said woorkes which are undertaken by the said Sheppard and the reste, be so inconvenyent and hurtfull to the haven as is pretended, and to certefie us your opinyons thereof." *Signed. Seal.*

1604, December 14. Rye.—The Commissioners of Sewers to the Lords of the Council.

Reporting that the inning of the marshes by William, son of Alexander Shepherd, is prejudicial to the haven of Rye.

1604[-5]. March 21.—Depositions of William Palmer of Rye, fisherman, that on the nineth of February last while sailing in his boat, as a passenger from Rye to Dieppe, and carrying with him Sir John Wentworth of the County of Essex, knight, at a place called the Sowe he came upon about five or six and thirty sail of French fishermen, one of whom, as he supposes, thinking he came to board them to see with what engines they fished waved their caps for this deponent and his company to come aboard, when this deponent saw ten or twelve men armed with muskets, calivers and pikes to spoil this deponent and his company if they came near.

1605, May 10.—Depositions of Peter Norry of Dieppe that being in his ship with his company and about ten passengers going from London to Dieppe, while lying at anchor right against "Landes Inde, strappinge his floude" there boarded him on the night of the seventh instant a boat wherein were about twenty Englishmen and "bestowed" this deponent his company and passengers, and took away all their money and left aboard them eight of their men. And in the morning the said pirates set sail on his ship and came athwart of "Farley" [Fairlight?]

and landed this deponent his company and passengers and carried away the ship and all their goods.

1605, June 7. Greenwich.—The Lords of the Council [to the Lord Warden].

"There hathe binne a practise as a kynd of trade used by Irishe people to transport themselves into France and there, by begging and theire nakednes, to moove the people to compassion to give alms unto them, and after they (by this begginge trade) have gotten some money, they retorne hither or their contry. Theise kynd of base people resorting thither of late in soe greate multitudes and their hipocrisie beinge espied there is order taken to banishe them out of that kingdome, by reason whereof they come over hither in great companies and nombers and soe come up to London and disperse themselves over all the realme, to the great annoyaunce of all men in those places where they doe come. To prevent this inconvenience and swarminge of theis idle, and sluttishe, and noysome people who maie live in their contry, where all thinges (at this present) are att reasonable rates, with more ease, but take theis beggerly and idle courses upon them onlye to gett money. We doe pray your good Lordship that you will give speciall direction to the officers of the Cinque Portes, that they suffer none of theise Irishe people to be sett one land in any sorte, whither they are transported in Englishe or Frenche bottomes, and to give further order that soe soone as they come into the Rodes they maie be searched what money they have, which may be ymployed for the sendinge of them by sea into their contry. But if they be brought hither in Englishe vessells, the same boates that bring them hither maie be enjoyed to retorne them backe or to undertake the transportation of them into Ireland; yf any Frenche vessell, and uppon searche made, they have money emongest them to paye for theire transportation, then order is to be taken there may be shipping provided with the money founde aboute them to convey them into Ireland, otherwise that they be not permitted to be sett one lande, which order wee praie your Lordships to cause dulye to be observed in all the Cinque Portes, members, and creeckes, and other portes of the coast and to cause certificatt to be sent to your Lordship of the names, surnames, sex, and age of those that shall be brought thither." *Copy.*

1605, June 16. Greenwich.—The Earl of Northampton to the Mayor and Jurats of Rye.

Objecting to his servant, Richard Portriffe, being sent as Bailiff for Rye to Yarmouth. *Signed, and Seal of Arms.*

1605, November 5. Whitehall.—The Lords of the Council to the Lord Warden of the Cinque Ports.

"Whereas upon the discovery of the most horrible treason that ever was intended against the person of the King's Majesty and the whole State of this Realme, it is thought expedient to make staie of all manner of passengers that shall offer themselves to be transported owt of this realme into forreine partes, untill the accesaries and parties unto this conspiracy maie be apprehended, who no doubte will make what shifte they can to fly the realme. Theis are to praie your Lordship to take order within your commaund of the Cinque Portes that no person be suffered to passe out of those portes, under what color or preteuxt soever, but that stay be made of all manner of shipes and passengers for a tyme, untill your Lordship shall receave direction to the coutrary.

And besides his Majesty's further pleasure is that you cause diligent searche and enquirey to be made within the precinct of those portes for the person of Thomas Percy, according to the deriction of the proclamation inclosed, and yf he shall be found and apprehended there, that order maie be taken for the safe custody of him and for the sendinge of him unto us at the Courte under sufficient garde." *Copy.*

1605, November [7]. Dover.—Sir Thomas Fane to the Mayor, Bailiffs, and Jurats of the Cinque Ports.

"Whereas I have this afternoone receaved letters from our right honorable Lord Warden in the name of all the Lordes of his Majesty's most honorable Privye Councell for the staying and aprehending of a certaine damnable traitor whose description I sende you hereinclosed, who hath bene actor in the most barbarous and divelish treason that ever was invented or put in practice in any state or kingdome. Wherefore these shall be very heartely to pray and desire you and in his Majesty's name streightly to charge and commande you that foorthwith you make presente and diligent searche everyone in your severall lymittes and precincte, for the apprehension of such a most traiterous and daugerous person, and that everyone of you be carefull for the stayeinge of all such as you shall have any cause to suspect, especially if in any sorte he answer this subscribed description, to send such person or persons so taken unto mee that I may foorthwith take instant order for sendinge them up to his Lordship and the Councell."

Postcript.—"He is a tall man with a great broad beard, a good countenance, the coulor of his beard and head mingled with white haires very much, and the head more white then the beard, his face is well coulored, he stoopeth somewhat in the shoulders, his legges small, his foote longe."

[1604–5.]—Orders concerning fishing.

Whereas by an order of the Admiralty court at Dover dated 17 August, 1602 it was set out that the trawl nets, commonly used by the fishermen of Hastings and other foreigners and fishermen, were reputed to be great destroyers of the fry and food of fish and should therefore be utterly prohibited and damned as altogether inconvenient. After further trial of the said nets it is ordered that they be no more used within the jurisdiction of the Cinque Ports under pain of forfeiture of the said nets and twenty shillings fine. It is further ordered that the "droitgatherer" of the Lord Warden do burn or cut in pieces all such nets found.

[1604–5.]—Declaration touching John Snepp.

That he affirmeth it was a merrier world when ministers might not marry, that now they ought not to marry and that their children are illegitimate that he absented himself from church at Northiham for half a year, and was a profaner of the Sabbath in entertaining men's servants in playing of cards and dice. That he threatened to pull Mr. Frewen out of the pulpit and spit in his face and made the said Mr. Frewen come to him on his knees, and threatened that songs should be made of him.

1605[–6], February 3.—The Mayor and Jurats of Rye to the Earl of Northampton.

Complaining that the French fishermen fished with unlawful nets and at unseasonable times upon the English coast, to the great destruction of the brood of fish.

1605[-6], February 9.—The Lord Warden to Sir Thomas Fane.

The matters I wrote to you about I am to recommend from the King's own mouth to myself. "I must require you with all speede possible to awake the Portes and charge them to putt on all their eyes of caution and curiouse observation whether any man do lande in port or creeke that is of little personage, a sharpishe nose, a shrimpishe face, a beard light auborne or somwhat more enclyninge to a reddishe yellowe, that he may be either stayed, till I have word or sent up, with sure garde of two or three, with so great care in the keepinge him from accesse or speeche of any man till he be brought to me as I may answer both for myself and for the diligence and discretion of those that are putt in the leike trust in my absence to have an eye to these occurrences under me. It is likely that he will not tell his name, but he is northerly, which circumstance in his tongue may geve you some light also wherby to gesse at the right man, yf it be so happy that he fall into their handes, that knowe the right waye howe to handle him." *Copy.*

1605[-6], March 11.—The Fishermen of the town of Rye to Sir William Twysden.

Requesting him to accept "a poore dishe of fyshe," consisting of "one codling, three gornards, one playse, one scalloppe, thirty rochettes, eight whitinges, and a thorneback" in consideration of his care in soliciting the suit for the amendment of the harbour of Rye. *Draft.*

1605[-6], March 23. Dover.—Sir Thomas Fane to the Mayors, Bailiffs and Jurats of the Cinque Ports.

"Wheras ther hathe byn a folysh rumor spred abrode withowt any sertan grownd of som dangurus and dyseasteras accident faling upon the person of his most excellent Majesty, I have this morning received letters from owr ryght honorable Lord Warden singnyfing that the same reportt is most false and untrue and that his Majestie, thankes be to God, is verie well, lustie, and in perfett hellthe, and fre from the touch of any such unhappie efeacktes, as have byn brutied, to the exeding grett joye and comfortt of all his Majesty's loving subjects. According to the tenor of his Lordship's saied letters I have hyld fytt for the which to aquaynt you wythe the premases."

1606, May 23. Whitehall.—The Earl of Northampton [to Sir Thomas Fane, Lieutenant of Dover Castle].

I hear that the commissioners for passage at Dover and Margate have been of late very remiss in suffering great numbers of Irish beggars to be brought over and landed here, contrary to the express directions from my Lords of the Council. I pray you let them understand from me that if it be true, as it is reported, they shall not only run into danger themselves by their negligence, but cause an imputation and blame upon me. *Copy.*

1606, July 18.—Deposition in a suit of Thomas Radforde against Abraham Kennett touching lands at Playden on the east and west sides of the Churchyard, described by bounds.

1607, September 26. "Moate."—Sir William Twysden to the Mayor and "his bretheren" of Rye.

The death of his friend Mr. Hamon causes a vacancy in Parliament for the town, "which (as I take it) is in your guyft." Recommends, therefore, "a gentleman, whome I much esteeme . . . . . for whom I can promise, as for myselfe, that he shalbe carefull for your good." If they expect direction from the Lord Warden, he asks them to withhold their election until he "may speake with his Lordship, which wilbe within a fortnight." He will send them the name of his friend when they tell him of the date fixed for the election. *Seal of Arms.*

[1607, September ?].—The Lord Warden to the Mayor and Jurats of Rye.

"Though I never meant to presse furder upon your curtesie in those thinges that belonge to your owne right then reasone moves, and then in your owne enclynation doth admitte, yet presuminge upon the kindnesse which I dayly more and more observe, to my comfort, towarde me, I make bolde to recomende to your acceptance my requeste for the choise of Mr. Hennage Finche into the place of Hamonde one of the Burgesis for your towne. The jentilman for his decretion and towardaesse in the study of the lawe shall be verie able to performe that service to the credite of the corporation that belonges to him and the place requires, and I am the rather induced to write in his behalf bycause he will be willinge in respecte of his aboad in this place to ease you of that dayly and large allowance which was befor allottid to the prediscessor; and bycause I have found both his father and Sir William Twisenden [Twysden], his brother-in-lawe, so kindly and constantly affected, to the furdernance of any good that my invention ore industry doth entende, ore can devise to drawe to your corporation. From myself, you shall ever expecte and be sure to receive as many lovinge and faythfull offices as my meanes can worke; and I think myself more happy in the love which I finde both in you and other members of my charge to my self then any fortune that I enjoye nexte to the Kinge's favour." *Seal of Arms.*

1607, October 12. Peckham.—Sir William Twysden to the Mayor and Jurats of Rye.

"At my attending on my Lord Warden, I did so præsent unto his Lordship your regard of him in this business [the choice of a candidate for Parliament], which naturally belonged to your selfes, that it hath wonne confirmation of his good affection unto you, as you may perceave by his owne letter of his consent herewithall sent . . . . The gentleman for whome I moved yee, is my brother Heneage Finche, Sir Moyle Finche's sonne, a barrester of the Inner Temple, who I will assure you is very willinge and able, not now only, but at any time heerafter, to advise as well as ayde and pleade for yee if neede shalbe." *Seal with Crest.*

1607, December 20.—Indenture witnessing the return to Parliament of Henage Finch, Esquire, as member for Rye in the place of Thomas Hamon, gentleman, deceased. *Copy.*

1607, December 21.—Order touching the trial of "Tramell Nettes."

The boat to be of Hastinge, the nettes to be provided equally betwine Hastinge and Rye. Yf it hapen that Hastinge cannot fyshe with tramells, that then the townesmen of Rye to yeald recompence for their nettes and to have them to ther oune usse. The Tryers to be iij Dover, viz.:—Gregory Michaell, Henry Tydde man, James Neales, Thomas Wallop of Heithe, Mychell Rycke, Thomas Lovett [and] Paul Hutson. The Tryers to retorne certyfycatt upon oth after the season of fyshinge ended, yf the fyshinge sesson prove nott proffitable then the tounes of Rye and Hastinge to make them recompence for ther hinderance as the Court shall awarde. To fyshe the whole seasson." *Copy.*

1607, December 31. Dover Castle.—Sir Thomas Waller, Knight, to the Mayor and Jurats of Rye.

"Notwithstandinge the course taken the last yeare by our most honorable Lord Warden in repellinge and beatinge those insolent and irregular fyshers which yearlie have used to come in swarmes from Deipe, Traporte, and the places nere adjoyninge, to the prejudice of your townsmen in their trade of fishinge, and soe consequentlie to the detriment of the whole state of your towne; and notwithstandinge that the French Kinge hath byn pleased by his late proclamation to inhibitt such their unwarranted fyshinge uppon paine of deathe, yet that there is a present preparation in seacrett and underhand in Deipe and more appertlie in Traport by some malignant spirits, that have neither sence of dutye to their Soveraigne's comaund, nor conscience to distinguish betweene theire owne interests and other mens, to thrust out against this approachinge season, dyvers boates in their wonted and unlawfull manner. Albeit, I doubt not but this is as well knowne to yourselves as to me; yet I could not chuse (in my affection to you and my dutie to the place wherein I serve) but recommend this preparation to your advised consideration wherein I would desire you to consider whether yee shall be able with your owne forces to preserve your owne fyshing, and whether yee will undertake the same, as I have been enformed by some of yourselves yee willinglie will doe, so as yee may have the one moyetie of the boates, nettes and ransom yee shall take soe unlawfully fyshinge, in leiwe of your chardge and adventure, which to my understandinge yee may safely undertake and to your proffitt performe by reason your neereness to the place and acquaintance with their manner of fyshinge, will give you oppertunity to surprize them in the night without your danger, they beinge then bysye at worke. I desire to receive your resolution in this pointe with your fyrst convenience which I exceedinglie [desire] maye be between this and Twelvetyde, for that yf yee shall finde this course inconvenient for you, that then some other may be thought on." *Signed. Seal of Arms.*

[1607–8], January 3.—Sir John Boys [and others ?] to the Mayor of Rye "and his bretheren."

"We wishe you to be well advised before you proceede to the execution of eny, uppon the statute of 1 Regis Jacobi, for that it is the onely statute now in force against such as doe use invocation or comunication of evill spirits or consult, covenant with, entertaine, feede or rewarde any such wicked spirit. In that estatute, power is given to any justice of peace to enquere, and although it were made one yere before the charter, yet the estatute [charter?] gevinge noe aucthoritie to any justice of peace to inquire of any such invocation nor any such wordes in your newe charter to inquire of it expresly, nor of eny other estatutes (*sic*), but of such as autoritie is geven by statute to inquire of by justices of peace (althoughe in the newe comission of the peace some wordes to leike effecte be inserted) yet you, not having eny such wordes, cannot as we thinke and are informed by the best lerned of these partes, inquire, heare and determyn them. And wee write soe much the rather unto you because we have byn requered to graunt a *certiorari* for the removinge of an inditment against Mr. Tayler's wife which is informed us to be done uppon former mallice and hope of gaine thereby, and thereuppon you have called an especiall Sessions which wee assure ourselves you will forbeare to proceede therein, untill it may be resolved upon that you may lawfully proceed therin lest some former imputations laid to your towne be verified. Thus wishing you not to proceede but to forbeare, as Tenterden doth, untill full resolution and order may be had for a due and orderly proceedinge therein." *Copy.*

1607[–8], January 24.—[The Mayor of Rye ?] to Serjeant Shorly.

"At my beinge at London the last tearme, I had your counsaile concerninge the triall of a woman imprisoned in our towne uppon the statute in the first yere of the King's Majesty's raigne against conjuration, witchcraft and dealinge with evill and wicked spirits, and accordinge to your advice, and with the direction of Mr. Thurbarne, at our last general sessions holden in Rye, we proceeded to the triall of her, where she was indited, arrayned and condempned to death but in regarde she is with child, execution is staid. Sithence which tyme wee have received this inclosed letter from Sir John Boyes, who certifieth us that we have no aucthoritie nor power by the said statute nor by our charter, to inquere of the said cause. Wherefore these are most earnestly to intreate and desire your advice and direction what is best for us to doe in this case. I have intreated Mr. Thurbarne to attend uppon you for our further resolution herein."

1607[–8], January [?].—The Mayor and Jurats of Rye to Sir Thomas Waller Knt. Lieutenant of Dover Castle.

The masters and chief fishermen of Rye are grateful to Waller for "the great love and care" that he has had for their poor estate in writing as to the French fishermen. The Rye fishermen "all protest and vowe that to the uttermost of their powers they are most willing to imploy their best indevors for the repellinge and beatinge awaye of those insolent and irregular French fyshers. But so it is right worshipful that the fyshermen of our toune doe thinke themselves altogether unable (without the helpe of a pynnys of his Majesty's to be aydinge and assistinge unto theire boates, at the sea) to suppresse and repell the force of the French fysher boates by reason that they are soe many in nomber and so strongly prepared, armed, and violently beat to defend their unlawfull proceedinges; for the whole nomber of our fisher boates which goe to sea this winter are not above sixteene and for the moste parte of our fyshermen they are forced to attend their fyshinge with great care, otherwise they shall not be able to maintaine their great charge of wyfe, children, and famelie, their estates beinge so poore. Besides they do assure themselves that yf it shall be knowen or intelligence given unto the French that the fyshermen of Rye shall take uppon them in warlike manner to suppresse and repell them from their unlawfull fishinge, without the ayde of his Majesty's ships or pynnysses to stande in their defence, that they of Deipe and Treyport will bend all their forces against them that they shall not be able to abide the seas in their lawfull fishinge without great danger of bloodshede. In consideration whereof and in regarde that the said French fyshers neither respect the feare of God nor their Kinge's stricte comandement to the contrary, our said fyshermen most humbly beseche your Worship that you will vouchsafe so farre to favor their distressed case that by your good meanes unto our most honorable Lord Warden, a pynnys of his Highnes may be graunted to come and lye in the harbor of Rye this present fyshinge season, to goe to sea, at tymes convenient, with our fysherboates, and they all doe faithfully promys that they will from tyme to tyme as occasion shall serve be redey to geve due attendance uppon the said pynnys and arme themselves for the apprehension of the said French fyshers, in the beste manner that they canne or may. And for their paines and sallery to be taken therein they most humbly submit themselves to be considered of by our right honorable good Lord Warden to receave for the same as they shall worthely merit and deserve. And this much they have intreated us to signifie unto your Worship."

Postscript.—"Wee have sithence the wrytinge of this letter bene very credably informed by one Henry Dunne (?) sayler, a master of one of our passage boates of Rye who came from Deipe about three dayes past, that Mr. Bellier (?) the Purveyor for the French Kinge, did send Dunn to informe our fishermen of Rye that there are twentye fysher boates of Deipe sent to Treport by certeine men of Deipe and their they are manned and sett forthe to fyshinge, notwithstanding the French King's proclamation to the contrary; and that they have alredey bene at sea afyshinge and doe bringe by horsbacke from Treyporte to Deipe sometymes 20 horse loades of soles and playce in a day; and that Mr. Bellier wold have advertised so muche by his letters but that he dares not to writt for feare lest he should be killed amongest them." *Copy.*

1608, March 10. (New style.)—Appointment by Clara Larder of Rye, widow, daughter and heir of John Vanvost, late Ypres in Flanders, deceased, of Tobias Streekeman of Rye, her son and heir, and William Dennys of Faversham, fisherman, her son-in-law, as her attornies to take possession of her property in Ypres. *Copy.*

1607[-8], March 15.—Circular letter from the Lord Warden to the Mayor Bailiffs and Jurats of the Cinque Ports and their members.

Requiring the observance of certain directions, given by the King under Privy Seal, respecting victuallers, tiplers, and alehouse keepers. *Copy.*

Enclosure:—Copy of the King's warrant, setting out that there is great abuse in the granting of victuallers', tiplers' and alehouse keepers' licences, and directing the observance of the following directions in granting the same for the future:—

(1.) The High Constables of Hundreds, and the churchwardens and constables of parishes are to present, at the next Easter Sessions, the number of necessary alehouses in their districts, and the fittest persons to keep them. All old licences are to be brought in.

(2.) Future licences are to be granted at the General Quarter Sessions.

(3.) Certain articles of "good order" for ale house keepers, are to be "conceaved" by the Justices of the Peace, and to be duly observed; these are to be reported to the Privy Council before the end of the next Trinity term.

(4.) Alehouse keepers are to be bound by recognizances against unlawful games.

(5.) All licences for ale house keepers are to be "sealed with a common seale, ingraven in brasse with a rose, and the inscription of the countie, cittie or towne-corporate haveing authoritie to hold sessions of the peace."

(6 & 7.) As to the custody of this Seal, the fees payable for licences granted under it.

(8 & 9.) A register of Licences is to be kept.

(10.) The number of alehouses is "not to be increased but diminished."

(11.) Justices of Assise on their circuits, and Justices of the Peace at General Quarter Sessions, are to inquire as to the due execution of those orders.

1608, March 26. [The Mayor and Jurats of Rye] to Sir Thomas Waller.

They have taken order with the masters of the Rye "fysher boates" for the redelivery of all such things as their companies have taken away from the French fishermen. The Rye fishermen fear attacks from the French fishermen who "fysshe for herrings and coddes in great barkes, and our men fysshinge by them in small boates, they may (as heretofore they have done) spoyle their nettes by ronninge over them, and so utterlye overthrowe their fysshinge for that Yermouth season, and leikwise for the Scarborow voyage, yf by some good meanes they be not prevented." The Rye men hope the Lord Warden will find means to protect them. *Copy.*

1608, March 28. The Mayor and Jurats of Hastings to the Mayor and Jurats of Rye.

They are ready to provide money for the purchase of "tramell" nets. The boat for the "tryal" is ready for the coming of the "tryers" according to the order. They have asked the Lord Warden to move the Mayor and Jurats of Rye to obtain these nets for them in Rye "our reasons are, that having never used here such kynd of netts (as you knowe) we are altogether unfurnisht both of such netts and stuff to make them, and also unskillfull how to make them as they ought to be."

1608, April 3.—The Lords of the Council to the Lord Warden.

Enclosing revised directions, as to licencing ale houses, made after conference with "divers principall gentlemen dwelling within the shyres neerest to this cittye"; these directions have been printed by public order. *Copy.*

1608, May 2, Dover.—Francis Raworth to the Mayors, Bailiffs and Jurats of Hythe, Folkstone, Romney, Lydd, Rye, Winchelsea, Hastings, Pevensey, Seaford, and Tenderden.

"The seals, that by certain articles concerning the licencing of victualers are appointed to be used to seale these licences, are made at the Kinge's ingraver's; he dwelleth in the lower end of Foster Lane over against the Goldsmith's Hall. He is to have 20*s*. for every seal by order and warrant under the late Treasurer's hand (which I did see) and so much I paid for one for this town, assuring myself I shall have allowance thereof again and would wish that your town clerks should send thither for their seals if they buy them [not] elsewhere, yet this engraver sayeth he is promised the 20*s*. for every county, city, and town, and therefore to his book he taketh the name of every person that payeth him to be subscribed with his own hand."

1608, July 22. Northampton House.—The Earl of Northampton, Lord Warden, to the Mayor of Rye.

He has received a petition on behalf of Anne Taylor who is kept a prisoner in the common gaol at Rye, "uppon the unjust accusation of a lewde woman and some pryvate displeasure conceaved by your selfe against her" though she has tendered good bail and is by law bailable.

"As I like at no hand that authority be made a maske to revenge private injuries, so ame I not credulous of every information I receave against the magistrates for due execution of justice, yet in this case I could be well contented in respect of her sex and her present state, beinge now with childe, and growen very weake by reason thereof, and the lothsomness of the prison, to afforde her all favour warrantable by lawe." Desires, therefore, that the charges against her be set down and delivered to her husband, whom he has appointed to attend Sir John Boys and Mr. Haddes that they may decide whether she is bailable. *Signed. Seal of Arms.*

1608, July 28.—The Mayor and Jurats of Rye to the Earl of Northampton, Lord Warden.

Concerning Anne Tayler, in her own examination she had confessed that she "was from tyme to tyme acquainted by one Susan Swapper (since that tyme before us tryed and condempned uppon the last statute of witchcrafte) with her conference and conversinge with spirittes, and that she, the said Anne, delivered to her divers thinges which she demanded for the said spirittes." At the last general sessions of the peace held at Rye, the said Anne was duly convicted for aiding and abetting the said Susan. Before Anne's conviction, but subsequent to her examination above referred to, her husband promised that she should appear when called upon; but, contrary to that promise she withdrew herself into Kent for half-a-year. Lately she came secretly to Rye and whilst making stay there, used "some outrageous behaviour" upon her maid servant, for which behaviour and for "divers other matters and suspicions concerning witchecraftes . . . . . . come to light since her departure," she was apprehended and committed to gaol where she hath remained a few days. No good or sufficient bail has yet been tendered for her. "It hathe not at any tyme heretofore byn used amongst us, or often hearde, that persons indicted for felonie, especially in suche cases where the benefitt of clergye is taken awaie, have byn bayled." Serjeant Shorley, the town's counsel advised that on apprehension she should be kept without bail. Still the Mayor and Jurats are ready, at the Lord Warden's request, to accept the said Anne's husband as her bail. *Copy.*

1608, July.—Memorandum that George Taylor of Rye, gentleman, had bound himself in the sum of 100*l.* for the appearance of Anne Taylor, his wife, at the next sessions of the peace.

[1608, July ?] William Angell to Thomas Higgions, Mayor of Rye.

He has recommended the Board of Green Cloth to write to the town to see that the fishermen are placed nearer the fishmarket "and the Ostes farther off," which was considered desirable "although it wilbe alleadged that tenants are not to be put out without sufficient warneinge, nor without their own likeinge, it may well be aunswered, that by reason of their common inconveniences, bred and offered by themselves, many waies, we are driven thus to doe, as well for the ease of the King's officer there, as also for betteringe the King's service, especiallye for keeping the markett betimes." *Seal of Arms.*

1608, August 6. [The Mayor and Jurats of Rye] to William Angell.

The contents of his letter has been communicated to the "Hostes and Fysshermen" who are willing to abide thereby. "In regarde that in the winter season every particular fyssherman hath his shoppe unto hymselfe, and in the somer tyme when they goe with tramells the whole company of one boat use but one shopp; for them, we thinke it most fitt that they should change shoppes with the hostes between this, and All Saints about which tyme the boats come from Yermouth." *Copy.*

1608, August 27. Dover Castle.—John Packenham to the Mayor and Jurats of Rye.

I have received a warrant from my Lord and master to give notice to all Ports that one Sir Nicholas Hales and Captain Henry Fortescue, on Thursday last, came out of London intending to pass over the seas and there to fight a challenge made here in England between them. These are to give you notice that you permit no such persons to pass but to stay them till further orders.

1608, October 8.—License by the Earl of Northampton to John Hangney of Dieppe, fisherman, with his boat and servants to fish at the place called the Sowe upon the English Coast out of respect for the service of the French King.

[1608, October].—Petition of the Mayor, Jurats and Commonalty of Rye to the Earl of Northampton, Lord Warden.

"Humbly shewing unto your honorable Lordship that of late by the violence of the sea thear is so muche sande broughte into our harbor and lyeth so highe that it causeth the sea (rowling over that sand) to fall with such an exceeding force upon our jetties, keyes, and caulseys and other defences thereabouts that it is very likely in short space to undermyne the same; the highe waye to the towne is almost eaten upp and the gate and streate that leadeth to the towne is almost undermyned, which in short time will growe to the utter ruyne and decaye of the whole towne if speedie remedie be not had. And your poor suppliants have alreadie byn at such chardge in seeking to amend the haven and to withstand the violence of the sea thear, that they have well neere spent the whole revenues of the same towne and so ympoverished themselves thereby that they are not able to doe any more by their owne meanes or abilitie; by reason they being but feu in number and very much ympoverished for wante of trade but onely fishing, and the houses there so meanly rented, and soe many standing emptie, that it seemeth a thing unpossible to levy uppon the saide corporation or of the lands and tenements within the same any proportionable some of money for the effectuall repayring thereof.

Nowe may it please your good Lordship in tender comisseration of our poor estates (and consideringe all meanes to helpe ourselves is taken from us) referring ourselves wholly to your Honor's protection, humbly beseech you of your accustomed goodnes to be a meanes to his Majestie for us for some speedy supply and releife in this our distressed estate, or els the whole towne is likely to be utterly ruynated and decayed, his Majesties service thereby neglected and a number of us very likely to be undone."

1608, October 17. Staple Inn.—John Cloke to the Mayor and Jurats of Rye.

I have received your letters by this bearer Goodman Baylye and upon receipt thereof we petitioned immediately to my Lord of Northampton who was very forward to do you any good, and willed us to petition the Lords of His Majesty's Council which we did. The answer from the Council consisted of two points first that if we could benefit ourselves by a Commission of Sewers we should have a new commission with as large words as we could devise and if this could do us no good the Lords of the Council would direct their letters to the country for our present relief.

1608, December, to 1609, March.—Correspondence touching a dispute between Rye and Hastings concerning the fishing "with traules and tramells."

1608[–9], March —— Lewes.—The Commissioners for levying of aid for making Prince Henry, his Majesty's eldest son, a knight, to the Mayor and Jurats of Rye.

These are to give you notice that we have appointed to execute our commission at Lewes on 25 April and to require you to warn and summon in every parish within your port and the liberty thereof, all freeholders that they be before us at Lewes aforesaid.

1609, March 25.—The Mayor and Jurats of Rye to Sir Thomas Waller.

We have received letters from the right worshipful knights of the County of Sussex concerning the levying of aid for making Prince Henry, his Majesty's eldest son, a knight, which for our part we are persuaded that we are clearly discharged from the payment of any aid by the Charter of the Ports.

1609, April 8.—Dover Castle. [The Lieutenant of Dover Castle] to the Mayors, Bailiffs, and Jurats of the Cinque Ports and two Ancient Towns.

"Whereas we have resceaved letters from our most honorable Lord Warden to cause present restraynt and staye to be made throughout all the Portes and members, of all such barkes as the copie hereinclosed dothe mention, and that noe person bee permytted to passe over the seaes with any of the saide barkes whatsoever. These are therefore to will and requier you the Maiors, Bailliffes and Jurattes of the severall Portes, twoe auncient townes and theire members to have an especiall care and respect to see his Majesties comandement in that behalfe most carefully obeyed." *Copy.*

1609, April 20. Dover Castle.—Sir Thomas Waller to the Mayor and Jurats of Rye.

"For that I perceave the pointe of fisheinge betwen the French and you ys lyke to bee exceedinglye pressed against you wherein I understand ther are above thirtye severall depositions taken on the other syde that will be enforced against you, and ther are only fyve deposed on your parte to proove that the Broad Smooth ys parte of the Sow and hathe ben tyme out of mind so reputed, and of the extent therof; least thys number should seeme to be sumwhat overwayed with multitude of opponants I pray you indelayedly upon the receyte heerof, yf therebe any others in your towne that out of their experience or by waye of tradition are able to depose to thatt point, that Richard Oake and the other two lately deposed before you, that you lykewyse take their depositions and haste them up to be without fayle att London att my Lord Privy Seale's house on Satterday night or Sundaye morninge att the furthest. You may be noe meanes fayle to have twoe men for the business of the petition as was formerly appointed." *Signed. Seal of Arms.*

1609, April 27.—The Mayor and Jurats of Rye to the Mayor, Bailiffs, and Jurats of the other Cinque Ports.

A circular letter as to whether the Ports have the power under the Charter of Edward IV. to try offenders under the Statute against conjurations or for other offences made felony since the said Charter.

[1609], April 28. Dover Castle.—Sir Thomas Waller to the Mayor and Jurats of Rye.

"The question between the French and yow for the right of fisheinge upon the Sow and Broad Smoothe, which to muche importes the state and lyfe of your towne of Rye, ys exceedinglye prest above by the French Embassador and to farr urged as yt behooveth, that yee be not sylent nor secure when your adversaries doe importune and are soe vigillant least the state should conceave ytt ys not so important to you as hathe been pretended, and our most honorable Lord Warden should growe weerye of carryeinge your burden yf yee shall nott be redye to sett to your helpeinge hande. Ytt ys conceaved to be more then convenient, most necessarye, thatt yee send upp 2 discreet parsons to be att London one Frydaye next which shall delyver a petition on Sondaye morninge to hys Majestie in the name of all the inhabitants of Rye. They that yee shall imploye in thys sarvice shall finde either Mr. Packnam or Mr. Warde at the Starr in New Fishstreet whoe shall delyver them the petition reddye drawne and shall directe them farther as occasion shall requyre." *Signed. Seal of Arms.*

1609, May 3. Doctors' Commons.—G. Newman to the Mayor and Jurats of Rye.

"I think you understood in generality howe the cause of fyshing went at the Counsayle table this last weeke, but now by this you shall know more particularly what was done. The Lords that then heard it agreed to referre the hearing and determining thereof to the Lord Kinlasse, Sir John Herbart, Sir Julius Cesar, Sir Thomas Parry and others; the Commission to that end I have drawn.

The French confesse the Sowe to be the King's wholly and promise never to use it more without leave, but when it cometh to be questioned where the Sowe lyeth and how much it conteyneth they allow us a peece of the sea about five miles from our shore and in length and breadth about some seaven myles, which as you know is not nigh the Sowe by many leagues, and this is so confidently avowched as yf it were most true. Those that be of counsayle with the French have shewed me the mapp that they have drawen to this effect, and for that parte which you accompte the Sowe they terme it the Vergoye and the Aleppo and soe with strange names they intend to put us quite besydes the Sowe. With this opinion they have fully possessed the French Embassador and their Counsayle, soe that of necessity you must take this course. You muste send, at the least, ten of your moste sufficient auntientest and wisest fyshermen to goe of purpose with a boate in the day time to sound and as they can measure the Sowe in this manner, they must observe for the length from east to west, right over to what parte of Fraunce the east end lyeth and to what parte of England; soe likewise right over to what part of Fraunce the west end lyeth and soe to England. Then for the breadth, to what part of Fraunce the nighest part of the Broadsmoth or the Sowe lyeth and howe nigh to that coast; then must they as nigh as they can gesse and observe the juste length of the Sowe from east to west and the juste breadth from south-east to north-west. This being done, they must come up hyther when I send for them to depose this upon theyr oathes, and soe I doubt not to procure an order for perpetuall quietnes by the honorable Commissioners that it shall remaine without question herafter. Nowe is the tyme to settle your quietnes in this matter for ever. Your Lord Warden is your most honourable Lord and most zealous patron herin. Therfore be not waintinge to yourselves nowe, and with all alacrity take the matter in hand which I have prescribed you and lett it be dispatched quickly, for there will be neede heere very shortly of the oathes of those men that shall thus surveye it.".

1609, May 28. Doctors' Commons. G. Newman to the Mayor and Jurats of Rye.

You lately wrote that the day after the date of your letter I should receive from you by Mr. Beveridge the plat which your fishermen had taken of the Narrow seas and the Sowe, but as yet I hear not either of Mr. Beveredge or it, for which cause I write desiring you to send it with all speed. *Seal.*

1609, May. Correspondence concerning right of the Mayor and Jurats of Rye to try Mrs. Taylor for witchcraft.

1609, July 19. London.—Sir William Twysden to the Mayor and Jurats of Rye.

"By my Lord of Northampton his meanes the Kings Majestie hath pleased to grant your petition for the Chanell of Apledore and the lands conteyned within it, and his Lordship hath geven order to Mr. Atorney for drawing the conveyance unto your Corporation with a clause of a yearly accompt to be made unto the Lord Warden for the time being of the imployment of the proffitt thereof unto the use of the haven in such manner as is expressed in your petition."

1609[–10], February 8. Northampton House.—The Earl of Northampton to the Mayor and Jurats of Rye and Hastings.

Whereas I have given license with his Majesty's privity to seven boats more to fish for the service of the French King for the reasons therein expressed. And whereas liberty is given to the French to begin their fishing the fourteenth day of February which is one month before the time limited by the constitutions, because that their Lent falleth out commonly before ours, therefore because I will have them enjoy no privilege whereof you shall not partake I am well content that you begin your fishing at the same time. *Signed. Seal of Arms.*

Enclosure. Copy of licence to the French fishermen granted at the request of Monsieur de la Bodery, late resident ambassador in England for the French King, Henry the fourth.

1609[–10], March 18.—Depositions of Richard Colbrand of Holborn in the County of Middlesex, musician. He says that while lodging at the house of Fraunces Daniell of Rye, innholder, he heard the said Daniell say, "We have a Puritan to our Mayor and therefore you may play as long as you will at his door, but he will give you nothing." And that was the occasion that they stayed from playing and showing their music unto Mr. Mayor.

1609[–10], March 20.—The Mayor and Jurats of Rye to the Earl of Northampton.

Asking aid for the advancement of a Bill in Parliament for the amendment of the haven of Rye. *Draft.*

1610, July 3.—Commission directed to Henry, Earl of Northampton and others to collect an aid within the Cinque Ports for making Prince Henry the King's Eldest son, a knight.

1610, July 18.—Depositions of Joan Bayly of Rye aged four score years and upwards. She saith that the child of Thomas Hart, fisherman of Rye, "had not all her friends about her" and she thought the child was bewitched, therefore she told Susan the wife of the said Thomas to get her a piece of red cloth, three score needles and a halfpennyworth of pins and by God's help she would cure the child. Which needles and pins being brough to her, she did stick them in the said red cloth and put the same on the fire upon the "emeryes" and stuck a dagger in the midst and she should know thereby the party that had bewitched the child, as the party that did the deed would come into the house if the child were bewitched. And she saith it was a long time before the said cloth was consumed and at length it did seem to be like unto a toad but no party came in nor does she know who bewitched the child.

1610, September 3.—The Mayor and Jurats of Rye to the Lord Warden.

The bearer "Mr. John Stoneham one of his Majesty's gard, and well knowen to be a very good and ingenious workman about the amendinge of waterworkes and havens" has, of late years, been largely employed at Dover (where his father was also employed) about the works upon the pier and harbour there. He has now taken in hand the amendment of the haven of Rye, assuring himself that by your honourable good meanes, there may be procured sufficient money for the repairs which will make Rye haven as serviceable as ever it was. He will suggest how such work is to be done, and how the requisite money is to be raised without charge to the town of Rye, "the which, he himself by your honourable favour will take upon himself, to effecte at his owne charge." *Copy.*

1610, September 7. Certificate by the Mayor of Rye that Henry Blackborne "chirurgion and occulist by his profession, about one yere nowe last past, by the helpe of Almightie God, his arte and skyll, did recover divers persons within the toune of Rye aforesaid that were blinde, unto their sight againe." Those restored to sight were Agnes Blakey of Rye, widow, 74 years of age who had been "darke and blinde" about two years; Jane the wife of William Hurlstone of Rye, fisherman, 65 years of age, who had been "blinde of bothe eyes" about ten years; and Alice the wife of Joseph Stare of Hastings, fisherman, 75 years of age also blind of both eyes. All these three persons are "yet alive, in good sort, can see, and goe aboute the toune without any guide." *Draft.*

1610, October 26.—Certificate by the Mayor and Jurats of Rye that, time out of mind, the citizens and free men of the City of London have paid to the Corporation of Rye the following duties. "Anchorage of all such shipps and barques of theirs as doe arive in the harbor of Rye," and also "keyage and wharfage" for their goods and merchandize brought from beyond the sea to Rye. *Seal torn away.*

1610, November 1.—The Mayor and Jurats of Rye to the Local Warden.

Begging his aid in obtaining an Act of Parliament granting to them, for "a certain tyme," tonnage at the rate of 3*d.* a ton (in like manner as had been granted to Dover) to be bestowed on the repair of their haven, which is so decayed that without repairs—for which the town can no longer afford to pay—"there is nothing to be expected but onely the losse of his Majesty's poore toune, which in very short tyme will be eaten and beaten doune by the rage of the sea, in regarde that our jetties and timber works are broken and worren awaye."

1610, November 20.—The Mayor and Jurats of Rye to John Griffithe, chief Secretary to the Lord Warden; James Thurbarne "at Grayes Inn in Holdberne;" Sir William Twysden "at his house in Reed Crosse Street near the Crosse;" and to Hennage Finch, and John Young, members of Parliament for Rye.

Stating that the Lord Warden had promised his aid towards obtaining for them an act of Parliament for granting to the town tonnage, at the rate of 3*d.* a ton "in suche sort as heretofore by Act of Parliament hath been granted to Dover haven" towards the amendment of this "poor decayed haven of Rye"; and begging the assistance of those to whom they write towards the passage of such a bill through the House of Commons. *Copies.*

1610, December 3.—Certificate made at "His Majesties Court," held in Rye, by the Constables and Churchwardens of Rye that they do not know or believe there are any "popish recusant, or other refusers of the Kinge's Majesties laws ecclesiastical" within the parish or liberties of the town.

1610, December 4.—Deposition of Francis Cossen of Cranbrook, Kent, to the effect that one Ralph Wood was never apprenticed to the trade of tallow chandler, though he dwelt with Francis Harris of Rye "who used to make candles, but was no chaundler or brought upp in that trade."

1610[11], January 2.—Depositions concerning William Wale of Plymouth "sworne to the othe of Alleageance."

Thomas Pretty of Rye deposes that he heard Wale say that "an Ireishe man was all ways as good as a Scotishman.". Pretty replied "that may not be, for wee have one Scotisheman [that] is better than any Irisheman," to which Wale answered "You make so much of your King." Pretty said again "Our King is supreame head [the words "of the church" are struck through] what say you to that?" Wale said "there was never an Irishe man but was as goode as the Kinge.' Pretty said "there may be Kinges in Irelande" to which Wale did not answer. Other depositions to a similar effect. Wale replies that if he used such speeches "he was in drink" when he did so. *Memorandum.*—The Mayor and his bretheren ordered Wale to be whipped for his "bad and lewde speeches."

1611, April 18. Dover Castle.—Letters of Henry, Lord Howard of Marnhull, Earl of Northampton, K.G., Keeper of the Privy Seal, Constable of Dover Castle, Keeper of the Chancery and Admiralty of Cinque Ports and their members, addressed to the Mayor, Jurats, and others of the toun of Rye; reciting the Kings Letters Patent of the previous 6th of March appointing Thomas Milward Esqre. of Lincoln's Inn and John Huggefford Esq. of Henwood, Warwickshire, to execute, for term of their lives, the office of Bailiff of the town of Rye. *Copy. On the back, is a copy of the King's Letters Patent.*

1611, April —.—Sir Thomas Waller to the Mayor and Jurats of Rye.

Informing them that he had received directions from the Lord Warden for the mustering of the Cinque Ports, and that on account of the infection at Sandwich he could not perform the same. Commanding the Mayor of Rye to give notice that the captains of the trained bands and their companies, and also the captains of the general and untrained bands are to appear before him (Waller) on the 7th day of May next to be mustered and their armour viewed. *Signed.*

1611, May 18.—A Proclamation against melting down of gold and silver coins. *Printed by Robert Barker.*

1611, June 4.—A Proclamation for the apprehension of the Lady Arabella [Stuart] and William Seymour, second son of Lord Beauchamp.

1611, June 23.—The Mayor and Jurats of Rye to the Lord Warden.

About seven years before they obtained, through his instrumentality and for the preservation of their harbour, and for "subpressing" or sundry parcels of salt marsh, "intended by diverse gentlemen to be inned," a Commission of Sewers which extended "from the enteringe of the sea to the Camber, and from thence to all manner of creekes, streames, channels, and sewers that then did resort to the said Camber or in tymes past have resorted or come to the same, and also from the entering of the sea aforesaid unto the Pudle of Rye, and so forthe to the towne of Rye" and the streams, &c., leading up to the country on both sides of the town, viz.:—that to Appledore, and so to Newenden and Robertsbridge, and that, on the other side of the town, to Udimer and Peasmarsh. A new Commission of Sewers has lately been granted, at the suit of certain noblemen and gentlemen of the county of Sussex, which extends to the whole county and is a *supersedeas* to the former Commission which has still three years to run, and, under it, much work upon the harbour is in contemplation. In the new Commission, the names of many, who, under the former Commission have done useful work, are omitted; amongst the persons omitted are the Mayors of Rye and Winchelsea. All this, the Mayor and Jurats consider may be very hurtful to them unless the Lord Warden looks after their interests, which they beg him to do. *Draft.*

1611, July 8. Northampton House.—The Earl of Northampton to ——————.

Out of the regard I have for the poor estate of the town of Rye I have made stay of a late grant unto Sir John Tufton, of the Hospital of St. Bartholomew of Playdon, in the Parish of Rye, and send you copy of the docquet of the said grant. I pray you to send me particulars of the estate of the Hospital so that I may know whether to give way to Sir John Tufton's contract. *Signed. Seal of Arms.*

1611, December 30.—Depositions taken at Rye concerning John Allen of Rye, goldsmith. Henry Damir deposes that he heard Allen say "there was a lible cast abrode which concerned the makinge of the harbor of Rye, and that the water should be cutt throughe St. Mary's marshe and the water should come out of Bridge well, and [that] the harbor makers were brewers, and bakers, shepherds, and silver-candlestick makers, carters, and hogschops (*sic*) and divers other bad speaches." Other depositions follow.

[1611.] Copy of a presentment by the Jury at the King's Court held at Rye that Susan, the wife of Roger Swapper, late of Rye, sawyer, on the 21 July, 1607, and on other days before and after, not having God before her eyes and led by diabolical instigation, at Rye aforesaid, wickedly, diabolically, and feloniously "did councell" with certain wicked and impious spirits, and the same wicked and impious spirits "did enterteyne and feed" in order to gain wealth, against the King's peace and the form of the Statute &c. Further presentment that Anne wife of George Taylor of Rye, gentleman, received abetted aided and comforted the aforesaid Susan knowing her to have committed the felony abovesaid. Written beneath, are the opinions of Counsel as follows:—"I thinke it is pardoned by the generall pardon—John Shurley. I am of Mr. Sergeant Shurley's opinion—Ja. Thurbarne."

1612, May 13. Whitehall.—Proclamation by the King offering a reward of 500*l.* for the apprehension of Lord Sanquair and 100*l.* for apprehension of Robert Carlisle, if alive, and 300*l.* for the body of the the former, or 50*l.* for that of the latter, if dead. Lord Sanquair is described as of "tall stature, pale faced, of a sallowe colour, a small yellowishe beard, one glasse or false eye, attended commonly with a Frenche boy"; and Robert Carlisle is described as of "an ordinarie stature, a handsome fellowe, his hayre of his heade of a flaxen redd, his beard something redde with a hayre scarre, or cutt on his lip up to his nose which maketh him snuffle in his speeche." The Proclamation recites that "one Turner" had been murdered on the previous Monday, by Robert Carlisle, a Scottish borderer a servant of Lord Sanquair, and Erwin, an English borderer, and that Lord Sanquair was a party to the murder. *Copy.*

1612, July 11. Northampton House.—The Lord Warden to "the Commissioners of Sewers and the Baylife of the surrounded levells upon the River Rother."

A decree had lately been made for stopping the "auncient and navigable river of Rother" near Thorney Wall; this the inhabitants of Rye and Tenderden consider will "utterly decaye" the haven of Rye and impoverish the ports of Rye and Tenderden. The Commissioners are, therefore, to forbear the execution of that decree till further enquiry has been made.

1612, August 20.—Licence granted by Henry, Earl of Northampton, Lord Warden, to Charles de la Mare, fisherman, of Dieppe to fish "at a place called the Sowe upon the English coast, and elsewhere upon that coast" for all sorts of fish, without restraint of season. The licence recites that the King had, at the suit of Monsieur de la Bodery, "late resident Ambassador in England for the French Kinge Henry the fowerth," consented to licences being granted to six French "barques," in addition to the number allowed in Queen Elizabeth's time, to fish on the eastern coast of England, "besides one other boate which his Majestie is pleased out of speciall favour to graunt personallie to Monsieur de la Bodery, in respect of his owne good carriage during his abode in these partes." King James stipulating that neither his Majesty of Fraunce nor any other his ministers that shall serve hereafter in this place will ever after this grant published, excuse or seek by their treaty to exempt from the punishment accustomed, any other fishermen of Fraunce whatsoever that shall presume to fish in these parts above this number. *Copy.*

1612[–13], February 13. Dover Castle.—John Packenham to the Mayors, Bailiffs, and Jurats of Rye, Winchelsea, and Lydd.

Ordering that the certificates of taking the oath of allegiance be sent in at once and complaining that they had not been sent in earlier. *Copy.*

1612[-13], February 16. The Mayor and Jurats of Rye to the Earl of Northampton.

We took the oath of allegiance of most of the inhabitants on 3 December and on the 14th instant we took the oath of the remainder, who were before at sea.

1612[-13], March 9. The Mayor and Jurats of Rye to Mr. John Harmon at Maidstone.

We are advertised by Mr. John Bracegirdle, our vicar, of the great love and favour towards our poor town of Rye in furthering the pretended works for the amendment of our decayed harbour, that you will vouchsafe to take such course with the Commissioners upon good consideration to give security for the affecting of the said work. Therefore these are to desire you to send us your answer by the bearer, Mr. Bracegirdle, whether it will please you to take upon you the charge of these weighty affairs or not, or what course you think is best to be done. *Draft.*

1613, May 15.—Verdict at a coroners inquest.

"Wee do find that on Thursday the thirtenth day of May and in the yeare of the raigne of our Soveraigne Lord King James of England &c., the eleventh, about fower or five of the clocke in the afternoone of the same day. Robert Mullenex of Farleighe in the County of Sussex, yeomann, and one William Lamperd of Farleighe aforesaid, gentleman, being in the house of Richard Barker of Rie in the County afforesaid, inholder, and playing at cardes at a game called newe cutt, and Edward Skynner of Rie standing by them and looking uppon them, the said William Lamperd dealing the cardes did turne up seaven and twenty for the said Mullenex and for himself eight and twenty, whereuppon the said Mullenex said the game is myne, and the said Skynner standing by and looking on them at play, said it was not his and thereuppon the said Mullenex said unto the said Skynner that hee did lie, whereupon the said Skynner suddainly tooke up a stone pott standing before him at the table with beere and did fling it at the head of the said Mullenex and strooke him on the lefte side of his head in such sorte as the said Mullenex did presently sincke downe and so with the said stroke did breake and perishe the scull of the head of the said Mullenex, by meanes whereof the said Robert Mullenex did laye and languish in the howse of the said Barker untill the next day being Friday, the fowerteenth day of the same moneth of May, untill three or fower of the clocke in the afternoone, and so died by meanes of the said flinging of the pott."

1615, August 31.—Certificate of the Mayor and Jurats of Rye to Lord Zouch that they have appointed Marke Thomas, Mayor, Richard Fowtrell, Thomas Ensinge, Mathewe Younge, John Galmer, and Richard Gibbridge, Jurats of Rye, to go to Shipway to do such service as to them pertains by the ancient usages and customs of the Cinque Ports at the solemnizing of the "Cerement or Promise" of the Lord Warden at his first entry into the said office.

1615, September 2. Dover Castle.—Lord Zouch to the Mayors and Bailiffs of the Cinque Ports.

"The Kinges most excellent Majestie hath bene graciouslie pleased to signifie unto me that the Kinge of Spaine, havinge a purpose to send men for supplies into Flaunders, hath by his Embassador resident here made request unto his Majestie that if any of the King of Spaines shippes appointed for conveance thether shoulde perhaps, ether by ill weather or by any other casualtie, be driven into any of his Majesty's

RYE MSS.

portes of his kingdome, they shoulde be fairely used and with such good respecte as the subjectes of a kinge that nowe is tied in a league of amitie with his Majestie is deserved and suffer them to furnish themselves with such thinges as they want, paying for the same, which his Highnes is well pleased to graunte and hath commanded me to geve directions accordinglie throughe all the Cinque Portes and landinge places within my government. These are therefore in his Majesty's name and in accomplishement of his directions therein to will and require you and every of you that if any Spanishe shippes or other vessels bound with men for Flaunders shall occasionally arrive into any of the portes, creekes or havons within the Cinque Portes or the members thereof and within your severall precincts you doe suffer them quietlie to land without gevinge any occasion of offence and permitt them for their monyes to supplie themselves of such thinges as they shall stande in neede of." *Copy.*

1615[–16], January 15, Phillip Lane.—Lord Zouch to the Mayors, Bailiffs, and Jurats of Hythe, New Romney, Rye, and Lydd.

"His Majestie hath beene of late pleased by his Letters Patents under the Great Seale of England to geve power and licence unto Sir Edward Howard, Knighte, to erect and sett up a light upon the Nesse near adjoyning unto you, intending it will be for the generall good of all marchants and others which passe that waye by sea, and I understandinge thereof and desirous to performe all worthy office of a carefull governor towards all his Majesty's subjects inhabitinge within the Cinque Portes, and not knowinge how prejudiciall or disadvantage the building of such lanthorne might be to you which dwell thereaboutes, have by my place interpassed and as yet stayed all further proceedings therein till I had geven my advertisement thereof, wherefore I praye you to enter into a serious consideration of the busynes and after mature deliberation and a necessarie consultation taken therein, to certefie me how you approve the course intended herein." *Copy.*

1616, May 1.—The Mayor and Jurats of Rye to Lord Zouch, the Lord Warden of the Cinque Ports.

"This day our Mayor, Mr. Marke Thomas, made known to us of your most honourable love to us towards the amendment of our poor decayed haven and withall advertised us of your great care therein in addressing your letters unto the Low Countries to very substantial and expert workmen well able to judge of such waterworks, as is to be done about these affairs. We pray you again to send over your letters unto those workmen that both or one of them may come over and view our decayed harbour." *Draft.*

1616, September 10.—The Mayor and Jurats of Hastings to the Mayor and Jurats of Rye.

We send you the Commission to the bailiff of Yarmouth to be sealed desiring you to send him such money as from either of your towns is due having respect therein to the last decree for increase of their fee. We pray you likewise to send unto him the names of your questmen, the names of your masters and barques which are gone to Yarmouth to fish, with the number of men in every of them.

1616, September 30.—A list of the Jurats and commons of Rye with facetious notes against each name. "Mr. Convars the ancientest townclarke in the Portes, John Walker the wisdome of Rye" etc.

1617, May 19.—The Bailiff and Jurats of Lydd to Marke Thomas, Mayor of Rye.

Whereas one John Skiptone, an inhabitant of Rye, about a year since took unto his service Joane Skiptone, his sister, and hath received three pounds of our overseers for keeping her during her life, hath forced her from his service and denieth her any maintenance, whereby she is likely to become vagrant, and then we shall be forced to send her unto you to be kept and provided for. *Seal.*

1617, July 12.—Certificate by the Mayor and Jurats of Rye, of the good behaviour of Thomas Maxwell, a musician, an inhabitant of Rye, formerly an inhabitant of Battle, who desires to go to Middleborough in the Low Countries to visit his brother, John Maxwell, a merchant there, and to take with him John, son of the said John Maxwell, Oliver Sanders, his servant, Michael Borne, an apprentice, and Ambrose Drury, one of his company, with their musical instruments and to return again to Rye.

1618, August 31.—Bond, signed with the marks of several persons who "goe to Yermouth for the fishinge this present yere" promising to pay to the Corporation of Rye, "out of every boate" half a share towards the repair of the "owter jettye at Stronde which otherwise will shortly by the violence of the sea be utterly overthroune and cast awaye."

1618, October 31.—The Mayor and Jurats of Rye to the Lord Warden.

The aid given by him in times past towards the amendment of the decayed harbour of Rye, emboldens them to entreat his further help towards effecting such works for their harbour as are needful for the support of the town and so for "his Majesties service of sea fisshe," and for "the bringinge upp of many navigators and saylers, fitt for the common weale of the land. They have appointed "——— Bacon Esquire," Captain of Camber Castle, to solicit their cause with the Privy Council to prefer to the King a petition for the amendment of the harbour. *Copy.*

1618[–19], January 29.—The Mayor and Jurats of Rye to "Mr. John Frewen (Minister of the Word of God at Norithm) in London."

An assembly of the Mayor, Jurats and commonalty of Rye have approved of the petition which he proposes to address to the Lord Chancellor "for the makeinge of the way or causy at Newenden." *Copy.*

1618[–19], February 4. Gray's Inn.—James Thurbarne to the Mayor and Jurats of Rye.

"For my own part I know not how I have deserved any ill opinion amongst you except I may be blamed for being faithful and over careful of you and yours." Advises them as to the *Quo warranto* issued against them by the Attorney General. *Signed.*

1618[–19], February 11.—The Lords of the Council to the Lord Warden.

"The leavinge [levying] of forces and the preparations made at this tyme almoste throughout all the partes of E[urope is] a sufficient motive in reason of state to induce his Majestie to carrie the like vigilent and carefull eye to the saftie of his oune domynions and people upon

. . . . . . and events, by requiring a more effectuall and speedie supplie of such defectes as are found in the armed forces of this realme, then yett hath been performed in the tyme of peace, notwithstanding the many and often addresses from this Boarde in that behalfe." The Council therefore, by the King's special command, desire the Lord Warden to cause a general view and muster to be had, within his jurisdiction, both of horse and foot and a perfect enrolment to be made of all the numbers both trained and untrained. The trained bands are to be made perfect and complete "by supplyinge the roomes of such officers and other persons as are either deade, insufficient or otherwise wantinge, as well with those of the better qualitie as with such other freeholders, farmers, owners of land or househoulders as shalbe fitt for the same." In the second place, the Lord Warden is to give special order "that the armes of those forces be good and servisable, *videlicet:* for the foot, muskets and pickes, compleate and fullie furnished, without admittance of anie other unservisable armes which heretofore have been too frequentlye shewed and tollerated uppon the musters there." As the horse men "through conivancye and neglecte," are, for the most part, defective in arms and horses, it is, the Council consider, high time at length, after so many admonitions, that the troops of horse be filled up and made complete with all provisions and furniture. From this service no person is to excuse himself, but such as are known to be His Majestie's ordinary servants in Court, such of the clergy "as are appointed to finde Armes," the Lord Warden shall—according to lists received by him from the Bishop—cause it to be "shewed and disposed amongest the trayned bandes and troupes of horse as shalbe meete." Above all the Lord Warden is to require all persons, belonging either to the trained bands or troops of horse, to be ready at ten days warning. The Council has often reminded him that provision of powder, match, bullets, and carriages is needful for the safety of the Ports, yet so little care hath been taken thereof, as there is scarce any at all to be found. For redress of this deficiency, it is the King's commandment, that, according to the proportion formerly allotted in the late Queen's time, the Lord Warden shall cause provision to be made and kept in the accustomed places in the Ports, of such quantities of match and powder as are expressed at the foot of this letter [viz.: "At Sandwich; powder, one laste : match, 500 lbs. weighte. At Dover . . . . powder, demye laste : match, 250 lb. weighte "]. Lastly, the Council call the Lord Warden's attention to the repair of the beacons "which are altogether neglected and decayed"; these are to be amended, furnished with material for firing, and duly watched. *Copy.*

1618[–19], February 11. Dover.—William Ward, Mayor of Dover, to the Mayors, Bailiffs, and Jurats of the ports and towns of Folkeston, Hythe, Romney, Lydd, Rye, Winchelsea, Hastings, Pevensey, Seaford, and Tenterden.

The Lord Warden desires that "a speciall Guestling or meeting of the Cinque Portes and two ancient townes" should be held at New Romney on the 23rd of February "by eight of the clocke in the forenoon" to consider a letter from the Lords of the Council as to a petition which had been received by the king from "the marchaunts and owners of shippes trading the Straits and other places" complaining of the spoils committed by pirates, "especially those of Argier and Tunio [Tunis?] who have grown to an extraordinarie height and strength of robberie and have taken from the said petitioners in a few years past above 300 sayle of shipps with their lading and merchandize, besides the captivating of many hundred of his Majestie's subjectes." Towards the suppressing of those pirates, the merchants and ship-owners of London "have freely and with all allacritie" offered to raise 40,000*l.* The merchants of the Cinque Ports are required by the King to state what they will contribute towards this service which it is expected will not be less than 200*li.* in money for the two years next to come, one half of this sum is to be in readiness by the 18th of April next "at the farthest," because the King is resolved that this service shall be undertaken this summer. It is hoped that all [*i.e.* all the inhabitants] of the Ports will contribute something, "other wyse it will be a verie small summe that can be rared (*sic*) from the marchantes and owners of shippes of the Ports, which are now growen to be very few in number in respecte of the little trade there—the citizens and marchantes of London ingrossing all." Concludes "You see what [it] is his Lordshippe requireth by his said lettres, and therefore I pray you lett those that shall comme from you be prepared accordingly." *Copy.*

1618[–19], February 23.—Minute of the proceedings at a Guestling held at Romney.

On consideration of the letter addressed by the Lord Warden's direction to the officers of the Ports, concerning pirates, the assembly grants the sum of 200 marks towards the service in question, the first 100 marks to be ready by the following 1st of April and the other during the next year. The said sum is "to be levied by way of shipping, viz:—22*s.* a shipp"; any town failing to send its portion is to forfeit double, to the use of the Ports and their members. It is also agreed that "a lettre be directed from this house to our Lord Warden in excuse of this small contribution, which falleth out by reason of the small number of owners and merchauntes in the Ports by meanes of their restraint of trading by divers companies of merchauntes incorporated, and likewise by want of harbours and havens." The letter is to be delivered by the Mayors of Dover and Romney and Mr. Ruck of Sandwich "who are desired to second the cause in their discretion"; 6*s.* a day each is to be allowed them, with 20*s.* additional to the Mayor of Dover for his horse hire, afterwards "in his chamber, because of his unwillingness to goe to London for so small allowance, by certain of the Mayors and others, it was made up the full of fortie shillinges, over and above 6*s.* a day". A statement showing the sum to be contributed by each town follows. *Copy.*

1618[–19], February 23, Romney.—The Mayors, Bailiffs, Jurats, and Commons of the Cinque Ports, two ancient towns, and their members to the Lord Warden.

In accordance with his request, relative to the extermination of piracy, they have enquired "what number of inhabitants and owners of shipps trading to or neere the Straytes are resident within the Cinque Portes." They find only one ship. She belongs to Dover, and is not above 50 (?) tons burthen, and is only freighted by two or three merchants of that town. All the residue of the ships of the Ports are of small burthen and only trade to Newcastle and the west of England with malt; some few are "passage boates," and employed for France, Holland, and Flanders. The writers, however, confess that of late "the masters and owners of diverse shippes of good burthen did inhabite within the said Portes, but for wante of trade and imployment there, were constrayned to settle themselves at London" where they have continual employment owing to the merchants of that city having of late been incorporated into several companies, thereby the merchants and other inhabitants of the Ports are "altogeather barred from that ordinary trade" formerly used. They continue :—" Yet not withstanding, out of the zeale and desyre we have to be helping unto soe worthy worke, we have agreed and most willinglye assent to contribute" to the charge mentioned in the Council's letter the sum of 200 marks "hoping that the merchants and owners of shipps of the said cittye of London wilbe as willinge and readye, upon occasion, to be helping unto us, if cause shall require." They ask the Lord Warden to urge their suit with the Council that they may as freely use "that trading within the Cinque Ports as auncientlye hath been accustomed, whereby the same Ports may be the better peopled" and the ancient number of ships for the King's service maintained. To obtain the Lord Warden's favour they have sent, as bearers of this letter Mr. William Ward, Mayor of Dover, Mr. Robert Wilcocke, Mayor of Romney, and Mr. Arthur Rucke, Jurat of Sandwich. *Copy*.

1618[-19], March 3. The Mayor and Jurats of Rye to the Lord Warden.

Once again they make known to him their "miserable poor estate" as "unto our only stay and refuge next under God and his Majestie." Owing to the decay of their harbour, and consequently of the fishing industry, a hundred of their fishermen are "ready to begg and starve;" many of them have forsaken the town, and "left their wives and children to a parish charge." The very few persons in trade, "of any abilitye to live," are so burdened by continual cesses and taxes that they are determined to leave the town. Thus the town, not long since of "good respect and importance" is likely soon—"if som gracious aspect shine not uppon it"—to be quite depopulated and abandoned. Of late by order of Council they have been "appointed unto that proportion of powder, lead [and] match, with carriages and mounting of ordinaunce," that in the late Queen's time "this toun was enjoyned unto," when "her Majestie's Ordinance was heere, which now is taken hence long since by commission." Their town was then in prosperity; but now their poverty is such that "though it be for that end and purpose wherein with willing harts, under his Majesty's and your honourable commaundment, wee are redy to spend our lives"—they pray that consideration may be had of their present state which they beg may be shown forth to this Council in order to obtain relief in respect of the proportion in question. *Copy*.

1618[-19], March 20. The Lord Warden to Mr. William Ward Mayor of Dover.

He has acquainted the Council with the Mayor's answer touching the contribution demanded towards the suppression of pirates, and has endeavoured to obtain the acceptance of his offer, but the Council will not abate their first demand. Encloses a letter he has received that evening from the Council, and hopes the Mayor will "not distast them in so small a mater." Begs he will communicate this enclosure to the other Ports. *Copy*.

Enclosure; 1618[-19], March 19. The Council to the Lord Warden. —"As your Lordship well knoweth the expidition now extended by his Majestie ageynst the pirates, which is assisted with the power and strength of six of his royal shipes, at his owen charge, hath not only relation to the benefit and advantage of London or any other parteckler place alon, as intumated by the letters from the saide Portes, but moveth especially from his Majesty's princely carre for the security of common trade which may be interrupted as well near [home?] as furder off, and for the saffty of his subjectes that haunt and frequent the seas by way of trafique and commerse, which hath been of late so infested by those sea rovers that the western portes of this realme have within this foure yeers lost neere four hundred sayle of shippinge." This being well known to those of the Cinque Ports "wee find it straunge that they should stick at so poore a thinge as a hundred poundes a year for two yeares for the making up of the contribution opon them, towards so worthy an enterprise." They cannot therefore abade "any one penny" of the assessment, and beg the Lord Warden to act accordingly. *Copy.*

1618[-19], March 22.—The Mayor and Jurats of Rye to William Ward, Esquire, Lieutenant of Dover Castle.

According to the order and decree made by the Guestling (held at Romney on the 24th of February last) concerning the payment of 200 marks towards the supression of piracy, they send by the bearer "for the five shipps that wee and the toune of Tenderden are charged to pay, towards the first payment"—*5l.* 10*s.* and 1*l.* more "towards the charges of presenting thereof" to the Lord Warden. They would have sent this money before, but waited for the payment by Tenderden of its share which they have not yet received. *Copy.*

1618-19. March 22. Dover Castle.—William Ward, Mayor of Dover] to [the Mayor and Jurats of Rye].

Has received the Lord Warden's letters requiring diligent execution of the Council's commands concerning the musters. Begs that "in those places where [there] be two bandes, that there, the sellected bande be compleated," and that rolls and certificates of the selected and general bands in every place, both of foot and horse—with their captains and officers and "distinctions" of each sort of arms and furniture, digested into good order and "faire written on parchment," each roll to be signed by the Captain of the band—be sent into the office of Dover Castle not later than the following 3rd of April, "together with true notes of your carriadges, and how your proportions of powder, shott and match, as well for the generall store of each place, as allso for each private man's provision, shall be by that time supplied."

Endorsed—

Officers of the general band.

Mr. Richard Gilbridg	Captain
Mr. John Pallmer	Lieutenant
Mr. Stephen Frencham	Engign
Mr. Anthony Worton	Marshall
Mr. Lansdall	Clarke
John Chestor Emanuell Dugard John Rider Nathaniell Holmes Peeter Bennett Francis Daniell William Lukas	Serjantes
John Rendell	Surgeon
John Skinner John Bredgat	Droms
Thomas Maxwell	Fife

The 4:
Thomas Mellow
Thomas Ashbye
Thomas Radforde.
Francis Homwod.

1619, May 1. Northiam.—John Frewen to the Mayor and Jurats of Rye.

Approves of their petition. Purposes to begin his journey on Monday about 9 or 10 in the forenoon "and to make a beginning of this busines upon Wednesday," therefore begs that the petition be sent back to him concluding with a request of a grant of letters patent "unto the sayd parishes or one of them" of licence to collect "good willes and benevolences" in London, Westminster, the boroughs and liberties adjoining and the counties of Kent, Essex, Middlesex, Sussex, and Surrey with the cities of Canterbury and Rochester and the Cinque Ports, towards effecting "so publick and necessary a worke." Prays, also, that he may receive without delay "the promised dorser of fish," and he trusts by the success of his pains to give a good account of the fit bestowing of it. *Seal.*

Enclosure.

Petition of the Mayor and Jurats of Rye to the Lord Chancellor setting forth that there "hath beene antiently a certayne wall or causeway raysed cross (*sic*) the levill of Newenden, lying in the parish of Newenden in the countie of Kent, and Northiam in the countie of Sussex, beinge a common passage betweene both the said counties and the usuall roade waye and thoroughfare betweene the Citye of London and the toune of Rye." And whereas the town of Rye has ever been, and is, very useful in serving with sea-fish both the neighbourhood, the king's court, and the City of London, and also the neighbourhood with salt, corn, and grain, especially "in tyme of dearth," which is brought from parts beyond the seas. The said causeway is much more overflowed than formerly, particularly in winter time, and much decayed by long standing and force of the weather and is consequently dangerous to all persons using it, including the many who daily arrive at Rye from abroad and have no other way by which to go to London or places beyond. All this tends to the decay of navigation, and of late years the "fisher boats" of Rye have fallen in number from forty to sixteen or eighteen, whilst merchant ships are "utterlie gone away." The Commissioners of Sewers "ymportune the said parishes of Newenden and Northiam forthwithe and speedilie" to repair the said causeway. The Petitioners think the necessary charge (400*li.* at the least) too great for the said parishes to bear, and they therefore pray—[ends abruptly without setting out the nature of the prayer]. *Copy.*

1619, August 6, Dover Castle.—Richard Marshe to the Mayors, Jurats, &c. of the Cinque Ports.

The Lord Warden has found it needful to hold courts of Admiralty within the Ports, yet he thinks that resort to each particular town, by his Lieutenant, Deputy, or officers, to hold those courts, "would draw very great and excessive charges uppon the inhabitants;" to ease them of such he has decided that one general court of Admiralty should be held at Dover, to which place every Port and ancient town shall send four—and "every other town corporate" two—inhabitants, "beinge marryners, merchants, or other persons of the best sufficiencie." Such persons being assembled, to be empannelled and sworn to enquire upon all matters concerning the Admiralty. The Lord Warden therefore appoints a court to be held at Dover "at the publique place called the Mount uppon the shore of the sea there" on the following 19th of August at 8 o'clock in the morning. *Copy.*

Appended is "A Schedule conteyning the nomber of persons required to appeare for each towne and place at the court of Admyraltie mentioned."

East Portes.		West Portes.	
Dover	4	Folkestone	2
Ringeswould and Kingesdoune	2	Hithe	4
St. Peters in the Isle of Thanet	2	Newe Romeney	4
St. John and Margate	2	Lydd	2
Burchington	2	Dengemershe	2
Sandwich	4	Tenderden Reading and Smalled	2
Deale	2	Rye	4
Walmer	2	Winchelsey	4
Ramsgate	2	Hastinges	4
Brightlingsea in Essex	2	Pevensea	2
Fordwich	2	Seaford	2
Feversham	2		

1619, October 9.—An account of a dispute between the Bailiffs of the Ports and the Bailiffs of Yarmouth as to the right of the former to meddle with the conduct of the free fair at Yarmouth.

1619, December 19.—" Phillip Lane."—Lord Zouche to the Mayor and Jurats of Rye.

Hearing your Town clerk is dangerously sick and not likely to recover I pray you admit the bearer Mr. Anthony Tuttisham, the younger, to discharge the office, if it become vacant. *Signed.*

1619[-20], January 20.—"Phillippe Lane." Lord Zouch to Mr. William Ward, Mayor of Dover.

I am given to understand that Sir Edward Bainton and Mr. Duns are purposed to cross the sea to fight. These are to require you to make search to apprehend the said persons. *Copy.*

1620, November 20.—William Angell to the Mayor, Jurats, and Commons of Rye.

Requesting them to choose his son, John Angell as one of their burgesses for the Parliament. *Signed.*

1620, November 28.—London. William Angell to the Mayor and Jurats of Rye.

I have in your behalf attended my Lord Warden about the French fishers and he is pleased to grant his letters, as well to Hastings as to your town, that some course may be taken that the said French may be brought in, boats, nets, and men, and kept in custody until his Lordship be certified thereof that further order may be made by his Honour, as hereafter they shall not dare to fish without special license. His Lordship well knowing my son, has written unto your town on his behalf to make him one of your burgesses, which altogether is in your own choice.

RYE MSS.

His Honour seemed very willing to have given him one of his particular places in the Ports had he not been so exceedingly pressed by great personages for them, because saith he "that both I and my son will endeavour together for the good of the town and that two is better than one." *Seal of Arms.*

1620, November 28. Clerkenwell.—Lord Zouch to the Mayor Jurats, and Commonalty of Rye.

Requesting them to elect the son of Mr. Angell, his Majesty's fishmonger, as burgess of their town for Parliament. *Signed. Seal of Arms.*

1620, December 1. Whitehall.—T. Edmondes to the Mayor, Jurats and Commonalty of Rye.

Requesting their favour on behalf of Mr. John Angell, to elect him one of their burgesses for the Parliament. *Seal of Arms.*

1620, December 2. Whitehall.—The Duke of Lennox to the Mayor Jurats and Commons of Rye.

Requesting their favour on behalf of Mr. John Angell, one of his Majesty's pensioners in ordinary, to elect him one of their burgesses for the Parliament. *Seal of Arms.*

1620, December 4. Tenterden.—Samuel Short to the Mayor, Jurats, and Commonalty of Rye.

Offering his services as a burgess to Parliament for the town of Rye. *Seal of Arms.*

1620, December 18. Clerkenwell.—Lord Zouch to the Mayor Jurats and Commonalty of Rye.

Whereas you have ever used, on the commendation of the Lord Warden, to elect one of the burgesses you are to choose for the Parliament, it hath been my care to find out such a sufficient gentleman as I thought would be forward, not only to advance the good of the Ports in general, but ready to do and stand for the good of your town in particular, his name is Mr. Emannuell Gifford, who (though peradventure not well known to you) is my ancient acquaintance. I think it needless for him to be sworn a freeman of your town. *Signed. Seal broken.*

1620, December 23.—The Mayor, Jurats and Commons of Rye [to William Angell].

According to your request we have chosen Mr. John Angell for one of our burgesses for the Parliament.

1620, December 25.—William Angell to the Mayor Jurats and Commons of Rye.

This present Christmas day about nine of the clock I received your most loving letter, wherein I understand you have made my son John Angell one of your burgesses for the Parliament, by which I perceive your loves, and return you many thanks. *Seal.*

1620[-1], February 9. London.—John Angell to the Mayor, Jurats, and Commons of Ryc.

Promising to forward their cause in Parliament concerning their haven and the unlawful fishing of the French. *Seal.*

1620[-1], February 21. London.—Emanuell Giffard to the Mayor Jurats and Commonalty of Rye.

Your free choice of me to be one of your Barons for the Parliament, and your admittance of me to be one of your corporation have so prepared my affection to all service in token of true and hearty thankfulness. God be thanked, we have a happy beginning of our Parliament and I hope the end will be suitable, and so great is the disposition of our whole House to do all the good we may, as it is not to be doubted but all good motions will be well entertained and speed well. *Seal of arms.*

1620[-1], February 27.—The Mayor and Jurats of Rye [to the Lord Warden].

We have acquainted the fishermen who took the French fishers of your Honour's bountiful gift bestowed upon them, to encourage them to take pains to take more of them. *Draft.*

1620[-1], March 3.—Lord Zouch, the Lord Warden, to Francis Wilford, Lieutenant of Dover Castle.

"I have received commandment from the Lords of the Higher House of Parliament for the present stay and apprehension of Sir Giles Mompesonne, knight, who, beinge accused for divers great offences, is fled from the custody of a sergeant to whom he was commytted. These are therefore strictly to will and require you to make all speedy and diligent hast in sendinge to all places, portes, and creekes within my government for the present apprehending and staying of the said Sir Giles Momepesonne if he shall come into any part of my jurisdiction, either to hide himself or to be transported beyond the seas."

Postscript.—"A discription of Sir Giles Momepesonne. He is a litle man of a black swart complection with a litle black beard and of the age of about fortie yeares."

1621, April 3.—The Mayor and Jurats of Dover to [the Mayor and Jurats of Rye].

"Letters were lately addressed hither from the right worshipful and our verie lovinge freind Sir Richard Young, knight, one of the Barons of the Parliament for this port, of the date of the 29th of the last moneth, whereby he signified that uppon the same daye the whole committee of so many of the Parliament house as were then in towne being commanded then to meete, to fitt and prepare matters for their next meetinge, fell into consideration of free trade, and thereuppon motion was made that the merchantes dwellinge in the Cinque Portes were much restrayned, contrary to their charter, in the coarse of their tradinge by particular societies in London, whereuppon it was ordered that on Twesdaye the afternoone next after Loe Sunday in the Exchequer Chamber at Westminster, the committees are pleased to hear what can be said of the Portes or any other to advance the libertie of free trade, and therefore he did thinke it verie necessary that some particuler persons which well understand the circumstances of this busines should be sent from Dovor and Sandwich and from other townes in that government which have trading to attend the commyttees at that tyme, bringing with them the old chartre by which we have freedome of trade togither with all other instructions and papers as may conduce and be of use to obteine libertie of trade.

And forasmuch as much tyme, labor and mony hath allready be[en] spent in the prosecution of this suit (as is well known unto you) we have taken consideration of the same lettres and, (as thereby is required) did communicate this busines to our loving brethren the Maior and Jurates of Sandwich and they and wee have thereupon resolved and given our consentes for the further followinge of the same suit uppon

RYE MSS.

assurance that if uppon this fitt occasion wee do not obteine our free trade, there wilbe little hoope hereafter to gaine it. And because wee are streightened in respect of the tyme appointed for hearinge as that wee could not send to you and receive your answer, wee have agreed that Mr. Rucke and Francis Raworth, town clerk of this towne, shall forthwith prepare themselves to attend the said Committees, being persons best acquainted in this cause having foremerlie followed the same, presuminge that you will not dislike of our election but that you will willinglie contribute to the charge, yet forasmuch as a busines of this nature will require best help that may be added to it in respect of the strong opposition that hath ben and is likelie to be, we think it verie meete, and our brethren of Sandwich desire, that you wilbe pleased to send one or more persons such as you thinke most meete, one of the west portes to joyne with the parties aforenamed in this suite who resolve and have agreed (if God so please) to meete in the middle ile of St. Paul's church, London, upon Sunday next ymediately after prayer there then to have communication of their meetinge and proceedinge on the next day to prepare for the daies work followinge, intending also in their jorney towardes London to have conference and to advise with Mr. Tharbanne upon the drawinge of the petition and otherwise as shall apperteine, it being wished that this day of attending the committees had ben appointed in the terme tyme where he might have stood us in greate stead in this suit."

1621, April 20. London.—Francis Raworth [to the Mayors, Bailiffs, and Jurats of the Cinque Ports ?].

Whereas it pleased you to appoint Mr. Rucke and me further to solicit our suit of free trade into all parts beyond the seas and for our free buying in Blackwell Hall in the City of London and elsewhere. And according to your directions in that behalf, we made our repair hither at the time prefixed and exhibited our petition for those two grievances, and by direction of Sandwich a third grief was therein inserted, which was to be free of prisages. The same petition was first read on Friday last in the afternoon before the grand committee, and then committed to a sub-committee who are pleased to hear us at large. The first will be opposed by the Merchant Adventurers who seek to keep all trade only to London and against them certain merchants of London, whom they call interlopers, oppose to have as free trade as they. The second grievance is for that we are forbidden to buy freely in Blackwell Hall in which we are likely to be opposed by the Lord Mayor and citizens of London. The third is to be free of prisage of our own proper wines for which we should venture, which is not denied us of such wines as we bring into the Ports but there is a special decree in the Exchequer against us, that we shall not hold this privelege for such wines as we shall discharge at London or other port. This privelege is very much opposed by Sir Francis Barnham, being Chief Butler of England, during the minority of Sir Thomas Waller's son, and he having many honourable friends in Parliament the obtaining thereof will be very difficult, and having had conference with Mr. Thurbane and Mr. Edwards of Faversham, they are of opinion we were better to leave out the third grievance so shall we speed better with the other two.

1621, August 28. Westminster.—The King to Lord Zouch, the Lord Warden.

"We have foremerlie directed our letters to our High Treasurer of England authorezing him to give order to all the officers of our portes to suffer any of our subjectes, that are willing to serve in the warrs of any prince or state in league or amytie with us, freely to passe thither without stay or molestation, wee havinge allwaies professed that indeferent and equall respect to all our frindes and allies as to leave our subjects therein to theire own liking and election, as wee have heretofore done in the warrs of Denmark and Sweden, of Poland, Venice, the United Provinces and divers others. Forasmuch as we are informed, that notwithstanding our said lettres and order thereuppon given by our Treasurer of England unto the severall portes, divers of our subjectes intending to serve our good brother the King of Spaine in his presente warres in the Low Countryes, and seekinge to transporte themselves thither at some of the Cinque Portes are stopped by our officers there for that they are not willinge to take the oath of supremacie and allegiance; it is not unknown unto us that for the most part such as shall offer their service on that side are not conformable to the religion professed in the Church of England and may therefore make difficultie to submitt themselves to that trial which other of our lovinge subjectes would not refuse; nevertheless our meaninge is not to make that equallitie which we professe to all other princes useles to our said good brother the King of Spaine, and that we professe to give libertie in shewe yt shalbe to none or litle in effect as to his service. Our will therefore and pleasure is that you shall give instantlie strict order unto the officers of our Cinque Portes that when any of our subjects shall repair thither to embark themselves for the partes beyond the seas to serve in the warres either [of] the said Kinge of Spaine or the States of the United Provinces or other prince or state in league or amytie with us, ye suffer them quietly to passe without exactinge from them any of the oathes aforesaid or without any other lett, trouble or contradiction of any person or persons whatsoever, unles any of them be persons against whom their may some other just cause of exception be knowne that may make them fitt to be restrained, especialle seeeng this libertie spareth them not from taking the oath at their retorne which is [to] them more necessarie in respect of the danger then at theire going out of the realme."

1622-[3], February 15. Barbican.—The Lord Warden to the Mayor and Jurats of Rye.

"Whereas it hath bene an auntient custome that the Lord Wardens of the Cinque Portes have ever used to have from your towne the choyse of the third fishe for his houshold provision, complaint is made to me that of late there hath not bene that forwardnes of respect given by the fishermen of your towne to such as I imploy to take upp the same for me, as hath bene used, and as I may bouldly say I have deserved. Wherefore I thought good hereby to give you this tymely notice that thoughe I shall not looke back to neglects past, yet I shall from henceforth expect (by your care) herein a reformation and to that end, I hereby will and requyre you to cause and commaund the fishermen of your towne to deliver unto my said officer such a proportion of fishe as hath bene used and att such reasonable rates as you shall thinke fitt, and if any shall refuse soe to doe, that you (on complaint made by my said officer) doe cause redresse therein, and if on your admonition any shall be soe obstinatt as to persist in his or their disobedience, I will that you send me a note of his or their names, and the manner of their contempt and neglect of me and my service." *Signed. Seal of arms.*

RYE MSS.

1623, October 24.—The Mayor and Jurats of Rye to Edward, Lord Zouch, Lord Warden.

Heretofore you were a principal means "for the setting upp of our lecture which now of late one Mr. Wittacre, curate unto Mr. Briant Twyne, our vicar, hath opposed of his owne authoritie, and will not suffer Mr. Warren, our lecturer, to goe into the church; wherefore we beseech your Lordshipp that you would be pleased to be a means that the lecture may still continue." *Draft.*

1623, October 29. The Mayor and Jurats of Rye to the Bishop of Chichester.

Upon their petition to the Archbishop of Canterbury they obtained his leave "for a lecture to be sett upp in our towne, and hath here continued the space of six years and upwards; which lecture of late Mr. Whitacre, curate unto our vicar, Mr. Twine, hath opposed. Of which thinge wee have thought good to certifie your Lordshipp, humbly besechinge you that so worthie a worke, so much conducing to the honour and glory of God, may not be suppressed, but by your Lordshipp's leave and approbation, may still continue. Yet we dislike not Mr. Whitacre for our curate, but desire his continuance here, for we hold him a sufficient preacher; who, beinge your Lordshipp's chaplaine, you can a great deale better judge of his learning than wee." *Copy.*

1623, December 29. London.—Sir William Twysden to the Mayor and Jurats of Rye.

"I cannot forget the old love which hath bene mutuall betweene your towne and myselfe as the many letters enterchanged betweene us can testifie; so also the good service done by my brother, Heneage Finch, when by me recommended, he was Burgesse for your towne in Parliament; and because the same affections remaine in mee I doe now write unto you againe not for any other but to entreate the same courtesie from you to be conferred upon meselfe in making me a Burgesse for your towne in this next Parliament; which kindnesse of yours shall both in the Parliament and out of it, with my best strenght and paines, make me endevour your good, and I hope as heretofore so still I shall be able to effect it." *Seal of Arms.*

[1623-4], January 12. Dover Castle.—The Lord Warden to the Mayor, Jurats and Common Council of Rye.

Nominating according to ancient custom Sir Edward Conway, the younger, as one of the representatives of Rye for the next parliament. *Signed. Seal of Arms.*

1623[-4.] January 14.—The Mayor and Jurats of Tenderden to the Mayor and Jurats of Rye.

Recommending the election of Samuel Short as member for Rye at the forthcoming parliamentary election.

1623[-4.] January 16. London.—William Angell to the Mayor, Jurats, Commons, and Freemen of Rye.

"It is but a small tyme since the last time of Parliament which you well know was short and without any acte passed therein, so as no man's service appeared what it was or would have beene unto the place he were Burgis of, to the great discontentment of those who aymed alltogether for the common good and the place they served, and as I conceave the very remembrance (besides their papers in their handes) of every theire instructions is still fresh and perfect. And now it pleaseth his Majesty to call another Parliament in February next for which you are to chuse Burgesses againe, and forasmuch as John Angell, my sonne, a freeman of you allready, was lately one the last time and then so well approved of by the whole house, I am confident thatt if you please to make him one in this (being alltogether devoted to your service) you shall surely find as good cause to thanke him for his endeavours as any other. It may be you are sued unto by many and such no doubt as would be worthy for the place, but seeing he was one before and no concluding act done, and being one without exception for his affection to you, lett me entreate and perswade your worthy freemen to consider you have begunne and made him a practiser for you in thatt honorable howse, leave him not now till he hath finished both his and your intended worke, which I doubt not of, and which not only myself but all my freindes will assist, and withall because your towne hath of all others moste neede of help. I desire when the time ys that you would send one to sollicite and prosecute as neede shall require and for your better ease and effectinge your busines I will entertaine him in my owne howse at bedd and board and every evening wee being alltogether may the better conferre and consider of the best way to doe you service." *Seal of Arms. Signed.*

Postscript. "I am entreated to write unto you thatt you would be pleased to make choise againe of Emanuell Jefford, who was the gentleman which my Lord Warden named unto you in the last and hee is allso desirous to doe you service in this Parliament, if againe by his Honor nominated unto you."

1623[-4], February 7. Theobalds.—Sir Edward Conwey to the Mayor, Jurats and Commonalty of Rye.

On the recommendation of Lord Zouch, made at his request, they have chosen the writer's son as their Burgess in the next parliament. They have, however, through his mistake in not sending the proper description of the candidate, elected his eldest son who is out of the Kingdom instead of his second son, Captain Thomas Conwey, who is with the writer. Begs that the return be amended. *Signed.*

1623[-4], February 24. Whitehall.—Sir Edward Conwey to the Mayor and Jurats of Rye.

"I take most thanckfully your favor shewen me in your choyce of my sonne Edward for one of your Barons for this Parlament. You shall dubbeliey ty me to you if you now choise this sonne which I have sent to you, and by me was at the first ment, but I take the falt upon myselfe. I will in eavery poynt be answerable to you for his care and dillegence in serving you, and whearin he shold be slack I will myselfe execute. Your buisnes left in my hands hear by Mr. Maior I have put in execution. I have drawne my Lord Admirall to joyne with me to the King soe that I doubt not but that you will have a good ende of it to your liking. If there be anything elce whearin you will command me eyther for your towne in generall, or yourselves in particular you shall eaver finde me with all ardency approove myselfe." *Seal of Arms.*

[1623-4], February 27. Dover Castle.—The Lord Warden to the Mayor and Jurats of Rye.

Not being acquainted "with any of Mr. Secretary Conwey's sonnes but this" [i.e. his eldest son, Edward], he recommended him for election as a Burgess of Rye, but the Secretary desired the election of his other son, Captain Thomas Conwey. A second writ has now arrived for the election of their "chiefe of Burgesses" and so he entreats them "to be as good they ment" and choose Captain Conwey, who he believes will give them "such a taste of his love and service" that they will "like well of him." *Signed. Seal of Arms.*

1623[–4], February 27.—The Mayor and Jurats of Winchelsea to the Mayors, Bailiffs and Jurats of Rye and the other Cinque Ports.

"Whereas many trobles controversies and debates have growne and fallen out amongst us the pore Corporation and inhabitants of the towne of Winchelsea by the disorderly and indirect course, carradge, and proceedinges of some willfull and headstronge persons rescidinge with us, who seekinge rather to please and satisfye their owne unruely passions then to doe anythinge for the furtherance or preservation of peace and tranquility, about the succession of the maioralty in this place, which though it was ordered by the right honourable the Lords of his Majesty's Prevy Counsell and the then Lord Warden, and since by a solleme decree ratified and confirmed by a generall consent of the wholl Corporation to be inviolably kept and observed for ever hereafter, and that there should not be any juratt or freeman sworne before they had subscribed to the allowance and mainteinance of the said decree, yet notwithstanding this soleme and solid decree and from soe high and eminent auctority, these fiery and turbulent spirits have wrunge, wrested, and perverted the true meaninge thereof to their owne imagination and idle construction, which appeareth to be noe lesse the sequell proovinge soe mischeevous. And therefore now to prevent and take away all occasions hereafter of any further trubles, vexations and unquietnes from ourselves and others, it hath pleased the right honourable our Lord Warden to commaund us to write unto you, our lovinge brethren, combarrons and freinds within all the Five Portes and the auntient towne of Rye to intreate your opinions, councell and advise in this busines of ours for the succession of the maioralty (for which our election is at hand) and as your worships shall advise us herein soe wee are to certefie unto his Lordship who in so noble and religious disposition and respect his Lordship hath to the maintenance of peace and quietnes, will take such order herein (that if it be possible) yet at the last a true peaceable goverment may be setled amonge us. By this decree of the succession of the maioralty (as by most of your worships it is not unknowne) the eldest juratt successively is to be chosen Maior yearely if there be no just cause or good reason first shewed to the then Lord Warden, and whereof his Lordship must approve and allow before there be any such proceedinge, contrary to the said decree of succession. And for that (as too lately wee have found by experience) by some colourable causes and reasons pretended and alleaged for the breach of the said decree, strong factions, much envye, hatred and malice ar crept in amongst us (and many have ignorantly suffered for the same) the better to prevent all future mischeeves in that kind (least wee may againe smart for it) we desire to have your worships opinions and to be resolved from you whether the eldest jurat (on whom the maioraltie by the decree of succession ought to be placed) by his discontinuance and now residency from this towne of Winchelsea, hath lost the benefitt of this decree of succession, yea or nay? And wee ar the rather imbouldened to move this question unto your worships for there is one Mr. William Channon, now eldest juratt, for the succession for the maioralty this years to come, who hath his abode farr distant from hence and from whence he hath discontinued these fower months at the least, neither hath he payed scott or lott or done any other duety to the towne or corporation. Now may it please your good worships, if wee shall strictly follow the bare letter of our said decree wee must then choose for our Maior the next yeare according to his seniority and whether he will come heither or noe before the election wee know not, neither [doth the] decree make any mention of resciancy or non resciancy of any juratt that shall soe have the maioralty by succession, and what confusion this may breed wee leave to your wise and judicious considerations. There is likewise one Mr. Danyell Tilden, one of our eldest juratts, who hath discontinued as longe as the other and paid as little scott and lott and done as little duety, and therefore the like question may be made of him, besides to skipp and leave out any of those elder jurats and choose the next jurats unto any of them in his senioreṫy wee ar in doubt for feare wee may erre (as some have done before us) in the one or the other. Our request therefore to your good worships is this, that you will be pleased by your opinions in writing (in some place of this paper) to advise us what wee shall doe in this cause that soe goinge on in a just and straight course orderly, wee may be assured from fallinge into any further inconveniences. And further wee intreat your worships' opinions in this one thing allso, whether any juratt or freeman forsaking this place and inhabiting in any other, doe not loose all theire benefitts or previledges of juratts or freemen, *ipso facto;* for wee ar a corporation and incorporatt body, and had need to have the members of this our body neer at hand to helpe the body, every member according to his place and use, and not to have the members disunited, cut off and severed soe farr from the body, or one member from the other whereby the body shall loose all the use and helpe of such members and soe grow weake and unable to helpe itselfe." *Copy.*

Reply to the above from Hastings dated the following day:—

"Our opinion and advise is that you observe inviolably the course injoyned by the Lords of the Counsell by successive election of your Mayor. And although this scruple be hatched by such turbulent heads favouring rather of faction then of a peaseable disposition, namely, that the bare letter of the Lords' order cannot be satisfied but by election of the senior jurate in succession, though non-resident, yet in our opinion the order ought to receive such benigne reasonable interpretation as may agree in equity and stand with the intent of the institutors of that order and law, otherwise the same intended for peace of your corporation may, by too nice inconstruction, be wrested to greater breach of the peace thereof then was before that order made. Wee ar of opinion therefore that they ought to be housholders and inhabitants at the election day and this accordeth with the opinion of the wholl Ports, at a brotherhood holden at Romney the 23rd of August, anno 19, Henry VIII, where it was decreed that the freemen of every election shall goe together and by the othe which they have taken at theire admittance to theire freedome, all favour love and dread layd assyde, shall elect, name and choose one jurate of the towne which shall be inhabitant and shall be one of the Maior's brethren and associate with him on the bench one yeare before the day of election, and such a one as you shall thinke most meetest and most able to exercise the office in the towne as the King's Leivetennant for the yeare following &c., which decree expoundeth the bare letter of the order in our opinion; for if an absent Maior not inhabiting in the towne be elected by common intendement (because for his non-residens he is not capable and cannot execut the office in person) the election is voyd, *ab initio,* and the old Maior must serve still, till a competent person be elected. Be pleased to read the decree for in our judgment it will give great [help] to clear this scruple. Wee ar allso of opinion that a jurate or freeman departing to inhabit out of the Ports *de jure* lose theire freedome and priviledge for the reasons alleadged by you unlesse of favor they be borne with in case they departe for awhile for theire earnest affaires or ease, intending in some reasonable time to returne againe and in the meanetime doe paie scott and lott and be liable to performe all offices and services as apperteyneth to theire place." *Copy.*

1623[-4], March 5. Battle.—Ro. Foster to the Mayor of Rye.

Has made, and sends, two drafts of an Act [concerning the Dungeness Light House]. "I have not expressed Mr. Lampley's interest, nor expressed lesse tyme to you, than for ever, for that, if you obteine this Act to passe, Mr. Lampley's interest will fale of itself, and for the present give him noe collour to oppose, or his friends to object, the King's interest; and yourselves (if you think for ever, to be too longe) may limit a shorter time . . . . . . I likewise wish you would make the Speaker as mutch yours, as you cann." *Seal, with Crest.*

Enclosures.

(1.) "The light at Dungen Nease was first projected about 12 yeares since by John Allen, a freeman of the ancient towne of Rye, one of the antient townes of the Cinque Portes, who did assaye to obteine this for the supply of the wants of the said towne, which John Allen wanting strength of frenndes to effect this suite, it was obteined by Sir Edward Howard and others and since transferred uppon Mr. Lampley.

The light is mainteined by the imposition of 1*d.* uppon the tunne of all such laded shipping as passe by the light and thereby receave a use and bennefitt by it.

That this light is needfull to be mainteined is proved for that the place is daungerous about it, that a shipp may be in 10 or 12 faddome water and in a quarter of an houres sale may runne uppon land, which would be an evitable danger in the night and dark weather if the light did not better direct the marriners. Besides experience showes that the steeple of Lyd, a towne neere by, doth unhappily present unto straungers uppon those seas, the forme of a sale of some tall shipp which hath binn a meanes oftentimes towards night to incourage marriners to steere their course confidently that way, the rather because it is all low land neere the said steeple which seems as sea afarr off, whereby many shipps have suddenly out of their false supposition of this sea and saile and deepe sounding neere the land when night hath come on, runn on ground and perished, which dangerous mistake this light doth prevent. And likewise before the erection of this light there were many and often shipwracks uppon those coastes, but since that time there hath perished but 2 ships and that as it is thought by the ill maintenance of the light, which is necessarie to be mainteined by a fier and not by candle.

Now that this light is a publick good and is mainteined by a publicke chardge it is fitter to be comitted to the chardge and use of a publicke place then a private, and if so, then to the towne of Rye before any place, for these reasons.

1. The light being first devised by the said Allen, a freeman of Rye, and erected within seaven miles of Rye and neere unto there viewe they will better oversee the sufficient maintenance of it then a private

man who trusts others to guide the light and cannott knowe of there negligence but by report, being absent from it.

2. This light is so good a guide into the harbour of Rye, which harbour, by the proffitt of this light, God may please to restore as fully as ever it was, that it will alwaies behoufe the towne of Rye as well for there owne good as the publicke good to have a dilligent and vigilant care over this chardge.

3. The towne of Rye hath binn of soe greate consequence to this State that it hath supplied his Majesty's howse and this parte of the kingdome with more plenty and store of fish then any two townes of England. It hath had such trade and traffick that it hath paid 2000*l.* a yeare custome in Queene Elizabeth's time. It hath binn a towne peopled with a greate number of able and true subjects and soe strongly furnished with shipping and marriners as uppon all occasions they have binn able to doe and have done the King and kingdome greater service then any of the Ports and is also soe convenient a harbour for releefe of succor of shippes in time of fowle wether as well of our owne nation as straungers, and likewise is the convenientest towne of England for passage into the harte of Fraunce, but of late yeares the harbour is much swarved with sand which the sea with fearce windes brings in for want of a sufficient fresh to drive it back to sea, by which meanes the towne is impoverished for want of trade and unpeopled, there being a hundred howses unhabited, there trade and shipping is decayed, to the releeving of which harbour they have not only disbursed much money out of there private purses but likewise soulde the towne landes, and now wanting meanes to proceede further in this good and hopefull worke, if the said light might be as fully confirmed to the said towne of Rye by Act of Parliament and they receave the proffitts thereof soe fully as Mr. Lampley doth, it will not only fully recover there harbour and thereby restore them to there auntient state and course of trading but also incourage many to inhabite the towne who now dayly fly from it by reason of the greate chardg the towne is at for the maintenance of the jetties, keyes, groines and sea walles. The which, yea even the towne itselfe, they will not be able to mainteine unlesse they be supplied by the benefitt of this light or some other chardge raised upon the commonwealth.

That the recovery of this harbour is feasable it plainly appeareth by the experience they have made of a small indraft and sluce which they finde hath donne such reall good that if they were enabled to undergoe the chardge of making and erecting more of such sluces aad indraftes they should undoubtedly sufficiently recover there harbour according to the judgment of the Commissioners of Sewers and all experienced seamen that have viewed it."

(2.) Draft of same with the following additional paragraph.

"Dunger Nease begineth at the mouth or entrance of the harbor of Rye and runeth alonge from thence out into the sea by the space of six or seven miles, beinge a verye dangerous place for shippinge passinge by everye waye whearupon many ships of great worth hath perished. For saufgard thearfor of all men it was devised by the towne of Rye and put in pracktise by John Allen to create (*sic*) a light on the utmost poynt thearof whear the light now standeth."

(3) "An Acte for the mainteininge of a fier light at the Dungen Nease and the regaininge of the harbour at Rie and repaire of the said towne.

"Maie it please your Most Sacred Majestie your ever faithfull and loyall subjects the Maior and Jurates of your Highnes towne and porte

RYE MSS.

of Rie in your Countie of Sussex doe humbly shewe your most excellent Majestie that whereas the said towne and harbour of Rye is one of the auncient townes of the Cinque Portes and hath binne of great consequence to this State both for the convenient scituation thereof for trade and greate provision of fishe, it havinge supplied your Majesty's howshold, the Cittie of London and the south easterne partes of this kingdome with more store of fishe then anie other sea towne uppon the said coaste, and the trade of traffique heretofore soe greate in the said towne as that in the raigne of the late Queene Elizabeth the yearlie custome of the said towne amounted to two thowsand pounds and upwards and was so strongly furnished with shipping and marrinners as uppon all occasions the said towne hath done the Kings of this realme as great good service as any of the other Portes. And the said harbour hath binne heretofore a greate releife and succour as well to our owne nation as straungers in time of stormes and fowle weather there beinge noe other safe roade or harbour for shippes to lie in betwixte the harbour of Portsmouthe and the Thames mouth, and the said towne is the most convenientest port of England for the passag into the harte of Fraunce. And of late years the said towne hath furnished to sea thirtie fisherboats and upwards manned with above fower hundred men and youth who have proved excellent marrinors and profittable men for this kingdome. Which said harbour of Rye is of late yeares much swarved upp with sand brought in by violence of wind for want of sufficient freshe to drive it backe to sea and is become exceedinge daungerous for shippes to come in, especially in the eveninge and darke weather, which danger is increased by the steeple of the church of Lidd, a towne nere by, which unhappily presents to straingers uppon these seas the forme of the sale of some toll shipp, and the land neere the said steeple beinge all lowe seemes a sea afarr of, whereby many marrinors having binne incouredged to steer theire courses that waye have by that daungerous mistake runn aground and perished, by reason whereof the trade and fishinge of the said towne is much decayed, the inhabitants impoverished, and the towne itself much depopulated, the shipping of the said towne, seafareing men and marranors muche deminished and many shipps uppon the said coastes for want of a sufficient harbour in tyme of stormes have perished. The restoringe of which said towne to the former prosperitie, and regaining of the said harbour, and preventinge the perishinge of shipps passing that waye, and safetie of such as shall in tyme of storme come into the said harbour may happily be effected by erectinge a convenient fier light at the dangerous passages neer the mouth of the said harbour commonly called Dungen Nease which might direct the seamen in cominge into the said harbour, and meanes raised for the openinge and preservinge the said haven by a contribution of such shipps as come in or passe by the same and may take benifitt thereof. May it therefore please your excellent Majestie that it may be enacted by your Majestie, the Lords Spirituall and Temporall and the Commons in this present Parliament assembled, and by the authority of the same that a convenient lighthouse and beacon or a stone worke with a fier light therein or thereuppon, be made, erected and mentioned (*sic*) at or neare the said place called the Dungen Nease being the mouthe of the said haven that thereby the shipps and vessels may passe with safetie as well by night as by day. And for the defrayinge of the necessary charges and continuall maintenance of the same, that it may be inacted by the authoritie aforesaid that there shall be collected and taken of and for every shippe that shall passe that waye, one pennie for every tunn outwards bound and one pennie for every tunne homeward bound, that is to saie, of the marchants an halfe penny and of the owner of the shipps, hoy or barke an halfe penny. And of such straingers as shall happen to passe thereby after the like rate as they shall putt into any port or harbour, allthough they do not unload and discharge any goodes there. And that for the erecting and continuance of the said lighthouse and beacon with a fierlight therein, and for the scouringe of the said harbour, that your Majestie would be pleased it might allso be . . . . . . by the authoritie aforesaid, they the said Maier and jurates for the time being of the said towne and port of Rie and theire successors for ever hereafter shall and may have free liberty, lycence power and authority from henceforth to make, build, erect, sett upp, continue, renewe and mainteyne, or cause to be builded, erected, sett upp, continued, renewed and mainteined in such place and plases of the sea-shores and uplands neere the sea coastes or free land of the sea, at, uppon or neere the entrance of the said harbour or place, commonly called the Dungen Nease, as to them shall seeme most needful and requisite, a convenient lighthouse and beacon or stone worke with a light of fier or coales to be continuallye burninge therein in the night season, whereby seafaringe men and passengers may take notice of the said daingers, and soe avoid and escape them and the shipps the better come to theire porte without perill. And allso that theie the said Maior and Jurats and theire successors may have, hold, exercise and enjoy the said libertie licence power and authoritie in as large and ample manner and forme and to all intents and purposes as the Maisters of the howse at Deptford Strond in the County of Kent or any other person or persons anie the like liberties, licences, power and authorities now have hold, or enjoy or may or might have, hold or enjoy in any other place or places within this your Highnes' realme of England. And that the said Maior and Jurates of the said towne and porte of Rie and theire successors may have and enjoy to them and theire successors for and towards the defray of theire said charges in erectinge, setting upp, continuinge, renewinge and mainteyninge the said lighthowse, beacon, or stone worke and keepinge the said fier light in or uppon the same, as allso for and towardes the cleansinge, scouring and newe making of the said harbour the said penny for every tunn soe to be collected and taken of every shipp, hoy and barke that shall passe that waye as aforesaid. And that it may alsoe be enacted by the authority aforesaid that all and every the customers, collectors and controwlers and all other the officers of the Customes of your Majestie, your heires and successors now being or which for the time being shall be in your Majesty's porte of London and in all and every other portes, harbours, roades and places within this your Highnes' realme of England to whome and where it shall or may apperteine, that they or some of them from time to time and at all times hereafter before such time as they or any of them doe give any cockett or other discharg, doe collect and receive the said contribution as well of all and every such marchants and straingers as of all and every such shipp, hoy or barke belonging to any marchant or stranger as shall arive or anchor within the Porte of London or any other the portes, harbours, roades and places within the realme of England. And that they and every of them doe and shall yeild upp and make due accompts and paiements of all and every such contributions some and somes of mony as by them everie and anie of them shall be soe collected and resceived from time to time to the said Maior and Jurates of the said towne and poarte of Rie to be by them the said Maior and Jurates and theire successors received and reteined by the said Maior and Jurates and

RYE MSS.

theire successors to the proper use and behoofe of the said towne and porte and for and in respect of theire charges in erectinge and mainteyninge the said lighthouse, beacon or stone worke and fier lighte to the use and purpose hereinbefore mentioned without any accompt or other thinge therefore or for anie parte thereof by them the said Maior and Jurates and theire successors therefore to be yeilded, made or given."

[1624, March.]—The Mayor and Jurats of Rye to the Lord Warden.

They think it their duty to tell him of the Bill they have preferred in Parliament for obtaining "the benefit that is made by the light that is erected and sett upp at Dungeon Neasse beinge at the entrance and mouthe of our harbour." They ask the Lord Warden's approval of their scheme. There have lately come to dwell in Rye "Mr. Abington and his wife, with his sonne and daughter, who are papists." Mr. Abington, they are informed, "was questioned in the treason of the gunpouder plott" and "nott yet cleared." They ask for instructions, if Mr. Abington and his family shall be suffered to remain in the town "for we desire not the company of any of that religion, if possibly wee may lawfully avoid them." They are sorry the Lord Warden has been lately often troubled "with so many complaints made unto you about the difference of our Ministers, for wee have had of late much controversie and devision between those that take Mr. Warren's parte, and others that are for Mr. Whitacre, to the greate disturbance and discredit of our town." They have bound some persons over to appear at the Sessions, and would have proceeded against others "where it not in such cases as perteine to the spirtuall Court, as wee take it." *Copy.*

1624, April 14. Dover Castle.—The Lord Warden to the Mayors, Bailiffs and others of the Cinque Ports.

It is thought necessary that the "forces and bands" within the Ports should be forthwith prepared for the general muster about to be made and due provision of powder and shot laid in. The Mayors, Bailiffs, and others are, therefore, required, on certain days, to bring before Anthony Hill "our muster master," all such forces to be by him "trayned, instructed, exercised and disciplined to use theire armes and weapons soe as at the ensuing musters they may be found able and prepared." Former muster rolls to be produced. *Copy.*

1624, April 29. Whitehall.—The Lords of the Council to the Lord Warden.

"Whereas his Majestie havinge taken into serious consideration the present estate of the Kingdome of Ireland, doth in his princely wisdome observe how great the quiet thereof and saftie of his loving subjects there inhabiting may be troubled and endagened (*sic*) especially in these doubtfull tymes, by those Irish, who beinge of turbulent spirit and ill affected in religion and otherwise, have been or are imployed in the service of forraine princes. Wee do therefore pray and require your Lordship by his Majesties express command to take present and effectual order that whatsoever Irish shall arrive in any of the Cinque Ports from any port beyond the seas, the magistrate of the place shall examine them, from whome they came, of what conditions they are, where they have spent their time and wither they intend to goe, and, withall, minister unto them the oath of allegaunce; and if they refuse to take the same, they shall then send them up hither in safe custody to be further examined and proceeded with as we shall find cause." *Copy.*

1624, April 30.—The Mayor and Jurats of Rye to the Lord Warden.

That day four fishermen of Rye, saw "to theire great greife" six "English traulers" fishing for "place" [plaice] within two leagues of the town in the usual fishing place. On the approach of the Rye men those in the trawlers "shot off twenty muskets of purpose to affrighte and terrifie them." The Mayor and Jurats request the Lord Warden's attention to the matter, "for the good of our poore town; for, if the travelers [trawlers?] be suffered in that place to traul, taking all the fishe, and our men labouring in vaine with tramell nettes, as they are every yeare more and more emporeshed [impoverished?], in short tyme the trade of fishing here wilbe utterly overthrowne." *Copy.*

1624, May 6.—The Mayor and Jurats of Rye to John Angell.

Thanking him for his attention to the Town's business in Parliament. "For the moving of the House, touching our sute, wee leave it to such a fitt and convenient tyme as in your judgment and discrecion shall seame most likely and avayalable . . . . for you, beinge continually present in the House, know the best opportunity for such a purpose. Concerning Mr. Bullocke, who saith that he was the first projecter of the Light [at Dungeness], it is easilie to be proved that John Allen, before ever Mr. Bullock knew of it, acquainted our Corporation with it, and moved often tymes the Corporation to sue for it." *Copy.*

Note.—On the fly sheet is the draft of a letter addressed by the Mayor and Jurats to "Mr. John Davies," a former inhabitant of Rye. They propose to prefer a bill in parliament for "obteyning for our toune the light at Dungen-Neasse, beinge more requisite to be granted to publicke use then a private." They therefore desire him to be their "friend" to the Trinity House, not to oppose the town therein "but rather helpe us that the benefit received by the said lights may be employed about the amending of our harbour."

1624, May 20. London.—John Angell to the Mayor and Jurats of Rye.

"The pattent for Dungen Neasse light hath beine in the House this month, and hath had severall hearings by Committee, but is not yett determined, but Fryday next is appointed to the Pattentees to make further defence of theire light by Councell. Now, after that the House hath determined theire right, then will be the time for us to make our request by bill, as I conceave, for certeinly the House will either take the pattent quite away from Mr. Lumley, or else soe moderate the imposition that he will be willing, for a small recompence, to yeeld his rights. But truly the businesses that are in the house at this time are of soe great importance and highe a nature, that these more ordinarie businesses are putt off from time to time and infinitly delayed, but I make noe question this Parlament will be of soe long a continuance that wee shall have fitt and leisurable time to effect our desires for you. I desire that you would strengthen me with some arguments against one Bullocke who intends, as I heare, to laye clayme likewise to this Light as the first projecter, which (as I take it) was John Allen." The writer will, however, pursue a different course if the Mayor and Jurats think proper. Sickness has lately made him "an ill member to the House and a bad servant to you."

1624, July 19.—The Mayor and Jurats of Rye to Captain John Halsey.

Thanking him for the gift of a house to be used as the house of correction.

1624, August 13.—The Mayor and Jurats of Rye to the Archbishop of Canterbury.

We have been again sued unto by a poor woman since our last letter addressed to your grace about poor captives, to certify unto you that she hath a son of hers in Turkey, one Thomas Grenaway, who being in a ship of Plymouth was taken by the Turks some three years since and not able to endure the great and cruel slavery, he has turned as she is informed to their religion. We beseech you that the said Thomas Grenaway may be remembered among such as are to be ransomed. *Draft.*

1624, November 28. Newmarket.—Secretary Conway to the Lieutenant of Dover Castle.

"His Majestie hath had information of a foule murther comytted upon the Duke of Croy in his own house at Bruxelles, and besides the intercescion that hath ben made to his Majestie for the discovering and apprehending the offender, in case he repaire into this kingdome, his Majestie, in detestation of so foule a fact and for the especiall estimation he had for the Noble Duke, hath ben graciously pleased to command me to give you direction in his name to cause speciall notice to be taken of all such strangers as shall land in any of the Cinque Portes or theire members, and to cause those that are any way suspicious (wherein you may uppon all occasions take the advice and direction of Monsr. Van Mal, agent for the Archduchesse) to be strictly examyned, and such other meanes used as your wisdome and discretion may direct for the finding out and apprehendinge that murtherer." *Copy.*

1624, December 22. Wallingford House.—The Duke of Buckingham to Sir John John Hippeslye.

Ordering the stay of several vessels laden with Newfoundland fish bound for Spain and Portugal. *Copy.*

1624[-5], March 12.—The Mayor and Jurats of Rye to the Masters of the Trinity House.

We are requested by the bearers John Dugard and Thomas Martin, masters of barques which were employed in his Majesty's service for the transporting of the soldiers into the Low Countries, to write to you that they may have their pay having performed the service with credit as appears by the testimonial of the Captains. *Draft.*

1625, March 27. Wallingford.—The Duke of Buckingham to Sir John Hippisley.

"These are to will and require you forthwith on sight hereof to cause good watch to be kept as well at all havens, portes, and creeks, as all other places which you shall thinke fitt or where watches have used to be kept within my government of the Cinque Portes on such importunat occasions as now ar happened, and to cause that at least double watches and wardes to be kept as well in Dover Castle as all other his Majesties fortes and castles within the jurisdiction of the Cinque Portes."

1625, **March** 27. Theobalds.—The Duke of Buckingham to Sir John Hippisley, Lieutenant of Dover Castle.

"These are to will and require you forthwith to cause that all the portes and havens within my government be shutt up soe as noe barke, boate, nor other vessell be suffred to goe forth of any of them untill you shall receive further dirrections to the contrary."

1625, April 1. Dover Castle.—Sir John Hippisley [to the Mayor and Jurats of Rye].

Discharging the restraint of the passage of all ships and vessels out of any haven or creek of the Cinque Ports. *Signed.*

1625, April 1. Dorset House.—The Earl of Dorset to the Mayor and Jurats of Rye.

Recommending as their burgess to Parliament, Captain John Sackeville, his dear kinsman. *Signed and Seal.*

1625, April 3. Clerkenwell.—[Sir?] James Ley to the Mayor, Aldermen and Commonalty of Rye.

Recommending them to re-elect Emmanuel Giffard as their burgess to Parliament. *Signed and Seal of Arms.*

1625, April 9. London.—John Angel to the Mayor, Jurats and Freemen of Rye.

Asking that they will again accept him as a burgess to Parliament. *Seal broken.*

1625, April 11. Whitehall.—The Duke of Buckingham to the Mayor and Jurats of Rye.

Recommending Sir John Franklin as burgess to Parliament for their town. *Signed and Seal of Arms.*

1625, April 11. Whitehall.—The Duke of Buckingham to the Mayor and Jurats of Rye.

Recommending Thomas Fotherley, his servant, as one of their burgesses to Parliament. *Signed and Seal of Arms.*

1625, April 11. Savoy.—Edward Nicholas to the Mayor and Jurats of Rye.

I have thought fit, as well out of my affection to your town as to my well-wishing of Mr. Thomas Fotherley whom my Lord has recommended to you for a Burgesship of your Town to this Parliament, to let you understand that he is one of my Lord's Commissioners for his estate and in very great esteem with his Grace besides he is Mr. Lieutenant's brother in law. *Seal of Arms.*

1625, April 18. Old Fishstreet, London.—John Halsey to the Mayor and Jurats of Rye.

Recommending his kinsman, John Angell, as their burgess to Parliament.

1525, May 14. Dover Castle.—Sir John Hippisley to [the Mayor and Jurats of Rye].

Order for the beacons within the Cinque Ports to be well provided and kept.

1625, June 6. Dover Castle.—Sir John Hippislye [to the Mayors, Bailiffs and Jurats of the Cinque Ports].

Whereas long time since, to the end the Commissioners of the passage within the Cinque Ports might better have certain knowledge what persons either were transported out of the kingdom or did come from foreign parts beyond the seas by way of the said Ports, there was a general order taken that all the masters of ships, barques and crayers and all inholders, victuallers, and hackneymen should enter into bonds with such conditions as were conceived fit for that purpose. These are in his Majesty's name to pray and require you to cause the said articles to be duly executed. *Copy.*

1625, June 10.—The Mayor and Jurats of Sandwich [to the Mayor and Jurats of Rye].

At Mr. Peke's going to London, he was assured by Mr. Nicholas, Sir John Burroughes, and other Secretaries that the Coronation was deferred till Michaelmas.

1625, June 22. Dorset House.—John Sackville to the Mayor and Jurats of Rye.

"Better late than never, and I hope my love and affection cannot come soe late but that it will be kyndly excepted by you, especially when you shall understand that when yours of the last of May came to towne I was out of towne and am but lately com to towne, otherwise I should have answered you sooner. As touching your desire for the procuring you a good curatt, know I have not bene unmyndfull of you, but have dealt with Mr. Twyne about it, and assure yourselves (if you please to have a little patience) I shall provide you of a sufficient one which I hope shall be Mr. Rogers, the man you desire. And as for Mr. Bell assure yourselves he shall not come there, doe Mr. Reve what he can, nor noe man els contrary to your good lykeinge. According to your order I swore Mr. Fotherly, as I hope he hath given you to understand not to trouble you any farther att this tyme. In a word beleve you shall have a sufficient curatt speedely, and as in it, soe in all other things you please to use me, you shall fynd me allways most ready to aprove myself." *Seal of arms.*

1624, July 3. Dover Castle.—Richard Marshe to the Mayor and Jurats of Rye.

Order for the arrest of Seigneur Antonio Brulati, late servant to the Ambassador of Venice. *Description attached. Copy.*

1625, July 13.—The Mayor and Jurats of Rye to Mr. Graines, minister.

Whereas we are at this time unfitted of an able and sufficient minister to keep this solemn and public fast commanded by the King, and hearing by some of our town of your worth, we earnestly entreat you (if you be not otherwise appointed) to let us have your company here upon Wednesday next so long as the fast shall continue to help and assist our minister to perform that pious and holy duty and for your pains we hope to give you that content as shall please you in every respect. *Draft.*

1625, August 22.—The Mayor and Jurats of Rye to ——

"We have thought good to certifie unto you of some injury and wronge, as we conceive, that is offered unto our towne by such persons as ar appinted to watch in the country; for wee are credibly informed that your watchmen takinge uppon them more then their commission is, or at least more then they ought to doe, resist and disturb not only such of our towne as ar sound and cleare from the infection to goe about their lawfull callinge and busines, but alsoe doe intercept others from cominge to our towne, usinge to them these threatninge wordes, that if they come to towne they must not retorne againe into the country. Also the ferryman of Guldford hath denyed some of our townesmen who were cleare of the infection to carry them over the ferry insomuch they have bene constrayned to wade over to the endangeringe of their health. And whereas we were lately promised that victual should be brought to the townes end to supplie our want at reasonable prizes, the first market after which was Satterday last, there was onely a small proportion brought, vizt.: butter and oatmeale, and the butter sold at five pence the pound, which is a greate price at this tyme of the yeare. As concerninge the houses infected, there are in our towne sixteene, and the number that have died both of the infection and other sicknesse in eight weekes since it first began are fortie, of which number wee praise God there died this last weeke of the sicknes but fower, so that the reporte in the country of those that die in our towne of the plague is tenn times more then it is. And the houses infected ar onely in two places at the Landgate alltogither, and likewise in the Watchbell Streate nere unto the Gungarden, alltogither. And whereas one died in the Butcherie that houshold removed into the Watchbell Streate; so that all other places in the towne elce, wee praise God, ar cleare."

1625, October 12. Salisbury.—The Lords of the Council [to the Duke of Buckingham].

We have received information from so many several parts of the bold and impudent speeches used by many Romish Catholics of this realm, declaring how much they are offended with the gracious satisfaction given by his Majesty to the Lords and Commons in Parliament in the points concerning the true and pure religion as it is at this day by authority practised in the Church of England. And having just cause to doubt that many violent misled papists through the instigation of the "Jesuited papistes" may be inclined to take part with such as we well understand at this time practise with the King's subjects to raise stirs and tumults which they do not only by persuasion and instigations, but with promise of assistance and seconding them by arms, their pretext being religion, but their ends conquest, pushed thereunto by an unlimited ambition to a general monarchy of which we have too large and too clear proof. And although we do not misjudge and condemn all his Majesty's subjects "Romish Catholics," but believe that many of them will employ their arms and lives in his service, yet because we are not able to distinguish between the well and worse affected we have seconded with our advice his Majesty's gracious inclination to take out of the hands of all Popish recusants, convicted or justly suspected, all such martial munitions, arms and weapons as shall be found in their houses. These are therefore to pray and require you to repair either by your self or your deputy lieutenants to the houses of all Romish recusants, convicted or justly suspected, within the precincts of your lieutenancies and take such arms where they be found belonging to such recusants. *Copy, enclosed in letter by Sir John Hippisley to the Mayor and Jurats of Rye.*

1625, October 15. The Court at Salisbury.—The Lords of the Council to Sir John Hippesley.

Whereas by a letter from this Board dated the twentieth of August last directed to the Lord High Admiral he was prayed and required for divers reasons to give order that no ships within his Majesty's harbours should be suffered to depart until his Majesty's fleet were first put to sea. In regard that the said fleet is now set forward we think it fit that the Ports be opened. *Copy.*

1625[-6], January 10. Whitehall.—The Duke of Buckingham to the Mayor, Jurats and commonalty of Rye.

Recommending as burgesses to serve in Parliament "Thomas Fotherley, esquire, a freeman of your corporation," and in the second place Mr. Thomas Allun. *Signed. Seal of arms, broken.*

1625[-6], January 14. Westminster.—The King to the Lords of the Council.

We having taken into our consideration the providing for the safety of our dominions and people by all the ways that may be taken, we have found that the trained bands of this our kingdom are so considerable in strength in respect of their numbers, serviceable persons of men, and their own particular interest, as the well experiencing of them in the use of their arms and fitting them for service would settle a great security at home and give terror to any our enemies. We have therefore often recommended to our Lieutenants of our several counties the putting in execution of those plain and exact rules which were formerly conceived and sent now unto them in printed books. And being resolved to peruse the same to effect, we have caused a certain number of experienced soldiers to be sent from the Low Countries hither, to be distributed into several counties there to teach the captains and other officers and leaders of files in each company the true modern use of their arms and order of soldiers, that the officers being well instructed may teach the soldiers. *Copy.*

1625[-6], January 17. Whitehall.—The Lord Warden to the Lieutenant of Dover Castle.

"Having this day received summons under his Majesty's privie Signet concerninge the coronation of the Kinge and Queene, I have thought good hereby to pray and require you presantly to geve order under the seale of the office of Dovor Castle to all the Cinque Portes and two ancient townes forthwith to make their election of such Barons as shall be fitt for performance of the service which apperteineth to them, and to cause them to be prepared and in a readiness at Westminster upon the second day of February next, which is the day appointed by his Majestie as by his letter (a copie whereof I herewith send you) appeareth. In the choise of your barrons for this service I would have you give directions that care be taken for the election of men of the meetest and comlyest personages and of the most sufficiencie, otherwise observing therein their ancient customes and priviledges as well for the nomber of men as otherwise." *Copy.*

1625[-6], January . . .—The Mayor and Jurats of Hastings [to the Mayor and Jurats of Rye].

Upon the return of a circular letter to the Ports concerning the coronation services "we were much perplexed by reason of the uncertaine answere of Sandwich from whence was cheiflie expected best instructions concerning this solicitation, Mr. Peke lately and others there foremerly, being therein solely imployed. Howbeit the service of such importance requiring both industry and speede, I, the Maier of Hasting, prepared myself accordingly to travell and for my better assistance intreated Mr. Thomas Brian, jurat here, to ryde with me. And so furnished with such instructions and recordes in that behalf collected in writting by our Towneclarke, we departed towardes London on Wensday the iiij[th] of January instant and arrived there the next day, and first acquainted Mr. Nicholas with our busines, whom wee found verie kind and effectionate, with readines and travell to preferre our suite, and then exhibited our petition to his grace as the inclosed copy appeareth, who graciouslie accepted and referred us to the Earle Marshall, the Erle of Arundel, who all so favourably vouchsafed to promise a privy seale to be presently directed to the Duke, his grace, for our service. Candlemas day by most voices is the day appointed for the Coronation. It is readily affirmed that no Liveries wilbe graunted to any in that service The Lord Steward was not yet certainely knowne neither yet when his Court wilbe appointed and held for allowances of services at the Coronation. And so wee returned hom on Satterday the xiij[th] of January. Wee are enforced to be breife in writtinge, the brevitie of the tyme requirith so, and referr our larger relation untill our next meetinge. In the mean tyme, we pray your opinion whither you think it fitt to assemble for further conference herein, where, when, and how many from every Town or elc (to spare charge and fowle travell) to forbeare such assembly untill sommons doe come which wilbe verie shortly. Whereuppon when everie towne have made their elections to that service those persons or some one of them from every towne may spedilie travell up to London as well to sue for allowance of their service at the Lord High Stewardes Court as allso to conferre about the manner of their execution herof and to furnish themselves with apparell."

1626, July 18.—The Duke of Buckingham to John Totton, press master in the County of Sussex.

Whereas you have received warrant for the pressing of one hundred and fifty seamen and mariners in the County of Sussex to furnish his Majesty's fleet at Portsmouth, now for that there are divers limbs and ports within the County which are members of the Cinque Ports so, as it is likely that upon notice of the press most of the mariners will resort thither to avoid the same, whereby his Majesty's service may be frustrated, these are therefore to require you to press in the Cinque Ports within the County of Sussex only so many able seamen and mariners as may respectively make up the said number of men which you have warrant to press. *Copy.*

1626, August 5. Whitehall.—The Lords of the Council to the Mayors, Magistrates and Chief Officers of the Cinque Ports.

"Wee have considered of your petition sent by John Pringle and John Nowell, wherein wee did not expect that our favour towardes you in our former abatement should have produced a request for a new abatement, which the condition of the publique safetie will not permitt. But wee are well contented as the said Pringle did desire, that you shall make provision your selves of the two shippes to be readie by the 4th of September next at the place appointed so as they be of the burthen of 200 tonnes a peece, and provided as is formerly directed. And wee do require and authorize you to leavie the charge (as is desired in your petition) as well uppon the inhabitantes of the said Portes and members as uppon the landes and goodes of those who are not there resident according to the abilities of the said inhabitants and value of the said land and goodes, as hath been betwen the said Ports and Members the year 1588 when the occasion of service was." *Copy.*

1626, September 12. Whitehall.—The Earl of Marlborough to the Customers and officers of Chichester, Lewes, Mechinghaven, [Newhaven] Shoreham and Pevensey.

"Whereas there have been divers orders made at sundry times by their Majesties by the advice of the Council of State to prevent the unlawful transportation of iron ordnance and shot, and to that end did reduce the making of such iron ordnance and shot to be made and cast within the Counties of Kent and Sussex, by John Browne, his Majesty's founder, and Sacvile Crowe, another founder, who are bound to his Majesty for the whole making thereof and bringing of it to the market place at London. And whereas also by Letters Patent his Majesty hath authorized Mr. Phillipp Burlamack and Phillipp Jacobson to be his sole agents for the transportation of all iron ordnance and shot. Of all which you cannot be ignorant, yet you have suffered divers quantities of shot to be shipped out of your ports which have been made without warrant by men unauthorised and no account given what is become of the said shot. These are therefore to require you that from henceforth you do not suffer any iron shot whatsoever to be shipped out of your ports but such shot as the aforesaid founders shall make and provide for his Majesty's service and the subjects as aforesaid." *Signed and Seal of Arms.*

1626, September 17. Denmark House.—The Duke of Buckingham to Sir John Hippesley.

"Whereas I have received order from the Lords of his Majesties Privy Counsell, that, in regard of the extraordinary preparations that are making in all partes in hostilitie with his Majestie and particularly in those nerest adjoyning to his Majesties dominions, no shippe shall be suffered to goe to sea without my knowledge, and that untill, uppon true certeficat for what place they are bound and wherewith they are freighted, I shall give them especiall licence. These are therefore to will and require you to give spedie and effectuall order throughout the jurisdiction of the Cinque Portes and their members to make stay of all shipps and barques of what burden soever belonginge to any of his Majesties subjects being now within any of the Cinque Portes or their members or shall come into them, and not to suffer any of them to departe without especiall licence from me under my hand, which restraint is to be so continued until you shall receive order to the contrary to the ende that his Majesties dominions may be provided and furnished with sufficient strength both for defence of themselves and the mutuall assistance ech of other against the attempts of any enimy." *Copy. A like letter addressed to the Earl of Nottingham for restraint of vessels within the County of Sussex.*

1626, September 21. Whitehall.—The Duke of Buckingham to [the Earl of Nottingham].

"Whereas as by a former lettre dated the 18th of this instant September I gave order to your Lordship for the stayinge of all shippes and barques within the Countye of Sussex whether soever bound, untill

I should give specyall lycence for their release. Now these are to pray your Lordshipp to take a present and discreet course for the releaseing of all shippes and barques which you have or shall stay by virtue of my said former letters that are bounde for any other kingdome, state, country or place whatsoever excepte only such as are bound for any parte of the kingdome of Fraunce, which are still to be restrayned untill you shall receive further order for their release. This letter and directions your Lordship is to keepe secreat as a matter of State and thoughe you release all other shippes yet your Lordship is to declare that those shippes which are bound for Fraunce are stayed onely by vertue of the former letters which you received for a generall restraynte. Your Lordshipp is also to take especiall care that this trust committed to you be carried verie discreetelye and secreatly and not abused nor made a matter of gaine and advantage to such as your Lordshipp shall ymploye in the execucion heereof." *Copy.*

1626, September 26. Dover Castle.—Sir John Hippesley to the Mayors, Bailiffs and Jurats of the Cinque Ports.

For the better ease of such as are stayed, upon their repair to me with a certificate whither they are bound from the Mayor or other principal officer of the Ports, I shall be ready to give liberty of passage during the time of the imbarment to any that I shall see cause for. *Copy.*

1626, September 29. Buckingham House.—The Duke of Buckingham to Sir John Hippesley.

"Whereas upon consideration of the great power and preparations of the enemy chiefly by sea, it hath pleased the Lords of his Majesties Privie Counsell to give me order, not onely to cause an exact survey to be taken of all shippes and vessells, but likewise a muster to be made of all sea men and marriners belonginge to everie Porte towne of England and Wales and certificates thearof speedylie to be returned. These are thearfore according to thear Lordshipes saide order to pray and require you forthwith to cause an exact survey to be presently taken and certified to mee, under your hand, of the number, strength and burthen of all the shipps, barques and vessells now in any of the Cinque Portes or thear members, or imployed at sea belonging to any of the Cinque Portes or thear members where you are particulerly to expresse what ordinance are aboard every shippe and what others they are well capable of, and whoe are the owners and parte owners of every of them, and likewise to cause a generall muster to bee forthwith made of all suche marriners, saylors, and fishermen, as are now remayninge or belonging to any of the Cinque Portes or their members, and to returne a true and exact certificate to mee under your hand of thear numbers, names, dwellinge places, and qualities as whether masters, pylotts, gunners, marriners or fishermen and any other considerable circumstance fitt to bee knowne." *Copy.*

[1626, October.]—A list of the barques and vessels belonging to Rye with the names of their owners and masters, and their burdens. The largest vessel is the *Guift* of 40 tons belonging to Thomas Martin, John Dugard, Joseph Dugard and Margerie Michell. There are 16 vessels in all.

1626, November 11.—The Mayor and Jurats of Rye to the Duke of Buckingham.

"We received a lettre from your Lordship concerninge certeine lands intended to be inned by Mr. Henry Pecke and Mr. Peter Farner and for that cause, as wee conceave, procured your Grace's letter unto us, that if it were not prejudiciall to our habor we should not oppose them. These are to certefie your Lordshipp that our auncestors and wee have found by experience for our own particulars that inning of lands nere and about our habour have ben a principall cause of the decay of our habor, which was a habor, before certaine landes nere unto it were inned, that a shipp of five hundred tonns might have [entered] at low water; and by the ining of the same land a verie good habour, called the Camber, within two miles of our towne is utterly decayed, and this land which now is intended to be inned, if it be suffered, will be the utter distruction of our habor and an inducement for the owners of many hundred acres of salt joining nere our harbor, to inne them, who may as well as they pretend that it will not hurt the same." *Copy.*

1626, November 25. Whitehall.—The Duke of Buckingham to Sir John Hippesley.

"Whereas uppon the hearinge and debatinge of the complaints of the merchants tradinge for Fraunce touchinge the arrests and seizures of their shipps and goodes lately made in severall partes of that kingdome, it hath pleased the Lordes of his Majesty's Privie Counsell to commaund that no shipps or goods belonginge to any the subjects of the Frenche Kinge should pass out of the port of London or any the out ports or members of the same untill further order. These ar, accordinge to their Lordshipps said order, to praye and require you to take a speedie and effectuall course that noe shipps or goods belonginge to any the subjects of the said French Kinge do passe out of any porte or other place within the jurisdictions of the Cinque Portes or their members, untill further order." *Copy.*

1626, December 18. Whitehall.—The Duke of Buckingham to the Mayor and Jurats of Rye.

"Whereas I am informed you have made stay of a French barque or boate of about fifteene or twentie tonnes belonginge to Treport in Fraunce, whereof Patron John is master, which onlie brought over a French gent who being wounded is nowe abidinge in the Towne of Rie, without anie manner of goods or merchandises, I have thought good hereby to pray and require you forthwith to release the said barque or boate together with the said master and companie." *Signed and Seal of Admiralty.*

1626, December 22.—The Mayor and Jurats of Rye to the Mayor and Jurats of Dover.

"We understand that there is of late brought into your habor a smale boat of Bridgis in which there is two men of the Archdutches subjectes. Our ernest request therefore unto you is that you would so compassionat a poore distressed neighbour of ours John Browne, who was taken by the Kinge of Spaines ships and carried into Ostend, that he may be ransomed for one of the men in your custody which wee hoope you will the sooner condiscend hereunto, for that he is a Portes man, and the men taken by one of the Portes shieps and for this curteosie shewed him wee shall be greatelie beholding to you and thereby you shall bynd him ever to acknowledge it for a great and speciall favor done unto him now in his miserie, havinge sixe smale children destitute of father and mother." *Copy.*

1626[-7], January 4.—The Mayor and Jurats of Rye to Mr. Petter.

Since you have left your ministry for the recovery of your health, we are informed that for the zeal of God's glory and the love you bear to our town, you will, if we desire it, come again to us. Therefore we pray you so soon as conveniently you can, let us be made happy by your presence. *Copy.*

1626[-7], January 9.—The Duke of Buckingham to Sir John Hippesley.

I would have you employ your best care to apprehend Adrian Payes, a subject of the King of Spain, and one John Neway, a saddler of London, who I believe met at Dover or Deal with intent to cross over to Calais or Bologne. [Descriptions of Payes and Neway.] *Copy.*

1626[-7], January 29.—The Mayor, Jurats and Commonalty of Rye to the Duke of Buckingham.

Petitioning that the Duke will be a means to procure from his Majesty a brief to help in defraying the expenses in repairing the sea walls, groines, jetties, and sluices, so broken and torn up by the extraordinary raging tides, great tempest and foul weather of late. *Draft.*

1626[-7], March 2. Dover Castle.—Sir John Hispieley (Hippesley) to the Mayors, Bailiffs and Jurats of the Cinque Ports.

"Whereas I have of late received credible intelligence that by reason of the scarcitie of victualls and meanes to sett the poore on worke in the Provinces under the Archdutches, there is a course there intended to send away those of the poorest and worst condition of French and other for Calais, to be thence by the Governour's assistance put aboard in such vessells as come for England, and there landed; by sufferance whereof not only the enimies of this kingdome may be holpen and these partes of his Majesty's dominions much pestered but many other inconveniences ensue. These are therefore to pray, and in his Majesty's name for the advancement of his service to require you, that noe Wallons, French, or other such necessitous people, as cannot give good reason of their imployment here or have not meanes to maintaine themselves without the pestering and burtheninge of this country, be suffered to be landed within any of your liberties, and if you find or know of any such persons allreadie landed that you give me speedie notice of their numbers and places of abod. And to the end that for the gaine of some one or more particuler men the enimies of this commonwealth may not in this tyme of their dearth be releived and so their strength maintained against this kingdome, these are to praye, and in like manner as before require you, that you have a vigilant care to hinder (as much as in you lyeth) the transportation of all corne and other victualls prohibited to be transported out of this country." *Copy.*

1626[-7], March 13.—The Mayor and Jurats of Rye to Sir John Hippesley.

"Whereas a yearly pay out of the Exchequer is paid to one that receives it, as gunner of Rye, who never doth any service nor resides among us, we have thought good to inform you, and with it beseaching you, to take into your serious consideration the urgent necessity of a gunner's presence here with us in these so dangerous times, and that now some speedy course may be taken through your furtherance to compel him to look to his charge here, which hath been so long time neglected." *Draft.*

RYE MSS.

1626[-7], March 17. Whitehall.—The Lords of the Council [to the Mayors, Bailiffs, and Jurats of the Cinque Ports].

"Whereas we are given to understand that there are observed dayly to come out of the Low Countries without leave from their commanders as well inferior officers as souldiers in great numbers, belonging to those regiments under his Majesties pay there, which having bene likewise made knowne to his Majestie, he hath commanded us to cause them to be apprehended and punished. These are therefore in his Majesties name straightly to wiil and require you to cause diligent search and inquirie to be made for all such persons, of the condition aforesaid, lodged and harboured within your jurisdiction and to cause them to be apprehended and detayned in safe custodie until you shall have acquainted this Board therewithall and received further order for the disposinge of them. And that you do the like from tyme to tyme for such others of them as shall come over and passe through anye the places within your severall jurisdictions."

1626[-7], March 23. Dover Castle.—Sir John Hippesley to the Mayors, Bailiffs, and Jurats of the Cinque Ports.

"Whereas by my letters of the nine and twentith of July last under the seale of my Lord Warden his Grace's office here, I acquainted you with his Majesty's pleasure and my Lord Warden's direction concerninge the continuance of John Withers and Samuell Helinge in their exercisinge and instructinge the trayned soldiers and others within your liberties, to which they had bene formerly appointed by his Majesty's command. I ame nowe credibly informed that many of the persons in the same your liberties [who] should be exercised and instructed according to the said directions, have of late neglected and refused to be exercised or receive any instructions from the said John Withers, who hath bene resident amongst them, whereby his Majesty's expectation of the benefitt which would have bene reaped by the said instructions is like to be frustrated and myselfe and you disabled to make that good accompt which will in this behalfe be required. These are therefore to pray and (by vertue of the authoritie by my Lord Warden his former command to this purpose given me) require you that you give strickt charge and command to all the persons within your liberties, which are appointed by the directions you have heretofore received, to be exercised or instructed that they faile not in their attendance at tymes convenient to be exercised and directed by the said John Withers accordinge to the intention of the severall commands of the Lordes of the Counsell and my Lord Warden, wherewith you have bene acquainted. And if you shall find any in this respect refractory that you take speedie course for reformation thereof or otherwise certifie their names unto me, whereby I may take such course with them as may best further his Majesty's service." *Copy.*

1626[-7], March 24.—The Mayor and Jurats of Dover [to the Mayor and Jurats of Rye].

As we are best acquainted with the occurances of these troublesome times as nearest to the troubles and dangers, so do we not omitt any opportunity to impart what may concern the Ports in general as ourselves in particular. First touching 116 tuns of wine brought to this harbour by the Ports' ships, the same was sold yesterday and all but 14 tuns thereof found to belong to French merchants, which said 14 tuns are professed to belong to merchants of Flanders the which will fall only to the Ports' share; and for the three ships and *Billinder* taken by the Ports' ships only the *Billinder* and 2 bags of flax fall within the compass of our letters of marque. We also hear of a warrant for a press of 200 seamen forthwith within the Ports and their members, which in these times of danger of so potent and ancient an enemy as the French, to be granted, is somewhat strange and likely to tend to our prejudice. For our parts we are yet sensible of our late losses of our men cast away in the three ships the other year on the coast of France near Calais, besides those in the transport of the soldiers of Count Mansfield and since of others taken by the Dunkirkers and of late of the absence of others with their ships at Bordeaux, and of others taken up for pilots all which have and do much depopulate this Township as it hath and doth other Towns of the Ports so that to prevent the utter ruin some speedy and sudden course must be taken.

1627, March 28. London.—Thomas Harrison to the Mayor, Jurats and Commonalty of Rye.

"You have made a complainte of mee to my Lord Duke of Buckingham his grace because I having a Gunners fee of 6*d.* per diem and am not resident with you in these so dangerous and perrilous tymes etc. To which I answere that I am sure yow know that this fee belongs not to the service of your towne, it being given by King Henry the VIII., who having warres with Fraunce placed a cannon of brasse in Rie, giving to a gunner for his atendance (only) thereon the said fee, and to be disposed of by the Lord Warden to whome hee should thinke fitt, the Towne ever having other gunners (besides) of theire owne for divers peices of brasse and iron ordinance. The said cannon was at the comming of the Spanish Armada, Anno 1588, sent for from Rie, either to her Majesties Navy or to the Campe at Tilbury and afterwards brought to the Tower of London, where it now is and hath ever since continued. And I nowe living heere am more ready to do service when soever I shal be commanded by the Master Gunner of England, and much neerer then if I should live in Rie, to which place I am not bound, except you can make meanes to have the said cannon brought back again or procure another. And then I shalbe very willing to give my best attendance and performe the utmost of my indeavour among you. Moreover although Mr. Ratliffe and Mr. Portriffe enjoyed the same fee which I nowe have for the space of 36 yeares and upwards, after the cannon was absent from your Towne, yet you had several gunners in those tymes, John Prowse, Robert Burdett and John Bayly, each of thease having theire pay out of the Chamber of your Towne." *Signed.*

1627, March 28. Whitehall.—The Lords of the Council to Sir John Hippesley.

"Whereas we are given to understand that there hath bene of late observed to be a greate resorte into this kingdome from forraigne partes of all sorts of strangers, beinge for the most parte of the meaner sorte, and those, in such numbers as may well be conceived to have bene purposely sent away to discharge and unburthen those places from whence they come, who as wee are informed are usually at their first cominge over, sett ashore in the severall Porte townes and places within that county. These are therefore straightly to will and require you to cause expresse order to be taken within the Cinque Portes and members of the same, or any landinge places within their jurisdiction, that either they suffer not any strangers of such condition as aforesaid to come ashore at all, or in case they shall be landed to cause them to be reimbarquet and sent back againe. And that for all such strangers and forriners of better qualitie as shall come over and happen to land in any the aforesaid portes or places and shall not upon examination taken, yeild sufficient reasons for their cominge over, so as you may find just cause to lett them passe, that you cause them to be stayed and deteined in safe custodie untill you shall have made certificates thereof to this Board and received our further directions therein. And that for suche of them as you shall suffer to passe as aforesaid, that you doe nevertheless make entry of their names and of the occasions by them pretended for their cominge over, as allso of the places where they intend to lodge at their cominge upp hither. And that you certifie the same to this Board from tyme to tyme."

1627, March 28. Dover Castle.—Sir John Hippisley [to the Mayor and Jurats of Rye].

"Whereas for the giving of certaine intelligence to the Commissioners for the passage within the Cinque Portes and their members, as well of such persons as were transported out of the kingdome as of those that were brought from beyond the seaes into the same by the way of the said Portes or their members, order hath bene taken by the honorable predecessor of my Lord Warden his Grace that all masters of ships, barques and craiors and all inholders, victuallers and hackneymen there, should enter into bonds with such conditions as were conceived fitt for the purpose above recited. And whereas the right honorable late Lord Zouch (for the better execution of the same order) did in his tyme add thereunto diverse articles wherewith he acquainted you, amongest which one was (as I doubt not you remember) that all Maiors and Jurates, Bayliffes and Jurates of the Cinque Portes, two auncient townes and their members should within fowerteene dayes after notice given from the office here, certefie into the same office, as well the names of the masters of all shipps, barques and crayors as the names of all inholders, victuallers and hackneymen within their severall portes, townes, members, and liberties, with a speciall note uppon every one of those who used more then one of the said trades to the ends, bonds might be prepared for them according to another of the said articles. Now forasmuch as our Lord Warden his Grace that nowe is (well weighinge how much the due observance of the said former and later orders conduce to the service and safetie of his Majestie and this realme and what danger might ensue by the omission of the same) hath well approved of the said orders and commanded that the said orders be from tyme to tyme within his government of the said Cinque Portes, townes and members, duly observed. These are to pray and require you that, in performance of one parte of the said orders, you forthwith send into his Grace's office here a true and perfect certificate as well of the names of the masters of all and every the ships, barques, and crayors as of the names of all the inholders, victuallers, and hackneymen within every of the severall liberties, with note whereby every of those which use more then one of the said trades may be knowne, and bonds here may be prepared for their sealinge as is fitt and hath bene heretofore accustomed." *Copy.*

1627, April 4. Whitehall.—The Duke of Buckingham to Sir John Hippisley.

Order to make stay of all ships and barques within the Cinque Ports. *Copy. This letter is almost word for word the same as that of* 17 *September* 1626.

1627, April 16. Dover Castle.—Sir John Hippesley to [the Mayor and Jurats of Rye.]

"I formerly received lettres from the Lords of his Majesties Privie Councell for the impressinge of 200 marriners and seafaringe men for his Majesty's service in his Majesty's fleete shortly to be put to sea, to send the same men so imprest to Chatham there to be put aboard such shipps as by his Majesty's officers shold be directed and appointed. These are to advertize you that I now lately received a letter from the Clerke of the Checkes according to my Lord Wardens command, by him received beinge now at Chatham, with a list of all those mens names which have appeared there, beinge prest, the true coppies whereof I herewith send you that upon the perusall thereof you may understand that divers of those men which soe made their appearance are since run away, and that you may perceive who they are by this marke as you shall finde it in the Clerke of the Checkes letter, as it is written in the margent of the aforesaid list against the names of those who are runawaies. Also you shall further understand that their was wantinge of the whole number 60 men which never appeared at all, beinge most parte of them prest. Wherefore I pray and require you that with all expedition you cause a strict and diligent serche to be made for the findinge out of those which are supposed to be runawaies and allso of those that never appeared beinge prest, and that you cause some of them to be exemplarely punished whereby the rest may take warninge, without the which undoubtedly his Majesty's service will suffer for want of men, and that you see the whole number to be made upp of what is wantinge accordinge to your former warrant and directions."

1627, April 17. Whitehall.—The Duke of Buckingham to Sir John Hippisley.

"Whereas I have received expresse order and comand for preventinge intelligence and for divers other important reasons of state that noe shippe, barques, or other vessells, whither belonginge to his Majesty's subjects or strangers, of what qualitie or burthen soever, which are at this presente or which hereafter shall come into or ride within any of his Majesty'e portes or roads, betwen this and the goinge forth of his Majesty's fleete nowe preparinge, shall be suffered to departe and putt to sea untill further order. These are accordingly to will and require you to cause a sure stay to be made of all shipps, barques, and other vessells whatsoever, whither belonginge to his Majesty's subjectes or strangers." *Copy.*

1627, April 26. Whitehall.—The Duke of Buckingham to the Mayor and Jurats of Rye.

"Whereas I am credibly informed that notwithstanding the striot order and commaund given for a generall restraint of all shipps, barques, and vessells, there doe dayly passe out of your porte or the members thereof aswell sloopes as barkes and other vessells to the infringement of the King's expresse comaunds and prejudice of his Majesty's service. Wherefore these are to will and require you not only to inquyre and certifye me what barques or vessells (since the said restraint) have passed out of your porte, and by whose directions, licence, helpe, and meanes, and whether they have gonne, but to take a more strict and vigilant course, that noe shippe, barque, sloope, or other vessell whatsoever of what quallity or condition soever, whether belonging to his Majesty's subjects or straingers doe by any meanes passe or goe forth of your said porte, roade, or harbor untill further order from me or the Lieutenant of Dover Castle." *Signed. Seal of the Admiralty.*

1627, April 28.—The Mayor and Jurats of Rye to Sir John Hippisley.

Whereas the Duke of Buckingham our Lord Warden has commanded us to make strict stay of all ships and vessels going forth of our harbour until further order be given, we have made stay of all fisherboats which go ordinarily to sea for the taking fish for his Majesty's provisions, which the King's house will fail of by reason of this restraint. Insomuch we have thought good to write you and to be advertised if we shall continue to stay them or suffer them to go to sea for taking of fish for his Majesty's provision. *Draft.*

1627, April 29.—The Mayor and Jurats of Rye to the Duke of Buckingham.

"Whereas your Grace is informed (as we conceive by your Honours letter of the 26th of this instant) that notwithstanding the strict order for a general restraint of all ships there do daily pass out of our harbour sloops and barques. These are to certify your Grace that since the restraint there hath not any sloop, barque, or vessel gone out of our harbour save only small boats as ordinarily go afishing but now we have given them strict charge to forbear to go to sea till we receive order to the contrary." *Draft.*

1627, May 1. Whitehall.—The Duke of Buckingham to the Mayor and Jurats of Rye.

As the King cannot be sufficiently supplied on fasting and fish days unless the fishermen of Rye may freely use their fishing, notwithstanding the restraint they may put to sea upon giving bonds for their return every tide into harbour and shall bring such fish caught to be disposed of for his Majesty's service. *Signed and seal of the Admiralty.*

1627, May 11. Whitehall.—The Duke of Buckingham to the Mayor and Jurats of Rye.

Commanding them to send to Dover "the Spaniards, Portugalls, and Dunkerkers" now prisoners at Rye that they may be exchanged for His Majesty's subjects prisoners in West Flanders. *Signed and seal of the Admiralty.*

1627, May 11. Whitehall.—The Duke of Buckingham to Sir John Hippesley.

"Whereas by former order from his Majesty and the Lordes of his Majesty's Privie Counsell I gave you formerly two severall strict commands not to permitt any shippe, barke or vessell, whither fisherboat or other to departe or passe out of any porte or place within the jurisdiction of the Cinque Portes without especiall licence from me under my hand, thereby to prevent all intelligence which otherwise might be given to forraigne states. Now forasmuch as credible information is given that notwithstanding such strict order and command there have many barques and other vessells, either throwgh negligence or conniviencie of mony gone out of severall partes of the Cinque Portes from by-crekes and places principally, whereby letters have bene carried into forraine partes to the great prejudice of his Majesty's service and the State. These are to pray and require you to take an effectual and strict corse throughout the Cinque Portes and their members not only to enquire after and certefie all such as have transgressed contrary to his Majesty's and their Lordshipp's said command but to make sure stay of all shipps, barques, fisherboates and other vessells of what qualitie soever belonginge to any of his Majesty's subjects or strangers beinge now within or shall come into any porte, harbor, rode, creke, or other place within the Cinque Portes or their members and not to permit any of them to departe or passe other then such as are in his Majesty's immediate service without especyall lycence and directions from me under my hand." *Copy.*

1627, May 27. Dover Castle.—Sir John Hippesley to the Mayors, Bailiffs and Jurats of the Cinque Ports.

"I have this day received letters from my Lord Warden wherein charge is given me accordinge to the order of his Majesties Privie Counsell to cause an able and strict watch to be kept throughout the jurisdiction of the Cinque Portes, two auntient townes and their members. These are therefore to pray and require you to cause his Grace's said command to be putt in speedie and punctuall execution in every particular accordinge to the purport thereof and if you shall finde any negligence or faulte in observanc of any point of his Grace's said command that you certefye me from tyme to tyme thereof whereby I may be able to give that accompt which is in this behalf required I should. And whereas I am informed that the watches within diverse of your liberties have bene heretofore performed by the poorest sorte of people and such as have least cause to be carefull of so greate charge as is commytted to them, these are to praye and require you as you tender the saftie of the state of this Kingdome and yourselves, that duringe these tymes of danger you appoint the most sufficient and ablest men within every of your liberties for performance of this service." *Copy.*

1627, June 9. Gray's Inn.—Samuel Shorte to the Mayor and Jurats of Rye.

Asking that he may succeed Mr. James Thurbane, who died "at Grays Inn on Wednesday last," as counsel for the Town of Rye.

1627, June 11. Dover Castle.—Sir John Hippesley to the Mayors, Bailiffs, and Jurats of the Cinque Ports.

I, being of late in London, obtained by special favour order for the opening and discharge of the restraint of passage of all ships, so that it is now permitted that all ships may pass and go forth putting in good bond that they shall not cross or pass the seas or have any connivance with Frenchmen or such like. *Copy.*

1627, June 26. Portsmouth.—The Duke of Buckingham to Sir John Hippisley.

Order for releasing the restraint of all ships and vessels in the Cinque Ports, excepting French ships which are to be stayed. *Copy.*

1627, July 16.—Proclamation by the Duke of Buckingham, Lord Warden of the Cinque Ports, for the mustering, surveying and exercising of the trained and untrained bands of the Cinque Ports, both of foot and horse, and for having all beacons furnished and provided with convenient materials for firing them if need shall so require.

1627, July 16. Dover Castle.—Sir John Hippesley to the Mayors, Bailiffs, and Jurats of the Cinque Ports.

I have lately received directions from one of his Majesty's Secretaries of State for the stay of the person, trunks, and other packs of one who is called by the name of Old Fraunces, a man of low stature, aged seventy years, and gray-haired. He hath now bought divers cloaks which he intends to transport, and under colour thereof he secketh passage to Flushing and thence to Calais. There is great blame laid in general upon the officers of the Cinque Ports for suffering some lately to pass which have done bad offices to the state as this Old Fraunces is suspected to do. *Copy.*

1627, July 17. Dover Castle.—Sir John Hippesley to the Mayors, Bailiffs, and Jurats of the Cinque Ports.

I have this day received letters from his Majesty's Secretaries of State whereby I am required to make stay of the body and letters of one, Short, who is now coming out of France with directions and letters for such as are agents here for that Country. *Copy.*

1627, July 25. Dover Castle.—Sir John Hippisley to Mayor and Jurats of Rye.

"Whereas there was lately a general restraint of passage from the Cinque Ports into any foreign parts, yet I am informed there was not only during that time of restraint a common allowance of men's passage from you into France, but also some barques, hoys, and other vessels, and in particular one laden with coals bound for France then suffered to pass out of your harbour, peradventure you had some superior authority for these things, if so it is well; however that I may be able to render the account which is required for these things I desire you to certify me by what authority those things were done. There hath also been lately a special command for the strict examination of such as resort into this kingdom from beyond the seas and apprehension of all that might be suspicious, how this service is performed by you I desire in like manner to be certified, for I have hitherto been informed of no man stayed by you, albeit I know there is many more passengers land with you than in some other Ports where good services in this respect hath been lately done." *Signed and seal of office.*

1627, August 29. Dover Castle.—Sir John Hippesley to the Mayors, Bailiffs, and Jurats of the Cinque Ports.

Ordering a strict examination of all such as seek transportation, in order to effect the stay and apprehension of one Martin Lucas, a Dutchman, lately escaped from prison. *Copy.*

1627, October 1.—The Captain of H.M.S. *Bonaventure* to Sir John Hippesley.

I am commanded by special order from the King and Council to haste away which I intend, God willing, with the first tide although I stand deficient of many sufficient men. Therefore I am forced to solicit you to command the men that have been pressed within your precincts to attend upon me. Of the 26 pressed by John Jacob, only 2 have appeared, of 10 pressed by Mr. Rabonet, only one has appeared. If I come not to anchor in the Downs I will make "2 or 3 bordes" before Dover and shoot three pieces, which shall be a sign for these men to come aboard there, in case I stop not at the Downs. The urgent occasion of this service, which is for the relief of my Lord Duke and his army, will I make no question invite you to be extraordinary careful in the performance of this service. *Copy.*

1627, October 10. Whitehall.—The Lords of the Council to Sir John Hippesley.

Whereas it is come to the knowledge of his Majesty and the Board that divers gentlemen and others inhabitants of the Cinque Ports have of late years, and do daily more and more, withdraw themselves and desert their habitations and dwellings in those parts, whereby the said Ports and places lying most in danger of foreign attempts and therefore needing the most population of defence are left naked and exposed to the invasion of an enemy. And whereas in regard of some late advertisement from foreign parts of the great fleet coming from Spain with intention to join with a good fleet prepared at Dunkirk, pretended to be in aid of the French King, it is found very necessary that the said Cinque Ports and members of the same and parts adjacent should be strengthened and secured all that possibly may be. We therefore by his Majesty's express command do hereby require you to summon and command all and every such persons, housekeepers, as have at any time within the space of three years last past had their habitation and dwelling within the said Cinque Ports, to make their immediate repair back together with their families to their several dwellings there. *Copy.*

1627, October 15. Whitehall.—The Lords of the Council [to Sir John Hippesley].

Whereas 60 men were lately impressed within the Cinque Ports for manning of His Majesty's ship commanded by Sir John Chudleigh there hath not been above ten of them appeared, whereby the service wherein the said ship is to be imployed is like to suffer if not altogether frustrated. We have thought good to require you to cause the full complement to be instantly supplied and sent aboard, and those formerly pressed who have not appeared to be apprehended and committed to prison. *Copy.*

1627, November 1.—The Mayor and Jurats of Rye to Thomas Partridge at Town Sutton, Thomas Webb at Canterbury and William Barnes at Peasmarsh.

We have received letters from the Lords of his Majesty's Privy Council to summon all and every such persons or housekeepers as have at any time within three years dwelt within the Cinque Ports to make their immediate repairs back with their families to their several dwellings there. These are therefore to command you forthwith to repair hither with your families. *Draft.*

1627[-8], January 21.—Writ to the Constable of Dover Castle for the election of Barons to Parliament.

1627[-8], February 1. Dorset House.—The Earl of Dorset to the Mayor, Jurats, and freemen of Rye.

Asking them to elect as burgess to Parliament his near kinsman Captain Sackvile, of whom they made choice for the two last Parliaments. *Signed and seal of arms.*

1627[8], February 7.—Brief from Charles I. empowering the Mayor and Jurats of Rye to collect alms and charitable benevolences within the Cities of London and Westminster and the Counties of Sussex, Surrey, Kent, Southampton, Dorset, Essex, and various other cities and counties for the repairs of the harbour of Rye. *Print.*

RYE MSS.

1627[-8], February 9. Wallingford House.—The Duke of Buckingham to the Mayor, Jurats and Commons of Rye.

Recommending Thomas Fotherley, esquire, for a burgess' place in the next Parliament. *Signed and seal of the Admiralty.*

1627[-8], March 2. Dover Castle.—Sir John Hippesley to the Mayors, Bailiffs and Jurats of the Cinque Ports.

Has received letters from the Lord Warden for the opening and discharge of the imbarment and restraint of passage of all ships. *Copy.*

1628, May 17. Whitehall.—The Duke of Buckingham to the Mayor of Dover.

Commanding that no ship or other vessel be put to sea from the Cinque Portes until further order.

1628, June 19. Dover Castle.—Stephen Monins, deputy to Sir John Hippesley, to John Jacobs, Serjeant of the Admiralty of the Cinque Ports.

Whereas by letters lately received from the Lord Warden according to order he hath received from the Lords of the Privy Council, I am required to impress forthwith twenty able pilots and one hundred and fifty mariners and seafaring men within the Cinque Ports and their members for his Majesty's service in his fleet, now preparing in the River of Thames, for the relief of Rochelle, and to send the same men into the Downs there to be put aboard his Majesty's ships there. These are therefore to require you "undelayedly" to impress seventy-two able pilots and seafaring men according to the proportions underwritten. Folkstone 6, Hythe 6 and 2 pilots, Romney 3, Lydd 6, Rye 20, Hastings 30. *Copy.*

1628, June 20. Whitehall.—The Duke of Buckingham to the Mayors, Bailiffs and Jurats of the Cinque Ports.

Releasing the stay of all ships and vessels. *Copy.*

1628, July 11. Whitehall.—The Duke of Buckingham to Sir John Hippisley.

I have received express order to prevent intelligence and for divers other important reasons of state, that no ships or vessels which are now within or which shall come into any Port or harbour within the jurisdiction of the Cinque Ports shall be suffered to go to sea, until further order. *Copy.*

1628, August 28. Dover Castle.—Sir John Hippesley to the Mayors, Bailiffs, and Jurats of the Cinque Ports.

I have this day received command from the Lords of the Council for stay to be made of all ships and vessels within the Cinque Ports. *Copy.*

1628, September 13. Lulworth.—The Earl of Suffolk to Sir John Hippisley.

By directions from the Lords of the Council you are to give order that all ships and vessels within the jurisdiction of the Cinque Ports (especially the men of war that belong to the States and United Provinces) be released and suffered to proceed in their intended voyages, having first paid his Majesty's customs and other duties.

1628, November 28.—The Bailiffs and Jurats of Lydd to the Mayor and Jurats of Rye.

"This nobleman is landed at Lydd out of one of the King of Denmark's ships of war by the help of a Hollander, and hath required of us to send them down ten men to help to bring the ship into the harbour as also a boat to bring some other of their company to land. The wind being contrary, our fishermen are not able to go to sea and thereby not able to yield them the help we would. We have thought good to write unto you desiring you to send with all possible speed a boat and ten men sufficient to supply their wants, as by his letter and this messenger's relation, you may see needful. The Dunkirkers have taken away ten of their best men and many more of the company are hurt and sick so that they are not able to weight their own anchor so that the ship in great danger of being lost for want of men."

1628, November 28. Lydd.—Lord Spencer "Colonell" to the Mayor of Rye.

"Mait pleis this presentt is to lat you know that I am heir areiffitt befor Leid in on of ye King of Denmarkis schipis, and hes matteris of grytt importance and hes lositt the best of our men vith the Dinkirkeris, and our boott, so that I maid my retraitt heir to this toone to the ballyeis heir and at thair request hes vreittine to you and your maigestrates vith you for asistanc of the nomber of tene sayllaris, or uthervayis ye schipe is in danger of losing both men and guidis. So loiking for your performanc as you vill be ansverabill to your King and mester, for be asuiritt I vill reportt your dilygenc or disobedienc as I sall tak atasstacione of all vith me to his Majestie."

1628, November 29.—The Mayor and Jurats of Rye [to Lord Spencer.]

According to your request (considering your extreme necessity) we have delayed no time, as you may perceive, but with all the diligence we could use, have provided and sent to you a boat and the number of men you wrote for, not doubting but that your Lordship will see these men shall be well satisfied for their service. *Draft.*

1628, December 24. Whitehall.—The Lords of the Council to the Lord Warden.

The occasions are more apparent and every day more frequent why all provident care should be used for the securing of the Cinque Ports from the danger and spoil of enemies, especially at the present his Majesty having had advertisement of some hostile preparations. And therefore we pray and require you to take effectual order for the careful watching and looking to, of the beacons of the Cinque Ports and their members. *Copy.*

1628[9], January 2.—The Mayor of Dover to the Mayors, Bailiffs, and Jurats of the other Cinque Ports.

I have received letters from the Lord Warden to use my best endeavour for the apprehension of one, John Shorte, lately a prisoner in the Tower and thence escaped, he is described to be a low man of little stature, his face pale and wan, his hair black, clothed in black "russesuite" and an old pair of russet boots. He pretendeth himself to be a Frenchman but speaketh perfect English. These are to require you that strict examination be taken of all persons seeking for passage in every of your several liberties that the said Short may by no means escape through any of them.

RYE MSS.

1628[9], January 6, Suffolk House.—The Lord Warden to the Lieutenant of Dover Castle.

According to the direction of the Lords Commissioners of the execution of the place of Lord Admiral of England. These are to require you forthwith to take survey of the ships, sailers, and mariners within the Cinque Ports.

1628[9], January 25.—The Mayor and Jurats of Rye to the Lord Warden.

These are to certify your Lordship of such ships, barques, and vessels as belong to our town with their owners and part owners, masters, mariners, or fishermen. *Draft. Certificate of ships and vessels in the Port of Rye with their owners, masters and mariners, enclosed. In all five ships (of which the two largest are of 60 tons) and 9 fishing boats of 14 tons.*

1629, May 1.—Sir Edward Deringe, Lieutenant of Dover Castle, to the Mayor of Dover.

According to orders received from the Lord Warden these are in pursuit of his Majesty's commandment to give you notice of the good agreement between his Majesty and the French King, and to desire you that you give order to the several Ports that ships of reprisal against the French go not forth to that intent and purpose. And it is his Majesty's pleasure that if any French do arrive or land within the Cinque Ports you give them all friendly and courteous entertainment as befitting his Majesty's friends. *Copy.*

1629, July 15. Whitehall.—The Lords of the Council to the Earl of Suffolk, the Lord Warden.

Whereas there was lately a great tumult in Fleet Street in which many insolent persons did in a rebellious manner resist the Lord Mayor and Sheriffs who were forced for the suppressing of them and the maintaining of his Majesty's peace, to employ the trained bands. Forasmuch as it may be doubted that some of them will seek to convey themselves out of the Realm we have thought fit hereby to pray and require you to give present order to all the officers of the Cinque Ports not only not to suffer any gentleman or any other person that may be likely to have had any hand in the tumult, to pass without special warrant, but also if any such person do seek to pass to stay him and take strict examination of him. *Copy.*

1629, September 21. Windsor Castle.—The King to the Earl of Suffolk.

The abuses and neglects of the trained bands of the several Counties are by connivence and want of due care grown so customary, as the directions of the State for reformation are commonly received for matters of form only, and so slightly executed as the wished and necessary effects are not at all produced. And since so essential a part of the strength and safety of the Kingdom consists in those bands, and in having them well chosen, well armed and well disciplined, and that neither the serious recommendations from us nor the iminent dangers of the times can serve for sufficient admonition, we are resolved to take a strict account ourselves of the performance of each man's duty in that so important service. Our will and pleasure is that you cause a general muster to be taken of all the trained bands, horse and foot, under your lieutenancies and that you make equal impartial and indifferent charge, according to the value of each man's lands and means, whether the owners be resident or not for finding horse and foot, and see the horse and arms so charged and sufficient men to ride the horses. Those that are to be enrolled in the trained lists are to be of gentry, freeholders, good farmers, and their sons, that are like to be resident in the country and ready to serve with the arms they bear and are trained in at the musters, and that the meaner sort of people and servants whose residence cannot be expected to be constant be avoided at least where any servant is enrolled it shall not be in his masters power to change or put him away without the licence of you, because by such changes the benefit of training and teaching the use of arms is utterly lost. *Copy.*

1629, October 28. Whitehall.—The Lords of the Council [to the Lord Warden].

Whereas we are informed that as well in Holland and especially in Amsterdam as also in France and more particularly in Rochell and in the Ports and towns of Brittany, there is at this present much contagious and pestilent sickness, whereof great numbers daily die, and that the said infection is already brought into the Isle of Scilly, we charge and command you not to suffer any persons or commodities to be landed until you have first fully inquired and informed yourselves whether the place from whence they come were free from infection or not, and if they have come from places infected that you cause them to forbear coming on shore till such course be taken by them for airing of their goods and so many days after their arrival as may give hope and likelihood they are free from danger and infection. *Copy.*

1630, May 10. Dover Castle.—Sir Edward Deringe to the Mayors, Bailiffs and Jurats of the Cinque Ports.

Forbidding that any corn be shipped out of the Ports notwithstanding any licence heretofore granted. *Copy.*

1630, September 15. The Court at Theobalds.—The Earl of Suffolk to the Mayors, Bailiffs, and Jurats of the Cinque Ports.

Orders for all masters of ships, barques, and crayers and all innholders, victuallers, and hackney men in the Cinque Ports to enter into bonds, that the commissioners of passage may have certain knowledge what persons are transported out of the kingdom or come from beyond the seas.

1630, September 20. Dover Castle.—Sir Edward Deringe [to the Mayors, Bailiffs, and Jurats of the Cinque Ports].

Notwithstanding the order forbidding the export of corn I am informed that divers persons daily ship and export great quantities of wheat and barley, that the store of corn in those parts is so far exhausted, and the prices so much enhanced that without some speedy remedy a great dearth is likely to ensue. These are therefore to charge you that no person be permitted to export or ship any wheat or barley. *Copy.*

1630, December 14. Dover Castle.—Edward Kempe to the Mayors, Bailiffs and Jurats of the Cinque Ports.

Requiring that the proclamation touching the peace agreed upon between his Majesty and the King of Spain be publicly declared throughout the Ports, and especially to all owners, masters, and officers of ships.

1630[-1], March 1. Dover Castle.—Sir Edward Deringe to the Mayors, Bailiffs, and Jurats of the Cinque Ports.

Order for the quiet sufferance of one hundred quarters of wheat lately bought by Sir Sampson Darrell in Sussex, for the supply of his Majesty's navy, to pass without interruption. *Copy.*

1630[-1], March 4. Dover Castle.—Sir Edward Deringe to the Mayors, Bailiffs, and Jurats of the East Ports.

Acquainting them with the intention of the Lord Warden to hold a "Court of Shipway," the holding of which Court had been discontinued.

1631, May 21. Dover Castle.—Sir Edward Dering to the Mayors, Bailiffs and Jurats of the Cinque Ports.

Requiring them to put in speedy execution the laws and statutes made for putting forth of poor children as apprentices, against unlicensed alehouses and divers other offences, according to his Majesty's late proclamation.

1631, June 19. Greenwich.—The King to Theophilus, Earl of Suffolk, Lord Warden.

Whereas upon motion made unto us on the behalf of our good brother the King of Sweden, we have given licence to the Marquis of Hamilton and to the captains and officers under him to levy and transport six thousand English voluntaries to be employed for that King in a war just and honourable, not undertaken for private ambition, but for the re-establishing of such Princes, his Majesty's allies, as have been wrongfully deposed, of which sort the distressed estate of our dear brother and only sister cannot but come near unto our heart, and for the general peace of Christendom and the enlargement of commerce. For the good esteem we have of our cousin who hath undertaken this charge, and for the benefit this kingdom will find in disburdening itself of so many unnecessary men, that want employment, and for that the season of the year requires expedition for the raising and transporting so many men into so remote parts, we do therefore instantly require and command you to employ your very best endeavours to the accomplishment of this service. *Copy.*

[1630-1631.]—Petition of the Mayors, Bailiffs, Jurats and Commons of the Cinque Ports, two ancient Towns and their members for a new Charter. *Copy. Note at the end to the effect that the petition was granted.*

1634, June 18. London.—Stephen Monins to Markes Thomas, Mayor of Rye, Speaker of the Ports, and the Jurats of Rye.

These are to acquaint you how our affairs stand, we have passed the Signet and Privy Seal and now our Charter is in the hands of the Lord Keeper, but we have not sufficient money. We expected that the eighty pounds we last wrote for would have given a full end to the affair. Our experience in passing these offices which we have already passed, doth show us that the particular charge of passing every office doth far outgo our expectation, moreover there is such notice taken of our said Charter with the greatness of the Port's corporation, as of so many towns incorporate, that there is such general expectation of expedition money in every office, and that of no small sum to gratify them, that unless we do somewhat deal after their expectation we cannot be looked on. Our Charter is grown already into so large an extent by reason of their small skins that we assure ourselves it will be ten or eleven skins at the least when we have passed the broad Seal and the fine we are to pay will be, according to the fine which was paid for King James' Charter which was four skins and came to eighteen pounds, at the least will be thirty pounds. *Signed. Seal of Arms.*

1634, August 22.—The Mayor and Jurats of Rye to Sir Thomas Sackville.

Whereas it is reported abroad in the Country that the infectious disease of the plague is in our Town which false rumour causes the Country to forbear to resort to our Town and repair to other places to provide and furnish themselves with such necessaries as they want, wherefore we have thought good to signify to your Worship that herein we are greatly wronged for, we thank God, our town is clear of that infectious disease, only (as it hath been in many other places) we have some few houses in our Town visited with the small pox, of which sickness to our knowledge there have not died above five or six persons. *Draft.*

1634, November 15.—The Mayor and Jurats of Rye to the Mayors, Bailiffs and Jurats of the Cinque Ports, ancient town of Winchelsea, and their members.

Having lately received the Kings writ to provide and furnish a ship of 800 tons, "in warlike manner for his Majesties service," they think it very requisite to hold a general meeting of the Ports and members at New Romney on the 25th of November to consult how to proceed. *Signed.*

Postscript.—"Pray pay this bearer ij*s.* vi*d.*, everie toune, for wee woald not gett any to goe scarcely for this price."

[Answers follow from the various ports and towns agreeing to meet on the day fixed.]

1634, December 31. Whitehall.—The Commissioners of Plantations to [the Lord Warden].

"Whereas it appeareth that greate numbers of his Majesties subjects have been and are everie yeare transported into those parts of America which have been graunted by patent to severall persons, and there settle themselves, some of them with theire families and whole estates, amongst which numbers theire are also many idle and refractory humers, whose only end is to live as much as they can without the reach of authoritie, wee, having—according to the power wherewith wee are intrusted by his Majesties Commission for matter of plantation—seriously considered how necessarie it is for divers waightie and important reasons to take carefull and effectuall order for the stoppinge of such permiscowus and disorderly departinge out of this Realme, doe therefore pray and require your Lordshippe to charge and command the severall officers in the Cinque Ports not to suffer any person beinge a subsidie man to embarque himselfe in any of the said Ports or any the members thereof for any of the said plantations without licence from his Majesties Commissioners, nor any person under the degre of a subsidie man, without any attestation from two justices of peace, living next the place where he dwelt last (or where he lived before, if he hath lived but a while there) that he hath taken the oth of supremicie and allegeance, and like testimony from the Minister of the parish

RYE MSS.

of his conversation and conformitie to the orders and discipline of the Church of England." Returns of those departing for the plantation to be made every half year. *Copy.*

1634[-5], February 15. Dover Castle.—Nicholas Eaton, Deputy of the Lord Warden to [the Mayors Bailiffs and Jurats of the Cinque Ports and their members].

Forbidding the departure of "any Irishe or English souldiers . . . . . to serve any forraigne prince whatsoever," without speciall order.

1634[-5], March 20.—Sir Edward Hale, Mr. Roberts, Thomas Culpepper, John Foule, John Culpepper, William Boys, and William White, Commissioners of Sewers (?) to the Mayor and Jurats of Rye.

As for making a bridge at Kent Wall, though mending the "greate Roade at Newenden," by them, is more advantage to the whole country, than the want of the bridge can be prejudicial, yet if a bridge can be made at reasonable charge one shall be undertaken. As for the question of navigation, "wee may take it for a certaine rule that in a mayne nothinge can be hurtfull to the harbor of Rye that is not likewise hurtfull to our wett marshes, neyther can there any thinge be good to the generall of the levells, but must likewise be good for your harbor; therefore wee neede the lesse be jealous one of another. Hitherto there is nothinge done but what was done by the hand of God, but when the sea shalbe let into the great quantitie of lowe landes of Wittersham, for which wee pay soe large a rent of purpose to make an indraught, wee have noe doubt but both wee and you shall receave the good we hoped for by our worke. Besides our charge and paynes, wee have had a greate deale of patience and wee must desire you to have a little, till our work be finished." *Signatures and Seal of Arms.*

1635, April 13. Dover Castle. Anthony Percivall to [the Mayor and Jurats of Rye].

Has lately received from the Lord Warden the King's Commission for a collection "towards the reparation of the church of Saint Paul, London, to be made in the Cinque Ports and members."

1635, May 18.—"At the Court at Greenwich." Order of the Council.

"Whereas notice has been given to his Majestie and the Board, by the Lord Warden of the Cinque [Ports], of the landing of great number of strangers at Dover who desire, in respect of troubles abrode, to retire for a tyme into this kingdom for theire better saftie, his Majestie commiserating theire estate, with the advice of the Board, was thereuppon pleased to give them passage, and to order and command that the said Lord Warden shall give expresse directions to all the officers of the Ports within his jurisdiction to make and keep a particular register of the names, surnames, qualities, and professions of all such strangers as [there] were, or [should] hereafter arrive, at any of the said Ports with an intent to reside in this realme; and that they shall from tyme to tyme send up a true copie or transcript thereof to the Board. And that his Lordship should likewise direct and charge the officers respectively not to permit the said strangers, so landing, to dwell or reside in any of the said Ports but to repair to the more inland townes and more remote from the sea." *Copy.*

1635, June 6. Dover Castle.—Anthony Pervicall to the Mayors, Bailiffs, and Jurats of Dover, Hythe. Romney, Lydd, Rye, Hastings, Winchelsea, Pevensey, Seaford, and Tenterden.

Desiring them to forthwith comply with a warrant by which they were required to send into Dover Castle, by a given day, now past, the rolls of the last musters taken, expressing the arms charged upon every particular man, together with the proportions of the general and private store of munition, and also the names of all persons in their jurisdictions not imbanded between the ages of 16 and 16 [60?] years.

1635, June 15. Whitehall.—The Lords of the Council to the Lord Warden.

They doubt not that their previous commands, sent to him on 27 April, have been put into execution; but as the King receives daily advertisment of further preparations both by sea and by land on the part of neighbouring Princes and States—they consider it necessary to give the following additional directions:—The Deputy Lieutenants are to keep particular watch on all the ports and places "apt for landing" in the Cinque Ports. Upon the first notice of appearing or approach of any foreign fleet upon those coasts, all the trained bands of the counties [Kent and Sussex] or as many as shall be found needful, are to be "drawn down thither to repulse the landing of any enemy." Landsmen are, from time to time, to be impressed for the King's ships. All musters are to be made near the coast. *Copy.*

1635, July 7. Dover Castle.—Anthony Percivall to the Commissioners and clerks of the passage at Hastings, Romney, Hythe, Rye, Winchelsea, Folkestone, Lydd, Pevensey, and Seaford.

A great offence has been committed by the clerks of the passage within the Ports, especially at Dover, "in suffering young persons by indirect meanes and without licence to be conveyed beyond seas to be trained up in the Romish religion, which, as a matter of dangerous consequence, his Lordship's [the Lord Warden's] chiefe care hath ever ben to prevent." Extra diligence is, therefore, to be observed in the future, and all the clerks of passage within his Lordship's government are to send him "a particular account of all persons whatsoever that have been allowed passage at any place or creeke within the jurisdiction of the Cinque Ports or their members within the space of three years last past."

1635, July 25. Dover Castle.—Henry Crispe to the Mayors and Jurats of the Towns of Hastings, Rye, and Winchelsea, and to the Bailiffs and Jurats of Pevensey and Seaford.

Enclosing letter from the Privy Council to the Lord Warden concerning the non-payment of 50*l.* of the tax assessed on the above-named towns towards the ship lately charged on the counties of Sussex and Kent. The sum in question is to be immediately levied and paid to the High Sheriff of Sussex.

1635, August 20. Whitehall.—The Lords of the Council to [the Lieutenant of the County of Sussex].

"Whereas his Majestie sent you his writt to provide one ship of five hundred tons to be furnished with men, tackle, munition, victuall, and all other necessaries to be sett forth for the safegard of the sea defences of the realme at the charge of the countie and corporatt townes or the greater parte of them, whereof the Sheriff of the Countie to bee one, shall within thirtie dayes after the receite hereof assesse and sett downe howe much every of the said corporate townes shall pay, and after to proceed on in the further execution of the sarvice as by the said writt appeareth. Wee are by his Majesty's expresse direction and commandment to lett you knowe that hee hath upon important and weightie reasons concerning not only his owne honor and the antient renowne of this nation, but the saftie of yourselves and all his subjectes in this troublesome and warlike times, sent out the aforesaid writt to you and the like unto all other counties, citties, and townes throughout the wholl kingdome, that as all are concerned in the mutuall defence of one another soe all might putt to there helping handes, for the making of such apparation as by the blessing of God may sarve this realme against those dangers and extremities which have distressed other nations and ar the common effectes of ware, whensoever it taketh a people unprepared; and therefore as his Majestie doubteth not of the redines of all his subjectes to contribute hereunto with cherefulnes and alacritie soe hee doth especiallie require youre care and diligence in the orderinge of this buisines soe much concerning his Majestie and all his people that noe inequalitie or miscariage may eyther retard or disgrace the sarvice, which in itselfe is soe just, honorable and necessarie for which cause wee have by his Majesty's lik direction sent you, together with the same writte, thesse insuing advises and instructions for your better proceedinges. First, therefore, whereas by the said [writ] you the said Hight Sherife are only of the quorum for making of the said assesments, it is to be understood by youe all that his Majesty's intention was and is that in case anie of youe, the maiors and head officers of corporate townes, desiring the ease of your owne townes beeyound that which is meete, should make a major parte and pluralitie of vote and thereby lay or leavie a greater burden upon any other of the corporate townes or upon the body of the countie then were fitt, that the Sherife, whoe is presumed to stand alik effected to all the corporat townes, might have some powre to ballance that inequallitie and alsoe might not bee overruled with the major vote to the prejudice of the countie which is the greater body but it likwise to bee understood that his Majestie expectes that equalitie and indifference in you the Hight Sherife that you neyther favor one corporat towne above another, nor the countie itselfe above the corporat townes, but that you use the power given youe by the said writt with such moderation as occasione the greater rediness in all to contribute and may give noe cause to any to grudg or repine for any purrialitie (*sic*) or inequalite in the assessment. Secondly, because diverse of you may bee unacquainted with the charge of such martan [maritime] preparation, and the mistaking thereof might hinder the sarvice, wee have thought good to lett youe knowe that upon a due and just calculation wee find that the charge of a shipe of that burden soe manned and furnished will be five thousand powndes, and to prevent difficultie in dividing the assessments upon the corporat townes wee have informed ourselves the best wee may of the present condition of the corporate townes and what proportion of that charge each of them is fitt to beare, doe conceive that Hasting with the members may well beare fowre hundred and tenne powndes, Chichester twoe hundred powndes, Arrundell thirtie powndes, Shorham twentie powndes, and the residue of the said five thousand powndes is to bee layed upone the rest of the countie, and thesse rates wee wish to bee observed rather then any difference of opinione amoungst youe of the corporations or beetwene you of the corporations and the Sherife of the countie, should retard the sarvice; howbeeit wee are so fare content to [*blank*] waie to the judgmentes which are upon the place that in case the major of you of the corporations shall agree upon any other rates, and that the Sherife of the countie shall approve the same rates sett by the major parte of you, and approved by the Sherife, shall stand, allbeit thay vary from those expressed in our letters, it being his Majesty's desire and the intention of his Lords that all things should bee done with as much equalitie and justice as is possible for us and you to discerne. Thirdly, when your some [having] agreed upon the generall assessments, what shall be done by every corporat towne and what by the rest of the countie, wee think it fitt you subdivid the same and make the particuler assessments in such sorte as other common payments upon the countie or corporate townes ar most usually subdivided and assessed, and namely that you the Sherife divid the whole charge laid upon the countie into hundreths, lathes, or other divisiones, and those into parishes, must bee rated by the houses and lands lying within each parish or towne as is accoustomed in other common paiments which fall out to bee payable by the countie, hundreths, lathes, divisiones, parishes, townes, saving that it is [his] Majesty's pleasure that wheare there shall happen to bee any men of abilitie by resone of gainefull trades, great stock of mony or other personall estate, whoe perchause have occupied eyther none or littel, and consiquently in an ordinary land scott would pay nothing or very littelle, such men bee rated and asseissed according to theire worth and abilitie, and that the monyes shall bee levied upon such may be applied to the sparing and easing of such as being eyther of weak estate or charged with many children or great debtes or unable to beare so greate a charge as ther land in theire occupation might require in an usuall and ordinarie proportion, and the lik course to bee held by youe in the corporate townes, that a poore man be not sett in respect of the usuall tax of his house or the lik at greater some then others of much more worth and abilitie and to them this may bee effected with much mor equalitie and expedition youe the said Sherife may send forth your warrants to the Counstables of the severall hundreds, requiring them to call unto them some discreete and sufficient men of every parish, towne, or tything and to consider with them howe the same, charged upon each hundred, may be distributed and devided, as aforesaid, and most equallitie and indifference, and to retourne the same to youe which beeing done you may give order for collection thereof by the Counstable and others usually imployed for collection of other common charge and payments, and when any shall bee by them retourned to you, eyther to refuse or to neglect to mak payment, you ar without delay to exicute the ritte upon them, and you, the Maiors and hed officers of the corporat townes observing your usuall distributions by wardes, parishes, and otherwise as is accustomed amoungst you for the common paiments for your parte to doe the lik by yourselves and your severall ministres under youe respectively as is before appointed to bee done by the Sherife, as fare fourth as may bee apte and agreeable to the course and state of your severall townes and corporations. And as concerning the clergie albeit his Majesty is resoulved to maintaine all theire due priviledges which they have injoyed in the time of his noble progenitors yet because it hath not hetherto bene madde sufficiently appeare to his Majesty or this Borde what priviledges have bene alowed them in former times touching paiements and sarvice of this nature, his Majestie is pleased that for the present youe proseed and texe and assesse them for this sarvice and receive and levie theire sessments as you are authorised to doe the rest of his Majesty's subjects with this care and caution that you and the ministers faile not to beare a due respect both to theire person and calling not suffering any

RYE MSS.

inequalities or pressures to bee put upon them, and such your assessments and proceedings his Majestie resoulveth shall not be prejudiciall in the future to them or any of their rightes and priviledges which upon farther search shall bee found due unto them. Lastly, to all other matters not particularly mentioned in theise instructiones you must upon all occurrantes governe yourselves according to the writte to you directed and as may best effect and accomplish the sarvice committed to youre trust." *Copy.*

Postscript.—Directs [the Lieutenant] to communicate this letter to the Mayors and head officers of the corporate towns.

1635[-6], February [5?]. Suffolk House.—The Earl of Suffolk to Henry Crispe.

"Whereas uppon notyce given by me to his Majestie and the Bord of the landinge of great numbers of strangers in the Portes within my government whoe in respect of troubles abord desyre to retyre into this kingdome for theire better safetie, his Majestie commiserating theire estate with the advise of the Bord was then pleased to admitt them passage and did in May last order and command me to give . . . . directions to keepe a particular booke or register of the names, surnames, qualities and professions of all such strangers as then were arived or from thence forward should arrive at any of the said Portes with an intent to reside in this realme, and that they should from tyme to tyme send up a true copye or transcript thereof. And that I should direct and charge the Maiors and others whome it should concerne not to permit the said strangers so landinge to dwell and reside in any of the said Portes [but] to repaire to any of the said inland townes and more remote from the seas. According to the purport of which order I did addresse my letters to the Porte townes in generall to put the same order in execution, and som of them did only make return unto me of the persons that landed, but have not caused them to departe the Porte townes; neither have they since theire last certificates in Michlemas terme last past made known unto me of the great numbers of people since arrived, wherein they deserve much blame no more to regard his Majesty's command in that behalfe, it beinge so dangerous to this kingdome that if any enimy should arise, the numbers of strangers might neere equalize if not exceede the strength of those townes, and secondly the tyme of yeare cominge on it is dangerous for infection of the plague and other infectious deseases, and thirdlie verie incommodious for theire owne inhabitantes in raysing the prizes of victualls; but not the least of all to myselfe in my accompte to his Majesty when I shall be called thereto, touchinge the performance of this service by them hitherto neglected. And therefore these are to praye and require you to send copies of this my letter unto all the Maiors of the townes within my government to require them that they spedilie put the said order in presente execution in all particulars. And that they shall also spedille give an accompt thereof, especially from the townes of Dover, Sandwich, Margate, and Rye. Nevertheles in respect of the great trade at Dover by merchant strangers by composition lately made for advancement of his Majesty's customes, yf the Maior can shewe me any sufficient reasons for the residence of some fewe in that towne only which are potestants and whole abydinge there, may be good for his Majesty's service, I would be ready to endeavour such theire accommodation; and that the remove of such persons may not be precipitately done nor in a tumultuous way, I leave the well orderinge thereof to the Maiors and heads of the townes after theire discretions, so as the delay therein be not to great. And of all this I require as speedy an accompt as may be, because I knowe not how sone I shall be thereto called myselfe."

Postscript.—"In the performance of this service, yf the Maior of Dover shall desire the stay of any, they must be protestante, and in that case he must take the advise of the ministers or preachers of the towne."

1635[-6], March 16. Dover Castle.—Henry Crispe to the Mayors and Jurats of Sandwich, Rye, and Faversham.

According to an order lately received from the Lord Warden signifying that divers certificates and attestations have been granted to many strangers, mariners, within his Lordships government by the Mayors and other principal officers of the Ports, whereby they are taken to belong to the Cinque Ports and so go free with their merchandise between Spain and Flanders, answering no composition for custom to the prejudice of his Majesty in his revenue, and requiring that the Mayors of the said Ports should not only forbear to give the like to any strangers hereafter without the consent of the farmers of his Majesty's customs but forthwith to call in all such as they have already given. *Copy.*

1636, March 25.—The Mayor and Jurats of Rye to "Mr. Montigny Governour of Deipe."

The Lord Warden has made an order for the transport of passengers from Rye to France, "appoyntinge only six vessels and theire severall masters and companies to attend carefully and diligently to that service." And because some persons of Rye, going with fish and merchandize to Dieppe, often take away the passage from those six persons, to their great damage, the Mayor and Jurats request the Governor not to permit any but the six authorized persons to bring back passengers from Dieppe to Rye.

1636, September 2.—Certificate by the Mayor and Jurats of Rye that William Bullock, gentleman, the bearer, had resided at Rye "about his necessary occasions and especially about the repayring of the Light at Dungeon Nesse;" and that the town of Rye, "God be blessed," is, and for many years had been, free from "the infection of the plague." *Copy.*

1636, September 5.—Similar certificate for Monsieur de la Grile, his wife, man and maid servants, and for James Cawsabor, gentleman, who had landed at Rye about a fortnight previously (since which time they had remained in the town) on their way to the Queen's Court. *Copy.*

1636, September 24.—Similar certificate for Paul Derby, John Whitway, Richard Davidge, and Thomas Dashwood, merchants, who had lately landed at Rye, on their way to Dorchester in Dorsetshire. *Copy.*

1636, October 17.—Similar certificate for Mr. Laurence Grene, merchant, and his servant, Mr. Danyell Cogill and Mr. Jordan Firfax, merchants, who had landed at Rye two days previously. *Copy.*

1636[-7], January 31.—Mark Thomas, Deputy Mayor of Rye to [the Bishop of Chichester].

Mr. Blackwood, the curate of Rye, has shown him a letter from the Bishop in which he sees that Mr. Norton, one of the churchwardens of the town, has informed his Lordship of "many abuses committed by divers persons in our toun against God's service, honor, and reverence due to holy and consecrated places, against the lawes, statutes, and canons of the Church, in makinge the chancell, arsenalls, prisons and places of execution of punishment." When this first began, "none now livinge in our Toune can remember"—but the south aisle of the chancel has for long been used "for a place to keepe Arteliry, which was sent thither from the Toure of London" for the safeguard, and defence of the town, "and the ordnance, guns, ingins, and other warlike instruments that have been in former tymes there kept, and those that now remaines, are his Majesties, of which ordnance and all other his Majesty's Arteliry," the Earl of Newport, Master of the Ordnance, during the last summer took an inventory, and left them for the town to keep "which part of the chancel thus used and employed for his Majesties service, wee cannot conceive or imagin that any would be so bold to sequester or use for this use and purpose but by order from some Lord Bishop of Chichester lyvinge at that tyme, and for good cause and consideration shewed him for the sufferinge and allowinge of it." Dr. Andrews [Bishop of Chichester 1605–9] when he visited Rye saw the use to which the part of the chancel was put and "did not dislike it for anything wee know, for it concerns not us so much as the Kinges Magistie, whose the ordnance and other Artilery be." This is all the "prophanation" of the place, except that some "unruly servant" has been in times past whipped there by the Mayor's orders. "Thus much wee have thought good . . . . . . for the clearinge ourselves of the aspersion layd uppon us, to signifie unto your Lordshipp." As to the complaint made against the curate "for omyttinge readinge the church service, and for preaching sometymes two howers," the Bishop is informed that "though often tymes he doth reade the Letanie, and tenn commandments, yett sometymes he doth omytt the reding thereof, through weakness of body, as he saith, and wee truly believe; and for the accusation of preachinge two howers long, we do assure your Lordshipp that the accusation is alltogether false; for the mostlie he keepeth himself to his howre, and sometymes preacheth lesse then an howre." Hopes this apology will satisfy the Bishop.

1636[-7], March 9. Suffolk House.—The Lord Warden to Sir Thomas Colepper, Knt., Lieut. of Dover Castle.

The King has granted to Sir John Meldrum Letters Patent concerning Lighthouses erected and to be erected upon the North and South Forelands. "These are [therefore] to pray and require you to give notice thereof to Maiors, Bailiffs, Jurats and other officers under my government within the jurisdiction of the Cinque Ports and their members" requiring them to be aiding and assisting Sir John Meldrum. *Copy.*

1637, April 1.—"From Richard David's house in Rye." Warrant from Thomas Freebody, constable, addressed "two the counstables or Hedborrowes or his Majesties officeres to whome it may com or concerne."

"These are therefore in his Majesties nome to make diligent scherch for to horse men, one a blacke tale man in sad coler coat with weppon by his side, the other a shorte man in a whit hate and a light coler sute, a young man with a silver belte and weppon by his side. These to men for breke into the house of John Colbeard and beat him and his wife wounding hem with a knife. These are in his Majesties name to atach them and safely to keepe to answer to his Majesties lawes in that case made and provided, and hereof faile you not as you will answer the contrary."

1637, April 29. Suffolk House.—The Lord Warden to the Mayor and Jurats of Rye.

The officers of the Customs at Rye complain to him "that divers watermen, porters, and other poor men that live by their labour about the waterside, refuse to rowe them to or from aboard shipps, to help them open or carry prohibited or uncustomed goods to his Majesties Storehouse" or to afford them other needful assistance. The Mayor and Jurats are therefore ordered to punish offenders and aid the Customs' officers. *Signed. Seal of Arms.*

1637, May 17. Suffolk House.—The Lord Warden to the Mayor and Jurats of Rye.

He has appointed and authorised George Merefeild of London, fishmonger, "to take present order" in all places within the jurisdiction of the Cinque Ports, "for collecting receavinge and takinge up for my houshold provision, all such respects, rights and priviledges of fish, by waye of pre-emption or otherwise, as have heretofore belonged unto the Lord Wardens of the Cinque Ports, my predecessors." *Signed. Seal of Arms.*

1637, June 7. Dover Castle.—Circular Letter of John Manwood to the Mayors and Jurats of Hastings, Romney, Hythe, Rye, Winchelsea, Folkestone and Tenterden, the Bailiffs and Jurats of Lydd, Pevensey, and Seaford, and the Commissioners for restraint of passage at any of those places.

Has lately received orders from the Lord Warden (in pursuance of instructions from the Privy Council) to obtain from all those to whom the letter is addressed "a perfect roll or list of the names, surnames, and qualities of every person which hath taken passage" for any of the American plantations, "since the last account;" the same roll or list is to be returned "into the office here." The writer further directs that a similar list be sent to him from each of the above places "half-yearly at the least." *Copy.*

1637, June 14. London.—Warrant signed by Edward Broomfeilde, Lord Mayor, addressed "to all Constables and other his Majesty's Officers and Ministers whatsoever"; for the arrest of Robert Edmondes for stealing from the lodging of Rodolph Gee in Chancery Lane, and other places, "one watch with a silver case, a scarlett coate with silver lace and divers other thinges to the value of 40*s*." Edmondes is described as being "of a middle stature," as having "a little blackisshe beard," and as being dressed in "a whiteshe gray suite and coate." *Seal of Arms.*

1637, June 21.—Examination of Robert Edmondes of the parish of St. Dunstan's in the West, London. He has known Randolph Gee, who is his wife's brother, but he (the examinant) was never his servant, though he had sometimes done business for him. Denies having the possession of Randolph's cloak or watch or any things of his, "but knowes that he had such a watch and scarlet cloak, which he hath pawned in Drury Lane for 40*s*." *Signed.*

1637, July 1. London.—Randolph Gee to the Mayor of Rye.

"Whereas Robert Edmonds is in prison in your toune of Rye, being apprehended by vertue of a warrant signed by the Lord Maior of London for stealinge from me one watch, one scarlet coate, and other thinges, theise are to certifye you that I have since that tyme heard of my goods againe, and find the said Robert Edmonds to be cleere of the said felony, although I had greate cause to suspect him in regard I lost my goods about the same tyme he went from me, besides goinge away without taking any leave of me."

1637, August 8.—The Mayor and Jurats of Rye to Mr. William Thomas.

We have in our gaol at Rye "a prisoner who being found guilty for having two wifes, praied his clergie, which we have granted him, but for want of an Ordinary to hear him reade, we adjorned our Sessions to an other day." They pray him to depute and appoint Mr. Richard Marten, the rector of Iden, Mr. Christopher Blackwood, curate of Rye, and Mr. Edward Gee, curate of Playden, to attend the adjourned Sessions and to hear the prisoner read. Mr. Blackwood will pay him what belongs to him for the commission. *Copy.*

1637, August 22.—Sam. Short to the Mayor and Jurats of Rye.

As to a sentenced felon, who—having being allowed the benefit of clergy—"was so unhappie as not to reade, so as he might have escaped the sentence of death." If there is any likelihood of obtaining the King's pardon, he thinks the respite of the felon's execution may be arranged amongst themselves.

1637, September 30. Hampton Court.—The Lords of the Council to the Mayor and Jurats of Rye.

We have been made acquainted with your letter to the Earl of Suffolk concerning the abuse of the searcher of your Town in suffering two English gentlemen to pass without licence, and have thereupon thought good to commit the said searcher to prison and thereby to give you thanks for that your care. It seems by your letters that it hath been a common practice amongst the officers of that port to suffer gentlemen to pass without licences upon slender excuse or upon a ticket only from the farmers of the Customs at London, which is such an abuse as cannot be answered and therefore we pray you continue your care and vigilancy to discover all such officers or others as connive at such passengers. *Signed.*

1637, October 23. "Retherfield."—Anthony Fowle, Sheriff of Sussex, to the Mayor and Jurats of Rye.

Ordering a meeting to be held at the sign of the Bull at Lewes on the third of November to make assessment for raising 5000*li* for providing a ship of war of 500 tons for his Majesty's service and defence of the realm. *Signed.*

1637, November 3.—The proportions to be paid by the maritime towns of Sussex towards the charge of a ship of war for his Majesty's service.

1637, December.—Correspondence concerning a petition for a royal pardon for Richard Died, condemned to death at the Sessions at Rye for bigamy.

1637[–8], February 20.—Commission directed to Sir Dudley Digges, Sir John Finch, Sir Charles Harbert and others touching the draining of 20,000 acres of marsh in and about the Romney Marshes.

1638, June 21. Suffolk House.—The Earl of Suffolk to the Mayor of Rye.

Complaining of certain persons of the Town of Rye who trespassed over the lands of his cousin Sir Henry Gilford at Winchelsea and took away the "olives and puetts" that breed there every year upon the beach lands and grounds. *Signed. Seal.*

1638, July 10. The Court at Oatelands.—Proceedings by the Lords of the Council ordering that a room shall be made and maintained on Dover Pier for serving the Customs.

1638, September 18.—Answers to certain articles as to the navigability of the River Rother and the Harbour of Rye.

1638, October 16.—The Mayor and Jurats of Rye to the Mayor and Jurats of Sandwich.

We make no doubt but that you are sensible of the grievance of the Ports concerning the impost and tax of fifty shillings upon all foreign salt brought into the Ports, which (as we conceive) might have been remedied if we had been vigilant to prevent it as other towns who by humble petition to his Majesty got themselves free, as all the western towns and Ports as far as Southampton. We think some course should be taken to take off this great charge. *Draft.*

1638, November 15.—The Mayor and Jurats of Sandwich to the Mayors, Bailiffs, and Jurats of the Cinque Ports.

A circular letter calling attention (as speaker of the Ports) to the grievances offered by the undertakers of the sole making of Salt, and desiring the opinions of the various Ports touching the prosecution for the freedom of the Ports from the same thraldoms. In the replies of the Ports, the Mayor and Jurats of Dover think the Ports should join with the fishmongers of London and that Mr. Lanesdale, town clerk of Rye, or some other of that town, should go to London to join in solicitation with the said fishmongers. The Mayors and Jurats of Folkstone, Hythe, New Romney, Rye, Hastings, and Winchelsea reply in the same terms. The Bailiff and Jurats of Lydd are of opinion that the sole making of Salt is a grievance of particular towns and does not concern them. The Bailiffs and Jurats of Pevensey, Seaford and Tenterden and the Mayors and Jurats of Faversham and Fordwich agree with the Bailiff and Jurats of Lydd.

1638, [November].—An humble declaration of the discommodities and grievances arising by means of the late undertakers for the sole making of Salt, together with the remedy for the same.

1638, December 7. London.—Samuel Landsdale to the Mayor and Jurats of Sandwich.

"After Mr. Mayor of our Town and his brethren received your letters and Mr. Hearnes' and other writinges theere inclosed, and there finding that I was chosen to joyne with the Fishmongers and traders in Salt of the Cittie of London and others of the Southwest Portes in the solicitation of the salt business against the intended patentees thereof, they wer verie ernest with me not to neglect any tyme, but with all speed to take my jorney for London and not to stay for any further approbation, the major part of the Portes and their Members havinge consented thereunto. Whereuppon I rid towardes London and uppon the xxij[th] day of November last betimes in the morninge came thither and repaired to Mr. Hearne, Mr. Cockram of our Towne going with me, where we met with Mr. Legey of Southampton; Mr. Hearne presentelie then sent for Mr. Davis, who [had] ben (as he said) a principall agitor in this busines. And being come to us, after we had conferred about our designes, we respited further communication thereof untill Satterday following, appointinge to meete together againe at the Mermaid in Breade streat with Waymouth men and others of the South-west Portes, where accordinglie we all met. Allso one Mr. Perott for Yarmouth and Mr. Cockram was there likewise present, where we of the Northeast Portes informed them of the Southwest Portes that we intended to farme the Salt busines at as easie a price as we could, demaunding of them if they would joyne us therein. But they utterlie rejected it resolving to petition the King for free trade, and said that they would shew sufficient reasons to induce his Majestie thereunto. We, seinge they would not be removed from theire grounded and setled resolution and opinion, moved them that we might all joyne together in one petition for free trade, which by no meanes they would graunt unto us, being yet free and exempt (as they said) from the imposition of 48*s.* 6*d.* the weigh for forreine salt imported upon the former contract. So they left us to petition by ourselves. Nevertheless we agreed then amongst ourselves to meete againe on Wednesday followinge in the afternoon, that we might have the sight of either of our petitions and be privye to each others proceedinges. At which time and place we met and there reading and perusing our severall petitions, reasons, and certificates, we concluded to deliver them on Sunday followinge to the Lordes of his Majesties most honourable Privye Counsell. And then after we of the Northeast portes were come on Sunday last in the afternoon to Whithall, we found there those of the Southwest portes, who certified us that they had delivered theire petition and hooped that it should be read that day. We forbore then at that tyme to deliver in ours for that we were promised a certeficat from the Trinitie Howse on our behalfe. But that day there was nothing done. Upon Wednesday last we all attended againe the Lordes and then delivered in our petitions. And after the Lords were risen wee understood that the petition of the Southwest portes was read and an order entred that they should attend the Board on Wednesday come seavennight. And thus farr we have proceded in our busines. And for so much as Mr. Hearne and Mr. Davis allwaies were since my cominge up and still continue of opinion, that neether they of the Southwest Portes or we of the Northeast portes shall obteine our suite for free trade being against the Kinges revenue and profet, which the Lordes so much stand for, they have often tymes and at this instant are vere ernest and importunate with me to write unto the Portes and theire Members that they would be pleased (if they shall like thereof) to give further Commission and authoritie to Mr. Cockram and myselfe by theire letters with all speede to fall upon theire first intended project, which they are allready acquainted with, it we cannot prevaile in our suite for free trade. And Mr. Perott hath to this end and purpose writ to Yarmouth, desiring them to send up two of the most ablest men of theire Towne to assist him herein. Thus havinge related to your worshipps our proceedinges hetherto in the Salt business I leave the determination and prosecution of the farminge of it to the grave and discreet consideration of the Portes and their Members, intending (if wee prevaile not in our suite for free trade) to proceed therein as I shall have warrant and directions from you. I have sent this messenger of purpose with this letter and our petitions and certificates there inclosed, desiring you with all convenient speede to send your answeres, allso that you would be pleased to writ unto everie particular Towne to send me their severall proportions of mony thought fit by Mr. Maior of our Towne and his Brethren (as appeareth by their answer to your letter) to be sent unto me for defrayinge all such needefull and necessarie charges as is incident to busines of this nature. And allso to order what everie Towne shall pay to this messenger for his travaile paines and hire of his horse rydinge through the Portes and theire Members and reterninge hither."

1638, December 19.—Order of the Lords of the Council assembled at Whitehall, that upon consideration of the several petitions presented in the name of the Cinque Ports and their members, and the Towns and Counties of Southampton and Poole, and the Towns of Weymouth, Melcomb Regis, the Town and Fishery of Great Yarmouth, Lewes and the traders in salt and fish in the City of London touching the making and vending of Salt made at the Shields, and upon hearing of the agents of the said Ports and their counsel and of the answer of Thomas Horth and the new undertakers of the Salt business, His Majesty and the Board conceiving it to be a matter of great advantage to the Kingdom that Salt made within his Majesty's dominions should be preferred and used before foreign salt and finding upon debate that salt made within his Majesty's dominions is sufficient for use if skilfully handed, did therefore order that the said business be forthwith established.

1638, December 22. London.—Samuel Landsdale [to the Mayors Bailiffs and Jurats of the Cinque Ports].

"In my foremer letter I signified unto you that uppon the reading of the petition of the Southwest Portes exhibited before unto the Lordes of his Majesties Privie Counsell an order was made that they should attend the Board the 12th of this instant. And our Petition was not then delivered because we staidd for a Certificate from the Trinite Howse, which beinge afterwards sent to us on Fryday the 9th of this present, we delivered our Petition and certificates, but could not have them then read nor the Sunday followinge, but by meanes of friendes on Tuesday at a private setting they were read and there ordered that the next day in the afternoone our petition and Certificates and the Southwest Portes petitions and reasons should be then taken together into consideration. Where we then attended, and after the rysing of the Lords we were certefied that they had deferred the haringe of our cause and greviances untill Wednesday followinge. The next day wee went for the Order in which we were injoyned that we should in the meane tyme deliver unto Horth and his Associates copies of our petitions and Certeficates. Upon the day assigned us to attend the Board we meete together at Whithall where in short tyme after we were come, we wer called into the Counsel Chamber where the King was presente. Mr. Recorder of London and Mr. Hearne being of our Counsel went in with us. And after Mr. Recorder had delivered and made knowne to his Majestie and the Lords the full scope and most material points of our petitions, reasons and certificates and throughly proved them, Mr. Horth in defence and approbation of the Sheilds Salt, delivered to the Board his answere in writinge to all that we in our petitions, reasons and certificates did object against the salt or against himself, which I send you here inclosed with the certificate of the Trinitie Howse and all the orders of the Lords concerninge the imployment of the Salt busines, whose answere both the King and Lords greately favored and approved, when whatsoever Mr. Recorder or we said was litle regarded. This busines thus argued and debated on both sides it

RYE MSS.

was thought fit by his Majestie and the Lords that Horth and his associates shall not be left to theire own libertie to sell salt, but the prize of salt shal be regulated by the Lord Treasurer and Lord Cottingdon which will be one chefe thinge in the order which is now to come forth, which we went often for but could not for that the King will first have the sight of it. Upon Fryday last I received from the Portes and Members their severall auswers about the farming of the salt wherein I perceive that the greatest part will not consent to the farminge of it although some are verie ernest and forward therein. But I havinge no sufficient warrant to proceede therein I surcease further to present it. And allthough that is not effected which we desired, yet seeinge the prize of salt will be regulated, the subject thereby shall be removed, which will recompence our charge and expences which else might have been otherwise.

1638[-9], March 16.—Depositions of George Goodwin of the City of London, carpenter, taken before the Mayor of Rye.

The deponent says that King James, neglecting to do justice, lost his right to the Kingdom, and King Charles going on in the same courses is an usurper and saith that if he had his right he should enjoy the Kingdom. "His ground for this is that in Ecclesiastes that better is a poore and a wise child then an old and folish King."

1639, April 4.—The Mayor and Jurats of Rye to the Lord Warden.

Of late one George Goodwyn coming to our Town said he was the King of England and had right to the Kingdom. He said he had been in Bridewell for these speeches and from thence to Newgate and at the Sessions he was, by the Lord Mayor, discharged. *Draft.*

1639, April 25.—The Mayor and Jurats of Rye to the Lord Warden.

Acquainting him that on the 23rd among other passengers that came out of France was one John Pulton who refused to take the oath of allegiance. *Draft.*

1639, October 11. Dover.—The Earl of Suffolk to the Mayors, Bailiffs and Jurats of the Cinque Ports.

"Accordinge to his Majesty's command latelie signified to me, these are to will and require you to take care and order within your severall liberties that if any Spaniardes or Hollanders shall, by reason of the present fight betwen them at sea on this Coast, be forced on shoare for succour, that you cause them to be received and accommodated with provisions of meate, drink, and lodging for theire mony in such convenient places and manner as may be without prejudice to his Majesties subjectes."

1639, December 7. Suffolk House.—The Earl of Suffolk to the Mayor and Jurats of Rye.

"Whereas his Majesty hath now resolved to call a Parliament and for that I intend to recommend one unto you in your election to be chosen one of your burgesses I have thought good to signify my intention to prevent your engagements otherways." *Signed. Seal.*

1639, December 14. Glastonbury.—William Roberts to the Mayor and Jurats of Rye.

Asking that they will choose him to serve as one of their burgesses to Parliament. *Seal of arms.*

1639, December 18. Suffolk House.—The Earl of Suffolk to the Mayor, Jurats, and Commonalty of Rye.

Having already written to you to spare your engagements to any other for one of your Barons or Burgesses places but to reserve the same for my recommendation, wherein I request no more than you have freely done to my predecessors, I do now accordingly recommend unto your election my beloved son, Thomas Howard, to be one of the Barons or Burgesses of your Town in this ensuing Parliament. *Signed. Seal of arms.*

1639, December 18. Broomham.—L[aurence] Ashburnham to the Mayor, Jurats, and Commonalty of Rye.

Asking to be elected one of their burgesses to Parliament. *Seal of arms broken.*

1639, December 24. Chilham Castle.—Thomas Diggis to the Mayor and Jurats of Rye.

"I am one who hath made means for your knightship this Parliament, but being like to be overborne by many powerful competitors in the west ports, out of an earnest desire notwithstanding to do my country service I look out for myself, and finding letters from your corporation to my late honoured father I am encouraged to commence unto you."

1639, December 31. Whitehall.—The Earl of Northumberland to the Mayor and Burgesses of Rye.

Recommending Sir Nicholas Selwin as one of their Burgesses to Parliament. *Signed. Seal of arms.*

1639[–40], January 8. Hollingborne.—John Culpeper to the Mayor, Jurats and Commons of Rye.

Requests in consideration of his affection to their town and harbour that he may serve them in Parliament. *Signed. Seal.*

1639[–40], January 9.—Assessment of the Ports and corporate towns in the County of Sussex towards the charge of one ship of war of 400 tons for his Majesty's service.

1639[–40], February 8. Suffolk House.—The Earl of Suffolk to the Mayor, Jurats, and Commonalty of Rye.

Recommending Mr. Reade, Secretary to Mr. Secretary Windebanke, as one of the Barons of their town to Parliament. *Signed. Seal.*

1639[–40], February 26. London.—Sir John Manwood to the Mayor of Rye.

Recommending Mr. Reade as a burgess to Parliament for his town *Signed. Seal of arms.*

1639[–40], February 27. Suffolk House.—The Earl of Suffolk to the Mayors, Bailiffs, and Jurats of the Cinque Ports.

Ordering the re-enforcment of the articles for binding mariners, innkeepers, victuallers, and hackneymen to make a return of all passengers.

1639 [–40]. February 28. Whitehall.—The Earl of Dorset [to the Mayor and Jurats of Rye].

Upon his Majesty's first declaration of a Parliament I recommended unto you for one of your burgesses Sir John Sackvill, my kinsman, but since his occasions are such that he cannot so act without much prejudice to his fortune, I shall desire you that you would be pleased to make choice of John White, Esquire, my Secretary. *Signed.*

1639[-40]. March 8. "My house in Drury Lane."—Sir Francis Windebank to the Mayor Jurats and Commonalty of Rye.

Recommending to them the bearer Robert Reade, his secretary, as a burgess to Parliament for their town, *Signed. Seal of arms.*

1639[-40], March 17. Westminster.—King Charles I. to the Earl of Suffolk.

"The great care we have had of the safty of this our Kingdom and the peace of our subjectes hath bine of late manefested unto them by the chardgable and warlike preparations we made to withstand the disroyall designes of such ill-affected persons (whoe as much as in them laye) indevored the disturbance of both. Nor is it at present unknowne to our subjectes howe just reasons we have to continewe the same preparations and to be in like reddynes as formerly, and therefore we have with the advice of our Privie Councel thought fitt and doe by these presentes athorize and requier you to cause 300 able and serviceable men to the warres to be levied in that our County of Cambrig, 300 men in our Cinq Portes, 600 men in our County of Dorsett, and 600 like able men in that our County of Suffolk under your leftenancie, and to observe in the choyce of the men and the ordering and disposeing of them, such directions as you shall herewith receive by letters from the Lordes and others of our Privie Councel, with such care and diligence as the importance of this present occasion for which these forces are to be levied doth requier." *Copy.*

1640, March 26. Whitehall.—The Lords of the Council [to the Earl of Suffolk].

By his Majestys letters sent herewith your Lordship will understand his pleasure and intentions for the levying of certain soldiers.

"We have thought good hereby to pray and require your Lordship to give present and effectual order to your Deputy Lieutennant in each County respectivelie forwith to meete and in the first place to distribute the numbers of men to be raised in the severall Hundreds of every particular County, and to take especiall care that there be a verie good choise of the men of the trained bandes there, that they be of able bodies, and yeares meete for this employment. Where any freeholder hath used to have his armes borne by an other man, that other man is to be pressed to serve if he be of able body, and where a freeholder hath served with his owne armes, and is not fitt or willinge to serve himselfe, he is to finde another able man to serve in his place, and if he cannot procure an other then your Lordship or your Deputy Lieutennant are to cause an other able man to be pressed to serve, and where any man hath used to beare the comon armes of the parisshe, if he be fit and able of body he is to be taken, but if he be unfit a sufficient man is to be pressed in his steed. Your Lordship is especiallie to take care that in the libertie given to change men to serve in the place of trained soldiers, there be not any rewardes or money taken which was an abuse to much practized in the last yeare in some counties and now in examination to recevie condigne punishment. As for the choise of men our verie good Lord, the Erle of Northumberland, Lord Generall of his Majesties Army, will forthwith send into those Counties Commanders to assist your Lordship or two of your Deputy Leiutennentes in the choise and listinge of them. And when they shall be in such manner listed, your Lordship is to take effectuall order that there shall be no alteration of any of them, without a particular warrant under the hand of your Lordship or two of your Deputy Leiutenantes. The men to be raised in each county are to be appointed to meet in companies of one hundred a peece at theire particular rendezvous in each County respectively most convenient for each hundred men, untill they shall be brought to the generall rendesvouze in the severall Counties to be weakelie exercized with false fiers or no fire by such Inferior Officers as the Lord Generall shall send downe to instruct them in, their postures and the use of their armes. To which purpose your Lordship is to cause the Armes of the trained bandes to be lent to them which shall be delivered back when they shall march out of the Counties. Your Lordship is likewise to take order that there be prest and sent with the said soldiers one drum to everie hundred men who shall enter into his Majesties pay as soone as the said soldiers shall march out of the Counties, besides each particular rendevouze where the severall companies of one hundred a peece are to make in those Counties, your Lordship is to cause a generall rendevouze to be appointed on the confines of each shire most convenient for the soldiers march towards the severall portes or places following (vizt.) The six hundred men from the County of Dorset unto Newcastle uppon Tyne, the three hundred men from the County of Cambridge and the six hundred men from the County of Suffolke to Yarmouth And the three hundred men from the Cinque Portes to Gravesend. To which generall randezvouze in each County respectively those of the County of Dorset are to come the 10th of May to remaine there till the 20th, then to march towardes Newcastle. Theise of the County of Cambridge are to come to the generall rendevouze of that County on the 25th of May to remaine there till the 5th of June then to march to Yarmouth, that they be there ready to be shipped on the 10th of June. Those from the County of Suffolke are to come to the generall rendevouze in that County on the 27th of May there to remaine till the sixth of June, then to march to Yarmouth that they may be ready there to be shipped on the eighth of June. Those of the Cinque Portes are to come to theire generall rendevouze on the one and twentieth of May to remaine there till the first of June, and then to march to Gravesend that they may be ready there to be shipped on the fourth of June. And they are all to be at the said generall rendevouze of the severall counties exercised and put in order for theire marche towardes the said portes and places by such Commanders and Officers as shall be sent thither by the Lord General, to whom your Lordship is to send present advertisment what places you appointe for each generall rendevouze for everie County. The soldiers are to be allowed at the charge of every County respectively 8[d] a piece *per diem* for everie day they shall be exercized at each particular rendevouze in Companies as aforesaid of 100 a piece in everie of the said Counties, as allso for the tyme they shall remaine at the generall rendevouze in their severall Countyes untill they march out of the County when they are to enter into his Majesties pay. Your Lordship or at the least two of your Deputy Leiutennants for everie County are to be at each generall rendevouze of the said Countyes by the tymes afore sett downe for the same as well to assist for the departinge of the men in order to take care for the receivinge back of the said armes from them and to deliver the said men over by Indenture to such Comanders and Officers as shall be appointed to receive and take charge of them." *Copy.*

1640, April 26. Fetter Lane, London.—Francis Raworth, William Richards, and Nicholas Robertes to the Mayors, Bailiffs, and Jurats of the Cinque Ports.

"We, yestorda had our pettition drawn and ingroced to his Maiestie in the names of the Maiors, Balyfs, Jurats, and Freemen, and Inhabitantes of the 5 Portes, 2 Ancient Townes and there Members by the advice of Mr. Sargent Finch and Mr. Short, and in the evening left the same with Mr. Read, servant Mr. Secretary Windebank, one of the Burgesses for Hasting, who promised to procure Mr. Secretary to get it redd at the Bord this afternoon for that he did know his Majestie wold make no order therein without the Lordes, my lord keeper, therle of Dorcet and Sir H. Fann, as favors were desyred therein, but the Spanish Imbassador being to have audience, his Maiestie and the Lordes did not sytt above 1 hower and rose, and so our pettition was not redd, but only profored by the clark of the Council to be redd, and refused, for that it was said there was an order therein allredy, of which I did tell him we never had notis. To morrowe morning we shall have coppi of it and then according to advice I shall tak other corse. Upon perusal of our Charter by our Councel we find we have not expresse and full wordes to free us of the service by land, by sea there is expresse wordes and yet you know seamen are daly impressed, howsoever we trust we shall get free of this required service, although not soe soone as you may expect it. We hope Sir John Manwood will doe the Portes the favor to forbeare the returne of certifficat in the buesnes some daies to which we doubt not but you will move it. We, this evening, received your letter touching which we here the Lordes gave full direction and that the choyce of the men is left to my Lord Warden and his lifftenant, so that Sir John Manwood is to be requested to do the same you write of. There is no hope here to gett the directions already given in the buesness altered in any port. We hope to do it in the whole and therein God willing shall doe our utmost indevor whatsoever it costes."

1640, May 20. Dover Castle.—Sir John Manwood [to the Mayors, Bailiffs, and Jurats of the Cinque Ports].

"Whereas accordinge to his Majesties Command and the directions of the Lordes of his Majesties most Honourable Privye Counsell given to my Lord Warden for the levying of 300 able soldiers within the Cinque Portes for his Majesties service, I latelie proportioned the certaine number of men to be raised out of everie Port, Towne, and place within your Liberties for that service, and gave directions for your respective levyinge of such monies as might be sufficient for the coating and conduct mony and other allowance to be made for the same 300 men, so that they may be at the generall rendevous completelie armed and furnished for his Majesties service at such tyme as I should signfie unto you. Theise are now in his Majesties name to will and require you in your severall Liberties to conduct and bringe or cause to be conducted and brought into the Towne and Port of Dover (where the generall rendevous for the said Soldiers is appointed) upon the first day of June next, before noon, the severall numbers of soldiers upon everie of your Portes, Townes, and places by me so as aforesaid proportioned and charged, amounting in all to the number of 300, as in a schedule annexed to my last letter in this behalf directed unto you set downe and expressed, takinge especiall care that the said soldiers be all able and well proveded for in theire armes, coatinge, conduct money, and otherwise."

1640, July 2. Dover.—John Pringle and Nicholas Roberts [to the Mayor and Jurats of Rye ?].

Upon certain notice of the Duke of Lennox, being Lord Warden of the Cinque Ports, to the Mayor and Jurats of this town, as to the employment concerning the taking of three hundred soldiers, and their charges being left to this town, the said Mayor and Jurats sent us to London in the name of the whole Ports therein to petition his Grace. Our petitioning his Grace in the business we found to be very well liked, and the effect of the business being understood by his Grace he said he would do us all the right he could therein, and afterwards attending for an answer to our petition his Grace willed us to draw a petition to his Majesty taking coach to Roehampton (his Grace being then to ride in the coach with him) so that he might on the way have conference with his Majesty therein, whose command we accordingly pursued and upon their return to Whitehall we waited for an answer. His Grace informed us that his Majesty would not take any of our priveleges from us. *Copy.*

1640, September 24. York.—Royal writ for the election of Barons to Parliament for the Cinque Ports. *Copy.*

1643, December 24.—The Mayor and Jurats of Rye to the Committee for Sussex.

"We have thought good to let you know that the Castle, called Camber Castle, neere to our towne is soe greatlie ruinated and broken that any man may goe in there and purloigne and take from thence the tymber and leade; and therefore it will be verie fitt (as we conceive) that some course may be taken that the leade and such tymber as may be easilie embeazeled be taken away from thence and put in safe custodie where you shall thinke fitt to appoint." *Draft.*

1643, December 27. Lewes.—The Committee for Sussex to the Mayor and Jurats of Rye.

Order for six of the biggest and most serviceable pieces of ordnance in Rye to be conveyed to Shoreham. *Signed.*

1643[-4], January 25.—The Mayor and Jurats of Rye to the Committee for Sussex at Lewes.

"Concerning the removinge of the lead in Camber Castle, the wheather hath ben so unseasonable that as yet there is but litle of it brought away but there hath ben a watch day and night for securinge it ever since order from you. And we intend, with all convenience, to bringe away the rest which when it is done you shall have spedie notice. We have received a letter from Nicholas Shinner, employed by us to convey our ordnance to Shorham which you sent for, referring him to us to pay the fraight and other charges, for that the last tax imposed upon our towne is not fullie paied in of which 53*l.* is paied in to the receivers at Battle and the residue cannot be collected by distresse, but by warrant from yourselfes to our collectors." *Draft.*

1643[-4], January 25.—L. Ashburnham to the Mayor and Jurats of Rye.

"We have this day receaved letters from the Committee at Lewes under the hands of Sir Thomas Pelham, Sir Thomas Parker, Collonoll Morley, and others, intimatinge that the Armey is in greate wante, by reason that the provision money is not sent in according to the time appointed. Wee desire you therefore with all possible speede to take

RYE MSS.

such order that the said mony and all the arearages thereof may be sent to Mr. John Aylwine of Lewes." *Signed and Seal.*

1643[–4], February 21.—The Mayor and Jurats of Rye to the Committee for Sussex at Lewes.

"Havinge so oportune a messenger to writ unto you concerninge a former letter we sent of the 25th of January last about our proposition mony and plate, and two hundred powndes that was ordered by the Committee towardes the fortification of our towne, of which, receivinge as yet no answre, we have thought fitt to put you in mynd of, the rather for that our forwardnes to pleasure the countie alltogether hath disabled us to fortefie our owne towne. Our humble request therefore is that the said two hundred pounds which was ordered by the Committee, as we have been informed, for and towards our necessarie fortifications may be allowed us, either out of the leade of Camber Castle or some other way, that our forwardnes in partinge with our mony and plate be not prejudiciall to us." *Draft.*

1644, June 5.—The Mayor and Jurats of Rye to William Hay.

"We have lately received a warrant from the Committee at Lewes concerninge an ordnance of Parliament for the Scot's loane beinge 13,500*li.* imposed upon our countie. We desire to be enformed from you whether the Portes are therein included, yf so whether there be no deference to be made betwen those that have been forward and others that have been backward. It is not unknowne to you what Rie hath done to the proporsitions beyond our estates, besides all taxes since. And the 200*li.* ordered to be deducted out of our porporsitions towards our fortifications hath not yet ben paied unto us, thoughe the Committee have been much importuned for it, nether are we any whit the more regarded for the 2,000*li.* worth of the leade of Camber Castle for which we were the only meanes to help the State to, which had been embeaseled had not our care prevented it. Our forwardnes hath exposed us to the verie scorne and obliquie of the county. We desire allso to be informed concerninge the Commissioners of the Rape of Hasting and there instructions, admyringe much that one put out of the Commission of the Peace above (as we heare) should be one of the Commissioners in so waightie a busines, who is the greatest enemie our towne hath and hath blamed us to our faces for taking so much. Yf noe care be taken for our poore towne we are like to be exposed to as great danger by our malignant neighbours as to a forren invasion which we expect dailie for our vesels which usuallie carry passengers for Deipe dare not adventure out for feare of surprisall." *Draft.*

1644, June 10.—The Mayor and Jurats of Rye to Robert, Earl of Warwick, Lord High Admiral.

"We have thought it our duties to signifie unto you that our towne of Rie beinge the ordinarie passage for Diepe where divers merchants of London and there goodes, merchant strangers and other passengers doe weekelie passe from hence thither, which bringes in a considerable somme of money to the State for custome and excise, latelie a barque of our towne was surprized by one of the Kinges men-of-warre of Waymouth, who had in her 3,000*li.* worth of goods, and persons of qualitie, two of them Mr. Arundell's sonnes, a member of the House of Commons, and Collonells Browne's son and heire, and divers merchants of good worth. We besech your Lordship to take this into your consideration and that you would be pleased to appointe a smale man-of-warre for the safetie of our passage barques to lie betwen our towne and Deipe Rode which will do good service for the State for there is store of ammunition weekelie shipt from Diepe for Waymouth by one Pinozeire." *Draft.*

1644, August 3.—The Mayor and Jurats of Rye to Richard Browne.

"The greate distres that our poore fishermen are now in, because they cannot goe about theire callinge for feare of beinge taken by the Kinges men-of warre, havinge this summer allready lost one gainfull voyage to the north seas to take fishe, and now not daringe (this season) to adventure to Yarmouth to take hearinges: theise two voyages beinge the greatest meanes of the yeare for theire maintenance, which, if they should be deprived of both, would prove there utter undoinge, not being able to subsist the next winter. Theire necessities therefore beinge so greate and they fearinge (not without just cause) will be greater, are determined to petition the honorable Howse of Parliament that they would be pleased to let them have safe convoys to Yarmouth, and theire to staie with them all the fishinge season. Our request therefore is that you would not only advise them how to drawe theire petition (if the draught which they shall present do not like you) but allso to give them your best assistance and furtherance that this theire desire may be effected which will not only be adventagious to them but to the whole kingdome." *Draft.*

1645, August 28.—The Mayor and Jurats of Rye to The Earl of Warwick.

Approving of Mr. Bastock to be one of their Barons for Parliament.

1645, September 7.—Writ from Charles I. to the Constable of Dover Castle, directing that whereas John White, lately elected a Baron for the vill of Rye to the present Parliament, being by Judgment of the House rendered incapable of sitting as a member, that therefore another Baron be chosen in his place.

1645, October 4.—The Mayor and Jurats of Rye to Colonel Herbert Morley.

"This morning two men of war who have lain in our Bay a long time have taken three or four boats, and our Yarmouth fleet being ready to come home, if some speedy course be not taken they will all be in danger to be surprised by those men of war. We beseech you that you would be pleased to take our lamentable condition into your consideration, and with all speed to dispatch a frigate for the rescue of our poor men who otherwise will be utterly undone."

1645, October 20.—The Mayor, Jurats, and Commonalty of Rye to Colonel Herbert Morley.

"We have sent you a petition by the bearer hereof Nicholas Shimer for the procuring a frigate or two to lie upon our coast for the safeguard of our barques, boats and fishermen entering into our harbour from the King's men of war. If the officers which shall go in her be not of our town we shall be little the better for it."

1645, December 3.—Depositions by Frances Royall, wife of William Royall, that about four years ago about twelve of the clock in the night there came a hound to the street door and made a great howling, and she looked out of the window and called out but the dog would not go away and goodwife Hownsell came and knocked at the chamber door, and presently (the door never opening) the said goodwife Hownsell came to

RYE MSS.

this deponent's bedside and took her left hand and said "Goody Royall you must go with me," and she asked "Whither?" and Hownsell answered "Home," and she said "she would not," then the said Hownsell vanished away and the deponent says that lately she came through a pane of glass while she was lying ill and afterwards departed in the same way.

1645, December 7.—Order by the Mayor of Rye and others for Martha, the wife of Stephan Bruff, and Anne Howsell, widow, being suspected to be witches, to be tried by putting them into the water.

1649, December 10.—William Hay to the Mayor and Jurats of Rye.

I understand you desire to have Mr. Russell to be settled with you. There hath been a solicitation from the brotherhood to solicit for a renewing of your charter, I see other towns have written to their members here for the prosecution of it but as yet I have heard nothing from you. *Seal of arms.*

1650, July 30. Dover Castle.—Thomas Wilson to the Mayors, Bailiffs, and Jurats of the Cinque Ports.

In the absence of Colonel Sydney, Governor of Dover Castle, I have received a warrant from the Council of State signed by the Lord President for the dispersing and publishing in all places within the jurisdiction of the Cinque Ports the Resolution of Parliament of 23rd of this month concerning such delinquents as have not paid in their fines according to compositions. *Copy.*

1650, August 6.—Order to the Mayor and Jurats of Rye to levy a rate in pursuance of an Act of Parliament for settling of the militia of the Commonwealth of England.

1650, August 12. Dover Castle.—Thomas Wilson to the Mayors, Bailiffs, and Jurats of the Cinque Ports.

In the absence of the Governor of Dover Castle I have received an Act to prohibit all commerce and traffic between England and Scotland and enjoining the departure of Scots out of this Commonwealth.

1651, September 2. Lewes.—Colonel Morley, John Fagge, and William Hay to the Mayor, Jurats, and Freemen of Rye.

"We think it our parts to acquaint you that your letter and desire to the Commissioners are granted, that your persons and arms shall remain at home for the service of the Commonwealth in the defence of your town, you listing yourselves and arms under the command of Capt. Fissenden, which will be an additional strength for the securing your corporation." *Signed, Seal of Arms.*

1651, November 14.—Order by the Trustees for Maintenance of Ministers.

"In pursuance of an order of the Committee for reformation of the Universities of the 15th of January 1650 grounded on an order of the Comittee for Plundered Ministers, it is ordered that the yearly summe of forty nine pounds sixe shillings eight pence be continued for increase of maintenance unto Mr. William Russell, minister of the Parish church of Rye in the County of Sussex, vizt. the yearly sume of 18*l.* reserved to the Deane and Chapter of Canterbury out of severall of their possessions in Ecclesham in the said County and the yearly sum of tenne poundes out of several of their possessions in Chislehurst, and the yearly sume of eleaven poundes, six shillinges, eight pence out of severall of the possessions belonginge to the Deane and Chapter of Chichester in Bexill, and the yearly rent of tenne poundes reserved to the Bishop of Winton' out of the impropriate rectory of Rye aforesaid, in all amounting to the yearly sume of 49*li.* 6*s.* 8*d.* as aforesaid, the said augmentation to be accoumpted from the 25th day of March last, the present maintenance belonging to the said minister being by the said order expressed to be but fourty poundes a yeare." *Copy.*

1651, November 20.—The Mayor and Jurats of Rye to Colonel Morley, Mr. John Fagge, and Mr. William Hay.

"Upon severall complaints of the poore tradsmen of this towne unto us made that many of the disbanded souldiers and other strangers did sett upp and exercisse pubike trades and callinges, to there great prejudice and apparent ruine, and desiringe redresse therein and withall being acquainted that divers of the said disbanded souldiers and strangers had wives and children which are like to bee a sudden and great charge to this place which is already so poore that the inhabitants are very much oppressed in beareinge the charge thereof (as also by the souldiers quarteringe in private houses, forcibly against the minds of the inhabitants) for remedy whereunto we did proceed accordinge to law and the priviledges of this Corporation for our own conservation, that we fall not into an irrecoverable mischeife, in manner followinge:—Firste, we have received into and permitted all such souldiers which were, now or at any tyme heretofore have beene disbanded, having formerly either beene borne or belonging to this place, to sett up and exercise their severall trades and callinges therein. 2ly. Wee have permitted all such disbanded souldiers which have married wives of this place also to sett up and exercise their severall trades and callinges therein. 3ly. Wee doe permitt and suffer many disbanded souldiers and others as also those which are in present service to worke as journymen under master workemen of this towne. Now upon the desires aforesaid we have proceeded with all such which are not comprehended in these severall qualifications aforesaid in this legall order. First, we gave them tymly warninge to desist the publique exercise of there callinges and depart this place and goe to there severall places of birth or last abode, there to use there severall trades, accordinge to Act of Parliament in that case made and provided. 2ly. After an expedient space of tyme expired, fynding them soe farre from observinge this order that they did not only stay but contempuously in there behaviour did abuse the Governors and Governement of this place, whereupon we directed our warrante to the Constables for the apprehendinge and committinge to prison of some of them for their misdemeanors aforesaid, in the prosecution of which we have found great opposition by Captain Farley (as we conceive by Captain Fissenden's instigation) who did rescue one of these, so committed, from our Officers as they were carrying him to prison under pretence that he was listed under him. Whereupon we desired a meetinge, and accordingly had, where wee desired of Captain Farly to know whether hee and the rest under committment were listed or not, whereupon hee ingenuously confessed that they were not, only he sayd he had promised Captain Fissenden to list sixe of his men next muster, but he did not know the names of them, only one of them he said he promised to list at the tyme above said, which is not the man soe rescued but one Dearinge, a man of evill behaviour and greatly prejudiciall to the poore tradesmen of this place whereby the course of justice is obstructed and the souldiers imboldened to despise and contemne all Government and ministers thereof. Of all which proceedinges we thought fitt to give you a true, full, and naked narrative thereof that you may be rightly informed of the premisees. Wee fearinge it may be presented to you in another dresse.

The premises considered we are in a sore and deplorable condition, poverty and misery cometh upon us like a armed man and wee are obstructed in the use of the remedy the law provided for the prevention thereof.

Wee therefore humbly begge your Honors would be pleased to take this our sad condition into your serious and speedy considerations (some of you being members of this opprest Corporation and so cannot but sympathize in our misery) and some way or other free us (who cannot as free men lye under soe great bondage) from our aforesaid obstructions, that we may freely execute the law committed to us by this present power on those that are offenders and contemne the Ministers thereof."

[1651]. "Visible causes threatening the destruction and ruin of this town if not prevented."

The causes may be summed up under the headings of the increase of alehouses and brewers, and allowing strangers pedlers and chapmen to sell their wares privately instead of in the market place, and the suffering of strangers to remain in the town until they become by law inhabitants, and in process of time a parish charge.

1651 [-2], March 13. New Romney.—Samuel Benbrigge to the Mayor and Jurats of Rye.

"Theis are to acquainte you that I beinge about my occasions this day heere at New Romney and being redy to take horse, I was attached by the Sarjant with a writte from the Mayor and Jurats for 9*li.* 6*s.* 3*d.* that our Towne of Rye was at the last Brotherhood ordered to pay in to the Clarke of the howse within six monthes then next ensuinge for the first defaulte of the westerne bayliffes defaulte in goinge to Yarmouth, which six monthes being now expired, I thought good therfore speedyly to send theis unto you, desiering you to take order for my inlargment untill which tyme I shall remaine heere in there custody."

1651[-2], March 22.—Certificate by the Mayor and Jurats of Rye that Louis Gilliart, a French Merchant, hath been and still is an inhabitant of the Town of Rye during twelve years and hath always behaved himself well.

1652, April 22.—Certificate by the Mayor and Jurats of Rye. Upon our petition to the Council of State for a free trade between this place and Dieppe in France, they have been pleased to grant an order for the furtherance thereof, that all vessels known to be of Dieppe shall quietly pass between this port and that, and not be interrupted. They have desired Colonel Popham, General in the Downs, to give notice thereof to all vessels under his command. John Manger is master of a vessel of Dieppe and has liberty to pass and repass according to the said order.

1652, June 3.—The Mayor and Jurats of Rye to Colonel Blake, General of the fleet in the Downs.

"We humbly certify that during the time of the late differences in this nation there hath always been a fair correspondence between this town and Dieppe in France, the Governour thereof behaving himself very civilly and courteously towards the friends of this State and denying entertainment to pirates, insomuch as upon our petition the right honourable the Counsel of State were favourably pleased to order free intercourse of trade between the said towns of Dieppe and Rye. And notwithstanding at Dieppe they were informed that two of their vessels (which only have commission to guard their fishing vessels from the Ostenders) were taken by some of our States men of war and now in the Downs yet have they since permitted an English barque of this place to bring over the greatest passage that we have known come over a long while, who arrived here this morning. All which we presumed to acquaint your Honour with, earnestly desiring those fishing guards might be released." *Draft.*

1652, June 9.—The Mayor and Jurats of Rye to Commissary General Whaley.

Requesting that Mr. Bendoll may be disengaged from the soldiery in order that he may be minister at Rye. *Draft.*

1652, June 19.—A true description of the present condition of the harbour of Rye.

"First, the harbour lyeth to the westward outward southwest in one channell and eastward east southeast outward in one other channell, and therefore is a good outlet for a ship to go to sea with the wind at east south east to the westward or to the eastward with the wind at south south west.

2ly.—When it flowes from foure to eight in the west channell, there is fourteene or 15 foot water on the shales, and betweene that time 24 and 30 foot water and in the East Channell is 10 or 11 foot water and betweene that tyme 20 and 24 foot water.

3ly.—The channell within the harbor in the narrowest place is a hundred fathom over and in lengtht is one mile and halfe navigable a quarter of a mile of which Channel is 4 and 5 fathome water at lowe water, the other mile and quarter hath part 3 fadome, part 16 foot and the rest 13, 14 and 15 foot water at low water in the ebbe of the highest springe tydes.

4ly.—There may lye afloat at lowe water 15 or 20 sayle of shippes which draw 3 and 3½ fathome water and have more water than they draw by 4 or 6 foot and at the same tyme further up in the Channell may ride afloat at lowe water 50 or 60 sayle of ships which draw 12 or 13 foot water all without prejudice one to the other.

5ly.—There is very good conveniency for ships to cleane and tallow, carreninge afloat or groundinge adry, which they please.

6ly.—There are boats alway ready to pilot any ship in when by any signe they shall make for the Harbor."

1652, September 22.—The Mayor and Jurats of Rye to the Council of State.

"Last night the *Marline* frigat arrived here and this morninge divers officers of the same complained unto us against there Captain, Peter Warren, for that yesterday at sea before they came into this place he killed one John Wright, a passenger in the vessell, and withall presented there captaine as a prisoner, desiringe he might be secured till further order. Whereupon taking severall examinations touchinge the premises and considering the nature of the fact we could do no lesse then committ him to custody untill your Honours pleasure should be knowne therein, which we humbly intreat for our further direction." *Draft.*

1652, September 22.—Inquisition taken on the body of John Wright, murdered by the Captain of the *Merlin*, frigate. *Seals of the jury.*

1652, September 24, Whitehall.—James Harrington, President of the Council, and John Thurloe, clerk of the Council, to the Mayor of Rye.

Order to send up to London in custody, the Captain of the *Merline* frigate, and also witnesses for giving evidence. *Signed.*

1652, December 22.—Depositions touching a debt owing to Edward Hoadley of Playden by John, James and Richard Shepherd.

[1652.]—Petition of the Mayor, Jurats, and Commonalty of the towns of Rye and Hastings for the preservation of their harbour.

1652[-3], January 31.—The Mayor and Jurats of Rye to William Hay, Esquire.

"In the vacancy of a minister you were pleased to recomend Mr. John Allin unto us, whom we find a man able and fitting for the place, and at a vestry he hath beene approved and chosen by the parish to be our Minister. We therefore intreat your Honor will be pleased to confirme and establish him here, and procure the continuation of the Augmentation unto him, for which with your former recommendations of him we shall we hope be ready alwaies to acknowledge as a great favour." *Draft.*

1652[3], March 19.—Order directed to the Constables of Rye. "By "vertue of an Act of this present Parliament for the better observation of the Lord's day etc., these are to will require you and every of you carefully and dilligently to make search and inquisition in all taverns, innes, alehouses, tobacko houses or shops, or victualling houses within this Towne of Rye and liberties thereof for the discovering and apprehending those which shall upon the Lordes dayes profanely dance, singe, drinke or tiple, contrary to the said Act and finding any soe to offend or otherwise by playing in the streets, working in there callings, selling wares, or merchandize or travelling etc. contrary to the said Act you cause the same to be apprehended and brought before me that they may be punished according to the said Act."

1653, March 29. The Mayor and Jurats of Rye to the President and Council of State.

"Upon the receipt of your order wee addressed ourselves unto the impressing men for the service of the fleet, but by reason that many of our Towne able and fitting to serve are in the service of the State already, and divers others at sea, this place at present affoordes none except unserviceable men, and for your Honors better satisfaction we have inclozed a list of such barques as are at present belonging unto this Towne and at home, with the Masters names and the men thereto belonginge, further assuringe your Honors that some of those men are not only aged as we have there certified but also sicke soe that most of our fisher Masters have soe few men that they have sent for out of France, some five and some sixe French men a piece to supply there wantes this fishing season, but as occasion offers men serviceable, you shall finde us ready and willing to officiate for the service of the state and benefit of this comon wealth." *Draft.*

Enclosure—List of ships belong to Rye.

1653, April 29. Dover Castle.—Thomas Wilson to the Mayors, Bailiffs, and Jurats of the Cinque Ports.

I have this evening received an order for the taking off the restraint lately made on the passage on your several ports. *Copy.*

1653, December 21. Dover Castle.—Francis Kelsey to the Mayors, Bailiffs, and Jurats of the Cinque Ports.

Order to proclaim the "Lord General Cromwell" as Lord Protector.

Endorsed. Proclamation was made on 24 December, 1653.

1653, December 27.—Certificate by the Mayor and Jurats of Rye that Louis Gilliart hath been an inhabitant of Rye for twelve years, where also his wife has lived and seven children have been born to him, and that he is a man well affectioned to this Commonwealth and never was in arms against the late Parliament.

1653[–4], February. Certificate by the Mayor and Jurats of Rye that about Whitsun week 1650 one John Parker, of Rye, fisherman, being in his vessel with eleven of his company off Dungeness to catch mackerel, was taken with his vessel by one John Welsh, an Irish Commander, and carried to Gravelines, where he was imprisoned for six days and afterwards was removed to Calais where he remained in durance four days longer, until he procured and paid thirty-five pounds. By reason whereof he and his family are greatly impoverished.

1654, March 28.—Depositions of John Savage one of the Footmen of the French ambassador, lately landed at Rye.

The Deponent says that last night being in the company of Captain Peter Borgaro in the house of Michael Cadman in Rye he heard the said Captain say that he wondered that my Lord Protector would suffer such a one, as my Lord Ambassador was, to be here for he came to cut the English throats. *Signed.*

1654, April 20.—Certificate by the Mayor and Jurats of Rye that Mark Heytman, master of the ship called the *St. Marke* of Straalsund, in Sweden, was taken at sea by one Captain Pedro Borgaro, of Dover, captain of a private man of war, and was brought into the harbour of Rye and that he hath lost out of his ship goods to the value of 50 *li.*

1654, May 21. Whitehall.—Henry Lawrence, President of the Council, to the Governor of Dover and others.

"These are to will and require you to suffer no person or persons whatsoever, without the speciall license of his Highnes or Councell obteyned, after the date hereof to passe the port of Dover or other places or precincts thereunto belonging to any the parts beyond the seas, for the space of fourteene dayes next coming. And for the better preventing their passing, as aforesaid, you are to appoint strict watches to be kept in the said Port and places and if any person shall come for the end aforesaid, you are hereby authorized to apprehend all such persons and others whome you shall have just cause to suspect to be enemies to the State, and shall remaine in the said Port and precincts and to give an account thereof hither. And all such persons as shall come from beyond the Seas within the said time, you shall make stay of and keepe them in safe custody, untill you signifie their names, and what else you thinke materiall concerning them to his Highnes or the Councell." *Copy.*

1654, May 24.—The Mayor and Jurats of Rye to the Council of his Highness the Lord Protector.

In pursuance of your order of 21st instant we have made diligent inquisition and search within this town and liberties thereof, and have only at present resident in this town bound for France ten persons whose names are hereunder written, whom we have detained till further order from your Honours. *Draft.*

The names are:—Thomas Gerrett, David Ford, Danell Dussieur, Edward Bew, William Simson, Henry Haulocke, George Copley, William Keeth, Jacob Corneuoan, and Edward Reguier.

1654, May 21.—[The Mayor of Rye] to John Thurloe, clerk of the Council, Whitehall.

According to your directions I have examined the two gentlewomen and have here enclosed the examinations. I have by your order also directed a messenger to attend them to London and charged him that no man might be suffered to speak to them till they have been before the Council.

Examinations enclosed. Mrs. Mary Lucey of London says that about eight weeks ago she did pass over to France to see a sister who lived at a place called Pontodame beyond Paris and this was the only cause of her travel.

Mrs. Frances Walpoole of London says that about two months ago she did go to France to bear a gentlewoman of her acquaintance, one Mrs. Mary Lucey of London, company, and she says she hath no other business than a desire to see the country.

1645, May 30.—Safe conduct by the Mayor and Jurats of Rye to Joseph Dugard, an inhabitant and mariner of Rye, a poor man, who hath had some losses by sea and hath four small children to maintain by his labour.

1654, June 1.—Writ to the Constable of Dover Castle for the election of Barons to Parliament for Dover, Sandwich, and Rye.

1654, July 4. Whitehall.—Henry Lawrence, President of the Council, to the Warden of the Cinque Ports.

"Whereas for the better preservation and security of the publique peace his Highnes and the Councell have thought it necessary that very great care and exactnes be used in searchinge all vessells coming to or goeing from any the Portes of this Nation for the better discovery of suspitious persons, whether in their way outward or inward and that a speciall and more then ordinary vigilance be used as to all the creekes and small outletts neare thereunto, whither dangerous persons will most probably apply themselves, you are therefore hereby strictly enjoyned and required to use your uttermost dilligence in the premisses within your Ports and all the creekes thereunto belonginge or adjacent and to apprehend and keepe in safe custody all persons of whom you shall apprehend grounds of suspicion, untill upon giving an accoumpt thereof to the Counsell, you shall receive other order from us." *Copy.*

1654, July 8.—The Mayor and Jurats of Rye to Col. Herbert Morley.

"Our high esteeme of your Honour and presumption of your acceptance hath put us upon the choyse of your Honour to be Baron for this Towne at his Highnes Parliament to be holden at Westminster, September 3rd next, which yesterday at the election was freely done at an assembly of this Corporation according to his Highnes writ and the instrument intituled, the Government of the Comon wealth of England, etc. Our intreaty is that your Honour will looke upon it as a signall of the good affections you deserve and wee beare to you, being in no other way capable to expresse our readynes to serve and honour you. We further desire to know your Honor's pleasure if your occasions will permit you to repaire hither within tenne daies to receive the oath of a Baron of the Portes, as is usuall in such case, if not, we shall commissionate some to administer the same to you." *Draft.*

[1654, July]. Glynde.—Col. H. Morley to the Mayor, Jurats, and Freemen of Rye.

"By letters from Ry of the 7th instant and by yours of the 8th I perceive that I am elected to serve for the Towne, in the ensueing Parliament, I doe acknowledge it a great honour that you deeme me capable of such a service, yet I so well know my owne inability and how unfitt I am for an employment of that consequence if I might fayrely deny to answer your expectacions, but since without my seeking or sollicitation, over ruling Providence hath by your free election devolved upon me, I shall not resist a call from heaven, but am the more free to enterteine the same. And I doe earnestly desire that we all may be frequent in prayer to Almighty God that he would so assist me with the Grace of His Holy Spirite that I may be qualifyed for this greate worke and enabled therby to doe Him, your towne and my country all faithfull service." *Seal.*

1654, July 13. Glynde.—Col. Herbert Morley to the Mayor, Jurats and Freemen of Rye.

"I suppose I neede not acquaint you what passed yesterday here, that I was elected by the county for one of their knights, so that it will be expected I should wave the election of the towne, which I do most unwillingly as not desirous to undervalue so undeserved a favour but though I doe not imediately serve for your towne in this Parliament yet my constant care shall not be wanting to doe you all the service I can, which you may rest confident of, and God willing shal be really demonstrated upon every opportunity." *Seal.*

1654, July 15.—Thomas Kelsey to the Mayor and Jurats of Rye.

Recommending Mr. Thomas St. Nicholas, the steward of the Chancery of the Cinque Ports, as their Baron to Parliament. *Signed. Seal of Arms.*

1654, August 30.—Depositions of Marke Hounsell of Rye, bricklayer.

That walking in the highway from Playden in May last he heard Anthony Norton say, as they were talking of the fighting at sea, that there were none but rogues that fought against the King, and that Cromwell and all that followed him were rogues. And he further saith that the reason he did not disclose these words to the Mayor and Jurats before, was because the said Anthony Norton owed him some money and he was willing to get his money before he revealed it.

1654, August 30.—The Mayor and Jurats of Rye to the Council of the Lord Protector.

On this present day at the Court of Record of his Highness the Lord Protector held before us at the suit of Anthony Norton against Mark Hounsell, there was tendered a declaration for scandalous words, which when we had read we found to reflect higher than the said Anthony Norton, to wit, on the honour of his Highness. Whereupon we instantly caused the said Mark Hounsell to come before us and examining him upon the same found him to justify the speaking of dangerous words by the said Anthony Norton." *Draft.*

1654, October 26.—Writ for the election of a Baron to Parliament for the Port of Rye. *Copy.*

1654, October 27. London.—Colonel Morley to the Mayor and Jurats of Rye.

"I hope the business about your harbour is put in a good way of preservation as Mr. Miller, your agent, will more particularly acquaint you with. If any service be further requisite I shall willingly appear in it as there shall be occasion. I cannot but acknowledge your favour in electing me for your burgess thereby demonstrating the great confidence you repose in me, wherein I hope you shall not be disappointed. And though I have now made choice to serve for the County, yet I shall be as faithful to your Town as any you shall employ in this second election. God direct you in your choice of which I shall say no more but that I entreat that the person elected may be of our own county." *Seal.*

1654, November 29.—The Mayor and Jurats of Rye to Nathaniel Powell.

"Whereas Col. Morley was lately elected one of the Knightes to serve in this present Parliament begune at Westminster September the third last, for the County of Sussex, and also a Baron for this Port, and hath made choyse to serve in Parliament for the County, we have lately received a writ for the choyse of another to serve as Baron in his stead, and this day proceeding to election, it has fallen upon your Honor, our desires are you will looke upon it as a segnall of the good affections this Corporation bear toward you." *Draft.*

1654[-5], January 2.—Certificate by the Mayor and Jurats of Rye that Lewis Gilliart and Claudius Gilliart, his brother, inhabitants of Rye, are both professors of the Protestant religion and the said Lewis has lived in Rye, with his wife and family, for thirteen years, and the said Claudius about two years and that they are men of good report.

1654[-5], February 20. Whitehall.—John Disbrowe and J. Lambert to the Mayors and Jurats of the Cinque Ports.

"We are lately given to understand that there is a sort of fisherman inhabiting within the Cinque Ports," called "trowlers and drawers by the water side" who by reason of the smallness of the "moakes" in their nets take up and destroy all the young fish which they meet with, to the great prejudice of the public. We desire you will forthwith cause public notice to be given that no person do henceforth use any such unlawful nets. *Copy.*

1654[-5], February 23.—Writ of *habeas corpus* directed to the Mayor and Jurats of Rye for Apolonia, the wife of William Churchey, late of Rye, merchant.

1654[-5], March 5. Dover Castle.—Thomas Wilson to the Mayors Bailiffs and Jurats of the Cinque Ports.

I have received a Proclamation of his Highness the Lord Protector prohibiting horse races which I pray and require you to cause to be proclaimed. *Copy.*

1654[-5], March 13.—The Mayor and Jurats of Rye to Mr. John Thurloe.

"Here is at this Port, desirous to pass for France, one Mr. John Barter, of London, of middle stature inclining to tallness, somewhat square, brown hair mixed with gray, about fifty-seven years of age. His business in France, he saith and we believe is, to put a nephew of his named Henry Barter to learn the French tongue. We have no cause of suspicion in him but because he hath no pass we desire to know your Honour's pleasure." *Draft.*

1654[-5], March 13.—The Mayor and Jurats of Rye to Mr. John Thurloe.

On the 11th instant landed at this Port from France these four whose names are under-written, whom, upon their security, we have permitted to pass to London to wait on your Honour, having found nothing suspicious about them.

John Chaumelle, of London, merchant, a short man, brown hair.

Abel Cherety, of London, merchant, a short man, black hair.

William Prandraicke, a tall man, brown hair, a Swedish gentleman.

Alexander Irving, of middle stature, bright hair, a Swedish gentleman. *Draft.*

1654[-5], March 14.—Order by Alexander Bennet to Richard Baseden, serjeant of the mace, to demand of every person within the Town of Rye such sums as are due to the Corporation and are yet behind and unpaid for Town's duties, malthood, quateridge, commonly called shop-window money.

1655, March 26. Whitehall.—Henry Lawrence, President of the Council, to the Warden of the Cinque Ports.

Order not to permit any ship or vessel to pass outwards from the Ports, except fishermen and coasters, till the third of April next. *Copy.*

1655, May 9. Dover Castle.—Thomas Wilson to the Mayors and Jurats of the Cinque Ports.

I have lately received several proclamations herewith sent (declaring his Highness' pleasure for putting in execution the laws against the Jesuits and priests, and for the speedy conviction of popish recusants) I hereby pray and require you that you forthwith cause the same to be duly proclaimed. *Copy.*

1655, May 29.—The Mayor and Jurats of Rye [to the Governors of St. Thomas' Hospital, Southwark].

Requesting that they will receive a child of William Cosbarre, seaman, of Rye. *Draft.*

1655, July 11.—The Mayor and Jurats of Rye to Thomas Marshall of the Spurre Inn in Southwark.

"By reason there are so many men of war on this coast (you know one of our vessels is taken already, [and] Capt. Cadman had like to have been taken going over Sunday night last) we thought good to petition the Lord Protector for a convoy, and we desire you to present the business."

Petition attached. Stating that whereas the seas on these coasts are much infested with men of war of the Royal party, and that the trade between Dieppe and this place is likely to be spoiled, the Mayor and Jurats pray that a small frigate may attend upon their vessels as convoy. *Draft.*

1655, July 11. Dover Castle.—Thomas Wilson to the Mayors, Bailiffs, and Jurats of the Cinque Ports.

I have lately received several of the proclamations for the relief of godly ministers against suits and molestations by persons sequestered, ejected, and not approved. I pray you forthwith to proclaim the same. *Copy.*

1655, July 23.—Thomas Wilson to the Mayors and Jurats of the Cinque Ports.

"I have lately received a proclamation for perfecting the collection for the relief of the Protestants inhabitants of the valleys of Lucerne, Agroma, etc. and also a proclamation giving notice that the remaining differences between the English and the Dutch stand referred to Commissioners appointed on both sides, who are to assemble at Amsterdam in Holland. I hereby pray and require you that you forthwith cause the same to be proclaimed.

Postscript.—I also send a proclamation against the further use of private letters of marque." *Copy.*

1655, August 24. Tenterden.—William Aldcroft to Mr. Samuel Jeake, Town clerk of Rye.

Touching the freeing of the town of Tenterden from charges at the Guestling or otherwise. *Signed.*

1655, August 31.—The Mayor and Jurats of Rye to Capt. Young, Commander in Chief in the Downs.

Whereas late upon petition to his Highness the Lord Protector, Capt. Sanckey was ordered to attend this port as convoy for vessels between this place and Dieppe, whom we have intelligence coming from Caen on Wednesday last was taken by a French man of war and carried into Boulogne. We desire your Honour will order a convoy, in the stead of Capt. Sanckey, for the safe conduct of vessels of this town laden with merchants' goods over to the said Port of Dieppe. *Draft.*

1655, September 18.—The Mayor and Jurats of Rye to the President of the Council.

"We have received your order for the prevention of the pestilence and what lies in us shall diligently do, for the safeguard of the Commonwealth."

1655, September 27. Dover Castle.—Thomas Wilson to the Mayors, Bailiffs, and Jurats of the Cinque Ports.

I have lately received a proclamation prohibiting Delinquents to bear office or have any voice or vote in any election of any public officer, I pray and require you forthwith to cause the same to be proclaimed. *Copy.*

1655, December 20.—The Mayor and Jurats of Rye to Samuel Gott, at Seddlescombe.

We have taken an opportunity by these to acquaint you that the middle aisle of the chancel here, which belongs to the parsonage of this parish, is very ruinous and one gutter, running between that aisle and the part inclosed to the use of the town, requires amending. We have received much damage by the rain, and although we have often solicited Thomas Morphet (who we understand doth hire the same of your Worship) that it might be repaired, yet will he do nothing nor without your help is anything likely to be done. *Draft.*

1655[-6], January 12.—The Mayor and Jurats of Rye to the Governor of Dieppe.

Complaining of the excessive fees charged on English vessels entering Dieppe contrary to the articles of Peace. *Draft.*

1655[–6], January 19. Whitehall.—Robert Blake and J. Lambert to the Mayor and Jurats of Rye.

There being a very great want of able mariners to furnish the fleet now setting forth to sea for the defence and service of the Commonwealth, we have thought it expedient to direct these our letters to you, authorizing and requiring you forthwith to impress within your town and membres, sixty able seamen, being above the age of fifteen and under sixty, giving to each man twelve pence press money and three halfpence a mile conduct to Dover. And you are to order them to repair before the Mayor of the said town, who shall take care for the sending them on board the State's ships in the Downs. The affair is of that concernment to the public that we shall expect a very strict compliance. *Signed. Seal of the Admiralty.*

1655[6], January 26.—The Mayor and Jurats of Rye to the Mayor and Jurats of Tenterden.

Whereas the necessity of seamen in the State's Service and our commands for their impressing within our town and member, we have thought meet to desire you that in case there be any seamen (as we hear there are some fled hence to secure themselves with you) within your Town and Hundred you would impress them, giving them their conduct money for Dover.

1655[–6], January 27.—The Mayor and Jurats of Tenterden to the Mayor and Jurats of Rye.

In pursuance of your desires we have this evening impressed eleven men, who we hope may prove good seamen and serviceable to the State." *Seal.*

1655[–6], February 6.—The Mayor and Jurats of Rye to the Commissioners of the Admiralty.

In pursuance of our Lord Warden's late order touching the impressing of seamen we have done our endeavours to impress the number of seamen required by the said orders, but some of our vessels being abroad and others laid up at home for this winter time, few seamen are to be found in this town and those that were upon suspicion of a prest (the messenger that brought the orders coming in the daytime) fled out of our Liberties and hid themselves in the Foreign, so that though we presently endeavoured their taking and since have searched divers houses yet cannot meet with enough to accomplish the number, nor believe the number of 60 can be found in Town, unless masters themselves and others incapable to do service should be added to the complement. *Draft.*

1655[–6], March 14.—Order by the Mayor and Jurats to the Constables of Rye to levy a distress of 26*s.* 8*d.* on Alice, the wife of Robert Batten, of Rye, seaman, for profanely swearing four oathes and in default of finding goods to the value of the fine, to set the same Alice in the stocks for twenty-four hours.

1656, May 7.—Circular letter from the Mayor and Jurats of Rye to the other Ports touching the right of the Ports to wrecks and findalls.

1656, July 10.—Writ for the election of Barons to Parliament for the Cinque Ports. *Copy.*

[1656, July 22.]—The Mayors, Bailiffs, Jurats, and Commoners, Barons of the Cinque Ports and two Ancient Towns to the Bailiffs of Yarmouth.

"Whereas by sundry Letters-Patents under the Great Seal of England and other edictes and ordinances of State, we the Barons of the Cinque Portes and their members were anciently assigned and appointed, together with you, the Bailiffes of Great Jernmuth, to be Wardenes and Governors of your free faire there, and to have with you the keeping of the prison and administration of royall justice there during the continuance of the said faire, which services have for many ages last past beene by us and our predecessors, Barons of Cinque Portes, and members duly and faithfully performed, and yet for ought we can finde by experience, little or no benefitt hath thereby redowned or is likely to redowne to the Comonwealth. In regard whereof we for our partes are contented, if you shall think it fitting and that it may be done without perill or prejudice either to you or us, to lay downe and relinquish upon reasonable and fitting termes all our power and authority any waies concerning the Government of the said faire, and to leave the same wholly to be acted and managed by you. For the better effecting whereof we shall desire (if you approve of this designe) that you would comissionate two or three to joyne with the like number to be by us comissionated to meet at London about the begining of this next ensuing Parliament, at a certain tyme and place to be by you prefixed, to treat, consult and consider how and in what manner and upon what safe and fitting termes we may be for the future, free and discharged from sending our Bayliffes to your faire for the performance of the services aforesaid and according to the oppertunity now putt into our hands to prepare and agree upon an Act to be presented to the high and honorable Court of Parliament, whereby we, the Barons of the Cinque Portes and their members, may be absolutely exempted for tyme to come from the said services and that the same may be transmitted and wholly settled and established upon you with fitting cautions and provisoes nevertheles that our Barons and inhabitantes of the Cinque Portes and their members may injoy their free fishing and free bringing in and selling of their fish at the said faire, and have den and strond theire, and all such other liberties privileges and immunities, as they or any of their predecessors have formerly had, used, or enjoyed in, at, or about the said faire or Towne of Great Jernemuth, either by sea or land. If you like of these our proposalls we shall desire your answer by the bearer."

[1656, July.]—Thomas Kelsey to the Mayor and Jurats of Rye.

Recommending Edward Hopkins, Esquire, one of the Commissioners of the Admiralty and Navy, for their Baron to Parliament. *Seal of Arms broken.*

1656, August 5. Glynde.—Col. Moriey to the Mayor Jurats and freemen of Rye.

Recommending Mr. William Hay, the elder, as a fit person to serve them in Parliament. *Seal.*

1656, August 13.—The Poll paper for the election of a Baron to Parliament for the town of Rye. William Hay, Esquire, Allen Grebell, Jurat, and Edward Hopkins, Esquire, candidates. William Hay elected.

1656, August 27. Great Yarmouth.—The Bailiffs of Yarmouth to the Mayors, Bailiffs, and Jurats of the Cinque Ports.

Concurring in the proposal of the Ports to relinquish the service of the Ports at the free fair at Yarmouth and suggesting a meeting of representatives from the Ports and Yarmouth at London to consider the matter. *Copy.*

1656, September 1.—Order by the Mayor of Rye to the Constables of Rye that in accordance with an Act of Parliament lately made for the better observance of the Lord's day &c., carefully and diligently on the said Lord's days to make search and inquisition in all taverns, inns, ale-houses, "tobacko houses" or shops and victualing houses within the town of Rye, for the discovering and apprehending those which shall on the Lord's days profanely dance, sing, drink, or tipple contrary to the said Act; and finding any so to offend or otherwise by playing in the streets working in their callings, selling wares, or merchandise, or travelling by land or sea, contrary to the said Act, to cause the said offenders to be apprehended and brought before the Mayor that they may be punished according to the said Act. *Draft.*

1656, October 21.—Certificate by the Mayor and Jurats of Rye that Lewis Gilliart and Claudius Gilliart, his brother, are both professors of the Protestant religion and that the said Lewis has lived in Rye fifteen years with his wife and family, and the said Claudius about the space of four years, that they have lived peaceably and are well affected to the Commonwealth. *Draft.*

1656[-7], January 6.—The Mayor and Jurats of Rye to Col. Clerke. Requesting that they may be reimbursed their expenses laid out in providing convenient guards, and also fire and candles during the abode of Capt. Smith and Capt. Hardyer. *Draft.*

1656[-7], January 7.—The rates that are to be paid for goods, wares and merchandise brought to or carried from Rye by water.

1657, April 24.—Order of the Court of Chancery for certain persons to be at the house of Michael Cadman, called by the sign of "Ye Maremaid" in Rye on 13 May to answer certain interrogatories.

1557, July 13.—The Mayor of Rye to the Governor of Dieppe.

I am informed that a barque, whereof one George Broadbridge was master, being surprised by the enemy was by some Frenchmen of your town together with the help of the barque's men regained and brought into Dieppe, and for their salvage they intend to make her their prize. The enemy have taken the master prisoner, and intend to set a ransom on him. Wherefore on the poor man's behalf I desire your favour that what may be reasonable for your men's salvage of the barque may be allowed and the barque restored. *Draft.*

1657, July 30.—The Mayor and Jurats of Rye to General Montague, Commander in Chief in the Downs.

May it please you to excuse our boldness in troubling you with these lines on the behalf of some merchants in this Town, to intreat your Honour to order a convoy for two barques which are here bound over with merchandise to Dieppe, and by reason of imminent danger and the late loss of a vessel of this place between the two ports, afraid to venture alone.

Postscript.—Since writing here is come to Town a post with a States' packet, who commonly passing by Dover with convoy, now finding his journey will be shorter this way to the English forces in France, is minded to pass this way and is fearful of venturing his packet without convoy. *Draft.*

1657[-8], January 12.—Petition by the Keepers of Taverns, Inns, and Alehouses in Rye to the Mayor and Jurats of Rye to advise them what lawful course to take to obtain payment for the billet and lodging of soldiers quartered upon them.

1657[-8], January 27.—The Mayor and Jurats of Rye to Col. Robert Gibbon.

"We have taken the boldness to present these to you not to tell you in generall of our good affections formerly to the Parliament or now to his Highnes and the present government, or in particular to yourselfe, nor of the poore estate and condition of this place, neither do we conceive we need so to do, yourselfe well knowing that as to the one we have obeyed, not only for feare but for conscience sake, and as to the other, we hope your experience will beare us wittnes in our absence, neither do we delight to trouble your Honor with unnecessary complaintes, but severall pressive burdens and inconveniences lying upon us, we are necessitated to be troublsome unto you at this tyme, which we hope you will favourably beare with. We have had quartered upon us as you know two companies of foot souldiers in your regiment above this twelve moneths (save a few that for some tyme past have beene at Hasting) and all this tyme they have had free billet, many of them at first upon the private houses and ever since the first upon the innes and alehouses (as by a copy of a petition lately to us presented here inclozed appeareth). And at their first coming did for a certaine tyme provide fire and candle for the guardes, of which we are not yet reimbursed. And since the beginning of November last, have at the request of the Captaines, alleadging an Act of Parliament in that behalfe, supplyed the Captaines weekly with money for the souldiers, whereupon, we have disbursed above 200*li*. And besides the souldiers by observing the strict rules of garrisons at their first coming by disarming gentlemen that came into Towne did cause an utter cessation of gentlemenes accesse hither, whereby the trade of this Town is abundantly decayed, but also of late the inhabitants have beene denied by the souldiers to goe up and downe the cliffes to and from their vessells though necessitie never so much require which is more strict then was ever used by any soulderes heretofore in this place. Now forasmuch as your Honour hath alwayes professed your love and good affections to this place and the souldieres are under your command, we thought meete to addresse ourselves to you, hoping that it may be in your power to redresse our grievances in the premises and intreat your answer therein by the bearer, desiring that our monies disbursed as aforesaid may be repaid, and the rest of our burthens removed, otherwise the people here are so poore and the trading so much decaped, that we are not able to subsist, but must as many already speake, leave the Towne and seeke a livelyhood elsewhere if no remedy therein can be had, but we hope we shall herein finde favour in your sight." *Draft.*

1658, April 7.—Petition of several artificers and tradesmen to the Mayor and Jurats of Rye praying a remedy to the practice of persons exercising misteries and trades to which they have not been apprenticed.

1658, April 17.—Whitehall.—Oliver, Protector [to the Mayors, Bailiffs, and Jurats of the Cinque Ports].

"We understand that there are several persons who doe daily land from beyond the seas as well in the Ports as in other creekes and by-places and by their wandering up and downe and other carriages, they show themselves to be dangerous persons, and come over with a designe against the peace of the Commonwealth. You are therefore upon the receipt hereof to cause some of your troopes to be allwayes upon the coast and neere these landing places with orders to apprehend and seize upon all such persons as shall land, or be found wandering up and downe in the country, and to cause them to be secured untill they be examined and can give a good accompt of themselves and their business. And all such as shall land in any of the Ports, the Officers of the Ports are required to make stay of them as aforesaid, and the same orders are to be observed, as to any that shall passe from hence to any parts beyond the Seas. And all Justices of Peace and other Officers, both military and civill, are to be aiding and assisting to you in these things, who are required to use their utmost indeavours to call all such persons as aforesaid to be apprehended and secured." *Copy.*

1658, June 9.—Thomas Marshall, Mayor of Rye, to Captain Jennes in Warbleton, Sussex.

"Att the request of your Quarter Master, Mr. Benbrigge, I have wrott these to acquaint you that all things are in a very quiet posture in these partes and for this particuler towne we are and shall remaine carefull to secure the same against all enemies of his Highness and the Commonwealth, with the utmost of our lives and estates, and since the time the soldiers went hence to the Leagure at Dunkirke, have given order to those which are listed under my command, by vertue of his Highness commission, to be ready with their armes, and intend to exercise them, and every night to keepe a sufficient watch in towne and if at any time any eminent danger should appeare I shall readily acquaint you therewith." *Draft.*

1658, September 4. Whitehall.—Henry Lawrence, President of the Council, to the Mayors, Bailiffs, and Jurats of the Cinque Ports.

"Whereas it hath pleased the most wise God in his providence yesterday about fower of the clocke in the afternoone, to take out of this world the most serene and renowned Oliver, late Lord Protector of this Comonwealth, to the unspeakable griefs of our hearts and the invaluable losse of these Nations, but in this sore affliction it doth much relieve our spirittes that his said late Highnes in his lifetyme, according to the humble petition and advice did appoint and declare the most noble and illustrious Lord, the Lord Richard, eldest sonne of his said late Highnes, to succeede him in the Government of these Nations. A person who hath given such eminent testimony of his faithfullnes and great affection to the cause of God and the publique interest of these nations hath given us aboundant cause of rejoycing that the Lord hath provided him such a successor to undertake the Government in whose prudence and moderation we may acquisce and under whom we have not only hopes but much confidence that the Lord will make these Nations happie. Wee therefore of the Privie Councell together with the Lord Maior, Aldermen and Cittizens of London, the Officers of the Army, with numbers of principall Gentlemen, have with one full voyce and consent, tongue, and hearte this day published and proclaymed the said noble and illustrious Lord Richard to be rightfully protector of this Comonwealth of England, Scotland and Ireland and the dominions and territories thereunto belonging, to whome wee acknowledge all fidellitie and constant obedience, according to Law, and the humble petition and advice with all heartie and humble affections. And therefore have thought fitt to signifie the same unto you, willing and requiring you to cause the same to be proclaimed in all the Townes within your jurisdiction imediately on receipt hereof, according to the form herein inclosed, *mututis mutandis*, with such solempnitie as becomes a busines of such a nature and to take all due care for the preservation of the peace and securing the same against all insurrections and disturbances that may be made by evill minded men upon this change." *Copy.*

Enclosing a Proclamation signifying his Highness' pleasure "that all men being in office of Government at the decease of his most deare father, Oliver, late Lord Protector, shall so continue till his Highnes further dirrection." *Copy.*

1658, September 22.—Order by the Mayor and Jurats of Rye to William Ducke, Collector of the duties for the maintenance of the "Lights, Boomes and Boyes" in Rye, to levy certain duties on ships and vessels coming in or going out of the harbour of Rye.

1658, October 16.—Depositions of Robert Covin, master of the *Francis* of Dieppe, and two of his Company who said that "about a moneth agoe they were at Flushing in Zealand and continued there the space of tenne daies, in which time these deponentes did observe that one man of warre belonging to the King of Spaine did bring into Flushing eight vessells taken prize from Englishmen, one of which eight was a vessell laden with seacoales, that did belong to Richard Oake of this Towne of Rye, and there did sell and dispose of them. Also these deponents during the time of there abode there at Flushing aforesaid, did see severall vessells belonging to the King of Spaine come in there with three or foure men, and in three or foure dayes tyme they were furnished with abut forty men apiece and were also fitted and supplyed with all sorts of provision needfull, which these deponents observed them to take aboard in the evening. And the aforesaid Robert Covin doth depose that severall persones that were formerly inhabitants in Dunkirke and other places in Flanders, seamen, do now dwell in Flushing and other places in Zealand and go to sea in the service of the Kinge of Spaine. And further he saith that when he was ready to goe to sea, he went to the Judges of the Admiralty there to desire them not to permit the King of Spaines men of warre to go to sea that tyed that he went to sea. And they answered him they could do no such thing they were as free as he (this deponent) was."

1658, October 18.—The Mayor and Jurats of Rye to Charles, Lord Fleetwood.

Requesting to be re-imbursed certain sums of money advanced to various companies of soldiers. *Draft.*

1658, December 9.—Writ for the election of Barons to Parliament for the Cinque Ports. *Copy.*

1658, December 9. Dover Castle.—Thomas Wilson [to the Mayor and Jurats of Rye].

I have lately received several proclamations for the better encouragement of Godly Ministers and others, and their enjoying their dues and liberty according to law, which I pray and require you forthwith to cause to be published and proclaimed. *Copy.*

1658, December 16. Glynde.—Col. H. Morley and John Fagge to the Mayor, Jurats and freemen of Rye.

"We, being informed of a speedy call of Parliament, conceive it oure duty as members of your Corporation to tender our assistance to you in that affayre, and to attend at the day of your election provided you doe fix uppon any day after the 3d of January which wee rather desire, because the day for the shire will fall uppon the 30th of this month of which you may hereafter have a more certayne advertisement. And in the meanetime consider of persons fitting for that employment, amongst whome wee offer to your consideration your old friend and burgess Mr. William Hay, and if you please to elect him for one and joine with him some honest and able Gentleman of your partes 'twill be a further encouragement both to him and us diligently to serve you, the former kindness received in affayres of this nature, justly meritt our gratefull acknowledgment which we hereby heartily tender unto you."

1658[-9], January 6.—Certificate by the Mayor and Jurats of Rye to Charles, Lord Fleetwood, Constable of the Castle of Dover, Lord Warden of the Cinque Ports, that they have unanimously elected William Hay, Esquire, and Mark Thomas, Esquire, to be Barons to Parliament. *Draft.*

1658[-9], February 28.—Petition of the Fishermen of Rye to the Commissioners of the Navy and Admiralty.

That whereas the petitioners usually in the spring and summer go to sea to catch mackerel, as they are now ready to do, but by reason of the danger of these coasts by the often approach of men of war they are likely to be prevented from their fishing, unless a convoy is sent to attend them.

1658[-9], March 24.—The Mayor and Jurats of Rye to the Lord Protector.

Two days ago one Robert Bouden, captain of a man of war by commission of the King of Sweden, brought into this harbour a vessel of Amsterdam, the master whereof hath petitioned us for relief conceiving himself to be free, as belonging to the United Provinces. On perusing Capt. Bouden's commission we find the extent thereof is only against the subjects of the King of Holand and Denmark, and therefore have made stay of the vessel aforesaid until your Honour's pleasure be known therein. *Draft.*

1659, May 18.—An Act concerning Commissioners of Sewers. *Printed by John Field.*

1659, May 26.—The Mayor and Jurats of Rye to Col. Morley and John Fagge.

"In September 1656 Capt. Smith and Capt. Hardyer with their foot Companyes marched hither and quartered here till the begining of January following, and then marched away, and Captain Cocker and Captain Lingwood with their Companyes came here and quartered here till June 1658 and when Captain Smith and Captain Hardyer first came this Corporation disbursed severall sumes of money for fitting of guards, some of the houses we also hired and payd rent for, also for candles and coales, till a good while after Captain Cocker came, to the sume of 32*li.* 7*s.* 7*d.* And could never be reimbursed thereof save only of 13*li.* 1*s.* 4*d.* which Colonel Gibbon paid to Mr. Marshall, so as 19*li.* 6*s.* 3*d.* thereof, is yet behind. Also since Captain Cocker and Captain Lingwood went away we have beene at some charge and still are for maintaining our watch both for fire and candle and for pay for Drums to set the match every night and for a Gunner and for pouder match and fixing of arms, as the bearer Mr. Marshall can further inform you. Now our Corporation being poore, our humble request is that you wilbe pleased to endeavour the reimbursing us of the 19*li.* odde money aforesaid, and also of procuring us an order for some satisfaction for our charge of watching at presente and future and other the premisses which we are willing to maintaine having beene alwayes and still are faithfull and well afectioned to the Comonwealth as you know." *Draft.*

1659, August 30. Rye.—[The Mayor Jurats and Commonalty of Rye] to the Council of State at Whitehall.

"Whereas the inhabitants of this place in generall ever since the beginning of the late warres have beene and still remaine cordially affected unto the Parliament and not only formerly have given evident demonstration theerof in raising both men and monies for the cause and service of the comon wealth, but lately upon Captain Marshall's receite of your Honer's orders' at the beat of the drum appeared 120 men to list themselves for you under him with armes provided at their owne charge, and continued in the constant and faithfull discharge of their duties night and day since these last commotions before any souldiers marched hither. And whereas on the 21st instant a party of the county horse came hither and the next day a 100 foot out of Kent commanded by Captain Heath in the regiment of Colonel Gibbon, who marching hither without money, the same day Captain Heath desired a loane of money of us and accordingly for the present some few did furnish him with 20*li.* for a weekes pay, hoping in the expence thereof he might receive some, which failing and that expended both he and we are in a great strait, the soldiers because their wants are necessitous the inhabitants because they (having lost much in the late warres with Holland and Spain, the great decay of trade, taxes increase of the parish poore etc.) are growne generally poore the perticular places where the souldiers quarter are not able to disburse money, complaine of their allowance of free billet and many of them, yet not reimbursed of above 20*li.* sent by them to Captain Owens souldiers almost a yeare and quarter since. Wherefore on the behalfe of the whole inhabitants we humbly pray your Honor to take the premises into your grave and piouse considerations and if you (to whose wisedome and care in those things we shall alway readily submit) shall see it meet for foot soldiers to remaine longer here (although we hope you have not and are confident cannot have any ground to suspect us disaffected) you wilbe pleased to make provision for their constant supply with monies that the burden thereof which we are not able to beare may be removed from us". *Draft.*

1659, September 6. Whitehall.—Colonel Morley [to the Mayor and Jurats of Rye].

The Company, lately sent to you, is to be removed. I hope you will take care for the safety of your town by continuing your watches as formerly.

1659, September 18.—Sir A. Johnston, President of the Council [to the Mayor, Jurats and Commonalty of Rye.]

"The Council, having given order for the Company of the army foot that quartered in your towne to march to Sandwich, have thought good although they doubt not of your care of your towne, the security whereof as it is of consequence to you soe of greate concernment to the whole nation, to desire that in the absence of the aforesaid Company you will give order for strict watch and ward to be kept, that all such persons as shall endeavour to come in or to goe out at your cost whom you shall suspect to be any way dangerous to the peace of the nation may be stayed and secured according to the former order you have received in that behalfe. *Signed and Seal of Arms.*

1659, September 19. Rye.—[The Mayor, Jurats and Commonalty of Rye] to the Council of State at Whitehall.

"Wee having lately made our humble suite to your Honour for removall of the foot Company heere quartered and obtained your favorable grant thereof, who accordingly marched hence the 12th instant thought it our duty heereby to returne you hearty thanks and also to acquaint you that upon their departure wee did revive againe our watch observed heere. *Draft.*"

1659, October 3.—Proclamation declaring the Continuance of Justices, Sheriffs, and other officers.

1659, November 12. Dover Castle.—Thomas Wilson to the Mayors Bailiffs and Jurats of the Cinque Ports.

I have lately received a Proclamation declaring the inhibiting of all meetings for the raising or drawing together of force without order of the Committee of Safety of the Commonwealth or the Lord Fleetwood, which I herewith pray and require you to proclaim within your liberties. *Copy.*

1659, December 19.—Certificate by the Mayor and Jurats of Rye that Thomas Chisewell of Rye, mariner, came before them and made oath that in the year 1650 he was master of a small vessel which in sailing from Dieppe to Rye was taken by one Utash Deniball of Calais, who pretended to be a King's man of war and further that he had no share in the said vessel.

1659[-60], March 19. "Aboard the *James* at Gravesend."—John Lawson to the Mayor, Aldermen, and Common Council of Rye.

"Understanding the late Parliament is dissolved and that they have ordered the speedy issueing off writts for electing a Parliament to assemble at Westminster the 25th of next month, I take the bouldnes to recomend unto you Generall William Penn (who is now att London) a person of such worth abilitie and capacitie to serve your Towne that if you please to pitch upon and elect him for one of your Burgesses I presume it will turne to the great advantage of your Corporation, I need not write much concerning his merits, hee being knowne to you, these Nations and other Nations and as hee hath beene in Chiefe Comand att sea noe douth he will be concerned in the Navall affaires again and soe bee able to doe your Corporation better service and in this as you will serve the Nation in generall soe your selves in particular."

1660, June 16.—The Mayor and Jurats of Rye to Lord Culpepper.

Sir Thomas Milward, the King's Water Bailiff for Rye, being dead, that there may be no obstruction in the execution of justice in the Court of Record, we petitioned the then Council of State and obtained an order that our Corporation might make choice of a person to officiate in the said office until further order of the Parliament. Since which, the King's Majesty being returned to the possession of his Kingdom and dignity, we humbly beg your assistance to procure the said office for the benefit of our Corporation. *Draft.*

1660, June 28.—W. Coventrye, Secretary to the Duke of York, to Marke Thomas, Mayor of Rye.

"Complaint hath bin made to the King of France by the fisherman of France of this restraint of their fishing on your English coast and taking their netts, pretending that they have alwayes bin permitted to fish for machárell on our coast, I desire you to examine as well the records of your towne as the ancient men thereof and to certify to his Royal Highness under your Towne seale what you find concerning it that soe wee may now justify our rights and privileges." *Signed.*

1660, September 10. Dover Castle.—R. More to the Mayors, Bailiffs, and Jurats of the Cinque Ports.

I have lately received a proclamation for the apprehension of Edmund Ludlowe, Esquire, commonly called Col. Ludlowe, and also an act of Parliament for the speedy provision of money for disbanding and paying off the forces of this Kingdom, both by land and sea, and I hereby pray and require that you forthwith cause the same to be duly published and proclaimed. *Copy.*

1660, September 26.—A Proclamation for speeding the payment of the arrears of seventy thousand pounds for three months assessment due and payable the first of August last past.

1660, September 29.—A Proclamation for the suppressing of disorderly and unseasonable meetings in Taverns and Tipling-houses and also forbidding Footmen to wear swords or other weapons within London, Westminster and their Liberties.

1660, October 5.—The Mayor and Jurats of Rye to Col. Robert Gibbon.

We hear the army is shortly to be disbanded, we desire you will please to certify us whether you will pay us the monies lent by this town to your soldiers in the companies of Captain Owen and Captain Heath while they quartered here, for if you will not, we must apply ourselves to the auditors of the army accounts or else lose our monies of which there is no reason. *Draft.*

1660, December 27. Dover Castle.—Francis Vincent to the Mayor, Bailiffs, and Jurats of the Cinque Ports.

I have received instructions from the Duke of York, our Lord Warden, to take care that such of his Majesty's loyal subjects as have formerly for their loyalty been displaced or hindered from the exercise of majestracy and other offices of trust in the Ports, may be restored thereto, and that such persons as have been unduly put in and are men who have been eminently active against the King, and especially such as expressed themselves in opposition to his late happy restoration, may be removed. *Copy.*

1660[-1], January 25.—A proclamation for observation of the thirtieth day of January as a day of Fast and Humiliation according to the late Act of Parliament for that purpose.

1660[-1], January 29.—A proclamation for the restraint of killing dressing and eating of flesh in Lent or on Fish-dayes appointed by the Law to be observed.

1660[-1], February 11. Glynd.—Col. H. Morley to the Mayor, Jurats, and Freemen of Rye.

By your favour I have formerly been employed as your servant in the Commons House of Parliament, it is now strongly reported that the King's Majesty shortly intends to call another Parliament, though I am conscious of my own weakness, yet if your corporation shall please to repose so great a confidence in me as to elect me for one of their burgesses, I shall readily serve them with my utmost diligence. *Seal.*

1660[-1], February 18.—Writ to the Constable of the Castle of Dover for the Election of Barons to Parliament for the Cinque Ports. *Copy.*

1660[-1], February 28.—Sir John Jacobs to the Mayor, Jurats, and Freemen of Rye.

"It is now above 20 yeares since you did mee the honor to make mee free of your ancient and worthy corporation by which I was made so happy as to serve in Parliament for one of your Burgesses. I cannot but believe that you esteeme that Parliament most unhappy, and that now you will indeavor not only to repair yourselves but even your old Burgess and hope that you will renew your old affections, and even in justice sett mee where I was, which honor if you shall be pleased to conferr upon mee, I shall study to deserve what those times deprived mee off and not only to your ancient corporation, but to any particular member, shall give both publique and private testimony of my gratitude in any thing within my power, which I hereby assure you shalbe manifested with such fidelity as becomes so great a trust where in as all occasions shalbe most wellcome." *Seal of Arms.*

1660[-1], March 5. Whitehall.—James [Duke of York] to the Mayor, Jurats, and Commonalty of Rye.

"The King haveing thought fitt to summon a Parliament in which (as the whole Kingdome in generall is highly concerned) soe it is probable there may bee concernements peculier to your towne as a member of the Cinque Ports. I have judged it agreeable to that care which I sought alwaies to have of you, to recomend to your election for one of your burgesses to serve you in Parliament, Richard Spencer, Esqre., of whose abilities, for the discharge of that service I have soe good assurance that I doubt not but you will find the advantage of soe good a choice, to which the merrit of the person may bee sufficient to encourage you, besides that I promise myself it wilbee an additionall inducement to you, that by makeing a choice soe advantagious to yourselves, you will at the same time doe a work very acceptable to mee." *Signed. Seal of arms.*

1660[-1], March 6.—The Mayor, Jurats, and Freemen of Rye to Sir John Jacob.

"We have received your letter of the 28th of February last and take notice therein of your readiness to serve us as a Burgesse in the next ensuing Parliament as also your favourable aspect to this corporation therein specified, and for returne, although we have very much respects for you, yet can say no more at present but that we shall take the premisses into our consideration." *Draft.*

1660[-1], March 7. Whitehall.—James, Duke of York, to the Mayors, Bailiffs, and Jurats of the Cinque Ports.

Whereas by my letter to you of the 23rd of June last I directed you to be very watchful to observe the motions and meetings of dangerous persons and to secure them, upon which many persons have been imprisoned as Quakers, within the Cinque Ports. I have received a letter from the Lords of the Council directing the discharge of all such persons as have been secured within the liberties of the Cinque Ports only on suspicion, in the late insurrection or at any time since, and do remain committed except only the ringleaders of faction among them. *Copy.*

1660[-1], March 7. Orpington.—Richard Spencer to the Mayor, Jurats, and Commonalty of Rye.

"I send you by this bearer his Highnesse Royall the Duke of York his letter which I thought fit to present to you with all possible speed. I shall onely say for myselfe that I have beene an ancient Parliament man, having served in two Parliaments in King James his dayes and in three in the late King's time of blessed memory." *Seal of arms.*

1660[-1], March 8.—A Proclamation declaring his Majesties pleasure touching His Royal Coronation and the solemnity thereof.

1660[-1], March 9.—The Mayor, Jurats, and Freemen of Rye to Richard Spencer.

"We have this day received a letter from his royall Highnesse the Duke of Yorke, our Lord Wardon, together with yours of the 7th instant proposing yourselfe both ready and willing to serve us as a burgesse in the next ensueing Parliament and although you are a stranger to us, yet we presume his Highnesse would present none to us on such accompt but a person of honour and merit, and therefore in respect to his Highnesse we shall take the premisses into our consideration, and desiring the Lord to dirrect us in the issue, can say no more at present." *Draft.*

1660[-1], March 19.—A Proclamation for the Publishing of an Act of Parliament late made for the better ordering and selling of Wines by Retail &c.

1660[-1], March 21.—Sir John Jacobs, to the Mayor, Jurats, and Freemen of Rye.

I must return my thanks for your letter of the 6th instant "Truly gentlemen I had ones the honor to be made a member among you and I am still ambitious to continue, not to challenge, but to deserve your favors, by some returnes both in generall and particular that may happily fall within my power, wherein you then so nobly ingage mee; what fell out afterwards I have forgotten and forgiven, and therefore now only resume my old devotion to this corporation, and hope that I shall have some occasion to give you some testimony that, I assert no other ends or interest but to serve you." *Seal of arms.*

1661, March 25. Orpington.—Richard Spencer to the Mayor, Jurats, and Commonalty of Rye.

"I give you many thankes for your great civilityes to me which I shall ever acknowledge with all thankfullnes, and I have very great desire to appeare before you all in person, which if the wayes were passable for a coach I should now have done, but my health is not so confirmed as yet that I dare travell out of a coach, therefore I desire your excuse and favourable construction for my absence at this time, which if you please to make me your servant in this Parliament I shall doubly repaire in the Parliament house, and if you please to make choice of me, what commands you shall please to give me I shall faithfully performe."

1661, March 26. Glynde.—Col. H. Morley to the Mayor. Jurats, and Freemen of Rye.

"I am by indisposition of health confined to my chamber, so that I cannot (as I intended) be present at your election (of which I thanke

Mr. Mayor he gave me very tymely notice) I have formerly enjoyed the honour of being your servant, if you please to elect me this tyme for one of your burgesses I shall endeavour to be diligent and faithfull in your service and upon all occasions be ready to expresse my further acknowledgments to you." *Seal.*

1661, April 2.—Copy of the claim of the Barons of the Cinque Ports to the office of carrying the canopy of the King at the Coronation.

1661, April 3. London.—William Parker, John Raven, and John Pepper to the Mayor and Jurats of Hastings.

"We had yesterday a hearing before the Lords Comissioners for claimes upon ours for the carrying the Canopy over his Majestie at his Coronation, and we having before obtained the favour of his Royall Highnes to send his Secretary to the Comissioners on the Ports behalfes, had judgment that thePortes should performe the service by such as they should appoint, but the Lord Chancellor declared that, as the King had done the Portes that honour to admit them to so noble a service, so he did expect they should discharge it suitable to the magnificence of such a solempne Coronation, and particularly gave it in charge that they should be proper men in respect of their persons that should beare the Canopy, and habited alike suitable to such a great solempnity. And had you heard as we did, how many persons of good quallity were put by from the personall performance of their services when they were such as were about the person of the King and allowed only to act by their deputies appointed by his Majestie, you would have despaired of getting the Portes personally to performe this service, but his Majestie, had so great a respect to the Ports and so expresst his pleasure and his Royall Highnes so improved his interest in the Comissioners, that we had our claimes (when we got to one) readily allowed under that charge. As to our discharge of it, the time for that service is so sudden that we fear that the Portes will be much strainted and therefore we offer it as our humble advice that letters be forthwith sent through the Portes to direct the imediate election of their members, and that therein you would appoint a certaine day for the Barons elected, or so many of them as shall be thought fitt to meete as some convenient place in the Ports next weeke to consult about the performing the service and to appoint a meeting at London, which must be in a short time for we conceive it will be a very difficult matter to gett your apparell made under a more then ordinary time in respect of the multitude of people that will prepare to apparell themselves for this solempnity. The allowance of the canopy staves and bells are referred to the Attorney General whom we are to attend this day and hope we shall speedily effect it but for the scarlett we heare that the King gives no liveries to any and then we cannot expect it for the Portes, but we shall endeavour this day to informe ourselves whether their be any hopes thereof and to get a Warrant from the Lord Chamberlaine for the providing the Canopy." *Copy.*

1661, April 10.—The Mayor and Jurats of Rye to Sir John Fagge.

"This day at an assembly we have made choise of our Maior and you, to be Barons for this Towne at the King's Coronation, to performe that ancient and honourable service of carrying the Canopy over him. And forasmuch as the time is short and the Portes have appointed their Barons to meet on the Exchange in the French Walke by ten of the clocke in the forenoone on Saturday next being the xiij[th] day of this instant Aprill, in order to the furnishing themselves with apparell suitable." *Draft.*

1661, April 11. Glynd.—Col. H. Morley to the Mayor, Jurats, and Freemen of Rye.

"I had not opportunity till now to return my thankful acknowledgments to you for the late favours and kindnes as you have reposed a great trust and confidence in me so you may rest assured of my reall endeavors to serve your Towne (as well in Parliament as on all other occasions) with diligence and integrity, and if at the begining of the Parliament you have particular comands for me, upon advertisment thereof I shal be ready to pursue your directions, in the interim with my prayers to God for the prosperity of your Corporation." *Seal.*

1661, April 19. Dover Castle.—Richard Masters to the Mayors, Bailiffs, and Jurats of the Cinque Ports.

"I have lately received several schedules containing his Majesty's proclamation prohibiting the planting, setting and growing tobacco in England and Ireland, which I desire you to have duly proclaimed. And inasmuch as the happy time of the coronation of his Majesty now approacheth, I desire you will use your uttermost endeavours that there be such demonstration of your loyalty and affection to his Majesty as may become such a solemnity, and that you will take care that more than ordinary watch be kept about that time that so any disturbance that may happen to be made at such time, when so many of his Majesty's loyal subjects are absent from this abode and at London, may be prevented. You will herewith also receive several briefs of a patent from his Majesty for a collection on a more than ordinary occasion and your furtherance thereof is desired." *Copy.*

1661, May 20.—A Proclamation for the observation of the Nine and twentieth day of May instant as a day of Publick Thanksgiving according to the late Act of Parliament for that purpose.

1661, June 6.—The Mayor and Jurats of Rye to the Lord Warden.
Touching the claim by the French fishermen to fish off the English coasts. *Draft, much torn.*

1661, June 7.—A Proclamation for a General Fast throughout the Realm of England.

1661, June 7.—Certificate by the Mayor and Jurats of Rye in consideration that three quarters of the lands within the parish of Rye lie without the liberties, some in the hundred of Goldspur and some in the hundred of Gostroe, thereby causing many difficulties, it is conceived fit that Colonel Spencer be entreated to use his interest in procuring his Majesty's charter for annexing the foreign part of the parish unto the liberties of the town. *Signed.*

1661, June 10.—A Proclamation against Exportation and Buying and Selling of Gold and Silver at higher rates then in our Mint: also against culling, washing or otherwise diminishing our Current Moneys.

1661, June 22. Whitehall.—James, Duke of York, to the Mayors, Bailiffs, Jurats, and Deputies of the Towns within the jurisdiction of the Admiralty of the Cinque Ports.

I am very sensible of the great and many abuses that have of late years been committed in the fishing on the English coast. "I do hereby strictly charge and command all persons whatsoever within the said jurisdiction henceforth to forbeare to use any unlawfull nettes or engines whatsoever for the taking or catching of fish or to do any undue or unlawful act, whereby the brood or fry of fish may bee any wayes prejudiced or destroyed, or to take or catch any fish at unseasonable tymes contrary to the lawe or the ancient custome in fishing affairs." *Copy.*

1661, June 24.—The Mayor and Jurats of Rye to Richard Spencer and Col. H. Morley.

We have received notice from some of the brethren of the Ports that they intend to write to their respective barons in Parliament to endeavour the exemption of the Ports and their members from future taxes imposed on the Counties, as they conceive they ought to be by virtue of their charters, which they are minded to send up to Mr. Thurbane of Sandwich, and therefore we desire no assistance of yours may be wanting therein and the rather for that when formerly upon the granting of subsidies the Ports instead of paying taxes usually received 500*li.* by way of billet, yet were they then in a far more thriving condition, their trade being very much decayed and places depopulated of late, so that without some such encouragement for persons to live among them their ancient and flourishing Corporations will in short time irreparably come to nothing. *Draft.*

1661, June 26.—Richard Spencer to the Mayor and Juratts of Rye.

"I received yours of the 10th of June which came to my hands when I was in the country, as soone as I came to Towne I was not unmindfull of your businesse, but meeting Mr. Coventry at the House enquired of him what was done in the proposition you sent to his Highnesse Royal, who sayd that there was a man of warre sent downe by his Highnesse Royall to hinder those abuses by the French fishing, that they had taken away divers netts and that his Highnesse Royall was sending another." I received last night another letter from Mr. Mayor and the Jurats "I know very well that the Ports are exempt from subsidies and if there be any tax I shall take care of you, but I do not yet heare of any. I must deale clearely with you. I do not think Mr. Thurbane a man so fit to do your businesse because he is not very well liked by many of the House and there is a petition against him, but if anything shall come to him from you I shall assist him the best I can." *Seal of arms.*

1661, July 9.—The Mayor and Jurats of Rye to Richard Spencer.

"For your further satisfaction about our billet money you may please to understand that before the raigne of King Henry the seventh the Kings did use to allow the Barons of the Ports, out of every entire fifteenth and tenth, granted by the Laity in Parliament, such reasonable sume as the Ports did demand, and for that some time differences did arise betweene the Ports and the King's Receivers the said King Henry stinted their demands to the some of 500*li.* and granted them a Privy Seale for the said sume upon consideration that the Ports should put in recognizance to demand no more, which accordingly they did, and so in the reignes of King Henry the eighth, King Edward, Queen Mary, and Queen Elizabeth received thereby the sume aforesaid, but about the latter end of Queen Elizabeth's raigne the Ports obteined her charter for the same which charter was confirmed by King James and King Charles the first. This sume of 500*li.* useth to be divided among the Ports and their members proportionally according to the number of the shipping which they are to finde by their charter, and every towne for the receiving of his proportion of the said 500*li.* did give bills under the seale of office of Mayoralty or Bayliage testifying the receit of so much money of certaine persons therein named for such land lying in Kent or Sussex or to that effect, which bills were delivered to the collectors of the subsidies and allowed to them upon their accompt in the Exchequer and this is called billet money or billiting." *Copy.*

1661, July 13. London.—Richard Spencer and H. Morley to the Mayor, Jurats, Freemen, and Commonalty of Rye.

"In answer to all your letters which we have considered you may understand that we doe not thinke the present tyme a fitt season to move ether the King or Parliament for annexing that part of Rye parish that lyes in the county to the Corporation for we are most confident it will not be granted, neither can we at present tell or advise what to doe towards augmenting the value of your vicaridge, the value thereof being 40*li* per annum, the parsonage but 18*li* and consequently not comprehended within his Majesty's direction to the Bishops and Deans for augmenting small vicaredges out of great parsonages, yet we had attended the Bishop to have tryed what might have bin down if he had not bin out of Towne, but in our opinion the only way to obtaine some advantage for you in that affaire were to endeavour to get a lease which if you desire we shall waite upon the Bishop about it." *Signed, and Seal of Arms broken.*

1661. July 14. Dover.—John Raven to the Mayors and Jurats of Hastings and Rye.

Asking them to send what evidences they have touching the matter of the claim by the French to fish off the coasts of the Cinque Ports. *Copy.*

1661, August 3.—A proclamation for the well ordering the making of white starch within this Realm and for the restraint of the importation thereof from foreign parts.

1661 August 9.—A Proclamation for discovering and preventing the many fraudulent practises of under-officers and others in stealing His Majesty's Customs.

1661, August 16.—A Proclamation to restrain the excessive carriages in wagons and four-wheeled carts to the destruction of High-ways.

1661, September 7.—A Proclamation for the calling in all moneys of gold and silver coined or stamped with the cross and harp and the circumscription *The Commonwealth of England* and for making the same to be current only to the first of December next and no longer.

1661, September 12. Whitehall.—James, Duke of York, to the Mayors, Bailiffs, and Jurats of the Cinque Ports.

I find by inquiry there is no particular commission issued for receiving the subscriptions for the free and voluntary present to his Majesty within the Liberties of the Cinque Ports, lest the service should suffer by delay I have thought fit to permit the Commissioners of Kent and Sussex to do it, and do desire you that notice may be given of this my permission through the Ports that none may pretend the defence of the liberties of the Ports for obstructing that service. *Copy.*

1661, September 27.—A Proclamation concerning the granting of Licences for selling and retailing Wines.

1661, October 1.—Warrant to Allen Eades, master of the barque called the *Anne and Elizabeth*, of Rye, to receive on board his said ship, bound for the Port of Dublin, William and Philip Watson, sons of Thomas Watson, clerk, sometime schoolmaster of the free grammar school in Rye, who were left behind by their said father in May 1658 and have been chargeable to the Parish. And whereas it is reported that the said Thomas Watson, their father, is living and settled in or near Trim, in the County of Westmeath these are to require the said Allen to convey the said William and Philip to Dublin and deliver them to the officers who by law are to convey them to their father to be by him provided for and maintained. *Draft.*

1661, October 2.—The Mayor of Rye to Mr. Richard King and others in Tenterdon.

As to a dispute concerning the payment of certain charges and services by the Corporation of Tenterdon to the Corporation of Rye. *Draft.*

1661. November 4. Whitehall.—James, Duke of York, to the Mayor, Jurats, and Commonalty of Rye.

"I understand that Mr. Richard Spencer whome I formerly recomended to you to serve you as a Baron in Parliament is lately dead, by which that place is become vacant, the same considerations which moved me formerly to recomend to you Mr. Spencer, prevailes with me now to recomend to you Sir John Robinson, Knight and Baronet, Lieutenant of his Majesties Tower of London, whom if you think fitt to elect I make noe doubt but you will be very usefully served by him." *Signed. Seal of arms.*

1661, November 8.—A proclamation requiring all officers or soldiers that served under the armies of the late usurped Powers and have been disbanded, cashiered or turned out to depart the cities of London and Westminster before the fourth of December next.

1661, November 11.—A Proclamation for restraint of killing, dressing and eating of flesh in Lent or on Fish-days appointed by the Law to be observed.

1661, November 19. Samuel Gott to the Major, Jurats, and Commonalty of Rye.

"I have been very lately informed that my noble friend, Sir John Robinson, his Majestie's Lieftenant of the Tower of London, hath presented himself unto you to serve in this present Parliament in the place of Mr. Spencer, your late Baron, deceased, I should not have opposed his intentions if I had known them before I declared mine own, yet as election ought to be free I shall most freely leave it to yourselves to arbitrate between us in this present competition. I highly value my friend and yet shall not undervalue your friendship if to those many other obligations wherein I stand ingaged unto you, you shall think fitt to add the choice of me to serve you in this great affair." *Seal.*

1661, November 20. A Proclamation prohibiting the importation of divers foreign wares and merchandizes into this Realm of England and Dominion of Wales and Sale thereof; and to repress the excess of gilding of coaches and chariots.

1661, December 7. A Proclamation that the moneys lately called in may nevertheless be current in all payments to or for the use of His Majesty until the first day of May next.

RYE MSS.

1661[-2], January 3. The Mayor, Jurats, and Commonalty of Rye to Monsieur Montigny, Governor of Dieppe.

"We are very sensible of the decay of the passage trade betweene this place and Dieppe especially since the imposing of the 50 solx per tonne, which we understand both at Dover and Callis the passage barques are freed from. And willing to promote (as in duty bound) the good of the place we live in, we desire your Honor will endeavour the getting off the said 50 solx per tonne from such vessells as come hence to your port with passengers and their goods, and we shall endeavour the taking the same off your passage vesselles that come here, which we hope may be obtained and desire to know that your Honor is affected thereto and whether you conceive it feasible." *Draft.*

1661 [-2], February 4.—A Proclamation for Prizing of Wines.

1661 [2], February 26.—The Mayor of Rye to Sir John Robinson.

"This towne being scituate on the sea coast and so surrounded with water that the markets with corne as well as other provision are not supplyed neither by reason of our limited jurisdiction (but part of our owne parish being within our Liberty) can we compell any corne to be brought into markett, and by reason some have ingrossed great quantities of corne in their handes and others keepe it up from sale, not only the price is greatly inhaunced, but the poore hereabout reduced to extreame necessity, and without some speedy provision will inevitably famish. And although my selfe and others in Towne would willingly make a stocke to lay in a store for the poore of this place, yet we presume if we should contract for anywhere it may be had, the people would not suffer us to bring it away without license, and if the Justices of the Peace should grant us a License, yet an information may possibly be preferred in the Exchequer for ingrossing, Therefore if your Honor judge it feasible and please to favour me, so as to procure an order from the Lordes of his Majesties most honorable Privy Councell or from his Royall Highnes the Duke of Yorke, our Lord Warden, that what Corne I or my assignes shall buy for the provision of this place, may be permitted to come thence and to be landed at this port, your Honor will do this place in generall an exceeding courtesie." *Draft.*

1662, April 15.—Petition of the Mayor, Jurats, and Commens of Rye to James, Duke of York and Albany.

That the said Town of Rye anciently had more great guns mounted than any other of the Ports (Dover excepted) which requiring a magazine as well of powder as of other ammunition, upon petition to the Lord Warden hath been favoured with supplies of powder out of the Tower. And whereas the said Town is so much impoverished and decayed that to maintain the carriages of the guns with other ammunition necessary is a very great charge, and yet it stands alike exposed to the often use of them, both for ornament upon festival and other public occasions, and for service as well sometimes for the stop of vessels which might otherwise steal out of the haven without payment of tonnage and customs, as for keeping of the peace when ships of war of several nations with their prizes happen to be together in the harbour and otherwise might quarrel there, contrary to his Majesty's peace, the safety of the Town and the law of nations. May it please you therefore to favour us with the procurement of some barrels of powder out of his Majesty's store in the Tower. *Copy.*

1662, May 30.—The Mayor and Jurats of Rye to the Mayors and Jurats of the Ports of Hastings, Sandwich, Dover, New Romney, and Hythe and ancient Town of Winchelsea.

By septenary revolution the speakership of the Ports is now returned to this Town. As our affairs now stand, is it requisite to convene a Brotherhood and Guestling at the next accustomed time?

1662, June 9.—A Proclamation concerning the Act for the Revenue on Fire-hearths and Stoves.

1662, June 22.—The Examination of William Foxery before the Mayor and Jurats of Rye.

He says that by virtue of the paper now shewed "at his examination he did goe to sea to take such vessells of Hollanders as he could meete with, which said paper he received of one Captaine Welsh aboute a moneth since, and he saith the vessell he went to sea in is about two tonnes, and that he went to sea with eleven men but he saith that hee never tooke any prize since he had the said paper, and that they came in to this Harbor to take in some of his men, which went ashore at the Nesse. This examinant further saith that they have aboord about 8 or 9 swordes, seven pistolls, five firelockes, and two matchcockes, a halbert, a halfe pike a small quantity of powder and bulletts, and that he this examinant is an English man."

1662, July 11.—The Mayor and Jurats of Rye to the Mayors, Bailiffs and Jurats of the other Cinque Ports.

"Having perused the late Act of Parliament concerning fire hearths and stoves, we find a vast disproportion betweene the way of raising his Majesties additional revenue by the said Act and the ancient parliamentary course of X^{ths} and XV^{ths} (which we hoped this Parliament would have revived) so that instead of receiving *500li.* upon every such taxe, nowe a sume well nigh (if not above) double thereto will yearely for ever be charged upon the Ports and members, if the said Act include us, which under correction we conceive we have some ground to scruple, considering the Cinque Ports are not specified verbally in the said Act, as in the late Act for regulating Corporations which the same Parliament made and intended should reach us, as well as other Corporations, and also remembering how often we and our predecessors in case of briefs, Comissions, &c. have conceived ourselves neither included or injoyned when not expressed, neither in the said Act can we finde any clause of *non obstante* whereby our liberties, customs and priviledges by the said Act should be impaired in this particular, and suppose the Towne of Barwicke upon Tweed had it beene omitted, although within the Kingdome of England would have beene free from this new kind of taxation. Wherefore although we are assured that you with us (as all loyall and obedyent subjects) are alwaies ready to contribute our due proportions to all publike assessments, when we clearly understand we are thereby duly charged, yet doubt not but you as we, are very tender of addmitting any other taxes or burdens (then by law clearly warranted) upon the inhabitants within your precincts and especially minding the Ports declining state, great decay of trade and poverty of the people, upon the meaner sorte of whom, neverthelesse, this taxe for the most part lyeth. Therefore (notwithstanding any presidents of contrary nature in the monethly taxes during the late times of usurpation, when partly feare of ruine and other preventions occasioned a submission thereto) yet we thought meete as Speaker *pro tempore* (least we should incurre your deserved blame for neglect thereof) to present these to your introspection and hereby brotherly pray your serious consideration of the premisses, and withall your opinions and subscriptions, whether it would not be expedient for us forthwith joyntly to petition as well his Majesty for his gracious resolution upon the said Act in this case, as his Royall Highnes, our Lord Warden, for his assistance therein and that one or two of each Towne may meete at Romney or such place and time as you shall think fitt, and agree upon for that purpose, with whom we shall willingly joyne or if you shall incline otherwise shall heartily acquiesce with you in paying thereof, yet apprehend we are not by the said Act obliged to send our Accompts to the Forrein Sessions or collect the monies or doe any other thing in pursuance of the said Act, by vertue of any warrant from the forrein Justices as we understand some intend."

W. J. Hardy.
W. Page.

A MANUSCRIPT VOLUME IN THE POSSESSION OF JOHN DOVASTON, ESQ., OF WEST FELTON, CO. SALOP.

The following is a Calendar of the contents of a large volume, which, according to a note at the beginning, was bought by John Dovaston, Esqre., at a sale of books after the decease of Mr. More, of Linley, in 1781, at Linley House in Shropshire, for *5s.* The book may have come into the possession of Mr. More's ancestor Col. Samuel More, who was a leading Shropshire Parliamentarian when Ludlow Castle was taken and dismantled in 1646.

f. 1. 1586, September 15, Windsor Castle.—Instructions given by the Queen to Henry, Earl of Pembroke, Lord President, and the Council in the Marches of Wales, perused by the Archbishop of Canterbury, William, Lord Burghley, Sir James Crofte, and Sir Christopher Hatton.

The Council is to consist of William, Earl of Worcester, Henry, Earl of Derby, Edmund, Bishop of Worcester, William, Bishop of Llandaff, William, Bishop of St. Asaph, Marmaduke, Bishop of St. David's, Herbert, Bishop of Hereford, Hugh, Bishop of Bangor, Sir James Crofte, Controller of Her Majesty's Household, Sir George Bromley, Justice of Chester, Sir John Perot, John Puckering, Serjeant at law and one of the justices of Sowales (*sic*), Thomas Egerton, Solicitor General, Edmand Walter, one of the justices of Sowales, Charles Fox, Her Majesty's Secretary there, Edward Leighton of Watlesburgh, Esquire, William Leighton of Plash, Esquire, one of the justices of North Wales, William Aubrey doctor of law, Fabian Phillips, esquire, one of the justices of North Wales, Henry Towneshend, one of the justices of North Wales and the county palatine of Chester, Elice Price, doctor of law, Richard Pates, esquire, Jerome Corbet, esquire, and Thomas Atkins, esquire. The Chief Justice of Chester and the Secretary of shall give continual attendance except as specified.

(The Instructions are based upon those of 1574 printed in *Documents connected with the History of Ludlow*, pp. 309–334, but they are somewhat fuller and not arranged in the same order. Those of 1574 are among the Lansdowne MSS. in the British Museum, No. 49, art. 82.)

f. 9. 1586-7, February 24, Westminster.—Commission to Henry, Earl of Pembroke, Lord President of the Council in the Marches of Wales, to be the Queen's Lieutenant in the Principality of South Wales and North Wales, the Marches adjoining and the counties of Worcester, Monmouth, Hereford, and Salop and all corporate and privileged places therein.

f. 9*b*. 1591, April 8, Ramesbury.—H. Earl of Pembroke to the Council in the Marches at Ludlow. Notifying his appointment of Henry Meirick to be Steward of Her Majesty's Household in the Marches.

f. 10. 1590, June 21, Greenwich.—The Queen to the Earl of Pembroke. Considering his indisposition of health and inability to repair

DOVASTON MS. to Wales to hold the session, Sir Richard Shuttleworth, the justice of Chester, has been ordered to repair to Bewdley for the purpose. Her attorney there has by some oversight been named one of the Council, and so at his will occupies the place of a judge. As it is inconvenient and not compatible for him to be both an advocate and a judge, the Lord President is by private letter to advise him to forbear from taking the place of one of the Council.

f. 10*b*. Memorandum that the Lord President wrote to Mr. Attorney accordingly.

f. 10*b*. 1590., July 10, Bewdley.—Order by the Council for the admission of Peers Madoxe to be one of the ordinary messengers and pursuivants of the Court in the place of Roger Gruff *alias* Barbor who desires to be removed on account of his age.

f. 11. Forms of oaths to be taken by the Attorney and the Examiner.

f. 11*b*. 1594, May 22. Greenwich.—The Queen to the Lord President and the Council. Order for the admission as Councillors, of the Bishops of Bangor, Worcester, Llandaff, and St. David's, William, Lord Chandos, Sir John Harington, Sir John Danvers, Sir Henry Poole, George Kingesmill, serjeant at law, Richard Atkins, esquire, "John Crooke thelder brother, esquire;" Richard Broughton, esquire, Thomas Cornwall, esquire, Richard Corbett of Moreton, esquire, and William Fowler, esquire.

f. 12. 1590, April 19. Baynard's Castle.—H. Earl of Pembroke to the Council in the Marches at Ludlow. On behalf of Peers Madoxe who has been recommended by Roger Barbor and others.

1590, July 12. Ludlow.—Roger Griffethes *alias* Barbor to the Lord President and Council. Notifying his agreement with Peers Madoxe and acknowledging the receipt from him of 40*l*. and a bond for the payment of 20*l*. more for the messengership.

f. 12*b*. 1590, December 16. Richmond.—The Queen to the Earl of Pembroke, Lord President. Order for the admission as Councillors of Edward, Earl of Worcester, Giles, Lord Chandos, Sir Thomas Lucy, Sir Richard Barkley,. Sir Thomas Throckmorton, Sir William Herbert of Swansey, and Thomas Owen, serjeant at law. (Printed in *Documents connected with the History of Ludlow*, p. 355, from draft in Lord Burghley's handwriting).

1590 [-1], January 18, Ludlow.—Memorandum of the admission of Sir Thomas Throckmorton.

1590, December 31. Ramsbury.—The Earl of Pembroke to Sir Richard Shuttleworth. Desires that Sir Thomas Throckmorton may be summoned to repair to the Court. Notifies his appointment of the bearer, Thomas Evans an old clerk of the Court to be an attorney in the place of Griffith Evans.

f. 13. 1590, November.—Petition to the Council by John Spencer of Penmarcke co. Glamorgan, yeoman, "beinge a poore servingeman," for a writ of error in an action of trespass brought against him by Anthony Maunsell, esquire, before the justices of Great Sessions in the said county; and subsequent proceedings thereon.

f. 17. 1596, December 10. John Fortescue to the Queen's woodward in the county of Hereford. Warrant, upon information from John Taverner, gentleman, surveyor of Her Majesty's woods, to deliver to the Steward of household of the Council of the Marches so many firewood trees out of Orleton wood as may make 600 loads of wood and coal, the said steward paying for the felling of the same, "provided alwayes that no tymber tree be falne by cullor hereof."

Memorandum of the delivery of this letter to Mr. Morgan, steward of the household, after registration.

f. 17*b*. 1589, August 13. Westminster.—Letters patent granting to Arthur Messinger, gentleman, the office of examiner.

f. 18. 1598, August 14. Wilton.—The Earl of Pembroke to the Council in the Marches at Bewdley. Order for the admission of Messinger to the office of examiner.

f. 18*b*. 1598, August 16. Bewdley.—Order for the admission of Arthur Messinger.

1598, September 24.—Appointment by Foulke Grevyle of Beauchamp Court co. Warwick, esquire, of John Powell to be his deputy in the office of clerk of the Council in the Marches.

1598, November 14. Wilton.—The Earl of Pembroke to the Council in the Marches at Ludlow. Order for the admission of John Powell to be clerk of that Council.

f. 19. 1598, November 20. Ludlow.—Admission of John Powell as above.

f. 20. 1602, July 7. Greenwich.—Instructions given by the Queen to Edward, Lord Zouch, Lord President, and the Council in the Marches of Wales.

The Council is to consist of Edward, Earl of Worcester, Master of the Horse, William, Earl of Pembroke, the Bishops of Worcester, Hereford, Chester, Gloucester, St. Asaph, St. David's, Bangor, and Llandaff, for the time being, Edward, Lord Stafford, William, Lord Chandos, John Herbert, esquire, Her Majesty's Second Secretary, Sir Richard Lewkenor, chief justice of Chester, Sir John Scudamore, Sir John Leighton, Sir John Harrington, Sir Richard Barkely, Sir Richard Bulckely, Sir Henry Poole, Sir Thomas Lucy, Sir William Herbert of Swansey, Sir Edward Wynter, Sir Thomas Mauncell, Sir Richard Treavor, Sir Thomas Jones, Sir Thomas Mostyn, Foulke Grevill esquire, Her Majesty's Secretary there, John Crooke esquire, one of the justices of South Wales, William Leighton esquire, one of the justices of North Wales, Henry Towneshend, esquire, second justice of Chester, Richard Atkyns esquire, another of the justices of South Wales, Thomas Coventree of Crome co. Worcester, esquire, George Wylde of Wicke co. Worcester, esquire, Richard Barker, esquire, another of the justices of North Wales, William Oldisworth, another of the justices of South Wales, Thomas Cornewall of Burford co. Salop, esquire, Richard Corbett of Moreton co. Salop, esquire, Herbert Croft of Croft co. Hereford, esquire, Francis Newport of Eaton co. Salop, esquire, Edmond Coles of Lighe co. Worcester, esquire, Roger Owen of Condover co. Salop, esquire, Roger Puleston of Emerall co. Flint, esquire, Richard Pryce of Cogarthen co. Cardigan, esquire, Hugh Hughes, esquire, Her Majesty's attorney in North Wales, and Richard Davies of Waterston co. Hereford, esquire.

Sir Richard Lewkenor, John Crooke, Henry Townshend, and Richard Atkyns, or three of them, of whom the said Sir Richard Lewkenor, chief justice of Chester shall be one, shall give continual attendance except as specified.

(The Instructions are based upon those of 1574 and 1586, but they differ somewhat from either.)

f. 30. N.D. Instructions given by the King to the Lord President and the Council in the Marches. (Enrolled on the dorse of the Close Roll, 7 James I.).

f. 44. 1616, July 19. Theobalds.—The King to Sir Thomas Chamberlaine, Chief Justice of the county palatine of Chester. Order to consider and determine the complaint of Richard Shirburne of Stonihurst co. Lancaster, esquire, holding an estate in Chirk co. Denbigh, lately the inheritance of John Edwardes, esquire, that sundry great parcels of the commons and wastes of that lordship have been wrongfully enclosed by Sir Thomas Midleton, Alderman of London, contrary to a charter of Henry VII. and other grants, and to orders made by the Council of Queen Elizabeth in the Marches.

Certificate by Sir Thomas Chamberlain and Sir Henry Towneshende, two of the Council in the Marches, that, at the term at Ludlow which began the Monday after Whitsun week and continued a month, they heard above 260 causes set down for hearing, concerning poor men, at a small charge to them and near their own country, besides as many rules and motions, and besides many misdemeanours. They thank the King for his mention of this Court in his speech in the Star Chamber. They likewise by this Court preserve his possessions in the Principality of Wales, both for his tenants, forests, chases, parks, deer woods, and all other profits, and punish the thieves and stealers of his deer there, and also those keepers who have neglected their duty.

f. 44*b*. [1621.] F. Viscount St. Albans, Lord Chancellor, to the Earl of Northampton, Lord President, and the Council in the Marches. He has always continued one man, consistent. "The Starr Chamber ought not to forerunne or preoccupate by dealinge in the collaterall pointe [of perjury], while the principall is undiscussed, but yf the plea be judged and determyned, then it is the birthright of the subject, yf the cause be worthy of yt, that he may complayne in the high courte of Starr Chamber for the grief he susteyned by perjurey or abuse of justice in those other courtes . . . . in the Kinges Bench, Common Pleas, Exchequer, Court of Wards, from which the provincial Councells may in noe sort be exempted."

f. 45. 1582–3, January 4.—Ludlow. Order by the Council for the creation of the office of Remembrancer, and assignment of certain specified duties thereto.

f. 46*b*. 1621, June 21. Westminster.—Letters patent granting to Richard Randall and Thomas Beale, gentlemen, and the survivor of them the office of Remembrancer in any court before the Council in the principality of Wales.

f. 48. 1609, December 4.—Bewdley. Ancient orders as to procedure, etc. in the Court, renewed with some additions by the Lord President and the Council.

f. 51. 1604, October 26. Ludlow Castle.—The Council in the Marches to Sir John Popham, Lord Chief Justice of England. He has awarded a writ of *habeas corpus* to the porter attending this court for sending up the body of one John Farely now remaining in ward in the porter's lodge, but by precedents of former times it appears that no such writ from any of His Majesty's Courts have been here allowed. On all occasions private letters have been written from the Courts at Westminster and answered to the good satisfaction of the same. The Lord President, who is in London, is well acquainted with the cause of this man's commitment.

1599, June 19. Westminster.—Letters patent appointing John Fleet of the Inner Temple Esquire to be attorney in the Principality of Wales and the Marches.

f. 52.—"A Kalender" of the names of the gentlemen admitted to the Council in the Marches who took their oaths according to the Instructions given to Lord Eure dated May 24, 1609 :—

Sir Thomas Cornewall Sir Edward Foxe	June 18, 1609.
Sir Francis Lacon	June 19, 1609.
Sir Randle Brereton Sir Robert Needham Sir Robert Vernon	July 28, 1609.
John, now Bishop of Man,	August 13, 1609.
Nicholas Overbery	January 14, 1610, (VIII. Jac. I.).
Sir Edward Herbert of Montgomery	May 22, 1611.
Robert Bennett, Bishop of Hereford,	May 26, 1612.
Sir Francis Eure Thomas Chamberlain, serjeant at law,	March 1, 1615.
Sir James Scudamore	June 1, 1617.
Sir John Stafford	June 13, 1617.
Sir Robert Vernon	October 5, 1626.
Sir John Scudamore, Bart., John Rudghill Esquire	October 13, 1626.
Sir Richard Foxe	Hilary Term, 1626.
Godfrey, Bishop of Gloucester, Sir William Sandes	February 17, 1626.
Spencer, Lord Compton,	July 10, 1627.
George, Bishop of Hereford,	July 9, 1640.
Timothy Litleton esquire, serjeant at law,	November 15, 1644.
Richard, Earl of Carbery,	February 20, 1644.

f. 53. 1603, June 30. Inner Temple.—Sir Edward Coke to Sir Richard Lewkenor, Chief Justice of Chester and the rest of the Council in the Marches. Desires them to admit the bearer, Mr. Bird, as deputy for Richard Cartwright gentleman, appointed by letters patent to the office of Examiner in the place of Arthur Massinger gentleman, deceased, but now otherwise employed in the King's service.

f. 53*b*. 1603, May 29. Westminster.—Letters patent granting to Richard Cartwright the office of Examiner.

f. 55*b*. 1603, June 30.—Deed of Richard Cartwright of London gentleman appointing Peter Byrde of Paynswick co. Gloucester, gentleman, to be his deputy in the office of Examiner.

DOVASTON MS.

f. 58. 1603, September 20. Shrewsbury.—Order by the Lord President and the Council concerning the manner of making oaths or affidavits.

f. 59. 1603, September 2.—Deed of Richard Cartwright of London, gentleman, appointing John Parry of London gentleman to be his deputy in the office of Examiner.

f. 60. 1603–4, February 8. Ludlow.—Order by the Lord President and the Council concerning the entry of appearances in Court.

f. 60*b*. 1607, November 10. Ludlow.—A further order concerning the same.

f. 61. 1604, March 28. Westminster.—Letters patent granting to Peter Byrd, gentleman, the office of Examiner.

f. 62*b*. 1604, August 2. Bewdley.—Memorandum that the signet of the late Queen Elizabeth remaining with the Lord President and the rest of the Council in the Marches was this day broken and defaced.

f. 63. 1606–7, January 15. Ludlow.—Order concerning the fees to be paid to Peter Byrd or his deputies.

f. 64. 1606, July 12. Westminster.—Letters patent appointing John Hooper gentleman to be clerk and receiver of fines and forfeitures, on the nomination of the Lord President.

f. 65. 1606, November 30. Ludlow.—Order for the admission of Piers Gruffith gentleman to the office of Messenger in the place of John Tullye resigned.

1606. December 3. Ludlow.—Admission of Piers Gruffith accordingly.

f. 65*b*. 1620–21, January 25. Ludlow.—Licence to Richard Jones esquire, serjeant at arms, to go to London remaining absent for a month.

1625, September 12. Deed of Foulke, Lord Broke, appointing Richard Cam and Thomas Crumpe to be his deputies in the office of Secretary and Clerk of the Council in the Marches.

f. 66. 1607, July 4. Westminster.—The King to Sir Richard Lewkenor, Chief Justice of Chester and the rest of the Council in the Marches. Concerning the manner of taking oaths or affidavits.

f. 66*b*. 1607, July 17. Westminster.—Letters patent for Sir Fulk Grevill.

f. 67. 1607, July 31.—Deed of Sir Fulk Grevil appointing William Bevan of Ludlow, gentleman, Thomas Coxe of Catstrey co. Salop, and Richard Cam of Ludlow, to be his deputies for taking oaths or affidavits.

f. 67*b*. 1608, June 28. Greenwich.—The Lords of the Council to the Sheriff of the county of Gloucester. There has been of late much controversy about the jurisdiction and authority of the Council established in the Marches of Wales, especially concerning jurisdiction in the counties of Gloucester, Worcester, Hereford, and Salop. Complaint has been made that the Sheriffs of these four counties have usually refused to execute process directed to them by that Court.

The King has caused the controversy between the Lord President of that Council and the chief judges of the realm to be brought before his Council, to be heard and determined in Michaelmas term. In the meanwhile his pleasure is that the Sheriffs are not to refuse to execute any process directed to them by the Council in the Marches that shall be agreeable to the instructions given by the King to the Lord President thereof.

f. 68. 1607, September 25. Hampton Court.—The King to the Treasurer, Chancellor, Chamberlains, Barons, and other ministers of the Exchequer. Warrant for payments to the receiver of the fines before the Council in the Marches.

f. 68*b*. 1608, August 16. Grafton.—The King to Lord Eure, Lord President of the Council in the Marches. Ralph Clare, Esquire, keeper of the King's house at Tickenhill "hath forgotten himself" in refusing to receive the Lord President and the Council without reserving some rooms to himself. He has been commanded to receive them immediately. As he has letters patent for the park and the herbage thereof, and the King is far from his learned counsel and has not many of his privy council in attendance, the consideration of that question is deferred until next term.

f. 69. 1609, May 29. Westminster.—Letters patent granting to William Vaughan, Esquire, the office of King's Solicitor.

f. 70. 1609, December 23. Westminster.—The King to the Lord President and the Council in the Marches. Warrant authorising Peter Mutton, Esquire, one of the King's Council in the Marches, and his Attorney there, in succession to John Fleet, Esquire, resigned, to prosecute all matters of misdemeanours, and also to practise, advise, and give counsel.

f. 70*b*. 1610, December 8. Westminster.—The King to the Lord President and the Council in the Marches. Warrant for the admission of Nicholas Overbury, Esquire, to the office of a Councillor in the place of Richard Atkyns Esquire, deceased.

f. 71. 1609–10, January 25. Bewdley.—Order by the Lord President and the Council that no attorneys or clerks shall offer suits to obtain commissions with the bills enclosed before the defendants shall have answered the matters contained in such bills, or offer warrants for signature until after the return of letters missive awarded therein, under penalty of committal to ward for the first offence and expulsion for the second.

f. 71*b*. 1610, October 20. Westminster.—The King to Lord Eure, Lord President. Warrant authorising his absence from Parliament.

f. 72. 1609–10, February 12. Westminster.—Letters patent appointing Sir Herbert Croft, the King's woodward in the county of Hereford, and his deputy, to do and execute certain matters specified in a schedule thereto annexed.

f. 73. 1576[–7], March 24. Westminster.—Orders set down by the Queen, with the advice of Her Privy Council, for the direction and reformation of her Court in the Marches. (*Printed in Documents connected with the History of Ludlow, pp.* 335–348.)

f. 77*b*. 1611, May 24.—Proceedings in a suit between John Hall and Elizabeth his wife, plaintiffs, and Richard Booth, defendant, concerning debt.

f. 78. 1611, September 9.—Deed of Rowland Scudamore of Cradock co. Hereford, appointing Richard Cholmley, gentleman, to be his deputy in the office of Porter before the Lord President and the Council in the Marches.

f. 78*b*. 1611, November 9. Shrewsbury.—Order that orders of continuance, etc. shall be submitted to the King's Attorney for signature.

f. 79. 1611[-2], January 20. Shrewsbury.—Order concerning the hearing of causes.

f. 79*b*. 1611, November 2. Shrewsbury.—Order for the admission of Robert Medcaulfe late of Staple Inn, gentleman, and now servant to Lord Eure, to be one of the attorneys in the Court of the Marches.

f. 80. 1613, November 3. Hunsdon House.—Ralph, Lord Eure, to the Deputy Lieutenants in all the shires of his Lieutenancy. Warrant for the exemption of Counsellors at the bar of the Court of the Marches from appearance at the musters.

1614, July 14. Hunsdon House.—Ralph, Lord Eure to Sir Robert Needham, Vice-President, and the rest of the Council in the Marches.

Enclosing fourteen letters, for the thirteen shires of Wales and the town of Monmouth, and a bundle of proclamations, for the supply of voluntary contributions to the King.

f. 80*b*. 1614, December 3. Ludlow.—Order concerning Sheriffs and bailiffs.

f. 81. 1614, December 3. Westminster.—Letters patent granting to Marmaduke Lloyd, esquire, the office of King's Attorney in the place of Peter Mutton, resigned.

f. 82*b*. 1617, August 9. Asheton.—The King to the Lord President in the Marches. Warrant for the admission as Councillors of Sir Francis Bacon, Lord Keeper of the Great Seal, George, Earl of Buckingham, Master of the Horse, Sir Gilbert Gerrard, Sir Peter Warberton, a justice of the Common Pleas, Sir John Crooke, a justice of the King's Bench, Sir Henry Yelverton, Attorney General, Sir Richard Mollineux, baronet, Sir Thomas Gerard, baronet, Sir John Peshall, baronet, Sir William Throckmorton, baronet, Sir John Stradlinge, baronet, Sir Peter Leigh, Sir Edward Lewis, Sir Walter Chetwynd, Sir Henry Williams, Sir William Thomas, Sir Roger Mostyn, Edward Fytton, Charles Gerrard, Thomas Price of the priory of Brecon, William Dutton, John Fleete and Richard Fowler. (Printed in *Documents connected with the History of Ludlow, p.* 360.)

f. 83. 1613, December 27. Westminster.—Letters patent granting to Thomas Powell, esquire, the office of King's Solicitor.

f. 84. 1615, November 25. Ludlow.—Order that the messengers shall be sent once only to disobedient persons.

f. 84*b*. 1615[-6], January 17. Westminster.—The King to the Lord President and the Council in the Marches. Warrant for the admission as Councillors of Thomas Chamberlain, serjeant at law, and Francis Eure, knight, in the place of Richard Barker, esquire, deceased.

f. 85. 1610, December 28. Westminster.—The King to the Lord President in the Marches. Warrant for the admission as a Councillor of Nicholas Overbury esquire, in the place of Richard Atkyns, esquire, deceased.

f. 85*b*. 1615, March 20. Whitehall.—Lord Chancellor Ellesmere, Ralph Winwood, and Fulke Grevill, to the Lord President and the Council in the Marches. Sir John Wynn, baronet, one of the Councillors in the Marches, has upon a sentence decreed against him in that court for misdemeanours committed by him and his servants, repaired to Whitehall, hoping to be relieved therefrom by petition to the King. Now, "in coulde bloud upon better advisement findinge his errors," he has resolved to submit. It is desirable in this case "to follow that course of grace and favor which is practised in the Starre Chamber, where, upon humble submission to the censure of that Court, both the tyme of ymprisonment is abridged and the fine imposed eyther whooly remitted or in the greatest parte (of course) abated." This gentleman's voluntary submission "soe strongly allyed in his cuntery and supported with soe powerfull freends in court, will add more grace and lustre to the authority" of the Lord President than if he had been at first apprehended and detained in prison. He should be favorably treated both as to the restraint of his person and the fine. The fine of 40*l*. allotted to John Conway, the relator, who was supposed to have been suborned by Henry Salisburey, esquire, and the allowance of 20*s*. a day to the serjeant-at-arms who sought Sir John Wynn in vain should be reduced, and the pursuivant's charges disallowed.

1616, March 29. Ludlow Castle.—Memorandum of the submission of Sir John Wynne of Gwithur in the presence of the Lord President and five other members of the Council.

f. 86. 1616, May 21. Greenwich.—The King to the Lord President and the Council in the Marches. Warrant for the admission of Sir Thomas Chamberlain serjeant-at-law, chief justice of Chester, and justice in the counties of Denbigh and Montgomery, to be a member of the Council "as in former tymes all justices of Chester have been."

1614, August 20. Woodstock.—The King to the Lord President and the Council in the Marches. Warrant for the admission of Rowland White and Thomas Alured to the office of Remembrancer.

1614, November 8. Ludlow.—Order for the admission of the above, Thomas Alured being present.

f. 86 *b*. 1618, June 12. Fleet Street.—The Prince's Council to the Lord President and Council in the Marches. Arrears of cordwood due to Sir Henry Wallop out of the forest of Darvall (i.e., Deerfold in Herefordshire) are to be made up to him. The underwood in the forest of Bringwood and the Chase of Mocktree are to be allowed towards fuel for his Majesty's use at Ludlow, and to be cut according to a constant proportion yearly.

f. 87. 1618, November 27. Fleet Street.—The same to the same. Thanking them for the progress they have made in reforming of sundry abuses offered to his highness by the Lessees of the Manor and

DOVASTON MS. Park of Bewdley, and praying "that the same may be prosecuted to effect in that Court [of the Marches] being in our opinion the fittest place of all others for that purpose." The grant to Sir Henry Wallop of 2,000 cords of wood yearly from the forest of Darvall has been resumed by his highness in regard of the great loss and detriment received thereby. A mill and dwelling house in the chase of Bringwood, and certain parcels of land in the forest of Mocktree the chase of Bringwood and the forest of Darvall have been let to Edward Danahan Esqre Steward of his Majesty's house at Ludlow for the rent of 100 marks yearly; and out of this six hundred cords of wood and 4,000 faggots are to be yearly assigned towards the provision of fire for his Majesty's house at Ludlow.

f. 87*b*. 1619, December 24th. Ludlow.—Order for the admission of Thomas Pingle to the office of messenger in the place of Peers Griffeth, gentleman, resigned.

f. 88. 1616, October 9. Westminster.—Letters patent being an *inspeximus* made at the request of the Lord President in the Marches.

f. 91. 1616, November 7. Ludlow.—William Connar, Deputy Ranger of the King's forest of Feckenham, to the Lord President and the Council in the Marches. Certifies that since he took office under Sherington Talbot, Esquire, two years before, he has supplied them with three bucks and three does yearly, serving them out of his friends' parks so as to increase the game in the forest, which has within that period increased by two hundred deer of all sorts.

f. 91*b*. 1608, May 23. Westminster.—Letters patent granting to Griffin Jones, gentleman, the office of porter (*janitor*) of Ludlow Castle.

f. 92*b*. 1618–9, February 8. Ludlow.—Order for the admission of Henry Trotman, gentleman, to be an attorney in the place of Robert Watkins, gentleman, deceased. *Signed by* W. Earl of Northampton.

f. 93. 1619, December 17. Fleet Street.—Order by the Prince's Council that whereas the Lord President and the Council in the Marches have been "most observante and respective to see his highnes revenewes and royalties and woodes in those partes carefullie kepte and maine-tained" they shall have "in some manner of acknowledgment and retribucion" all woods and underwoods, except timber trees, in the chace of Bringwood and forest of Mocktree, for the provision of fuel for his Majesty's house at Ludlow, and "that a warren shalbe erected upon some parte of the comon of Mocktree" for the provision thereof.

f. 93*b*. 1620, June 15. Theobalds.—W. Earl of Northampton to Sir Thomas Chamberlain, Chief Justice of Chester, and the rest of the Council in the Marches.

"Whereas Mr Alured hath verie unadvisedly written a lettre against the match with Spayne, the which the King and his Councell hold to be a grate presumption in him and therefore hath comitted him to close prison in the Fleete," and the scattering of copies thereof may mislead the simple and ill-affected, it is his Majesty's pleasure that all such shall be sent to the Lord President with the names of such persons as shall be found to have them or to divulge them.

Postscript:—"The Kinges pleasure is that you take care that the Lottery shall be presently removed from Beawdeley and that it con-tynue noe longer within the Marches of Wales to the ympoverishing of his subjectes there unles it be in some greate and wealthy towns or citties, with speciall care of the governors that the poore be not suffered to venture, or ells to be absolutely dismissed and forbidden according as you in your discreacion and wisdome shall think fitt."

1617, May 21.—Memorandum that this day in full Court, in sight and presence of the whole assembly, the Lord President, humbly kneeling upon his knees, took the oaths of supremacy and allegiance ministered to him by the Chief Justice of Chester. He then caused to be openly read two several Commissions of Oyer and Terminer, one for the Principality of Wales and one for the counties of [left blank]; and also one other Commission of Lieutenancy from the King's Majesty to his Lordship directed for the Principality and Marches of Wales and for the Counties of [blank] excepting only [blank]. And immediately after the said Sir Thomas Chamberlain and the rest of the said Council (all kneeling on their knees) took the said oath of supremacy and allegiance and the oath by his highness' instructions set down and appointed to be taken by all such as are ordained of the said Council.

f. 94. 1616, April 6. Ludlow Castle.—Lord Eure to Lord Chancellor Ellesmere. Announces the death of Sir Richard Lewkenor. Recommends that his place be conferred on Serjeant Chamberlayne, "only herein I beseech your Lordship to do me the honour in the eye of the world that he (or whomsoever it be) be not brought in without my privity." Recommends his own brother Sir Francis Eure to succeed him, in the circuit of North Wales. (Note at foot of letter) "Sir Richard Lewkenor died at 7 of the clock this Satterday the 6 of April."

f. 94*b*. 1616, April 26.—Lord Ellesmere to ———.
I have sent you two patents for Serjeant Chamberlen for the office of Justice of the County Palatine of Chester and of Flintshire in Wales which Sir Richard Lewkenor lately had, in the terms of the former patents to Sir Richard Lewkenor and Sir Richard Shuttleworth and other their predecessors, to be presented to his Majesty for his signature. "This gent. hath such a generall commendation for his late services in the provinces of North Wales I never knew Judge have the like."

f. 94*b*. 1616, July 17. Hunsdon House in the Blackfriars.—Lord Eure to Sir Thomas Chamberlen Knight, Chief Justice of Chester and of his Majesty's Council established in the Principality and Marches of Wales. Congratulations on the report that is spread of his worthy doings in advancement of His Majesty's service in every place. Has appointed Sir Francis Eure Chief Justice of North Wales to keep the Court at Ludlow until he begins his circuit which will be about the 6th of August.

f. 95. 1616, May 23. Hunsdon House.—Lord Eure to the Council of the Marches. Sends the King's letters for the admittance of Sir Thomas Chamberlen. Sir Thomas Cornwall and Mr. Harley are to be sent for to administer the oath, and to assist the Chief Justice in disposing of the Court's business, as the term begins on Monday morning next. The officers and ministers of the Court are to go out on Saturday after dinner to meet the Justice on his first coming. The pursuivants are to take the enclosed letters from the Lords of the Council and himself to the Deputy-Lieutenants, for general musters.

f. 95*b*. 1616, May 21. Manor of Greenwich.—Warrant to appoint Sir Thomas Chamberlen to be of the Council. Another copy is on f. 86, *ante*.

DOVASTON MS.

f. 96. 1620, May 24. York House.—Lord Verulam, Chancellor, to Sir Thomas Chamberlayn. I have received his Majesty's pleasure signified by my Lord Marquis Buckingham that you should be made one of the Judges of the King's Bench.

1620. June 22. York House. The same to the same. His Majesty is pleased that you accept. You can hold your present circuit as fixed, and take your seat in the King's Bench at the beginning of Michaelmas term.

f. 96*b*. 1620, November 3. Palace of Westminster.—Warrant to the Earl of Northampton Lord President and the rest of the council, in the same form as above, to appoint Sir James Whitlock, Chief Justice of Chester, &c., one of the Council of the Marches; and memorandum that he took the oath accordingly 8 Nov. 1620 in presence of the Lord President, Sir Henry Townshend, and Sir Francis Eure.

f. 97. 1610–11, January 10.—Letters patent to Thomas Alured for the office of Groom of the Wardrobe within the Principality and Marches of Wales, and of making the Bills of Complaint for matter of debt to be exhibited before the Council there, in reversion after the death of Thomas Stevens, for his life.

f. 98. 1621, March 30. Ludlow.—Thomas Stevens having lately died and various persons claiming a right to succeed him, Thomas Burghill is appointed to the office of keeping the wardrobe, and William Bowdler to that of making of bills of debt, until further order is taken by this Court. Signed by James Whitlock.

f. 98. 1621. May 8. Savoy.—The Earl of Northampton to Sir James Whitlock Chief Justice of Chester and the rest of the Council, at Bewdley. I have consulted Mr. Attorney General, who is clear of opinion that Mr. Alured hath the sole right to the above offices, so I have given them to him, and leave you to determine what is reasonable as to the claims of others.

f. 98*b*. 1621, May 20. Bewdley.—Order, after recital of letters patent to Thomas Stephens and Thomas Alured, and judgment in a *scire facias* setting aside a former grant of the said offices to James Ambler, and the above letter of Lord Northampton, that Thomas Alured be admitted to the offices in question. Signed by Hen. Townshend.

f. 99. Trinity Term, 1621. Bewdley.—"The coppie of a Report made by those whose names are underwritten for the explaining of a Clause in the present Articles of His Majesty's Instructions, published 12 No. 1617, (of saving of his place to the Chief Justice of Chester as aunciently hath been used). [For the Article, see Rymer's *Fœdera* xvii. 30.]

"We whose names are underwritten do affirm upon our knowledge that the Chief Justice of Chester hath allwaies had place and precedence at the Counsell in the Marches of Walles, as well out of Court as in Court, next to the Lord President, and above such bishops and Noblemen of the said Counsell as have resorted thereto for his Majesty's services.

I Henry Townshend Knight one of his Majesty's Counsell there affirm this to be true upon my personal observation for 44 years last past."

Signed also in similar form upon personal observation for about 30 years, Edward Littleton Esqre. one of His Majesty's Counsell there.

37 years. Brian Crowther, Esq[re] Counsellor at the barr there.

30 years or thereabouts. Richard Smith, Esq[re] Counsellor at the barr there.

26 years. Edward Waties, Esq[re] Counsellor at the barr there.

18 years. Richard Blunt, Esq[re] Counsellor at the barr there.

18 years. Thomas Eyton, Esq[re] Receiver of his Majesty's ffines.

20 years. Richard Jones, Esq[re] his Majesty's Serjeant at Armes.

14 years. George Leigh, Yeoman Usher of Counsell Chamber.

49 years. Richard Cam, gent, attendant in the office of the Clarke of the Counsell. He adds "I have also observed out of the Records of the Court there, and out of the Counsell Chamber books, that in all decrees in Court, and in all letters written from the Counsell table, the name of the Chief Justice is subscribed next after the name of the Lord President, and after the Chief Justice the names of Bishops and noblemen that were present.

58 years. Roger Bradshawe, gent, attendant in the said office of Clarke of the Counsell.

50 years. William Aston, gent, attendant in the office of Clarke of the Signett at the Counsell in the Marches.

f. 100. 1613–4, February 10. Ludlow.—Writ of Error. Walter Jones of Tregyb [in the Parish of Llandilovawr] in the County of Carmarthen complains that one Roderic William has recovered Judgement in an Action of Debt for 500*l.* against him in the Great Sessions of the said County of Carmarthen before his Majesty's Chief Justice of the same great Sessions, and has sued out execution thereon, and that there are manifest errors in the proceedings; whereupon the Justices of the said Great Sessions are ordered to send the whole proceedings to the Council of the Marches that they may reform such errors if any; and the Sheriff of Carmarthen is forbidden to proceed with the execution until further order taken in this Court. Signed by Sir Henry Townshend, Knight.

f. 100*b*. 12 Jac. 1. Apr. 5. Ludlow—By M[r] Justice Sir Henry Townshend K[t]. Walter Jones appearing before the Council, and the Council being satisfied that he has used all diligence to bring the Record into Court, but no return or Certificate of the former proceedings has been made to this Court, it is ordered that letters like the last letters be sent to the Justices of the Great Sessions of Carmarthen, returnable in this Court on the 1st of July next.

——— 12 Jac. 1. July 8. Salop.—By Richard Lewkenor, K[t]. Chief Justice, and M[r] Justice Barker. Plaintfff and Defendant appearing by Counsel, a Certificate was produced from Nicholas Overbury and Richard Payton Esq[res] Justices of the Great Sessions of Carmarthen to the effect that a special verdict had been found in the case and judgement given, both parties being represented by Counsel, that they forbear to certify the Record until the Plaintiff in error can show them some matter of error fit to be examined, as by law required, which he has not done, and it appears he is only now aiming at delay. Thereupon it is ordered that a writ of Supersedeas be sent to the Sheriff ordering him to execute any writ of execution which may be sent to him hereafter against the plaintiff, but this writ is not to be delivered to the Sheriff till after the next great Sessions of the County, to give the

DOVASTON MS. Plaintiff an opportunity of satisfying the Justices that there is a case of error which may be argued, and if he can do so then the writ is not to be delivered until the errors are examined in this Court. And it appearing by the affidavit of Griffiths ap Ivan that he duly delivered the alias writ of error to Nicholas Overbury Esqre. who hath not yet sent or satisfied the said Record, it is ordered that a pluries writ of error be directed to the Justices returnable 10 Nov. next.

f. 101. 12 Jac. 1. December 5. Ludlow.—By the Vice President Sir Henry Townshend. A *Plus Pluries* writ of error sent, returnable 27 January next;

———————— 10 Dec. Ludlow.—Form of the said writ.

f. 101*b*. Record of the trial before Nicholas Overbury and Richard Payton Esq^{res} at Carmarthen on the 23rd March in the 9th year of Jas. 1.

f. 103*b*. 23 Jas. 1. February 23. Ludlow.—Appointment of William Skirme to be an attorney in this Court in the place of Richard Boult, gent., deceased. He has taken the oath accordingly. *Signed by* James Whitelock, H. Townshend.

f. 104. 23 Jac. 1. Dec. 5. Ludlow.—" Whereas great contention and grief is like to arise within the County of Carnarvon touching the election of a knight of the parliament within the said County at the next County Court, in which election it is feared, if factious persons be suffered to carry weapons in the town when the said election shall be, that blood and breach of his Majesty's peace may ensue therein if great care be not had to prevent the same" it is ordered that His Majesty's letters be sent to the Sheriff and Justices of the Peace of the said County to be present at the said election, to see the peace preserved, and that the said County Court be held in the open and public place where the Great Sessions of the County are usually held, and that the Sheriff cause proclamation to be made in the said Court before the election that no one except the Sheriff and his servants in livery and officers do bear any weapons in or to the said Court during the said election. If any do so, they are to be bound over to appear in this Court on the 22nd January next, or to be committed to gaol if they refuse to be bound.

Signed by Wm. Northampton, James Whitlock, Henry Townshend.

The like letter to the Sheriff Justices of Peace and Bayliffs of the County of Worcester.

104*b*. 1620, last of February. Savoy.—The Earl of Northampton to Sir James Whitlock at Ludlow Castle.

"The chief and only business that is moved in the parliament house concerning Wales is a general desire of the Knights and Burgesses of the Principality to repeal the clause of the Act of 34 Henry 8, as I take it, whereby the King hath power to reform all manner of former ordinances and ordain what other he will beside, whereby all such laws and ordinances to be hereafter made devised and published by the authority of this Act by the King's Majesty in writing under his great seale shall be of as good strength virtue and effect as if they had been had and made by authority of Parliament. Now how this may be prejudicial to the King's power or government or validity of our Instructions I am not yet satisfied, but before the Act pass I will be well informed by the King's Counsell, and do desire that I may receive instructions from you and the rest of the Counsell if you doubt anything in it. The petition for His Majesty's allowance for repealing this clause was delivered within these two days, the consideration whereof was referred to my Lord Chancellor and myself. I have no more at this time, but commending myself most heartily unto you and your associates, do rest your very loving friend, Wm Northampton."

f. 104*b*. 1620, March 8. Ludlow Castle.—Sir James Whitelock, Sir Henry Townshend, and Sir Francis Eure. We have considered the above letter. All of us have been heretofore present at the debating of this matter in former Parliaments. We have consulted with his Majesty's Attorney, with Mr. Crowther, Mr. Littleton, Mr. Waties and Mr. Blunt; "and first for whether of the King's honour and prerogative why he should not be trusted with this clause as well as four of his predecessors, having never yet given any occasion of distrust therein, we leave that to better consideration, but we are all fully resolved that if that clause be repealed, there must be special saving and provision for the full upholding and maintaining of the King's power of altering, adding, and administering the Instructions for this Court and government, otherwise there will ensue great damage thereby."

f. 105. 1620, March 3. Savoy.—The Earl of Northampton to Sir James Whitlock, Chief Justice of Chester, and the rest there. Sir Giles Montparsons Knight, who was committed to the custody of the Serjeant, has escaped. A conference has been had between both houses, and it was resolved that the Lord High Admiral, the Warden of the Cinque Ports, and the Lords President of York and Wales, should direct their warrants and letters for search to be had within their limits. Therefore you are to send your letters to the Ports within the Principality and Marches of Wales to apprehend him.

f. 105. 1620, March 1. Ludlow Castle.—Sir James Whitelock, Sir Henry Townshend and Sir Francis Eure to the Earl of Northampton.

Have sent out letters for the apprehension of Sir Giles Montparsons, and for bringing him up before the Council in the Marches, to the Sheriffs of Salop, Hereford, Worcester, Gloucester, Monmouth, Glamorgan, Brecon, Radnor, Carmarthen, Pembroke, Cardigan, Montgomery, Denbigh, Flint, Merioneth, Carnarvon, Anglesey.

f. 105*b*. 1620, March 17.—At the Counsell table in Ludlow Castle. The same to the Justices of Assize for the County of Salop.

The bailiffs of Shrewsbury lately informed us of seditious speeches not long since uttered by one John Evans of Coleham in the suburbs of Shrewsbury, and sent us a copy of an examination which they had taken of him. We thereupon sent letters to the Sheriff of the County, and to the bailiffs, to apprehend him and bring him before this Council, but as they have not yet found him we commit the further consideration of this Cause to your Lordships, you being in Shrewsbury, that upon conference with the Sheriff and bailiffs you may take such order at the Assizes as may be fit.

f. 105*b*. 23 Jac. I. March 20. Ludlow.—Order to Arthur Winwood and Thomas Pringle the messengers of the Council, to go to the wood of Bringwood and Darvall [*i.e.*, Deerfold] in the county of Hereford and bring before the Council any one whom they shall find cutting or spoiling the said wood, Thomas Harley, Esqre one of the said Council having given information that great waste is being committed there.

"Signed by James Whitelock, Hy Townshend, Francis Eure, Nicholas Overbury, Francis Lacon."

f. 106. 23 Jac. I. March 23. Ludlow.—The Council desires to remove one George Boulton late of Madeley in the County of Hereford Schoolmaster, now in Hereford gaol, to Montgomery gaol. Therefore a letter is to be sent to the Sheriff of Herefordshire to bring him to Bucknall on the confines of Hereford and Shropshire at 12 at noon on 20 April next; to the Sheriff of Shropshire to bring him thence to Ednop on the confines of Salop and Montgomery; and to the Sheriff of Montgomery to take him thence to Montgomery gaol. *Signed by* James Whitelock, Hy Townshend, Francis Eure.

f. 106. 1620, July 11. Fleet Street.—The Prince's Council to Sir Thomas Chamberlain and the Justices of the County Palatine of Chester.

One Watkin Jenkyns "a most lawless and disordered person" has committed great waste in his Highness' forest of Kilgairne [Kilgarren] in the County of Pembroke, under colour of a lease of certain lands called Kevendrun, and the herbage of the forest of Kevendrun parcel of the lordship of Kilgairne. As he goes from County to County, and the sheriffs have therefore not been able to apprehend him "and it is very unfitt to suffer a fellow of his quality and condition any longer to commit such disgraceful misdemeanours" the Council in the Marches is to take steps to apprehend him and put a stop to them. Signed by Henry Hubarte, James Ley, James Fullerton, Richard Smith, Thomas Trevor.

f. 106*b*. 23 Jac. I. March 22.—Minute to send orders accordingly. Signed by James Whitelocke.

1620. Ludlow Castle.—Sir James Whitelock, Sir Henry Townshend, and Sir Francis Eure to the Bishop of St. Davids.

On 10 February last we wrote to tell you the sentence of this Court concerning Jane Gwyn "by which you might perceive the notorious misbehaviour of David Morgan Gruffith both against common government and this Court. We therefore thought fitt in our friendly respect to your Lordship as a brother and companion with us in this service, by our Letters from the Table to putt you in minde of the great prejudice will grow to the Infant (if she consent to this marriage) by the forfeiture of the profitte of her lands during life." The Bishop is desired to take present course to hand her over to Gruffith Henry and Jenkin Franclen, two of the Tutors appointed by her Father's Will (John Price the 3rd Tutor to avoid all suggestions made by David Morgan Gruffith desiring to be spared therein). "Your Lordship's power of detaining her as a sequestrator is now determined by the sentence of this Court; and if your Lordship shall not take present order herein we must be enforced forthwith to put the sentence of this Court in execution."

1620, March 12. Westminster.—The Bishop of St. David's to the Council of the Marches.

He was desirous that the Infant's delivery might have been delayed till his return from Parliament, but as the Council think this would be to cross or defeat the sentence of Justice "and to savour of some favour shown to that audacious malefactor whose precipitate and exorbitant courses in these affairs I did ever dislike" he has sent word to his wife and family to deliver her to the parties named. "It hath been untruly suggested unto you that a great part of her estate is in my hands by way of sequestration whereas indeed I never had any pennyworth of her goods since she came into my custody, and therefore I doubt not but that it will be thought fitt in your discretion her entertainment should be paid for before her departure from my house." DOVASTON MS.

f. 107. 1621, March 29. Ludlow Castle.—Sir James Whitelocke, Sir Henry Townshend, and Charles Fox, to the Lord Chancellor. Francis Haslewood, David Morgan Griffith and William Symonds, against whom decrees have been made in this Court, have fled to the City of London. The Lord Chancellor is desired to authorise the Serjeant at Arms by his warrant to apprehend them and send them to this Court to deal with.

1621, March 26. Ludlow Castle.—The same to the Bishop of St. David's. Giving him notice that John Price and others have laid an Information against him concerning Jane Gwyn an Infant lately sequestered by this Court unto his custody, and suffered to be eloigned and taken away contrary to the trust in him reposed by this Court, which would not have happened if he had taken order for her delivery according to the decree of this Court.

19 Jac. 1, March 27. Westminster.—Commission of Dedimus Potestatem to Sir James Whitelock, and note of his being sworn in as Chief Justice of Chester before the Earl of Northampton and Sir H. Townshend on 4 April, 1621.

f. 107*b*. 19 Jac. I. June 19. Bewdley.—Order, on death of Thomas Stephens, various persons claiming to succeed him as keeper of the Wardrobe, that, without prejudice, George Bett, Steward of H.M. Household in the Marches of Wales, shall exercise the office of keeping the wardrobe, and William Bowdler shall collect the fees of 4*d*. upon every bill of debt by way of sequestration, and John Jones and Thomas Alured who have received such fees since Thomas Stephens' death shall pay them over to William Bowdler, who shall account for them. Signed by James Whitelock, Henry Townshend, Francis Lacon.

f. 107*b*. 1621, May 19. Bewdley.—Warrant to be sent to all forresters &c. in the several Chases and Forests under-mentioned to send forthwith to the Council for provision of H.M.'s household the under-mentioned number of bucks.

Ockley Park [Oakley, near Ludlow] 3 bucks.
Bewdley Park [Worcestershire] 3 bucks.
Houlte Park [Holt, Denbighshire] 3 bucks.
Malvern Chase [Worcestershire] 3 bucks.
Corstane Chase [Corston, Shropshire ?] 3 bucks.
Bryngwood Chase [Herefordshire] 3 bucks.
Shotwick Park [Cheshire] 3 bucks.
Mocktree Forest [Shropshire] 3 bucks.
Feckenham Forest [Worcestershire] 3 bucks.
Deane Forest [Gloucestershire] 3 bucks.
Dalamore Forest [Delamere, Cheshire] 3 bucks.
Kyngswood Forest [Shropshire] 3 bucks.
Maxfield Forest [Macclesfield, Cheshire] 3 bucks or 3 stags.
Snowdon Forest [Carnarvonshire] 3 bucks or 3 stags.

The like warrants to go out in season for does and hinds to all the places aforesaid.

Signed by James Whitelock, Henry Townshend.

DOVASTON MS.

1618, June 4. Westminster.—Warrant under the King's signet that William Lord Compton, Lord President, and the rest of the Council of the Marches, may have out of every Park, Forest, and Chase within the Principality of Wales and the Counties of Gloucester, Worcester, Hereford, Chester, Salop, and Monmouth, 3 bucks of the season in summer, and 3 does of the season in winter, and also 3 stags of the season in summer and 3 hinds of the season in winter where red deer are to be taken and may themselves hunt and kill the same with their bows hounds or greyhounds, or other ways at their liberty.

Form of warrant to a forester to send a buck.

f. 108*b*. 1621, July 2. Council Table at Bewdley.—James Whitelock, Francis (Bishop of) Hereford, Henry Townshend, Nicholas Overbury, to the Bishop of Worcester asking him to be present with them on Wednesday morning to assist in the execution of H.M. service.

19 Jac. 1, May 23.—The King to the Earl of Northampton and the rest of the Council. Appointment of Edward Litleton, Esq[re] to be a member of the Council in place of Sir Francis Eure deceased.

Note that Sir Edward Litleton, now Knight, was sworn accordingly at Bewdley 18 July 1621, present the Lord President, the Chief Justice, and Justice Townshend.

f. 109. 1621, September 29.—Sir James Whitelock and Sir Henry Townshend to the Lord President. Names of persons fit to be appointed Sheriffs and Escheators for Denbighshire and Montgomeryshire.

1621, October 27.—Sir E. Litleton to the same, as to the Counties of Merioneth, Carnarvon, and Anglesey.

f. 109*b*. 1621.—Lists of Sheriffs and Escheators for Glamorgan, Brecon, and Radnor, signed by Walter Pye and Andrew Howell, and the like for Carmarthen, Pembroke, and Cardigan, signed by N. Overbury and J. Hoskyns.

f. 110 to 121*b*. No date [1617].—Instructions to the Council of the Marches. There are 55 articles, of which 45 are printed in Rymer's Fœdera, XVII., 28. Here the first 3 and part of the 4th are missing. In the 4th and 33rd the names of Sir James Whitelock, Sir Henry Townshend, Sir Francis Eure, and Sir Nicholas Overbury were first written, but the first three of these have been scratched out and the names of Sir Thomas Chamberlain, Sir Marmaduke Lloyd and Edward Waties substitued in another hand; and in the 21st and 34th instruction the name of Lord Brooke has been similarly substituted for that of Sir Fulke Grevill K[t]. In 51 "Lord Compton" is struck out and Earl of Northampton inserted, and at the end after "granted" is inserted "by the late King James." The following are the Instructions omitted by Rymer:—

33. And H. M.'s further pleasure is, and his highness doth by these presents give full power and authority to the said Lord President or Vice President for the time being and Counsell as aforesaid or any 3 of them whereof the Lord President or Vicepresident or in their absence or vacancy the chief Justice of Chester to be one, by their warrant signed under their hands, to give order from time to time to the Clerk or Receiver of the fines for the time being, for payment as well to the said Sir James Whitelock of the sum of 100[l] as to every of the said Sir Henry Townshend Sir Francis Eure and Sir Nicholas Overbury of the sum of 100 marks a piece per annum before by these presents

to them appointed. And to H. M.'s secretary there his ancient fee of 13[l] 5[s] 8[d]. And to H. M.'s Attorney there his ancient fee of 13[l] 6[s] 8[d]. And to H. M.'s Sollicitor there for his fee the sum of 10[l]. And to all other persons such fees and allowance as are by these instructions appointed to be paid out of the said fines, as also the aforesaid sum of 6[s] 8[d] per diem to such of the Counsell learned as shall be called to attend there as is before appointed for the time of his said attendance, with the like sum of 6[s] 8[d] by the day for and towards the charge of every such Counsellor which shall be sent for to attend there in riding from his house directly to the said Counsell and home, and for no more time nor in other sort. And that so much of the overplus as is behovefull may by the discretion of the said Lord President or Vice President for the time being and Counsell as is aforesaid or any 3 of them whereof the Lord President or Vice President or in their absence or vacancy the Chief Justice of Chester to be one be employed and bestowed in manner and form following (that is to say) first in the satisfying and discharging of such duties and sums of money as have been or shall be laid out or disbursed by warrant of the Lord President or Vice President for the time being and Counsell as is aforesaid or any 3 of them whereof the Lord President or Vice President or in their absence or vacancy the Chief Justice of Chester to be one by any person or persons for H. M.'s service in the service of the said Court, and then in discharge of necessary foreign expenses, utensils of H. M.'s household there, and such other things as shall be behovefull for H. M.'s honour and better service there, and not otherwise, and upon necessary reparations of H. M.'s Castles or houses within the limit and jurisdiction aforesaid, and other needfull causes for H. M.'s service as occasion shall require and as the Lord President or Vice President for the time being and Counsell as is aforesaid or any 3 of them whereof the Lord President or Vice President or in their absence or vacancy the Chief Justice of Chester to be one, shall see to be requisite and expedient. Provided always and H. M.'s pleasure is that no person or officer of the said Court who hath any constant fee by the year for his service or attendance there (other than the Counsellors before in these instructions appointed for continual attendance) shall have any manner of allowance for his riding charges in coming to or riding from the said Counsell, except at such times as he or they shall be specially employed or sent for or for H. M.'s service. And the said Lord President or Vice President or Counsell as is aforesaid shall not call any of the said Counsellors learned in the laws, or who are to expect their allowance or pay of money by the day to come and attend, but at very needful times and when the greatness of the affairs shall so require, and then they the said Counsellors so called to have continuance and abode there for the time of the said great and needfull affairs only and for no longer time with or upon any manner of allowance or entertainment at H. M.'s charge there. And H. M.'s pleasure is that for such fees allowances and payments aforesaid to be made, these H. M.'s Instructions shall be a sufficient warrant and discharge to the said Lord President or Vice President and Counsell as is aforesaid in form as is before remembered against his highness his heirs and successors for the payment of the said sums of money and fees out of the said fines, and likewise a sufficient warrant for the disbursement of the same to the Clerk of the fines of the same Court.

DOVASTON MS.

34. And H. M.'s will and pleasure is that the Attorney, Sollicitor, and all other officers whose attendance shall be found needfull to that Counsell (except Sir Fulke Grevill, Knight, who is to attend there at

DOVASTON MS. H.M.'s pleasure) shall give their attendance accordingly without departing from the same, except by licence by 3 or more of that Counsell whereof the Lord President or Vice President or in their absence or vacancy the Chief Justice of Chester to be one. And the same Attorney, Sollicitor and other officers shall have their diet in the house for themselves and such servants and such fees answered and paid unto them as heretofore hath been accustomed.

39. And H. M.'s further pleasure is that there shall be one learned minister allowed being a graduate in divinity or Master of Arts and not having any benefice with cure of souls, to preach and to use the Common Prayer with due administration of the Sacrament, for the said Lord President and Counsell for the time being as is aforesaid and whole household, which person so learned and qualified and using the office of a preacher, shall have the yearly fee of 50[l] with diet for himself and one servant in the household, and shall be always resident with the said Counsell, and not to be absent to serve any other cure or function.

40. This is identical with the corresponding clause in the Instructions of 1633 printed in Rymer's *Fœdera* xix., 461, and there numbered 35.

41. And H. M. is pleased and contented that the keeper of the armoury and artillery at Ludlow shall continue his wages and diet after the rate of 6[d] per diem; and if he shall not diligently do such things as to his office appertaineth then he shall be defaulted of his wages and diet at the discretion of the Lord President or Vice President for the time being and Counsell or any 3 of them, whereof the Lord President, Vice President, or Chief Justice of Chester to be one.

43. And the King's Majesty's pleasure is that the household shall be kept and continued by the Lord President or Vice President for the time being for the diet of himself and the rest of the Counsell there as is aforesaid, and for such others as are by H. M. allowed to have their diet there. And that the Lord President or Vice President for the time being shall from time to time nominate and appoint a substantial man to be Steward of the household, and shall also name all other officers necessary for the said household, and at such time as there shall be no President or Vice President there, in their vacancy the said household shall be kept and continued and the said Steward and other officers named by the said Chief Justice of Chester for the time being, and that the Counsellors there attendant shall have in diet and household their number of servants hereafter mentioned (that is to say) the Chief Justice of Chester to have in household 8 servants and a chaplain or preacher, and that all and every person of the said Counsell before named and appointed by these Instructions to continual attendance, or any other when they shall be called to attend, shall have in household 3 servants. And H. M.'s pleasure and express commandment is, That no Counsellor before remembered other than such as are appointed to continual attendance shall (without being sent for by his highness' letters under the seals of that Court) come to the place of service there to sit in Counsell or in any sort to deal in the service of the Court. Nevertheless such of the said Counsell as are men of estimation and livelihood, though not learned in the laws, nor having fees for attending, may (for the greater honour of the Court and dispatch of H. M.'s service in term time) be appointed some certain times by turn to repair to the said Counsell, at the places meetest for their resorts in respect of their dwellings. Provided always that if any of the said Counsell other than as aforesaid shall come thither not being sent for as is aforesaid, that then he shall have no allowance of diet or otherwise, nor be

received to sit in Counsell without the special license and allowance of the said Lord President or Vice President and Counsell or 3 of them, whereof the Lord President or Vice President or in their absence or vacancy the Chief Justice of Chester to be one.

44. And H. M.'s pleasure is that there shall be a warrant dormant signed by his highness to H. M.'s general Receiver of South Wales and North Wales now being, or that hereafter for the time being shall be, for the payment to the said Lord President for the diet of himself and the rest of the Counsell after the rate of 20[l] sterling by the week, and over and besides that, for foreign expenses not appertaining to the diet there yearly the sum of 100 marks sterling, which diet money the King's pleasure is that the said Lord President or Vice President for the time being and Counsell shall have only for the maintenance of an honourable household there, without yielding any account to H. M. for the same, foreseeing that the charges of the said diet exceed not the said allowance whereby the profits of the fines should be thereby chargeable.

45. And H. M.'s pleasure is that the said 20[l] by the week shall be employed for the household and diet of the said Lord President or Vice President for the time being and Counsell as is aforesaid and that no fees of the said Counsell or any other shall be deducted or paid out of the said diet money, save only the wages of the officers of the household, who shall be yearly paid out of the same, and that the Steward of H. M.'s household there to be nominated and appointed as aforesaid shall receive the said sums of money as well for the said diet as also the said sum of 100 marks yearly for their foreign expenses, and shall disburse the same and yearly yield account before the said Lord President and Counsell or 3 of them at the least whereof the said Lord President or Vice President or in their absence or vacancy the Chief Justice of Chester to be one, for all such sums of moneys as by him shall be received for the said household. And for the further and better ordering of the said expenses of the said houschold the King's Majesty's pleasure is that the Steward or Clerk of the Kitchen shall once every week declare and make before the said Lord President or Vice President or in their absence or vacancy before the Chief Justice of Chester, and 2 of the said Counsell resident at the least if so many shall be there a true and just account of the expenses of the said household for the week, which account shall be entered into a book to be provided for the same, and subscribed weekly with the hands of the said Lord President and Counsell as is aforesaid or such of them as shall be there present.

51. And forasmuch as his highness doth hold it very convenient that it be made known to his good subjects within the limits and jurisdiction aforesaid what care he hath taken to have them relieved in their causes necessary, the Lord President and other of the Counsell there shall give direction to all Mayors Sheriffs Bailiffs and all other officers as they shall think fit within the limits and jurisdiction aforesaid, that they shall by a proclamation to be made in H. M.'s name cause to be published that H. M. hath presently granted sufficient commissions and instructions to his right trusty and right well beloved William Lord Compton Lord President and others of his highness' Counsell there for the hearing and determining of causes, and executing of all the like authorities for the relief of his people as is ordained by the late Commissions and Instructions granted in that behalf.

f. 122. 20 Jac. 1. April 6. Westminster.—Warrant appointing Marmaduke Lloyd to be of the Council in place of Sir Henry Townshend deceased; and note that he was sworn in 22 Apr. 1622 at Ludlow Castle before the Lord President, the Chief Justice, and Justice Litleton.

f. 122*b*. 1622, April 14.—Wm. Earl of Northampton and Sir James Whitelock to John Bishop of Lincoln, Lord Keeper of the Great Seal.

Sir John Pryce, Sheriff of Montgomery is dead. The Summons for the great Sessions is already out and the Quarter Sessions is presently to come on. The late Sheriff has made all provision, and we recommend that his father Sir Richard Pryce be appointed for this year, as it will be very chargeable and troublesome for anyone else to undertake it.

The following three names of possible Sheriffs are appended,

Richard Pryce, Kt.
Rowland Pughe, Ar.
Evan Glyn, Ar.

f. 123. 19 Jac. I. Feb. 9.—Appointment of Thomas Taylor of Ludlow, gent., to be a messenger or pursuivant attending the Lord President and Council, in place of Arthur Wynwood, gent., resigned; both of them being now present. "Signed by Wm Northampton, James Whitelocke, Nicholas Overbury, Edward Litleton, Edward Fox."

f. 123*b*. 19 Jac. I. July 9.—The King to the Council.

"Whereas by a late trial and experiment made by our own commandment of the rich proportion and yield of silver found in the lead mines of Cardiganshire, we hold it fit for our honour and necessary for the public good of our realm that the said silver should be separated from the lead and extracted out of it for supply of bullion for our own use, and not exported into foreign parts under colour of the ordinary merchandize of lead, to the enrichment of strangers with our own native commodities; and are therefore desirous that our well beloved subject Hugh Middleton, Esqre, farmer of our mines royal in that County, should have all lawful favour" &c., the Council is to give him all assistance.

f. 124. 20 Jac. I. Apr. 11. Westminster.—Appointment by the King of Sampson Eure, Esqre, to be his Attorney in Wales and the Marches.

f. 124*b*.—Note that he was sworn in before the Lord President, Chief Justice of Chester, and others (undated).

f. 125. 1622, July 11. Bewdley.—James Whitelock, Nicholas Overbury, Edward Litleton, Marmaduke Lloyd, to Sir James Lea, Chief Justice of the Pleas. The Chief Justice has issued a writ of *Habeas Corpus* to bring before him one Francis Olliver who is a prisoner here for contempt in refusing to answer an Information against him, and also in execution for a debt of 20*l*. to the King. Such prisoners have not hitherto been removed, lest His Majesty should thereby lose his debt, and they hope they need not have the trouble of sending him, but will do so if desired.

f. 125*b*. 19 Jac. 1. January 30. Ludlow.—Order to the Sheriff of Worcestershire to apprehend Thomas Haslewood, Elizabeth his wife, and Francis Haslewood, of Wicke, and send them to the Council, they have resisted apprehension at their own house by the Serjeant at Arms. If he cannot he must proclaim them rebels in the towns of Evesham, Pershore, and elsewhere in the County. He is also to seize all their lands and goods within the County, and to make a return to the order on 8 February next. Signed by Wm. Northampton, James Whitelocke, Nicholas Overbury, Thomas Cornwall.

f. 126. Same date.—Arthur Wynwood and Thomas Pyngle, messengers, are to take this order to the Sheriff. Signed Wm Northampton, James Whitelocke.

f. 126*b*. 19 Jac. 1. Feb. 20. Ludlow.—Thomas Haslewood, Esqre, appearing before the Council is bound over in 500*l*. to appear with his wife and son on 30 March next. Signed by James Whitelocke, Edw. Litleton, Thos. Cornwall, Thos. Harley.

f. 127. 20 Jac. 1. Sept. 16. Bewdley.—Humphrey Briggs, not having yet performed certain orders made upon him in a suit, is ordered to pay on 20 October next 20 marks for costs to His Majesty's Attorney, and 5*l*. being the costs of a sequestration of his cattle executed by the Sheriff of Salop, and 20 nobles for costs to the Serjeant at Arms, and 6 marks to the messengers; and shall make his submission in writing, as previously ordered, before November next. Signed by James Whitelock.

f. 127*b*.—Note that he did so on 28 Oct. 1622.

f. 128. 1622, Nov. 17. Ludlow.—A difference which has arisen between the Aldermen Bailiffs and Burgesses of Denbigh about the interpretation of their Charter devolves on the Council to decide "as a matter concerning government." They give their opinion that Thomas Lavie was duly elected a Bailiff by the major part of the Capital Burgesses at the end of the year, notwithstanding there was no Alderman nor Bayliffe who gave voice with that major part. At the election of Bailiffs the nomination of four by the Aldermen and Bailiffs shall continue. Present the Lord President, the Chief Justice, Justice Overbury.

f. 128. 20 Jac. 1. Nov. 12.—Appointment of Thomas Harvey of Sandhurst in the County of the City of Gloucester to be an Attorney attending the Council, in place of Charles Weaver resigned; both being now present. Signed by Wm Northampton, J. Whitelocke, N. Overbury.

f. 128*b*. 10 (?) Jac. 1. Sept. 30. Hampton Court.—Order that fines, bonds, forfeitures, &c., certified into the Court of Exchequer by the Council of the Marches in order that they may be more easily levied, shall be paid over by the Exchequer to the Council and accounted for by them.

f. 129. 20 Jac. 1. Jan. 22. Ludlow.—In a suit between William Watton and Richard Watton plaintiffs and John Lane defendant, John Lane entered into a bond for 300*l* to perform the order of the Council, but as he has now gone out of their jurisdiction, the bond is given to William Watton, to sue on in the Exchequer. *Signed by* Wm. Northampton, James Whitelocke, N. Overbury, Mar. Lloyd.

1622, Jan. 22.—Certificate of the above to the Lord Chief Baron.

DOVASTON MS.

f. 129*b*. 20 Jac. 1. Jan. 22. Ludlow Castle.—Writ in the King's name empowering William Watton to sue on the bond.

f. 129*b*. 1622, Aug. 16. Weston. Lionel Lord Cranfield, [Lord Treasurer] to the Earl of Northampton.

The wood and timber in Altons Wood, Sir William Welshe's Parke, the forest of Wyre, and the Manor of Bewdley, is all wasted and consumed, partly by pretended claims of estovers, partly by negligence of H. M.'s officers. He desires the Lord President to stop all falling of wood, whether by the tenants or the King's officers, without special warrant from the writer, when H. M.'s own immediate service shall demand it, and he hopes the Lord President's own purveyor will set a good example and take only dry wood and that in very moderate proportion for the use of the Household.

f. 130. 1622, January 22.—Lord Northampton, Sir Jas. Whitelocke, Sir N. Overbury, and Sir M. Lloyd, to the Lord Chief Justice of the Common Pleas, asking that a prohibition to the Court of the Marches to hear a case of bribery and extortion against Walter Powell late deputy Sheriff, and Roger Evans late Sheriff of Monmouthshire, may be withdrawn, the case having already been partly heard.

f. 130*b*. 20 Jac. I. Feb. 21. Westminster.—Appointment of Edward Waties to be of the Council in place of Sir Edw. Litleton deceased; and note that he was sworn in 13 March 1622, present the Lord President, Chief Justice, Justices Overbury and Lloyd.

f. 131. 21 Jac. I. June 30. Greenwich.—Appointment of new Councillors, viz. Sir John Tracy, Sir William Sandis, Sir Thos. Estcourt, and John Bridgeman, Esq[re], in Gloucestershire, Sir Samuel Sandis, and Robert Bartley, Esq[re], in Worcestershire, Sir Richard Newport, Sir Richard Fox, and Edward Litleton Esq[re] in Salop, Sir John Scudamore K[t] and Barronett, Sir John Hanmer K[t] and Barronett, Sir Robert Harley and Sir Roger Mostyn in Hereford and Flint.

Notes of the swearing in of Sir John Scudamore 25 Aug. 1623, at H. M.'s house of of Tyckenhill, before the Lord President, Chief Justice, Sir N. Overbury, and Edw. Waties; of Robert Bartley, Esq[re] "Recorder of the City of Worcester, a man of good parts and learned in the laws" on 13 Oct. 1623, at Worcester, in presence of the Lord President, Lord Spencer Compton, and the Bishop of Worcester; and of Sir Richard Newport and Sir Richard Fox on 29 Jan. 1623, in open Court, before the Lord President, the Chief Justice, Sir N. Overbury, Sir M. Lloyd, and Edw. Waties.

f. 131*b*. 1623, July 30. Chelsea.—Lord Middlesex to the Council. The compositions which have been made by commissioners for the carriages and provision of H. M.'s household do not affect the right of carriage given by the Instructions to the Council, which will still be due from those who have compounded; but it should be required in moderation and no purveyance at all must be used but for that which the necessity of the King's service requireth.

f. 131*b*. 21 Jac. I. August 6. Salisbury.—Order that, whereas it is convenient that the Justices of Assize within the four counties be members of the Council of the Marches, Sir Humphrey Smith and Sir William Jones be admitted accordingly.

f. 132. 1623, July 6. The Duke of Richmond and Lenox to the Lord President. The compositions are for H. M.'s own particular house only, and in no way affect your right to carriage.

21 Jac. 1. June 7. Bewdley.—Order for admittance of Richard Phillipps to be an Attorney in place of his father Thomas Phillipps deceased. *Signed by* Wm Northampton, J. Whitelocke, N. Overbury, M. Lloyde, Ed. Waties.

f. 132*b*. 1623, Aug. 30.—Lord Middlesex to the Lord President. The inhabitants of Bewdley are committing great waste in the Bewdley Woods, and especially in the wood called the Lord's Park, where Thomas Smith, his wife and daughter, have been carrying away black poles, and being opposed by one William Fidoe, they set upon him and beat him very sore and said they would never cease cutting wood there whilst there was any standing; and many of the magistrates of that town, that should right the King against such apparent wrong, do trade money in things wrought out of such black poles and wood. The Lord President is asked to punish these misdemeanours and stop them for the future.

1623, Sept. 10. Bewdley.—The Lord President to John Bishop of Lincoln, Lord Keeper. Request to arrest Rowland Badger Esqre. who disobeys the process of the Court on an action of debt brought by Robert Ramsey, and has removed out of the jurisdiction.

f. 133. 20 Jac. 1. Feb. 17. Westminster.—Patent to Griveth Gibbs of office of gentleman porter (*i.e.* gaoler) to the Court of the Marches; and f. 133*b*., mem. that he was admitted accordingly on 21 Sept. 1622 at Bewdley, before the Lord President.

The names of the Sheriffs for Wales, Cras Animarum 1623.

Montgomery, Sir William Owen, Kt.
Denbigh, Thomas Pryce Wynn, Ar.
Flint, John Broughton of Broughton, Ar.
Carnarvon, Ellis Brynkow, Ar.
Anglesey, John Bodithen, Ar.
Glamorgan, Lewis Thomas, Ar.
Brecon, John Madocks, Ar.
Radnor, Wm Fowler, Ar.
Carmarthen, John Stedman, Ar.
Pembroke, James Bowen, Ar.
Cardigan, John Pryce, Ar.

f. 134. 20 Jac. 1. March 21.—Return to *Habeas Corpus* respecting Francis Olliver, that he was committed to the porter's lodge, for a debt of 20*l*. to the King.

f. 134*b*. 21 Jac. 1. Nov. 7.—Order of the Court of Wards and Liveries that the Court of the Marches be requested to send Edward Lingen of Stoke Edith in Herefordshire Esqre either to Stoke Edith or to his other house of Sutton, he being and having long been a prisoner for contempt in the porter's lodge prison, but having now been found a lunatic and committed to the care of Sir John Scudamore, baronet.

f. 135. 21 Jac. 1. Dec. 11. Ludlow.—Order accordingly that he be sent to Stoke Edith in care of Cæsar Hawkins, Lewis Phillipps, and Edward Disney or any two of them. Signed by the Earl of Northampton.

DOVASTON MS.

f. 136. 1623, Jan. 2. The College at Westminster.—The Bishop of Lincoln (Lord Keeper) to the Lord President sending writs of summons to Parliament by John Shockledge, to be delivered with all possible speed.

—— Jan. 11.—Receipt for the writs, viz. 12 for the 12 shires of of Wales, one to the Town of Carmarthen, one to the Town of Haverfordwest, one to the Lord Bishop of Bangor, and one directed "Custodi Spiritualitatis Episcop. Asaph ipsa sede vacante.

—— Note that they were delivered to Thomas Pyngle and Thomas Taylor, messengers.

f. 136*b*. Jac. I. March 17. Ludlow.—Order that next Trinity term shall begin 10 June and end 7 July, and no cause shall be entered for hearing after 10 June. Present the Vice President, the Chief Justice, Sir M. Lloyd K^t^, Edward Waties, Esqre.

f. 137. 1623, March 10. Westminster.—Thos. Trevor, Speaker of the House of Commons, to the Council. Proceedings before the Council have been taken by Edward Brooke and Edward Baldwyn, two customary tenants of Sir Thomas Thynn's Manor of Stretton in Shropshire, to compel Francis Phillips, under Steward of the Manor, to hold a Court to admit them to certain copyhold tenements which they claim, but which Sir Thomas Thynn claims to be his own freehold. As he is a Member of the House, and the business will not permit his absence, the House has ordered that he have privilege of Parliament for stay of all proceedings until he is at liberty to defend himself.

———————————The same letter to Edward Brooke and Edward Baldwyn, of Stretton in County of Salop.

f. 137*b*. 22 Jac. I. Nov. 1 Royston.—The King to the Council. Re-appointment of Sir Thomas Chamberlayne to be Chief Justice of Chester.

f. 138. 1624, Nov. 20. Ludlow.—Many Informations Books and Records have been found to be missing out of the Council Office. John Peers, Attorney, and his clerk, Edward Morgan, who had detained many, are pardoned as it is their first offence. John James a clerk of the Court, who has committed other offences also, is committed to the Porters Lodge prison, discharged from practising before the Court, and an Information is to be laid against him by H.M.'s attorney. Thomas Tryte, another clerk, was lately discharged from practising, but drew up an order to re-instate himself and got it signed by Mr Justice Overbury without telling him the contents of it; therefore he is committed to the Porters Lodge during the pleasure of the Council and for ever hereafter banished from this Court. Signed by Wm Northampton, Tho. Chamberlyn, N. Overbury, M. Lloyd, Edw. Waties, Wm Herbert, Tho. Cornwall, Rich. Fox.

f. 138*b*. 1624, Nov. 20, Ludlow.—10 Rules, headed "To be observed for preservation as well of faint prosecutions of misdemeanours as of secret compositions taken by delators and others for the same." They provide for all steps in the proceedings passing through the Remembrancer's office, for keeping proper records there, for sending information of certain things to the King's Attorney, and substituting other delators &c. if necessary, and fining those who do not do their duty.

Signed by Wm Northampton, Thos. Chamberlaine, N. Overbury, M. Lloyd, Ed. Waties.

f. 139b. 1625, Thursday the last day of March.—Proclamation of King Charles the First at Ludlow by Sir Thos. Chamberlayne.

——— No date.—Copy in MS. of Proclamation of King Charles by the Lords Spiritual and Temporal, the Privy Council, with numbers of other principal gentlemen of quality, with the Lord Mayor Aldermen and Citizens of London." The first signature is Jo. Gore, Maior, and then follow G. Cant., Jo. Lyncolne, C.S., &c. "Imprinted at London by Benham Norton and Jo. Bell, Printers to the King's most excellent Majestie, 1625."

f. 140. 1625, Apr. 1. St. James'.—Warrant to change the date of the patent to Sir Thos. Chamberlain as a Justice of the Common Pleas so as to give him the precedence he would have had if he had not in James 1st's time been removed from the King's Bench to be Chief Justice of Chester.

f. 140. 1 Car. 1. 31 March. Westminster.—Letters patent authorising use of seals of the late King until new ones are made.

f. 141. 1 Car. 1. 2 Apr. Westminster.—Letters patent to Sir Thomas Chamberline of office of Justice of the Bench.

3 July (no year). Savoy.—Earl of Northampton to Sir N. Overbury authorising him to act as Vice-President, the Earl having been summoned to Parliament.

f. 141b. 1625, 23 Oct.—Formal appointment of Sir N. Overbury accordingly, for the term beginning 27 Oct.

24 Jan.—The like, with no limit of time.

f. 142. 1 Car. 1. 9 Feb.—The King to the Council. Appointment of Sir John Bridgman to be Chief Justice of Chester in place of Sir Thos. Chamberlaine deceased.

Memorandum that he took the oath, 3 March 1625, present Robert Viscount Killmorey Lord Vice-president, Justices Overbury, Lloyd, and Waties.

f. 142b. 1626, Nov. 4.—Writ to remove all proceedings by Edward Wolrith against John Thynne and others from the Council of the Marches to the Council in London.

1626, July 20.—Opinion of Wm. Jones on a case stated, that a pardon issued by the King at his coronation did not remit a fine which had been previously imposed, and for the payment of which bonds had been entered into, on the ground that the offence was res judicata, and fines and bonds were not expressly released.

f. 143. 3 Car. 1, June 8. Westminster.—Letters Patent appointing Timothy Turnour, of Shrewsbury, to be solicitor in the Court of the Marches, at a salary of 10*l.* per annum.

f. 143b. 3 Car. 1, Nov. 20. Ludlow.—As names of attorneys and clerks practising in this Court have been counterfeited and set to various documents, any one doing so in future will be debarred from practice and banished from the Court, and be punished by fine and

DOVASTON MS. imprisonment. Signed by Jo. Brydgeman, N. Overbury, M. Lloyde, E. Waties.

f. 144. 3 Car. 1, Nov. 20. Ludlow.—Replications must not be put in after causes are set down for hearing. Signed as the last.

f. 144. 1627, Dec. 13. Ely House.—Sir Thomas Coventry, Lord Keeper, to Sir John Bridgman. Sending him a petition of Walter Vaughan to the Star Chamber for protection against arrest on process obtained from the Court of the Marches, by Owen Jenkins and Grindy, with whom he has litigation in the Star Chamber. The Lord Keeper says he does not grant letters of privilege, but he requests that the gentleman may not be disturbed in his travels to and fro to attend his affairs before the Star Chamber.

f. 144*b*. 1628, May 20.—Order of the House of Lords that Nicholas Bowyer of Kidderminster, Attorney, shall ask pardon at the Bar for scandal spoken by him of the Lord President and Council of the Marches, and shall also ask pardon of the Council; and memorandum that he made submission accordingly at the Bar of the House.

4 Car. 1, July 24.—Order that no more than 20 causes be entered for hearing in one day during the first fortnight in each term, nor more than 16 in one day during the rest of the term. Signed by Jo. Bridgeman, R. Overbury, M. Lloyde, E. Waties.

f. 145. 1628, October 28. Ludlow.—Admission of Sir Adam Newton, Baronet, as Secretary and Clerk to the Council, and of Ralph Goodwin as his deputy, on the decease of Lord Brooke the late Secretary, and by virtue of a patent from the late King to Sir A. Newton. Signed as the last.

f. 145*b*. 4 Car. I. Oct. 1. Hampton Court.—The King to the Council, requiring them to swear Sir Adam Newton of the Council, and admit him to the office of Secretary.

1628, Oct. 3. Deputation from Sir A. Newton to Ralph Goodwin.

1628, March 14. Deputation from Robert Thornes to Thomas Watkies of Ludlow, to administer oaths and take the fee of 4*d.* thereon in the Court of the Marches.

f. 146. 11 Jac. I. Oct. 3.—Letters Patent to Robert Thornes of New Inn in the County of Middlesex Gent, for the same office.

f. 147*b*. 4 Car. 1, Feb. 27. Ludlow.—Order to put a further check on the putting in of replications and rejoinders after the date of the orders of issue, and to fine attorneys who do so.

" Signed by Ro. Killmorey. Jo. Bridgeman. N. Overbury. Marmaduke Lloyde. Edw. Waties.

f. 148. 4 Car. 1, Feb. 20. Westminster.—The King to Sir Marmaduke Lloyd, Sir N. Overbury and Justice Watyes. Under colour of a grant to them by the late Lord Brooke they have prevented Robert Thornes from executing his office and receiving the fees thereof. They must do so no longer, as the death of Lord Brooke terminated their right to the office.

Note at foot.—These letters were delivered at the Counsel. Table att Ludlow Castle the ix day of March 1628 after dyner.

f. 148. 5 Car. 1, July 11. Westminster.—The King to the Council. DOVASTON MS.

The petition of some of the Judges respecting the fees for affidavits has been referred to the Lord Keeper and other Judges. Meanwhile the letter of 20 Feb. ought to have been obeyed. As it has not, all fees received since that time must be brought into Court until the royal pleasure is known.

f. 148*b*. 1629, Aug. 31. Bewdley.—Certificate of order made by the Council against Charles Bowen Esq[re] Lord of the Manor of Manorbeer in Pembrokeshire and W[m] Jones his Steward to admit John Marishurth to a copyhold tenement therein on the surrender of David Thomas. M[r] Bowen was fined for neglecting the order "and for very contemptuous words against the Court, which fine was quallified upon his submission to a very small sum." Signed by W. Northampton, John Bridgman, N. Overbury, Edw. Waties.

f. 149. 1629, July 22. Bewdley.—Order to admit Humfrey Wynne, one of the Clerks of the Court, an Attorney, in place of David Moses Esq[re] resigned on account of old age. Signed as the last.

f. 149*b*. No date. Petition to the Council by Thomas Crumpe, Robert Vaughan, and John Andrew, "three of the ancient Attornies attending your Lordships, on behalf of themselves and the rest of the Attornies there," against a grant said to have been made under the privy seal to Robert Tyrrwhitt Esq[re] of a new office "for making of billetts to serve defendants before your Lordships," and for receiving a fee of 3*d*. on each billet. They say the attorneys have hitherto made such billets for nothing, and the office will be a needless charge on the subject, and a monopoly for the private benefit of the patentee.

There follow 6 "reasons against the billett office," to the effect that the billetts will be useless, and expensive, and will cause delays, and that they are against the Statute 21 Jas. 1., c. 3. Signed as above.

f. 150. No date. "Answers to the reasons" [of the petitioner for the patent] "expressing why the speciall Billett Office shall not be established for the Court houlden before the Lord President and Counsell in the Marches of Wales." Further arguments against the office. Signed as above.

f. 150*b*. 1629, Nov. 13. Ludlow Castle.—Sir J. Bridgman, Sir N. Overbury, Sir M. Lloyd, Edw. Waties, [to the Lord Keeper? no address]. Sending the above petition and reasons against the proposed office, the erection of which they hear is still on foot, though it had been referred to them to report upon and they had reported against it.

1629, Nov. 11. Reference to the attorneys as to whether where one defendant has appeared and the other has not, evidence of witnesses already examined against the first is good against the second when he appears. They give their opinion that it is not, on the ground that the King might lose some fines if evidence were thus taken in the absence of some of the defendants. Signed Thomas Crumpe, Robert Owen, Robert Luther, Thomas Noade (?), W. Andrew, Rees Jones.

f. 151. 5 Car. I. Jan. 16. Westminster.—The King to the Council. Order to admit Lord Goringe, Master of the Horse to the Queen, and John Verney, Counsell at Law, of the Middle Temple, Esquire, to be members of the Council and to "the office of our Secretary Clarke of the Signett and Clarke of our Counsell in the Marches of Wales" in the place of the late Sir Adam Newton Baronet deceased.

DOVASTON MS. Mem.—That Lord Goringe was sworn and admitted; and R. Goodwin was sworn and admitted as his deputy, 22 January 1629, in presence of Sir J. Bridgman, Sir N. Overbury, Sir M. Lloyd, and E. Waties.

f. 151*b*. 4 Car. 1, July 5. Danbury.—Patent to Arthur Wynwood of the office of porter.

f. 152. Memorandum—That the validity of the letters patent to Robert Thornes "before entered verbatim in this book" was referred by the King to the Lord Keeper Coventry, the Earl of Northampton, President of the Council, Sir N. Hyde, Chief Justice of the King's Bench, Sir Thos. Richardson Chief Justice of the Common Pleas, Sir John Walter Chief Baron, and justices Sir R[d] Hutton, Sir W[m] Jones, Sir James Whitelocke and Sir Henry Yelverton, who on hearing counsel on both sides decided it to be void.

6 Car. I, July 6. Westminster.—The King to the Council. Announcing the above decision, and that oaths are to be taken by the judges, and the fees divided among them.

Memorandum.—That, shortly after, Robert Thornes delivered up his patent accordingly.

f. 152*b*. 5 Car. 1, Oct. 26. Westminster.—Letter under Privy Seal erecting the office of Clerk of the Billets for Wales and the Marches, and appointing Robert Tirwhitt Esq[re] to it, during pleasure. The fee to be 2[d] for each Billett.

f. 154. 6 Car. 1, May 12. Westminster.—The King to the Earl of Northampton and the Council, requiring them to admit Robert Tirwhitt accordingly, and to enrol the above privy seal in their Court that all persons may take notice thereof.

Note at bottom of letter:—It is our will and pleasure notwithstanding the death of the Earl of Northampton that you the judges proceed according to this our letter. St. James', 1 July, 6 Car. 1.

f. 154*c*. 1630, July 9.—Deputation of the office by R. Tirwhitt to Thomas Hanmer Esq[re], during R. Tirwhitt's pleasure. Witnessed by Philip Willoughby, Hen. Shuter, John Cresswell.

f. 154*d*. 1634, June 22.—Appointment of William Haughton of Haughton in Cheshire gent., and James Haughton his brother, to be R. Tirwhitt's deputies for 3 years, and revocation of an appointment of William Langton. Witnessed by John Essington, Henry Shuter, Edw. Bosden.

f. 155. 1630, Nov. 11. Ludlow.—Order that if leading interrogatories are administered in future, the Counsel Attorney or Clerk who drew them, or, if not drawn by them, the party on whose behalf they were issued, shall be fined. Signed by Sir J. Bridgeman, Sir N. Overbury, Sir M. Lloyd, Justice Waties.

f. 155*b*. 6 Car. 1, Feb. 20. Westminster.—The King to the Council, requiring them to admit Richard Wigmore, gent., as deputy of Lord Goring, to the office of entering of causes in hearing and making of warrants of attorney, which office the King had granted to Wigmore under the privy seal, but finding that it was part of Lord Goring's office as secretary, he requested Lord Goring to appoint Wigmore his deputy.

1630, Feb. 31.—Deputation by Lord Goring to Richard Wigmore accordingly.

f. 156.—Form of oath taken by Richard Wigmore. DOVASTON MS.

1630, March 12. Ludlow.—Orders for the hearing of causes must be served on parties dwelling in other counties than Salop, Hereford, Worcester, Monmouth, Montgomery and Radnor, six days before the day of hearing instead of three days as heretofore. Three days are sufficient for the Counties named. Signed John Bridgeman, N. Overbury, Edw. Waties.

f. 156*b*. 1630, March 19. Ludlow.—Appointment of Rowland Higgins to be messenger or pursuivant in place of Thomas Taylor deceased. Signed (autographs) by Jo. Bridgeman, Nich. Overbury, Marmaduke Lloyde, Edw. Waties, Ric. Foxe.
Memorandum that R. Higgins took the oath 20 March, 6 Car. I.

f. 157. Another copy of the order of 12 March 1630 about serving orders of hearing.

1631, July 8.—Order that as "divers of the inhabitants of the towns of Shrewsbury and Wrexham have lately died of the plague and the infection there is dangerous" none of the inhabitants of those towns be allowed to appear in this Court till further order, and no advantage is to be taken against them in their absence; and any Counsel, Attorney, Clerk, or officer of the Court admitting such inhabitants to their office or company shall be suspended from practice. Signed by Jo. Bridgeman, Nicho. Overbury, Mar. Lloyde, Edw. Waties.

1631, July 16.—J. [Earl of] Bridgewater to the Council. He has received their letter about a prohibition granted out of the King's Court upon the information exhibited by Mr. Eure Her Majesty's Attorney by the relation of John Turnor of Coddington against John Turnor of Colwall. He agrees with the Council in disliking the multitude of these prohibitions, and the clashing of the different Courts, and will do what he can to check it, but hopes that the Council will be careful in pursuance of their Instructions, which will of itself tend greatly to the result desired. Counsel and Attornies applying for such prohibitions improperly should be admonished.

f. 157*b*. 6 Car. 1. Dec. 6.—The King to the Council.

Price Holland of the County of Flint has avoided service of processes issued against him by Thomas Roe for debt. The Council are to find him and make him appear in their Court and answer T. Roe's complaints.

f. 158. 7 Car. 1. June 20.—Trinity Term. Order by Court of Exchequer. Robert Wynne, Sheriff of Denbighshire, and his under-sheriff, had been attached and imprisoned by the Court of the Marches for executing an extent out of the Exchequer upon the body of Piers Holland, Esqre. Thereupon the Exchequer issued an Injunction to stay the proceedings, and a Certiorari to remove the bonds the Sheriff had had to enter into, and a conditional attachment against Mr Justice Waties and Richard Jones the Serjeant at Arms. The case was argued in the Exchequer by Mr Calthrop and Sir Thomas Roe and Mr Littleton and it is now ordered that all the above orders be made void and the whole cause left to the Council to deal with.

Petition of the said Robert Wynne and of Edward Williams his deputy to the Earl of Bridgewater, Lord President of the Council and to Sir John Bridgman and the rest of the Council, that proceedings

DOVASTON MS. against him may be stayed and his bond cancelled, and confessing his mistake in arresting Piers Holland who was already under arrest of the Serjeant at Arms of the Court of the Marches.

Note by the Earl of Bridgwater recommending him to favour "if the course now taken be such as was agreed on in my presence by Sir John Bridgeman for the satisfaction and reparation of the Court of the Council of the Marches and in particular of Mr. Waties."

f. 158*b*. Another copy of the same petition, with note at foot. 3 Sept. 1631. Petitioners bonds to be delivered up unto him. Signed J. B., N. O., M. Ll., E. W.

7 Car. 1. Sept. 3. Ludlow.—Formal order for delivery up of the bonds accordingly. Signed M. Lloyd.

7 Car. 1. Jan. 29. Ludlow.—Leave of absence to M[r] Tournour, H.M.'s Solicitor, and appointment of John Robins Esq[re] as his deputy in his absence. Signed by John Bridgeman, Marmaduke Lloyd, Edw. Waties.

f. 159. 1631, Jan. 23.—Orders to be observed by Attorneys and Clerks, in addition to the orders of 4 December, 7 James 1.

1. Attorneys being allowed two clerks each, the clerks must not have the keeping or carrying of any record of this Court until they are sworn and inrolled; they must write in their master's chambers, and get no one but their masters to put their hands to their bills, pleadings, and orders, unless their master is out of the town.

2. Counsellors' clerks are likewise to be sworn, and to return all books.

3. Clerks must not themselves keep clerks.

4. No examiner or officer of the court may practise as attorney or solicitor.

5. No attorney or clerk shall deliver any Record of the Court to any one but a Counsellor, Attorney, or Clerk sworn.

6. Attorneys and Clerks must carefully restore all Records to the office of Clerk of this Council.

f. 159*b*. 7. Interrogatories must be signed by a Counsellor or Attorney or in his absence by a Clerk.

8. Bills of Stay must be signed by an Attorney or a Clerk before they are presented to one of the Council.

9. Bills must be complete in the office on the day fixed for appearance to them.

10. Attorneys or Clerks getting books delivered to them without cause shall pay a penalty.

Signed Jo. Bridgeman, N. Overbury, M. Lloyd, Edw. Waties.

1631. 7 Car. 1. June 26. Greenwich.—The King to John, Earl of Bridgewater appointing him to be President in place of William Earl of Northampton deceased.

f. 160. 7 Car. 1. July 24. Oatlands.—Warrant granting deer to the Council, in the same form as that of 16 James 1, on f. 107*b*.

f. 160*b*. 1633, Oct. 28.—Earl of Bridgewater to the Council, sending the new Instructions.

1633, Nov. 26.—Memorandum that Sir John Bridgeman, Sir N. Overbury, Sir M. Lloyd, and E. Waties, Esq[re] were sworn in open Court according to the new Instructions.

1633, Nov. 27.—Mem. that George Bridgeman Esqre. was sworn one of this Council.

f. 161. 9 Car. 1. May 12. Theobalds.—The Earl of Bridgewater's Instructions. (Rymer's *Fœdera* xix., p. 449. Of the 10 articles there omitted, Nos. 33, 34, 39, 41, 43, 44, 45 and 51 are the same as those herein before printed from the Instructions of 1617; and 37 and 38 are identical with those in the Instructions of 1617 printed in Rymer's *Fœdera* xvii. 39).

f. 178*b*. 9 Car. 1. Nov. 30. Ludlow.—Order for payment of 40*s*. a year to Edward Bulstrod for being of Counsel to this Court in all occasions at Westminster. Signed Jo. Bridgeman, N. Overbury, Edw. Waties.

9 Car. 1. Jan. 28. Ludlow.—"Process to bind" shall not henceforth be granted unless the allegations contained in it are verified on oath; it having been found that they are often untrue though verified as true by the signature of the attorney or clerk.

f. 179. 7 Car. 1. July 24.—The King to the Council. Prohibitions from Westminster have become too frequent. The Council must be very careful not in anything to transgress the Instructions, "which layd for a ground we then further charg you to see that our Subjects bee not deluded nor delayed in their just remedies, but that you cause our decrees to be fully and speedily performed by all such ways and means as is used in our Court of Chancery, notwithstanding any prohibicon to be granted to the contrary, to stay such your proceedings warranted by our said Instruccons." "In all questions of jurisdiction, assuming the judgement thereof to ourself, wee will ever bee ready to hear and judg equally betwixt the Courts," "it being indeed most proper to our self (as most indifferent) to settle those differences than any other person concerned therein either in extent of power or point of benefitt."

The original MS. ends here; but the owner of it at the end of the last century inserted some original documents and copied some others into the book. These are:—

f. 179. 1. An original petition from the borough of Ludlow to the Master of the Rolls to vacate the Inrollment of a Deed surrendering their Charter, enrolled in 1684. The petition is undated, but endorsed for hearing on 25 March 1690.

f. 179*b*. 2. 8 Car. 1. Dec. 20. Copy of Patent appointing Commissioners to remove obstacles from places within two miles of London where Archery has customarily been practised.

f. 180*b*. 3. 40 Eliz. June 29. Copy of Patent, being an exemplification of Charters relating to the neighbourhood of Dudley and Wolverhampton &c., made at the request of Richard Colbourne, Richard Hammett, Richard Shaw, Oliver Dixon, Nicholas Bradley, John Hodgett, Richard Jevon, and Robert Hodgett; and headed "A Copy of the Charter with Queen Elizabeth's seal annexed in the hands of Mr. Daniel Shaw of Dudley."

f. 183*b*. 4. No date. "The officers in household to the late Viscount Mountacue with their several charges and order for the government of his Lordship's house."

5. Extracts from a book entitled "A brief treatise to prove the necessitie and excellence of Archerie" &c. by R.S., 1596.

6. "Extracts from a MS. of Richard Podmore A.B., Rector of Copenhall in the County Palatine of Chester and Curate of Cundover in the County of Salop, made by him in 1765." These are printed in *Documents connected with the History of Ludlow,* but without the Author's name.

f. 191*b*. 7. Copy of "A remonstrance of the Justices in Ordinarie in the Marches of Wales to the Right Hon[ble] the Lord President of the Council." It recites some of the Instructions, and cites a number of facts to show that the Lord President has usurped to himself authority over the household, and made a profit out of it, which properly belongs to all the Justices; among other things he has "carried the King's plate and linen to Golden Grove [seat of the Earl of Carberry, Lord President 1660 to 1672], a thing never heard of"; and "command has been given to search the lodgings, to see if we have any of the King's goods there, and to bring them away, and our servants slandered and abused, and some of them by the Lady's order commanded out of her house; its well she cannot carry the Castle with her." It ends—If the Lord President "were somewhat admonished I think he would not be so apt to ill treat us, nor his Lady neither, and to tell us in effect we have nothing to do in the government of the household, as his Lady writes, who no doubt had it from himself." Addressed "ffor my hon[ble] friend Sir Job Charlton K[t] Serjeant at law, Chief Justice of Chester." No date.

In the margin of the page on which this is copied is written;—"The following extracts are made from authentic papers (found at Park near Oswestry the house of the descendants of the Chief Justice Charlton of Ludford, Chief Justice of Chester) by me in anno 1789. The originals are in this book or in a bundle in the bookcase."

f. 192. 8. Services done by H. M.'s Keeper of Ludlow Castle and his servants.

f. 192*b*. 9. 17 Car. 2, Nov. 29, and 18 Car. 2, May 14. Further Instructions to the Council as to the taking of oaths.

10. 8 Car. 1, Oct. 10, and 9 Car. 1, Oct. 23. Proceedings on an information exhibited by the Attorney General against Edw. Jones and others Bailiffs and Burgesses of Ludlow about 5 Mills in Ludlow which had belonged to the Prioress of Acconbury in Herefordshire and came to the Crown by the dissolution of the Monasteries, but have ever since been detained by the Defendants. They are headed "Anno nono Reg. Caroli Marturii," and "Reg. Caroli Martis."

11. 23 Car. II., Feb. 12. Copy of exemplification of some of the proceedings in the last mentioned case.

f. 193. 12. 1662, July 13. Appointment of Robert Milward, one of the Justices of the Great Sessions within our Counties of Carnarfon Merioneth and Anglesey, to be of the Council of the Marches.

f. 193. 13. Undated.—Petition of Sir Job Charlton Kenrick Eyton George Johnson and Francis Mayley, Justices of the Council of the Marches, that their salary of 100 marks may be increased, as to Sir Job Charlton to 200*l*. and as to the rest to 100*l*.

f. 193*b*. 14. 1663.—Account of fees received by Sir Job Charlton in 1662 and 1663 (original inserted in the book). DOVASTON MS.

f. 194. 15. 1627.—"Articles of the evil behaviour of Richard Longwall of Wydbach [Woodbach] in the County of Salop now standing bound for his good behaviour exhibited and proved the 19th day of October before Humfrey Walcott Esqre and Richard Moore Esqre J. P's for the said County to the end that he may continue so bound." He conspired with Richard Latward and Thomas Longwall to charge Mr Justice Doddridge with partiality in a trial before him on 17 July last, and was committed to prison for it. He was drunk in Bishops Castle 17 Aug. last. He is a perverse and troublesome fellow and turbulent amongst his neighbours. He has been vehemently suspected and accused of causing the death of Philip Wall by beating him.

Opinion in margin signed W. Littleton that proceedings must be taken before Justices of the Peace of the neighbourhood, not in the King's Court.

f. 194*b*. 16. Notes (pasted into the book) on the "State of the Tynfarmers' Case." Their patent provided for the rent to abate in case of civil war or other destruction of the preemption. The King by patent in 1642 discharged the rent, which they paid up to January 1642. The Parliament nevertheless by imprisonment of the farmers and of their "Casheire" did force 8,000*l*. from them. Afterwards in 1643 the said farmers lent the King 11,530*l*.

17. 1642. Jan. 16.—Order of House of Commons that "Mr Overinge cash keeper to the Tynfarmers be forthwith summoned in safe custody, and that such moneys as be in his hands that belong to the Tynfarmers be seized by Colonel Mainwaringe.

18. 1642. Jan. 17.—Order of House of Commons that 1,600*l*. of the money seized of ~~the Tynfarmers~~ by Capt. Thomas Player be paid to Mr Dicks "as part of the brotherly assistance."

f. 195. 19. 1 & 2 Philip and Mary. Oct. 10.—Copy of deed by which Jane Fox grants to the Bailiffs and Burgesses of Ludlow a burgage and tenement in Ludlow worth 23*s*. 4*d*. a year on condition of their keeping up certain masses for the souls of Richard Downe, Agnes his wife, William Fox and Jane his wife and their parents, and to make certain payments to the poor in St. Giles' almshouse; and if any law should hereafter make the masses illegal, then the whole sum to go to the almshouse.

The original of this deed, but without the seal, is inserted in the book.

f. 195*b*. 20. No date. Copy of Address of the Speaker of the House of Commons to Charles II. on his election, "their former Speaker being honoured by your Majesty into an incapacity of further serving them as Speaker."

21. A paper inserted in the book headed Mr Baxter's Expositions upon the New Testament, and endorsed by Mr Dovaston (about 1790). "These were the charges against Mr Baxter's Sermons for which he was imprisoned. I found this paper among Judge Charlton's papers" [viz. at Park, near Oswestry, which belonged to the Charlton family].

DOVASTON MS.

f. 196*b*. 22. Undated.—Copy of Thos. Alured's letter to the Marquess of Buckingham (about the treaty for Prince Charles' marriage with Spain).

A contemporary copy of the letter is inserted in the book.

Various printed proclamations of Charles II.'s time, &c., are inserted at end and beginning of book.

R. LLOYD KENYON.

THE MANUSCRIPTS OF THE CORPORATION OF HEREFORD.

HEREFORD MSS.

The records of the city of Hereford are for the most part stored in sheepskin sacks, which have been the means of keeping them almost entirely free from damp and decay. There are upwards of a hundred of these sacks, of which some, however, are in a very tattered condition. Through a long series of years the charge for the sack annually appears in the city accounts, the price rising from 8*d.* in the time of Henry VIII. to about 3*s.* 6*d.* at last. But the contents of the sacks were found on examination to be in the utmost confusion, documents of the 14th and 15th centuries being mixed with papers of the 18th and 19th. They appear to have been partially inspected (as attested by occasional endorsements) by a Town Clerk in the early part of the present century; but were more generally overhauled by his successor, Mr. Richard Johnson, who copied many documents, which he published in 1868 in a book entitled *The Ancient Customs of Hereford*, of which a second edition appeared in 1882, after his death, but whose transcripts unfortunately can by no means be depended upon for accuracy. It would seem that, after he had examined the bags, their multifarious contents were stowed away promiscuously just as the bags and the papers came to hand, so that verification of any particular document was rendered impossible. But the records had met with worse treatment than this. A woman who had the charge of the old Town Hall before the year 1830, and who thus had access to these stores, sold many of the documents for waste paper, and amongst them the oldest existing Council Registers, although happily two volumes of these were recovered, as noted below. Whether it was through her thefts, or by some more definitely planned and intelligently carried out robbery, that all the papers of the Civil War period disappeared, cannot now be ascertained, but it is a most disappointing fact that the years from 1642 to 1650, which it was hoped would prove rich in notices illustrating the war and the Scottish siege, and the King's relief of his faithful city, present a total blank. Not a scrap of any kind belonging to that time appears to be preserved. A further destruction of papers took place at a much later period, but it is believed that these were all first carefully examined and found to be worthless. It is singular that the cases of the two corporations of Reading and Hereford with regard to preservation of their records are totally different. At Reading the Files for routine business and official papers, on which much was entered of interest and value, have all perished while the Registers are perfect; at Hereford, the Files are for the most part preserved with all the writs, warrants, bonds, petitions, &c., while only a portion of the Registers has escaped destruction. But now it is hoped that all danger of further destruction is over. The work of the agent of the Historical Commission was gladly welcomed, and he desires to acknowledge not merely the personal courtesy of the Town Clerk, Mr. Joseph Carless, but the warm interest that gentleman takes in the records under his charge. The city is also greatly indebted to another gentleman, Mr. R. Paterson, for unwearying labour in sorting, cleaning, smoothing, and arranging the vast mass of dirty and crumpled papers; a self-imposed labour of love which he has not relinquished until the years have been all duly arranged in their proper order, and the papers of each year rendered easily accessible. That these papers well deserved examination and care the ensuing notes will abundantly prove.

I.—Royal Charters, &c.

In an iron chest are preserved the following royal charters and documents:—

1. 1189, Oct. 9. Charter of Richard I.

"Ricardus Dei gratia Rex Angl. Dux Norm. Aquit. Com. And., archiepiscopis, episcopis, abbatibus, comitibus, baronibus, justiciariis, vicecomitibus, ministris et omnibus fidelibus suis Francis et Anglis totius Angliæ, salutem. Sciatis nos concessisse civibus nostris Hereford in Wallia villam de Hereford tenendam perpetuo pro xl. libris reddendis per annum ad Scaccarium. Ita quod ipsi auxilium præstabunt ad claudendam villam. Et ipsi pro hac concessione dederunt nobis xl. marcas argenti. Et ideo præcipimus quod prædictam villam illam habeant et teneant perpetuo per prædictam firmam, cum omnibus libertatibus et liberis consuetudinibus suis, et cum omnibus pertinentiis suis. Ita quod Nullus vicecomitum Nostrorum intromittat aliquid super eos de aliquo placito vel querela aut occasione vel de aliqua re quæ ad prædictam villam pertineant. T., H[ugone Pudsey] Dunolm. episcopo, W. de Sancto Johanne. Dat. apud Westm. primo anno regni nostri, ix. die Octobris, per Manum W. de longo Campo Elien. Electi Cancellarii Nostri." This charter measures 5½ inches by 4½. Seal lost.

2. 1227, March 23, 11 Henry III. Westm.—Grant to the citizens of a three days' fair, on the feast of St. Denis and the two days following. Seal almost entirely lost.

3. 1256, August 8, 40 Hen. III. At Worcester.—Grant of return of writs. Seal lost.

4. 1256, Aug. 8, 40 Hen. III. At Worcester.—Grant of exemption from arrest for debt in cases where they are not bail or principal debtors unless they have means sufficient to satisfy their debts; and that the goods of persons dying intestate shall not be confiscated; &c. Fragment of green seal.

Of this charter there is a duplicate, with a small fragment of the seal.

5. 1265, July 24, 49 Hen. III. At Hereford.—Grant by the King to Thomas son of William Thebaud of Hereford of all the land which was Mansell the Jew's in Bischopesgate in Hereford "in recompensacionem dampnorum quæ idem Thomas sustinuit occasione amocionis domorum suarum quas extra portam de Ighene Hereford prestravit per preceptum nostrum." Witnessed by Simon de Monteforti, Hugh le Despenser, Peter de Monteforti, Giles de Argenten, Roger de St. John, Walter de Crepping, Stephen Soudan, Bartholomew le Bygod. Fragment of green seal. This charter was granted by the King while a prisoner at Hereford.

6. 1267, Oct. 23, 51 Hen. III. At Monemuth.—Pardon from Prince Edward to the men of Hereford. "Pardonavimus . . . . . . omnem iram et rancorem quos contra eosdem habuimus pro quibusdam transgressionibus nuper factis et illatis per eosdem contra nos, videlicet

a prima turbacione nuper in Anglia mota usque ad festum Omnium Sanctorum proximo venturum." Small fragment of green seal.

7. 1268, 6 March, 52 Hen. 3.—Writ of Hen. III. to the citizens of Hereford to admit Roger de Clifford. "H. Dei gratia Rex Angliæ Dominus Hiberniæ et Dux Aquitaniæ, ballivis et probis hominibus suis Herefordiæ, salutem. Sciatis quod concessimus dilecto et fideli nostro Rogero de Clifford quod moram faciat in villa nostra Herefordiæ ad eam defendendam ad modum obsidionis Troiæ, a die Pasch. proximo futuro in unum mensem, de gratia nostra speciali. Et ideo vobis mandamus quod prædictum Rogerum villam prædictam ingredi et ibidem morari permittatis in forma prædicta. In cujus rei testimonium has literas nostras fieri fecimus patentes. Teste me ipso apud Westm. vi. die Marcii, anno r. n. L. secundo." This writ (which measures $6\frac{5}{8}$ inches in length by $1\frac{3}{4}$ in breadth) is now placed in the box with the royal charters; it was found amongst miscellaneous papers of late date. The extraordinary expression "ad modum obsidionis Trojæ" is very puzzling. If the date of the writ had been but a little subsequent to the time of the King's captivity at Hereford it would have seemed to be a far-fetched allusion to the wooden horse; one of the King's partisans was to be admitted to defend the city, in order that thereby he might the better secure it for the King. But it is issued three years after that captivity, when no one was disputing his sovereignty. And yet no other interpretation suggests itself.

8. 1271, Feb. 8, Hen. III. At Westm.—A renewal of the grant of July 24, 1265 (*ut supra*), in the same terms; witnessed by Robert Aguillun, Elias de Rabayn, William de St. Cremina, William Belet, Richard de Monet, Ralph de Bakepuz, William de Faukeham, Roger de Wauton. The larger portion of the great seal remains, in white wax.

9. 1298, June 6, 26 Edw. I. At Wartre.—Grant to the bailiffs and citizens of Hereford of the right of levying numerous tolls for five years for the purpose of walling the city for its security and safeguard. Seal lost.

10. 1307, Sept. 21. 1 Edw. II. At Lincoln.—*Inspeximus* of a charter of Edw. I. dated at York, Sept. 16, 1280, confirming the charter granted by Hen. III. at Worcester, Aug. 8, 1256, with regard to arrest for debt, and the goods of persons dying intestate. Green seal, nearly perfect.

11. 1314, Sept. 16, 8 Edw. II. At York.—*Inspeximus* 1, of the charter of Rich. I. in 1189; 2, of a charter of John, granted at Clarendon, July 10, 1215, granting "gildam mercatoriam cum hansa," and "quod si aliquis nativus alicujus in præfata civitate manserit et terram in ea tenuerit, et fuerit in præfata gilda et hansa, et loth, et schot, cum eisdem civibus nostris per unum annum et unum diem, deinceps non possit repeti a domino suo, sed in eadem civitate liber permaneat"; 3, of a similar charter of Hen. III., dated at Westm., March 23, 1227; 4, 5, of the charters for the fair and return of writs, *ut supra*. Granting also further privileges with regard to pleas, with the right of Utfangenethef. For this charter and for the following a fine of 100*l.* was paid. Fine and perfect seal, in green wax.

12. *Same date.*—Charter generally to the same effect as that of Sept. 21, 1307. Green seal, broken.

13. 1327, July 15, 1 Edw. [III.] . At Durham.—*Inspeximus* of the confirmation-charter of Edward II. granted at York, Sept. 16, *an.* 8. Green seal, imperfect, but exhibiting the greater part. Also a duplicate, with part of the seal.

14. 1331, Jan. 28, 5 Edw. [III.] At Hertford.—*Inspeximus* of the same charter of Edward II.; granting also exemption from murage, panage, kayage, and picage throughout England, in addition to the freedom from tolls granted by Henry III. Green seal, nearly perfect.

15. 1333, July 26, 7 Edw. [III.] At Berwick-on-Tweed.—Pardon to John Pyteman of Holme Lacy. "Sciatis quod de gratia nostra speciali et pro bono servicio quod Johannes Pyteman de Lacishomme nobis in instanti guerra Scociæ impendit, pardonavimus ei sectam pacis nostræ quæ ad nos pertinet pro omnibus feloniis et transgressionibus per ipsum in regno nostro tam contra pacem domini E. nuper Regis Angliæ patris nostri perpetratis, unde judicatus, rectatus seu appellatus existit, ac eciam utlagarias si quæ in ipsum his occasionibus fuerint promulgatæ, et firmam pacem nostram ei inde concedimus, *excepta secta nostra pro morte dicti patris nostri*, necnon erga illos qui homines de regno nostro ceperunt et eos detinuerunt quousque cum eisdem redempciones pro voluntate sua fecerunt. Ita tamen quod stet recto in curia nostra si qui versus eum loqui voluerint de feloniis et transgressionibus prædictis, et quod idem Johannes in obsequium nostrum ad vadia nostra proficiscatur quociens et ubi super hoc fecerimus præmuniri. In cujus rei testimonium has literas nostras fieri fecimus patentes. Teste me ipso apud Berewicum super Twedam, vicesimo sexto die Julii anno regni nostri septimo." The greater part of the seal remains; white.

16. 1383, Jan. 18, 6 Rich. [II.] At Westm.—Grant to the bailiffs and citizens of Hereford, "in auxilium et emendacionem pontis civitatis nostræ prædictæ, qui dirutus est et confractus ad grave dampnum et periculum hominum per pontem illum transeuntium et ad eandem civitatem veniencium," of the right to levy certain specified tolls upon all articles brought over the bridge for sale, for the term of ten years next ensuing. White seal, partly imperfect.

17. 1383, Jan 29, 6 Rich. [II.] At Westm.—Grant to the commonalty of Hereford of thirty oaks from the King's forest of la Haye, near Hereford, for repair of the bridge "ultra ripariam de Waye apud Hereford, qui quidam pons jam tarde per cursum et impetum aquæ prædictæ confractus extitit, ut dicitur"; and also of forty perches of stone from the quarry within the said forest, as much as may be wanted for the same purpose. Fragment of white seal.

18. 1383, Nov. 5, 7 Rich. II. At Westm.—Grant to the citizens of Hereford, at the request of John Burley, knight, that the bailiff for the time being shall be named Mayor, and shall be annually elected as in time past. Part of the seal; green.

19. 1393, Feb. 2, 16 Rich. [II.] At Winchester.—License to the Mayor and commonalty of Hereford, because they have no house, as they say, within the castle or city of Hereford in which the sessions of the justices of assize or of peace, or the pleas of the city, can be held, to acquire in mortmain the messuage, worth sixty shillings annually, which belongs to Thomas Chippenham, William Bowode and Thomas Hoppeleye, and is held of the Crown in free burgage by the annual service of 18*d*. Green seal, nearly perfect.

1392, Sept. 28, "die sabati pr. ante f. S. Mich. Arch.," 16 Rich. II. At Hereford.—Grant by Henry Cachepolle, citizen of Hereford, to Thomas Chippenham, William Bowode, and Thomas Hoppeleye of the tenement called Bothehalle; [being that to which the preceding license refers]. Good impression of a seal with a merchant's mark; "Sigill' Heurici Cachepol." Two of the witnesses are William Breyntone and John Troney, then bailiffs. In the same box with these charters.

20. 1394, 3 Sept., 18 Rich. II. At Hereford.—Translation (written at the beginning of the 16th century), of a charter granted by Rich. II. to the Mayor and citizens of Hereford, that whereas they have complained of frequent wrongful arrests for debts when passing through the lordship of Wales, although the persons arrested be neither debtors nor sureties, whereby they are compelled to cease passing through Wales for the practising their occupation of merchandise, and procuring of fish and other victuals, it shall be lawful for them hereafter, when such arrests are made and no deliverance follows, to arrest in like manner any persons belonging to the lordship of Wales found within the city and the liberties, until satisfaction be made for the losses sustained.

21. 1399, June 23, 23 Rich. II. At Westm.—Contemporary copy of a charter granting to the Mayor and citizens, in consideration of the receipt of 100*l*., the goods of felons, deodands, fines, etc. This is certified by Thomas Lee, clerk to Sir John Borough, and by Richard Ravenhill and Thomas Seycill, on Feb. 16, 1636, to agree with the record in the Tower.

22. 1399, Nov. 20, 1 Hen. IV. At Westm.—*Inspeximus* of a charter of Edw. III. dated at Westm., June 20, *an.* 23, confirming previous charters.

23. 1457, Oct. 16, 36 Hen. VI. At Westm.—Charter exempting the citizens from being chosen collectors of any tenths, fifteenths, taxes or subsidies, granted to the Crown, except within the city and its liberties. Fragment of green seal.

24. 1463, Nov. 18, 3 Edw. IV. At Westm.—*Inspeximus* of a confirmation charter of Hen. VI. of Nov. 20, *an.* 1, 1422, confirming also the preceding charter of 1457. Green seal, nearly perfect.

25. 1536, July 20, 28 Hen. VIII. West.—Charter granting license to the city to acquire lands to the value of forty marks. Good impression of the seal, broken but nearly perfect. In a tin box.

26. 1553, June 8, 7 Edw. VI.—Exemplification in Chancery of the privileges granted to the city. Poor impression of seal.

27. 1597, Aug. 19, 39 Eliz. Westm.—Charter of incorporation, and confirmation of former charters. On four sheets of vellum. Seal lost. In a tin box.

28. 1619, July 12, 17 Jac. 1. Westm.—Similar charter, on six sheets of vellum. Seal perfect. This charter is now kept in an embossed leather box said in Johnson's *Customs of Hereford* to belong to the preceding charter.

29. 1682, Apr. 28, 34 Car. II. Westm.—New charter, upon the surrender of the old one; in which the King reserves to himself the confirmation of the appointments of steward, aldermen, and town-clerk. Seal broken. In a tin case.

30. 1690, Apr. 5, 2 Will. and Mar.—Charter granting a three days' fair at Easter, with a court of piepowder. Seal perfect. In a wooden box. The seal is said by Mr. Wyon, in his work on the Great Seals of England, to be the most perfect impression known of the seal of these sovereigns.

31. 1697, June 14, 9 Will. III.—Charter from Will. III. on nine sheets of vellum; seal perfect. In a wooden case.

32. 1836, June 3, 6 Will. IV. Westm.—Charter granting a court of quarter sessions. In a wooden box.

II.—Corporation Registers.

The Registers now remaining are :—

1. A paper volume in quarto, containing 274 numbered leaves (not always in chronological order), bound in very unsuitable modern half-roan binding. A few leaves here and there are missing. This contains the minutes of proceedings from 15 Dec. 16 Hen. VII., 1500, to 12 Dec., 22 Hen. VIII., 1530.* There is little in it besides entries of recognizances. But at f. 176, under the year 1503, is given a list of the Corpus Christi pageants, which, although it has been printed (without reference) in Johnson's *Customs of Hereford* (p. 118), is worth reproducing here, especially as in that copy very many mistakes are made.

"The paiants for the procession of Corpus Christi.

Furst, Glovers - -	Adam, Eve. *Cayne and Abell* (erased).
Eldest seriant - - -	Cayne, Abell, and Moysey, Aron.
Carpenters - - - -	Noye ship.
Chaundelers - - -	Abram, Isack, Moysey cum iiii[or] pueris.
Skynners - - - -	Jesse.
Flacchers - - - -	Salutacōn of our Lady.
Vynteners - - - -	Nativite of our Lord.
Taillours - - - -	The iii Kings of Colen.
The belman - - -	The purificacōn of our Lady, with Symyon.
Drapers - - - - -	The . . (*blank*) deitours goyng with the good Lord.
Sadlers - - - - -	Fleme Jordan.
Cardeners - - - -	The castell of Israell.
Walkers - - - -	The good Lord ridyng on an asse ("judging at an assize," in Johnson!) with xii Appostelles.
The tanners - - -	The story of Shore Thursday.
Bochours - - - -	The takyng of our Lord.
The eldest seriant -	The tormentyng of our Lord with iiii tormentoures, with the lamentacōn of our Lady [and Seynt John the evaungelist : *faintly added by another hand*].
[Cappers - - - -	Portacio crucis usque montem Oilverii : *added by the second hand.*]
Dyers - - - - - -	Jesus pendens in cruce [*altered by the second hand from* Portacio crucis et Johanne evangelista portante Mariam].

* One leaf, which evidently belongs to this volume, of 12 Edw. IV., 1472, has now been prefixed, which was found thrown aside in a drawer.

Smythes - - - -	Longys with his knyghtes.
The eldest sariant -	Maria and Johannes evangelista (*interlined*).
Barbours - - - -	Joseth Abarmathia.
Dyers - - - - -	Sepultura Christi.
The eldest seriant -	Tres Mariæ.
Porters - - - - -	Milites armati custodes sepulcri.
Mercers - - - -	Pilate, Cayfes, Annas, and Mahounde. [*This last name has been partly erased.*]
Bakers - - - - -	Knyghtes in harnes.
Journeymen cappers -	Seynt Keterina with tres (?) tormentors."

Instances of disfranchisement occur. In 1491 one Roger Draper is disfranchished "pro inobedientia sua contra majorem," and in the following year Robert Nowell, "causa inobedientiæ suæ contra officiarios domini Regis," but he is subsequently restored. On June 6, 1514, Robert Carpenter is disfranchised "for as moche as the seid Roberte beynge one of the Councell house of the seid cite made affray upon one Thomas Tailour an other of the seid Councell house in the highe causey, and for reformacōn thereof in example of other mysdoers he was ordred by the seid Councell to content and pay xxs. towards the reparacōns of the walles and yates of the seid citie, uppon peyne of forfeture of his franches, which he utterly refused. Ideo, etc." Other cases occur in 1530. Extracts from ordinances in this volume are printed, but without references, in Johnson's *Customs of Hereford.* On the cover is this note: "N.B. This was one of the books stolen by Esther Garstone (who was convicted of larceny at Hereford Spring assizes before Baron Bolland, 1830), sold by her to Wm. Beniams, grocer, Eign Street, and recovered from him 1 Jan. 1830."

2. "The great Black Book"; a folio volume, bound now in rough calf, with 468 numbered leaves of paper; of which the first is wanting. It contains the minutes of proceedings from Oct. 35 Hen. VIII. (1543), to 31 May, 34 Eliz. (1592). Prefixed on four quarto leaves is a table of the "acts and ordinances made at law-days and other special matters," by Griffith Reignolds, Mayor, 1685. And on the cover is this memorandum, "N.B. This book was stolen by Ester Garstone (who was convicted at the Spring assizes at Hereford, 1830, before Baron Bolland), and recovered 1 Jan. 1830 from Wm. Beniams, a grocer in Eigne Street." The chief contents of the book, in addition to ordinances made from time to time, are enrolments of recognizances and conveyances. Many extracts are given (but without reference to their source) in Johnson's *Customs of Hereford.*

The subsequent registers only begin at the year 1800, in consequence, as it seems, of the depredations committed upon the records referred to above.

One folio volume contains the Chamberlain's accounts from Mich. 1732 to the end of 1769.

A thin folio volume, in parchment cover, somewhat dilapidated, which was written in the 17th century, contains:—

1. The customs of the city, as established in 1486. This is printed at length in Mr. Johnson's book, pp. 11–45. Another and better copy is in the custody of the Town Clerk.
2. Notes of the city lands, rent-roll, and gifts (to about 1639).

III. Early Title-deeds.

A number of early deeds of title are contained in 12 small oak boxes and paper parcels.

1. Box containing 13 deeds relating to a house in Northgate, Hereford, from 9 Jan., 34 Hen. VI. [1456], to 5 Oct. 7 Hen. VIII. (1515). They begin with a release from John Griffith, of Hereford, glover, son of Gruffin ap Jornard, of Boughereden, tailor, to Henry Oldecastell, Henry ap Griffith, and others.

2. Box containing three deeds relating to Staunton-on-Wye, seven to Llangarvan, and five to Hereford, English Bicknor, Leominster, and Bishopstone.

3. A few deeds of property in Fownhope, Over Litton, Hardwick, &c., and Hereford, *tempp.* Edw. III.–Hen. VI., in a box containing bonds and a few other miscellaneous documents. In one dated 1457 mention is made of *le Brode Cabage lane* in Hereford. Another, in 1389 (witnessed by Richard Skydmore, mayor, and John Trowe and William Faks, bailiffs, amongst others), is dated "in festo S. Thomæ de Cantalupo," the canonized bishop of Hereford who died in 1282. There is also a parcel of 16 deeds relating to Great Cowarne from about 1220–30 to 21 Hen. VII. (1506). The earliest is a grant from Randulph the tailor ("cissor") to Adam son of Hugh Hereford of a meadow in Wyhammedene, "apud superiorem Flodyhate," near the land of the church of Cowre. A deed of 1292, which is a grant by Roger the carpenter of three acres as a marriage portion to "Hauwicæ nutrici Ricardi presbiteri de Magna Covera," has in its date the peculiarity of specifying the hour at which it was executed: "acta die Jovis proxima ante festum S. Michaelis, anno r. r. Eadwardi xx°, apud Magnam Couwernam, circa horam primam."

4. Box containing 39 deeds relating to the manor of Elton (including Stocklow, near Staunton on-Arrow, Newton, and Stewart's Hide), near Bromyard, from 15 Edw. III. (1341) to 38 Eliz. (1596). The property belonged in some portions to the Croft family. The first deed is a release from Sir Hugh de Crofte, knight, to his brother John of 38*s.* of annual rent from his inheritance at Stokkelowe, granted to the said John by Sir John Tronwyn, Knt., and Pernia his wife, mother of the said Sir Hugh. Hugh's son John in the same year (1341) also makes a grant of the same, to which his seal of arms is attached; quarterly, a fess indented, in dexter chief (a lion's head ?). A conveyance, dated at Teddesterne (Tedstone) 29 Sept., 16 Hen. VII. (1500), of the messuage called *Stywards Hyde* is from "Humfridus Doore, valectus Regis de sua corona." The last document in the parcel is an indenture of sale by the mayor and commonalty of Hereford to Sir Herbert Croft for the sum of 20*l.* of two messuages in Croft, "whereof one is called Drake's thinge," paying annually 21*s.*; 3 May, 38 Eliz.

5. Box containing 38 deeds relating to property in Widemarsh Street, Hereford, from 44 Edw. III. (1370) to 8 Eliz. (1566). In one of the year 4 Hen. V. (1416), as also in other deeds, there is mention of a tenement in "Malyerestrete inter tenementum pertinens hospicio vocato *Goodknavesinne*," etc. One of 8 Edw. IV. (1469) has a good impression of the seal for recognizances described as being "sigillum officii majoris."

6. Box containing 15 deeds relating to a messuage at Wye-bridgegate (noted as being afterwards called *The Saracen's Head*) from 33

Edw. III. (1359) to 18 Hen. VIII. (1526). The first of these and one dated 1394 are sealed with almost perfect impressions of the civic arms, probably the oldest extant, viz., Three lions courant, "S'. Ballivorum Civitatis Herefordie." The original silver matrix of this seal, in perfect condition, has just been very happily recovered for the city by the Town Clerk, after being in private hands for many years. At the same time two other silver matrices have been obtained: one, the seal for recognizances, bearing the King's bust, with a lion couchant beneath, on either side a castle, surmounted on the dexter side by the sun and on the sinister by the moon, "S' Edw' Reg' Angl' ad recogn' debitor apd' Hereford'"; the other, the seal of the hospital of St. Katherine, representing the saint holding her wheel, under a canopy: "Sigillum scē Katerine."

7. Box containing 18 deeds, of which 12 relate to a tenement in "Cokenrewe," Hereford, from 46 Edw. III. (1372) to 18 Apr., 26 Hen. VIII. (1535). One of the boundaries mentioned throughout from the first date to the last is a tenement belonging to the Prioress and Convent of Acornbury. The first deed (1372) is a grant from Thomas de Grendon, of Hereford, "fourbour," to David son of John Rythyd, of "Glomargan, fysshere," which, though said to be sealed with the grantor's seal, has an armorial seal, checquy, with an indistinct inscription resembling "S' Ardilvpi . . . . iensis." It is witnessed by William Collynges, William de la Mere, and John Goldsmyth, "tunc ballivis domini Regis civitatis Hereford." These in Johnson's list of the bailiffs are assigned to the years 1373, 1376, and 1374 respectively. In 9 Rich. II., 1385–6, Henry le Cachepol is Mayor, and Richard Skydemore and John Trone (misprinted *Trovie* in Johnson when mayor in 1395–6) bailiffs.

8. A parcel containing 26 deeds relating to property without Widemarsh gate, and about 50 relating to the manor of Eton [Eyton] and Caldwell, near Leominster. The former extend from the time of Edward III. to Henry VIII.; the latter begin towards the end of the reign of Henry III. The earliest of these Eton deeds relate to a family named Ernieht or Arniet; and one which is perhaps the first (*circa* 1260) is a grant from Hugh Hakelutel to Hugh Ernyeht of an acre of land in Crowemore, extending from the way leading towards Leominstre to the water called Chetene, which has a seal of arms, a bar between three axes, "S' Hugonis Hakelutela." This name of Hakluyt occurs frequently in this century. A deed of about 1270 has among the witnesses three named Hugh le Pelerin, Henry le Turc, and William le Jongehosebonde. Measures of land called "curselliones" and "cursiones" occur several times; and a measure of corn occurs in the words "quindecim truggis bladi" (truck-loads ?).

9. Twenty-five deeds relating to lands at Burghill, and chiefly concerned with a family named Furge or Forge, 12–28 Hen. VIII. (1520–1536).

10. Ten deeds relating to houses in Malierestrete (now Maylard's Lane) in Hereford. They include a release from Richard Gardyner, custos of the college of Vicars Choral, dated "in domo nostra capitilari" (*sic*) 2 Jan., 17 Edw. IV. (1478), which has a good impression of the college seal, the B. Virgin and Child under a canopy: "Sigill' coē vicarioȓ ecclesie Herefordie."

11. The box so numbered formerly contained a few deeds relating to "Langston and Treville," but none such are now found in it. It now contains one deed of 6 Rich. II. (1382–3) relating to a tenement in "Bewalstrete," and three, of 12 Edw. IV. and 11 Hen. VII. (1472, 1495

–6), relating to houses in Widemarsh Street, in one of which a tenement belonging to the chantry of the B. Virgin in the church of All Saints is mentioned.

12. Two deeds of 12 Nov., 8 Edw. IV. (1468), of a demise by William Pershore, chaplain, to Thomas Molde and Isabella his wife of land in le Morefelde, Hereford.

IV. Bailiffs' and Mayors' Rolls, and Rolls of Cases in the City Court, to the end of the Reign of Henry VII.

1264–5, 48–9 Hen. fil. Joh.—Roll of receipts of tolls for 14 weeks from the f. of St. Denis (Oct. 3) to the Purif. B. M. V. (2 Feb.), and of expenses for 10 weeks. The tolls are from Way Gate, Bishopstreet Gate, St. Owen's Gate, Zizene Gate, and Widmarsh Gate. The name *Zizene* (*al.* Ighene) appears now in the form *Eigne;* but its derivation seems to be unknown. In the payments are the weekly wages to the gate-keepers, who appear under the name of *Insidiatores:* "tribus insidiatoribus tempore nundinarum at portam Waye, vi*d.*," and so at the other gates. The wages of labourers are 1½ per day; to four labourers working at repair of the wall. three shillings are paid for a week, and to one working for three days 4½*d.* To a smith for making a chain for a gate, 5*s*.

1270, 54 Hen.—Receipts for 24 weeks from f. of St. Peter in Cath. (22 Feb.). These accounts are very interesting as showing how the traffic varied at the different gates; *e.g.* in the first week in March "De porta Waye, nichil. De porta de Igene, v*d.* De porta de Wythm[ersh] 11*d.* ob. De porta Episcopi, vii*d.* De porta Sancti Audoeni, 11*d.* Summa, xvi*d.* ob." But in the first week in July, "die Sabati prox. post festum beati Petri et Pauli," the receipts (the highest in the 24 weeks) are, "De porta Waye, 11*s.* viii*d.* De porta de Igene, xx*d.* De porta de Withm[ersh], xv*d.* De porta Episcopi, xx*d.* De porta Beati Audoeni, vi*d.* Summe, vii*s.* ix*d.*" The total sum in the 24 weeks is 4*l.* 18*s.* 5*d.*

1273, 1 Edw.—Compotus of John Seym and Walter le Wanter [bailiffs], the Wedn. after Mich. Day. A very short summary of their accounts. With this is a very tattered small fragment of an expense roll some time in the reign of Edw. I.

1275, 3 Edw.—Court roll, of six courts held from July to Sept. John de la Felde, chaplain, sues Richard de Swynefeld, prebendary of Berton, for debt.

1276, 4 Edw.—Receipts and expenses, in two rolls, of Reginald Moniword (bailiff)]. The receipt roll has been carefully mounted on linen, being mutilated. The receipts are chiefly derived from fines. The majority of items in the expense account are of wine (a sextary and a half, a sextary, or half a sextary) sent to the following persons: Roger Barbastre, J. Saym ("in adventu suo de Lond."), J. de Meus, Sir Giles de Berkeley, Sir Walter de Rudmarleye, Sir W. de Heliun, Sir Edmund de Mortimer, Sir H. de Moutfort and Salamon his companion, John de Gernemue (*i.e.* Yarmouth) "inquratori (*sic*) bonorum Flandriæ," Richard the clerk "in adventu suo de Lond.," the Seneschal of Goderich Castle, Sir Richard de Hereford, Robert prior of Hereford, and the Bishop of Hereford, to whom also were given an ox and four pigs. For a breakfast ("jentaculo") for four persons going to London for some inquest, 12*d.*; for the expenses of a messenger sent to London only 2*s.*, but to Richard the clerk for his expenses on a like journey, 24*s.*, and "ad expensas proborum hominum versus Lond." (probably the four mentioned above), 51*s.* 10*d.*

1277, 5 Edw.—Account of the same Reginald Moniword on one roll (mounted on linen). The total receipts are 9*l.* 2*s.* 2*d.* The expenses are not summed up; but the gifts of wine are far fewer (as well as other gifts) than in the preceding year, being only to the wife of Rich. de Hereford when she came from London after his death, to Salomon de Roff' [Rochester? Ross?], to the Sheriff of Hereford, and to W. de Helion. Half a mark was paid for the carriage of a tun of wine from Gloucester.

A tattered court roll for the same year.

1279-80, 8-9 *incip.* Edw. — Mutilated expense roll of John le Gaunter; the first part of every line wanting; (mounted on linen). Some special persons mentioned are Sir Roger de Norwode, Master Will. de la Marche, Rob. Fulk, "——duxerunt Thomam Turbevile extra villam."

1281, 9 Edw.—Receipt roll of William Godknave, John le Gaunter, and Gilbert Blod; a short summary, mutilated; (mounted on linen). To this has been recently attached a roll of receipts from fines and rents which has no evidence of year, and may or may not belong to this account.

Enclosed with this is a writ from the King to the Sheriff of Hereford respecting a plea of disseisin brought by Sibilla, daughter of John Monyword against various parties, dated at Westm., 10 May, *an.* 9, which is endorsed with a return of persons giving bail for appearance, &c.

1282, 10 Edw.—Receipt and expense rolls of John de Strettone and John le Gaunter. (Mounted on linen.) The receipts are not added up; the expenses amount to 51*l.* 4*s.* 5½*d.*; but the roll being mutilated all the separate sums are lost. There are several journeys to London, as before, for payment of the rent of the city into the Exchequer. Three horses are provided for the bailiffs and two servants ("garciones") who have shoes allowed them. The presents are, wine to Sir Roger de Northwode, Sir N. de Castell with three cheeses, and the same to Rich. de Stayvorde, the Bishop with two pigs, Will. de Hay, Sir Hugh Burnel, the Sheriff, Sir Walter de Helion, Sir Rob. Fouc, Sir Roger de Mortimer. Two pigs are sent to the Dean, and also two sextaries of wine "in celebratione novæ missæ" (?).

1284, 12 Edw.—Receipt roll of John le Gaunter. The receipts from the market stalls are 13*s.* 6*d.*, and the large sum of 50*s.* is received "de quodam homine de Crikhowel pro recreantis'" [regrating?].

1285, 13 Edw.—Receipt roll of Will. H . . . el; name and date almost entirely effaced. This is a very long and interesting account, with receipts of rents under the several parishes and from tenants outside the city. The fines "pro pace fracta," "pro bateria," and "pro sanguine effuso" are extremely numerous, showing that there must have been frequent riots; and amongst those who are amerced are 10 or 12 persons from Lugwardine, Newton, and Withington. Several are fined for digging in the King's highway; Will. Hondy 12*d.*, "quia recettavit in domo sua mercandisiam contra libertatem"; several for brewing without license; "de Gilberto Saym pro clamore et utesio" (hue and cry) vi*d.*; one offender was allowed to compound, "de Willelmo de Wynton quia non est prosecutus, xii*d.*" The first mention of Jews which I have seen in these accounts occurs here in the following entries; "de Judæis, xii*d.*; de Johanne Bibol (?) quia vendidit carnes Judæorum, xii*d.*; de duabus filiabus Cok Judæi de introitu, ii sol."

1287, 15 Edw. I.—Roll of pleas in the city court, chiefly in cases of debt. Roger Cunyng sues Joan wife of Thomas Hamond, because she "contra pacem noctanter fregit laticium suum ad dampnum ipsius Rogeri dim. marcæ," which she is ordered to pay, and is fined. A writ from the King is recited respecting a complaint of Thomas Cope and Joan his wife against John of the Halle in the matter of the will of Hugh of the Halle.

Account-roll of John le Gaunter; three membranes sewn together, of which the receipts fill more than two. The profits of the fair of St. Denis amount to ix*s.* xi*d.* The receipts are chiefly, as usual, from fines (including some for forestalling), fees for admission into the city of comers from other parts (which include one from Oxfordshire, "de Willelmo filio Johannis de Wyteneye, pro introitu, xii*d.*"), and fees for the gild. Among the fines are, "de Cecil. le Bolter de Presthemede attach. cum quadam tunica furata de blueto, de qua tunica vocat warantum et non invenit, iii*s.* iii*d.* De Rogero le Gaunter de Kaynham pro gratia habenda inveniendi warantum suum de pellibus domorum, et non invenit, iii*s.* De Roberto de Sonursete pro clamore et hutesio, vi*d.* De Johanne de Radenovere pro litera habenda de aveyamento,* ii*s.* De Johanne de Wormebrugge pro habenda litera ad curiam Leominstre, dim marc. De Stephano Knoyl pro indictamento capcionis piscium de fossato, iiii*s.*" The curious Christian female name of Danecosa occurs. The total receipts are 16*l.* 15*s.* 3*d.* Among the outgoings are the expenses of J. le Gaunter three times to London, for the first time 25*s.* for himself, 4*s.* for hire of a horse, and 4*d.* for shoes for his servant; for the second time, 41*s.* for himself, 3*s.* for a horse, and 8*d.* for a servant; and for the third, 19*s.* 6*d.*, two horses 6*s.* and servant 8*d.* Wine is sent to Robert Crevequor, and also 18*s.* 1½*d.* "ad perficiendam pacationem Roberti Crevequor," and "clerico marscalli pro allocacione R. Crevequor, xii*d.*" Wine is also sent to the sheriff several times, and bread and wine "uxori vice-comitis ad pur[ificationem] suam"; wine to Rob. Fulcer, Sir Will. de Heliun, Will. de Haya the Chancellor's clerk, Sir Peter de Huntingfeld "marscallo Comitis," Adam de Wynton, Sir N. de Castell, and Rob. de Wallisford, clerk of the Exchequer; and bread and wine to Sir Roger Loveday, to the Earl of Cornwall "in adventu suo," to Sir Will. de Hamiltone (twice), Sir Ralph de Hingham, Sir Robert Fulk, to the Abbot of Gloucester "in adventu suo," and to Will. de Mortimer. The year was a year of law-suits; besides that noticed above with Sir R. de Crevequer, there were disputes with the abbot of Reading,† at Hereford itself, on some business connected with the Jews, and other matters. For the Reading dispute there are these entries: at the King's Bench, "ad impetrandum rotulamentum judicii abbatis de Redinge, ii*s.*; lib. vice-comiti Hereford pro summonitionibus Scaccarii de Reginaldo Moniword, Johanne le Gaunter et Johanne clerico pro placito abbatis de Redinge, xxiiii*s.* viii*d.*" For Hereford, "lib duobus attornatoribus coram domino R. de Hyngham pro communitate versus

---

* For a license to come to Hereford? "Aviamentum, itio, aditus." Du Cange.

† These arose out of the fact that the priory of Leominster was dependent as a call upon the abbey of Reading.

episcopum, decanum et capitulum, vis. viiid." (To the bishop a salmon was sent on Easter Eve, which cost 4s.) Entries relating to the Jews are these: "in vino misso Absoloni * in adventu suo de London, viiid.; in vino misso domino Macolino in adventu suo ad faciendam deliberationem de catellis Judeorum, xvid.; Ade de Wynton, clerico Judaismi pro breve recreando de contemptu ballivorum, iis." Other notices connected with law-suits are, a journey to Leominster "coram Rob. Fouk et sociis suis," a journey to London "propter placitum domini Edmundi," a journey to Worcester "coram domino Thoma de Weylonde," "item, justiciariis pro gratia habenda, iis."; a journey to Gloucester and a journey to London not only for the half-yearly proffer to the Exchequer but "ad computandum de subsidio Johannis de Kyrkeby." Among miscellaneous entries are these: half a mark given to Sir Robert de Lutlebure and also to Sir Nich. de Castel ["de Castro"]; "ad emendandum fossatum circa villam, iis.; in uno novo rete empto, iiis. iid. ob.; in viginti ulnis linee tele emptis ad opus domini Ricardi de Staunford, viis."

1291, 19 Edw.—Similar roll of John le Gaunter, in duplicate; one copy mutilated and mounted on linen; the other perfect. The receipts from stallage at St. Denis' fair were xs. vd., and from fines at the same ("amerciamenta nundinarum") which are entered separately, xxiiiis. vid. The "summa de claro" of receipts was 24*l*. 6*s*. 10*d*., and of expenses 19*l*. 11*s*. 3*d*. The law suit with the Abbot of Reading is continued. Presents are very frequently made to two sheriffs of the county, whose names are now first mentioned, Sir Roger de Burhulle and Sir Henry de Solers. Other gifts in wine, bread and cheese ("formagio") are to Sir Will. de Assheburne, clerk of the Wardrobe, Reginald Moniword, Sir Roger le Rous "et sociis suis" (judges), Sir John de Metingham, Will. de Louth ("Luda"), Bishop of Ely, the sheriff of Glamorgan, Rob. de Kriketot, seneschal of the Bishop of Bath, Rob. de Tipetote, the Lord Treasurer, Sir Nich. de Castell, the Countess of Gloucester,† Nich. de Warewik, serjeant at the Bench, Sir Peter de Leycestre (8 cheeses, xix*d*.), Sir John Butetourte, a judge, John Theubaud xxis., and Sir Will. de Mont Reuel, xs. The sheriffs were on several occasions entertained at breakfast "ad tabernam."

1292, 20 Edw. (Called in the heading "anno undecimo nono.")—Part of the expense-roll; containing seven weeks' expenses in work (quarrying, labour, carting, and smith's work) "circa panag." [a bakehouse?‡], expenses at law, and a few other items. The suit with the Abbot of Reading is continued, and there is one on the part of John le Gauter *versus* the Master of the Temple. "Lib. vic. Hereford die dominica, invencionis Sancte Crucis, anno r. r. E. xx pro lib. civitatis per manus Roberti de Dik et Hugonis Clote, tunc temporis ballivorum domini Regis, xiii*li*. vis. ob. Item, lib. Roberto de Dik ad pacandum domino Joh. Boutetourte pro quadam fine facta, xiiis. iiii*d*. Item, lib. eidem Roberto de Dik ad emendum meremium ad furcam ad aventum (*sic*) justiciariorum domini Regis in itinerant. (*sic*), xv*d*. Item, die dominica post festum Sancti Jacobi apostoli lib. fuit Rob. de Dik et

* He was, it seems, an officer of the city bailiff, probably a converted Jew. In 1291 shoes are given to him and William the clerk at Christmas.

† In one copy of the roll this is entered as "Com. Glouc.," in the other, by interlineation, "Comitisse Gloue."

‡ The wages of the labourers slightly vary, but are for the most part still 1½*d*. per day; three labourers receiving xxi*d*. per week. The master has 2*s*. per week and his companion ("socio suo") 1*s*. 6*d*.

Johanni Ethelman ad deliberandum duas cartas de manibus Roberti de Ratford, vis. viiid."

1293, 21 Edw.—Account-roll of the receipts for 11 weeks from the tolls at the gates. The Eigne gate appears under the names of "Zeyne" and "Zyne."

1299–1300.—Account-roll of Henry . . . . of the weekly receipts of tolls at the city gates from the feast of St. Denis, 26 Edw. I. to the same feast in the following year.

1306, 34 Edw.—Receipt-roll of Richard Monyword (somewhat mutilated, and mounted on linen), and the expense-roll, as it seems, of the same (much injured by damp, and mounted), in which many of the payments belong, however, to the preceding year. The former roll is endorsed with the gild receipts, which include some of 35 Edw., and 12*s.* 10*d.* "de Rogero Penkes conballivo meo in recompensacionem liberacionis firme." Amongst the expenses are frequent breakfasts provided for the judges, and wine given to Sir Miles Pychard the sheriff, and to Sir Will. de Mortimer.

1314–5, 8 Edw. II.—A tattered roll of pleas in the city court. The Eigne gate appears under the form "Zezene." One of the plaintiffs bears the name of Warin Oldecrist. A complaint is brought by Alice la Lymbernere as executrix of the will of Sir Richard le Lymberne [*sic*], chaplain of B. V. M. in the Church of St. Nicholas, against the prior and convent of Llanthony.

1316, Oct. 10 Edw. II.—"Placita in nundinis Hereford die sabati in festo S. Dionysii et aliis diebus subsequentibus." A short roll.

1318, May–July, July–Oct., 12 Edw. II.—Two rolls of the city court, without the names of the bailiffs. The first of these is much mutilated and very tattered.

1319, July–Sept., 12 (ending) and 13 Edw. II.—A similar roll. Two actions brought by executors run through the greater part of it, viz., one brought by Master Richard de Hamenashe and Roger le Taylor, executors of the will of Master William de Caple, against John de la Maudeleyne, chaplain, and the other by Osbert, vicar of the church of St. Peter, Hereford, Will. de Orleton, Roger de Maddeleye, and Walter de Paris, executors of the will of Richard de Cruce, against Cecil. de Amyas. These cases are continued in the next rolls.

1319, Feb.—1321, 12–15 Edw. II.—The same; on 13 rolls. In 1319 there is a case of seizure of goods for rent. A. le Engleys complains that Ralph le Gurdeler came to his house in Cabage Lane, which he rented of the said Ralph, and took away "unum tapetum, unam supertunicam, unum firmaculum, quinque paria sotularium, et duo paria des enpeynes qui vocantur *embles*," to the value of 30*s.* Gurdeler replies that he had let the house at 3*d.* per week, and that the rent was 17*d.* in arrears, and that he therefore took these things (but not the "firmaculum," brooch), as he was well entitled to do by the custom of the city. In Oct. 1319 the court was held before John de Brompfeld, the Bishop's steward, and the bailiffs of the city. In 1320 James de Henleye, a canon of Hereford, brings an action for debt. "La Mercerierewe" is mentioned in an action in 1321 as the street in which certain cloth was bought. Walter de Lugwardyn, a citizen of Oxford, becomes bail with Hugh the butcher of Wormbrugge in Oct. 1320, for payment of one mark for Walter of Oxford, a citizen there, who had been arrested "pro una cloca" of Hugh de Moutton's, a citizen of Hereford, which was found in the house of John Sat, also a citizen of Oxford, and which had been carried away the Sunday before Michaelmas Day.

1319, Mich.-1320 Mich., 13-14 Edw. II.—Account of Philip le Worror (called in the preceding court-rolls Werrour), bailiff, in three rolls of five membranes. Thomas Tope accounts for receipts as bailiff of the toll-house ("tolneti") and Will. Godknave as bailiff and collector of the King's rents. The receipts for stallage at the fair of St. Denis are only 4*s.* 6*d.* "De Glodythe, serviente Cecil. Amyas, pro sanguine, xviii*d.*" John Wade the clerk had one mark for his robe, and Roger de Hull 40*d.* for his fee. Two marks are paid to Hugh de la Hull "communi attornatori civitatis pro feodo suo." The customary gifts of bread and wine are very often sent to John de Carewe; they are also sent to Sir Rich. de Wottone, to the sheriff, Roger de Elmrigge (who is also twice entertained with wine in the house of Will. Godknave), and to the judges, Sir Henry Spigurnel and Adam Herwyntone. There are expenses in connection with, apparently, a confirmation of the city charter; "ad impetrandum unum breve pro libertatibus allocandis," and payment to Rich. de Westbury "pro auxilio præstando ad cartam allocandam." "In expensis ballivi, clerici, et sub-ballivi per duodecim dies in quibus generales inquisitiones tenentur, xx*s.*" The "compotus" of Henry de Orleton, "collector muragii" (a tax for the city walls which was granted by Edw. I. in 1297 for five years, but must have been renewed) is attached on a small separate roll. The receipts are 30*l.* 16*s.* 9*d.*, and the expenses these:—"Liberavit Thomæ de Strettone per preceptum civitatis, iii*s.* iiii*d.* Item liberat. Willelmo de Aylmestone pro prosio (*sic*) faciendo apud Ebor. termino Mich. anno xiii, vii*s.* iiii*d.* Item lib. eidem Willelmo de Aylmestone in reditu suo pro labore suo, vi*s.* viii*d.* Item in expensis duarum feriarum, xvii*s.* viii*d.* Item in expensis omnium janitorum Hereford, xxxix*s.* Item in salariis facientes (*sic*) signa, 11*s.* Item in cariagio et operacionibus et aliis expensis circa paina (?) xxvii*li* ix*d.*"

Throughout the long reign of Edw. III. there is not a single roll of bailiffs' accounts now found. In the 27th year, 1353, there is a county justices' roll containing a list of all the fines inflicted, with the names of those who were bail for the offenders, which is thus headed: "Civitas Hereford. Hec indentura facta inter Ricardum Talbot et socios suos, justiciarios ad transgressiones et excessus operariorum, servientium et artificum in com. Hereford assignandos, et Thomam le Brut, chevalier, et socios suos, collectores xv^{e} et x^{e}, juxta ordinacionem domini Regis et consilium anno regni sui vicesimo septimo." But there is a large, though nevertheless very incomplete, series of the rolls of the city court, as follows:—

1329, 3 Edw. III.—Four rolls.

1334, 8 Edw. III.—One roll.

1335, 9 Edw. III.—One roll. Walter le Cachepol is bailiff. There is a plea of debt against Master John de Orleton as executor of the will of Master Thomas de Orleton.

1336, 10 Edw. III.—Four rolls.

1343, 16, 17 Edw. III.—One roll.

HEREFORD MSS.

1345, 19 Edw. III.—One long tattered roll. The Friars Minor of Hereford do not make appearance in a plea of debt, and are therefore distrained upon to the extent of one horse and one [bushel?] of meal; afterwards they appear and give bail. The curious name of *Vygorous* occurs in this roll, as also before.

1351, 25 Edw. III.—Six rolls. The following royal acknowledgment of a loan is entered:—

"Edwardus &c. Noveritis nos recepisse per manus Thesaurarii et Camerariorum nestrorum quinquaginta libras de Communitate villæ Hereford, quas eadem Communitas nobis pro expedicione arduorum negociorum nostrorum salvacionem et defencionem regni nostri Angliæ contingencium mutuavit, nos igitur volentes præfatæ Communitati de summa prædicta satisfieri prout decet, concessimus et assignavimus eadem Communitati dictas quinquaginta libras percipiendas de exitibus custumarum et subsidiorum lanarum, coriorum et pellium lanutarum quæ eadem Communitas vel alii extra regnum nostrum Angliæ educet vel educent, in quibuscunque portubus ejusdem regni eligere voluerit, in duobus annis post festum S. Michaelis proximo futurum proxime sequentibus, per equales porciones, per manus custumariorum vel receptorum custumarum et subsidiorum eorundem. In cujus rei, &c.

1353, June–Sept., 14 Edw. III.—Two rolls; no names of bailiffs. To these is attached a writ from Richard de Brugge, sheriff of Herefordshire, with a copy of a writ from the King respecting an action for debt, with his seal of arms (checquy) attached.

1356, 30 Edw. III.—One roll.

1358, 32 Edw. III.—Three rolls. Thomas Dun (*alias* Don) is bailiff.

1359, 33 Edw. III.—Four rolls. The Prior of St. Guthlac's, Hereford, is sued by Reginald Monyword for taking and detaining a silver cup with a cover, and, together with William Blokkeley, a monk, by Thomas, parson of Newington, near Banbury, on a plea of trespass.

1366, 40 Edw. III.—Nine rolls.

1367, 41 Edw. III.—One roll.

1374, 48 Edw. III.—Fourteen rolls; (one of these was found amongst papers of 1764–5).

1375, 49 Edw. III.—One roll.

The City Court Rolls then continue as follows:—

1377–8, 1 Rich. II.—Four rolls, "Tempore Hugonis Osebarn," of which one is much rubbed and in parts illegible; and a fragment of one on paper. John Penny, chaplain of the Chantry of B. Mary, in the church of St. Nicholas, sues John Yattone, prior of Lanthony "in Wallia," and the convent, for debt.

1378–9, 2 Rich. II.—One roll.

1379–80, 3 Rich. II.—One roll. Richard Pallmere, bailiff.

1391–2, 15 Rich. II.—Six rolls. Thomas Chippenham, mayor. The title of mayor was first granted by the Charter of 7 Rich. II.

1392–3, 16 Rich. II.—Three rolls; one on paper.

1406–7, 8 Hen. IV.—Fragment of one roll.

1407–8, 9 Hen. IV.—Nine rolls. One plea of debt is interesting from the information it affords of the price of armour and complete fitting out of a horseman-at-arms. Roger Atfurton sues Thomas Leynham for "1 loricam, prec. xiii*s.* iiii*d.*; 1 brestplate, 1 paunce, prec. ix*s.*; 1 bassenet, 1 ventaille, prec. ix*s.*; 1 paire gloves de plates, prec. ii*s.* vi*d.*; 1 paire quysshers, 1 paire greves and saboters, cum 1 paire de bourges, prec. x*s.*; 1 paire vaumbras and 1 paire de rerebras, prec. vi*s.* viii*d.*; 1 pollax, prec. xx*d.*; 1 paire de trussyng cofres, prec. xx*d.*; 1 equum nigrum, prec. xxx*s.*; 1 curt' tog' cum capucio (*short cloak with hood*) viridis coloris cum liliis, prec. xx*d.*; 1 huyke, prec. ii*s.*; 1 curt' tog' (*the scribe here wrote* gou, *but crossed it out before adding* n) viridis coloris cum 1 capucio de ray, prec. xii*d.*; 1 toga de ray furur[ata], prec. vii*s.*; 1 som^csadull (?), prec. xx*d.*; 1 chalover, prec. xii*d.*"* One other case of debt is a plea of Thomas Burghull, John Hale, and Will. Waryn, "procuratores et supervisores operis et fabricæ ecclesiæ de Wythintone," against Michael Checkeley for 10*s.* 6*d.*, "quos ex sua propria voluntate promisit et concessit novæ fabricæ companarum dictæ ecclesiæ, et quos solvere debuisset, etc., et quos nondum solvit licet inde sæpius fuerit requisitus." The defaulting Michael denies the promise; and, on giving bail, the trial is postponed.

1409–10, 11 Hen. IV.—Nine rolls. John Mey, mayor. The churchwardens ("procuratores") of St. Owen's sue Sir John Nokes, because after he and John Adam, chaplain, had on the f. of St. Cecilia, 10 Hen. IV., altogether submitted themselves in a matter in dispute to the arbitration of John Mey and three others, and had been ordered to pay 6*s.* 8*d.* to the work of a certain window in the said church, he refuses to do it. Robert Walker, vicar choral of the Cathedral, is sued because on 18 April he by force and arms took away a horse from the house of one Henry Nowel. Lewis Breules is mentioned as being Warden of the Friars Minor. William Smyth (whose trade is not mentioned) brings complaint against Grono ap Jevan that after he had engaged him on the Sunday before the feast of St. Martin to serve him as an apprentice for one year, then for two years, and that then in the fourth year, if they suited each other, he should give him 30*s.* for his wages, the said Grono left him on the Wednesday in Easter week; to which the latter replies that the agreement was conditional, upon their mutual liking.

1412, 14 Hen. IV.—Roll for the months of Oct. and Nov.; John Falke, mayor. Sir Leonard Hakeluyt has a plea of debt against Will. Hosey of the parish of Maurdyn.†

1414–5, 2 Hen. V.—Three rolls. John Mey, mayor. Walter Eton is prior of St. Guthlac's, Hereford. A plaint of debt is brought by William Hemmyng, one of the vicars choral. The name of Walter Bookbyndere occurs, which affords the first mention of that trade which has been here noticed. . . . .

---

* This list may be compared with one of the time of Hen. VII. or VIII. found in a small parcel of early bills of the same kind (now bound up in a volume of selected papers) for the supply of "harness."

"John Whytewood. The coste off the harnessynge of a man. In primis, a jacke with slevys, viii*s.* Item, a apurne and a gurgytte of mayle, ii*s.* Item, ii. swyrdys, v*s.* iiii*d.* Item, ii. dagars, xii*d.* Item, ii. swyrd gurdyls, vi*d.* Item, a salett, ii*s.* Item, a hawbert, xvi*d.* Item, for the scorynge of the salett and the mayle, xii*d.* Item, a shotynge glove, ii*d.* Item, a braser, i*d.* Item, for v. yardys and a halfe of whyte clothe, pryce the yard, xiii*d.*, summa v*s.* xi*d.* ob. Item, for bokulles and thinges for the brygtreyers (?), ii*d.* Summa, xxvii*s.* vi*d.* ob." Another parcel of similar bills, without dates, is among the papers of 1521–2.

† As an example of the utter confusion in which all the papers were found, it may be mentioned that this roll was discovered in a parcel of pleas, &c. endorsed as belonging to 1782.

1415, June–1416, 3, 4 Hen. V.—Eleven rolls. May 4, Walter Eton, prior of St. Guthlac's, sues Hugh Lukas, vicar of Felton, for 20s. for tithes granted to him at Felton, and 20*d.* which he had paid for the said Hugh to the clerk of the abbot of Gloucester. June 23, one is prosecuted for assault who "vi et armis jacuit in agaito in Cabouche lane."

1434–5, 13 Hen. VI.—Three rolls, "rotulus primus," "tercius," and "sextus," John Fuster, mayor.

1439, Oct.–1440, Oct. 18.—A paper book of eighteen leaves. On 30 Apr. John Hauler and John Pewte sue Thomas Sporyour "de placito detencionis unius libri de lusionibus, prec. iis. iiii*d.*," for which detention of a playbook Thomas is arrested.

1441, July–Aug., 19 Hen. VI.—One leaf, tattered.

1446, Oct.–1447, June 13.—Nich. Falke and John Fuster, mayors. One roll.

1473, 13 Edw. IV.—Cases on Aug. 9. One leaf.

1475, 14 Edw. IV.—Cases on Jan. 4. One leaf. "Item, presentant pro nyghtwalkyn cum gladiis Thomam Carver, clericum, Johannem Lloid, clericum, Johannem Bolter, clericum, Johannem Swanstone, et Thomam diaconum de Priorye. Item presentant Thomam Bullocke pro raptione unius puellæ. Item presentant Johannem Cariour of Lemster pro malo regimine in receptione mulierum. Item presentant Johannam vocatam *feyr Jenet* pro borderia." Presentments of this last kind are unusually numerous about this time.

1475–6.—Six leaves, being a fragment of a paper book of cases in the Mayor's court.

1477, Oct.–1478, Oct. 17, 18 Edw. IV.—Paper book, chiefly containing pleas of debt. On the inside of the parchment cover at the end is a list of the wardens of the trade guilds at the time, viz., bakers, drapers and hosiers, painters, butchers, smiths, fellmongers, and shoemakers.

1478, 18 Edw. IV.—Eleven leaves of presentments at the sessions. "Item, presentant quod Ricardus Taillour et Ricardus Hugyns, capellani, sunt communes pervigilantes per noctem, ac jactant lapides aureos (*sic*) per vias, etc." Several persons are presented for selling "metheglyn pro viii*d.* contra proclamationem domini Regis." Amongst several cases of adultery, &c., are these: "That Sir Jon Tanner, vycarye of Allehaloue, holds comyn bawdry with Ales Bath, the wyffe of Water Bath. Item, Sir John Glover holds comyn bawdry with Elenour . . . . Item, præsentant Margeriam Catour quod ipsa tenet borderiam cum Willelmo Chestourfelde, fratrum Prædicatorum."

1482, 22 Edw. IV.—View of frankpledge on 17 Sept. One paper leaf.

1490, 6 Hen. VII.—Cases on 4 Oct. One paper leaf.

1492, 7 Hen. VII.—Among many presentments at the Easter sessions for street affrays, one is made against Roger Draper, a draper, for shooting two arrows at the mayor, Thomas Draper, and wounding him.

c. 1500.—A mayor's account-roll, torn, and wanting name and date; but evidently about 1500 from Sir Rich. Delabere, knt., being named as Steward and John Goodman as Clerk.

1502, 18 Hen. VII.—View of frankpledge, 26 Sept. Three paper leaves.

1503-4, 19 Hen. VII.—Fragments, on three tattered leaves, of the court roll.

1506, 22 Hen. VII.—Accounts of the chamberlains (Robert Carpenter and John Mower), Dec. 21. The total of the receipts is only 17*s.* 4*d.*, and of payments 18*s.* 11*d.*, which are almost entirely for repairing "Fryerne Yate," and for gilding the swords. On paper.

Court-rolls, Aug. 31–Sept. 3.—Thomas Newent, sub-prior of the house of St. Guthlac, Hereford, is presented for breaking into the house of Robert Williamson "vi et armis," and one Excetour, a monk of the same house, for being a common nightwalker.

1507, 23 Hen. VII.—Accounts of the chamberlains (Robert Carpenter and Maurice Davies). The total of receipts is 39*s.* 8*d.*, and of payments 29*s.* 4*d.*, of which 19*s.* are "paied to the vicars of the quere." One paper leaf.

1508, 24 Hen. VII.—A long paper roll of the Michaelmas Sessions.

All these earliest rolls of court and of accounts are placed together, in an iron box, together with the earliest mayors' inventories. The later court-rolls and presentments are with the parcels of papers of the years to which they belong; but the rolls of account are all placed together in the box.

Mayors' Inventories.

1475, Oct, 20, 15 Edw. IV.—The first MAYOR'S INVENTORY is of this date. The outgoing mayor, Thomas Brynles, hands over to his successor, Thomas Mey, "duos libros, videlicet unum librum de Statutis, alt[e]rum de consuetudinibus civitatis prædictæ; item, duos alios libros de recognitionibus et memorandis ibidem, unam lagenam æneam; item, . . . corpus Johannis Mosley condempnati ad sectam Hugonis Williams in xlvi*s.*," with four other prisoners, of whom three are for numerous debts and one for felony and murder.

The next inventories of persons and things handed over by one mayor to another which have been met with are of the years 1522, 1528, 1530, 1531, 1549,* and 1554. That of 1557 may be taken as a fair representative of the general character of these lists at that period, and is as follows:—"Three swordes, called the King's and Quenes swordes, with theire three scabards . . . . . one hatte of purple velvet . . . . . . the seale of the offyce of the meyralte . . . . . one statute book of customs and three bokes of recognysances and remembrances of the courte of the saide citie; and also . . . . fouer maces of sylver, one pollaxe, one case of tymber gylte to putt in the saide swordes, and also two scochyns of sylver berynge the armes of the saide citie, with two roses of sylver to the saide scochyns pendente weyinge thre onces and half, a quarter scante, and two halberds; and also [*etc.*] three peire of boltes, seven peire of gyves, three iron cheynes, three necke collars, one peire of armeboltes and eighte peeis of brasen weightes remaynynge in the handes of John Kynge, and one keye of the Tolsyende dore of the said citie; and also [*etc.*] the harnes remaynynge in the said Tolsyende, that is to saye, two peyer of harnes for horesmen, one peire of Almen [*i.e.*, Almayn] ryvetts without splyntes, fouer peire of splyntes, one aperne [apron] of mayle, twelve salettes, one scull, nyne

* There is no list of prisoners in this inventory. The sum of 24*l.* is handed over for the maintenance and expenses at Parliament of Thomas Havard and William Barekeley, citizens.

swordes, fyve sworde gyrdelles, two bowes of yewe, three sheffes of arrowes, thre gyrdelles, nyne gloyves, eighte daggers; and also [*etc.*] one brasen metynge yarde, a gallon, a quarte, a pynte of brasse, nyne weightes of grete and smale of troy weighte, the letter H graved on them, also thre quarters of a pounde of Abberdepoys,* and ten peces of ledden weightes; and also [*etc.*] in the Kynges and Quenes gayole of the cytye of Hereford the bodies of all thes prysoners whose names hereafter folowethe: [fourteen, for felony, larceny, trespass and debt; and also fourteen bonds of persons out on bail. Signed by the outgoing mayor, Thomas Havard].

The next year's inventory, that of 1558, adds in an interlineation "one key of the common coffer"; the list of harness is omitted; the prisoners (among whom are two women mentioned in the preceding indenture, convicted of felony but reprieved on the score of pregnancy in Jan. 155 7/8, and who continue still mercifully reprieved†) are twelve, of whom four are for debt. The bail-bonds are 26. The other inventories met with up to the end of the century are for the years 1564, 1580, 1585, 1589, 1591, 1594, 1596, and 1600. In 1585 the scabbards are described as "three chapes of sylver guilte"; there are two hats, one of black velvet, the other of red; the escutcheons become four "scochyngs of sylver, being the armes of the said citie," with four roses. The prisoners are only two for felony, three for debt, and one, Thomas Hall, committed by letters from the Privy-Council, "in that he departed from his captayne after he was by him receaved to serve in the Lowe Contries of his owne voluntarie free will." The prisoners cease to be mentioned in these inventories towards the end of Q. Elizabeth's reign.

V. Miscellaneous Documents and Papers.

1362, July 8.—Deed of sale by the executors of the will of William le Fourbour (viz., his wife Joan, and Thomas de Breyntone and Richard Marcet, chaplains) of a messuage in Hereford; reciting that whereas it is the custom used in the city of Hereford, and granted and approved by the Kings of England, that every citizen may leave all the property acquired for himself to whomsoever he will, and the said Will. le Fourbour directed that the proceeds of the sale of the messuage should be given to those who celebrate for his soul in the church of All Saints, they have therefore sold it to Sir Robert de Prestone, perpetual vicar of the cathedral church (No. 2 in the box numbered 3).

1378, Thursday after feast of Assumpt. of B. V. M. [Aug. 19].—Will of John Verbum, cook and citizen of Hereford. Leaves his body to be buried in the cemetery of St. Ethelbert, under the north chapel; to the work of the cathedral 20*s.*; to the high altar of the church of St. Peter for tithes and oblations forgotten and omitted, 13*s.* 4*d.*; to the work of the same church, 40*d.*; to the Friar Preachers, 10*s.*; to the Friars Minor, 10*s*; to each chaplain of St. Peter's and All Saints' coming to his funeral, 4*d.*; houses and shops to his children Cecilia and Thomas and his wife Cecilia; the proceeds of the sale of a croft to be given to the chaplains celebrating for his soul in the church of St. Peter. "Item, lego loricam meam, 1 par de plates, cum cirotecis de

* In the inventory of 1554 this word is disguised under the form of "*haberd price.*"

† A fragment of the inventory for 1576, which was found to be used as the cover for a book of bonds, contains a similar instance of a merciful reprieve, in the case of a woman who had been originally reprieved in Sept. 1573.

plates, 11 bollas argenteas, 1 caminum de ferro, 11 sheemsadles, 1 rode-sadle, totum focale de shoppis meis, et carbones, et tabulas meas, et quinque patinas servientes shoppæ meæ, et cathenam argenteam, et ii equos meos, et 1 sellam . . . equinam, et c lb. et dimid. ceræ, et omnes cudos servientes arti meæ, et arbores jacentes in Widmersshestrete . . . . [et] totum mel quod habeo," to be sold for the carrying out his legacies. Proved 6 Aug. [*sic*, probably by mistake for 6 Sept.]. (In the box numbered 3.)

1390, Sept. 1.—Certificate by Geoffrey, vicar of Longhope and dean of Forest, to John [Trefnant], Bishop of Hereford, in pursuance of a mandate from him of Aug. 30, that he has inducted John Walton to the parish church of Aston Ingayne on the presentation of William de thston; having, on enquiry by citation of the rectors and vicars of the Aeanery of Ross, published in the chapel of Lake ("de Lacu"), found dhat the vacancy began on Aug. 24 in the said year by the death of Sir Thomas, then rector, who had been presented by Sir Thomas de Astone, knt., that William de Astone is now the true patron, that the value of the church is nine marks, that the presentee is in priest's orders, of good life, and not elsewhere beneficed. [It is rather remarkable that the death of the last rector, the presentation of his successor, the mandate from the bishop, the enquiry, and the induction, are all within eight days !] The official seal of the rural dean is attached; apparently two herons or cranes. [No. 10 in the box numbered 3.]

1393, Sept. 28, 17 Rich. II. At Dynbioghe.—Writ from Roger de Mortemer, Earl of March and Dulvestier, addressed to the stewards of all his manors and lordships, informing them that he has granted to the citizens of Hereford exemption fram distraint for any trespass or debt for which they have not become bail. In French. Fine impression of seal, but the border broken off and lost. [This document is very incorrectly described in Johnson's *Customs of Hereford*. In the box with the Royal Charters.]

1433, Oct. 19.—Will of "Willelmus, Anglice Smytht." Leaves his body to be buried in the cemetery of the cathedral church of St. Ethelbert; to the fabric of that church 6*d.*; and to that of All Saints 2*s.*, and to the vicar 3*s.* 4*d.*; his smithy ("unam fabrillam") to his son Thomas, etc. (No. 11 in the box numbered 3.)

1445–9.—A small parcel of seven bonds, with two writs to Mayors from Sheriffs of the county, transmitting writs from the King; i. from Sir Walter Devereux, knt., for the attachment of Henry Brasher to answer to the churchwardens of St. Nicholas for 10*l.* for some damages, May 18 [1448]; ii. from Sir Walter Sculle, knt., for the attachment of William Hemmyng, clerk, for 40*l.* due to Thomas Sherrard, a servant of the Chancellor, Feb. 1 [1449].

1459, Apr. 10.—Judgment by Walter Eckeley, sub-dean of Hereford, in a suit by Walter Rogers of the parish of Presteheinde (Presteign), against his wife, Ellen Porter, of the parish of All Saints, Hereford, for restitution of conjugal rights; by which the marriage is annulled and the parties divorced, on the ground that the said Ellen had never consented to the marriage, but had been forced into it by relatives. [No. 12 in the box numbered 3.]

1464, Sept. 27.—A lease of a messuage in Malyerystrete to John Andrewe, hosier, at an annual rent of 6*s.* 8*d.* payable to the Custos of the College of Vicars Choral, gives the names of the Vicars forming the College at that time. They are Maurice Jones, John Dore, John Dyny, Hugh Mylle, Thomas Carpynter, Roger Were, and William Panyers, clerks. The seal of the College is broken. (No. 8 in the box numbered 3.)

1470, Dec. 31.—Will of Margaret Godwyn, of the parish of Llangaren. To be buried in the parish church there; leaves 6*s.* 8*d.* to the fabric of the Church of B. Mary of Ketyre, and lands in Llangaren for wax lights to burn before B. V. Mary and *St. Daniel* in the Church of Llangaren; bequests to two daughters both named Sibilla, and her sons Thomas, John and William ap Gl̃i, and for works of charity for the souls of herself and her husband, Meuric ap Jevan. Proved Nov. 22, 1473. (No. 13 in the box numbered 3.)

1472, Apr. 4.—Will of Richard Mathew, citizen and tanner of Hereford, "languens in extremis." To be buried in the churchyard of the Cathedral; 3*s.* 4*d.* to the Vicar of All Saints for tithes forgotten; property in Wydmersche strete, &c. to his wife Cecily, his sons Thomas and Henry, and his daughter Agnes. Proved Apr. 23, 1472. (No. 14 in the box numbered 3.)

1485, Sept. 20.—Will of Richard Benthlowd, tanner. Leaves his body to be buried in the cemetery of the monastery of St. Ethelbert; to his curate for tithes forgotten, 2*s.*; to the fabric of the cathedral church, 12*d.*, and to that of the Church of All Saints, 20*d.*; to the Friars Preachers 3*s.* 4*d.*; to the Friars Minor 3*s.* 4*d.*; to his brother John his russet gown; the residue to his wife Cecily and Richard Tayler, his executors. Proved, 2 Nov.

1498.—Account (on one leaf) of receipts and expenses of Richard Pole, esq., steward of the household of Jasper, Duke of Bedford, to 22 Dec., the day of the Duke's death, showing a balance in the steward's hands of 30*s.* 6*d.*

[*c.* 1500 ?]—A letter from Edward Grene to the Mayor, whose name is not given, asking him to perform a feoffment of trust in which he and Sir William Mylle, chaplain, had been put for the writer's wife, Jane; so "that she and I have no cause reasonable forther to complayne by the same token that your maystership and I wente to Mordeford the morowe after the churche mynnynge daye" (*sic*). "Wrytten at the monastery of Saynt James of Wigmor the Sonday after Saynt Markes the evaungelyst daye."

[1500–1520 ?]—A petition from the journeymen shoemakers relative to their part in the procession on Corpus Christi day and its profits.

"To the ryght worshypefull mayer of the cytey of Hereff̃ord and to hys bretherne. Shewythe unto your good mastershippes your umble orators the persons subscribed beyng jornemen of thoccupacion of corvesers within this cytey haue obtayned of your mastershippes predecessors mayers and aldermen of the seyd cytey a composysyon whereby your sayd orators were bound to bryng furth certen torches in the procession on the day of Corpus Christi yerelye, and that your said orators be also bound to paye yerlye to the wardens of the sayd occupacion at xiii hall dayes within the sayd cytey yerelye to be holden xiii*d.* for the mayntenaunce of the sayd torches and for the relyeffe of the pore bretherne of the sayd occupacion beyng sycke or in decaye within the sayd cytey, and for to burye suche pore bretherne as shuld happen to dye within the same. Whyche good laudable orders have alwayes bin kepte from the makyng thereof untyll nowe of latte that the wardens of the sayd occupacion, and certen other frowarde persons in a cedule hereunto annexted named, of theyre perverse mynd dyd dystribute and geve away the torches of the sayd occupacion att theyre plesure, and that the sayd wardens have alwayes hetherunto refused and do refusse to make and yelde to your sayd orators an account of the receipte of theyre charge, contrary to theyre othe thereffore taken, and contrary to theyre olde custome thereffore used. And that they also wolde breke dyvers ordynaunces in the sayd composicion comprised and by the lawes of the realme or custome of the sayd cytey not forbydden, which ys to the utter impoverishyng of your sayde orators and contrary to all ryght and consyons. Wherefor hytt may plese your good mastershippes to commaunde the sayde wardens to make redeliverye of the sayd torches and to yelde theyre sayde accounte according to justyce, and that your sayde orators may enjoye all suche grauntes and libertes in the same composicion mencioned and by the Kyngs Magestie and his moste honorable Councell nott abrogatt, accordyng to the porpotte of the sayde grauntes to them made. And your sayde orators shall dayli pray to God for the prosperous estatte off youre good mastershippes long tyme to endure." There are no names subscribed nor is the "cedule" annexed; the paper is therefore probably a copy.

An ordinance made in Dec. 1549 with regard to the substitution of annual payments for the pageants is printed from a copy in the *Black Book* (f. 27) at p. 119 of Johnson's *Customs of Hereford*.

1503, March 7.—Will of Richard Aythene, of the parish of St. Martin; *English*. Bequeaths his body to be buried "in our Lady herbary" before the cros there; to his curate for tithes forgotten xii*d.*; "also I wolle that y have aboute my herse the day of my sepulture in waxe vi tapyrs weynge iii lbs. apece, of the whyche y wolle have ii tapyrs to remayne to Seynt Martynis church to brenne in tyme of dyvyne service, one afore Seynt Martyne and another afore the ymage of Seynt Kateryne; also y wolle that y have iiii torches of Seynt Martinys churche toward the mynstre aboute my herse, paynge for the waste of them iiii*d.* a torche; also y wolle that the vicary and prests of Alhalous, Seynt Nich[olas] and Seynt Martyne with ther clerks be at my Dirige, havynge for ther labours aftre the custome of the citee of Hereford." (In the box numbered 6.)

One of the boundaries of the property to which some of the preceding deeds relate is frequently described as "viam vocatam Rody-pot quæ ducit versus le Watryng-place."

c. 1510–20.—In a fragmentary paper of presentments are the following entries: "We gre and present the Koke of the coledg and the queer for forsstawlyng of the markedd for byyng of chese, bottor, and eges, with other vettels, the whyche is yll soford. We gre and present a sarvaunt of Tomase Wellkokes, on Wyllyam a Wode, for the seyde game at cayles at the chapell of Elyntry. We present a sarvaunt of John Howell for that seyde game aforeseyd."

1512, Sept. 25. Hereford.—Decree of arbitrators (Rich. Judde, clerk, Rich. Draper, clerk, and John Baker, gent.) in a suit respecting the free chapel of Ogystone [Hoggestone] in the diocese of St. David's, enjoining that Sir William Mendus, clerk, shall pay to Sir Thomas Adys, clerk, 6*l.* 13*s.* 4*d.* on condition that the latter deliver up to him a letter of presentation of the said Sir William to the said chapel, directed from John Devereux, knt., lord Ferrers, to the Bishop of St. David's. (No. 15 in the box numbered 3.)

1514, Jan. 4, *an.* 5 Hen. VIII.—An instance of a thief availing himself of sanctuary for saving his life is afforded. "Richard Meredith otherwise called Boweer, of the citie of Hereford, bowier, asked the privilege of the churche of Seynt Peter within the seid citie, for savegard of his liffe, and called for a croner to here his confessione, and theruppone George Honour, meire of the citie of Hereford and cronour of our soveraigne lorde the Kyng within the citie aboveseid, came to the seid churche to here the confession of the seid Richard Meredith, and then and ther the seid Richard Meredith knoweleged and confessed before the seid croner that he robbed and stale a coverlete of the goodes of John ap Rees, and therfor he toke the privilege of the churche, and for none other cause."

1514.—A curious information is laid on Apr. 20 against a poor tinker for talking about the battle of Flodden with commendation of the Scots and their artillery.

"The xx day of Aprell, the v yere of the rayne of Kynge Harry the VIII, Thomas Grayngar, of the citei of Hereford, peutrer, cam before George Owonour,* meyre of the citey of Hereford, Thomas Weles, purcyvant of your sayd soverene lord Harry, Chypman Squyer, Thomas Gybbons, Wyllyam Scudamore, and Robert Fystuer, and then and there was examynyd of certeyne wordes and langegees that were spokyne by one John Browne the tynkere. The wyche Thomas Granger sayd for troyth that the sayd John Browne, tynkere, was yn hys howse in the company of one John Gode the Wenysday or Thursday before Paume Sunday last past, and there the sayd John Browne talkyd of the Shotyse fylde, and sayd thoughe the Scotes lost there kynge they lost no fylde. Item he sayd that he had seyne and knew the kynges of Scottes ordinance, wyche were as godly ordynances as any was in the worlde, and thoughe they were lost they wolde have as good agayne. Also he sayd that the Scottes wolde come agane into Ynglond unto Hamtone." There is another short deposition to the same effect.

On June 6 William Hunt comes before the Mayor and others, "and ther confesseth that one Phelipe Morgan shuld sey that he hadde broughte a lre from the kynges grace to the seid maior to prepare mene, for my lord Harry Buck. is gon out of the land and iiii^{m} men with hym; and also that ther was poysened ii lordes in London; and also he seid to the prisoners in the kynges geyle of the shere and also of the seid citie, Be mery, ye shalbe shortely all delyvered so that ye that (*sic*) be here for murther. For the whiche wordes by the commaundement of the Kynges Councell he sate in the stockes, and a pauper aboute his hedde with diverse wordes."

1514, Apr. —.—Petitions of Agnes Baker, of Bodenham, to the Commissioners of the Marches against her son, Harry Baker, for wronging her in her farm by the support of Sir John Lingen, knt., and his wife, with replies and order thereon.

July 10. London.—Rouland Brugyes, M.P. for Hereford, to the Mayor, etc., about nonpayment of his allowance.

"Ryght worshipfull master meire and worshipfull masters your bretherne and to other the ryght honest of theleccion and comyne councelle of the citie of Hereford. In my righte herty maner I re-

* In the printed lists of mayors, this mayor's name is erroneously given as *Bonner*. It was *Honour*, as appears from various papers of the time.

commend me unto you desiryng your welfares and also of the seid citie, and where ye are in controversie for the expences of the money for me and Reignold Mynours my felowe elect for you and by you for alle the last long parliament so oft proroged and as yet in parte not fynyshed as M. Ridalle kane telle you, in parte I gretely marvele that ye of your gentilnes wull not se no better for thexecutyng of the Kynges writte made for the leveying therof as right is and as you and other where (*sic*) agreed at the tyme of eleccion, whiche in parte was this, that I shuld have but xxs. of the comynalte for myne expences therof yf the seid parliament wer not proroged or further adjorned, the wiche parliament was ofte proroged to my grete cost and charge at diverse tymes. Trustyng and also desiryng you that with your good wysdomes to se suche convenyent ordre herein to me as ye have done to other in tymes passed, so that I have no resonable cause to seke for forther remedye herein, for I will be conformable to all good ordre and reasone though it be parte to my grete losse, the wiche a comynaltie might better susteyne then I; and as for the first being and sittyng of the said parliament, the wiche continewd fifty dayes or therabonte, I shall rebate all that to the xxs. and other promises made for the same, so that I be welle dealed withall in the remaynent as right and conciens wull, and what ye wull do in the premisses I desire you of answere. And Ihū save the citie and you. Writene at London the x day of July, aº 6 H. 8.

Your assured to his pore power,
ROULAND BRUGYES."

The other member also writes on the same subject, but in a much more indignant strain. Unfortunately the beginning of his letter is wanting. "——— and where as ye have elected Rowland Briggs and me for your citie at the parlament, we the v day of February have apperid for you and taken the charge on us, the wiche for my parte was for by cause I was sworoun to meynteyn the citie of Hereford to my power, and therfor I wold not suffer ye the citiez[ens] to be amerced, and for no kyndnes shewed on your partiez. It is an holde sayng, he that doith for a comonalty schall have litille kyndnes and thankes, and so I have that hathe spente my money in your serveces in yeres passed, and cannot be payd of my wages. I ensure you of the lawe will I will (*sic*) have it every peny, and as shortly as I can, and I will discharge me of my nothe (mine oath), and wheras ye writte that I schulde be bounde to saffe you armeles at the parlament, and that the quenys tenaunt geythe free of tolle by an acte at the last parlement, as to saffyng of you harmeles, wyemene may know when we have entred into the parlement we have taken the charges on us, and at the last parlament ther passed no acte that queneys tenaunts schall goe free for payng eny tolle, but ther was an acte what landes the quene schuld have to hir joyntour, and Marcle was parte of quene Elizabeth joyntour, and it is not unknowyn to you how hyr tenaunts used theym. And he that caused you to writte thes ii articles hath don your citie litill good and knowith well that mater, and if he could devise no othir thynges for your citie he may spare pauper (paper), for I entend the same... Written at Lyncolles Inne, the viii day of February. REYNOLD MEYNOURS."

Several persons are presented in 1513 and 1514, as well as in other years, for putting hops in ale.

1519, Aug. 7. xi Hen. VIII.—Decree of arbitrators for settlement of disputes respecting the will of Thomas Jaxsone, the elder, deceased, which begins by providing that Thomas Jaxsone "shall desire his mother of hur blessynge, and she for to geve hur blessynge to hym."

1520, Jan. 7.—Notification by William Burghill, commissary of Charles [Booth], Bishop of Hereford, "in remotis agentis," of the excommunication of John Grigge, chaplain, for contumacy.

Feb. 14, St. Valentine's day.—Notification that John Gregge, chaplain and rector of the parish church of Little Birchis, is absolved from the sentence of excommunication.

1520.—A letter from "the Custos and his compeny, vicares of the chore of the cath. chirche." "Charytabully shewyth" to the Mayor and Council "that where they and their precessors and predecessors for the tyme beinge, tyme owte of mynde prescryved, haue be yn possessyone of the receyte of a certayne annualle and sacke rent of ixs. vid. by yere owte of an howse or mese place callid the Bothhalle in the saide cyte purchased and gevyne to the saide Custos and compeny by one Sir Roger Barbour, whose sowle God pardon, to thaugmentacōn and ffyndynge off towellys whann necessyte shalle requyre, and the saide Custos and compeny haue peaseably receavyd the saide rent off ixs. vid. off the chamberlaynes of the saide cyte for the tyme beinge, tyll now of late by the space of v or vi yeres hitt hath be wrongfully withholdene, agenst goode conscyens and ryght, into the grett prejudice of the said Custos and compeny, lettynge of the last wylle of the said Sir Roger Barbour, in his lyffe tyme beinge one of the saide compeny, and evyll example off other good Crystene people. Wherefore this premysse consydered, hitt may please yow maister meyre and your honorable company to se restytucōn made of the saide rent for the tyme hit hath be vnpaide, and duly to be contynued hereafter. And ye soe doynge shall bynde vs to pray for your preservacōn and alle the hole cyte. And to know your pleasure in this behalfe and answere we hartely desire, trustynge to allmyghty God and oure holy patrones Seint Ethelbert and Seint Thomas that we shall haue no cawse further to complayne. And this as lovynge neighbours we desyre in the way off charyte, as ys before rehersed."

Several persons are charged in this year for night-watching and playing at cards and dice, and a woman "pro subauditione sub fenestra." Cases of fines for such eaves-dropping occur also in other years.

[*c.* 1520–30 ?]—Letter from seven prisoners in Bisters Gate to the Mayor praying for protection against a fellow prisoner named Hugh Detlare, who is ready to kill one or other every day, and who says that when he comes out of ward he will impeach the mayor of high treason and murder and extortion, "for he thynke to undo all the cettey with hys sottoll lawe and falssete." One of the seven petitioners, John Bedowe, writes also a letter praying the mayor to release him from prison where he has been for nearly half a year, and he will be sworn not to come again within the franchise of Hereford while his master ives.

1521, 13 Hen. VIII.—John Duppa* sues William Lewcas for 4*s.* damages for not having delivered to him "quandam imaginem pictam de beata Maria virgine" which he had agreed to give in exchange for a shirt valued at 2*s.* 6*d.*

William, abbot of St. Peter's Gloucester, sues Thomas Huet for 13*s.* 4*d.* lent to him by Edward Wotton, prior of St. Michael's, Ewenny,

* On a member of this family of Duppa in the following century, Thomas Duppa, who died suddenly in Hereford in the house of a victualler, a coroner's inquest was held on 9 May 1654.

and a monk of Gloucester, Dec. 20, 1519, which he agreed to repay on demand, but which agreement he now repudiates.

1521, May 22 and June 18, 13 Hen. VIII. Salop.—Orders of the Commissioners for the Marches of Wales upon a petition from Thomas Hervy against John Kidermynstre; signed by G[eoffrey Blyth], bishop of Cov. and Lichfield, and — Uvedale *serv.* [serj.-at-law], with a letter from Richard Phelips, Mayor of Hereford, to them, dated June 17, that he has directed the parties to appear before them, upon Kidermynstre's desire, as the latter will in no wise be ordered by his neighbours.

1521, Sept. 23, 13 Hen. VIII.—At the View of frankpledge various persons are presented (*qu.* ale-sellers ?) "for usyng of unlawfull potts of erthe and not sealyd"; and also "all the bochers for sylling ther vittelles contrary to the statute, and also for ther acte that they have made contrary to the comen weale, that is to wete, that none of ther occupacion to kylle freshe mete tyll they have sold ther stale mete kylled byfore tho hit be incorporate (*sic*) and not holsome for manys body."

Petition to the Mayor and the three inquests representing that the whole commonalty of the city have great enmity amongst them "in preferryng the Bishoppes officers rather then the thynge that shuld serve to the profite of this citie in pynnynge of catell," in that the owner of every beast which is pinned within the palace shall pay 5*d*., which is a great impoverishing to the commons, who have a pinfold upon the King's fee; wherefore they desire that every citizen and every man that dwells upon the King's fee shall bring all trespassing cattle to the King's pound anent the castle upon pain of 6*s*. 8*d*. for every default.

The second and third inquests allow this bill.

1522.—Petition to the Commissioners for the Marches from Richard Hill, of Tillington, about a suit with Walter Hill, of Hereford, with an order thereupon dated 16 July, and signed by G. Co. and Lich., Uvedale serv., P. Newton, and B. Bromley.

Letters and orders from the Council of the Marches are of continual recurrence up to the time of James I., relative to actions for debt and various ordinary causes, but only in the above two instances are they found with signatures of Commissioners.

1524.—Vincent Warminster produces in court on 14 March, as a bar to an action brought against him by one Richard Barret, a protection granted to him by the King on 23 Feb. *an.* 14, on account of his going o Calais on the King's service in the train of Sir John Bourchier, knt., Lord de Berneye, Governor of Calais.

1529.—Printed broadside containing two Acts of Parliament, made in the Parliament beginning Nov. 3, 21 Hen. VIII., and prorogued to 26 Apr. following: i. Act against killing of calves; ii. Act limiting the price of hats and caps brought from beyond the sea.

1530, June.—Printed proclamations of Hen. VIII., printed by Tho. Berthelet.

i. The proclamation, issued with the advice of the primates and learned persons of Oxford and Cambridge, condemning the books called *The wicked Mammona*, *The obedience of a Christen man*, *The Supplication of Beggars*, *The Revelation of Antichrist*, *The Summary of Scripture*, and divers other books made in the English tongue and imprinted beyond the sea, as containing pestiferous errors and blasphemies [&c.];

and also forbidding that the Scripture should be in the English tongue and in the hands of the common people as unnecessary, the permitting or denying thereof depending only upon the discretion of the superiors, and therefore ordering all the copies thereof [as well as of the books above mentioned] to be given up to the bishop of each diocese within fifteen days. [In clean and perfect condition. Johnson has reprinted this in his *Customs of Hereford.*]

ii. "A proclamation . . . . . . for punisshinge of vacabundes and sturdy beggars," enjoining their being sharply beaten and scourged. [In clean and perfect condition.]

1530, Aug. 17.—Certificate of the delivery of certain gipsies to a Justice. "This indenture made the xvii day of Auguste in the xxii yere of the reigne of Kyng Henry the VIII. betwene John Cantourcelly, meyre of the citie of Hereford on the one partie, and Roger Millewarde, gentilman, on the other partie, witnessith, that the seid meyre hath delyvered to the seid Roger Milleward one Antony Stephen of the countrey of lytyll Egipte as hedde and capytayne of xix persons of men, women and chylderyn named them selfes pilgrims, the whiche came to the seid citie of Hereford the viiith day of Auguste the seid xxii yere of the reigne of Kyng Henry the VIIIth, and soo taryed there by the space of ix dayes and ix nyghtes, and in the seid citie dydde no hurte as I can perceve as yet, savying only there was persute made after them by one Thomas Phelipes of Ludlow for a certeyne sume of money to the sume of iiii*l.* vii*s.* vi*d.* taken by certeyne of them owte of the house and chambre of the seid Phelips contrary to the Kynges lawes. And soo I the seid meyre have delyvered to the seid Roger Milleward the seid capytene with all his compeny, to the nombre in all with the seid capytyne, as men, women, and chylderyn, of xix persones, with bagge and baggayge, and the seid Roger to use them after the Kynges commaundement. In witnesse wherof I the seid Meyre and Roger Millewarde to this present indenture entyerchangeably have put to our seales the day and yere above seid. [*Signed*] Per me Rogar Mylleward."

1530.—Petition to the "Pryncesse Counsaill" (the Council of the Marches of the Princess Mary) from "Sir William Hunt, pryst, oone of the Vicars of the quere in the cathedrall churche of Hereford, that is to say, vycar of the vicaraige called Wynmyllhylle," setting forth that whereas there are two shops in the "Narowe Gaheige lane," of the annual value of 8*s.*, belonging to the said vicarage, one Philip Baskervile, esq., has occupied them for the space of three years, refusing to pay any rent, and has added them to his own house adjoining, making one of them a porch, "manysshyng your orator yf he will medle therwith or seke any distresse that he will kyll and sle, and also he is a strong gent there that your poor orator is not able to opteyne remedye agaynst hym." He therefore prays letters to the Mayor to examine the matter. A letter from the Council follows dated 17 Jan. *an.* 21, directing the Mayor to bind over the defendant to appear before them on 6 Feb.

1531, Sept. 7, 23 Hen. VIII. At Chelsehith.—Writ to the Sheriff of Herefordshire directing him to publish throughout the county a proclamation in English which is subjoined, forbidding the exportation of provisions to other countries, "per ipsum Regem et de data auctoritate parliamenti." Forasmuch as the King by his high wisdom foreseeth and in experience knoweth divers persons so to regard their own private lucre and advantage, as without regard to the violation of his high commandment heretofore given to the contrary, or consideration what damage they do therin to the residue of his grace's people, and consequently to themselves, they only intend to apply all their policies daily how to convey out of this realm into other countries victuals in great quantities, By reason whereof, this present year not being so fruitful as was trusted, and in many parts of this realm by unseasonable weather fails, this realm should be shortly brought into extreme necessity and penury of victuals requisite of the sustenance of man's body, unless by dreadful penalties the covetous affection of such persons were therein in time restrained, For these causes his highness straitly chargeth that no man born under his obeisance or stranger, of what estate, degree or condition soever he be, do convey or cause to be conveyed out of England or Wales into any other country, by sea or land, any manner corn, butter, cheese, tallow, bere, beeves, muttons, or other victual, unless it be for the necessary victual of their ship, crayer, or boat, under pain of forfeiture of all so conveyed. [Notice of transport of any victual above the value of 40*s*. from one port to another to be given to the customers, etc. Rewards to informers.] Seal lost. [In the box with the royal charters.]

1531, St. Andrew's day [Nov. 30]. James Gawey to the Mayor. —Has received the money from Thomas Hamtone for which he distrained upon him for the King's rent.

1532, 23 Sept.—At the View of frankpledge the Jury present "the Priour of the Black Fryours for afray and blodshede uppon James Ga . . . . ," and "Richard Grene, chapleyne, for pety larceny."

1533.—In the Court papers of 25–6 Hen. VIII. there are presentments in Nov. 1533 against various persons "quod custodiunt lusores ad cartas et tesseras in domibus suis contra formam statuti"; and "for playing at the tabulls for money" and in 1535 persons are also presented for playing at "le poyche" (pitch ?) and "pro custodiendo le boullynge."

1534, Aug. 26. 26 Hen. VIII. Salop.—Order in the King's name from the Commissioners for the Marches to the Mayor and Aldermen of Hereford, that whereas they are credibly informed "that by meane of gadering of Commertheas* and other like exactions, and for affrayes and estries used in those partyes our pour subjects be not only gretlye impoveryshed and endamaged but also put in grete feair and jeperdye of their lyves, by means of mysruled persons (contrary to our lawes and peas) vsing to weyr cotes of diffence, and demaund siluer of our poure subiects by thretnyng wordes, so that for drad therof they dare not applye thair busynes nor attende thair merketts, as our true lyege people ought to do, whiche we ne wold shuld contynue, but that the same shuld be redressed with spede: Therfore we and our said Counsailours and Commyssioners woll and charge you and everye of you that frome hensforthe ye mak open proclamacions in fayres, merketts, sessyons, courtes and churches where ye shall seme most expedient, that no maner person or persones shall frome hensforth gadre any Commertha within our said Cytye of money, corne, catell, or other unlawfull colleccion, nor assemble nor gadre any our subiects to any love ales or bydden ales, nor suffer any

---

* *Commorth* was a contribution customarily collected at Welsh weddings, on behalf of the persons married; and the custom is still in part kept up in districts of Wales. It was forbidden by Statute 26 Hen. VIII., cap. 6.

person or persones to weyre any cotes of diffence nor other harnes contrary to our statutes in suche case provyded"; persons offending to be committed to ward pending the Commissioners' further order.

1535, July 3.—Letter from John Meredith, the Mayor of Hereford, "to the Kings most honorable Counsell nowe being at Glouc." He has now in sure custody certain rude persons who have here of late misused themselves in counterfeiting of the letters of the King and of the Council (which letters he sends enclosed) respecting a debt due from one Thomas Walle to one M. Powell of Bristowe.

On July 6 the Council of the Marches write from Gloucester their reply, in the King's name. "Forasmoche as John Bedo of our citie of Herford of late of his craftye and vntrue disposicion procured one William Blast to falsyfye our lr̃es dyrected to one Thomas Wall of Herford forsaid, and delyveryd sealed with the seale of an old lr̃e from our Commyssioners in our marches of Wales hertofore to an other person dyrected, and one James Watkyns of counsaile with the same Bedo in delyvery of the same forged lr̃e to the said Wall: Therfore it is ordered and determyned by our said Commyssioners that the said John Bedo, James Watkyns and William Blast shalbe conveyed to Herford at this tyme and delyveryd to you, to the entent ye at the next markett day in tyme of most congregacion of people shall cause the said John Bedo to be put on horsebake, his fase towards the horse taile, and the said James Watkyns and William Blast to lede his horse throughe the markett place and stretes of the said citie, and the forsaid John Bedo to have papers aboute his head with a scripture in gret lr̃es theron writen conteynyng these words, This were I for falsefying the Kinges lr̃es. And after the said thre persons shalhaue passed the said stretes in maner aforsaid, then the said John Bedo for his further punyshment to thensample of others to be put on the pyllarye there to make his abode during the spase and tyme as the said markett endureth, and the said James Watkyns and William Blast to stand by at the same his punyshment; and the same premysses executed accordingly, ye to deteyne theym in warde till the next day after, and therupon to enlarge theym to thair liberties."

There is one leaf of accounts of money received by the said Mayor, and of money spent by him upon the hat "that the wsordeberer (*sic*) werith"; which is as follows:—

"Item, for a elle of welvett - -	xv*s*.
Item, for a nayll of blak welevett and a halfe for to rebounde the hatt abowt -	xiiij*d*.
Item, for iii. ells of bockeram for to make paste for the seyde hatt - -	xviij*d*.
Item, for iii. quarters of fustyane -	vi*d*.
Item, payd to Herry Boules for the makyn of the seyd hatt - -	11*s*. iiij*d*."

Amongst the papers of this year, not dated but written to the same Mayor, are these letters:—

1. From John Wyddyns (or Myddyns) "dwellyng with Humfrey Cawfyes (?), clerke of the signet," to his "ryght worschipfull unkowll," John Meredith the Mayor, sending him a copy of a bill of complaint which has been made on 20 Sept. against him, John Welsfood, and John Hackluet, esq.

2. From William Croft, of the town of "Preschende" (Presteign), on behalf of a man of Presteign who is being prosecuted for some

affray made upon a "pardoner," with which the writer certifies he had nothing to do, and will bring with him the best of the town to prove it and then the plaintiff will have to pay their costs.

3. From Richard Warmecombe, dated at Wormysley.—He was told to-day that a jury is empanelled for trying this afternoon an action between Sir Thomas Flemmyng and M. Cole; desires that the case may be adjourned, as Ogle is a man of honour, and is now far out of this country but intends to be here at Michaelmas, "and besides that he is as now without lerned counsell, forasmoch as the citie is so vexed with the plage that there is none wolle comme there, as Jesu knoweth, who cease the seid plage when his wille is."

4. From George Herbert (without the name of the Mayor to whom he writes) dated from Bergavenny, 12 Oct.—Whereas an action has been brought by a burgess of Hereford, called Roger Spicer, against the bearers for being sureties for one William Herbert "of this country," against whom he presupposes an execution to be had, he desires that the case may be dismissed from the Mayor's Court; and let Spicer come to the writer and to the court here, and according to the law he shall have the execution.

1540.—Inquests are held on three persons who died in prison in April and June "de quadam infirmitate vocata *a consumption*."

——, Nov. 19, 32 Hen. VIII., at Westm.—Writ from the King to the Mayor and Bailiffs, ordering publication in the several wards, parishes, and other places of the following proclamation:—"Where the Kinges moste roiall Maiestie, at his graces grete costes and expenses, hathe a long tyme susteyned and maynteyned and yet kepyth a grete armye in his lond of Irelond, aswell for conservacyon and defence of the sayd lond as for the annoyaunce of suche his highnes enymyes as attempt dayly great displeasures agaynst his subiectes of the same, and for the mayntenaunce and relief of the sayd armye and subiectes, by his most excellent wisedome hath ordered a coyne of money aswell of grotes as pens of two pens to be curraunt only within his sayd lond of Irelond, beryng the prynte of the harpe of the one syde therof, whiche coyne dyvers and sundrye persons haue lately transported and brought out of the sayd lond and vttered the same within this his realme of Englond, not only to the greate detryment and hurte of his sayd gracys lond of Irelond and of the sayd armye and subiectes of the same, but also to the grete deceyt of his highnes louyng subiectes of this his realme of Englond: For remeydye wherof his Maiestie by this his proclamacyone straictly chargeth and commaundeth, that no person or persons of what astate, degre or condicyone soeuer he or they be shall from hensforth transporte or bryng out of his sayd highnes lond of Irelond eny of the sayd coyne of grotes or pens of two pens ordayned to be curraunt for and within the sayd londe, nor vttere or paye for eny payment within this his realme of Englonde, Wales, Berwyke, Calyce, or the merchies of the same, eny of the same coyne, vpon payne of forfayture of the treble value of the sayd coyne brought transported or vttered for payment contrarye to this proclamacyone, and ouer that to suffre ymprisonment and make fyne at his gracys will and pleasure."

1541.—In the jury presentments for this year very many persons are presented, and fined 4*d.* and 6*d.*, "pro custodiendo joca, videlicet cartas, in domibus suis contra formam statuti, et contra proclamationem inde factam," others (fined 8*d.* and 4*d.*) "pro custodiendo in domos suas (*sic*) joca, videlicet tabulas et alias contra formam statuti," many persons (fined 6*d*., 4*d*., and 2*d*.) "pro eo quod ludebant ad cartas," and others (fined 4*d*.) for keeping "in domo sua tenys pley," and "quod custodiunt pilam pedalem vocatam Tenis pley."

1546, Oct. 17.—Will of Edward Tayleare of Much Cowarne, Herefordshire. To be buried in the churchyard there; leaves to the mother church of Hereford 4*d*.; to the high altar in his parish church, 8*d*.; "to owre Ladys syngs" there 3*s*. 4*d*.; the residue to his wife Agnes, his son Richard, and his three daughters. Proved 20 Jan. 1546–7.

1547, Dec. 27.—Notification to all justices, &c., by the brothers and sisters of the house for leprous persons in Hereford, founded in the worship of St. Anne and St. Loye, of their appointment of George Whyte and Richard Collyns to be their proctors to gather alms for the said house, in pursuance of letters patent from K. Edward VI. authorising such gathering. On parchment.

Undated Papers.

The following undated papers belong for the most part, if not altogether, to the reign of Henry VIII., but some may possibly be a little later.

Jan. 21. "At Beaudley." The Princess [Mary's] Council of the Marches, in the King's name, to the Mayor of Hereford.—To our no little marvel you have not certified the Council of our dearest daughter the Princess whether Thomas Baskervile, Esq., be in danger of his life through such hurts as he sustained in the affray in the city of Hereford between him on the one part, and Thomas Vaughan, George Walwyn, William Walwyn and others, on the other part. You are therefore, upon sight hereof, putting apart all favour, affection and excuses, in writing to certify the Council by the bearer in what case the said Thomas is, and whether he may be in peril of death, that the Council may further proceed according to justice.

Apr. 2. At Ludlow Castle.—[In the name of] The Prince [Edward] to the same, thanking him for his diligence and toward disposition with the Council of the city for furnishing 24 persons to be ready to attend on the Prince to do his most dread lord and father the King service. Touching Roger Gibbys and John Breynton, is content that they and all other citizens shall conform themselves as they have been used in times past with the city, in such case.

Unsigned petition about a watercourse and drains. "To the right worshipfull Mr. Mayor of the citte of Hereford. Yf yt may please yow of yowr gentilnes to remember the matter that I schowde to yowr Maystyrshipe ysturnyghte, who [*how*] that Jhon Bellynyame hathe ii dragthys and a place to kyppe a bore on the Kynges dyche, dyrectely agenste my gardyng, and on John Flemyng, alias Carver, hathe ther an odur dragthe, so that the watter maey not nor cannot have his frey curse but oftemys dothe drownde my gardyng, and the savour of the fylthynes of the same dragthis ys so nowsaime that no man may abyde yt, nor cum to my gardyn, and yt ys vere hurtfull and contagyus to all the inhabytens ther, buttyng gret bondedayge yn the Kynges dyche, wiche of ryght owghte to be frey, as yowr goodnes dothe ryght well know. Wherefor the premissis of yowr gentylnes consydreyd, wher as yow of that yowr goodnes dothe and haue redressyd odur fauttes within the citte, I pray yow of remedy, for the love of God."

Letter to Hugh Gebonys [Gebons], recorder of Hereford, from Hugh ap Rece, priest, "vycary" of Skynfraythe [Skinfrith, Monmouthshire], requesting him to conduct a lawsuit for him.

Petition, unsigned, of complaint against the Chaplain of St. Giles' Hospital.—"To the ryght worshyppfull Mr. Meyre hys Bretherne and the thre inquestes. Shewethe vnto yowr good Mastershipps that whear John Perkes, clerk, now pressent beyng amyttyde chappleyng of seynt Jyllys within the sothebarbes of the cytye oght to be by the fundacyon to be sworene to be all weys contynuallye dayly sarveys within the sayde chappell, as hytt in the fundacyon dothe more at large aperyng, notwithstandyng, good Mastershipps, that at Ester last past, lytylle regardyng hys duty and sarves vnto the pore allmes men, went into the contrey and ther servyd alle the Ester tyme, so that ther wass no servies within the said chapelle, nor dothe lytyll regard hys said duty therin, unles that yowr good Mastershypps do se some reformacyon therin acordyng to ryght and eqwytte, for God's love."

Another undated and unsigned petition to the Mayor and his brethren relating to the same Hospital and its chaplain (which was found among some papers of 1572–3, and is now placed, as well as the preceding petition, among the bound *Special Papers*), is as follows. It may possibly be of the year 1567, as a Chaplain was then removed for neglect of duty. See *infra, sub anno.*

"For as muche, Right Worshipfull, that ther ys a great nombre of the cytyzens and other poore inabytaunts of the same cytye beyng housholders are very aged, impotent, and fawlene into decay and extreme poverty, the more ys to be pytyed. and as lytyll relyffe for them as yet provyded as in any cytye of Yengland, may it therfore please yow to be moved with compacion as God's stuards to concider the same by yowr wysdomes and som charytable meanes, som helpe and remedy therin. And to pute yow in remembrauns for that purpas, there ys a fundacion parteynyng to Saynt Giles in the sothbarbes of the said cytye concernyng certeyne articles tuchyng the admytyng of the chaplene therof, and that none oght or maye be inductyd or admyted chapplene therto but suche as shuld be ther recydent bothe nyght and day, dwellyng and prayne [praying] with the bedmene, as hathe bene of owld tyme usyd and acustomed, untyll now of late that by an inderecte and unknowne meane ther ys one crept in to the sayd chaplenshipe, and injoyethe hit at his wyll and plesure, not beyng resydent nor abydynge ther, acordyng to the trwe meanyng of the sayd fundacion. And nevertheless he hathe the howsse, orchard and gardene ther, and that unocapied, beyng worthe by the yere xx*s.* and more, and also hathe fyve markes yerely for his wages, and as it were all together for the only countenaunce and name of the Chaplene of seynt Gyles; all wyche ys cleane contrary to the true meanynge of the sayd fundacyon, auncyent costom, usage, and all good dyscrosion, and so the sayd induccion and admision ys bothe in lawe, ryght and concience uterly voyd, and now ryghtfully in yowr dysposyssion. Wherfore that the chapell and the sayd Beadmen are within the parishe of seynt Owen's, and a lytylle dystaunce from the parishe churche, therfore it may please yowr worshipes to take order and dereccion that the parson of seynt Owen's may be ther chapplene, gyvyng him for his paynes xx*s.* to sarve the pore allmes men at tymes convenient, and that the said howse and gardene may be devided into too parts, and that there may be too othere pore mene ther placed, and that they may have seven nobles betwene them yef yow thynk so good. And forther, som order to be takene for the cyvyle order for the good behavyor for the sayd bede mene, that they go not comynly beggyne dayly, contrary to the lawes of the realme, and that they be not comene haunters of alehowses, and to be dayly drounk, as they are presently dayly nowe, and for theire reformacione a ponyshment devysed by yowr worships for thos that wyll not be ordered, that dothe breake suche good orders as yowr worships by yowr good dyscresion wyll devyse, and they to be hadd before yow as sone as yow convenyently may, and they that deny to stand to yowr orders may be dysplaced, and other sett in theyr places." To this petition these answers of the inquests are subjoined. "The second Inquest both agre that the pore allms men shall not be removed to here serveys any ells wher but only in the chapell at saynt Gylles, accordyng to the owld custome, and that the chapleyne shalbe bownd to saye serveys at suche howers as hath ben accustomed, and to have for his paynes iii*l.* vi*s.* viii*d.* and the howse and garden therunto belongyng: and also doth desyer Mr. Mayor to deveyse some ponysment and refformacion that the pore allms men may not goe abrod a beggyne aftur gentylmen to our dyscredyt. The iii Inquest dothe agree as the seconde Inquest have done before rehersed. The furst Enquest dothe agre likewise."

May 8. At Rychemount.—Letter from Will. (?) Devereux to the Mayor, commending the bearer, Henry Wenstone, to him, who has determined to make in the city "a game or a geve aill after the custome of the contre," and desiring him and the aldermen "to be favorable and good maisters vnto hym, as in gevyng hym leyff to kepe the same game or geve aill, and that it may be as moche to hys provytt as you may cause." Written by a secretary, and only signed by Devereux very indistinctly.

Aug. 15. Exeter.—Letter from John Tronge, esq., to the Mayor. An indignant complaint that certain stuff of his which one of his servants had with him in Hereford has been detained, until the writer sends a testimonial to prove his ownership. He does not go a begging, nor does he like a snail carry all that he hath upon his back, for his possessions are not of so small a value; but he desires the Mayor at once to make delivery of his goods without any further business, or he will make him answer in the law to the contrary with all his costs and charges, or else it shall cost him 100*l*.

Feb. 26. "Under our signet at our Manour of Hampton Courte."—Letter from Henry VIII. to the Bishop of Hereford and others, directing them to levy the tenth and first-fruits of the spiritualty granted at the last session of Parliament. With the King's signature, apparently impressed by a stamp.

Inventory of the goods and chattels of Robert Croweleye, clerk. Specifies all the furniture, &c. in the parlour, the chamber wherein he did lie, the inner chamber, "the grete chamber next the Cabage lane," the outer chamber, another chamber, the "calerne" (cellar, containing a hogshead and a barrel), the buttery, the "hale" (hall), and the kitchen. There is also "a chamber of boks," of which unfortunately the contents are only described thus (a description, however, which shows that Crowley's library was large):—"Item, xxx greate books with claspes. Item xli other books with claspes. Item cxlvi books without claspes."

Petition to the Mayor and his brethren from some of the citizens against the admission of strangers to trade, which ends with a remarkable and spirited threat of nonpayment of taxes.

"Sheweth vnto your Mastershyppes your pore neyghbores citizens and artificers of the cite forseid, that wher the custome of the cite is and owt of tyme of mynde hath ben that no man shulde bye ne sell, nor make no maner of marchandise but he were in skotte and lotte vprisynge and downe lyenge, dwellynge and abyddyng in the same cite, which laudable custome hath bene full well meynteyned be the right worshipfull fathers which hade the gydynge of the cite in tymes past to the worshippe of the cite and to the wele and profete of the inhabytans of the same, So it is nowe that one Robert Sandewyche whyche dwelleth in the towne of Lychefeld ocupieth the mystere of Sadelers crafte to the grete hurt of our consitezens the sadelers, and to the evyll example of other strangers to sette vp any other crafte at ther will. Wherfor we beseche your mastershippes and other of the Councell to see the remedy accordyng to our customes, that we have no cause further to complayne, and in eschewynge of other inconvenyens that myght ensewe. For we assertene you ef we may not enjoy suche preveleges and customes whiche the Kynge and his noble progenitours hath granted vnto the citezens of this cite, we will not be contribetours nor ber scotte nor lotte to the confirmacion of our Chartour nor to non other maner of charge when we be called vppone."

Among the papers of 1535–7 is a Writ (stamped with the King's signet and dated "at oure manour of Rychemount the xx[th] day of May") for the strict execution of the Act against vagabonds, there being a "gret multitude of idle sturdie vacabonds that woll by no good meane or commaundement applye themselfes to labour and travaile for their lyvyng"; ordering also that watch be duly kept from 9 o'clock at night until 5 in the morning until Michaelmas next, and that one of the watch, at least, shall be a householder of the honestest and best sort.

An undated order, of the middle of the 16th cent., enjoins the ringing of one bell in the church of All Saints at 4 o'clock every morning from the vigil of All Saints until the feast of the Annunciation, for half an hour; the ringer of the bell to have 10*s*. yearly.

End of the undated papers.

1549.—Presentment is made by the second inquest of all the bakers in the city for taking a penny instead of the customary halfpenny for baking a bushel of "wyven"; of the Vicars Choral for not repairing Barr's Bridge and the way leading to it; of Richard Hu[n]tyffylde because "he wille not fylle a quart of alle for halpeny"; and of William Haskett "for kypyng of card pleyng and manteyning men servants in hys howse to pley at cards." Similar presentments respecting card-playing are of frequent occurrence in other years.

1550, 4 Edw. VI.—Richard Huntyfield is again presented for selling ale at a penny a quart, and is amerced in 12*d*; whereupon follows a representation from the jurors of the inquest to the mayor and his brethren that "wee perceve the sayd Huntyfeld ys offendyd with us, and dothe opynly declare that wee are all false harlots and noughty harlots, to the gret sclaunder of your sayd pore neybours"; and evidence is taken thereon, but Huntyfield denies it all *in toto*. And all the bakers are again presented for doubling their charge for baking a bushel of "wyven bred," taking a penny "wher the cytesens were wont to pay but an ob." Seven persons are presented for putting hops in ale. John Higgins is indicted for seditiously inciting other persons to break up inclosures, saying that by the King's proclamation all inclosures were to be broken up.

1552, Dec. 15, 6 Edw. VI.—Copy of an agreement made under the authority of the Council of the Marches between the mayor and commonalty on the one part and the tenants and inhabitants of certain neighbouring places on the other, respecting the rights of pasturage on Widemarsh Commons.

Cf. Johnson's *Ancient Customs of Hereford*, pp. 155–6.

——Examination of a wandering tailor who had come from Ireland, and before that had served two years in Guienne, and five years at Boulogne under Capt. Walter Bromwich.

1553, Jan. 19, 6 Edw. VI.—Writ from John Scudamore, Esq., sheriff of the county, to the mayor, Thomas Havard, for the election of two burgesses for parliament.

1553, May 15. At Hereford.—Letter to the mayor desiring him to release Sir Thomas Fawkener, clerk, servant to Sir George Cornewall (one of certain Commissioners sent on some duty not specified), who has been arrested by some of the mayor's serjeants; signed, Jo. Prise, George Cornewall, and Thomas Dansey.

[1554], Jan. 23. Letter to the Mayor, William Smothie from John Hill.—"Yt maye please yowre mastershipp to be advertised that one Wylliam George lyeinge in my house in the cytye of Oxford at the singe (*sic*) of the Swann there, the xxiii of Januarye laste paste (*sic*), there beinge wyttnessys presente as shall followe, conveyed in the presens of them a letter being clapssyd in a booke, and so hyd the said letter under the forsaide George his saddle, so that I with the reste of my geste beinge desyeryd and movyd of right to testefye the trwethe have the daye above wrytyn signed this byll to be of a trwethe. From Oxenford the xxiii of Januarye. Yowre frende to his powre

JOHN HYLL.

Wytnessys, John Calloweye, gent., Edwarde Curtis, Cristover Edwards, with maynye moo."

1554, Jan. 25, *an.* 1 Mar.—Copy (directed to John Scudamore, Esq., at Holme Lacy) of a circular letter from the Queen to the Council of the Marches, sending a copy of the marriage articles with the Prince of Spain to be published throughout the county, since "certen yll disposed personnes, meaninge vnder the pretense of myslykinge this mariedge to rebell againste the Catholycke relligion and divine service restored within this our realme, and to take from us ther Soveraigne Ladye and Queene that lyberty whiche is not denied to the meaneste woman in the choyse of ther husbands, cease not to spreade manye false vile and vntrew reportes of our saide Cousyn and others of that nacion": the authors and spreaders of these false braits and rumours are to be apprehended and punished.

1554, Feb. 1. Homelacy.—Letter to Will. Smothye, mayor of Hereford, signed by John Scudamore, sent with the preceding letter and a copy of the marriage articles, and desiring him to execute the instructions therein.

1553–4, Feb. 4. Newenham.—John Pollard to Mr. Smothy, mayor, and Mr. Havard, urging them to help the vicar of Holmer in some dispute with one Will. George about tithe-corn.

1554, Feb. 7. At Ludlow Castle.—Order from the Council of the Marches to the mayor, that there be due watch kept nightly within the city, and that the gates be closed and kept safe in convenient time, for "the chouring" of the misorder that might ensue, and for the apprehending of such as would attempt the same.

1554, Feb. 9. At Ludlow Castle. — Order from the same to the same that whereas Morgan Daires and John Hawle have complained that there hath been time out of mind a corporation in the city of goldsmiths, blacksmiths, cutlers, plumbers, glaziers, braziers, pewterers, and cardmakers, and that the plaintiffs being chosen wardens of the said crafts for this year, have received their oath according to the custom of the city, yet nevertheless the said mayor has refused to deliver to them the charter of the said corporation and the stock belonging to the same, he do minister justice in the said matter as he will answer at his peril.

1554, Feb. 25. At Ludlow Castle.—The same to the same and his brethren, straitly charging and commanding them, for special reasons, to have such care and regard to the keeping of the watch nightly within the city thet every night there may be a substantial watch kept, and the same to be of the most honest sort of men, and in a good substantial number, as they will answer at their extreme perils.

1554, March 21,—Indenture between the mayor (Will. Smothye) and sheriff (Sir John Prise) of the election of Thomas Havard, Esq., and Thomas Bromwiche, gent., as burgesses for the city in the parliament to be held at Oxford on Apr. 2.

1554, Aug. 24. "Barthilmewe daye." At Estmore.—Letter to the mayor, William Smothe, from Thomas Clyntone, informing him that he has non-suited the plaintiff in a case submitted to his decision between Thomas Careles and Roger Farre.

The blacksmiths present a petition in this year, setting forth that whereas they had admitted the goldsmiths, pewterers, cutlers, plumbers, braziers, cardmakers and glaziers into their fellowship and company of smiths, these the Sunday after Epiphany elected two wardens, of whom, contrary to custom, neither was a blacksmith: they pray therefore that they may be dissevered, and made again one fellowship of themselves. Their prayer is granted, on paying 6*s*. 8*d*. to the city.

1554, Oct. 13.—A circular letter from Nicholas [Heath], Bishop of Worcester (signed by him), filled up for Hereford, and addressed to the Mayor and Burgesses, about election for parliament.

"After my ryghte harty commendacions. Where for diverse causes tending principally thadvauncement of Godes glory and the common wealthe of this Realme, the Quenes maiestie hathe thoughte convenient to calle her maiesties highe courte of parlyament againste the xii[th] of November next comminge, and hathe for that purpose addressed furthe the king his and her maiesties writte to the Sheref of that countie of Hereford: Forasmuche as I knowe assuredlie that her hyghnes pleasure is to have suche elected to be of that house as be of the wise, grave, and Catholique sorte, and suche as in dede meane the true honour of God with the prosperitie of the common wealthe, And for that her highnes by her maiesties speciall letters hathe commaunded me within all my rule to admonishe on her highnes behalf all suche as have thellection of knights citezens and burgenses to chose suche, being eligible by order of the lawe, as may be of the sorte before remembred;

HEREFORD MSS.

Therfore, myndinge the due accomplishment of her highnes said pleasure, I have thoughte good to geve you notice herof, and on her maiesties behalf to require you to have suche a vigilente eye and erneste care to this matter that those maye be chosene for that citie as be of good Catholique religion, and suche as may answere thexpectacion that her maiestie hathe in you and thinhabitants of that citie; and lyke as by your erneste endevour in following her maiesties pleasure in this behalf you shewe whate good hartes you bere towardes her highnes, whiche I assure you cannott but be thankfully takene by her maiestie, so shalle you geve me iuste occasion to remember the same and to make reporte therof bothe to her maiestie and her highnes moaste honorable Privey Counsaill. Thus eftsones praing you earnestlie to consider this matter, and so to travaile therin, I bid you hartely farewell. From Ludlowe the xiii^th^ of October, 1554.

Your verey lovinge frende
NICO. WIGORN.

Postscript.—I have thoughte mete to commende unto you Thomas Havard, esquier, and Thomas Bromyche, gent., being as I am credibly enformed mete men for the purposes forsaid to serve the Quenes maiestie at this present."

On 18th Sept. in the following year Bishop Heath, now signing as "Nico. Ebor. electus" (having been elected to York at the end of February, but not receiving the pall until 3 Oct.), and Adam Mytton write again on the same subject; that whereas the King and Queen's majesty have appointed their parliament at Westminster on 21 Oct. next, and their pleasure and expectation is that such be chosen "as be grave men and of good and honest haviour (*sic*) and conversacion, and specially of Catholique religion, whiche sorte of well ordred men are most mete to consult upon the good order and state of the Realme," therefore they give notice thereof, and require the mayor, aldermen, and burgenses to bend their travail so that persons of the sort aforesaid may be chosen (&c., *as in the preceding letter*). Dated from Beaudeley.

1554, Dec. 6.—Inhibition from the Court of Canterbury to the diocesan court of Hereford, on account of an appeal, to proceed further in a case concerning tithes, against John Stapeley, claiming to be vicar of Holmer.

[1555], March 20.—Letter to the Mayor from Anthony Wasseburne, Thomas Smythe, Will. Unet, and John Harford, commissioners appointed by letters patent of the King and Queen "for and concernyng theire affaires and necessary busynes to be by us done" within the county of Hereford, requiring him to admonish all parsons, vicars, curates, and churchwardens of every parish in Hereford, and also two or three honest and substantial men of every parish, to appear before them in the chapter-house of the Cathedral Church on Friday, 22 March, at 9 o'cl., there and then to do that shall further to their duties appertain concerning the contents of the said letters patent; [apparently to inquire concerning heretics].

1554–5, 1 and 2 Phil. and Mar.—A long paper roll containing ordinances for the markets made by the Mayor, Hugh Welsh, and justices; 1, that no persons bring weapons with them to any market or fair, saving that a knight or squire may have a sword borne after them; 2, that the bakers make good and able white bread at 4 loaves, 2 loaves, or 1 loaf, for a penny, and 4 wastells for a penny or penny three-farthings; and wheaten bread of 2 loaves or 1 loaf for a penny, of able weight according to the middle price in the market; and horse-bread, 3 loaves for a penny of beans, peason and "fachers" without bran; 3, regulations for ale sellers and vintners; a cester of ale for 20*d.*; a gallon of good "metheglen" to be sold for 12*d.*; 4, for butchers; no bull flesh to be sold "untyll the tyme hyt be slaughter[ed] with houndes"; no beasts to be slain in the streets, &c.; 5, forestallers; 6, sale of fish; 7, sale of corn; "provyded allwayes that no person havyng suffycyent corne of hys owne to fynde hys familye and to sowe hys landes shal be force of thys ordynaunce have any lybertye to by corne in the sayd markett oneles he brynge other corne or grayne into the said markett of lycke kynde and value there to be solde"*; 8, sale of candles; the pound of good lights and able for 2½*d.* and no dearer; 9, tallow; 10, sea-coal, to be only sold in the market; 11, tanners; 12, timber not to be left lying in the streets; 13, "that no man cast oute dounge nother mullock, neyther cley at hys dore neyther in any other place within the cytye other then in comyn myskeyns appoynted for the same," and that all persons clean the streets directly against their own doors upon pain of forfeiting, *toties quoties*, 3*s.* 4*d.*; no swine to go at large, upon pain successively of 4*d.*, 8*d.*, and 12*d.*, and then of forfeiture of the swine; nor ducks, upon pain of forfeiture the first time; 14, no man to walk in the streets after 9 o'cl. "and the common belle ronge in the nyghte but yef he be of good name and good fame and have lyghte with hyme", upon pain of imprisonment and fine; and all who have been mayors or who are of the Common Council, and all innholders, vintners, tallow-chandlers and candle-sellers, shall from the vigil of All Saints next to the feast of the Purification have and maintain every night, except the nights that the moon doth shine, a lantern and a candle burning at their doors, the candles to be lighted at 6 o'cl. and to be burning until 8, under penalty of 4*d.* each time of default; 15, salters not to bring their wains with salt above the Tolsend, to remove their wains within three days after the fair or market, and to make clean the street where they stood; 16, no persons who buy any sea fish, shell fish, or other, may retail the same; 17, no horses to be left standing in the market-place.

1555, May 13.—Examination taken before the Mayor and Justices. "Raffe Coles, of the cytye of Hereford, carpinter, saithe, repoortithe, and is redie to depose, that apon the feast of the Invention off the Holye Crosse last past [3 May], as the canons and mynisters of the cathedral church of Hereford and the mayor and cytezenes of the cytye of Hereford apon information to them then geven that the quens maiestie was brought to bedd of a prince, went in solempne prosession in the said cytye, renderynge therfore lawde and praise to God, accordynge vnto theyr most bounden duetye, one John Gillam of the cytye of Hereford carp[ent]er there, and then spake to this examinate theese words followynge, *scilicet*, Now that there is a prince borne his father will bringe into this realme his owne nation, and putt out the Englishe nation, etc."

* A list is found in the same parcel of papers of persons returned for infringing this ordinance. It is headed, "Thys be the names of the baggars that bye corne without lycence or necessitye." The names of twelve persons are given (amongst them two with double Christian names, John Nycolle Phellyps, and Richard John Jevan), with a valuation of their land, stock, or goods.

1555, June 20.—Order by the Mayor and Council that no victualler take of their guests at meals "in theyr gales and parlors" above 4*d.* for every man, they having two dishes of boiled meat and one roasted, and not above a halfpenny for one foot man's bed, and not above 4*d.* for one horse grass of the best for one day and night, and not above 2*d.* or 3*d.* day and night for other grass; and "yef any shuter wyll call for a penye worthe of ale in a vitaylynge house within the sayde cytye that he shall have three pyntes for a penye and no lesse."

1555.—A petition from fifteen "cappers" to the Mayor against certain "master cappers" who endeavour to secure a monopoly: "whereas other master cappers to the nomber of vii hathe made [agreement?] within themselves that noe poore man one to another shall not worke noe pece worke but he shalbe preasented and lose vii*s.* vnless he worke the same in one of there shoppes, to the vtter vndoinge of your poore oratours," &c.

——.—Petition from William a Prise, tailor, who has been a long time detained in ward in "Bouthe hall," complaining that he has not the liberty that other prisoners have of "goeinge withe a freeman to the churche to here the devyne service of Almyghtie God, and so withe hym to warde agayne, whiche hathe bene accustomed tyme oute of mynde."

—— May 22. — Memorandum that John Brayne, clerk, Will. Smothye, Rich. Perteryche, Walter Marshe, Anth. Browne, and Rich. Davyes, mercer, have declared unto the Mayor that Sir Roger ap Rees, clerk, has unjustly taken out of St. Peter's church these parcels of the ornaments of the said church: "Inprimis, one vestment of rede chamlett of selke with a glove, one whyte awbe, one stole, and one fanell with the appurtenances. And two alter clothes of dyaper. Item, one paynted clothe hangyng affore the alter."

—— Sept 28.—Letter from Thomas Kerry to the Mayor about the re-erection of fulling-mills.*

"Right worshipfull, after moste hartie commendacions. Where I have undertaken (as ye right well knowe) the newe erecting and edifieing of the late-suppressed mylles upon Wye, whereunto I understand all men willing, considering howe it may advaunce that comonwelthe of yours, and no enjury to any others, and forasmuche as the same wilbe to me before it be fynished bothe paynefulle and chargeable, so will the successe be unto you all and your successors greate welth and comodite, for your poore peple hereby shalbe relyved, and your ydell men shalbe sett on worke, whiche cannot but bringe to the citie moche wealth and quiett; and having for the zeale I beare my naturalle contrey travayled by all meanes possyble howe after thereccion of the same mylles they myghte stand for ever, at lenghte by frindes am perswaded to erect the same by Parliament, whereunto I must pray your ayde, whereof allmost I counte myself assured, for that I knowe thernest good wills ye owe unto ytt, and therefore am the bolder to pray you, good master mayor and the rest of my masters your brethorne, to consyder the particulers of a bill herein enclosed, whiche I have caused to be don by advised counsaille; and yet I know yt cannot be so welle perfyted here as by you, unto whom every braynche therof is apparaunt; whiche considered by you at good leynghte, and corrected

* The mills had been destroyed by order of Hen. VIII. See Johnson's *Ancient Customs*, where, however, this letter is not noticed.

where nede requirethe, my petycion is, that if the same shalle seme to you alle convenient and requisite, I may receave by your Burgenses (whom I truste you will instructe depely on this case) the same fayre writene in parchement under your hands and comon seale to thentent the said Burgenses, and suche as I shall require to be my good lordes and masters herein, may the bolder and rather exhibite the same to the parliament howse, and overthrowe suche as shall blyndely obiect any matier against yt. Wherein like as you shall chiefly deserve thanks at God's hand, muche benyfytt your common welth, and justly receave the good name due to the furtherers of so godly an acte, to the perpetualle fame of you all and your posteritie, so shall you bynde me and myne to be yours, and fynde me and my service likewise ready to reacquite the same at any tyme (occasione serving) accordingly; as knowith thalmyghtie, to whose tuecion I commett you. From London the xxviiith of September, 1555. Yours to commaund assured,

THOMAS KERRY."

—— 4 Sept.—A letter from the burgesses of Leominster to the Mayor of Hereford, requesting that two victuallers who had gone from their town to buy wheat in Hereford market (corn being insufficient at Leominster because the farmers at this time of harvest do nót much frequent the market), and were there stayed after purchasing it under colour of the statute of regrating, may be allowed to bring it away, the statute not applying to them as they are no farmers.

—— Friday, *no day of month.*—Letter to the Mayor from his "pore frynd assuryd, Gabryell Bleytso," dated from Massyngton, earnestly urging him at once to give judgment in the case between him and Jauncy, according as the xii men gave their verdict, for Jauncy hath laboured out such things that he hath given the writer the overthrow. "My lady Morton sende you and your bedfelow harty commendacions."

—— Oct. 14, 2 & 3 Phil. and Mar.—Copy of a charter of incorporation granted by the Mayor and commonalty to the goldsmiths cutlers, pewterers, braziers, plumbers, cardmakers, and glaziers [formerly united with the blacksmiths. See under Aug. 24, 1554.]

[1557.]—Directions for providing accommodation for the coming of the Lord President and the Council of the Marches of Wales to Hereford, with the arrangements made thereupon. [From the mention of the Mayor's name, Thomas Havard, it is seen that this visit must have been in 1556–7, and, from the abundant provision of fuel required, in the winter of those years; probably at the beginning of the latter. These papers are now in the bound volume.]

"In primis that ther be preparid within that citie of Hereford the fairist house and of most easment, whiche requirithe to have one lodginge for my lord with ij severall roromes (*sic*) for hime sealf, one chambre for his l. gromes, and one chambre for his apparell if this maybe.

Item, my lord lodgid iij of the Counsaill, to be next placid at the least.

Item, the steward, the gentill man usher ore [har]binger, the usher of the haule, with butt[eler, pantl]er p . . . verer, with k . . . rer and porter . . . . . within the . . . . . if hit be posyble [*some words lost*].

Item, xxx^{tie} feather bedds with all thinges belonginge to the same for my lord, the counsaill and their men, at the lest.

Item, vi hogsheds or tenne barrells good beere.

Item, x large wain lodds goad fewell woodd to be had and takine out of the Queenes Majesties wood in place most necessary, and if ther want of her highnes wood then to mak other proviseone as necessarylye as you may.

Item, stables, hey, provandre and litter for xx^tie horsses or mor.

Item, grasse for lx gealdinges and nagges for my lord and the counsaill, or mor.

Item, viij large table clothes, iiij towells, iiij cupurd clothes, vj dosine of napkines, and xxx^tie candillstickes ether of pewter or lattin, as you may gett them.

Item, one gret pote or cawdrone to boyle beefe ine.

Item, iij lesser potes and iiij pannes of great and smale.

Item, one gridyrone, one frynge panne, and one chafingdishe.

Item, one payre of raks and iiij broches.

Item, xlviij platers, xlviij dishes, and xlviij saucers.

Item, one bryne tubbe or vesell to powdre beef ine.

Item, bucketts and tubbes, with other necessary veassells for water."

"The order ffor the provysyon of my lorde presydent and the counsaill.

In primis, Mr. Lusons* howse ys appoyntted ffor [my lorde presydent and, *struck out*] two of the counsaill, viz. [ffor Mr., *struck out*] and ffor iiij beddes [with the steward, gentyllman usher and buteler and cooke, *struck out*].

Item, Mr. Doctor Baskervyle† ys howse ys appoynted ffor [Mr. Justice *struck out*] one other of the Ciunsaill and ffor two beddes.

Item, [the sewar and harbinger, *struck out and some words lost by the paper being torn*] appoyntted [ffor one of the Counsaill, *struck out*] the . . . . rd and the master [?] porter.

Summa of bedes to be provyded within the Close, xiiij bedes.

Item, John Parteryche ys appoyntted to ffynde stable rome ffor xij horses and two beddes ffor the horse men.	xij horses
Item, John A Thomas ys appoyntted to ffynde stable rome for viij horses, and two beddes.	viij horses

[Item, Harrye Grene to ffynde two beddes, *struck out*.]

Item, Wylliam Benett to ffynde one bedde in hys howse.

Item, Hughe Kynesham to ffynde one bedde in hys howse.

Item, Mr. Rychard Patteryche, junior, to ffynde one bedde in hys howse, one ffyne table clothe, a dossen napkyns, and foure candyll-stycks.

Item, John Hydde to ffynde one bedde in hys howse.

Item, Thomas Meredythe to ffynde one bedde in hys howse.

Item, Thomas Davyes to ffynde one bedde in hys howse.

Item, Meryane Owyane to ffynde one bedde in hys howse.

Item, Thomas Marble to ffynde a bedde in hys howse.

Item, Mr. Carewyddyn to ffynde a bedde furnysshed into the palyce to Mr. Justice chambor.

Item, Thomas Churche to ffynde one bedde furnysshed into the palyce for hys gromes into the warderoppe. A cossen of sylke.

Item, Roger Gruffythe to ffynde a bedde.

Item, John Gybbes one bedde.

[*One short line lost.*]

---

* William Lewson, Prebendary of Church Worthington 1540–1583, and Treasurer of Hereford Cathedral 1558–1583.

† Edward Baskerville, Chancellor of Hereford Cathedral from 1555; died in 1566.

[Item], Wylliam Sy . . es one bedde.
Item, Edwarde Walewene one bedde.
Item, Thomas Benett a gredyorne.
Item, Wylliam Russhell a broche and reckes.
Item, John Shelfard to ffynde a bedde furnysshed into the palyce in the chambor over the kychyn.
John Darnell to ffynde a bedde furnysshed into the palyce in the chamber over the kychyn."

[*Then in the same hand, on a separate leaf, come the following additional arrangements for accommodation.*]

"The order for the provysyon for my lorde Presydent and the Counsell.
In primis, Mr. Mayre, Thomas Haverd, esquyer, a bedde of dowle, a bolster, two pyllywers with pyllowe beres, a peyre of ffustyan blankettes, a peyre of shettes, a fether bedde.
Mr. Hughe Welshe to furnyshe one bedde ffor Mr. Justyce.
The gentyllman usher and the clerk of the kychyne and buteler and panter to be placed in the palyce with Harrye Grene in two chambers.
Item, Mr. Cressett to ffynde the beddes ffor the usher of the hale [*hall*] and the eweres.
Thomas Bromewhyche, gent., one ffyne table clothe ffor my lordes table.
Mr. Webbe one ffyne table table (*sic*) clothe, a dossen of napkyns and a bedde.
Mr. Rawlyns a ffyne table clothe, a towell, a dossen of napkyns.
Rychard Parteryche, senior, a table clothe and a dossen napkyns.
Harrye Dudeson a longe table clothe, a [tow]ell and a dossen napkyns.
Mr. Rouland Rees a table clothe and a dossen of napkyns.
Rychard Bromewhyche, gent., a longe table clothe, a towell, and a dossen of napkyns.
Rychard Veale ffower candyllstyckes.
John Searle [?] a table clothe [*altered from* a fayer arryes clothe], a towell, a dossen of napkyns.
John Barkeley two arryes clothes."

In the files for this year several Welshmen are indicted for selling "quoddam genus vini vocatum le Metheglyn" for fourpence the sextary contrary to royal proclamation. Inquests were held on the bodies of eleven persons who had died in prison in "Bystrers Gate" in the months of April and May of the sickness called "the new disease," either gaol-fever or the plague. Many persons are presented for playing at the unlawful game of "the boules" in a bowling-alley in the garden of Gregory ap Res, Esq.; but a much larger number had been indicted at the sessions in 1552, *an.* 1 Mar.

1557, 16 Jan, 3 & 4 Phil. & Mar. At Greenwich.—Writ to the Bishop, Mayor, and others, sending the copy of an Act passed in the Parliament begun 1 Oct. 1555 for a subsidy, and directing the same to be put in effect. A fine copy of the Act, printed by John Cawode (16 ff.), is attached; and the assessments follow made within the several wards, which exhibit the names of all the inhabitants and the values at which they were assessed in lands or goods. Amongst the papers for this year is a long paper roll of ordinances made by Walter Carwardyne, Mayor.

HEREFORD MSS.

1557[-8], March 2. Copy of the Will (in English) of William Hyllar, clerk, of the parish of St. Mary Magdalene Hereford.—Leaves his body to be buried before the altar of our Lady in the church of St. Mary Magd.; to the works of the Cathedral, xx*d.*; to the parish altar of St. Mary Magd. a vestment of red purple velvet with the alb and apparels belonging to the same, a corporas with a case, two altar cloths, two cushions with silk, two panes, one of the image of Jesus and the other of the burying of Christ, and xx*d.* in ready money to help to fetch home a vestment that lieth in gage with Mr. Meye for iiii*s.*, the which vestment pertains to the said parish; to the church works of All Saints, xx*d.*, and of St. Peter's xx*d.*; to the parish of St. John Bapt. xii*d.*; to the vicars of the quire to be a brother with them, iii*s.* iiii*d.*; to the church of Davyswalle a corporas with a case, "a fyne shethe for the sepulture" (a burial pall?), a vestment of tawny velvet with the alb and apparels; to Thomas Philips a portuas and a mass book, and xiii*s.* iiii*d.* to pray for his soul and all Christian souls; to Sir Will. Scryven a portuas; to Sir Rob. Preston a black box much like unto a coffer; to Harry Loryman ii angels in gold and vi silver spoons, upon condition of giving xxx*s.* towards his funerals on the day of his burial; to Eliz. wife of the said Harry ii angels in gold, a painted cloth with the image of St. Francis and three panes of the Passion of Christ; [money to various individuals, a frise gown, a best frise gown "of mantyll fryse," the hangings with the tester about his bed, a short frise gown, a black short gown faced with russell worsted, to a poor child a coat lined with blue buckram, an old gown with white lining, an old frock]; to the prison house within the "Palys" to remain to the prisoners there to lie upon, a flock bed, a bolster, a pair of blankets, a coarse pair of sheets, and a coverlet; to poor people, where most need is, on the day of his burial in bread xx*s.*, and all his goods to be sold and similarly distributed. A list follows of debts due to him, including 6*s.* 8*d.* from Archdeacon Sparcheford and 55*s.* from Dr. Baskervyle (being 30*s.* for six ounces of silver at 5*s.* the ounce, 20*s.* of old debts, and 5*s.* for an angel he had of him, and for which he gave a broken French crown*), as well as other sums from others for which he has a pall, a girdle, and silver spoons in gage. "Also I have certen small pieces of silke and suche other stuff that did perteyne to vestments and churche stuff, the whiche I will that it shall be geven to the churche agayne to helpe to mende where nede ys." Proved 1 April, 1558.†

1558, Apr. 17, 1 Eliz.—The company of Smiths and Cutlers petition the three inquests of the city against certain persons who forestal and regrate the sea-coals that come to the city, to their utter undoing, and desire that no man be allowed to buy coals in the market until the smiths and cutlers are first served. The petition is granted, with the stipulation that 12 o'cl. be the hour allowed.

1560-1.—Printed copies of five proclamations issued by Q. Elizabeth respecting the coinage, one dated 2 Nov. 1560, the second year, one 19 Feb. in the third year, one 23 Dec. and two without date, of which the second is imperfect. The proclamations are printed by Jugge and Cawood. A MS. copy of a proclamation issued by the Council of the Marches against those who refuse to take the teston, dated 21 Nov. *an.* 3 is attached.

---

* The bond given by Baskervyle for this debt, signed by him and dated 10 March 4 & 5 Ph. & Mar. [1558], is in a parcel of bonds filed in 5-8 Eliz., 1563-5.

† This will is printed, with some mistakes, in Rich. Johnson's *Ancient Customs of the City of Hereford*, second edit. 1882, pp. 86-88.

1561, 31 March. At Ludlow Castle.—Letter from the Council of the Marches to the Mayor and Steward of the City, forwarding a bill of complaint on the part of one Thomas Handbache of Hereford against Thomas Cubley in a money dispute arising out of an unsuccessful attempt on their part to recover as concealed chantry-lands some small property in Marden formerly belonging to the chantry of the B. Trinity in Marden church. The pleadings in the case are subjoined.

1565, Oct. 22.—It is ordered that the brethren and council of the city, being 31 in number, shall attend upon the Mayor when he goes to the Cathedral or elsewhere to hear any sermon, or to receive the Justices of Assize or any honourable person, or to the burial of any honourable person or one of the brethren or council, or to do any other thing for the worship of the city, under penalty of 2*s*., if there be no lawful excuse for absence. In another copy of the order, in a shorter form (omitting burials &c.), the penalty is fixed at 12*d*., and it is ordered that the brethren shall on such occasions wear their tippets about their necks. It is also ordered that from henceforth that part of the book of Customs which concerns obedience to the Mayor (who represents the Queen's presence) in all things lawful and honest shall be observed, upon pain of incurring the penalties in the said book comprised.

1565, Dec 16. Hereford.—Letter from Thomas Havard to John Scudamore, esq., one of the Council of the Marches, and Steward of the city, complaining of infringements of the ancient and laudable laws and customs of the city which the freemen are bound to observe under pain of perjury, whereby the Common Council are grieved, and the body of the citizens, being the best occupiers are offended, in "that certen lighte promoutours be of Mr. Mayor [William Rawlings] receaved by popular accions to molest the fryse men and Welshe clothiers of the Marches of Wales repayringe with theyr fryses and white Welshe clothe to the seyd cytye ther to be uttred to the inhabitants of the same, wherby, as it is reported, fewe fryse men do of late repayre to the seyd cytye, so that the occupyers of the seyd cytye be driven to geve metinge out of the libertyes," specially to the hindrance of the farmer of the Bouthall who made the best part of his rent from the packs coming to the Bouthall with such cloth. And though these enormities have by divers sage persons been revealed to the Mayor, yet he by ignorance neglects to reform the same. Wherefore the writer appeals to Scudamore as bearing the second office in the city to advertise Mr. Mayor to amend such abuses in time.

—— Dec. 18. At Home Lacy.—Answer by Scudamore to the preceding letter, subscribed "By your owne assured," but not signed. "Havynge receved your gentle lres I perceue that there is some mysgouernment of the citee. I am right sorry to here yt, you beinge the auncyent father of the citie." Will be ready, according to his bounden duty, to wait on Mr. Mayor and him and others when commanded. "And thus I commytt you to God, who send you a mery Christemas, and many."

1566, May 28. London.—Pass signed by Francis Earl of Bedford, lieut. gen. of the frontiers towards the north parts, governour of Berwick, &c. for Thomas Twynborowe, soldier under Capt. Reade, who is licensed to be absent from service in Berwick for six weeks.

Printed in Johnson's *Ancient Customs*, &c., p. 163, where for "far anent Scotland" read "for anempst Scotland."

1566, June 5. Everisley.—Letter from James Baskerville [Steward of the city] to the Mayor, William Rawlyns. It is reported to my lord visc. Hereford that the Mayor has stayed two horses ("hosses") upon the proclamation of one George Mantell. Prays him to let them be sent by the bearer, "for I wold not wyshe you to stay them yf you did knowe howe he his favored with the Quenes majesty and the nobles of this realme; and yf they be contrary to the proclamacion my lord vicount will se them reformed, that there may be no more don in the matter."

1566, June 13. Dewles.—Letter to the same from John Parry, certifying that he has received a sum of forty marks for which one John ap Jevan had been arrested.

1566, Nov. 11, 8 Eliz. Ludlow. The Council of the Marches to the Mayor of Hereford.—Having received intelligence that it hath pleased Almighty God to visit the inhabitants of the city of Hereford with the plague of pestilence, they desire him to make proclamation that none of the said inhabitants repair to the place where the Council are nor to the fair of Ludlow now approaching without special license, under pain of imprisonment, since such resort may tend to great danger of infection to the inhabitants of divers parts, and to fix these letters, or a true copy, in some public place.

A copy of the Mayor's reply follows, intimating that he has made proclamation and has fixed a copy of the letters upon a post standing in the market-place, but that, after conferring with his brethren, he finds that [few]* persons have [lately]* died of all manner of diseases, "so that who so ever dyd gyve unto you any other knowledge is not a just man."

[1566?]—Statement by William Rawlyns, mayor, of his reasons for specially summoning his brethren for their advice respecting wrongful enclosures of common land, with diverting of a water-course, made by Gregory Pryse, esq., John Garmons, gent., and Richard Veale. He is bound by oath to maintain the customs and liberties of the city, and all citizens are bound to help him; but although these offenders have been indicted at the Queen's courts, yet they contemptuously proceed in their wrong-doing, and he of himself cannot reform their enormities; therefore, following the laws of the Book of Custom, he causes his fellow-citizens to be convented before him for their advice and help. In a clerk's hand, with numerous corrections and additions by the mayor himself. W. Rawlins was mayor in 1551–2 and 1565–6; and this paper was found among documents of the latter year.

1566–7.—A list of 36 Acts which passed both Houses of Parliament in the second session begun Sept. 30, 1566, and ended Jan. 2, 1567.

1566[–7], Jan. 9. Westminster. W. Smyth to the Mayor and Burgesses.—After hearty thanks for your gentle token, on my part undeserved, whereas Mr. Grene, one of your burgesses in parliament, has by order of the Privy Council received at my hands some sharp words, and after received again in parliament, for coming to parliament when the plague is in Hereford, and commandment had been given him to remain at home, yet as he hath in the election, for anything I can understand, behaved himself honestly, orderly, and like a good burgess, I have moved their lordships that he might have such ordinary

* Blanks are left for the number and the time.

allowances as are made in semblable cases, which their lordships have thought fit to allow. I therefore signify this to you, praying you to have consideration hereof.

1566–[7], 28 Feb. At Ludlow.—Letter from the Council of the Marches to the Mayor, enjoining that the Queen's late Proclamation for the reformation of the unreasonable excess of apparel ("whiche having of late yeres dailie encreased is nowe in thende growen to such extreme disorder as in no wise is any longer to be suffered") be not only observed in their own families, but also at Sessions and other assemblies be put in execution with all earnestness and severity, without any particular respect or partiality. And of their doings and proceeding herein they are to certify the Council before the last day of March next ensuing at the farthest.

1567, Aug. 9, 9 Eliz.—John Barkeley, mayor, with the advice of his brethren, removes Sir Giles Snell, who had been lately appointed Chaplain of St. Giles, from his office, because he hath of long time neglected to do divine service in the chapel, and appoints Sir John Rawelyns, clerk, to be chaplain in his place. (This is copied in the *Black Book* at f. 203. Rawlins died in 1568, and Sir Robert Lovard was appointed chaplain on Apr. 15; *ib.* f. 215. Lovatt (*sic*) surrendered the chaplaincy July 12, 1569, when Sir Richard Mason was appointed (*ib.* f. 229), who in his turn surrendered it July 31, 1583, and was succeeded by Sir Luke Prosser; *ib.* f. 404.)

1569.—A long examination of one Rich. Taber, a shoemaker of Trowbridge, suspected as a thief, is entered in the Court Book, to which is attached a certificate signed by John Plumple, parson of Trowbridge, that the said Richard was licensed to depart from his master's service and had liberty to serve elsewhere, according to the Statute in that case made.

1570, Sept. 26. Presteign. Edward Holland to Matthew Geffrey, Mayor of Hereford. — Where[as] the bearer my friend happened, as I am given to understand, to break a man's head, being thereunto provoked against his will, I shall heartily desire your lawful favour towards him, as if a Glamorganshire man should chance to hurt one of my neighbours.

1571, July 25. — The Privy Council to the Council of the Marches, enjoining that on 20 Aug., 12 Sept., and 12 Oct. ensuing, from 7 o'cl. at night until 3 the next afternoon, strict watch be kept in the whole shire, for the apprehension of all rogues, vagabonds, and sturdy beggars, who are to be punished by stocking and sharp and severe whipping. *Copy*.

Aug. 7.—The Council of the Marches to the Mayor of Hereford, enclosing the preceding.

1577.—A pass from the Lord Chancellor of Ireland. "By the Lord Chauncellor of her Highnesse realme of Irelande. Whereas John Asheton my servaunte ys presentlye to departe this realme into England uppon earneste and necessary affayers in furtheraunce of her Maj. service, These are therefore to will and straightly to chardge you and every of you quietlie to permitt and suffer hyme to passe and repasse without any your letts molestacions or any other impediment as you and either of you will answere to the contrary uppon your extreme perill. Dated at my howse at Dublin, the xxv[th] of Marche, a° 1577, a° Reg. nostre Eliz. xix. Will. Gerard, Cancell.

To all Mayors, Shyrriffes." [etc.]

On a day in March of this year which is not stated, a lengthy order was made by the Mayor and Common Council, to which twenty-six signatures are attached, respecting the payment by all the members of their shares of the expense of city banquets, in consequence of the Chamberlain's being "dryven to demaunde allowaunce of a certeyne chardge by them disbursed and leyde out towards a banckett in eatinge of venyson." It is therefore ordered "that at all and every solempne assemblie and meetinge of the Comen Councell or ellection of the said citie uppon sommons to eate venyson or otherwise to banquet and make mery as there have beene accustomed and used to doe," every member, present or absent, shall pay his share, unless some good excuse be given.

Regulations made by the Mayor, Gregory Prise, for the city and markets, fill a small paper roll.

A fragmentary paper contains notes of an estimate for powder and shot, and for the expenses of ten days' training of the trained bands. "Twentie bulletts for the calyver of the Tower is just a pounde weight, and one pounde of powder will make xxv[tie] (*sic*) shott allowinge [a] quarters weight of powder to every bullett, and the over[pl]us after that rate is v shott more, which is for touch powder. [So] that in the whole xx[tie] bulletts are to be made of the pownde, and xxx[tie] shott to the pownde of powder, whereof v allowed for touch powder. For xvi persons after viii[d] the day for x dayes, £v vi*s*. viii*d*. For x dayes for powder after xvi[d] the pounde for xvi persones, £iii. vi*s*. viii*d*. For bulletts, xxix*s*. viii*d*. ob. Towards the trayning about xx*s*."

1578, 18 Eliz. — Printed Act of Parliament [in a folio book of 18 leaves] for the levy of two fifteenths and one tenth and one subsidy, granted by the temporalty. With this is the assessment of the city for the purpose, and writs and letters thereupon. All these are much injured by damp.

(1578.)—In the accounts of the Mayor (Richard Bromwiche) for this year, in a very long list of "fines transgressionum," occurs the entry of a fine of 4*l*. imposed on John Baskervile, gent., Walter Baskervile, gent., Simon Dansey, gent., and Henry Watkin, "pro quadam riotta et aliis malefactis et offensis commissis 1 et 2 Oct. anno xx apud civitatem prædictam." xxvii*s*. viii*d*. were paid "diversis lusoribus in enterludiis diversis generosis."

1578[-9], Jan.—John Halle complains grievously to the mayor and his brethren "that one Rychard, servant to Thomas Bere, dyd under pretence and cowler of frindschyppe abbusse hymselffe to me longe tyme before I cowld perceve hytt, as in glasse wyndowes spiyng, waulle herkenyng, evys droppyng, and standyng in corners in my howsse behynd dors, to sherche for to cari the secrettes of me and my frindes, to my great hyndrance."

1580, Oct. 12, 20 Eliz.—Bond in 200*l*. from a sergeant-at-mace on his admission to office. Among the rolls of court is a familiar letter from Walter Caradyne [*al.* Carwardine] to his brother-in-law George Harryes, dated at London, Nov. 20, 1580.

1582, 24 Eliz.—A short vellum roll contains a list of annual subscriptions promised for the relief of one who had been mayor twenty-four years before. It is headed, "The benevolence and goodwill geaven unto Mr. Richard Partriche, gent., sometimes maior of the city of Hereford by the maior, his bretherne, and other good-disposed people towardes his relief and findinge, agreed and concluded uppon xx° die Junii . . . . to be paid quarterlie . . . . and in respect thereof he surrendreth and yeldeth up his rome of aldermanship." Twenty-nine persons promise sums varying from 2*s.* (in 21 instances) to 10*s.* (Gregory Price, esq.). Twenty-four names follow to which no sums are attached.

1582, Oct., 24 Eliz.—A petition is presented for a second time by John Garnons and Symon Wolffe (supported by others) to the Mayor and Corporation praying that John Eliote, gent., and Richard Davies, fishmonger, may be disfranchised and removed out of the Common Council as being not favourers, obeyers, and followers of the Gospel or of the Queen's laws and proceedings, nor good preservators of the commonwealth, nor men worthy of their worships' society, but rather slanderers of the same. They refuse to come to church to hear the divine service there set forth by public authority, and have been at divers times indicted for the same, and have been excommunicated by the Bishop. Sir Henry Sidney, knt., Lord President of the Council of the Marches, has most painfully, charitably and learnedly used all godly means to reconcile them, but all in vain. Sir James Croft, the high steward, did most godly and honourably advise herein not long ago; and if the said Eliote and Davies and all such other disobedient persons having any place or voice in the Council be not expelled, the petitioners' further suits will be to the Lords of the Privy Council. See *infra*, under 1585–6.

1583[–4], Feb. 4. At the Court.—Letter from Sir "Jamys" Croft, [Steward of the city] to the Mayor and Aldermen. Has received their letter of 19 Jan. respecting a *quo warranto* brought against the city; will not fail to confer with the Queen's Attorney, of whose lawful favour he has no doubt. And if they will send him by the bearer the draught of their book concerning larger liberties, he will not fail to further it as time may serve.

1584, Apr. 6. Westminster.—Warrant from the Privy Council authorizing John Walley, of the county of Chester, gent., to make collections on behalf of the town of Nantwich, where by misadventure on 10 Dec. last 800 houses were burned, with most part of the goods of the inhabitants, whereby the town has become waste and desolate; to the relief of which poor afflicted inhabitants her Majesty has herself contributed to a good value.* *Copy.*

1584, June 17. At our Castle of Ludlow. The Council of the Marches in the name of the Queen to the Mayor and Justices of Hereford.—Our Council in the Marches are informed that there are sundry outrages, unlawful assemblies, banding of people with sundry kinds of weapons, as swords, bucklers, morris pikes, dags, privy coats, and other munition and armour daily walking up and down the cities and towns in the county, "facing and brasing" our quiet subjects, and specially in the city of Hereford many assaults, affrays and tumults have been committed, and no punishment hath ensued; you are therefore to repair to

---

* Hereford appears to have contributed 58*s.* 4*d.*; *cf.* Johnson's *Ancient Customs, &c.*, p. 148.

HEREFORD MSS.

the city on all market days, fair days [etc.], and to bind over all persons found culpable to appear before the said Council.

1585, March 25, 27 Eliz. At our Castle of Ludlow.—The Council of the Marches to the Mayor of Hereford, ordering him to proclaim Richard Parker, Richard Bryan, Richard Partridge the younger, and Jenkin Scandrett as rebels, and to search for them and apprehend them as rebels, and bring them before the Council on 22 Apr. to answer to such matters as shall be objected against them by John Price.

——, Apr. 12, 27 Eliz. Westm.—Writ to the Bishop, Mayor, and others, ordering the levy of the first payment of a subsidy granted by a recent Act of Parliament, a copy of which Act is transmitted herewith. Seal lost. (In box with the royal Charters.)

——, June 20. At Greenwich.—Copy of a letter from the Privy Council to the Council of the Marches, ordering the suppression, in accordance with the Queen's Proclamation, of traitorous and slanderous books and libels, especially of one against the Earl of Leicester, [viz. Parsons' *Leicester's Commonwealth*].

"After our verie hartie comendacons. Upon intelligence given to her majestie in October last paste of certaine seditious and traiterous bookes and libelles covertlye spredd and scattered abrode in sondrie partes of her realmes and dominions, yt pleased hir highnes to publishe proclamations througheout the realme for the suppressing of the same, and due punishment of the aucthors, spredders abrode, and deteignors of them, in suche sorte and forme as in the said Proclamacion is more at large conteigned. Sithens which tyme notwithstanding her highnes hathe certenlye knowen that the very same and divers other suche like most sclaunderous shamefull and divelishe bookes and libells have byn contynuallye spread abrode and kepte by disobedient persones, to the manifest contempte of her majesties regall and soveraigne aucthoritie; And namelye amounge the rest one most infamous, conteigning hatefull and sclaunderous matter against our verye good lorde the Earle of Leycester, one of her principall noble men and chieffe counsailors of estate, of whiche moste mallicious and wicked imputacions her majestie in her owne cleer knowledge dothe declare and testifye his innocencye to all the worlde, and to that effecte hathe written her gratious lettres signed with her owne hande to the lorde maior sheriffes and aldermen of London, where it was likelye thes bookes wolde be chiffelye caste abrode: Wee therffore, to followe the course taken by her majestie, and knowing manifestly the wickednes and falshood of thes sclaunderous devises against the said Earle, have thoughte good to notifye her pleasure and our owne consciences to you in this case. Firste, that as in trothe her majestie hathe noted greate necligens and remisnes in the former execucion of her comaundement, forasmuch as the said sedicious libelles have byn suffred since that tyme to be disperced and spilled abrode, and keapte by contemptuous persones without severe and due ponishment inflicted for the same, soe nowe upon the seconde chardge and admonicion given unto yow, shee verely loketh for the moste strickte and precise observacion therof in the sharpest maner that may be devised, testifying in her conscience before God unto yow that her highnes not onlye knowethe in assured certentye the libelles and bookes against the said Earle to be moste mallicious, faulse and sclaunderous, and suche as non but the Devell himselffe colde deeme to be trewe, but alsoe thinkethe the same have proceded of the fullness of mallice, subtilli contryved to the note and discredit of her princely goverment over this realme, as thoughe her majestie shold have failed in good judgment and discrecion in the choise of soe principall a counsailor about her, or be without taste or care of all justice and consciens in suffring suche heynous and monstrous crymes as by the said libelles and bookes he infamouslye imputed to passe unponished, or finallye at the leaste to wante either good will habillitye or curraige, yf shee knewe thes enormityes were trewe, to calle enye subjecte of hers whatsoe ever to render sharpe accompte for them, according to the force and effecte of her lawes. Alle which deffectes (God be thanked) wee and all good subjects to our unspeakeable comfortes doe knowe and have fownde to be far from the nature and vertue of her moste exelent majestie. And of the other side bothe her highnes of her certen knowledge, and wee, to doe his Lordshipp but righte, of our sincere consciences must nedes affirme, thes straunge and abhomniall (*sic*) crimes to be raised of a wicked and venomous mallyce against the said Earle, of whose good service, sinceritye of religion, and all other faithefull dealinges towardes her majestie and the realme wee have had longe and trewe experiens. Whiche thinges considered, and withall knowing it an usuall trade of trayterous myndés, when they wolde render the prince's goverment odyous, to detracte and bring out of credit the principall persones about them, Her highnes, taking the abuse to be offred unto her owneselffe, hathe comaunded us to notifye the same unto yow, to the ende that knowing her good pleasure yow maye procede therin as in a matter highely touching her owne estate and honor. And therfore wee wishe and requier yow to have regarde therof accordingly, that the former negligens and remissenes shewed in the execucion of her majesties comaundement maye be amended by the dilligens and severitie that shalbe hereafter used, which amendement and carefullnes in this cause cheffely her highnes assuredly lokethe for, and will call for accompte at your handes. And soe wee byd yow hartelie Farewell. From the Corte at Grenewich the xx[th] of June, 1585.

Your verey lovinge frendes,

Tho. Bromely, canc.	W. Burghley.	G. Shrewsburie.
Hen. Darbie.	J. Bedforde.	C. Howarde.
H. Hunsdon.	F. Knollys.	H. Sydney.
C. Hatton.	F. Walsingham.	Wa. Myldemay.

To our verey good L. the Lorde President, and in his absence, To our verey lovinge frendes Sir George Bromeley, knight, and the rest of the Counsaill established in the Marches of Wales. T. Sherer."

This is printed at pp. 170–172 of R. Johnson's *Customs of Hereford*, but with very many mistakes.

1585, July 5.—Memorandum (signed by Edw. Threlkeld) that when Thomas Davies, Mayor, and Edward Threlkeld, doctor of the law and J.P., went to the house where William Luston, clerk, lately died, "to view a force," they were violently thrust out by James Parry, esq., and others, armed with daggers and a hatchet.

[1585.]—Articles exhibited against Thomas Wilkoxe. i. He is indicted for felony before the Mayor of Hereford. ii. He is excommunicated, and disquieteth the parish in the time of divine service. iii. He is a horrible usurer, taking 1*d*. and sometimes 2*d*. for a shilling by the week. iv. He has been cursed by his own father and mother. v. For the space of two years he hath not received the Holy Communion, but every Sunday when the priest is ready to go to the Communion, then

HEREFORD MSS.

he departeth the church for the receiving of his weekly usury, and doth not tarry the end of divine service thrice in the year. vi. He is a common breaker of his neighbours hedges and pales in the night time. vii. On Sundays and other holy days when his neighbours are at church, and likewise when they are in bed, he useth to keep his cow and horse in their corn fields and pastures. viii. He hath most beastly, filthily and lewdly abused the common well from which his poor neighbours drew all their water. ix. He bribed one of the serjeants at mace in Hereford on 20 Oct. last, 1584, [with several other charges].

The files of this year are stitched to a fragment of a fourteenth-century breviary, with musical notes to the responds. See under 1615–6.

1585–6.—In the files of this year (a large parcel) several papers call for notice.

Gregory Prise, esq., brings an action as holding the rectory of St. Peter's, Hereford, against William Hosier, the vicar, for payment of a customary annual pension of *5l.*

A case of seizure of a number of Roman Catholic books deserves transcription at length :—

"*Jhesus.** Johannes Eliott, generosus, queritur versus Philippum Hall in placito transgressionis. Et unde idem Johannes per Georgium Penry, attorn. suum, queritur quod prædictus Philippus xxviii die Marcii anno regni dominæ Reginæ nunc vicesimo octavo, vi et armis bona et catalla (videlicet, unum librum intitulatum ***Alphonsus de Castro,*** unum alium librum intitulatum ***Opus aureum, per Magistrum Antonium*** [ ], unum alium librum intitulatum ***Confutatio cavillationum*** [per Steph. Gardiner, Episc. Winton] unum alium librum intitulatum ***Textus sacramentorum*** [cum commento] ***Magistri Johannis C[h]aneysii*** [Lugd. 1505], duos libros intitulatos ***Titulmanni*** [Tilemanni Smelingi], ***Segebergensis de Septem sacramentis*** [Col. Agr. 1538, *etc.*], unum alium librum intitulatum ***Exegesis*** [Evangelicæ veritatis] ***autore Johanne Adevantrea*** [*i.e.* a Daventria, Colon. 1537], unum alium librum intitulatum ***Defentio regiæ assertionis contra Babilonicam Captivitatem*** [Jo. Fisher, Episc. Roff., 1525], unum alium librum intitulatum ***Johannes Capnion*** [*i.e.* Joh. Reuchlinus], unum alium librum intitulatum ***Demonstrationum Religionis Christianæ ex verbo Dei*** [libri tres] ***per Franciscum Sonnium*** [1557 et 1563], unum alium librum intitulatum ***De originis peccato disceptatio per Theodorum Beltarum*** (*i.e.* Peltanum, Colon. 1576], unum alium librum intitulatum ***Johannes Garretius de universali ecclesia*** [ ], unum alium librum intitulatum ***Theologiæ misticæ Henrici Herphii*** [Harphii libri tres, 1538, *etc.*], unum alium librum intitulatum ***Johannes Hessells Probatio*** [Corporalis præsentiæ in Eucharistia, Lovan., 1564], unum alium librum intitulatum ***Diacosio Martirion Johannes Whytte*** [Episcopi Wintoniensis, Lond. 1553], unum alium librum intitulatum ***Petri Lizecii Alverni Montigenæ adversum pseudo-Evangelist heresin*** [Par. 1551,] unum alium librum intitulatum ***Hierarchiæ ecclesiasticæ assertio per Albertum Pighium*** [Col. Agr. 1572], unum alium librum intitulatum ***Brevis et Catholica symboli Appostolici explicatis, autore Johanne Hessells*** [Lovan. 1562], unum alium librum intitulatum ***Loci communes Johannis Caspari*** [Rutlandi, Colon. 1560, etc.], unum alium librum intitulatum ***Psalterium Davidis in Latina,*** et unum alium librum vocatum ***A paper booke of notes***) precii v*li.* xiii*s.* iiii*d.*, ipsius Johannis Elyote hic apud civitatem

* This invocation of our Lord heads many of the law papers throughout the century.

Hereford infra jurisdiccionem hujus curiæ inventa cepit et asportavit, et alia enormia intulit, ad grave dampnum ipsius Johannis, et contra pacem dictæ dominæ Reginæ nunc, etc., unde dicit quod deterioratus est et dampnum habet ad valorem x*li*. Et inde producit sectam, etc."

These books doubtless belonged to some priest who was lodged in Elliott's house; and the latter may have been emboldened to bring his complaint from the fact that no missal or breviary was found among them. The names of the panel for the jury follow, and only eight were marked, many doubtless being challenged; then "decem tales" were summoned out of whom two were taken; and the list is endorsed, "xxi die Junii, ad ix^am^. Dicunt pro querente, et ass. dampnum prædicti querentis ad v*li*., et pro misis et custagiis suis, vii*s*. Ideo judicium, xiii. Julii."

The Mayor, William Maylard, issues in this year a "proclamation" straitly charging all manner of persons, of what estate, degree, condition and calling soever, that they keep the Queen's peace, and by advice of the judges of assize commands that all men coming to the city shall not bear or wear any armour or weapon in the streets to the terror or fear of any of her Majesty's subjects, or bring any unlawful weapons as long forest-bills, main-pikes, and such other, within the gates, but shall leave the same at some convenient place without the gates, except the Sheriff and the justices of the peace and their servants, and others travelling through the said city upon their lawful business; and also that none seek, stir, or pick, any quarrel against any person or persons, but lawfully demean themselves, upon pain of fine and imprisonment; and that none receive and take into their houses in any secret or undecent order any unlawful weapon or weapons. And the mayor openly publishes that if any, of what state, degree or condition soever, offend or are found culpable in any respect, they shall be presently committed to gaol until they enter into sufficient bonds to appear before the Council of the Marches.

John Hampton sues Hugh Morris for 18*s*. due out of 33*s*. 4*d*. for glazing the windows of Old Radnor Church, according to an agreement made 20 Sept., 14 Eliz. (1572); to which the said Hugh replies that the case had been already heard before the Council of the Marches on 7 June, 22 Eliz. (1580) and dismissed.

William Davies sues John Catchemaie for 8*s*., the price of "unum bumbardum, Anglice vocatum *a callyver*," which it appears was supplied to the Bishop, and which the defendant was to pay for out of money which he owed to the latter.

A letter from the Council of the Marches, dated at Ludlow, 24 Nov. 1585, and signed by Charles Foxe, H. (?) Touneshend, and The. Atkyns, requests the postponement of a case of debt for four silver spoons against Edmond Scrope, one of the clerks in attendance upon the Council, because he is unable to appear at short notice.

The weavers of the city present a petition representing their distressed condition, partly due to the admission of strangers, and of persons not duly apprenticed, whereby they are like to fall into utter ruin.

An instance of a double Christian name occurs in the case of one Thomas William Parry.

1586, Nov. 8, 28 Eliz. Ludlow Castle.—Order from the Council of the Marches to the Mayor that, whereas letters have been received from the Earl of Pembroke, Lord President of the Council, that divers persons naming themselves Jesuits and Seminaries, or rather to be called Massing priests, have of late under colour of that their feigned religion become most wicked traitors to the State, and most hurtful poison to [the Queen's] true and loving subjects, as not long sithence hath manifestly appeared unto the world by the writing and inventing of divers treasons, and whereas also they are given to understand that divers evil-disposed persons, not contented with this quiet state of government, for the disquiet thereof, the dishonour and danger to [the Queen's] person, the slander to the Privy Council and others in principal place of service, have and do daily spread abroad false tales and rumours, he is to cause diligent search and enquiry to be made for all such offenders, and them to apprehend, and to bring forthwith before the Council of the Marches, and the Privy Council to receive advertisement thereof; and he is to put this service in execution from time to time by all good means and policy, with secrecy.

1587.—In May the freemen and guild-merchants present a petition to the Inquests of the wards (to which the Inquests agree) that whereas no porter of any gate, by ancient custom of the city time out of mind, should presume to arrest any freeman or guild merchant unless he had previously disobeyed some summons, "notwithstandinge this good, lawdable and auncient custom heretofore used, the porters now adaies do not only procure fees of men, but lieth in bulks and holes to snatche and arest them, not only the worst but those that are of credyte, as thoughe theye were the fugitives persons that might bee, which is moste detestable, and clene contrary to the owld and auncient custome of this citie"; wherefore they pray that the old customs may be renewed and put in ure.*

——, June 4.—Letter from the Mayor (Luke Garnons) and aldermen of Gloucester to the Mayor &c. of Hereford, enclosing questions to be put to one Thomas Williams, a surgeon, respecting discourse had by him with an intimate friend John Reade, a surgeon at Gloucester, about a marriage proposed for Reade, whose first wife died at Bath at Whitsuntide last, "not by the visitation of God, as it is thought, but rather by his devilish practise."

——, Aug. 28, 29 Eliz. Ludlow Castle.—Order from the Council of the Marches to the Mayor that, whereas they have received letters from the Privy Council "purporting aswell the greate plentie of corne and grayne which yt hathe pleased God to blesse this our realme withall this present yeare, as alsoe the necessarie relief of the poore after soe harde tymes paste," he is therefore to have vigilant eye and due care and regard to the sizes of bread, ale and beer, and to see the same proportioned according to the statute, whereby the poorer sort may be the better relieved.

1587, Sept. 6, 29 Eliz. Ludlow Castle.—Order from the Council of the Marches to the Mayor, that whereas proclamations have been lately made for the preservation of hares, pheasants, partridges, and other wild fowl, and for the preventing of the spoil and destruction thereof with guns and other engines, and keeping of greyhounds, and nevertheless there is daily unlawful spoil and destruction of the said games by some evil-disposed persons, he is from time to time to call suspected persons

* This is printed, with some mistakes, in Johnson's *Ancient Customs of Hereford*, p. 108.

before him, and them to swear and examine, and to bind over such as he shall find faulty to appear before the Council.

——.—Roger Squyre petitions for the place of musician and head wait of the city, void by the death of William Jackson. He has "from his youthe byn broughte up in musycke, and dothe presently keepe and meynteyne servaunts in the arte of musycke to play on divers instrumentes," and if admitted "he trusteth that in shorte tyme he will attayne to suche knowledge in the instrumentes of shalmes and lowde noyce as shalbe to your good lykinge and contentacion."

1588, Feb. 14, 30 Eliz. At Hereford.—Order from the Council of the Marches to the Mayor, that, whereas none are suffered to sell within the city any flesh killed, or bread baked, out of the city, nor any candles unless they be free within the city, which may breed great scarcity there during the time the President and Council make their abode there, by reason of the great assembly of people resorting to the Council, he shall therefore make proclamation that it shall be lawful during that time for all persons, of what country or place whatsoever, to resort thither on Wednesdays and Saturdays with any kind of wholesome victuals, as flesh, fish, bread, and candles, with hide and tallow therewith, to be sold, free of molestation.

—— Feb. 23.—Order from the same to the same that, whereas by some evil and lewd persons the preceding order has been misconstrued, and speeches given out that liberty was given to the citizens and others to eat flesh in Lent time, which was not the meaning of the Council, but that the Lent and all other days prohibited from flesh should be strictly kept, he is to proclaim that all persons shall abstain according to the laws, and that all persons found faulty shall be sent for to answer the same.

——, May 21. Westminster.—Letter, signed by W. Burghley, Wa. Mildmaye, and Roger Manwood, to the Mayor, desiring him to send, before the feast of St. John Bapt. next ensuing, some sufficient person to the Exchequer, to receive, according to the Queen's proclamation of Dec. 12 last, the standard weights provided by the Court of Exchequer, viz., a pile or case and box of Troy weights, and a suit of great weights and a pile of small weights of Avoir de poiz, provided as good cheap as could be had, and rated according to their true valuation at 9*l*. 8*s*. 11*d*., viz., the Troy weights at 3*l*. 8*s*. 1*d*. and the Avoir de poiz at 6*l*. 0*s*. 10*d*.

[1588], June 29. Bewdley. Charles Booth to the Mayor, Paul Philpots.—Desires his immediate resolution about the purchase of the Katherines; Mr. Harford's demand was forty marks, but it may be had for twenty; Harford is about to be delivered out of ward, and perhaps it will be dearer then than now. Twenty loads of hay must be laid in, and wood, for "my lord and ladie bothe meane to remaine with you all the winter, soe that provision must be made accordingly."

1594, July 11, 36 Eliz. Westm.—Writ to the Bishop, Mayor, and others, ordering the levy of the second of three subsidies granted by a recent Act of Parliament, of which Act a copy is sent herewith. Fragment of seal in white wax. (In box with the royal charters.)

1596.—On the application of William Wellington, a tower of the city wall in the back lane behind St. Owen's gate is granted to him at an annual rent of 6*d*. on condition of keeping it in repair.

The toll-accounts of the Keepers of Widmarsh gate are found in this year, and again in 1603, and in a few other years; but are wanting in many.

Petition from the Clerk of St. Peter's Church asking for increase of wages for ringing the bell called the Commons bell from the feast of All Saints to the feast of the Annunciation, from 8 to 9 at night, for which he is paid 11*s*. 8*d*. (viz., 2*s*. by the Mayor, 4*s*. 8*d*. by the Chamberlains, and 5*s*. out of Widmarsh money), which is a very small wage, for when this was granted every thing was more plenty and better cheap than it is now, and he has to pay three halfpence every night for the ringing, and to repair the baldrick. The second inquest agrees to allow him 5*s*. more, but the third inquest refuses.

1597, Aug. 13. Plymouth.—The Earl of Essex to the Mayor, Aldermen, &c., desiring to have the nomination of burgesses for Parliament. "After my verie hartie commendacions. Being heere at Plymmouth expecting a good winde, I am advertised that her Majestie is resolved presentlie to call a Parliament: which geveth me occasion before my departure to intreat this curtesie of you, that you will be contented to graunt me the nominating of your burgesses, nothing doubting but I shall be returned from the present expedecion for her Majesties service in tyme convenient for this nominacion, which if you doe leave unto me assure yourselves I will be carefull to preferr unto this verie woorthie and sufficient men. I pray you send your aunswer of this my letter to the Court, to my secretarie Edward Reynolds, whome I have appointed to receave the same against my returne, that I may therbie understand your resolucion. I will take your readines to satisfie this my request in verie thankefull part, and deserve it upon all good occasions. So I committ yow to Gods protection. From Plymmouth the 13 of August 1597.

Your verye assured frend

ESSEX."

Only the signature is autograph.

1600. On 12 and 15 Oct. the Welsh servant of a tailor and William Cowper, a stationer and book-binder, are examined very strictly about "a popishe ballett" (unfortunately no further described) which the former found, sealed, one morning upon opening his master's stall, and took to the latter to read for him, who kept it in his pocket.

1600. Memorial from Thomas Kerry to the Mayor, Aldermen, and the three Inquests, for the letting of some land whereon to build some addition to his almshouses.—"Whereas Thomas Kery, of London, esquier, being borne in this cytie, hath of late for the benefite of the poore thereof erected an hospitall for three men and xii women to contynue for ever, praieth to have the fee ferme of the garden or voide grounde betwene Byster's gate and Saint Owen's gate, and also of the garden by Eigne gate now in the tenure of John Gery, to be to hym graunted at doble the rent is nowe paide for the same, and upon reasonable covenants therein to be conteyned, to thende he maie theron make some necessarie buylding for the ease and commoditie of the said poore, who will daily praie for your worships and the rest of this cytie, wherein you shall further this good work alredie begon." Subscribed with the consent of the inquests in this form—

"The . . . Inqueste dothe spare this bille"

1601[-2], March 13. At Dublin.—Pass signed by Sir Christopher St. Laurence, knt., capt. of 150 footmen in Ireland, addressed to all mayors, sheriffs, &c. for Francis Voughan, a soldier discharged by reason of grievous hurts and wounds, desiring that he may be assisted to lodging and relieved in his necessities. Subscribed with a certificate by Will Vawere, mayor of Bristol, that he landed there on 21 March, and was allowed to pass to Welshpool.

temp. Eliz. Not dated.—Letter from "Blancsh" Parry [a maid of honour to Q. Eliz.] to the Mayor and Aldermen, thanking them for their courtesy and goodwill, "beseechinge yowe to doe my comendacions to all your wyves, wishinge yowe and them with mee to take parte of your one gift."

1604, Dec.—William Goulston brings an action against James Berrowe, gent., for breach of covenant, alleging that the latter engaged him to attend from 1 Sept. to Michaelmas Day in the house of John Berrowe, gent., upon the said John and other persons, who were sick "de pestilencia vocata *le Plague*," for the sum of 5*l.*; that he went accordingly and remained the whole time, but has only received 46*s.* 8*d.*, the said James refusing to pay. To this James Berrowe replies that Goulston left at the end of two weeks, accepting 46*s.* 8*d.*, and refusing the 5*l.*, and went to the house of Will. Morgan, of Killpeck, gent.

1608, July 21.—Various persons are examined concerning "a libel" dispersed in the city, but the contents of which are not mentioned; one copy was fixed on Mr. Pembridge's door with wax, and was thence taken, and copied by several persons; another copy had been brought by a butcher two months before, written in a fair hand; a third was picked up in the market-house, which had been thrown down by a Welshman.

1610, May 28, 8 Jas. I.—Bond from Humfrey Walden of Bromsgrove, chirurgion, to John Havard, of Kinnerton, Radnorshire, gent., that in consideration of the sum of 3*l.*, he will by the help of God cure Sibill, wife of Matthew Maddock, of Evengeob, Radnorshire, and Elizabeth Havard, sisters to the said John Havard, of the several diseases wherewith they are grieved, by the feast of the Nativity of St. John Bapt. next ensuing, and that they shall continue whole and perfectly cured until the month of March next; failing which he shall repay the sum of 3*l.*

1612.—The name of a bell-founder at Hereford, Thomas Stone, is met with in this year. He is questioned about the pawning of a silver spoon.

1613.—Jury presentment against Thomas Dansey, late of Brynshoppe, gent., Thomas Smyth, of the same, gent., Robert Smyth, of the same, gent., Leonard Wallwene, late of Hereford, gent., with 24 other malefactors unknown, for assembling in warlike array on 17 April in the city of Hereford, armed with swords, reaping-hooks, sticks, knives, and other weapons offensive and defensive, "riotose, routose, et modo novæ insurrectionis," and attacking one Lewis Burche, a constable, whom "riotose et routose verberaverunt, mutulaverunt sive maihaverunt, vulneraverunt et maletractaverunt, ita quod de vita ejus desperabatur." The cause of the riot does not appear.

There is a similar presentment against four tradesmen, with ten other persons, for like assembling on 22 Apr., and breaking into the house of one Michael Nicholson and there assaulting Katherine Leath.

1615–6.—The Court-book for this year is stitched up in a fragment of a breviary of the 14th century, for the 2nd and 3rd Sundays after Easter and the Rogation days.

1617.—In October the butchers' company petition that the country butchers may not be permitted when they come to market to remain all day in town, but that they may be limited from 8 o'clock to 1, as it is in Worcester and Gloucester, and promise that, whereas they have been asked to contribute towards the renewing of the charter, they will give 10*l.* if this limit be fixed and enrolled in the charter. The freemen also petition against foreigners coming in to inhabit and to set up malt-making and brewing, and desire that no foreigner may be admitted as a freeman but upon allowance of the Council and inquests, and on payment of 10*l.*

1619.—In the month of August, Philip Trehearne, an innkeeper, one of the Common Council, was sent to prison by the Mayor, for revealing the secrets of the Council to outsiders, and for refusing to pay his assessment towards the expense of procuring a renewal of the charter, and encouraging others to do the like, saying that it was but faction and of purpose to serve private men's turns, saying he would appeal to the Privy Council. In October he was again brought up before the Mayor from prison, but still obstinately refused to yield. The conclusion of the case does not appear upon the Files.

1622–3, Feb. 7.—Hugh Nicolls and Rob. Major, chapmen, examined about certain clippings ("crippings") of gold coin, which they had offered for sale to Francis Hyde, a goldsmith, say that they bought the same of Mrs. Ralings in Monmouth, who said she had had them since the time that her husband was sheriff of the county, and they gave her in exchange 1*l.*, and 3 bales of tobacco value 9*s.*

1623–4.—In the Court files:—"Mr. Mayor. I praye you to lett Leonard Stephens depart out of the warde, for he and I have agreed—

But noe moe monie as yet I have
Which you may easie finde.
Therefore I praye you no longer him
Into your book to binde.
And if that Barabas be kepte close
Yet Belzebub's abroade;
And rather than that hee shall lacke
Shall steale yet manie a loade."

1625, Sept. 30.—Philip Millward, baker, is fined 13*s.* 4*d.*, and bound over to appear at the Sessions, for having sent a man privately to the city of London when that city was so grievously infected [with the plague], that no one therein knew himself free from the said infection, and by the return of the said person he might have endangered this whole city and the people therein.

1627[–8], Feb. 26.—A list of the names of those who made choice of Sir John Scudamore, bart., and John Hoskins, esq., serg.-at-law, to be burgesses in Parliament for the city of Hereford, being 38 in number, who attach their own signatures. With the indenture of election.

1628, Oct. 6.—The Mayor's accounts (a parchment roll). The total of receipts is 38*l.* 2*s.*, of which 15*l.* 8*s.* 5*d.* are from fines, and 10*l.* 10*s.*

in payments from the "gildæ mercatorum." The payments appear to largely exceed the receipts, but the total sum is obliterated.

1632.—In the presentments for this year the jury present as the default of James Carwardine, gent., that "a paire of buts usuallie to bee kept in the Greene Lane haue beene carried away, and presented formerlie, and as yet not repaired."

1633.—Frequent presentment is made that the High Cross in the market-place is in decay in default of the chamberlains of the city, and "that the *barlingams* or common washing place is in decay in defaute" of the same.

1635.—In the calendar of the gaol delivery on 9 Apr. there is the following charge of witchcraft.

"Elizabetha Williams de Kenchurch in com. Hereford, vidua, capta apud civitatem Heref. et commissa per majorem, videlicet, pro practizando et exercendo quasdam diabolicas et nequissimas artes detestandas, Anglice, inchauntmentes, charmes and sorceries." She was bailed by Richard Howells of Muchdewchurch, yeomen, and David Phillipps, of Rowlstone, weaver, in 20*l.* each, and herself in 10*l.*, and Francis Smith was bound over in 10*l.* to prosecute. But nothing more is found about the case.

1636–7.—Jonathan Bryden, vicar of St. John the Bapt., and parson of St. Owen's, petitions the mayor and justices on behalf of some poor children for apprenticeships. "Whereas the sayd Jonathan Bryden doth find in the sayd parishes many poore children whose parents are no wayes able to bring them up, and whereas the sayd Jonathan doth believe that he is bound by virtue of his pastorall charge to take care of the poore to his best power, the sayd Jonathan doth humbly intreate your worships, according to a statute in that case provided, to commend these poore children undernamed as apprentices to those whom your worships know to be able men and fitt to take them, and upon there refusall, according to the statute, to command them." The names of thirteen children are subjoined.

The mayor in this year, Thomas Church, has for his seal a church with a steeple, together with his initials.

1642[3], Feb. 22. The Commissioners of Array, Francis Conyngesby, W. Croft, and Wm. Rudhale, to the Mayor of Hereford.—Whereas all persons summoned to bear arms in pursuance of his Majesty's commission of array ought to have free egress and regress without molestation, we are given to understand that one Thomas Watkins, of Bridg-Sollers, summoned to appear before us this day to do such service as he should be enjoined for his Majesty, is by some of your officers attached in an action of debt; these are therefore to require you to set him at liberty forthwith, if he be detained for no other cause.

1644, Dec. 22.—Certificate (on vellum) by Herbert Croft, dean of Hereford, that Richard Ravenhill, senior, of the parish of St. Owen, had been cited as a recusant in 1639, had been excommunicated for non-appearance, and remains excommunicate at this time. In 1676 and in other years before and after that date, Richard Ravenhill, gent., probably the son, occurs amongst those who are presented by the city inquests for non-attendance at church. They were Roman Catholics.

1650–1.—A large parcel of returns by petty constables, &c., of letters respecting charities in the county, and of petitions respecting the same, addressed to the Commissioners for Charitable Uses. The places concerned are the following:—

Marden and Sutton; will of Jane Shelley, 1609.
Maunsel Lacy.
Winterton.
Ross; Rudhall's Hospital; Almshouse; Miscellaneous Charities.
Hereford: Vicker's Charity, Chin's Charity, Price's Hospital, Kerry's Hospital, will of Rich. Bromwich, with bequest to the poor of St. Giles, 1606; Trinity Hospital; Shelley's Hospital, parish of St. Nicholas.

Moccas.
Stanton-upon-Wye.
Erdisland.
Pembridge.
Whitchurch.
Meincell Gamedge [Mansel Gamage].
Bromwich.
Crasswall.
Goodrich.
Llansillo and Rolston.
Ringsland.
Llandinaboe.
Cannon Pyon.
Pipe.
Leominster.
Weston subtus Penyard.
Bishopston.
Kingscaple.
Hentland.
Stretton.
Much Cowarne.
Kynton.
Sellack.
Much Dewchurch.
Brampton Abbots.
Eton Tregos.
Vowchurch.
Wormbridge.
Bodenham.
Brainton.
Shobdon.

Ledbury; Chantry lands of St. Anne, Holy Trinity, and B.V.M., in 1638.
Dewswall.
Grendon Bishop.
Briddenbury.
Putley.
Warton.
Thornbury.
Taddington.
Almeley.
Clifford.
Lanwarn.
Upton Bishop.
Yatton.
Walterston.
Mordiford.
Holmer.
Caldicott.
Dore.
Hope-under-Dinmore.
Eastnor, with a return of all the moneys laid out in 1644–7 from the parish rents.
Bacton and Newton.
Erdisley or Yardisley.
Lugwardine.
Lynton.
Colwall.
Sutton.
No Charities. { Brombury. Kinnersley and Letton.

These are followed by some similar papers in the year 1664, in return to inquiries about charities misemployed, for the following places:—

Bosbury.
Clifford.
Longtown.
Weston. } Nothing to return.
Marstowe. } Nothing to return.
Yarkhill. } Nothing to return.
Woofferlowe.
Crasswall.
Calowe and Turford.
Lanwarne. } Nothing to return.
Madley. } Nothing to return.

Mordiford.
Langaran, nothing to return.
Vawchurch.
Hereford; Trinity Hospital; Shelley's Hospital.
Brainton.
Bullingham. } Nothing to return.
Garway. } Nothing to return.
Bodenham. } Nothing to return.
Moreton-upon-Lugg.

At the end is a list written out some time after 1692 of the sums of money left by various benefactors to the city of Hereford.

1651, Apr. 26. Mintridge. W. Bridges to Thomas Dannett and the rest of the trustees for the parish lands in Bosbury.—I have received your letter of Apr. 23, importing power given to you by the Commissioners for pious uses in the county of Hereford, to demand of me and other the late feoffees intrusted for the free School in Bosbury, all decrees, deeds, and other writings touching the same. I desire first that you will let me see your order and give me a copy, and then that you will appoint some day and place convenient at Bosbury, that I and my fellow-trustees may deliver over to you our trust. (This and the following letter are with the returns of Charities.)

—— Apr. 21. Kington. Mich. Broughton to Thomas Raulins, esq., Thomas Seaborne, gent., and other the commissioners for charitable uses in Herefordshire.—It is presumed by the executors of Charles Vaughan that there is due to them from my uncle Broughton 200*l*., but what part of this supposed debt is given by Charles Vaughan to charitable uses I cannot acquaint you.

1651, Oct. 9.—Printed broadside of the Act for the increase of shipping. Much torn.

1653[-4], Jan. 10.—Petition to the Protector from the High Sheriff, justices, grand jury, mayor, aldermen, etc., praying that divers weirs placed in the rivers Wye and Lugg, whereby floods are caused, may be removed, and the current of the rivers may have free passage.

1654, March 29 and Apr. 3.—Depositions against Mr. Matthew Lock as being a papist. On March 22, he, with one Henry Wall, accompanied one Thomas Walton, who was to be hung for murder, and who was not known to be a papist, to the gallows, speaking to him on the way; and being come to the place they all three kneeled down several times for the space of a quarter of an hour at a time, Walton sometimes reading in a prayerbook and sometimes falling on his face; and shortly after Walton declared that he was a Roman Catholic, and well confirmed in that religion, and desired all his friends that loved him to live and die in that religion, which was the only and best way to heaven. Also, on Mr. Lock's being told that a Jesuit affirmed that it was as good a faith to believe that Toby's dog did wag his tail as to believe that Christ died for sinners, Mr. Lock answered that it was so because one Scripture was to be believed as well as another, or words to that effect.

1655.—In a presentment of one Thomas Swayles for keeping a disorderly ale-house, where tippling and card-playing went on during the Lord's day, the old form of words "at the time of divine service and sermon," which was originally written, is twice altered into "at the time of divine exercise and publique sermon."

1656, Oct. 17.—Will of John Walter, citizen and draper of London, with numerous legacies to parishes in London; proved May 7, 1657. An official copy made in 1706; 14 folio leaves.

1660.—On the Court files of this year is a short series of depositions sworn on 5 June and 12 July against the Puritan minister of Staunton-upon-Wye, Mr. Edmund Quarrell, and his wife, which are well worth transcription in full.

1. "The deposition and information of John Dickes, of the parish of Brobury, in the county of Hereford, sworne and examined before me Walter Wall [justice of the peace in Hereford], 6 June.

This deponent sayth, That about eight yeares since he beinge a servant in the house of one Mr. Quarrell, minister of the parish of Staunton upon Wye . . . he did heare Mary, the then and now wife of the said Mr. Edmond Quarrell, say these words followinge, viz., Kinge Charles is the son of a papist whore, and that he woulde never be in quiet untill he came to the death that his father had, meaning the late Kinge, and that one Philip, a souldier belonginge to the garrison of the castle of Hereford, was then present and in heareinge of the said words. And this deponent sayth that he did acquaint severall persons of the speakeinge of the words aforesaid by the said Mary in manner and forme aforesaid, but durst not question her the said Mary for the said words by reason of the then dangerous tymes and then governement.

2. "Walter Freeme of the parish of Staunton . . . . sworne . . . . This deponent sayth that aboute eight or nyne yeares now past, or there aboutes, he beinge in the house of Mr. Quarrell . . . . . when John Dickes was then a servant to the said Mr. Quarrell, and upon some discourse then which this deponent had with Mary the then and now wife of the said Mr. Quarrell, concerninge the cominge in of the Kinge, she, the said Mary, replyed that if he (meaninge the Kinge that now is) did come in he should be served as his father was (meaninge as the late Kinge was served). And this deponent beinge demanded wherefore he did not discover the words and person that spoke them as aforesaid, he sayth that he durst not by any meanes devulge the same in respect of the then tyme of governement, for feare of his the deponent's life and fortunes.

3. "Richard Meredith of Staunton . . . sworne [&c.].

"This deponent sayth, That in and aboute the latter end of December last past, this deponent was at the house of Mr. Quarrell . . . . . where upon some discourse had betweene the said Mr. Quarrell, Mary his wife, and this examinant, concerninge the Kinge, he, the said Mr. Quarrell did say, as followeth: Alas you poor Cavialiers! you doe thinke to have a Kinge to rule here, but you shall never see it; to which this deponent replyed sayinge, I hope we shall see a Kinge to rule here, otherwise we shall never have any peace in England. Whereupon the said Mr. Quarrell to his wife said, Did I not tell you, Sweethart, what a stronge Cavialer the butcher was? meaninge this deponent.

4. "Edward Baker and Walter Freeme, of Staunton, sworne in Court, doe say that the said Edmond Quarrell did mayntaine half a dragoone for the Parliament for foure yeares or thereabouts.

5. "The examination of the said Edmond Quarrell taken the 6th day of June . . . . .

"The said examinant being examined whether about the time abovementioned or at any other time he did speake any such words as above are specified and layed to his chardge, utterly denyeth that ever hee did speake the same or use or utter any such words concerning his Majestie to the best of his remembrance. But sayeth that the said Richard Meredith hath byn oftentimes in this examinant's house, for that he did usually imploy him in slaughtering of his catell, he being a butcher by trade. EDMOND QUARRELL.

6. "The deposition of Thomas Hunt, of the parishe of Staunton-upon-Wye . . . . before Walter Wall, esq., 12 July.

"This deponent saieth that in and about a yeare agoe this deponent being att church in the parish church of Staunton, where he did heare one Edmond Quarrell, then minister, preaching in his pulpitt, said, That in Hell there is a cassie [causeway] pitched with Kings' sculls. Further, this deponent saieth that hee being in companie att the dwelling howse of Richard Merrickes in the parishe of Staunton with Edmond Quarrell and others, whoe did then heare him saie, as hee was discourseing with Humphery Baker, that the divell did make the booke of Common Prayer; and further deposeth not.

7. "The deposition of Thomas Vaughan [&c.], 12 July.

"This deponent saieth, That in or about seaven yeares agoe hee being in the barne of Mr. Edmond Quarrell's, in the parishe of Staunton, a threashing, did heare Marie, the wyef of the said Edmond Quarrell, speake and utter these words, That itt was not fitting such a bastard to inheirett the land, meaneing the King that now is; and further saieth not.

8. "The deposition of Humphery Baker, gent. [&c.], 12 July.

"This deponent saieth, That in or about a yeare agoe this deponent haveing divers conferences to and with Mr. Edmond Quarrell, minister of Staunton's parishe, concerning the reading of the booke of Common Prayer, that hee the said Edmond Quarrell then replyed and answeared him, this deponent, That it was the divell's worke, and therefore hee would never reade itt; and further saieth not.

9. "The deposition of Anne Clarke, wyef of John Clarke, of the parish of Staunton in the countie of Hereford . . . . This deponent saieth that about seaven yeares last past comeinge from church upon sabboth daie with somme other of the nighbours shee prayed for the Kinge, whereupon somme of them that were there in her companie and heard her pray for the Kinge did, as shee heard, aquainte Oliver Chambers thereof, whereupon the said Oliver did goe to Mr. Quarrell and Mrs. Quarrell, and complained to them that the said Anne Clarke prayed for the Kinge, whereupon the said Mr. Quarrell and Mrs. Quarrell did within a short time after ride to the city of Hereford, and there procured a warrant from the then Governour and Mr. Rawlings, which warrant was directed to the constables of Staunton upon Wye to bring the said Anne Clarke before them forthwith, which the said constable did, and there was in the said warrant the names of Lucy Baker and Susanna Chambers to testify against her, and after her examination before the said Governour and the said Mr. Rawlings, shee confesseing the words before them, that shee prayed for the King, shee was then by them required to procure a freind to engage for her not to offend against the States (*sic*), whereupon Edward Baker, beinge then the constable of Staunton aforesaid, said hee would engage for her to the value of one hundred pounds that shee should not offend in that kinde, whereupon shee, the said deponent, was discharged; and further saith not."

Quarrell is then bound over on his own recognizance in 500*l*., and with two sureties, Matthew Price of Hereford and James Whiting of Dorston, in 100*l*. each, to appear at the sessions when called upon; but the bond is marked at the foot, "Discharged."

HEREFORD MSS.

1660, Mich.—The Mayor's accounts from Mich. 1659 (a parchment roll). The total of receipts is only 22*l.* 14*s.* 4*d.* Besides the ordinary fee of 10*l.* the Mayor "craveth allowance for one besance in the Exchequer, 2*s.*" "For wine and other gifts bestowed uppon strangers comming to the citty uppon the publike service this yeare, 1*l.* For candle light and other extraordinary expences concerning the late troubles, and guifts to the messengers that brought proclamations, 2*l.* 10*s.*" The total of the payments is 55*l.* 19*s.* 9*d.* The entries in the Mayors' accounts for many years from this time forward are only of the most ordinary and routine character.

1661, Nov. 19.—John Giles of the parish of St. John's, Smithfield, London, tailor, being taken as a wanderer and examined, refuses to take the oath of allegiance, saying that he could not swear that the Pope has no power to dispose of his Majesty's kingdoms, or to discharge his subjects from their allegiance, "for that, for ought he knows, the Pope hath power so to do."

1662.—John Cule is presented for keeping a billiard table.

Jane Merrick petitions for relief, who when the Scots besieged the city was wounded by a cannon shot in the leg as she was doing service for the city in making up a breach in Wigmore Street; his late majesty, of ever blessed memory, promised that she should be taken care of. A second petition from her is found in the following year, which is noted with an order that she should have 20*s.* out of Wood's money.

Mary Hodges, a widow, is informed against for keeping a disorderly alehouse, and for frequently railing at and cursing her neighbours, but chiefly as being suspected "to forespeak," or bewitch, cattle, one horse having died suddenly and another being sick which belonged to a person whom she had cursed. This appears by "her usual and frequent manner of witchcraft privately in her house, for at night when her household is gone to bed, and she as is conceived going to bed, she is observed to take the andirons out of the chimney and put them cross one another, and then she falls down upon her knees and useth some prayers of witchcraft, and (with reverence to the court be it spoken) she then makes water in a dish, and throws it upon the said andirons, and then takes her journey into her garden. This is her usual custom night after night, which doth occasion fear that she intends mischief against . . . her neighbours." She is bound over to good behaviour.

1663-4.—Among petitions for relief in these years are several from men who had served the King at the defence of Hereford and elsewhere. And amongst them is one from a brickmaker named Henry Traunter, aged 91, who upon the entry into the city of Charles I. "had a verbal and personal grant" from him of leave to build a small cottage on the waste of the castle, which he accordingly did, but which was afterwards demolished by order of Wroth Rogers, governor of the castle and city, and carried away to the College to repair breaches there. In 1684 there is a petition from one John Evans who served as a foot-soldier in Prince Rupert's regiment and company, and was taken prisoner at Naseby fight, and conveyed with others to London, where he was detained in thraldom of misery for sixteen weeks, being likewise maimed and wounded in the service. Fourpence a week is allowed him.

1665.—In the presentment of the Jury at the sessions on 13 July, there is reference to the Plague then in London. "Seeing the heavy hand of God doth lye uppon the citty of London by visiting them with the plage, which without care may inevitably by the carriers that goe to that place, and passengers with them comeing downe, come into our citty, wee humbly pray that the Maior and Justices of the peace of this citty may take care therein. And for prevention thereof wee pray that any person or persons whatsoever that doe keepe any swyne within this citty may suddainely bee compelled eyther to keepe them up close in the house or to send them out of the citty, upon every default 6*s.* 8*d.* fine. Item, wee pray that the inhabitants of this citty that have pumpes in theire house or backside may bee ordered during the tyme of hott weather to keepe the pumpes goinge for halfe an hower and all at a prefixed tyme, soe that the channells and gutters of the streete may bee cleansed, and our citty preserved from nastiness which may produce infection, and that every inhabitant doe make cleane before theire dores and water it twice in every day. And that all persons within the citty doe within 6 days remove theire miskens out of the streets and back lanes, *sub pena* 6*s.* 8*d.*, and after proclamation made within 24 howers next after proclamation." On the same day orders are made by the Justices that during the hot weather all the inhabitants that have pumps in their houses shall pump for half an hour every day to clean the channels and gutters, and shall make clean before their doors and water twice in every day, with orders also for removal of miskens and keeping of swine; seeing that the heavy hand of God doth lie upon the city of London and other places by visiting them with the plague, which without care may inevitably fall upon this city.

On 7 April nine poor prisoners, "free denizens of this nation," petition the Mayor and justices to allow them a daily portion of bread while awaiting trial, an interval which they say "usually lyes undetermined"; they represent themselves as being unable to support life, while the alms which some of them beg from commiserating Christians "sufficeth not to sustaine our weake and hungry natures."

William Raynolds, a blind freeman, aged 65, petitions for an almsman's place, and says that heretofore in the time of the Scottish siege of the city he withdrew himself into it for defence thereof, whereby he lost all his goods by the Scottish plunder. His petition is marked "1*s.* a weeke untill an hospital fall."

And Richard Landon, blacksmith, petitions for help, who in the time of Charles I. was impressed for service in Ireland, where he continued for five years under the command of the late hon. Col. Meend [Mynne,] sometime governor of Hereford, "with whom your petitioner was upon service at Ridmarley [in August, 1644], where his said collonell was slaine, and your petitioner by the adverse party there upon service receaved a perillous maime with the violent blowe of a muskett upon his lefte arme, which did not much trouble your petitioner till of late yeares." 6*d.* a week until the next sessions. He petitions again in 1675 when about 80 years of age and in 1682 (*q.v.*) when he says he is aged 92. In the next year, 1666, there is a petition from one Thomas Reynolds who served in the defence of the city against the Scots, and was wounded in the head and left arm upon a sally out against them.

1667, Oct. 3.—W. Mallowes to the Mayor, etc. Whereas I have caused one Wendland to be bound over to good behaviour, I desire that I may have liberty to demand of his master Roberts or of him what offence I have ever given unto them that they should make outcries and hooting after me, and my servant when I came to market and whether the recognizance is not forfeited by calling after one of the witnesses, and setting on others to run after me in the streets. As they have made me a *ridiculum* through city and country, I desire to have the favour granted me of saying on what false grounds they build their clamours, with a few considerations which aggravate their crime: 1. I am a gentleman by birth: 2. A minister by profession, 30 years in holy orders: 3. I have preached once yearly for seven years in the Minster: 4. I have lived in the county 16 years in good repute: 5. And in the neighbourhood 7 without offence: 6. I have expended 100*l*. in the shops of the city since that time: 7. If I may not have quiet ingress and regress for my servants, we must try another place, where we may make better markets. Lastly, I desire that Wendland may continue bound until next sessions.

1668, May 7.—Albon Willis, yeoman, of Clifford, deposes that upon his discoursing this day with one John Bullock about some money to be returned from London, the said Bullock demanded some further security for its return, alleging as a reason that the city of London would lie in ashes by the tenth day of May, and that the French would invade the kingdom with 150,000 men. Bullock is committed till he finds security to appear at the sessions. The paper is endorsed with this note: "Mr. Gipps his lre dated the 2 of May from London intimated to Mr. Morgan Thomas that London was like to bee fyred upon the Munday before that."

1668–9.—John Howells, a tailor, aged 67, petitions for relief as being a maimed faithful soldier in the service of K. Charles I., in the regiment of the late Sir Ralph Dutton, under the command of Lieut.-Col. Hawkins, at the fight of Edgehill, "ould Brainford," Newbury, Naseby, Bristol, Ciceter, "and upon the siedge against the Scotts here, and in diverse other fights elsewhere." The petition is attested by Owen Greeneley, who had been clerk to Sir R. Dutton's regiment, Francis Rawlins, "one of the gentlemen of the pyke," and Thomas Whitney, being "some of the marching soldiers living in this city."

1673.—Four parchment rolls of fines imposed on frequenters of conventicles in May. These probably afford the names of all the known non-conformists in Hereford and the neighbourhood at the time. In 1669 59 persons were presented for non-attendance at Church; in 1686, 47.

——, Nov. 26 and Dec. 1.—Depositions by some of the bakers of Hereford against William Morse, one of the wardens of the Company, for not attending with the Company at evening quire prayers on Nov. 5, and not entertaining them at his house that night according to ancient custom, which is a night solemnized by an Act of Parliament.

1675.—Presentment is made of the need of providing buckets, hooks and other instruments necessary for preventing the danger of fire. While this city has been preserved, other places have been deeply sensible of such calamity, which not only calls on the citizens to bless God for their own preservation, but to endeavour the use of all lawful means for prevention.

Various persons are examined respecting a traitorous libel reflecting abusively on the King and Government with regard to the excise, which had been received from one Ely Walwin in London, and sent from Hereford to Gloucester.

Philip George, a cooper, aged 76, petitions for relief. He was apprehended and kept some time in prison when Col. Birch invaded the city, for keeping the secrets of the city, and was unmercifully handled and burned in both his arms and legs for not disclosing great concerns, whereby he has been since troubled with the dead palsy. He was a sergeant in arms for the defence of the city when the Scots beseiged it, and served the King in Ireland as well as in England upon perilous adventures. Seven pounds are granted to him "out of Harper's money." He petitions also again in the same year to be settled in a hospital.

Richard Landon, aged 86, petitions for relief on the ground that he was impressed for the service of his Majesty's father and amongst others sent to Ireland to fight against the rebels in the time of the mayoralty of John Powell,* under the command of Col. Meend, whose regiment was brought back to serve the King in England, where at Ridmarley the petitioner was shot and maimed in his left arm. Fourpence per week is allowed him.

Presentment is made of the condition of the city-gates, which it is desired may be repaired, Widmarsh gate having neither covering nor gate, and the roof of Eigne gate being in such danger that it may cost the life of some passenger, the archwork being in decay through there being no covering on the top to keep out the rain. Weybridge gate had been presented in preceding years, and was again presented in this.

1677.—Dr. Brigstocke Harford (M.D.) is presented on Oct. 23 for ploughing up an ancient way in the Portfield, and is pained in 39*s.* if it be not thrown open by Nov. 30; the presentment is repeated on May 7 in 1677 and in other years. In the presentments for 1684 his name often appears for turning a water-course, stopping up two paths, &c.; and he is ordered to amend his encroachments under heavy penalties. In 1686 a maid-servant petitions the magistrates for recovery of wages due from him.

1677, May 7.—It is ordered that every person that inhabits within the city who shall ride on the gallop along the streets, except it be when the horse is exposed to sale, shall be pained 2*s.*

1678, Sept. 29.—Grant from the Mayor, Aldermen, and Common Council to Thomas Mathewes, esq., late Mayor, whereas he has been lately put to great charges in new erecting of the High Cross of the city, of all the tolls received for standings in the markets and fairs until he has been reimbursed the sum of 60*l.* 14*s.* 9*d.*, with ordinary interest, and one year's receipts over and above that sum. (In the box numbered 3.)

.—Examinations are made of several persons respecting libellous verses circulated in Hereford entitled *A public vindication of Paul Foley, esq., to be left at the coffee house with the letters*, and respecting which one Godwin Aubrey of Hereford said to a person who remarked that there was neither wit nor sense in it, "If that be not enough you shall have ten times more, for we can rip up more old stories." Col. Birch, Samuel Saunders, and others, were mentioned in it.

1682.—Petition from Richard Landon, aged 92, who was impressed out of the city to serve in the army of Charles I., and was sent into Ireland in the regiment of Col. Meend, formerly governor of Hereford, and who lost the use of his left arm by a bullet-shot; he has only an

* Powell was mayor in 1650–1. The petitioner's memory therefore was at fault, or else he served not the King but the Parliament.

allowance of $4\frac{1}{2}d$. weekly out of the parish of St. John Bapt. See under 1665.

In a general presentment of all persons who do not frequent their parish church, it is said that all connivance or indulgence "upon any pretence is a ready way to bring in popery," and that "popery and phananticism (*sic*) are equally dangerous to the government by law established." The parishioners of St. Owen's are bound to go to the church of St. Peter, the former church being demolished and the parishes being united.

1683, 19 Apr.—An order is made at Quarter Sessions that whereas the chief and petty constables in the several parishes are not well known and distinguished from other persons as they are in other cities, by constables' staves for security of their persons and as a badge of their offices, the churchwardens of each parish do forthwith take care to provide such staves, with the King's and city's arms upon them, the chief constables' staves not exceeding the value of 5*s*. and the rest not exceeding 3*s*. This order is among papers of 1685, in which year it was renewed.

In April, at the quarter sessions, a presentment is made of "all wandering persons, especially Scotchmen, who under pretence of trade go as spies about the country having no habitation, nor paying his Majesty any tribute, but subverting his Majesty's subjects by taking their trade out of their hands. And if a rebellion should happen, which may God forbid, they would prove very dangerous to this nation, as this city and county can affirm by woeful experience."

1684[–5], Jan. 9.—Stephen Arundel, a shoemaker, is informed against for saying "that he hoped to hear of the King's death before his own, that the government might be better settled, and drank the Duke of Monmouth's health;" he is bound over to appear at the sessions. And in July George Langford, a glover, is indicted for saying on June 23, when the King's troops were marching through the county on their way against Monmouth, "I am sorry to see such men go to fight against the son of a King, and I would not for the room full of gold hurt the hairs of Monmouth's head, nor for the city of Hereford touch him."

1685, Oct. 14.—Thomas Parry deposes that one Oliver Whitney being at his house the day before "spoke these scandalous and libellous words, viz., That he would drink the Duke of Monmouth's health, and that the Duke was not dead yet."

——, Nov. 15.—Deposition by the Sergeants at Mace of their arresting six quakers at a conventicle held in the house of James Exton, of Burghill, yeoman; with the record (on a parchment roll) of the conviction of the said persons before the Mayor, and their being fined 5*s*. each, (three of them being ordered to pay the fines for the other three, who were unable so to do), Exton being fined 20*l*.

1687, Sept. 8. Badminton.—The Duke of Beaufort to the City Council. The remoteness of Mr. Marshall Brydges' usual abode from the city, and the indispensable occasions that frequently call him into Somersetshire, render him unfit to serve the city in those public capacities which his station will require. I therefore desire you will take from him the resignation of his Council-man's place. It is no want of loyalty or readiness to serve his Majesty, and the corporation that makes him decline it, but purely the reasons aforementioned.

In a parcel of petitions of this year is one from a glover, James Carwardine, who, being a drummer in the company of Major Cornwal, had one of his legs broken in his return out of the West in Monmouth's rebellion.

1689.—In pursuance of the Act of Toleration passed in this year, "the people of God called Quakers" make a return on Oct. 10 that they have one meeting place for religious worship in the city suburbs without Fryne gate in the parish of St. Nicholas "so called."

1691.—Presentment by the Grand Jury. "Wee present all the constables as well chief as petty within the said citty of Hereford and liberties thereof for suffering idle vagabonds and sturdy beggars to wander about the streets of the said citty, and desire they may be punished according to law for that their neglect of their office. And whereas the best of laws are but as a dead letter without being put into execution, and the best of customes useless without being rightly upheld, Wee, the representatives as well of the inferior better and capitall cittizens of this citty humbly desire Mr. Mayor our head, not only to putt these our presentments, but all other good laws and customes, in execution, for the incouragement of vertue and orderly living and disincouragement of vice and ill mannerrs. And wee doo most heartily congratulate our present Majesties safe arrivall, who under God was the reformer of our religion, laws, liberties, preserving our lives and antient customes from the greedy jaws of Popery and slavery, and ever since hath been our royall champion and preserver of the same, whom God graunt long to raigne, and lett all the people say Amen."

1692.—Nathaniel Preist is held to bail in 40*l.* for drinking the health of K. James and his Queen and wishing her a safe return home; he also offered to drink the Pope's health "as he is a prince and a gentleman.

1693.—Various persons are presented and fined for having wooden "fimbrills" in their houses for chimneys, very dangerous for firing. Presentments of this kind are found under several other years.

1694[-5], Jan. 17.—An alehouse called the Catherine Wheel, kept by Bridget Andrewes, is suppressed, on account of a riot which occurred there on Jan. 12, with some soldiers there quartered, upon which depositions are made which prove that "divers persons disaffected to the present government do weekly and daily resort thither, and read private, false and seditious news letters to corrupt his Majesty's subjects." Upon one of the soldiers drinking the health of William III., one Rowland Andrewes began another health "to him that had lost fifteen shillings," saying "Three crowns was good money," and wishing that if ever it came into his hands again he would play his game better. Hereupon a general fight followed, in which the landlady, her daughter and her servant all took part against the soldiers, as well as one Mr. Timothy Geers, who said he was a stranger and a gentleman of the gown, Mr. William Bowdler, Mr. Richard Traherne and Mr. Richard Bell. These are said to usually meet at the alehouse three times a week and drink the health above mentioned, and read private news letters, and while they are reading the maid-servant would commonly stand sentry at the door to give a caution, often using the words "Have a care."

1695.—Inventory of the stock of Roger Williams, bookseller, seized for debt and appraised. There are 42 volumes in folio, eight in quarto, and 120 volumes or parcels in octavo, chiefly English theology, history, and school-books; with the prices at which they were valued. The debt for which they were seized was one of 40*l.* but the total amount raised by stock and goods was only 35*l.* 6*s.* 7*d.*

1706.—At the April sessions a labourer was presented for going through the city in the week before Easter, being Passion week, clothed in a long coat with a large periwig, with a great multitude following him, sitting upon an ass, to the derision of our Saviour Jesus Christ's riding into Jerusalem, to the great scandal of the Christian religion, to the contempt of our Lord and his doctrine, and to the ill and pernicious example of others. He was bound over to appear at the next sessions.

1708.—Persons are now presented, not for not going to church but "for not going to some place or other of worship on the Lord's day," and the constables for not suppressing the boys for gaming and sporting on the Lord's day, and the Mayor is humbly desired to mind them of their duty. The commencement of the disuse of an old word is seen in a presentment for erecting "a miskin *or* dunghill."

1713, Aug. 1.—Indenture (on vellum) of the election of Hon. James Brydges and Thomas Foley, esq. as members of Parliament for the city.

1715.—Some evidence is taken on 13 July of some design for pulling down the meeting-house in the city, but what the house was, whether of Quakers or others, is not specified. On the next day William Carpenter of the parish of Hampton Bishop is prosecuted for keeping "an unlawfull game commonly called skittles or a tenne pins," and also he with others for an unlawful game "lately found out being called by the name of *Rooley Pooley*."* A labourer is mentioned in 1714 who had the singular Christian name of *Patriarch.*

1723.—The porters of the gates of the city present a petition, "That whereas there are five porters belonging to the gates of this city, and according to the custom of the same city each porter usually attended on the worshipful the Mayor, Aldermen, and chief citizens to church and other places with decent sticks, clubs or staves, which by length of time or otherwise are lost or mislaid, there being only three old sticks left, your petitioners therefore humbly pray that they may have new sticks made, for the use aforesaid, which your petitioners presume will be ornamental to their masters, as your petitioners walk in procession before them, to and from church and other places."†

1737, Dec. 24.—The Mayor and late mayor to the Duke of Argyll [Commander-in-Chief], regretting that an inquiry was made into a recent little scuffle between some citizens and two or three troopers. The parties were only bound over in order to show that none were exempt from the civil power, and to obviate any colour of pretence for returning supposed injuries. We have hitherto lived in good friendship with all officers and soldiers quartered amongst us, and shall endeavour to continue the good understanding, and to do justice

* In 1676, 1688, and other years about that time persons are presented for having nine-pins (called in 1677, nine pigs) and shuffle-board.

† Two of these "sticks" are still in use, together with four maces.

to your troops now quartered here. We have no manner of cause to complain of them, for their behaviour in general is very good.

1753, Aug. 3.—Faculty from the Vicar General of the diocese, assigning a certain seat on the south side of the middle aisle of the parish church of All Saints, containing in length 8 feet 9 inches, and in breadth 2 feet 6 inches, to the Mayor and his successors in office "for the Mayor's wife for the time being, to sit stand and kneel therein to hear divine service and sermon." (In the box with the Royal charters.)

1759, July 20.—Agreement (on vellum) by the Mayor and Corporation with the Bishop of Hereford, that the room which is about to be built with the aid of private subscriptions for a Guildhall in the place of the present ruinous hall shall be free for the meetings of the choirs of Hereford, Gloucester and Worcester whenever requested by the stewards thereof. (In the box with the Royal charters.)

1760, Oct. 16.—Letter from William Underwood to the Mayor and Corporation, offering to give *4l. 4s.* per annum for the farm of the Hop fair.

This fair has long since ceased to be held.

WILLIAM DUNN MACRAY.

THE MANUSCRIPTS OF THE CORPORATION OF HASTINGS.

HASTINGS MSS.

Unfortunately the earlier records of the town and port of Hastings are missing, whether they have been lost, stolen, or destroyed is unknown. Those that remain are now carefully preserved under the charge of the town clerk.

I. Charters, etc.

There are a few charters among the Corporation muniments, some of which have been lately presented by a gentleman interested in the history of the town.

16 Edward I., June 17.—Royal Charter to the Cinque Ports.

22 Edward I., Sunday the Feast of St. Benedict the Abbot.—Grant by Petronilla de Cham of Hastyng, widow, to the Brothers and Sisters of the Hospital of St. Mary Magdalene of Hastyng, of five acres of land in the parish of St. Margaret in Hasting for the healthful estate of her soul and of the souls of Godard, Matilda, Robert, Robert, Robert, William, Richard, and Henry, and of her heirs, parents and friends. Witnesses, William de Waldern, then Bailiff in Hasting, William Yrlond, Laurence de Wyndesor, Stephen Sprot, James le Plonter, Richard, Robert, Gilbert, Roger, Robert Baldelot, Nicholas le Banek, Henry le Meleward, John Sconyn, William de Dalinton, serjeant, John de Wych, clerk, and others.

21 Edward III., April 15.—Grant, with certain covenants, by Richard Large of Winchelsea to the Bailiff and Barons of Hastings, of a ship called the *Guodbizete*, for service in the King's fleet.

38 Edward III., July 1.—Confirmation Charter to the Cinque Ports. *Portion of Seal.*

47 Edward III.—Grant by Henry Brette, of the Parish of All Saints in Hastyng, to Thomas Starculf, of the same place, of a messuage in the said Parish bounded by the highway leading from the sea to Winchelse on the east, the land of the heirs of William Dean on the south, a watercourse called la Bourne on the west and the land of John Benet on the north. Witnesses, William Haylman, then Bailiff, John Knolle, Richard Mechyng, Robert Ro . . . . Deghere, John Oleve, John Scot, and others.

4 Richard II., February 1.—Charter to the Cinque Ports. *Portion of Seal.*

4 Edward IV., November 6.—Grant by John Benener to William Levett, de Ballo [Bello?] son of Thomasine Parker, late deceased, of one tenement called Richardadamys Place in Hasting, which tenement he, together with Henry Hammer, lately deceased, had of the gift of the said Thomasine. Witnesses, John Honywode, Richard Levet, Richard Byrche, William Yreland, Thomas Lydderland, and others.

15 Henry VII., December 30.—Grant by Edward Gibbes, son and heir of John Gibbes, while he was alive of Hasting, to Thomas

Twaytes and John Nutkyn, churchwardens of the parish of All Saints in Hastyng, of two tenements in the parish of All Saints, bounded by the tenement of Richard Taylour, in right of his wife, towards the south, by the High Street there leading from the high sea to le Menewes, towards the west, by the tenement of William White, towards the north, and le Tegill Wey, towards the east. To hold to the use of the said church for ever. Witnesses, John Flouer, Bailiff of Hastyng, Richard Levet, John Waterman, Henry Benenere, William Nepshame, Edward Franke, John Long, William Wattes, and Richard Taylour, jurats. *Seal.*

31 Henry VIII., June 11.—Grant by John Gille and Thos. Lese, churchwardens of St. Clement's Church in Hastyng, to Edward Durrante, of a tenement in the same parish. Witnesses, Thomas Whitte, John Hollond, and William Hulle, carpenter. *Seal.*

31 Elizabeth, February 14.—Charter of incorporation to the Barons and inhabitants of the vill and port of Hastings.

17 James I., December 18.—Grant by Nicholas Staplest, of the Town and Port of Hasting, to Daniell Easton, of Bexhill, of an annuity issuing out of certain lands in Hastings called Castle Meadow, and other lands in the Parish of St. Mary of the Castle.

10 Charles I., June 26.—Confirmation Charter to the Cinque Ports reciting charter of 2 James I.

2 James II., February 11. Charter to the Corporation of Hastings.

9 Anne, July 11.—Exemplification of a decree in the Court of Chancery touching the payment of an annual composition from the town of Pevensey to Hastings.

7 William IV., July 15.—Grant of a Court of Quarter Sessions of the Peace to the Borough of Hastings.

II. Court Books.

Containing records of the pleas heard before the Bailiffs (after Queen Elizabeth's Charter of incorporation, before the Mayors) and jurats of Hastings. These volumes begin in 1585 and continue irregularly to 1685. *7 volumes.*

III. Hundred Court Books.

These contain entries of the proceedings at the assemblies of the Corporation such as the election at "le Hundred Place" each year of the Mayor, jurats, common clerk, chamberlain, serjeant-at-mace, auditors, "perewardens," "keykepers," bailiffs of the Bourne, leather searchers, representatives to attend the "Brodhulls" guestlings, Yarmouth Free Fair, members of Parliament, etc., admission of freemen, and also entries of the proceedings at the gaol deliveries, sessions of the peace, the enrolments of Fines, Recoveries, private deeds, wills, recognizances, indentures of apprenticeship, etc. This series commences in 1595 and continues irregularly under the titles of Minute Books and Record Books (which last also contain proceedings before the Commissioners for the Land tax) down to nearly the end of the eighteenth century. The following entries from these volumes have been noted.

17 September 1594.—"It is decreed and graunted that for the present nedeful supplie of such powder, lead, di. c. sacre shott, and wheeles for carriage, as are charged and proportionated to this town, one shott [scot]

HASTINGS MSS.

of 25 *li.* shalbe forthwith taxed, levied, had, and made of all the freemen, comons, and inhabitantes of this Town and the liberties thereof by sessement."

"It is further decreed that Mr. Maior and his brethren or any iij or ij. of them with him shall forthwith make demaund of such sommes of mony as are due to this towne by composition from the Towne of Winchelsea touching the charge of the ship sett forth in her Majesties service in the yere 1588, and, if upon such demaund they shall refuse to make payment thereof, that then it shalbe lawfull to Mr. Maior and his said brethren to commence sute against the Maior, Jurates, and Commonalties of the said Towne or against such as under their hand have bound themselves for performance of the said composition."

1595, October 30.—Enrolment of a conveyance of a tenement and garden in St. Clement's Parish, Hastings, by Mark Barrie, son and heir of Thomas Barrie, and Isabella wife of the said Mark, to Richard Porter.

1595, December 11.—Order by the Mayor, Jurats, and Commons of Hastings that Christopher Cowper, in consideration of the release of his right and title to a concealed house and garden in All Saints' Parish in Hastings, shall have for his natural life one tenement by "the Bourne syde" beneath the Court Hall in All Saints' Parish for one penny yearly.

1595[-6], January 2.—Martin Life, jurat, and Melchior Rainolds, common clerk, nominated to ride to Dover and appear for the Port of Hastings on the 7th instant, to have conference with the residue of the Cinque Ports, then and there to be assembled, upon the letters lately directed to the said Ports from the Lords of her Majesty's Council and from the Lord Warden and his Lieutenant, touching and concerning four ships imposed upon the Cinque Ports to be set forth for five months from the last of March next, against the intended invasion of this Realm by the Spaniards and then and there fully and freely to conclude in that behalf in the name of the Town and Port of Hastings.

1595[-6], January 11.—Whereas at the late meeting of all the Ports at Dover it was fully agreed that the East Ports, viz.:—Sandwich, Dover, and Hythe, with their members, should find two of the four ships of 160 tons a piece imposed on the Ports for her Majesty's service, as aforesaid, and Romney, Rye, Winchelsea, and Hastings, and their members, should find the other two ships, and whereas at that time it was further agreed that those of the West Ports and their members should meet at Rye on the 15th of this January, to have conference touching the sub-division and apportioning of those two ships allotted to them, Richard Life, Martin Life, John Conny, and Melchior Rainolds, are elected and appointed to appear at Rye on behalf of the Town and Corporation of Hastings.

1595[-6], January 18.—At the meeting of the West Ports held at Rye it was agreed by Romney, Rye, Winchelsea, Hastings, and Seaford, the other members there dissenting, that a ship of 160 tons should be prepared for her Majesty's service, viz.:—Romney to bear the charge of 40 tons, Rye 50 tons, Winchelsea 15 tons, Hastings 40 tons, and Seaford 8 tons, and if the balance could not be obtained from the dissenting members it should be supplied by the aforesaid assenting towns. It was therefore agreed that a "shott" of 300 *li.* be taxed upon the commons and inhabitants of Hastings so that one moiety be collected by the first of March.

1595[-6], January 26.—The debt of Winchelsea, due for the ship set forth in 1588, to be submitted to arbitration.

1596, April 24.—Memorandum that about the 2nd of March 1595[-6] "the peere of Hasting was begonne to be reedified by certen Westerne men sent for of purpose from the Cobb (*sic*) of Lyme. And by them was built a highe woorke without thold pere, full south, all of huge rockes artificially pyled edglong one close by another of a great hight but without any tymber, yet to men's judgement unremoveable it grew to so huge a pile; but notwithstanding, the first wynter flow, overthrew it in a moment and dispersed the huge rockes lyke thin plankes. And so that cost was lost. But the next year after other woorkmen of better knowledge (as was thought) were called thence and by general consent the lyke pece of woorke was begon to be again built with the like huge rockes. And for more suerty, by advise of the master woorkman, it was thought best (because they judged the decay of the former was for want of some tymber) to lay the foundation of this new worke within the tymber woorke of thold peere and so to contynue with tymber braces and barres, crosse dogges, and such like up to the top. And this woorke was with singular industry and arte brought above the full and by All Holloutyde 1597 well nere finished, viz.:—xxx foote high and c foot long at least, bowtyfull to behold, huge, invincible, and unremoveable in the judgment of all the beholders, amounting to a great charge, wherunto the whole shire and divers beholders were contributaryes of benevolence, besides the Towne's great expenses. But behold when men were most secure and thought the woorke to be perpetuall, on All Saints' daie 1597 appeared the mighty force of God, who with the finger of his hand at one great and exceding high spring tyde with a south east wynd overthrew this huge woorke in lesse then an hower to the great terrour and abashment of all beholders, to the great discredit of the like woorke hereafter with the Contry and to the manifest undoing of the Towne which by reason therof was left greatly undetted. By theis presidentes let the posterity (for whome I record this) beware they never attempt to build them a pere with rockes only, without a mighty frame of tymber to be seled, and then belasted with rockes; alwayes remembring that about such woorke, tymber must not be spared."

In the margin is—*Per exempla periculosa antecessorum caveat posteritas.*

1597, January 10.—William Piddlesden of Bexhill, labourer, living at the Sluice House within the Liberties of Hastings, fined for neglecting to watch upon the sea coast.

1596[-7], February 20.—Order for the work of the pier to be continued, and towards the maintenance of the charge thereof, a whole share is granted by the fishermen, and a half share of the Scarborough voyage, and a quarter share due to the Town is also granted.

1597, April 17.—Order that the Act or decree made in this Town in 7 Edward III., touching this point or article only, viz.:—That he that was chosen bailiff one year should not be bailiff the year following again, shall be from henceforth repealed abrogated and frustrated, any confirmation thereof since renewed or had to the contrary thereof, notwithstanding.

1597, October 8.—Richard Life and Edmond Pelham, "our learned counsell" chosen Barons to Parliament.

1597, December 26.—Richard Life, Mayor, Thomas Lake and James Lashe, jurats, Melchior Rainoldes and Michael Stunt, chosen to ride to Rye to the guestling to be held there on 3 January next.

1597[-8], February 26.—Order, in consideration of the great debts which the town oweth, for the auditors to survey the Town's debts and report the best means of discharging the same.

1597[-8], March 5.—Order for the Mayor's fee or wages to cease, and in regard thereof the Mayors to be discharged from giving the supper on their election day and the breakfast on Christmas day morning, heretofore accustomed.

1598, June 18.—Order for taking away poundage from the Chamberlains and the fee or wages from the Mayor.

1598, July 28.—Summons for six, five, or four jurats to appear before the Lord Warden at Beakesbourne in Kent on the 24 August at 8 o'clock in the forenoon where the said Lord Warden intends to make "solempne serrement and promise to uphold and mainteine the liberties and priviledges" of the Cinque Ports.

Opinion by Serjeant Nicholas Barham "that wrecks happening in Pemsey, Seaford, etc. belong to Hasting by the general chartre of the 5 Ports."

1601, October 4.—Richard Life, jurat, and Sir Thomas Sherley, Knight, chosen barons to Parliament.

1601, October 13.—Hundred Court held at Beakesbourne in the County of Kent, a member of Hastings, before James Lasher, Mayor of the vill and port of Hastings.

Edward Pordage elected deputy or bailiff of the vill aforesaid; election of serjeant at the verge and admission of freemen.

Enrolment of the Will of Richard Calveley of the Parish of Oer.

1602, April 25.—Enrolment of claim by John Luch to a footway through a parcel of land heretofore used in times of necessity as a church-yard to the Parish Church of St. Clement for the burial of the dead, and now employed for garden plots, bounding on the highway from Marlepet field to the said Church on the south, the barn and field of Thomas Young on the west and north, and the backsides and gardens of the said John Luck, yeoman and Mary Barley, widow, on the east. Depositions in support of the said claim.

1602, June 20.—Order that an entry shall be made into a new shop lately erected on the stone beach by Martin Harrison without consent or grant from the corporation, or else the same be removed by him, because it is set to the annoyance of James Mitchel's shop and "the common weyne way there."

1602, June 11.—Election of Thomas Nicholl as bailiff of the Bourne with instructions to have diligent care for those that lay their filth above the full sea mark. Richard Life, "bailiff to Yarmouth," to have a tun of beer in further regard of his charges.

Mem.: This summer the Court Hall was repaired, and the new stairs and gallery newly built.

1603, March 28.—Proclamation of James I. as King of England.

"It is reported that her Majesty departed on Thursdie the 24 of March 1602[-3] about 3 of the clock in the morning, and that about 9 of the clock the same daie before noone this proclamation was made and proclaymed in London by all the said noblemen, read by Sir Robert Cecill and pronounced by a harold with sound of trumpet."

1603, April 6.—Order—to avoid the great inconveniences which by common experience are found to be by reason of the election of the

Mayor of this Town abroad is the public view of the whole multitude not only of inhabitants but also of many strangers assembling at such elections in the open Hundred place, whereby all matters of counsel are disclosed and may not be kept secret—that from henceforth all the elections of the Mayors of the Town shall be solemnised, made, done, and performed in the Court Hall of this town as a place more decent, apt, and secret for such affairs to be done and used, any old custom usage or decree to the contrary notwithstanding.

1603, May 29.—Whereas at a Hundred Court held on Saturday 19th of January 4 Edward IV., it was agreed by the Bailiffs, jurats and commons that from henceforth if any inhabitant within this town be chosen a freeman, and of wilfulness refuse it, he shall pay every year "duble maltot and doe in all things to duble" or else be fined 20*s*. to the use of the Town. The mayor, jurats and freemen at the present Hundred assembled—considering the small number of jurats and freemen of this town, and pondering on the necessity of the King's daily service and the bond of duty wherein every good subject is obliged to perform to his power such office and services as he is fit for to his Prince and Country, and for the better continuance of the ancient manner of government of this town by succession of magistrates and their assistants—have assayed to furnish those wants by supply of other able inhabitants in the void rooms of jurats and freemen according to the old customs and decrees. Which good intent has not obtained their wished for effect but often frustrated by reason of too small fines and penalties of those former decrees. It is therefore ordered and decreed that if any inhabitant chosen jurat or freeman refuse to act as such, he shall be fined at the discretion of the Mayor and jurats; which fine shall not be less than 100*s*., and upon refusal to pay, he shall be committed to prison.

Order that "whereas this our Hundred hath heretofore been accustomed to be held on the second Sabbath daie next after our election day which by reason of the multiplicities of business there handled, tending to the profanation thereof, and the great trouble of many men, therefore from henceforth our Hundred shall be yearly held on the Monday fortnight after our usual election of the Mayor, that is, on the third Monday after the said election day and at such place as shall be thought most convenient."

1603, July 7.—Letter from the Lord Steward to the Lord Warden, for the Barons of the Cinque Ports to be prepared for the services belonging to them at the Coronation.

1603, July 11.—Richard Life, Mayor, Martin Life and William Bysshop, jurats, elected barons to carry the canopy over the King at his coronation.

Memorandum:—"There ought to be 16 barons in all, 3 Hastings, 3 Sandwich, and 2 the residue of the other towns."

Memorandum:—That by decree of the Brotherhood now lately holden for this purpose especially, all the 16 barons are to be thus apparelled, viz., "Scarlet gownes downe to the ancle faced downe through before with crymsin satten, crymsin satten dublettes, crymson satten Gasgoing hose, crymsin silke stockings, crymsine velvet shoes, and black velvet broad cappes.

And by like decree in consideration of their wholl charge which they must of themselves beare without any contribution from their townes in any sort they are to enjoy the canopy amonges them to be devyded as they shall agree, and are to mete altogether in Poule's Church on the 22 of July to have conference for order and their manner of going and carrying of the canopy."

1603, July 17.—Upon letters of intelligence that the Queen shall also be crowned with the King, James Lasher, Richard French and Richard Ellys, jurats, are chosen to carry the canopy over her Grace.

1603[-4], March 1.—Richard Life and Sir George Carew, knight, chosen barons to Parliament.

1604, August 4.—Order that during every sessions of the present Parliament, the Baron to that session returned, shall have 2*s*. a day for his wages.

1604, August 18.—Lease to James Hunt of the house, barn, and lands, called the Mawdlyn.

1605, July 16.—John Shurley, esquire, sergeant-at-law, retained counsel for the town and 40*s*. paid him for his fee.

1605, October, 19.—Sir Edward Hales, knight, and Mr. James Lasher elected barons to Parliament, in the place of Sir George Carew, created a Baron and therefore having a place in the Upper House, and Mr. Richard Life, deceased.

1606, October 4.—Order for a scot to be levied towards conveying water to the town in lead pipes from the Bourn, beginning at such nearest place as shall be clear of the water falling out of the highways, the water of the Bourn in the Town having become corrupt.

1606, October 11.—Thomas Lake, jurat and Captain of the trained bands (*selectorum militum*) of this Town, died. Note in the margin "This man was captain of one of the ships of the Ports under the Earle of Essex at the sacking of Cales, where he fought manfully with many great Spanish ships and galleys to his great renowne. And that monument hanging in the south chancell of St. Clement's Church he brought from thence out of one of the Spanish ships."

1607, March 29.—A chamber over Mr. Young's shop appointed for a common school house for this town.

1611, April 14.—Order for the pier to be repaired, it being in ruins.

1611, June 9.—A decree of the Court of Chancery against Steven Porter concerning the common fine upon foreigners lands.

1611, August 7.—Order that inhabitants refusing to labour at the pier are to forfeit 12*d*.

1612, May 2.—The order that one man may not be Mayor twice together, revived and made perpetual.

1612[-13], January 16.—A list of inhabitants who took the oath of allegiance to King James I.

1613, July 29.—Thanks of the assembly at the Hundred Court to Sir Thomas Glover who proposed to become a suitor to the King for his royal assent to making a haven at Hastings, at his own own charge.

1613–14, March 7.—Election of Sir Edmund Seals and James Lasher, as Barons to Parliament.

1614, August 30.—Enrolment of the Will of Thomas Rogerson of Hastings, fisherman.

1620, June 12.—Order for Nathaniel Lasher, Jurat, to ride to London with the three patents lately granted by the king to the Town concerning the pier, and there to cause briefs to be printed.

1620, December 25.—Samuel Moore and Captain James Lasher elected Barons to Parliament.

1621, July 29.—Orders concerning the rebuilding of the pier.

1621, September 22.—Nicholas Lopdell, a retainer of Captain James Lasher, Baron to Parliament, arrested on a plea of debt, prayed to be discharged.

1621, October 3.—Letters from Sir Thomas Richardson, knight, Speaker of the House of Parliament, being shown forth for the discharge of Nicholas Lopdell, he is thereupon discharged.

A parcel of waste ground on the stone beach granted to John Sargant for 8*d.* yearly rent for ever.

1625, March 25.—Order for the Mayor to travel to London to sue for satisfaction of the charge of four barks of Hastings lately employed about the transportation of soldiers from Dover to the Low Countries under conduct of General Count Mansfield.

1625, August 10.—Order for watch and ward to be kept to restrain strangers repairing to the Town in order to avoid the danger of infection from the plague now universally raging in divers parts of this kingdom.

No persons strangers or town dwellers shall be suffered to drink or tipple immoderately.

Grant of a parcel of the waste stone beach.

1625–6, January 21.—Letters touching the Coronation services due from the Cinque Ports, John Barley, Mayor, Richard Wytheris, Richard Waller, Richard Boys, John Brett, and Thomas Brian, jurats, chosen barons to carry the canopy at the Coronation.

1625–6, March 8.—A scot ordered for the proportion of powder, shot, match, mounting of ordnance, reparations of gates, walls, fortifications, and such like.

1626, July 29.—A scot to be levied for the share of Hastings towards the two ships of 200 tons a piece to be set forth for the King's service by the Ports and their members.

1626–7, March 9.—"For that the imminent danger of the enemy suddenly expected upon these coasts" it is ordered that a strong watch be nightly kept and the fortifications repaired.

1627–8, February 22.—Order for the Town Gunner to go to London to receive the ordnance granted by the Lords of the Council for the defence of the Town.

1629, July 29.—Order for William Barkes, Mayor, and others elected to attend the Lord Warden at Shipway in Kent where he intends to "make solemn sacrament" to maintain the liberties of the Cinque Ports.

1631, August 5.—Order that the offer of the vill of Beakesbourn, a member of this Town, to make composition for all scots, charges, and payments to be hereafter imposed, by an annuity of 40*s.* be accepted.

1635–6, January 22.—Order for an able Surveyor to view the place for making a haven at the "Priorie."

1635–6, February 15.—Henrich Cranhalls, a Dutch engineer, upon survey, reports that a very good haven may be made.

1637, April 11.—A scot to be levied for the haven.

1639, May 28.—Enrolment of the will of William Parker, clerk, minister in the Parish of All Saints Hastings.

Proceedings in Chancery touching the free-school at Hastings.

1656.—An order against the immoderate drinking of hot waters.

That two guns be mounted for the defence of the Town.

1665–6, January 29.—Order that a petition be sent to his Majesty and his Council, or the Lord Warden, for assistance to put the town in defence against the intended invasion to be attempted by the French and Dutch.

1674, May 20.—Order to join with the Corporation of Rye in a petition to his Majesty concerning a dam made in and across the River Rother by the Commissioners of Sewers, to the great prejudice of the harbour of Rye.

1677, April 14.—Orders concerning fishing.

1680, April 16.—Letter from the Lords of the Council to the Mayor and jurats of Hastings requiring an account how the statute of 13 Charles II. for regulating Corporations, has been executed.

1685, June 3.—Letters, dated from London, from Col. Strode to the Mayor, jurats, and commonalty of Hastings acquainting them that no progress can be made in the grand charter of the Ports, till the private and particular charters of every corporation therein be surrendered. "It is therefore expected that you will forthwith surrender unto the King's hands the particular charter of your town and all rights which you enjoy thereby, and thereupon your charter will be regranted to you with all such rights, privileges, and advantages as you can desire and are fitting for the King to grant."

1685, June 11.—Order for the surrender of the Charter of Queen Elizabeth into the hands of the King.

1685, October 20.—Order for the "feeters or dosser makers"* to make their dossers according to an assize viz.: 12 inches wide in the yoke "between the bores," 7 inches deep, and 17 inches "between bayle and bayle."

1685–6, March 6.—Further orders touching the assize of dossers.

1691–2, February 29.—Order for the impressing of seamen for their Majesties' service.

1693, August 8.—Letter from Henry, Viscount Sydney, to Col. John Beaumont, Lieutenant of Dover Castle, stating that he had signified his intention of going to the Cinque Ports to be sworn Guardian thereof, but having lately received the King's commands to repair to his Majesty in Flanders, he will not be able to be at Dover at the time appointed.

1694, April 13.—Summons to meet the Lord Warden at Braidenstone Hill in the Liberty of Dover where he intends to make solemn "serement" to maintain the liberties of the Cinque Ports.

---

* Note in pencil that these were the large baskets in which the fish of the Town was carried to London on the backs of 10 or 12 horses in a line, under the charge of one man.

1694, June 5.—This day, the Earl of Romney, Lord Warden of the Cinque Ports, was pleased to visit the town of Hastings with Col. Robert Smith; and the freedom of the Port was conferred upon them.

1706, October 23.—Agreement between the Mayor and jurats, and the justices of the Peace, that only two freemen be made in each year, the one to be nominated by the mayor, and the other by the majority of the bench.

1709, July 5.—Summons from Lionel Cranfield, Earl of Dorset and Middlesex, Constable of Dover Castle, to the Mayor and jurats of Hastings, to attend a court of shipwey at Braidenston.

1724–5, February 20.—Orders concerning the making of freemen. (*See also proceedings at later courts.*)

1733, November 9.—Enrolment of the Will of James Saunders of Wittersham in the Isle of Oxney and now of the Town of Winchelsea, yeoman.

1733, November 9.—A Proposal by the Mayor and jurats of Hastings for supplying the town with water.

IV. Chamberlains' and Pier Wardens' Accounts.

The Chamberlains' accounts contain the entries of the receipts of fines, rents for lands belonging to the Corporation (including "the stone beach"), forfeited recognizances, scot levied upon the inhabitants (whose names are set out under their occupations as bakers, brewers, barbers, etc.), and the entries of payments of wages or fees to the Mayor, the town's counsel, town clerk, sergeant-at-mace, water baily, "boader" and other officials. On the Pier Wardens' accounts are entered the sums received from the fishermen for "pier shares" for their "shott nettes," for "flewers," "petty duties" etc, and the amounts paid for repairs to the pier. The following entries have been selected as illustrative of the Chamberlains' accounts.

1642–3.—Payments to Richard Pecke for keeping the "townes dyall" and Thomas Haines for keeping the "towne clocke." To the boader for bringing letters for the stopping of "Oneale." For repairs to the courthall and for dressing the town hall with boughs at the election and Hundred-day. To Steven Whales for carrying the hurt Frenchmen to Dieppe, 12*d.*

1643–4.—To a poor cripple with a pass, 6*d.* For mending the watch bell 10*s.* To an Irishman and his wife and four children, 6*d.* To William Geery for the "hundred's dinner," 2*li.* 4*s.* 10*d.*

1645–6.—To George Chambers for carrying a hue and cry for breaking open Guestling Church 6*d.* Other payments for hue and cry and for making a gallows and executing a woman.

1651–2.—Payments for the conveyance of pressed soldiers, "for the grand jury drinking," etc.

1652–3.—Payments for quartering Dutchmen. To Robert Marshall for dressing eight wounded Dutchmen.

1653–4.—To the Mayor of Rye for Rye Harbour, 6*li.* 13*s.* 4*d.*

1659–60.—To the musketeers on the proclamation of the King 1*li.* 10*s.* 9*d.* "More upon them in white wine the same day 10*s.* For

HASTINGS MSS. half a barrell of beere and bread to the ringers *5s. 2d.* More to the ringers upon the Thanksgiving day, *2s.*" Allowed and paid to William Bagg for the King's arms in the Court hall, *3li. 5s.*

1692–3.—Arrears of Pevensey for the Coronation of King Charles II., James II. and his Queen, King William and Queen Mary.

1713–14.—Paid for tar and tarring the pillory *1s. 7d.*

1714–15.—Paid Mr. Stephen Gibbon for mending the maces.

1715–16.—Payments to Robert Evernden for mending the halbert. Several entries for drumming.

1716–17.—To Mr. Gibbon for mending the maces, *6s.* For beer, bread, brandy, tobacco, and pipes going the bounds, *1li. 4s. 6d.*

1717–18.—Received of the mountebank *10s.* Paid to William Smith for the town's seal, *1s.* Payment for whipping three people.

1745–6.—Payment for expenses about the watch erecting the beacon and watch house also for expenses for the 5th November, the Duke of Cumberland's and the Prince of Wales' birthdays, and for the volunteers.

V. Rolls of the admission of freemen 1700 to 1811. 3 *rolls.*

VI. Declarations against the doctrine of transubstantiation taken at the General Quarter Sessions of the Peace 1751 to 1762.

VII. Papers relating to fines and estreats 18th and 19th centuries.

Thanks are due to Mr. George Meadows, the Town Clerk of Hastings, and his staff for giving every facility for the examination of the muniments under their charge.

W. J. HARDY.

THE MANUSCRIPTS OF SIR THOMAS BARRETT LENNARD, BART., OF BELHUS, ESSEX.

The documents described in the following report were selected from a very large collection of deeds and papers chiefly relating to the estates of the Barretts and Lennards. Sampson Lennard married Margaret Fynes, who upon the decease of her brother Gregory, Lord Dacre, claimed the title. This was after much delay awarded to her. She was succeeded by her son, Sir Henry Lennard, whose grandson, Thomas Lennard, Lord Dacre, married the eldest daughter of Chas. II. and the Duchess of Cleveland, and was created Earl of Sussex. The earl died only leaving two married daughters, viz., Lady Barbara Skelton and Lady Ann Barrett (who had married her cousin the eldest son of Dacre Barrett), and on the death of the former without issue the Barony of Dacre devolved upon Lady Ann Barrett. With the exception of the paper describing Frederick the Great and his Court in 1752 there is nothing to which special attention need be called in the few letters printed, which, for the most part, contain interesting comments on public and social events, tempp. Geo. I. and Geo. II.

1700. July 30th.—Richard Barret to his father Dacre Barret at Belhus (written probably from Eton). "The court here at Windsor is in great lamentation for the Duke of Gloucester who died here this morning about one of the clock. He was took ill on Friday last as the Doctors, namely Hans and Ratcliff, [say ?] of a fever and sore throat, but since he died the small-pox came out . . . . My Lord Paston has shot the Lord Portland for refusing to marry his sister Mrs. Howard to whom he had promised marriage. My Lord Paston challenged him first but he refused, and so was shot."

1700. Sept. 1st. Eaton.—The same to the same. "I received the suit of cloaths which you sent me for which I return you thanks; they fit me very well and are of a very genteel colour. I believe that the Mildmays are quite down in the mouth for I never hear Cottrell bragging as he used. Sir Charles was here at election and took his son to Sir William Trumball's, but did not see me."

N.D. [1714. Sept.] Russell Street.—Richard Barrett to Dacre Barrett at Belhus. "After I parted from you I went to Gravesend and saw the King pass by there and afterwards went to Greenwich and had the honour yesterday of kissing the King's and Prince's hands where was abundance of company of all parties. The King landed not till dusk by torch light. The Duke of M[arlborough] met him at his landing; the King spoke in French to him thus "my dear Duke I hope you now have seen an end of all your troubles." He was made Captain General the next day, and Lord Townshend who is Secretary of State, met the Duke of O[rmonde] as he was going in to see the King, and told him his Majesty had no further service for him . . . . The King and Prince are neither of 'em taller than yourself, the first is well set."

MSS. OF SIR T. BARRET LENNARD.

N.D. [about 1714.] Richard Barrett to Dacre Barrett. "I intended to have wrote this last night after a visit to the Bishop [of L. *sic* in another place] but coming there found old Lady Cowper and two other ladies who told us there was to be a great drawing room and the Princess would appear. So Lady Lee engaged me to go thither and bring an account. I found a numerous appearance of both sexes and saw the Princess and her two children. All these are charmed with her conversation which was in English, very good for a foreigner, and [she] addressed herself to every Lady there without want of words of subject of discourse. Her dress is very different from ours, high and full of pleats, hair fair and wears abundance of it and loaded with flakes of powder. She is taller and bigger than the Prince, she played at pique with Lady Pembroke . . . . . I believe it would give you the spleen to pass by the Exchange and hear the brawling libels . . . . . . The town wonders at the reports of Lord Orford having refused the Garter, which they cannot like; though all allow him to have acted well as to the Navy. Lord Hervey is to be Earl of Bristol, Lord Pelham Duke of Clare, Sir R. Temple a Baronet and other promotions which I cannot recollect . Judge Coote is reduced to Mr. Coote, and his son suffers here by soliciting for him. I met Sir A. Cairns at court who obliged me to dine with him. . . I cannot but tell you I saw old Mildmay at Saint James's in a red coat which provoked laughter."

1714. Aug. 10th. "Sunn Tavern behind the Royal Exchange." The same to the same.—"This day's courant contains the chief news. I send it lest Caster should omit. The King has been proclaimed with great joy at Edinburgh where all things are quiet and no disturbance. An express from the King is just come to the Regency thanking them for their care, and that he making all haste over. The Lords are adjourned and Commons have voted a supply, the sum not yet named. The gentlemen of Essex met at Pontack's last night to concert matters against a new election. . . . . . The French King has declared no prince shall be more ready to compliment and own our King George than himself."

N.D. [1715]. June 21st. H. Drysdale (apparently a lady) to Mrs. Jane Barrett at Belhus.—"They are now upon the Duke of Ormond in the House of Commons. Mr. Stanhope opened the case. It is the opinion of all that come from the House that it amounts to High Treason, there is an end of Tory mobbing here, for the Whigg mobb being headed by officers and gentlemen has quite silenced them. Mr. Freman the member for Hartfordshire is converted by knowing the villainy of the proceedings and many other gentlemen."

1715. July 30th. The same to the same.—"Lord Oxford is close confined in the tower at General Compton's whom I heard speaking of this last night. The reason of his being there is the representations of the Doctors, for he is really very ill and takes vast quantities of laudanum. Three more articles against him are expected daily to be brought into the House.

"A passage happened yesterday; this is the fact. One Montague formerly a captain in Dragoons but by the by no ways related to the Halifax family, but out of the City; known to most gentlemen at this end of the town; reputed to be a civil sober man, ingenious and good principles, and in good circumstances, came yesterday to Jerusalem Coffee Hous in Speck Alley, of a sudden struck a gentleman who knew him a severe blow on the eye; immediately after, drawing his sword, ran out through the Alley cross Cornhill still with it drawn;

and at the South entrance of the Exchange uttered words to this effect, that he was come in the face of the Sun to proclaim James the third King of England, and that only he was heir. He knocked down another gentleman who happened to be there, knew him and spoke to him. The gentleman I heard relate the story at Tom's Coffee house, Covent Garden, last night. The mobb immediately were for knocking him down, only this gentleman interfered and told 'em the man was struck with madness, as indeed he discovered all the symptoms; foamed at the mouth, grated his teeth, &c. It was the work of five or six men to hold him in a coach. He was carried to justice raving, but thought fitter for a mad-house than Newgate, to the which place he was carried."

N.D. Richard Barrett to Dacre Barrett. On private matters principally.—"The Princess came in a chariot to St. James's at 5 this evening with 4 or 5 coaches and some guards, the women were rendered very disagreeable by their headdress such as I never saw, sort of night clothes. Her 2 children are the finest . . . . I have sent you this pamphlet said wrote by the Bishop of R[ochester] . . . . I supped last night at Mr. Milner's who is Superintendent of the Sick Cattle and has given a recipe the Dutch used which Dr. Sloane approves of. He has already distributed about 1,000*l.* of the Government's money to sufferers. The King has by Mr. Stanhope signified to Mr. Iberville he shall esteem the Canal at Mardike an infringement of the late Treaty."

[1715, Sept.] Richard Barrett to Dacre Barrett.—"Last night ten of the short spikes which stand between your iron rails next Lady B. Norton's were wrenched out and carried off. They have done this without either bending the long rails or damaging the stone work. The whole number of them in front was 42, whereof ten are stolen. Lord Lemmon's house was broke a week ago and they took linen out of the kitchen, the footman was the greatest sufferer whose money and clothes were all carried off . . . . Here is no news worth sending. The French king is certainly dead but Lord Stair has as yet sent no account of it; they believe all messengers and letters were stopped."

N.D. "Court of Requests." The same to the same.—"The report yesterday of Pendennis Castle being siezed and Mr. Boscawen's house burnt by the mob is false."

1752. Idée de la personne et de la manière de vivre du Roi de Prusse et de sa cour.

Il est de la taille de cinq pieds deux pouces, assez proportionné, pas bien fait seulement quelque chose de gauche, acquis par un maintien contraint, la figure agreable et spirituelle, de la plus grande politesse, un son de voix gracieux, même en jurant, ce qui lui est aussi familier qu'à un grenadier, parlant plus correctement le François que l'Allemand, ne parlant jamais sa langue qu'a ceux qu'il sait ne pas entendre le François, d'assez beaux cheveux chatain clair, et toujours en queuë, il se frise et s'accomode lui même, et assez bien, jamais il n'a eu de bonnet de nuit, robe de chambre, ni pantoufle, un mauvais manteau de toile fort crasseux pour se poudrer, toute l'année en habit uniforme de son premier battaillon des gardes qui est de drap bleu parements rouges, brandebourgs d'argent en façon de point d'Espagne des houpes au bout lené Brandebourgs jusqu'a la Taille, veste jaune unie, chapeau point d'Espagne d'Argent plumet blanc, bottes aux jambes toute l'année, et ne sait pas marcher avec des souliers, ni porter son chapeau sous le bras, cette bagatelle lui donne un air contraint singulier; pour briller au mariage prochain, il vient de faire un uniforme de Gros de Tours. Il se leve tous les jours à 5 heures du matin, travaille au moins est-il en son particulier jusqu'a $6\frac{3}{4}$, il s'habille à 7, on lui remet les lettres, placets ou memoires ensuite les lettres des particuliers, et missives venuës de la poste dont il fait decacheter et lire plus ou moins, a 9 heures ses Ministres ou plutôt ses gens d'affaires viennent jusqu'a 11 qu'il sort et va sur la Place ou se monte la parade de la Garde, il fait faire lui même l'exercise sans jamais y manquer. Personne ne la commande à moins qu'il ne soit incommodé, à la demi il rentre chez lui. Reste 4 or 5 minutes dans un salon pour voir si personne n'a rien à lui dire, et rentre en son cabinet en faisant des reverences penchés, n'y aïant que ses gens dans la chambre elles paroissent d'habitude on dit que c'est ce que lui a tourné la taille. Il reprend son travail seul ou avec ses Ministres, s'il n'a pas fini avec eux avant la parade. Il se met à table a midi $\frac{1}{4}$ presque toujours avec les officiers de son premier battaillon; sa table est de 24 couverts, jamais on ne sert plus de 16 plats de cuisine, potage, bouillis, hors d'œuvres, entrées, rots, entremets, et tous 16 ensemble. S'il y a plus poisson de mer ou gibier, il le païe de sa poche, son fruit est un peu elegant. Le diné (*sic*) dure une heures après quoi presque toujours il prend un de ceux qui ont diné et cause en se promenant environ un quard'heure (*sic*) et rentre chez lui avec ses reverences; il arrive assez souvent qu'il fait rentrer avec lui quelqu'un de ses geunes gens, tout ce qui l'entoure est fait à peindre et les plus jolies figures. Il reste renfermé jusqu'a 5 heures que son lecteur vient, c'est ordinairement le Marquis d'Argens, la lecture dure jusqu'a 7 heures, elle est remplacée par le concert qui dure jusqu'à neuf. Le Roi est grand musicien, joue de la flute superieurement, son concert journalier n'est presque composé que d'instruments à vent qui sont les meilleurs de l'Europe. Il a 3 chatrés, une haute contre et Mademoiselle Astona, Piemontoise, ce sont des voix uniques, il ne peut souffrir le mediocre, mais rarement il fait chanter à son petit concert, il faut être dans la plus intime faveur pour y avoir entreé par çi par la quelque jeune seigneur s'il en trouve. A 9 heures viennent les Voltaires, Algarotti, Maupertuis et autres beaux esprits jamais plus que 8, le Roi y compris et un ou 2 mignons, à la demi ils soupent et le service est de 8 plats; le soupé (*sic*) dure presque toujours jusqu'à 11 heures après se fait la belle conversation, à minuit frappant le Roi se couche. Toute l'année voila l'emploi des 24 heures de chaque jour surtout pendant les 9 mois qu'il reste à Potzdam, à moins qu'il ne survienne quelque incident, comme dans le tems çi pour les revuës. Il ne peut souffrir aucun jeu ou spectacles, chasse ni promenades encore moins les beaux cercles. La depense de la cuisine est fixé à 33 ecus d'Allemagne (équivalent à 5 guineés et demi) par jour, il a pour cette somme 24 couverts 16 à diné et 8 à soupé (*sic*), 24 couverts le matin et 8 le soir jamais plus, à moins de ces extraordinaires. S'il y a plus de 24 couverts l'exedent est païé 1 ecu par couvert à celui qui a l'enterprise de la cuisine. Par exemple au futur mariage tout ce qui exedera ne sera païé qu'un ecu, mais tout le gros poisson et le gibier le Roi le païé de sa poche. Sur les 33 ecus l'entreprenneur païe le bois charbon entretien de batterie de cuisine, table linge de cuisine et generalement ce qui a raport à la cuisine, à l'exception des gages de cuisines que le Roi païe lui même, il en a 4, un Francois, un Italien, un Austrichien et un Prussien chacun lui fait 4 plats à diné (*sic*) et 2 à souper qu'il y soit ou non il donne toute l'année à diner aux officier, deson 1er battaillon. Ils out pour boisson aujourd'hui de la biersre demain une bouteille de vin pour deux. Il donne aussi tous les jours à midi 3 grands plats de viande bouillie, ou rotie, du pain et de la bierre pour les officiers des deux autres battaillons de ses gardes à pied, Ils y vont manger s'ils veulent, c'est un espece de halte le prix en est fixé. Jamais l'officier ni le soldat en garnison à Potzdam ne sort de la porte même pour se promener sans un billet signé de lui, ce qu'il accorde rarement, en general toute ce qui est à Potzdam, n'en peut sortir sans permission, même les Princes ses frères qui que ce soit ne peut non plus y aller sans prealablement en avoir obtenu la permission; Messieurs de Borchese (*sic*) n'ont pu l'obtenir. Les honnêtes gens qui connoissent ce lieu y font le moins de sejour qu'ils peuvent il y est peu de moments où la pudeur ne patisse (?). Il y a 5 battaillons en garnison qui ne sortent jamais. On n'y voit que soldats dont on exhale les horreurs. Il n'y a que quelques femmes d'officiers et de soldats qui à peine osent sortir de leurs chambres, on voit l'insulte et le mal très rarement et qui n'a pas le gout du Maitre en est peu fêté. Il a beaucoup d'esprit pas autant de connoissances qu'on veut lui en donner; il n'excle (*sic*) que dans le militaire, dont il est capable de tirer tout l'avantage possible, un travail aisé, facile, expeditif, comprenant ce qu'on veut lui dire premier mot, ne prenant ni ne voulant de conseil, ne souffrant jamais de repliques ni de remonstrances, pas même de sa mère, se connoissant assez aux ouvrages d'esprit soit en vers soit en prose brulant de de (*sic*) faire l'un et l'autre, sans pouvoir arriver au sublime, s'il n'est etaïé. On pretend que dans un moment d'humeur son squeletre d'Apollon dit il y a quelque tems *quand est ce qu'il ne m'enverra plus son Linge sale à blanchir* (sic). Assez mauvais plaisant piquant qui ne lui plait pas, manquant souvent de politique, n'entendant point la partie des Finances, encore moins celle du Commerce, ne tirant que l'argent qu'il aime beaucoup, ne sachant, ni ne voulant semer pour receuillir, traitant presque tout le monde en esclave, tous ses sujets sont tenus avec des entraves dures et terribles pour la moindre faute ou son interret seroit lesé; n'en pardonnant aucune de celles qui tendent á l'exactitude du service militaire, n'aïant à sa solde que des gens utiles et en état de bien remplir leurs devoirs, dès l'instant qu'il n'en a plus besoin il les renvoie avec rien, mieux servi que tout autre avec moins de depense, donnant peu d'appointemens à tout ce qui est grande charge de la cour, qui sont toutes *in partibus* à peu de choses près n'aïant dans tous ses Etats aucun gouvernement de Provinces ni de Villes, il commande seul dans les Provinces et dans les Villes, ce sont les Commandans des regiments qui y sont en garnison. Il ne ne (*sic*) païe aucun Etat Major de Place, ses 3 articles sont immenses chez les autres Potentats. Un militaire qui pendant 30 ans a servi dans tous les grades jusqu'a parvenir à celui de General à son rang, s'il en est content il lui donne un regiment. Le grade de Capitaine aïant une compagnie le met à son aise, sans qu'il en conte au Roi, c'est la justice que l'on rend aux soldats qui fait la fortune du Capitaine, par example les compagnies sont de 110 hommes, après la revuës (*sic*) le Capitaine peut donner 60 congés pour 10 mois, le Capitaine touche la païe toute l'année comme s'il étoit complet, et le soldat n'a rien pendant tout le tems qu'il est absent. En ce qui s'apelle le Maison Militaire il y a à Potzdam et à Charlottenbourg 160 cavaliers à qui l'on donne le nom de Gardes du Corps qui n'ont que la païe et l'habillement de cavaliers et qui reçoivent autant de coups de baton: le reste de sa Garde ce sont des soldats un peu mieux vetus avec la païe ordinaire, les Reines, les Princesses, et les Princes ne savent ce que c'est d'avoir des gardes et dès que le Roi est sortie de Potzdam il n'en a point non plus. Il a un chancelier qui ne parle jamais, un grand veneur qui n'oseroit

Voltaire

tirer une caille, un grand maitre qui n'ordonne rien, un Echanson qui ne sait pas s'il y a du vin dans sa cave, un grand Ecuyer qui n'a pas le pouvoir ce faire seller un cheval, un Chambellan qui ne lui a jamais donné la chemise, un grand maitre de la garderobe qui ne connoit pas son tailleur. Les fonctions de toutes ses grandes charges sont exercés par un seul homme qui s'apelle *Friderickdorf* (*sic*) qui de plus est valet de chambre, ordinaire du quartier, gentilhomme de sa chambre et sécretaire ordinaire du Cabinet.

Tous le Grands sont paié avec le titre d'Exellence (*sic*) toute sa Chambre consiste en 8 pages autant de laquais de Chambre, 4 coureurs et 6 jeunes gens avec l'habillement de differents orientaux, mais tous en couleur de roses chargés de galon. Le reste de sa Livrée n'y ressemble pas du tout, en general il n'aime que les couleurs douces, dans tous les apartemens qu'il occupe, les meubles sont couleur de rose ou Lisla (*sic*) pale; pour lui, les 2 Reines, et la Princesse Amelie, il n'a pas 300 chevaux, pas une seule voiture, pas une seule voiture (*sic*) qui vaille 300 ecus; feu son père aimoit la chasse, avoit un equipage vaille qui vaille, celui ci à son avenement au trone ordonna au grand veneur qui aimoit la chasse à la folie de supprimer tout et qui en representant que c'étoit au benefice pour le Roi, en continuant à vendre le gibier comme par le passé, s'avisa de dire au Roi qu'il perdroit 20,000 ecus de revenus (*sic*) en supprimant la chasse, le Roi lui dit, je vous abandonne dans le moment tout mon équipage mon gibier et la peche de mes rivieres, et vous me donnerez 20,000 ecus par an; le pauvre seigneur n'osa refuser et il a payé jusqu'asteure (*sic*) en se ruinant, il n'a plus de bien, plus de gibier plus de poisson; les gens dans le secret m'ont assuré qu'il étoit à bout et qu'il ne pouvoit païer cette année. Gare Spandau, Spandau est notre Pierre encise avec la difference que l'un est beaucoup plus peuplé que l'autre, les 20,000 ecus ont leur destination manquant il faut un revirement de parties et un nouveau tableau, dont plus d'un souffriront; il faut que cette somme ventre par quelques moïens et toutes les cordes sont si prodiguesement tendues qu'il est dangereux de toucher à aucune. Les subsides imposés sur les sujets sont forts et proportionnés aux revenus des particuliers, suivant les contracts et beaux et a que le sujet fait valoir par lui même sans égard pour ceux qui-devoit (*sic*) hors du nouveau plan, par exemple, j'ai 10,000 livres, mes creanciers jouissent de 5 ou 6 même plus il faut pourtant que je païe autant que mon voisin qui jouit en plein de 10,000 de rente. Tous plaignent les gens de condition en Silesie qui desertent successivement du païs en abandonnant ce qu'ils ne peuvent emporter. On veut que le Maréchal Schwerin ait osé lui dire dans le temps *si vous ne comptez pas de garder cette Province vous en tirez suffisemment, si vous devez la garder beaucoup trop* (*sic*) il lui a tourné le dos et ne lui a jamais pardonné. Pour faire vivre les cordonniers dont le païs est rempli, il vient de defendre de faire, ni de porter des sabots, qu'en resulte t'il, la moitié de ses sujets vont pieds nuds. Il permet d'assommer les hommes à coup de batons, et il defend de fouëtter un cheval de poste. Ce ne sont pas des contes, rien n'est plus vrai. Les gens qui l'approchent le plus veulent que sa politesse ne soit pas naturelle que c'est un reste des temps qu'il avoit besoin de tout le monde contre les persecutions de son père, il n'a point fait de bien à ceux qui se sont exposés à etre pendus pour empecher qu'il n'eut le cou coupé. Il n'a point fait de mal à ceux qui ont opiné qu'il eut la tête tranchée. Il respecte sa mère, elle est la seule personne pour qui il ait une sorte d'attention. Il estime sa femme et ne peut la souffrir, depuis 19 ans de mariage il ne lui a pas encore adressé la parole. Il y a peu de jours qu'elle lui écroit une lettre pour lui demander quelque chose dont elle avoit un pressant besoin, il prit la lettre avec son air riant, gracieux, poli qu'il se donne quand il veut et sans la decacheter devant elle il la dechira, fit une grande reverence et lui tourna le dos. La reine mère est une bonne grosse femme qui va et vit tout rondement. Elle a 100,000 ecus par an (qui font 17,500 livres sterlings) pour l'entretien de sa maison. On pretend qu'elle thesaurise, quatre jours de la semaine, il y a apartement chez elle où les gens du pays ne vont qu'après être invités. Ces jours il y a une table le soir de 29 couverts sur laquelle on sert 8 plats indecemment servis par 6 petits polissons de pages, hommes et femmes y mangent. C'est le grand maitre qui prie, à 11 heures tout le monde se retire, les autres jours la Reine mère mange seule. La grand (*sic*) maitresse, le grand maitre et les 3 filles d'honneur ont leur (*sic*) tables ou l'on sert 2 plats pour tout. Elle est indecemment logée au chateau; son *Mon Bijou* (*sic*) qui est à la porte de Berlin seroit assez joli pour un particulier, elle y passe quatre mois de la belle saison. La Reine regnante est la meilleure femme du monde, toute l'année elle mange seule, elle tient appartement le jeudi, à 9 heures tout le monde se retire, ses morceaux sont coupés, ses pas comptez (*sic*) et ses paroles dictées, Elle est malheureux et fait ce qu'elle peut pour le cacher, à peine à t'elle le necessaire. À la cour elle est logée au second etage, Schönhausen sa campagne à l'exception (*sic*) du jardin que est assez joli. Nos messieurs de la Ru Ste. Honoré s'y trouveroient assez mal logés. La Princesse Amelie est assez aimable. Elle a souvent de l'honneur parcequ'elle voudroit respirer un autre air et que l'etat de fille n'est rein moins qu'agreable dans cette cour. Elle est logée nourrie avec sa mère et a 1,500 ecus par an pour son entretien et ses menus plaisirs. Le Prince Ainé et successeur est dans les mêmes sentimens, et façon de penser que le Roi, son despotism ne sera pas plus doux, son gouvernement sera tout aussi militaire, encore plus interessé s'il est possible, infiniment moins d'Esprit et de connoissances, capable de faire regretter le Roi à ses sujets, sa femme est aussi genée. Elle n'a pas plus d'agrémens que sa soeur. Elle a 2 enfans males. Le Prince étoit le favori du feu Roi, qui pour lui prouver sa tendresse de père n'a jamais voulu qu'il aprit à lire ou à écrire; ce n'est que depuis la mort de son père qu'il l'a appris; son pere lui avoit donné en mourant ce qu'il apelloit son petit trésor, et lui en avoit remis la clef, mais dès qu'il fut expiré le premier soin de son successeur fut de s'en emparer. Le petit trésor contenoit trente millions, le Prince a 120,000 ecus pour lui, sa femme et sa maison. On dit qu'il a du reste qu'il épargne beaucoup. Il commerce, c'est le plus fort marchand de bois des etats de son frère. Le Prince Henri qui va epouser la Princesse de Hesse est le plus agreable; il est poli, genereux, et aime la bonne compagnie. Il a 80,000 ecus de revenus (*sic*) que son Père lui a donné de son vivant des biens confisqués de ceux à qui il a fait couper la tête, et fait mourir dans les fers. Si en se mariant son Frère qui le deteste ne lui donne rien, il ne sera pas à son aise. On lui meuble une maison de particulier ou il logera après son mariage. On le dit Potzdamiste! Pauvre Princesse que vous allez vous trouver decuë (*sic*). Le Prince Ferdinand est un petit chafouin, crapuleux a l'exces que tout le monde evite, personne n'en dit du bien. Il a 100,000 ecus de revenus aussi des biens confisqués. On lui donne un argant considerable. Il est logé chez le Roi, va vivre ou il ne lui coute rien et fait ce qu'il faut pour avoir beaucoup d'argent, tous les trois jours en bottes et habits uniformes. Ils (*sic*) faut qu'ils passent 3 mois àl eurs Regiments comme des Particuliers, la façon de vivre est etonnante pour le peu de depense.

Endorsed: Some Ideas of the King of Prussia and his Court.

1765. Nov. 19th. Gibraltar.—Mrs. Irwin to Lord Dacre. "Mons. de Crillon who commands the Spanish lines is a descendant of Harry the 4th's Crillon, and is lively and agreable . . . . . . He made an entertainment on the King of Spain's name day which was very magnificent and where I was overwhelmed with honours. I was much amused by observing the manners of the Spaniards especially the ladies (as to the men my curiosity had been fully gratified before, almost all the officers had been here; they are handsome and well made, but very few of them can read or write; but they can all play on the guitarre with which accomplishment they seem perfectly contented). There was above three hundred and but one tolerably handsome. *Cicisbeos* are full as much the fashion as in any part of Italy I have heard you describe, with this difference that there is not quite so much delicacy in changing them, and it is consequently more frequent. They are coquette and forward in their behaviour, talk horrid loud and shrill, and keep the men in great subjection; they sit at their feet or else kneel when they talk to them. To complete the matter they all dance Fandangos which is an exceeding indecent dance, so much so, that I felt ashamed of being in the room, although they assured me they are the very same that are danced at the court of Madrid."

1767. May 24th. Grosvenor Square.—The Duke of Grafton to Lord Dacre. Asking Lord Dacre to be in the House on the following Tuesday as a critical division will probably take place, and the House being in Committee, proxies will not avail.

1767. Oct. 25. Great Foster House, Egham.—Thomas Irish to Lord Dacre. Is about to continue the business of boarding and endeavouring to cure all persons afflicted with insanity relinquished by Mr. John Irish. The writer's father David Irish, surgeon and apothecary at Greenwich, has joined him in taking Great Foster House for the purpose. He hopes for the continuance of Lord Dacre's favour, and reports to him on the state of the health of Captain Moore, one of his patients.

1768. Feb. 22. Radway.—Sanderson Miller to Lord Dacre, with particulars of an old chimney piece obtained by Mrs. Nugent from a Manor House at Halstead in Essex. The house belonged to Lord Tilney and the chimney piece, which contained effigies of Henry VII. and his Queen, bore also the arms of Vere, Blount, Howard, Stanley, and Brackenbridge.

1768. May 6th. Knightsbridge.—The Marquess of Granby to Lord Dacre as to promotion for Lieut. Taylor of General Lambert's regiment.

1771. Aug. 11th. Copped Hall.—John Conyers to Lord Dacre; as to the pedigree of the writer. "You are very good my Lord in your friendly assistance and I will cease tormenting you with my Grimgribber."

1773. Nov. 7th. Easton Mauduit near Castle Ashby, Northamptonshire.—Dr. Thomas Percy to Lord Dacre. "I have written very urgently to Mr. Chambers not to delay the delivery of the Bristoll manuscripts, so that I flatter myself they are by this time safely deposited at your Lordship's house in Bruton Street or soon will be. The desire I have not to delay writing any longer to your Lordship makes me defer at present animadverting on Mr. Barett's letters which I here enclose to your Lordship. But as I hope to be in town next month, if your Lordship will then permit me to give them a second perusal I will make some remarks upon them with a view to the final decision of this affair, and I could also wish your Lordship would postpone the delivery of the manuscripts back till then."

[1774]. April 13. Cardigan.—G. H. to Lord Dacre on election matters. "I have paid my labors (*sic*) (and mere porter's work it has been) with almost 100*l.* of dry cash without a pennyworth of credit or a possibility of it. However I am crank and jolly upon the whole, and have escaped the gaol fever and every other disorder which the Taffies might have communicated."

1775. Sep. 12th. Bloomsbury Square.—Charles Plumptre to Lord Dacre as to the explorations of Cook and Fourneaux in the Southern Pacific, enclosing a track which "begins from the Cape of Good Hope; the track explains itself by the course of the arrows. At the end of the first red line the ships were separated by a storm, and the place of rendezvous in that case was to be at New Zealand. They met there, set out both for Otaheite and returned again to Zealand. Why now they took thence different routes I have not learnt. Fourneaux came home and seems never to have got very much towards the Pole. Cook then pushed South; and reached the Antartic, and expatiating again swept the Pacific Ocean, and in a different longitude again ran his ship, not against the Pole, but as nigh as he was able which was to the latitude of 71½ degrees almost. There the consolidated plain of ice put a stop to all farther attempts that way. But this hero was not yet content tho' advanced far towards Cape Horn and homewards, but steered the contrary course, and wide, thro' the immense Pacific in search of what he could find. His ambition brought him again to Otaheite thro' parts unknown before. After a supply of provisions (hogs), exploring yet unknown tracks, he light upon a large and long island placed there towards Terra del Espirito Santo. The land cultivated and plentiful, the inhabitants gentle. He gave to it the name of New Caledonia; adulatory; that the most distant climes might venerate their namesakes, so venerable in these days. Thence proceeding a third time to New Zealand, he returned homeward, and seems to have found considerable islands elsewhere . . . . Captain Phipps reaches ten degrees nearer to the North Pole than Cook did to the South."

[1776, May.] Harley Street.—H. I. de Salis to Lord Dacre. "At the very time that news of the utmost importance was in town, I said boldly to your Lordship that there was none. Quebec is certainly safe; General Carleton repulsed the assailants with very considerable loss (what day of April I forget) and has since been reinforced. General Howe is likewise safely arrived at Halifax, and Governor Tryon writes word (so do many others particularly an officer of the *Phoenix* man of war or frigate) that a report prevailed and was generally credited, that General Lee had fallen into General Clinton's hands, and that the Americans think he had betrayed their cause. This last many people doubt about, but I understand that the King and all the Court believe it. I do not myself conceive what business he had within Clinton's reach, neither do I think treachery at all consistent with the character of the man. I was at the drawing room this morning which was brilliant and crowded. After all the Duke of Montagu (not Lord Bruce) is Governor to the Prince; the latter however was so for two days. Col. Hotham is sub-governor, and a Mr. Arnold of Cambridge sub-preceptor. Lord Hyde kissed hands this morning upon being created Earl of Clarendon. . ."

1776. May 29. Harley Street.—The same to the same. "I cannot help mentioning the news of the day to your Lordship which surprises everybody, even those *who are the nearest to the Gods*, and which may possibly be a secret to the writers of the evening papers as it was to those of the morning ones. Lord Holdernesse and the Bishop of Chester and Mr. Sweet and Mr. Jackson are removed from their posts about the Prince of Wales; and Lord Bruce (to be created Earl of Aylesbury) and Dr. Hurd Bishop of Litchfield and Coventry are named Governor and Preceptor. The particulars of the fracas are not known out of the precincts of the Queen's House; so much only transpires that Mr. Jackson was the person who made the éclat and was displaced so long ago as yesterday se'nnight. . . . . . . People who are not in the secret speculate much upon the trip which Messrs. Stanley and Jenkinson have made to the Continent just at the time that the French Ministry is changed in part and still farther changes are talked of. They speculate too upon Mons. Necker's sudden departure from hence. If M. de Choiseul should be restored to the supreme power in France, which is much apprehended by some, this gentleman would be his *controleur* general. At present he is out of all business, yet he was sent for. Both he and his wife, who is *bel esprit* and *savante* were *fêtés* by all parties, and Garrick played six times extraordinary for Madame."

1776. June 3rd, Harley Street. The same to the same. "Nothing transpires relative to these unaccountable changes about the Prince's person. The Bishop of Chester and Mr. Jackson were spoken to very graciously at the Levee on Wednesday last, and Lord Carmarthen is a Lord of the Bedchamber. Those who frequent Lord Mansfield's say that Jackson has been the cause of the whole disturbance. Lord Holdernesse's people also say that the Bishop of Chester and Jackson have a great deal to answer for; and Lady Holdernesse says it is a secret the world never will know. If your Lordship can make anything out of this, it is more than people in general can. There is however evidently both a disturbance and a secret . . . . . . It is very true that Wortley Montagu is dead, and that the cause of his death was a wound in his gullet occasioned by the breast-bone of a small bird, which mortified. Padua was the place were he died. It seems he came into possession of an estate in fee by the death of the Duke of Kingston in right of his brother, the entail not having been cut off by neglect or oversight. The value of it 1,500*l.* or 2,000*l.* a year: of this he disposes in his will in the following manner. He leaves the bulk of it to his eldest son Edward now in the East India Company's service; he gives to his daughter Mary a nun in a convent in Italy 500*l.*, and 20*l.* a year. He gives to his youngest son Fortunatus (by an Arabian woman, and almost black) 5,000*l.* and 400*l.* a year. He appoints Lord Sandwich and the Duke of Bedford's Palmer executors to this will; to the former he gives 50*l.* and a cameo ring of Jupiter Capitolinus; to the latter 500*l.* and 100*l.* a year out of Fortunatus' legacy till the year 1783 when he comes of age; this to indemnify him for the trouble of the boy's education which he is to superintend. There are besides a variety of legacies, particularly one of 500*l.* to an old Mr. Anderson who travelled with him. I am heartily sorry he has left us at this time; whether the consequence of his return might or might not be marriage (upon any terms) I wish England could have been the resting place for his ashes."

1776. June 10. Harley Street.—The same to the same, as to news from America. The repulse of the assailants of Quebec confirmed. Refers to the cures effected by a "certain high German Doctor" Meyersbach. "Mr. Boehm told me the other day that the Banker with whom this Doctor keeps cash had told him the day before that he remits to his shop 1,000*l.* a month. He lives in Hatton Street, Hatton Garden, administers his own (*i.e.* he makes them up all himself) medicines, and takes no money from the poor. He is a man of a certain age, yet has married an English girl of 18. He has been here two years. It is prodigious what vogue he is in amongst the people of the very first rank." In a postscript is:—"A friend of mine met George Selwyn to-day and asked him if he had heard of this glorious success [at Quebec]? He answered he had, and moreover that the new Lord Clarendon was to write the History of it."

1776. Nov. 4th. Downing Street.—Lord North informs Lord Dacre that the latter's nephew has been appointed a writer in the East India Co's. service.

1777. Feb. 1st. Limerick.—Mr. Gilbert or Silvester O'Halloran to Dr. de Salis, enclosing a portion of the introduction to his proposed "General History of Ireland" for criticism.

1779. Nov. 26th.—E. Capell to Lord Dacre on literary matters, but not interesting.

1781. May 17. Brasennose College [Oxford].—Dr. Thomas Barker thanks Lord Dacre for a drawing of the ancient arch and door of Brasennose College at Stamford. "The beauty of the drawing itself as well as the relation it bears to the College in Oxford will always render it a valuable possession to the Society."

1783. Aug. 2nd. Melvill House.—Lord Leven to Lord Dacre, acknowledging a present of Stillingfleet's Tracts.

1784. August 17. Harley Street.—H. I. De Salis to Lord Dacre. "Next I am to speak about Foreign newspapers and in particular of *Le Courier du bas Rhin* and my father's reasons for preferring that paper to any other.

"First. It is written in a very good style and secondly it conveys good information. It is published under the protection of the King of Prussia at Cleves and speaks with the utmost freedom and great ability of all occurrences that do not immediately concern the Prussian Majesty.

"Every foreign paper has some object *qu'il faut ménager* and the Secrets of the Cabinet of the Belgians are not those one cares most about at present . . . . .

"Your lordship will not want to be told what is new in the political world particularly by a person so many hundred miles from the door of the Cabinet; I will, however, obtrude my political views upon you, and your lordship may treat it as you will.

"It is said and confidently said that Lord Shelburne is coming again into place; and to descend from anything so high to anything so low Parson Bate has offered himself to Government upon condition that they make him a Baronet. It has been likewise much said that a change is likely to be made in the Government of Ireland and that Lord Cornwallis will be the Duke of Rutland's successor.

"The late riot in Dublin has been somewhat exaggerated in the newspapers; but the outlines of the story related there is true. I have seen a letter from a gentleman much connected with the St. George family which says that the officer of that name is very dangerously wounded and that his recovery seems to be almost impossible. Lord Bristol has outdone his own outdoings; as your lordship will admit when I shall have told you that he has ordained his nephew FitzGerald, the FitzGerald who for years had been a nuisance to Society here, and when England was grown too hot to hold him went over to Ireland, seized his own father, confined him, set the whole civil power of the country at defiance, and was the cause of a great deal of bloodshed. He has fought one duel even since he has been in Orders. Church preferments to the amount of 2,000*l.* a year are given to him or intended for him. I think this to be much the most indecent thing, not to say the greatest outrage to Society that has happened in my time.

"The French Ambassador is going and I am heartily glad of it for I know that he was complained of from hence and I began to fear that as a considerable time had elapsed and I had heard nothing further that we had not credit enough in the French Court to get him recalled. On the Prince's birthday however I saw evidently that he had been told by his Court to hold his hand, for his house was not illuminated and one of the papers to-day contains an advertisement desiring all persons who may have demands on him or his domestics to apply before the 25th inst. I trust he goes to return no more for I think it an unpardonable offence in an Ambassador from that Court in particular to interfere in our domestic politics."

1784. Sep. 7th. Kirkhill by Edinburgh.—Lord Buchan to Lord Dacre, upon various artistic subjects, giving a list from memory of Royal Historical Portraits in Scotland.

1784. Nov. 19th. Haigh.—Lady Bradshaigh to Lord Dacre as to a portrait in the writer's possession, said to be of the Countess of Sheppey. and other pictures originally belonging to Viscount Bayning and divided among his children (among which was a picture of Our Lord and His two disciples at Emmaus, by Titian).

(N.D.) Paper endorsed: "Schedule of the papers deeds and letters in the Great Writing Table."

Among the papers scheduled the following are of the greatest interest:—

"Life of John Lennard with a pedigree of the family both written by Sampson Lennard Esq. his son."

"Some Antiquities and papers relating to the Dacres, Lennards, and Barretts."

Bundle 14 contains among others:—
Catalogue of pictures at Penshurst.

"Historical and Architectural account of the Westminster Abbey and its necessary repairs in a letter from Sir Christopher Wren to Dr. Atterbury, Bishop of Rochester."

Bundle 18 contains:—"Two Letters from Sir Francis Walsingham to John Lennard Esq."

Bundle 19 contains:—"Curious papers concerning the wrongs done to Margaret Lady Dacre by her sister-in-law Anne Lady Dacre."

Bundle 20 contains:—"Letters from Sir Henry Wotton to Edward Barrett Esqre. (afterwards Lord Newburgh)."

Bundle 21 contains:—"Copy of last will of Isolda de Belhouse dated 1353."

Bundle 34 contains:—"Letter from Sir William Herbert to Mr. Morgan containing a challenge."

The contents comprised:—

"The slanders about the Exors. of Archbishop Parker at Lambeth." Since put in the Red book.

Bundle 36 contains:—"Lord Buchan's last address to Scotch Barons and nobles &c."

W. O. HEWLETT.

THE MANUSCRIPTS OF CAPTAIN F. C. LODER-SYMONDS OF HINTON WALDRIST MANOR, BERKSHIRE.

MSS. of Captain Loder-Symonds.

At Hinton Waldrist is preserved a small collection of papers of Col. Henry Marten, the regicide. The manor belonged early in the seventeenth century to Sir Henry Marten, Knt., Judge of the Prerogative Court and of the Admiralty, and passed out of the hands of his son Henry towards the end of the Commonwealth period, by purchase, to John Loder, a gentleman of the neighbourhood. All the property of Col. Henry Marten (which included estates in Derbyshire and Herefordshire) had become heavily encumbered with mortgages through (as it seems) his extravagance, and the great majority of the letters are concerned with debts and difficulties which pressed upon him, and which led to his confinement for several years within the Rules of the Upper Bench. These letters were brought to light upon examination of several boxes which for the most part were filled with old leases, conveyances, and other law papers, and although there is not much of political or historical importance in them they were found well to repay examination. Probably upon the Restoration much of the Colonel's correspondence may have been destroyed to save it from falling into unfriendly hands; or, possibly, what has now been discovered, and which is all more or less in soiled and crumpled condition, may only be a remnant saved by chance out of much that may have been regarded as mere waste paper when the house at Hinton changed hands. The fragments of drafts of political tracts, the illustrations of the close relations of intimacy between Major Wildman and Marten as being two of the leaders among the Levellers, and the characteristically out-spoken letter from John Lilburne, are specially noticeable. Another interesting item is one which does not relate to Marten but belongs to the Loder family; a valuable farm and household account from 1610 to 1620, which cannot be surpassed in minuteness of detail.

In the following Report I have arranged these papers under the following heads:—I. Early Deeds. II. The Loder Account-Book. III. Miscellaneous Papers and Letters. IV. Petitions. V. Orders of Parliament, &c. VI. Family Letters and Papers. VII. Fragments of Political Tracts. VIII. Letters of the Chambre Family. IX. Harley Papers.

Upon the Marten papers follow, under a ninth heading, two which came into the possession of the Symonds family of Herefordshire from the house of the Harley family at Eywood in the same county. The first is that narrative of the death of John Hampden in which the fatal wound is attributed to the bursting of his own pistol. The paper appears to be a copy made, not with perfect accuracy but in a very legible hand, from some other paper, or, it may be, from dictation, and is probably of a date about 1720. The story is first mentioned in Laurence Echard's *Appendix* to his *Hist. of England*, fol., Lond. 1720, where Echard relates it in a few lines with the words "as I am assur'd by a great man", no doubt hereby referring to the Earl of Oxford. It is next said to be told at length in the *St. James' Chronicle* for 1761, as "found written on a loose sheet of paper in a book bought out of Lord Oxford's family," being very likely the very paper now in Capt. Loder-

Symonds' possession. The substance is given in Noble's *Memoirs of the Protectoral house of Cromwell*, 1787, vol. ii., p. 71, and it is noticed in Lord Nugent's *Memorials of Hampden* only to be discredited on the authority of Henry Pye, the poet laureate (who was the grandson of the Sir Robert Pye who figures in the story) as being unknown to him. The narrative, however, is so circumstantial in its details, and as an invention so purposeless, that it appears to deserve more consideration than it has hitherto received, and which it may have partly missed from no direct source for it having been hitherto distinctly traced. Both this and the following letter of Swift's, as well as several of the Marten papers, have been framed and glazed for their better preservation; and together with this one is framed the envelope of a letter addressed and franked by Lord Oxford, which was found in the same box with this paper, but the handwriting is not the same.

The second Harley paper is a very characteristic letter from Dean Swift, which is without address, but was written to some member of the Earl of Oxford's family. The care shown by the writer for the due and efficient maintenance of the choir of St. Patrick's Cathedral, while confessing (in an original way) his own entire want of musical knowledge and taste, reflects some credit on him in a particular in which it might not have been anticipated, but the *naive* declaration that it was more important to secure a good singer for the cathedral than a good parson for a church-living affords on the other hand a contrast which is thoroughly Swiftian.

I. A small parcel of *Early Deeds* is of interest. It consists of these :—

1. Grant by William de Bocl[an]d to William de Meletune of one virgate of land in Berecote [in the parish of Buckland] formerly held by William son of Britihild, with a garden, and one acre in Wicroft. Large green seal, with a knight on horseback; inscription effaced. Fifteen witnesses, Roger de Kingeston, Reg. de Meletune, Hugh Mansell, Reg. de Abendone, &c. Date about 1160–70.

2. Grant by Isabella de Boville, widow, to Sir William de Ulchote, knt., in marriage dowry with her daughter Helizabeth of the mill in Glosthorp called Londmilne. Oval red seal; a Roman gem representing a foot-soldier with sword and shield, with inscription on a broad margin of the setting, "+ Frange, Lege, Lecta Tege." Witnesses: Adam de Risinges, Reg. de Geytone, Will. le Nugun de Wykes, Thomas le Sire, Roger de Saldeford, Gilebert son of Warin, Will. de Potesford, Thomas de Risinges, John de Batesford, clerk, Peter de Bertone. Beautifully written: *c.* 1230–40.

3. Grant by Fraric son of Roger Esprinkyn to the Lady Elizabeth de Burnham, daughter of Richard Mauduyt, of $5\frac{1}{2}$ roods of land called Coneres Croft between the land of Juliana daughter of William and Floria daughter of Sabina, abutting on the water running from the east and the lands of Fraric son of Matilda and Symon son of Wlfketel, in the village of Burnham [Bucks]. Witnesses, Sir Geoffrey de Oyri, Sir Richard Mauduyt, Sir Peter de Peleville, Ralph de Beaufo, Thomas de Holcham, Tho. Crakefeld, Symon de Kerebroc, Roger de Loges, Reg. le Moyne, Barth. de Northgate, William Underburt, William de Angre, Roger de Saldeford, John de Grotener, clerk. Small fragment of seal: ". . . . Esprigk —" *c.* 1250.

4. Grant by John de Hulekote to Will. de Muletone son of Walter de Muletone of one virgate in Berekote which Henry le Frankeleyn formerly held, for the sum of fifteen marks. Witnesses, Sir Henry de Pesie and Sir Robert de Krafford, knts., Will. de Wrthe, Will. de Wycumbe, Reg. sub Gardino, Elyas de Neweutone, Richard Sewale, Peter le Blund, Will. de Wythone, bailiff of Boclond, Roger Gymel, William Hyeche of Kerswell, Roger de la Cumbe. Fragment of seal: "S' Joh'is Hu . . . .". *c.* 1260–70.

5. Grant by John de Claypol, dwelling in Newerk [Notts] and Avicia his wife to Matthew de Bakewell and Matilda his wife and his daughter Dionysia of a toft and buildings in Newerk in le Carter gate, between the toft of William Coag and the highway called Baldertungate. Two oval white seals: "+ S' Avecie fil' Hvgon' de . . . ;" 2 "S' Joh'is de Cleypol." Six witnesses. *c.* 1300.

6. 1309 [Feb. 16].—Sunday next after the feast of S. Scolastica, 2 Edw. II. Grant by Roger atte Flete of Wolfrissetone and Dionysia his wife, co-heiress of Alice who was the wife of Will. Roberd of Harewell to Milo de Mortone of 5½ acres in Westhakeburne. Witnesses, Thomas and John de Saundreville, Rich. Huscarl, Will. de Makkene, Rob. de Sottewelle, Manser de Mortone, Walter de Chiltone, Rich. le Oyselur, William de Walyngford, clerk. Two green seals: "S' Reggeri (*sic*) ate Flete:" "S' Dyonis' ate Flete."

7. 1348 [May 18].—Sunday before the feast of St. Dunstan, 22 Edw. III. Grant by Rich. Alayn of Harwell and Christina his wife to Walter Houghchild of Harwell of a cottage in Westhakeborne. Witn. John de Aula, John Brunz, Will. Bayllol of Harewell, Sir Rob. Dagenhale, chaplain, &c.

8. 1366 [Nov. 23].—Monday, the feast of St. Clement, 40 Edw. III. Grant by John atte Crouch of Harewelle to William Edward of the reversions of land &c. held by William Houchild and Margery his wife, Stephen Body and Alice his wife, and Matilda le Fort, in Harewell.

9. 1370 [Feb. 7].—Thursday after feast of Purification B.M.V. 44 Edw. III. Grant by Agnes le Waihol wife of Master Walter Howchyld to John Ket of Westhakeborne of land in Harewelle.

10. 1376, Apr. 13.—Easter Day 50 Edw. III. Bond from Thomas de Newentone, son of Elias de Newentone of Bokelonde to Elias de Thorp, citizen of London, in 60*l.* for the enfeoffing the latter in certain lands in Boclonde of which he is entitled to the reversion.

11, 12, 13. 1514, 1521, 1523.—Three leases from John Underhill, dean of the College of St. Nicholas in Wallingford Castle, and the Chapter to Richard Lowder (*al.* Loder) of Prince Harewell, of the manor of Harewell, for the term of 60 years, at an annual rent of 10*l.* The third lease is in English, and is granted to Rich. Loder and Alys his wife. The seal of the College is nearly perfect in each instance, the inscription only being broken: "S' coē decani et sub-decani collegii infra castrum de Waling[eford]."

14. 1530, 10 Feb. 21 Hen. VIII.—Appointment by the same dean and the fellows of the College, of the office of steward of their manors of Annersfee in Chepynge Wycombe and of Harwell to William Yonge and Roger his son, with an annual salary of 66*s.* 8*d.* The seal is nearly perfect; and the names of all the members of the College are subscribed, written (as it seems) by two hands: "per me, Ricardum Randall, clericum, subdecanum hujus collegii; per me dominum Hamonem Grosvenor, socium hujus collegii;" Sir Thomas Augustine,

Richard Adene, James Broughton, Thomes Crowche, Richard Lane, John Adene, John Carver, and Robert Bateman.

15. 1548, May 26.—General pardon from Edw. VI. to Richard Holcote, esq., senior, of Bercote. Great seal, broken.

16. 1572, Dec. 13.—Lease from John Fysher, of Longworth, gentleman, to Richard Aldworth, of Pusey, warrener, of his lodgehouse and warren of coneys in Longworth, for seven years, rendering annually thirty score couple of coneys and rabbits; and should the lessor need more coneys in the year, he may have them at 8*d.* the couple.

17. 1604, April 10. 2 James.—Copy, on vellum, made about the beginning of the present century, of letters patent of William, lord Knolles, as High Constable of the Castle of Wallingford, reciting (in English) letters patent of Henry III. exempting the tenants and residents of the Honour of Wallingford, now Ewelme, from payment of all tolls and customs, and declaring all the tenants and residents in Hinton who are of the said Honour to be thereby consequently exempt from tolls. (There is also a copy of this document on paper, made in the 17th century.)

II. 1610–1620.—A folio book of 78 leaves, closely written, containing a minute account of farm produce, cost, and profits, in each year from 1610 to 1620, with household expenses. Unfortunately neither the name of the writer nor the name of the place occurs, but the book evidently relates to some Berkshire property of the family of Loder.*

It is probable that the farm concerned was at Harwell, and may have belonged to Richard Loder, father of the John Loder who subsequently came into possession of Henry Marten's Hinton estate. The writer states that he was 21 years of age in November 1610, when he assumed the management of a part of the farm, and was then a bachelor, but three or four years later he speaks of his wife and daughter. The minuteness of detail renders this account book one of great interest and value in connection with the history of agriculture and prices. As brief specimens I add the following extracts:—

"In anno 1614

"Money payd servants for theyr wages at faithtide† in anno supradicto.

Inprimis, to Robert Androwes my carter, for his, - - - - -	iij^{li} vj^{s} viij^{d}.
Item, to John his brother as boy to goe to plow - - - - - -	xxiiij^{s}.
Item, to Johan Colle my maide, - -	xlvij^{s}.
Item, to Mary my other maide, - -	xl^{s}.
Summa tota of theyr wages is - -	viij^{li} xvij^{s} viij^{d}.

* It is worth noting that from 1651 to 1658 the series of letters from the bailiffs of the manor of Hartington in Derbyshire, and from the steward of the manor of Leominster in Herefordshire, Thomas Deane, as well as from other business agents (Will. Wardley, John Cleveland, &c.) to Colonel H. Marten, is extremely full, and the letters afford complete details of the management of the estates, the difficulties with tenants, &c. during that period. There is a quarto book containing a "Survey of the Lordship of Leominster," made in 1651, which gives the names of all the several pieces of land in the several farms, &c., with their measurement, and a table of all the tenants, with the yearly values. On one sheet are notes about Leominster written early in the 17th century, containing two charters copied from the Reading Chartulary in Cotton MS. Domitian III. about the church of Leominster, granted by Richard Bishop of Hereford in 1123, and by Bishop Hugh, with extracts from Leland's Itinerary and Collectanea. These are interesting as being probably the earliest extracts made from Leland's MSS., while they were in Burton's possession.

† This date occurs in several places. It would seem to mark the octave of Michaelmas, the sixth of October being St. Faith's day.

Memorandum that every of these spent me in meat and drink (as by my notes in anno 1613 I may reade and perceave) one with another, xij^li. a piece and a little above. Soe that I judge it were good (in such deare yeares) to keep as few servants as a man possibly can by any meannes convenient. To effect which I know no other meannes but by putting forth a man's land to tillage, or at a rent, or els keeping them at borde wages."

"How the prices of wheat went [in 1616].

"Inprimis, in September of redwheat at 3*s.* 2*d.* a bushell, taking one time with another. In October therof for 3*s.* 5*d.* In November, sould soe. In January whitwheat for 3*s.* 4*d.* In February therof at 3*s.* 11*d.*, the redwheat then for 4*s.* 3*d.* In March therof for 4*s.* 1*d.*, and whitwheat at 3*s.* 6*d.* In Aprill sould of the redwheat at 4*s.* 1*d.* In May therof for 3*s.* 8*d.* In June therof for 3*s.* 9*d.*, and of the whitwheat at 3*s.* 5*d.* In August at 4*s.* and 4*s.* 2*d.*

Mem. that vij and viij sheves of redwheat did ordinarily yeld a bushell.

"How the prices of wheat went [in 1617]. Inprimis, in October I sould whitwheat for 5*s.* 4*d.* the bushell. In November redwheat at 4*s.* 4*d.* In December therof (taking one time with another) at 4*s.* In February at 3*s.* 11*d.* In March at 3*s.* 10*d.* In Aprill at 4*s.* 4*d.* redwheat. In the begining of May whitwheat at 4*s.* and 10*d.*, and 5*s.*; at latter end therof the same for 4*s.* 4*d.* and 5*d.*, and some 2*d.* In June at 4*s.* 2*d.* the same whitwheat, and redwheat at 3*s.* 8*d.* and 7*d.* In July, the begining therof, the same redwheat at 3*s.* 9*d.* and 10*d.*, and at latter part therof for 4*s.* 1*d.*; and whitwheat at 4*s.* 1*d.* at beginning of July, for yt was all cleane without smutte, the red being all smuttie. In August of the redwheat at 4*s.* and 3*s.* 10*d.*, and of the whitwheat at 4*s.*"

Eight bushels are reckoned to the quarter in this account, as now; not nine, as reckoned by Adam Smith for that period.

In 1619 wheat was much cheaper. "In October I sould my best at 3*s.* 3*d.* and 3*s.* 2*d.*, and the worst at 2*s.* 11*d.*" In the course of the year the price goes down to 2*s.* 2*d.* at the lowest.

The orchards of apples (pippins, russets, &c.) pears and cherries were very profitable. In 1618 of cherries the writer had six thousand four hundred and two pounds for sale, besides what were given away and consumed in his own house. The pigeons also were a great source of profit.

In the accounts for 1618 there are these items:—

"Rice spent was but 1^lb which cost - - iiij^d.
Sugar was vj^lbs dim. which cost - - viij^s v^d."

The writer ends each year with expressions of thankfulness to Almighty God for his goodness to one so unworthy of it as himself.

III. The *Miscellaneous Papers* commence with a few which belonged to Sir Henry Marten, the Judge of the Prerogative Court. Amongst these is a commission, on parchment, signed by Archbishop Whitgift, empowering Sir Daniel Dun to hold a visitation of All Souls' College, Oxford, in the Archbishop's stead, dated at Croydon, 8 July, 1601; and a parcel of twenty-one papers, which belonged also to Sir D. Dun, relative to the case of Samuel Palachio a Jew, a born subject of the King of Morocco, and employed as his agent in the United Provinces, where he had been authorized to raise men for the service of Morocco, who, having put into Plymouth with a ship called the Sun, was arrested on complaint of the Spanish ambassador, on charges of piracy against the subjects of the King of Spain. On report from Sir E. Coke, Sir J. Cæsar, and Sir D. Dun, the Privy Council decide on 20 March 1614–5 that he is not subject to any criminal action for his acts, there being actual war between Morocco and Spain, and is theretore ordered to be released. The papers include a short letter from Sir Ralph Winwood to Sir D. Dun, dated 20 May, in which he says that he does not understand the merits of the case, but requests "that the Ambassador may receave as much favour as law and equity can permitt"; a letter, in Spanish, from Palachio to the Lord Admiral, dated at London, Dec. 20, 1614; and a declaration by Lewis de Halinge, in Latin, that the ship at Plymouth was made and bought in Holland, and employed in the service of Morocco.

[159 . .] May 22. London.—Letter from Edward Grey to John Fisher, at Longworth. Could not answer before, by reason of being at the Court. Has imparted his letter to Sir William Russell, who takes it very kindly, and desires him to hold on his course, "because he will procede in the sute, for the Queene saied within these tenne daies that he shuld have it, and did bid my Lo. of Essex to tell the deane as muche. . . . . The deane will be at Oxford very shortly, where I would wishe you to mete him."

1600, March 14, 42 Eliz.—Declaration signed by John Stocton, Rob. Davys, and Rob. Newman, that a hound bitch being locked in a chamber in the house of John Fisher, esq., of Longworth, Berks, where he and John Stocton were a little before conferring, did eat and tear certain writings and spoil the seals thereof.

1604, Feb. 6. Longworth.—Letter from John Fisher to —— Yat, respecting some dispute at law with Sir Edward Fiennes.

n.d.—Draft of a petition to the King from the ecclesiastical judges and civil lawyers in respect to a petition from Convocation with regard to prohibitions; with part of an argument on the same subject.

1614–5.—Notes of proceedings in the case of one Marsh of Southwold, charged by the Danes with piracy.

1617, Nov. 20.—Warrant from the Ecclesiastical Commissioners (signed by the Archbishop of Canterbury, Bishop of London, W. Byrde, G. Newman, and Tho. Edmondes) for the arrest of Sir Edward Lewes, of Vann, Glamorganshire, and his wife's sister, Anne Morgan.

[1619?]—Statement, and argument, on behalf of the Dutch East India Company respecting a ship called the "Black Lyon," taken and accidentally destroyed by the English East India Company in December, 1618.

1622, May 9. "At my house at St. Paul's."—Letter from Dr. John Donne to Sir H. Martin. "Sir, I wayted upon you heretofore when a cause which concernd me was brought before you and others, in another way, as Delegates. It ys for a pretended resignation of the churche of Keiston, upon which pretence one Mr. Silliard procured a superinstitution. To my L. Keeper I have declard the direct truth of the whole proceedinge for matter of fact; and for matter of law, I have told him, and them, That if any man learned in eyther law, of Mr. Silliard's own counsayle, would say that the church upon such a resignation was voyd, I would relinquish yt. And now, I am informed that my L. Keeper hath referrd that poynte to you. If I had not come home from Bedfordshire late and weary, I would have wayted upon you, but it had been onely to salute you, not much to solicite you (for that I know needs not) that you wyll be pleasd to take that poynte into your good consideration; and so, Sir, I rest

Yours ever to be dispisd,
J. DONNE."

The letter is endorsed with a rough draft of Marten's report on the legal points of the case, dated 13 May.

[Between 1620–30.]—Petition to Sir H. Marten from Joseph Ewer, curate of St. Mary Somerset, London under Mr. Thomas Burton, for a share in the gift of Mr. John Browne, deceased; with a note of the gift of 4*l.* [Burton, the rector, died in 1631.]

1623, Sept. 23. Farmon, co. Cork.—Letter from Richard Fisher to Sir Hen. Marten. He has bought the place of King's Attorney of Munster for 300*l.*; but is pressed by debts in England, and is unable to complete the payment; begs the loan of 30*l.* for two or three years without interest.

1626, Nov. 7. }
1627, Apr. 23. } Receipts by Will. Bigmore and Tho. Tuer, bursars of St. John's College, Oxford, for rents due from Sir H. Marten; in the second case received by the hands of William Chillingworth.

1628.—List, on seven parchment rolls, of all the inhabitants in the hundreds of Hormer, Ock and Murton in Berkshire, and the towns of Abingdon and Wallingford, assessed for payment of two out of five subsidies granted by Parliament; delivered to Robert Loder, junior, of Harwell, gent., for him to gather.

1628, Apr. 4.—Report of the speeches of the King and the Duke of Buckingham "this daie", on the report being made at the Council Board by the counsellors of the Commons' House of the grant of the preceding subsidies.

1629, Hil. term, 4 Charles I.—Copy of writ for recovery of a debt of 200*l.* due from John Fisher of Longworth deceased to Sir Edward Stanley of Ensham; with a receipt signed by Sir "Kenelme Digby" as administrator of the will of Sir E. Stanley, deceased, of the sum of 150*l.* from Sir Henry Martyn, in full satisfaction, 12 July, 1639.

n.d.—Copy of a memorial of the French ambassador concerning a ship called the *Hope* of Calais captured by an English ship of war commanded by Sir Edward Steward when coming with a cargo from Spain. The margins of the paper are filled with the draft of a letter on the case to the Secretary of State from Sir H. Marten, in a postscript to which he recommends Dr. Ryves, his Majesty's Advocate, for promotion.

1632, Aug. 8. Maidencott.—Letter from Seymour Lile to Joseph Nixon, respecting some suit for tithes with one Stroud. Seal of arms.

[1633.]—Part of the draft of an argument by Sir H. Marten against the legality and validity of Sir Edw. Coke's will.

1638, June 11.—Acknowledgment by Sir Francis Popham of the receipt of 180*l.* from Sir Henry Marten for threescore trees out of Littlecote woods.

On the same leaf is an acknowledgment by Henry Marten on behalf of his father Sir Henry of the receipt from Thomas Boyland on 13 June of 320*l.*, being the remainder of 500*l.* given by Lord Craven for the repairing of Shrivenham Church.

1639, June 15.—Declaration signed by Robert Veysey and others that Mr. Alderman Pratt's bank in the parish of Buckland, now questioned to be cut by the Commissioners of Sewers, has stood time out of mind, and that the inundations thereabouts do not proceed from it but from the narrowness of the Thames below it, belonging to Rob. Veseye, of Chimney, esq. (the Thames being there only 27 feet broad, but next Mr. Alderman's ground 36 feet), as also from the stopping of a common water-course called Boylake in the lordship of Sir H. Martyn.

1642, Dec. 26.—Return by Samuel Warcopp, bailiff of Southwark and keeper of the Compter Prison there, of the names of the persons committed to his custody, with copies of commitments and discharges annexed.

Peter Turner, M.D. - }
Robert Terrant, his servant }
Mr. Joab Weale - - } In custody.
Sir Anthony Percivale - }

Henry Asquith, a delinquent, in custody, by warrant from the Speaker of 29 Oct. 1642.

Mr. Roger Clarke discharged by the Lord Mayer.

Mr. George Gildon discharged by order of the House of Commons.

Mr. Henry Booth - }
Capt. Collins - }
Mr. John Ryding } Discharged upon bail by the committee for the
Mr. Vaughan - } safeguard of the kingdom, 23 Dec. 1642.
Mr. William Wade }
James Frost - }

"Thomas Tiser in custodie, who made an escape the 14th of December, and is taken againe this 26th of December."

Annexed are copies of warrants, &c.:—

1. Order of the House of Commons on 20 Sept. 1642 that Capt. Fotherby, Capt. Robert Bolles, Robert Rookes, George Drewell, Lieut. John Bellano, Peter Turner, M.D. and Robert Terrant his servant, be committed to several prisons at the discretion of the Sheriff of Middlesex.

2. Order of the House, 24 Oct., for the committal of Mr. Roger Clarke, Mr. Joab Weale, and Mr. George Gildon "for being refractory to the propositions for raysing of horse money or plate."

3. Order of the House, 31 Oct., for the committal of Thomas Tiser, master of the ship that brought officers and soldiers to Yarmouth.

4. Order of the House, 12 Nov., for the committal of Sir Anthony Percivall, Capt. Collins, Mr. John Ryding, Mr. Vaham (*sic*), clerk, Mr. Henry Booth, Mr. William Wade, and James Frost.

5. Order of the House, 24 Dec., referring a petition from Roger Clarke, grocer, to the Lord Mayor and Sheriffs, with an order from the latter the same day for his discharge.

1642, 22 Dec.—List of prisoners committed on Friday, Saturday, and Tuesday last to Lambeth House by my lord mayor and some of the trained bands; viz.:—

Edward Crosse, a thread dyer,
John Adams, citizen and weaver,
Humphrey Swan, an embroiderer,
John Horden, hosier in the Exchange,
John Swale, cheesemonger at Billingsgate,
Henry Mosse, of London, scrivener,
Mr. Edward Trussell, mercer in Paternoster Row,

Thomas Fryer, ammunitioner and chandler in Tower Street,
Thomas Heb, citizen and butcher,
Mr. Valentine Beale, merchant,
Mr. Edward Cuthbert, a woollen draper in Paul's Churchyard.

"These severally say they know not for what they were committed, unless for subscribing the late petition for peace. (*In another hand*) But by the order of the House the cause is expressed for being suspected to have bene active in the late tumults in London."

[1642.]—Charge signed by Vavasor Powell, John Williams, and David ap Rees, of Radnorshire, against Capt. Charles Price, Hugh Lloyd, High Sheriff of the county, and Brian Crowther, esq., for having executed the commission of array on Sept. 15, proclaimed the Earl of Essex traitor, for saying the Parliament was a silly and simple Parliament, &c.

[*c.* 1642 ?]—List of "reformado" captains, lieutenants, ensigns, and quartermasters, appointed by warrant of 13 Dec., and of captains, lieutenants, ensigns, and cornets, appointed by warrant of 16 Dec.

1642.—List of the "command men" in Wood Street, Compter, committed by order of Parliament.

Thomas Newtervill, committed 9 Feb. 1641, till he should give good caution not to go into Ireland.

Capt. Thomas Ketleby, 11 Oct. 1642, for high treason. [See Clarendon, *Hist. Reb.*, v. 381.]

Sir Edward Radney, knt., 12 Oct. 1642, for levying men against the Parliament.

Capt. William Hudson, Capt. Henry Bradneux, and George Jackson, 1 Dec. 1642, for levying war against King and Parliament.

1643, May 23 "1 of the clokke," Layton.—Col. Samuel Luke to Col. Marten.

"Sir, That you may see what necessity there was of an order of Parliament for the raysinge the payment for the dragoones, I cannot but lett you know that some townes whoe haue these 3 months brought in their dragoones with pay, and that with cherfullness, are now diswaded by some gentry, and told that it [is] without order of Parliament, soe that they would haue the world [believe] that your orders and his Excellency's for the raysinge of forces for the defence of the Kingdom are but vaine syphers. If the Parliament desire to know their names they shall be informed by me, though they haue bin my friends and neighbours. I pray, Sir, lett me heare your opinion in it, and what the house will doe, for our honest gray-coated countrymen ar as forward as hart can wish, and none backward but such as haue both their persons and their goods now in London, whoe will doe very little, and that they doe with as ill a mind as may be. Thus with my service presented to you, and assuring you that none shall be my friend longer then he is a friend to the Commonwealth, I rest,

Yours in all serviceable respects,

SAM. LUKE."

1642–1646.—Two sheets with full particulars of the taxes paid by tenants of Col. Marten at Hinton for the two armies of the King and Parliament, and of the losses sustained by both; mentioning the regiments of Prince Maurice, Lord Wilmot, &c., the army of Sir W. Waller at Newbridge, and Gen. "Cromell's" army.

1647, Aug. 27. Preston.—Letter to the members of Parliament for Lancashire enquiring whether Parliament has issued an order (as reported) for disbanding all the soldiers of that county except the garrison of Liverpool; signed by Alex. Rigby, John Starkie, Ri. Haworth, J. Fletewoode, and Rob. Cunliffe.

—— Nov. 1. Charing Cross.—Letter from B. Kingesmille to Col. Marten representing the request of Lady Woodward that she may not be called upon to pay again back-rents which were received by the King's garrison, by whom she was totally plundered and a great part of her house pulled down.

1649, May 3. London.—Letter from Thomas Oinatt to John Dove asking him to assist Capt. Meservy in recovering some satisfaction from Parliament for goods of Oinatt's taken by their ships in 1643.

1648–9, Jan. 12.—Letter from Lucy Richmond to the same, asking him to assist his old neighbour Mr. Thornton to regain his place of Chaff-Wax.

[1649.]—Mr. Rich. Warde, mayor of Lincoln, having stayed a brief which came there about 16 June on behalf of Farringdon, together with one on behalf of Torrington, pretending that that for Farringdon was unjustly obtained, Col. Martin and the Knights of the shire are desired to certify that the aspersion charged upon the brief is false.

—— Oct. 31. Bristol.—Letter from George Bishop to Col. Marten about the difficulty of completing the business of the Forest [of Dean] Commission.

—— Nov. 8. Aldersgate Street.—Just. Povey to the same, asking him to pay a debt by purchasing for the writer some crown land of which he is tenant.

1649, Dec. 12. Belfast.—Copy of a letter from Sir Charles Coote and R. Venables to the Speaker of the House of Commons, desiring relief for the poor English inhabitants of Lisnegarvy, the town having been burned and pillaged by Col. Monro and Sir Phelim O'Neil.

1650, Apr. 22. Edmunton.—Letter from Clement Oxenbridge to John Wildman at Col. Marten's about some private business.

—— Apr. 29.—Letter from Henry Anderson to Col. Marten begging him to assist a petition which the Speaker will present to Parliament, for his release from imprisonment for debt: his own children have procured a sequestration against him; he has never done anything against the Commonwealth.

—— June 2–6.—News letters, in French, from Paris and Bourdeaux.

—— June 30. Bourdeaux. — Letter from D. Batailhey to his brother Joseph Batailhey, a merchant in London, with particulars of the proceedings of the French army. *French.*

—— July 10.—G. Crouche to Col. Marten, begging him to be in Parliament when the business of some ladies is brought on.

—— Aug. 30. Plymouth.—Edward Blagge to Col. "Fitzeames" [Fitzjames]. Desires to acquaint the Council of State "that Ashton whoe is governor of Antigua hath proclaymd Charles there, King of England, Scotland and Ireland, and courted very strongly Nevis and St. Christopher's to doe the like by letters to that very effect from Willoughby; whoe have returned this reply both to Ashton and Willoughby, that they will take nether partye, but allowe free trade to all commers. Ashton hath a maine designe to put Barbadoes upon forming a fleete of shippes under commaund of Plunkett."

—— Aug. 20. Saumur.—Walter Blount [to Marten?] desiring advice how best to secure himself against a charge of delinquency likely to be made against him through his uncle Richard.

—— Nov. 13. Wittlesey.—[The Earl of] Portland to the same, congratulating himself, "my deare Lo. Lovelace, and I thinke all my freinds and acquaintance, that you are in the chaire for letting loose the law into the contry, wherein I am certaine you will be as carefull for debtors as for creditors," but especially "for the safe arrivall of my lord embassador, or rather dove George, for I heare he comes with an olive branch." Subscribed, "Your most affectionate servant."

—— Nov. 13. Dover.—Letter from Francis Simpson, serjeant of of the Admiralty, complaining that the Mayor and Jurats of Romney have stopped his proceedings with regard to salvage of a Dutch ship which ran on ground near Romney, alleging that exclusive jurisdiction belongs to them by charter.

—— Nov. 26. Inner Temple.—Th. Taylor to the same, urging the calling upon all the sheriffs to bring in accounts of escheats and forfeitures.

—— Dec. 10.—Theo. Taillor to Marten, on behalf of Lady Arundel, whose estate has been sequestered and she brought into debt; and for himself, that he may be relieved with the money which is in Marten's hands, that he may not perish.

1650?—Long list, on 7 folio leaves, of the names of persons that have moneys due to them upon the public faith, with the amounts; apparently supplemental to a list made in Sept. 1650.

165$\frac{0}{1}$, $\frac{\text{Jan. 7}}{\text{Dec. 27}}$. Paris.—A short letter signed C. Besse, doubtless a fictitious name, being apparently an intercepted letter from a royalist. All names are in cipher. "For newes I refer you to 1125, to whome I write constantlie twise a weeke. . . . . Lett the superscription [of letters] be as is annexd to the cypher, or thus, à Mons. Mons. Desarte a la rue de Parcheminene à Paris."

1650[-1], Jan. 26.—John Bodvill [to the same] asking his help to prevent the confiscation and sale of his estate in Anglesey, he having long since compounded and paid his proportion.

—— Jan. 31. Strand.—Henry Marten to Sir Thomas Essex, Bart., desiring his success in some business he is engaged upon, and regretting he cannot help him with the money he wants, for it is about twenty times more than he has by him. (*Framed and glazed.*)

—— Feb. 4. Saumur.— — Desverrans to Marten, in French. Capt. Stocal writes to him that many officers have obtained special orders from Parliament for an allowance for their horses during the time they served in the armies of Essex and Waller; begs Marten to assist him to obtain a like order.

1650[-1], March 19. Inner Temple.—Fabian Hicks to the same, asking him to assist Mrs. Gipps who attends at the Parliament door with a petition, "which wilbe of great concernement to the State. Shee is wife to one Thomas Gipps, a rich citizen's sonne latly dead, whose husband is a servant in the Barbadoes, and sent thither by Alderman Bunce his brother in lawe, which alderman is a delinquent, and nowe in Holland, and to whom the state of old Mr. Gipps and his sonnes, being much in money, wilbe made over if it be not suddenly prevented. I heare that the alderman hath lately furnished the King of Scotland with forty thousand pounds towards his charge of a warre with this State, and his wife hath little lesse then halfe as much by the decease of her father Gipps, which she will with the first opportunity, as is conceaved, make over to her husband."

1651, Apr. 9.—Joseph Nixon, "your poore and much afflicted servaunt and kinsman," to the same. "I am much afflicted in myselfe to informe you how much I have [been] and am deceyued in desiring you to putt Mr. Pecke into the parsonadge of Shifford," Oxon [*i.e.* to let him become lessee for the rectorial tithes], for he refuses to observe any of the agreements that were made.

—— Aug. 4.—Ed. Fisher to the same recommending John Pescodd for the place of messenger to the trustees for the sale of delinquents' estates.

—— Sept. 27.—Copy of a warrant from John Bradshaw, as President of the Council of State, to the Lieutenant of the Tower, to receive into his custody the Earl of Cleveland, to be kept close prisoner for treason in bearing arms against the Parliament and people of the Commonwealth of England. (*Framed and glazed.*)

—— Nov. 13. Ashbury [Berks].—Th. Fox (?) to Marten, asking for 5*l.*, and to send a commission for Will. Harrison to keep an inn, for which he and "the whole towne of Ashberrie" will be very thankful.

—— Nov. 20. Genoa.—Jean Nicolas Sfranchi to H. Marten, in French; thanking him for a letter of 3 Oct., which contained some notice of Marten's late father (the judge).

1652, May 3. Serjeants' Inn.—Hen. Rolle to the same, giving him notice that a bill of Middlesex has been taken out against him at the suit of George Savage, esq.

—— May 5. Chastre.—Intercepted letter, unsigned, from an officer serving with the army of Turenne, giving an account of an attack made by the latter upon the town of Estampes, and of the gallantry exhibited by the Duke of York.

—— May 6. Deptford.—John Holland to Marten, about a warrant to the Treasurer of the Navy for a payment.

—— June 1.—Copy of the letter, in Italian, from the Senate of Venice to the Parliament of England, accrediting Lorenzo Pauluzzi as their agent.

—— July 8. Tower.—Sir Will. Davenant to Marten; a letter of compliment and thanks. "I would it were worthy of you to know how often I have profess'd that I had rather owe my libertie to you than to any man, and that the obligation you lay upon me shall for ever be acknowledg'd."

—— July 17. Shefford.—Letter from the sequestrators of the living to the same, in the name of all the parish, desiring the appointment of Mr. Milcot (?) as minister.

—— July 30.—Joanna Savile to the same, urging the pressing forward Mr. Chidley's business as to the way for paying the public-faith money and the soldiers' arrears by means of discoveries [of delinquents?], and praying him not to offer any obstruction.

—— Sept. 8. Shifford.—Henry Hull to the same, applying for appointment as minister of Shifford. Refers to Dr. Barnard, preacher at Gray's Inn; is approved by the major part of the parish.

—— Sept. 8.—Letter from John Lilburne to the same.

"Honored Sir, Being yisterday in Zealand, and comming home by sea, in the ship hearing a good resolut English toung, as soone as with conveniency I might I maid towards it; and found it to be the masters mate of one of your lait taiken frygaits, missarabelly plundered and desperaitely burnt, yit with an other wounded comrade of his comming for England in a very poore and low condition, and a littell discoursing with them I found they had bene extraordinarily hard used, and one of them turnd away without a penny money to beare his charges, and haveing traveld with them after our landing at Sluse to Bridges 9 myles one foot, I promised the masters maite, this bearer, called Edward Brooks (who I found a good inteligabell resolut blad) to write a few lins to you in his behalfe, being he is resolued to addrese to the Parliament or Counsell of Staite for some reperations, haueing lost about 20^{li} besids the wounds of his body. In which regard, in the first place, although I be bannished from England and cut of from its commonwealth, giue me leue to say that in my apprehention the seamen of England are instrumentally your present bulworks, and I am affraid your present trobells will nesessitaite you to maike more use of them then it is posable you may immagen; and therefor it behoues you to maike much of them, and to giue them resonable incorradgment you can; in which regard I maike it my humble request to you, in the first place, that you would lend this honest bearer your efectually assistance in his just sute to the Parliament or Counsell of Staite.

2^{ly}, I propound it to your serious consideration, whether it be not fit for yourselues or your admirall to taike notice of the hard usedge of your men, and either to write to there admirall or the staites about setling some kind of method about the ciuill usedge of prisonners, or at least to desire that to Flushing you by bill of exchange may returne some moneys to some there you can trust well to keep your sicke and wounded men while such; and 2^{ly}, to bring them away, some being now forst to stay behind, as the bearer informs me, for want of a littell money to inabell them to trauell. Sir, I write not this out of any designe to cury fauour with you or the rest of your brethren; noe, Sir, I scorne it, for if keeping close nakedly to downeright right and truth will not bring me backe againe to England, I neuer desire againe to see it; but the only end I write, it is to discharge or manifest a peace of that English sperit that is in me, and if you please so to judge it, I shall be very much obliged to subscribe myself, Sir,

An honest Englishman at the hart, and your most
faithfull seruant,
JOHN LILBURNE.

Bridges, this 8 Sept. 1652."

Addressed: "For the hon^{ble} Coll. Henry Marten, a member of the Parliament of the commonwealth of England, at his howse in Chennell row neare Whitehall, in Westminster, these presents."

1652, Oct. 6.—Proceedings at a meeting of the Governor and Council of Barbadoes at which, upon certain articles of charge, Capt. Bayes was adjudged unfit to continue public treasurer of the customs and excise; in the handwriting of John Jenninge, deputy-Secretary.

—— Nov. 22.—Anna Windsor, wife of Samuel Windsor formerly farrier to Marten's troop (now farrier to Col. Okey in Scotland), to Marten, praying for payment of money due upon debentures from the committee of the county of Berks.

[1653.]—Part of a copy of a letter to Cromwell (with alterations in another hand) from one who had been invited by him to take part in the government after the forcible dissolution of Parliament on 20 Apr. (probably as a member of the new Parliament), declining, in very plain terms, to have anything to do with it.

Four pages folio, which probably may have formed half of the whole paper.

1654, May 3.—Acknowledgment by Henry Griffin, schoolmaster at Longworth, of the receipt of 2*l.* 10*s.*, paid out of Edward Southby's rent, as a gratuity from H. Martin for the encouragement of the school at Longworth.

1654.—"The account between Col. Martin and Anne Richmond, widdow, concerning the rent of the parsonage of Ashbury, Berks," 1650–4. It was let at 200*l.* per an. About 60*l.* had been laid out in repairs "of the howses, which were almost destroyed by gunpowder blowne up in the howse by the souldiers in the warre."

1654[-5], March 24.—[Sir] John Pettus to [Marten], respecting settlement of some money matters.

1655, May 2. Ashborne—William Wetton to the same strongly recommending Dick Peeters, Marten's Derbyshire agent.

—— Oct. 9. Wilton House, near Whitehall.—Arthur Samwell to R. Peeters, claiming payment of a fee-farm rent of 97*l.* 17*s.* 6*d.* out of the Colonel's estate.

1656, July 1. Buxton.—Rowland Heathcoate to Marten, asking for return of money lent to Peeters.

? Jan. 15. Buxton.—[The same ?] to the same, complaining that Peeters has commenced an action against him and a friend for hunting a hare in the manor of Hartington.*

1656, Dec. 22. Chimney [Oxon].—Robert Veisey to the same, asking him "as it hath bine alwayes your desier to doe workes of charitie and mercy," to grant a reversionary lease of "a smale thinge" in Shifford to a poor man.

1656[-7], March 15. Hurley [Berks].—John Lord Lovelace to "neighbour Whitfeild" authorizing him to agree with his brother [in-law] Marten and his son [-in-law] Wildman about such securities and settlements as may conduce to his safety against the Colonel's debts with the least prejudice to the latter.

1657, May 17.—Franc. Messenus (?) to Marten, in French, desiring a meeting with him for settling some business with "Sir George."

—— June 3.—Sheffeild Stubbs to Thomas lord Morley and Mounteagle, pressing for repayment of a loan. "Play not with a man's necessityes." Seal of arms: a bend between three pheons, thereon three buckles; crest, an eagle displayed.

1657[-8], March 1.—The constables of George's parish Southwark to Marten, desiring him to pay the bearer 5*s.* for watching for him 15 nights in 15 months, at 4*d.* per night.

1658, Sept. 16. Moorfields.—Samuel Bathurst [to Marten], asking for 20*l.* to start the writer's cousin Chambre on a voyage to Barbadoes.

—— Sept. 27. Adston.—Enigmatical letter to Marten, who is addressed as "My O" by one who signs as "his owne A.", [*i.e.* Major

* The signature has been torn off, but the two first letters of the Christian name remain, "Ro—." The writing somewhat resembles that of the preceding letter, but not very closely.

MSS. OF CAPTAIN LODER-SYMONDS.

Wildman] referring in disguised terms to some proposition from Sir John Lenthall who has "made me his turnekey," but of whom the writer appears to be very suspicious.

Another letter of the same kind is without date; in which the writer says that "a note signed with a single O [is] of much more power than if it were signed with O.P." [*i.e.*, Oliver Protector], therefore he will attend at the hour mentioned, and desires that Sir John Pettus may be asked to meet them "to despatch that businesse some way or other as he pleaseth." It appears from the cipher copied below at p. 18 that, Major Wildman is designated by A. and Marten by O.

1658[–9], March 24. Faringdon.—Thomas Phelps to [Marten]. A business letter, but mentioning that Mr. Francis Blagrove, of London, departed this life on Monday last in the afternoon and was buried yesterday.

165$\frac{8}{9}$, Jan. 11. Leominster.—Thomas Deane (Marten's agent) to Marten, respecting the approaching election for Parliament. "Here is a very great dicision and much seekeinge, the Burgimasters playing their game variously, and the rest of the towne the licke. They are so compounded and so divided that alltbough it might seeme so much the more hopefull yet it is so much the more uncertaine, insomuch that the best of my witts invitts mee not to begge, hunt or crave with much earnestnesse, but only to make it knowen that if their loue bee so much towards you as to make choyce of you, that you will bee willing to serue them. The choyce is this Thursday."

1662, Trin. Term, 14 Chas. II.—Plea on behalf of John Loder, in regard to proceedings upon the outlawry of Henry Marten in Jan. 165$\frac{4}{5}$ upon a plea of debt, at the suit of George Savage, Esq., setting forth that on Jan. 20, 165$\frac{8}{9}$, he acquired from Maria Pratt, widow of Francis Phelips and Philip Owen, the executors of Henry Pratt, deceased, the manor of Barcott, that having been mortgaged to them by Marten before his outlawry. The Sheriff's return in 1655 of all the property held by Marten in Berkshire is recited at length.

Papers without date:

Representation of the case of Sir Hugh Owen of Pembrokeshire against Col. James Lewis, formerly in arms for the King, for obtaining a sequestration of Sir Hugh's estate and leasing it to his own brother-in-law Capt. Thomas Woogan.

Apr. 20. Wanting.—Letter from Mrs. Anne Lyford to [Marten] asking for 40*l.* or 50*l.* to apprentice her son. (There is also a letter from Ben. Lyford, dated from Peasemore, pressing for the rent of some land.)

Clement Writer ("your true frind and servant") to the same, about a petition from the former.

Letter in French to the same, from Paris, signed "885 461," about some young friend whom he was desired to see and assist, but whom he found "infecté par ces diables de P. . . . . . J'ay vous ay escri une lettre pour (cy trouvez propre) la montrer aux comitties d'Oxon." Some public news follows, with all proper names in cipher. Lettere will reach him if addressed "A Mons. Desverrans," provided it be sent "chez Mons. Moore." See a letter from this writer *supra*, under date of Feb. 4, 1651.

William Edline to [the same ?], during the Civil War. Although he has set forth two horse upon his own charge, and lent the Parliament 10*l.* in money, and has been himself and four men at Tring, yet he is in danger of being plundered of all his team of horses and goods, and is afraid to lay his seed in the ground ; desires therefore to have protection.

July 20. Haddon.—The Earl of Rutland "to my noble and honored frende" Henry Marten. It troubles him to see that the malice of knaves must be completed by those who pretended much *honesteté* to the public and friendship to himself; but is the more sensible of his happiness in being still in Marten's good thoughts. "I fonde heer-upon much comfort, knowing my innocencye and your *integrité*, which will shame them if tried and sought into; if not, yet it comforts, and sustaines mee for the present: and at least, at last, will transport mee to the Elisian fields, whear I shall bee past their reach." His wife presents her hearty thanks and best respects. "Your oulde and true freinde, J. Rutland."

Oct. 5. Haddon.—The same to the same, thanking him for letters, in warm terms, and signing as "Your true and ancient freinde and serviteur." The following postscript is added: "Whiles I have right and Henrye Martin on my syde I fear no mineurs nor other unjust scandels which are throwne on me, as false as it is true they are soe, and shall so continue. I humblye thanck you for answering in my behalfe. Adieu." (*Framed and glazed.*)

"Austton," July 23.—Letter to Marten from a lady who signs as "Augu" Havard, thanking him for his care about her husband's commission to be a justice of the peace for Gloucestershire, which she desires to have down before the "esies" (assize); hopes to see him when he comes into Gloucestershire at the "pore hovs of mine" at "Austton"; begs him to subscribe to a letter her grandmother sent him, which "wos a leter of recomendasen for my hosbon and Mster. Robarts to the governor of Gloster."

Dec. 20. Covent Garden.—Jo. Denne (?) to [the same], addressed as "Signior illustrissimo." The character given by him to L. Com. Leile brought the broad seal immediately to the writer's suit; begs the same influence may be used with Col. Morley with respect to the tithes of the writer's living of Hartfield, Sussex, where one has been put in by the Committee to officiate, who may be continued.

[1652 or 1653], June 29. Whitehall.—Letter, in Spanish, unsigned, respecting an application made on behalf of the King of Spain to the Council of State for license to transport out of Ireland some of those who have borne arms against the Commonwealth, for the Spanish service.

Isabel Westrop to Marten, asking for money; begs that he and Major Wildman will speak to her lawyer.

John Jorden to the same, upon the latter's having been arrested for debt, which the writer had endeavoured to prevent; hears that he owes 29,000*l.*

Jane Langston to Marten, recommending the bearer to be appointed a physician in the army.

Vincent De La Bare to the same. "Wee have shipt for St. John's Bay, neer Bologne, 4,000 soldiers, and 2,000 more are shipping, all gallant olde soldiers. They will mack a highe rackett in Flanders, so wee expect daily to heer of great actions." He has a parcel of tortoise-shells come from West India, and desires to know what they are worth the pound.

Jane Brook to the same, begging him, as one of the Committee for examination, to procure the bailing of Mr. Webb.

R[alph] Brideoakes [then Lenthall's chaplain, and afterwards Bishop of Chichester] to the same, introducing the bearer, one Stowel, "an honourer of your little great philosopher Epictetus and you." Is just going to Oxford.

Thomas Laurence to the same, asking him to write on his behalf to Lieut.-Gen. Fleetwood, who has the appointing of Col. Claypoole's officers.

"Humble proposals" for raising a national revenue by the registration of lands, and the establishment of banks of credit in connection therewith.

"The humble representation of the case of the collectors for prize goods" with respect to the Dutch prizes.

"The Lord Baltimore's case concerning his plantation in Maryland," with reference to a Petition and Remonstrance against him preferred to the Council of State by one Capt. Ingle.

Rough ground-plan of a house, with short description in Italian, headed "Per casa di Parco in villa di Cervo," *i.e.* For *Park House in Hartington !*

The two last leaves (ff. 33–4, 4°) of a dialogue on polygamy, between O. and T.; [being a translation of the tract by Bern. Ochinus. A translation which verbally differs from this, was made by Francis Osborne, and printed at London in 12mo in 1657 ; this fragment begins at p. 87 of that edition.]

A list of the freeholders of Berkshire, in alphabetical order.

IV. *Miscellaneous petitions.*

1. Petition of the minister, churchwardens and inhabitants of St. Andrew's in the Wardrobe, London, to Sir H. Marten, asking for help to repair the church which is in great decay. Noted that 20*l.* were given, and 5*l.* to the poor.

2. Application from Lady Killigrew for an order from Parliament to the Committee of Rutland to pay her an annuity of 200*l.* which had been assigned to her by the Duke of Buckingham when under age.

3. Petition to Parliament from freeholders, farmers and labourers in that part of the county of Bucks adjoining Windsor Castle, transmitting a petition delivered to Sir T. Fairfax, against the free quartering of his soldiers upon the petitioners, twenty and thirty being sometimes quartered in one house, whereby all alike are becoming ruined. There are twelve leaves of signatures, numbering in all some hundreds; and of the parish of Chesham there is a fragment of a distinct list.

4. Petition to Parliament from Robert Tokeley for payment of 7,110*l.* 10*s.* 8*d.* for freight of ships employed in the King's service at Cales, the Isle of Ree and Rochelle in 1626–9.

5. Petition to the Commissioners for Compositions from Clare James, widow of John James, of Smarden, Kent, esq., praying that a sequestration laid upon her as a popish recusant may be taken off, she being certified by the minister &c. of St. Giles in the Fields to be no recusant; Oct. 1650.

6. 1651.—Petition to Parliament "of the well-affected gentlemen, ministers and others in the countie of Lancaster," praying that the Earl

of Derby, who "was the first and principall incendiary of war in this countye," and who "most inhumanely and unworthily at that horrid massacre at Bolton with his owne hands murthered Capt. Bootle, a religious, worthie and thrice valliant man after quarter given," may not be admitted to compound, for "our countie thus defiled with blood cannot otherwise be purged then by the blood of them who shed it." Sixty signatures are attached, of which 14 are with marks.

7. *c.* 1651.—Petition to Parliament from those who have shared in the draining of the level of Hatfield Chase against the riotous proceedings of persons headed by Daniel Noddell, an attorney, Lieut.-Col. Lilburne and Major Wildman, who have laid waste all the land, and burned the houses, &c.; "and on the 29 of October last, beinge the Lord's day, Lilburn came with a great number armed to the church" of Epworth, which had been built by the petitioners, "and there forced away the minister and congregation, saying he should not preach there unlesse they weare stronger than hee, and now makes it a place to lay his hay, and a slaughter-howse to kill cattell in."

8. Petition to Parliament from Col. John Fox praying for an order to enable him to have the benefit of an Act with regard to his sequestration.

9. Petition to Parliament from Mary wife of Maurice Awbert, that whereas her husband is declared a delinquent, but being a servant to the Queen is attendant upon her in France, he may have license to come to England to attend his own affairs, and then to return back again.

10. Petition to the Council of State from Henry Turner, of London, merchant, for license to transport some wool grown in Ireland.

11. Petition to the Council of State from Huntington Hastings Corney, gent., for license to remain in London to follow some suits at law, he having taken the Engagement.

12. Petition to H. Marten from William Roberts, praying him to present to Parliament as speedily as possible a petition of Sir William Thomas, Bart., "a gentleman of greate worth and eminencye in North Wales," who has done and still does to the said Roberts great favours and courtesies, and has acted nothing prejudicial against the Parliament, save only his non-appearance there, his election being voted undue.

13. Petition to the Council of State from Alice Powell, widow of Major John Powell, of Radnorshire, who served Q. Elizabeth, King James, and the late King, in the wars in the Low Countries, France, and Spain for forty years, and 35 years ago was allowed, in consequence of his many hurts and maims a pension from the county of Radnor of 10*l.* per an., which was suddenly stopped eight years ago; he being now dead, she prays for payment of the arrears of 80*l.* Noted, "Recommend it to the Judges, viz. Eltonhead and Norbury, who sit at Radnor on Munday come fortnight, viz. 1 April."

14. Petition to the Committee for Plundered Ministers from "divers well affected inhabitants of the towne of Redinge" on behalf of Mr. William Erbery. He has been accused of denying the deity of Christ and the satisfaction of His death, and an order has consequently been made that he shall not preach at Reading or elsewhere; but the petitioners affirm that they have both publicly and privately heard him assert both points, and "consideringe his former sufferings by the prelates for the Ghospell and a good conscience sake, and his affections to the Parliament and present government, and the many good services formerly done by him, and his holy and humble conversation," they pray that the order may be repealed.

15. Petition from William Lord Craven to the Parliament praying to be heard by counsel against his sequestration. On the information of Major Richard Falconer (who confessed that he, with another, drew the petition to the King of Scots against the Commonwealth, but said that the petitioner promoted the delivery), and of Capt. Thomas Kitchingman and one Hugh Reyley, that he was at Breda with the King, it was ordered on 6 March 1650 that his estate be confiscate; whereas he had gone beyond seas with consent of Parliament before the war began, and hath been there attending his charge ever since; the King came to Breda while he was there, and he did not go to him; the material charge depends on a single testimony, and that mainly disproved and contradicted; and he has never engaged or in the least manner appeared against the Parliament of England.

16. Petition to the Council of State from Harry Tyrrell, gent., praying for release from prison upon bail.

17. Petition to the Council of State from Col. William Eyre, who has faithfully served the Parliament and been greatly zealous for the good of the nation, though misguided therein and mistaken in the good purposes of others, praying for payment of arrears, that he may go with his family into Ireland, to take possession of his wife's estate there.

18. Petition to Gen. Deane and Gen. Popham from Thomas Wadland, who has been a master and mate in service for eight years, praying for the command of one of the boats now to be employed in the Commonwealth's service.

19. Petition to Mr. Reynolds and Col. Marten from the prisoners for debt in Newgate, praying for the speedy passing of an Act, nearly perfected, for their relief, but which is opposed by lawyers, the "infernall brood of Symon Magus," who offer a bribe of 100,000*l.* to stop it, and enslave the country to their infernal wills and corrupt minds. The petitioners for these many weeks have fed upon dogs, rats, and ox-livers being their festival food, and are allowed but 13*s.* 4*d.* a week amongst a hundred persons.

20. Petition to the Duke of York from Sir William Pargiter, knt., Philip Ward, gent. and Thomas Holt and Thomas Gunter, esqs. that, whereas the estate of Henry Marten (who stands attainted) was granted by him at the desire of the King to John Lord Lovelace in consideration of his sufferings, and of his having advanced 8,000*l.* upon the security of the said estate, and now has been conveyed by Lord Lovelace to them in two parts, the Duke will be pleased to pass new grants to them in particular.

V. *Orders of Parliament, &c.*

1642[-3], March 13.—Order of the House of Commons that the sheriffs of London and Middlesex and the committee for the militia do forthwith take into custody the Capuchins at Somerset House for the speedy sending them away to France; the former orders made for the demolishing of superstitious monuments in the Chapel to be executed; Mr. Martyn, Sir Peter Wentworth, and Mr. Gourdon appointed to see the orders carried out; the Earl of Warwick to provide shipping for the transportation.

1643, May 8.—Order of the House of Commons for the speedy payment of 10,000*l.* to Lord Fairfax.

1643, Aug. 19.—Order that a Committee of nine members of the H. of Commons, or any three of them, examine what moneys Col.

Marten hath received and disbursed, and report the whole state of the accompt.

1645, June 7.—Order of the H. of Commons that when this unnatural war shall be ended, the town of Lancaster shall have 8,000*l.* out of the estates of such papists and delinquents within the said county as were at the burning of the town; with an order of 23 Dec. 1647 that those inhabitants whose houses were burned shall for the year ensuing farm 2,000*l.* worth of the said estates.

1647, Oct. 6.—Order of the Committee of Lords and Commons for the advance of money &c. for the army that Benedict Hall, of Highmeadow, esq., have a month's time allowed him to examine his witnesses upon the information laid against him, and to cross-examine the witnesses for the State.

1649, July 9.—Order of Parliament that whereas it was ordered on 3 Apr. 1648 that 500*l.* per an. should be settled on Col. Hammond Governor of the Isle of Wight, and his heirs for ever; and whereas he, out of a real sense of Capt. Richard Pechell's good affections and losses for the service of the Parliament, hath voluntarily offered that 100*l.* out of the said 500*l.* should be settled on the said Pechell, the Committee of the revenue shall pay 400*l.* to Col. Hammond and 100*l.* to Capt. Pechell, by half-yearly payments, until those amounts be settled on them out of papists' and delinquents' estates.

1649, July 17.—Order for referring an Act for the enlargement of poor prisoners for debt, reported this day by Mr. Marten and read a first and second time, to a committee of 22; any five to meet, and to report with all speed.

1650, June 12.—Order referring a petition of Anne daughter and heir of Sir Robert Loftus, and grandchild and heir of Adam viscount Loftus of Ely, to a committee of 21 (of whom Marten is one), any five of them to meet.

1650, Aug. 6.—Order of the Council of State appointing a committee of nine (of whom Marten is one) to consider the drawing instructions for the better ordering of the business of the staying in town of such Scots as are here, and to consider such petitions as are offered by Scots for their staying.

1651, June 17.—Order of Parliament that Thomas Fanshaw, esq., son and heir apparent of Sir Thomas Fanshaw, K.B., being of the age of 19 years, be admitted to suffer a common recovery of the manor or farm of Westbury, and the farm of Tickingham Grange, in Essex.

1652, May 19.—Copy of an order by the Commissioners for compounding, allowing a deed dated 14 May 1643 by which Lord Morley conveyed the manor and castle of Hornby, Lancashire, to William Habington and John Harryes as trustees, for payment of his debts; and ordering payment of the rents from May 1650 to May 1653 to the said trustees.

1652, June 15.—Order of the Council of State appointing a committee to consider the several petitions desiring Irishmen for the service of foreign parts; with a subsequent order of 19 June adding Col. Martyn and Col. Purefoy to the committee.

1657[-8], March 11.—Order of the Committee for preservation of the Customs and regulating the Excise that Col. Henry Martyn do forthwith pay into the Treasury for prize goods the sum of 20*l.* for one tun of French wine by him bought of the late Commissioners for prize goods, for which the moneys were due at days long since past; or in default that he appear personally to show cause why he paid not for the same.

VI. A parcel of *family letters and papers*, of little importance.

1. Six letters from Marten to his agent at Leominster, Mr. Thomas Deane, and three to his agent in Derbyshire, Mr. Richard Peeters, in 1656–7, chiefly written from "The Rules," while confined for debt.

2. Two letters from him to his sister Lady Rogers, at her house at Bray.

3. One letter from him directed "to Mrs. Frances Ward at the Thatched House in the Rules, Southwark; for her sister," who is addressed as "my dear," "my love," and "my heart." Written from "The Holy Lambe in Abingdon," 12 July 1654. "They are now chusing knights of the shire in the market-place."

4. Letter to Marten from his sister Lady Mary Rogers, dated at Bray 11 Apr. 1648. "I thinke I shall have your daughter Betty at Eaton with hir sister Jane, which she will chuse rather then Hurley. . . . This day I cary Hal to his Mr., and Jane to hir Mrs., Rebeckey."

5. Five letters to him from his brother George Marten in Barbadoes, 1652–7. In the first, dated 28 March, 1652, he says, "Sir George [Ayscue] has performed the trust layd on him by the Parliament with greate honor, justice and wisdome; hee has delivered us from the Lord Willoughby and those that with him meant to have raised their fortunes upon or by the ruines of this place, has left us in a willinge and cherfull obedience to the Parliament, the supreme authoritye of England, and has caryed with him what wee humbly desire from that authority," which is chiefly the sanctioning the defraying losses and charges by the only means which the Governor, Council and Assembly can find possible, viz. the "continuinge the custome of 4 and 2 per cent. upon all the goods of the groweth of this place exported, 4 upon what goes off upon the merchants' accompt, 2 of what goes off upon the planters'." In the next letter, of 11 July, 1656, he introduces the bearer, Major Anthony Rouse, "whoe is my very kind and lovinge freind, and a person of as much honesty and honor as I have ever mett with in these perts. Hee has lately married a rich widowe heere, and with her some troble, which hee will acquaint you with." In the last letter, 20 May, 1657, he desires his brother to help "Susan," apparently his wife, to come out to him.

6. Letter to him from his sister Eliza Edmonds, and one in Latin from his nephew, her son, Charles Edmonds ("dab. e musæo Oxon, 17 cal. Julii, an. 1652"), in which he thanks him for his "prodiga munificentia."

7. Two letters to him from his son Henry Marten, in 1657, reminding him of a promise to send a coat for his master's son, who is five years old; "pray lett it bee laysed, or else it will not bee healfe soe pleasing." Asks him also to endeavour to obtain some scholars for his master, "for hee heath nothing but what hee doeth gitt by his teaching, except twenty pounds a yeare, and that hee heath no longer then his wife liveth. . . . Their are many men now at mens estate which doe give him many thankes for his care and panes."

8. Seven letters to Marten from his daughters, Jane, Anne, and Frances; viz.—

March 31 [1657].—Jane Marten to her father, "at his house in the Rules in Southwarke."

"Sir, The hopes I have had of seing you every day hath made me forbear to trouble you with writing till now. I am very sory to hear you are so incumber'd with fresh troubles before you are rid of the old. I whish with all my heart I knew how I might be so serviceable to you as that I could be capable of doing you any good, for indeed it is a very great trouble to me that ther is none of us is able to doe any more then wish and pray for your happy deliverance out of your troubles, and according to your comands bear it out till it shall pleas God either to make me more serviceable or less burdensome to you. So with my humble duty I rest,

Sir, your most obedient child till death,

(*Framed and glazed.*) JANE MARTEN."

Four letters from Anne (one in a hand unlike the rest), chiefly about money difficulties, and the non-receipt of 30*l.* which he had sent her by Major Wildman; "You will be plesed to consider that I can not keepe house without mony."

Two letters from Frances; one in a formal copy-book hand (in 1657) unlike the other. In the second, which is about her father's troubles she says, "Oh how unworthy is Mr. Louder! His mouth is an open sepulchre, and what he spaketh is of noe reputashon."

9. Letter to him from Tho. Parker, who signs as "Your faythfull and dutyfull sunne," dated at Hornby, 28 Jan. 1654 (?), apologizing for some quarrel at Whitchurch, "for which I was much to blame, in expressing myselfe so largly att your table, for beeing in soe much passion I was nott myselfe, for the which I hope it will be your goodnesse to pardon mee. Soe for the other businness conserninge the fallinge out, and the deffrence betwixt Mr. Warde and myselfe, was in refference of the respects and love that I bore unto your only sonne. Seeing him soe grosly abused, I could nott but vindycat in the honnor and respect I bore to you, withall hee giveing mee a boxe of the eare, which provocked mee to pattion, and to doe that which I would nott willingly have dun." Begs assistance for payment of debts due on 25 March. Intends to be in a few days with his wife at Chelton in Oxfordshire.

10. Schedule by Sir Henry Marten, knt. (father of the Colonel) of various legacies left by his brother, William Marten, of the city of Oxford, esq.; viz. 400*l.* for pious uses in Berkshire, out of which 100*l.* had been paid for Eaton Hastings' highway; to Sir Henry's wife Elizabeth, to Alice, Mary, and Robert Bonithon, and to others; lastly, to some sufficient and full minister that shall instruct and catechize in points of religion the younger people and children of Kennington and in the chappell there once every week upon Sunday or holiday, during the terme of 7 yeares, sixe pounds yearlie, to bee paid by equall porcions quarterlie."

11. Proposals and particulars for the sale of the manor, &c., of Hartington, sent by Marten to Mr. Savile, from the "Rules," 1 March and 22 March, 1658–9; in the first paper offering the whole for 9500*l.*, and in the second for 9000*l.*

12. Statement of the whole remaining unsold estate of Henry Marten, after his attainder. Whole annual value about 1000*l.*; of which 400*l.* for his wife's jointure, made before marriage, above 20 years since, out of which 2000*l.* are to be raised for portions for his two eldest daughters; 300*l.* per an. for the jointure of George Marten's wife, which is only Henry Marten's so long as he has issue male, he having now only one son; and the remaining 300*l.* is leased for 500 years without rent, for a full and valuable consideration. There is in judgments, statutes, and mortgages upon the said 1,000*l.* per an. about 30,000*l.*; and the

creditors desire to purchase from the King the reversion of the remainder although the encumbrances are about 15,000*l.* more than the whole estate can be sold for.

VII. A parcel of fragments of unfinished drafts of various *political pamphlets* in H. Marten's handwriting.

1. Fragment (4 pp.) of a tract in reply to J. Lilburne, of which the title has been written and re-written several times, and crossed. The following is part of the title: "Rash censures uncharitable . . . . in answer to a discourse . . . . of Lieut. Col. Jo. Lilburne, by way of epistle to Henry Marten, dated ult. May 47, but never seen by him until 26 June following when hee met it in the street." The following passage occurs near the beginning: "When . . . . I, adhering to my first principles had frequent occasion to deliver my conscience not only against the K. but against his countreymen, against the Lord M., Ald., and Common Councell of this greate, riche and faithfull citty, against the Assembly of godly learned and orthodox Divines, against the wholl House of Peeres, and the major part (as it proved) of the House of Commons, I could not but expect to bee reproched and inveighed against by almost every pen and tongue that would take notice of so mean a subject. Accordingly I have oftentimes mett my name bespattered in songs ballads and pamphlets, yet never troubled my head with framing of any counter-song, anti-ballad, or vindication, till I found Lieut. Col. John Lilburne firing upon Henry Marten."

2. Fragment ($1\frac{1}{2}$ pp.) of a reply to some Scotchman, addressed as "Jockey." "A man would think that our brethren of Scotland are not very fond of the King's person, because they do not carry him into his native Kingdome, which they might as easily do, and with as much leave, as they did carry him from Newark to Newcastle, neither doth it follow that the Parl. of England supposeth the company of this King to be a benefitt because they conceive the disposall of any King in this kingdom to be their right."

3. "The rights of the People of England, considered both in the masse, as they are inhabitants of one countrey gatherable into a body, and in litle, as they are represented at the House of Commons; published by Henry Marten, of Berkshire, esq., dated 4 or 5 yeares ago, upon occasion of certain collections set forth lately by Mr. Selden, and entitled *The Priviledges of the Baronage of England when they sitt in Parliament.* 1647." Title, and address to the Reader, 3 pp.

4. "Observations of Henry Marten's upon Mr. [Thomas] White's *Grounds of obedience and government*"; 3 pp. A prefatory note is prefixed, dated at the "Rules," Aug. 1655.

5. "An answer to the author of the Captious Questions"; 3 pp. The questions are "Whether we are willing to be healed?" and "Whether men know what they would be at?"

6. "History of independency; To the mistery of the 2 Juntos and the designes of O.C. etc.;" being one page of remarks on [Cl. Walker's] book so entitled. "It is clear to me that a wholl Parliament can have no plott at all; they are so numerous, and so mingled in temper and education, age and interests, that so great a party as hee calls Independants could not drive on any project of that bulk, so long a brewing, with secrecy sufficient for such an enterprize. And it is not clear to me that the single person you speak of did lay those eggs, or sett a brood upon them, which we see hatched indeed to his advantage. He was a man of a high spirit

from the beginning, very active and vigilant; he had got a crew about him of blades that would follow him through any other fire to avoid the fire of persequutions."

7. Description and vindication of the Levellers; one page. "I am more mistaken then I use to bee (which needes not) if the most mistaken thing this day in England (Religion allwayes excepted and foreprized) bee not the doctrine of those who rather by others then themselves are termed Levellers."

8. "The Considerations on Mr. Harington's *Commonwealth of Oceana* reconsidered by H. Marten, and made up in a letter to their Author;" one page.

9. A manifesto against the Scots; two pages. "We the P[eople] of the C[ommonwealth] of E[ngland] have bene not onely ey-witnesses but fellow-feelers of so many affronts, indignityes, and reall wrongs, in designe, in language, and in open act, putt upon this nation by our neighbours of Scotland."

10. Commencement, on one page, of remarks on the right of the people of England to choose their own representatives in the House of Commons, without which they become perfect slaves.

11. Title of a pamphlet: "Αντικρητισμός, or Satisfaction dissatisfying, in seventeen aunswers to as many Queries, calling themselves sober and serious (but being the first queries that ever went about to satisfy) of J.G., calling himself (instead of setting down his name at large) a cordiall friend, nay, a well-wisher, to all men he doth not say, but to the interest of all, except fighters and adventurers for the Commonwealth. There is likewise to 3 Queries more in a postscript of the same pamphlet a proportionable number of answers." J.G.'s tract was published in 1654, under the title of "Συγκρητισμός, or dissatisfaction satisfied, in seventeen serious queries, tending to allay the discontents of persons dissatisfied about the late revolution government."

12. Twenty-four lines of Latin verse of glowing panegyric upon Oliver Cromwell on his assuming the Protectorate:

"——ille, inclytus ille
Cromwellus, implet solium, acclamante Britanno."

They begin thus:

"Cedite (sic Anglûm Parcæ voluere benigne)
Heroes pariter veteres pariterque recentes."

They end:

"Quicquid id est, Deus est qui nos victricibus armis
Ductu Hujus, qui nos Hoc Protectore beavit.
Dicite Io Pæan, et Io ter dicite Pæan."

13. A key to a cipher; one page. This I subjoin in full. "For King, G; Parliament, T; speaking of the T write him, of G write them. For Cromwell write L, for Ireton N, for Fairefax X, speaking of him write her. For Col. Martin write O, for Wildman A, for Wallwin B, for Petter E. For the House of Lords D, House of Commons F, for the city of London H, for the Scotts C, for Commissioners in gen[eral] J, for Committee K, for the Frensh M, Irish P, the Welsh Q, Dutch R, an Army S, for Col. Overton V, for Col. Rainesbrough W, for the Isle of Ely Y, for Poole Z, for Ammunition &. For Money OO, for Numbers the Romane figures in small letters, for Men EE, for Harrison's JJ, for Col. Eyre's AA, for friends in generall AJ. For a Regiment OJ, a Company EJ, a Troop AO. For the General's

regiment of horse 1, for L.-G. Cromwell's regiment of horse 2, Ireton's regiment of horse 3, for Whaley's regiment 4, Fleetwood's 5, Harrison's 6, Tomlinson's 7, Riche's 8, Scroope's 9, Horton's 10, The General's regiment of foot 1, Col. Deane's 2, Pride's 3, Heuson's 4, Baxstead's 5, Constable's 6, Hammond's 7, Lilburne's 8, Skippon's 9, Overton's 10, [Okey's dragoones 20, *struck out*] Sir Hardresse Waller's 11."

VIII. A small parcel of papers relative to a family named *Chambre* [of Denbighshire and Wicklow].

1. Six letters from Kathren Chambre to her husband Calcott Chambre, about 1653–4. Complaining of neglect and poverty, and relative to some proposed sale to a Mr. Worsley.

2. Two letters from Calcott Chambre to his wife.

3. One letter to C. Chambre from his sister Ester Chambre at Barbadoes; this is the sixth letter she has written without receiving one in reply; she wants not any earthly thing, for God has raised up friends that she may term her father and mother.

4. To the same from his sister Judeth Chambre, dated at Harlston, 23 Oct. 1653. God has provided for her quite contrary to her expectation by those she never thought would have regard of her; she has so endeavoured to carry herself in a pleasing way to the Earl and Countess [of Meath?] that they have concluded to take her sister Elizabeth "My bro. Georg is the most unnaturall to us that ever I knew; I feere he is seduced by some unsantified creature."

5. Two letters to the same ("cosen Chambre") from John Datie, begging for repayment of money; 1654.

6. To the same from T. W.; 31 March, 1654.

7. To "Capt. Chambre" from William Newman, about remittances from Ireland; 18 Aug., 1653.

8. "Ma. Meath" [*i.e.*, Countess of Meath] to "cosen George" Chambre; has desired her cousin Bathurst to give him 50*s.*, he having written to her for clothes and about his learning arithmetic, and telling her of the kindnesses received from and promised by her cousin Col. Marten, "to bind you prentes to a marchant; he is a very good frend; doe not make il use of his frendship, but ease his charge by your humility, diligenc and industry"; 18 Feb. 1656–7.

[Edward Brabazon, the second Earl of Meath, married Mary, younger daughter of Calcot Chambre, Esq.]

9. Letter from Thomas Ward to his cousin George Chambre, written from Ballasore 29 Dec. 1655, with account of his voyage to the East Indies, &c.

There is also a letter from the same to Henry Marten, written soon after setting sail from the Downs "from Smythick in Cornewall," 22 Jan. 1654–5, and one without address, but probably to Marten, from one Rob. Ward, while at sea on 26 Jan. 1657.

10. Letter of extravagant adulation from George Chambre to one whom he addresses as "Most reverend Sir and cheife patron of good lear[n]ing." "The splendor of your singular goodlines hath not onely brightened my hands by the receipt thereof, but alsoe made my tongue to speake most elegantly whilst that I read them, O thou most learned man," &c.

IX. *Harley Papers.*

i. Narrative of the death of Hampden.

"Sir Edward Harley happened to go out of town towards his seat in Herefordshire with Sir Robert Pye of Faringdon; they were relations, and both of them lived at that time pretty near one another at Westminster. Sir Edward went in the same chariot with Sir Robert as far as Faringdon, and both of them having been military men entertained one another with the relation of many adventures of that kind; and amongst other matters, Sir Robert, who had married Mr. Hampden's daughter, acquainted his companion with the true history of his father-in-law's receiving his death wound on Chalgrove Field. When they were at supper at Faringdon, Sir Edward requested his kinsman Sir Robert Pye to repeat the account he had related on the road before his son Robert [now* Earl of Oxford] and one of the Foleys then likewise in company with them, as a matter of fact, which it might be usefull to curious persons to know, and upon the certainty of which they might depend, and you are to read the following account as coming out of the mouth of Sir Robert Pye, addressing himself to his kinsman after this manner. 'You know,' says he, 'it is commonly thought that my father-in-law dyed of a wound he receiv'd from the enemy in Chalgrove Field, but you shall hear the exact truth of the matter as I had it from my father himself some time before he expired. The Earl of Essex lay at that time with his army before Reading, and Mr. Hampden attended him there as one of the Committee from the Parliament, who were always to be with the General. Major Gunter was with a considerable party quarter'd towards Thame and Chalgrove and those parts. The General had intelligence that Prince Rupert was going to make an excursion from Oxford, by which he would very probably make great havock amongst Gunter's party with his horse, if timely care was not taken to prevent it by immediately dispatching proper succors. Upon this a councill was called, and Coll. Hampden voluntarily offer'd himself to command the detachment to be sent on the expedition, being a person very particularly acquainted with those countrys through which Prince Rupert was to pass, for he had been a very great sportsman in his time, and had often traversed those countrys as such. His proposal was accepted, and away he went. Prince Rupert came, and did the havock and execution design'd, and which could not by this intelligence and precaution be intirely prevented. In a skirmish on this occasion Mr. Hampden drew one of his pistols, and as it gave fire it burst to pieces in his hand, and shatter'd his arm in a very dismall manner. Upon this he made the best of his way off; he was very well mounted as he always used to be. When he was come to a considerable rivulet, as there are many such in those parts between the hills, he was much put to it what to do. He thought that if he alighted and turn'd his horse over, he could not possibly get up again, and how to get over upon him he could not well tell. But he resolv'd at last to try what his horse could do, and so clapt his spurs to, and got clean over. As soon as he possibly could he sent for me; he was in very great† pain, and told me that he suspected his wound was mortal; but what makes it still more grievous to me, says he, is, that I am affraid you are in some degree accessary to it, for the hurt I have receiv'd his (*sic*) occasion'd by the bursting of one

* Altered by another hand to "afterwards." Possibly this alteration may show that this paper was used by the printer of the *St. James' Chronicle* in 1761, and that the word was then changed.

† This word is supplied in the margin by the other hand.

of those pistolls which you gave me. You may be sure I was not a little surprized and concern'd at hearing this, and assured him they were bought from one of the best workmen in France, and that I myself had seen them tryed. You must know it was Mr. Hampden's custom, whenever he was going abroad, always to order a raw serving boy that he had to be sure to take care that his pistolls were loaded, and it seems the boy did so very effectually, for when ever he was thus order'd he always put in a fresh charge without considering or examining whether the former charge had been made use of or not, and upon examining the remaining pistoll they found it was in this manner quite filled up to the top with two or three supernumery (*sic*) charges. And the other pistoll having been in the same condition was the occasion of its bursting, and shattering Mr. Hampden's arm in such a manner that he receiv'd his death by the wound and not by any hurt from the enemy.'

Compare this story with Lord Clarendon's account, vol. II., p. 264."

ii. 1719, Feb. 9. Dublin.—Letter from Dean Swift.

"Sir, I was twice disappointed with your letter. When I saw your name on the outside I thought it had been a civility you had done to some friend to save me postage; when I saw the same name after opening I was in hopes to hear something of you and your family, my Lord Oxford, Lord Harley, and your son, and I wish you had sayd something on that head by way of postscript. I desire you will ask my Lord Oxford whether his brother Nathaniel understands musick; if he does, and recommends Mr. Lovelace particularly from his own knowledge, something may be said. I have the honour to be Captain of a band of nineteen musicians (including boys), which are I hear about five less then my friend the D. of Chandos, and I understand musick like a Muscovite; but my quire is so degenerate under the reigns of former Deans of famous memory, that the race of people called Gentlemen Lovers of Musick tell me I must be very carefull in supplying two vacancyes, which I have been two years endeavoring to do. For you are to understand that in disposing these musicall employments, I determine to act directly contrary to Ministers of State, by giving them to those who best deserve. If you had recommended a person to me for a Church-living in my gift, I would be less curious; because an indifferent Parson may do well enough, if he be honest, but Singers like their brothers the Poets must be very good, or they are good for nothing. I wish my Lord Oxford had writ to me on this subject, that I might have had the pleasure of refusing him in direct terms.

If you will order Mr. Lovelace to enquire for one Rosingrave my organist now in London, and approve his skill to him, on his report I shall be ready to accept Lovelace, which is the short of the matter that I have made so many words of, in revenge for your saying nothing of what I would desire to know; and I must desire you to put my Lord Oxford in mind of sending me his picture, for it is just eight years last Tuesday since he promised me. If you had said but one syllable of my sister Harriette I could have pardoned you.

Pray believe that there is no man who can possibly have a greater respect for you and your family than myself. Nothing but a scurvy state of health could have hindred me from the happiness of once more seeing you all. I am, with great respect, Sir, your most obedient and most humble servant, J°. SWIFT."

WILLIAM DUNN MACRAY.

REPORT ON MUNIMENTS IN THE POSSESSION OF EDMOND R. WODEHOUSE, ESQ., M.P.

THIS collection was originally, and is still for the most part, contained in a large chest, and numbers some thousands of books, rolls, deeds, and papers, chiefly relating to the families of Buttes, Bacon, and Wodehouse, and their estates in the counties of Norfolk and Suffolk. Some of them refer to Sir Nicholas Bacon, Lord Keeper, and there is a grant of arms to him in 1568; but none of his correspondence is preserved here. The agreement on the marriage of his son Nicholas with Anne Buttes, in 1561, deserves notice, not only as an early specimen of an elaborate marriage contract, prepared doubtless under the supervision of the Lord Keeper himself, but also as indicating the manner in which these estates passed from the family of Buttes to that of Bacon, though in reality the devolution was very complicated.

The period covered by these muniments extends from the reign of Henry III. to the beginning of the present century. They appear to be very valuable from a topographical as well as from a genealogical point of view. The amount of information they contain with regard to many families of Norfolk and Suffolk, and especially those families to which they more particularly relate, is considerable. Ample illustrations of local manners and customs, and of manorial rights and privileges, such as rights of common and fishery, may be gathered from the unusually extensive series of court rolls, bailiffs' accounts, and rentals, which commence as early as the first half of the fourteenth century. Attention may especially be drawn to two custumals of the manor of Ryburgh Magna.

Very little correspondence is comprised in this collection, but there are two letter-books containing copies of numerous letters between the King and the Privy Council and the Lord Lieutenant, Deputy Lieutenants, &c. of Suffolk, between 1608 and 1640, and between 1664 and 1676. They relate to matters of general historical interest as well as to local affairs. Some long letters from "J. Nixon" to Miss Bacon, giving an account of his travels in England and France in 1745–1750, are curious. A few more letters exist among the miscellaneous papers, but are of small importance.

Several handsome rolls of pedigrees and arms of the Bacon family, and other families related to it, are preserved in the chest.

Only a few manuscript volumes not connected with the families above named and their estates have been discovered. These are: (1) a copy of Higden's Polychronicon; (2) "The Statutes of the Garter"; (3) a Report relating to Daniel Archdeacon and Francis Mowbray, in the time of James I; (4) a Summary of Proceedings in Parliament, &c., 1625–8; (5) a poem entitled "The Calidonian Forest"; and (6) an heraldic MS.

These muniments were found in great confusion, without any kind of order or arrangement. In the year 1888, on the recommendation of the late Mr. Walford D. Selby, and as a preliminary step, the earlier deeds were selected from the other documents, and placed in envelopes, which were numbered and arranged in boxes in the manner now adopted at the Public Record Office. Of these deeds a catalogue was subsequently made.

After this was done, it was thought desirable that the remainder of the manuscripts should be put in order, and accordingly they have been arranged in the classes to which they respectively belong. The rolls and modern deeds and papers have been placed in thirty bundles, but some of the rolls of pedigrees are too unwieldy to be treated in that manner. A brief catalogue of the bundles as thus arranged has been made. The books have also been inspected, and ample notes taken from the more important of them.

The collection can therefore now be described more particularly, but before doing so it is needful to explain how by one marriage the Bacons acquired the possessions of three branches of the Buttes family, as well as of three coheiresses who married into that family, in order to make this collection intelligible. To do this we need go back only two generations in the Buttes pedigree preceding the lady with whom it ended.

William Buttes, or Butte, "doctor in medicinis," or "doctor artis medicæ," born about 1485, was the "dilectus serviens et medicus" of King Henry VIII., and an early member of the College of Physicians. The numerous notices of him which occur in the State Papers show that he was employed in affairs of State as well as in those connected with his profession, and that the part assigned to him by Shakespeare was not altogether an imaginary one. He was clearly in active sympathy with the King's new schemes of church reformation, though he is said to have given the King some advice with regard to the Princess Mary which was not agreeable. Sundry references to his recipes and fees are to be found in the recent edition of his contemporary Thomas Vicary's "Anatomie."

The earliest proof of the royal favour to him was shown in a grant dated 9th August 1529 of the wardship of the four daughters and coheiresses of Henry Bures, of Acton, Suff., Esquire, son and heir of Robert Bures, Esquire, Robert having deceased on 10th July 1524 and Henry on 6th July 1528, the latter being only 26 years of age. The Bures estates consisted of the manors of Acton, Reydon, and Wharsted in Suffolk, and other lands in that county and in Essex. Twelve bonds, still extant, given by the Doctor to the Treasurer of the King's Chamber, show that this wardship was far from being a free gift. Soon after, on 10th November 1529, Dr. Buttes had a grant of an annuity of forty marks out of these estates during the wardship; and subsequently his three sons married three out of the four coheiresses.

In later years Dr. Buttes obtained still more substantial concessions from his royal patient, consisting of manors, lands, and advowsons in various counties, partly in reward of his faithful service in the King's "affairs," and partly in consideration of extremely large sums of money. Some of the grants were in fee; in others provision was made after his death for his younger sons. His evident intention was to found three independent families of his name in the county of Norfolk, but his expectations were doomed to disappointment. With the lands in question he of course acquired the more ancient of the rolls and deeds to be described hereafter; it will be well therefore to give some particulars of these grants.

1. On 2 Sept. 1532 the King granted to him and the heirs male of his body the manor of Panington with appurtenances in Wharsted, Suff., which had belonged to Cardinal Wolsey, whose attainder is referred to at some length in the grant.

2. On 1 July 1536, for the sum of 900*l.*, he had a grant in fee of the manor of Thornage, with the advowsons of the churches of Thornage and Brynton, Norf., formerly belonging to the See of Norwich.

3. On 30 March 1538 there was a grant to him and Margaret his wife of the manor of Thornham, Norf., formerly belonging to the See of Norwich; with remainders after their deaths to Edmund Butte, one of his younger sons, in tail male; then to Thomas Butte, another younger son, in tail male; then to the heirs male of the Doctor.

4. On 10 March 1539, for the sum of 1,000 marks, the King made a similar grant to Dr. Butte and Margaret (Bacon) his wife of the manors of Great Ryburgh and Woodhall in Little Ryburgh, which had belonged to the priory of Walsingham, and of a messuage and lands in Great Ryburgh, late of the priory of Hempton; with remainders to Thomas Butte, a younger son, in tail male; then to William Butte, the eldest son, in tail male; then to Edmund Butte, another younger son, in tail male; then to the right heirs of Dr. Butte.

5 & 6. On 24 July 1540, he had a grant of the mansions and buildings within the site of the White Friars, London; and on 24 Nov. 1541, he and Anthony Denny obtained the next presentation to a prebend in St. Stephen's, Westminster.

7. On 3 March 1545, for the sum of 767*l.* 12*s.* 6*d.*, he obtained a final grant in fee of the manor of Edgefield, Norf., formerly belonging to Bynham Priory, and of other possessions in Norfolk and other counties, and in London; but soon afterwards he obtained licence to alienate some of these.

Besides the lands acquired by royal letters patent, the Doctor purchased others, such as the manor of Melton Constable, from private individuals. He also had "lands and tenements" in Fulham, but how he obtained these has not been ascertained.

Dr. Buttes made the house of the late Whitefriars his residence in London, and Thornage his principal seat in the country. He was knighted in 1545, but lived only a short while to enjoy the dignity, as he died on 22 November in the same year, according to his inquisitions, but on the 17th according to the inscription on his tomb in Fulham church, as usually quoted. In a letter of Paget's it is stated that the Doctor, "after a long and grievous sickness of a dooble febre quartane, is departed in an honest and godly sorte to God." Some account of him is given in Dr. Munk's Roll of Physicians, Wood's and Cooper's Athenæ, Faulkner's History of Fulham, in the Proceedings of the Society of Antiquaries, 2 S. xiii. 152, and in the Dictionary of National Biology.

By two inquisitions Sir William was found to have possessed the manor of Panington, Suff., the manors of Thornage, Edgefield, and Melton Constable, and lands in Brynton, Briston, Birnyngham, and Borough, Norf., mostly held of the King by knight service and by various rents; but Melton Constable was "held of the barony which had lately belonged to the bishopric of Norwich." Nothing is said about the manors of Thornham and Great and Little Ryburgh, no doubt because Lady Margaret, who had a life interest in them, survived her husband and remained in possession, as appears by the probate of Sir William's will, at Somerset House; but there are deeds in this collection which show that Thomas Buttes was lord of the two latter manors as early as 1546.

Sir William Buttes left three sons: William, his son and heir, afterwards knighted, Thomas, and Edmund. These brothers had married three of their father's four wards, the coheiresses of Henry Bures above-mentioned; viz., William = Jane, eldest daughter; Thomas = Bridget, second daughter; Edmund = Anne, third daughter. The youngest of the four daughters, named Mary, born in Dec. 1519, became the wife of Thomas Barrowe, Esquire, and had five sons and four daughters, viz., Thomas, who died *s. p.*, William, Henry, Edward, John, Anne, Bridget, Elizabeth, and Mary.

Edmund seems to have been the youngest of the three sons, though he died first of them all. He and his wife Anne obtained livery of *her* lands in or about February 1543, but portions of the Bures estates were then still held in dower by Anne (Waldegrave), widow of Henry Bures, and by Robert Buck and Joan (Higham) his wife. He died in 1549 or 1550, his will being proved in the latter year. Gage's History of Suffolk gives the inscription on the brass of an Edmund Buttes, who died 7 May 1542 (?), and was buried at Barrow, but the date is badly printed, and may be wrong. He probably succeeded his father in the manor of Thornham, but there is no inquisition after his death. As he left no son, it would go to his brother Thomas under the entail. This Edmund must not be confounded with another Edmund Buttes, nephew of Sir William, who is mentioned in both the wills above referred to.

Anne, wife of Edmund, was born 28 Oct. 1517, and survived him for sixty years, but did not marry again. She died at Redgrave, the seat of the Bacons, on 22 Dec. 1609, in her 93rd year, possessed of a moiety of the manors of Whersted, &c., William Barrowe, second son of Mary, having the other moiety.

Edmund and Anne had an only daughter, also named Anne, born about 1550, and married to Nicholas Bacon, son of the Lord Keeper, at Redgrave, on 2 May 1562. Even at that early date it was foreseen that she would become heiress of her two uncles and their wives, as well as of her mother, for they were all parties to her marriage settlements, and to the seven royal licences of alienation which were necessary to give them legal effect. At the time of her mother's death, in 1609, she is returned as then living at Culford, aged 59 years and more.

William Buttes, eldest son and heir of Sir William, was born in 1513, He and his wife Jane obtained livery of her inheritance on 9 Dec. 1538. He had livery of his father's lands on 7 Nov. 1546, and was knighted in 1547. He was commissioner for musters in Norfolk in 1569–1574. In 1571 he was one of the commissioners appointed to take an inventory of the attainted Duke of Norfolk's goods, and to establish a household for the Duke's children. The date of his death is variously stated as 20 Nov. 1580, and 3 Sept. 1583, the latter being the correct date according to "A Booke of Epitaphes" written in praise of his virtues both in the field and in counsel, and edited by Sir Robert Dallington. It contains verses by the editor and many other writers in Latin and English, including a few by Thomas Buttes. Sir William was buried at Thornage, a monument being erected to him in the church there. He is returned as owner of the manors of Thornage, Melton, Cockfield, Edgefield, Panington, &c. As he left no issue, his younger brother Thomas became his heir.

Lady Jane, wife of the second Sir William, was born on 12 April 1514, and died at Thornage on 25 Nov. 1593; her heirs-at-law being her sister Anne Buttes, widow of Edmund, and her nephew William Barrowe, son of Thomas and Mary; but according to the settlements of 1561, a moiety of Lady Jane's property passed to Sir Nicholas Bacon (the second) and Lady Anne his wife, to the exclusion the latter's mother, one of the heirs-at-law, who of course however continued in possession of her own fourth purparty.

Thus Thomas Buttes remained as the last male representative of Dr. Buttes. He was born in the year 1516. He had livery of his wife Bridget's property on 28 May 1541. On his mother's death, probably in 1546, he would succeed at once, without the usual livery, to the manors of Great Ryburgh and Woodhall, in accordance with the terms of the royal grant. Then, by the death of his brother Edmund, he became entitled to the manor of Thornham; and on the death of his eldest brother, Sir William, he succeeded to all the rest of the Buttes estates. He died without issue on 20 Jan. 1593, at Catton, Norf., being 77 years of age. Before his death he had conveyed the manors of Great Ryburgh and Woodhall, Thornham, and Pannington to Sir Nicholas Bacon and Lady Anne his wife in consideration of certain annuities payable at Redgrave. This partly accounts for there being no inquisition after his death, when, in default of issue, whatever possessions he retained would descend to his niece Anne, daughter of his brother Edmund, and wife of Sir Nicholas Bacon. An inquisition was however taken in respect of the lands of his wife Bridget, second daughter of Henry Bures, finding that she held a fourth part of the manors of Whersted, Reydon, Martyns, and Sulveyes, Suff., and of other manors in that county and in Essex. She was born 19 June 1516, and died at Ryburgh, 7 Feb. 1572; but her inquisition was not taken till 1594, after the death of Thomas. A moiety of her possessions likewise went to her niece Anne above mentioned, to the exclusion of the latter's mother.

In this tortuous manner all the Buttes estates, as well as two-thirds of the Bures estates, became vested in Sir Nicholas Bacon the younger and Anne his wife; excepting of course Pannington and Thornham, which would revert to the Crown under the limitations of the grants, though Sir Nicholas Bacon had purchased them from Thomas Buttes only the year previous, 1592.

Nicholas Bacon, son of the Lord Keeper, was born in 1548, and according to the dates given he was only fourteen and his wife only twelve years of age at their marriage in 1562. He was knighted in 1578, and was the first baronet created in 1611. Besides the succession of inheritances which accrued to him from his marriage, he enjoyed the large possessions left him by his father in 1579; but as very few of the earlier of these muniments relate to the lands acquired by the first Sir Nicholas, it would be out of place to describe the various means by which he obtained them. The Lord Keeper made his principal seat at Redgrave, Suffolk. There will be found sundry references to that manor, which was given by Henry VIII. to Nicholas Bacon, then solicitor of the Court of Augmentations, on 21 April 1545. The letters patent were enrolled twice, in pursuance of two warrants, an unusual occurrence, which is accounted for by the following memorandum: "The cause of the said two warrauntes was for that the King beinge sicke, the one of theym was offered to hym to be signed, and thother to the Commissioners that hadd authority to passe suche billes vnder the Kynges Stampe, and it happened so that at one tyme the Kynge signed thone, and the Commissioners signed thother with the saide Stampe." Mr. Solicitor Bacon was clearly as great a favourite of King Henry as was "Mr. Doctor Buttes," and no doubt their frequent meetings at Court originated a friendship between the two families, resulting in the marriage which proved so advantageous to the Bacon family.

The further particulars as to the descent of the Bacon family are well known, but only a few of the above particulars as to the Buttes family are given by Blomefield in his History of Norfolk. For his accounts of many parishes in the county he had access to private collections, but as he did not make use of the present one, though he wrote his name on the manuscript containing the Statutes of the Garter, his description of Great and Little Ryburgh, and the other manors to which these documents relate, is comparatively meagre and unsatisfactory.

It must be mentioned, to explain the devolution of these muniments to their present possessor, that Sir Edmund Bacon of Garboldisham, sixth Baronet, left four daughters and coheiresses, of whom the eldest, Letitia, married Sir Armine Wodehouse, and the third daughter, Sarah, married Mr. Pryse Campbell, of Stackpole Court, Pembrokeshire. Part of the estates referred to in this report fell to the share of the second daughter, Mary, who died unmarried, and by her will they descended to her nephew Thomas Wodehouse (third and youngest son of Sir Armine), who had married her niece, Sarah Campbell, sister of the first Lord Cawdor. These muniments passed with the property bequeathed by Miss Mary Bacon to Thomas Wodehouse, who was the great-grandfather of their present owner.

The classes into which the collection has been divided are these:—

- The early deeds.
- Court rolls, bailiffs' accounts, surveys, &c.
- Old and modern papers.
- Royal letters patent.
- Wills, plans, &c.
- Modern deeds.
- MS. books.
- Pedigrees, &c.

A description of each class will now be given, followed by appendices of the more important documents.

The early Deeds.

In the course of arranging the rolls, papers, and modern deeds, numerous early deeds were discovered, in addition to those which had been selected, and they have been added to the series. There are now twelve boxes full of such deeds, which are numbered from 1 to 700, and extend from the reign of Henry III. to the 17th century. When the catalogue was completed, the entries were sorted under the names of the places to which the deeds refer, and it was found that more than half of the deeds relate to the manor of Great Ryburgh and Woodhall manor in Little Ryburgh, with the advowsons of the churches there, and lands belonging to those manors in the vills of Great and Little Ryburgh, Gateley, Guist, and Testerton. The manor of Great Ryburgh belonged successively to the families of Monpinzun, Walkefare, and Felton, then to the Priory of Walsingham, then to the families above named. Besides the manorial evidences, there are still more numerous conveyances by freeholders of lands in the same townships, which are all in Norfolk.

Another large portion of the deeds refers to the manors and freeholds in Briningham, Hunworth, Melton-Constable, Stody, Harthill, Little Burgh, Briston, Brinton, Thornage, Holt, and the neighbourhood, also all in Norfolk.

Lists of the names of persons mentioned in connexion with all the above-named localities will be found in Appendix A. They will serve as a guide to the court rolls and surveys of the respective manors as well as to the deeds. Although the two groups of places are so close together, it will be seen that the lists differ greatly.

There are also sundry deeds relating to Egmere manor, tenements in North Elmham, and messuages belonging to the Mercers' Company in Thames Street, London; and a few relating to the following places: Tatterford, Little Narryngge, Walsingham, Hemelamstede, Pudding Norton, Causton, Harpley, Burhalle, Risborough in Wighton, Kedington *alias* Ketton, Brunham, Hockwold, Thornham, King's Lynn, South Lynn, Bynham.

Most of the deeds are ordinary conveyances of land from party to party, though locally interesting because they so frequently mention field-names and landmarks, and describe boundaries: such as manors and their demesnes, churches and their glebe lands, churchyards, mills, rivers, commons, heaths, fields, furlongs, acres, closes, and the lands of ecclesiastical and lay owners. Some of the deeds are however remarkable in one way or another, and will be noticed in Appendix A.

To many of the deeds *Seals* of arms and other devices are attached, mostly in good condition, a few being the seals of religious houses. These are well worthy of the attention of the student of heraldry, and of persons interested in particular families.

Some *Wills* are placed with the early deeds, being those of the following testators:—

John Haliday, 1362.—No. 551.
John Trendil, c. 1377 ?—No. 516.
John Rust, 1392.—No. 510.
Richard Harneyse, 1503.—No. 395.
Margaret Hervy, 1508.—No. 308.
Edmond Buttes of Barrow, Suffolk, Esq., 1550.—No. 366.
William Startweight, 1559.—No. 502.
Robert Harvye, 1566.—No. 451.

There are also a few royal letters patent of the reigns of Edward II., Henry VI., and Elizabeth (Nos. 228, 324, 424, 431, 627); some having portions of the Great Seal attached, and one being under the seal of the Court of Exchequer, specimens of which are uncommon.

Court Rolls, Bailiffs' Accounts, Surveys, &c.

There is a very large quantity—some hundreds—of Court Rolls, Bailiffs' Accounts, Estreat Rolls, Rentals, Surveys, Custumals, and miscellaneous rolls, which have been placed in bundles numbered from 1 to 12, the contents of which are as follows:—

Bundles 1 to 5.

Court Rolls of Great Ryburgh, Little Ryburgh, and Woodhall in Little Ryburgh, from the reign of Edward I. to the 18th century; with Estreat Rolls, Copies of Court Rolls, &c.

Bundle 6.

Court Rolls of Stody, Briningham, and Melton cum Briningham Bacons, from Edward III. to Charles I.; with Estreat Rolls, &c.

Bundle 7.

Court Rolls of Hunworth, Harthill, and Chosells, from Edward II. to Charles I., with Estreat Rolls, &c. Little Stody is also mentioned.

[*Note.*—Sundry Court Books of Ryburgh, Stibbard, Horsham St. Faith's, Walsingham, Harthill in Hunworth, and other places will be found in the list of Books.]

Bundles 8 and 9.

Ministers' Accounts of the Manors of Great and Little Ryburgh and Woodhall, from Edward II. to Elizabeth. Some of these are in a decayed state.

Bundle 9.

Ministers' Accounts of Stody, Hunworth, Harthill in Hunworth, Briningham, Thornage, &c., from Edward III. to Henry VII.

Bundles 10 and 11.

Rentals, Surveys, Valuations, &c. of Great and Little Ryburgh, Gateley, Woodhall, and the Manor of Paveleys in Little Ryburgh, from Edward II. to Elizabeth.

Bundle 11 also contains a separate parcel of rentals, &c. of Thornegge and Chossells, Stody, Harthill in Hunworth, and Briningham, from Henry VI. to Charles II.; with a few of Little Walsingham, Brinton, Edgefield, &c.

[*Note*.—Other Rentals of Ryburgh, Gateley, Guist, Stibbard, &c. will be found in the list of Books.]

Bundle 12.

Miscellaneous Rolls, viz.:—

Two Custumals of Great Ryburgh; c. 1300. They give the names of the tenants, the extent of their holdings, their rents in money and kind, their works in ploughing, mowing, hoeing, &c., and with horses and carts. The earlier of the two rolls begins thus: Custumarium de Ryburg' Magna.—Johannes Palmere et parcenarii sui tenent de Domino xii. acras terræ. Many other similar partnerships are mentioned. A few persons paid rents of capons for pasture in the common of Great Ryburgh.

Estreat Roll of the Hundred of Brothercross, temp. Hen. VII. (?)

Copies of Court Rolls of Gateley, Henry VII. and VIII.

Court Rolls and Estreat Rolls of Thornegge cum membris, from Edward VI. to Charles I.; with a few estreat rolls of Edgefield Bacons, temp. Chas. I.

Copies of Court Rolls of the Manor of North Elmham, relative to certain tenements therein, 1565–1697; with an estreat roll of the same manor, 35 Henry VIII.

A few Estreat Rolls of Wortham Abbots, Westhall in Rickinhall Inferiore, Wiverston, Walsham, and Walsham Churchhouse, 1616–1624; and of Tattersett and Tatterford cum Sherford, 1634–1640. (Paper.)

Copies of Court Rolls of the Manors of Little Walsingham, Walsingham ad Grangias, &c., from Henry VIII. to Elizabeth.

A roll headed: "Cartæ et Fines Domini Roberti de Walkefare,—de Ryburgħ, Ingolestorp̄ [Norf.], Balidoñ [Essex], et Iselham [Cantebr̄]." This contains copies of a large number of deeds and a few royal charters relating to the above-named places, and to Skyrbeck [Lincoln], temp. Edw. II. and III. (Parchment, 14th cent.)

"Account of Henry Smyth, Receiver of the First Fruits of the Rev. Father in Christ Walter, Bishop of Norwich, in the Archdeaconry of Norwich and in Norfolk, from Benefices taxed therein, from . . . . 10 Edward IV. to the feast of All Saints next following," &c. This large roll really extends from about 30 Henry VI. to 11 Edward IV., as it gives the names of Rectors and Vicars instituted within that period, and charged with the payment of first fruits. The names number several hundreds. The title and first few lines are damaged, but have been repaired.

Account of Catherine Violett *alias* Wadson, relict and administratrix of John Wadson, of King's Lynn, merchant, 1579. This is a parchment roll of three membranes, with a portion of the seal of the Prerogative Court of Canterbury.

Old and Modern Papers.

These have been placed in four bundles, the following being a description of their contents.

Bundles 13–16.

Papers chiefly relating to the families of Buttes, Bacon, and Wodehouse, and their estates in Norfolk and Suffolk, from the middle of the sixteenth to the beginning of the nineteenth century. They consist of—

Numerous documents and memoranda by Thomas Buttes, Esquire, lord of Great Ryburgh manor, concerning his estates, in the reign of Elizabeth; written in a very neat hand, in which also many of the papers in this collection are endorsed. He was evidently an industrious and methodical man of business, with a turn for versifying.

Law papers and proceedings in several suits, with a few depositions; including the Answer of Robert Bacon, Esquire, to the Information of William Noye, Attorney General, 1633.

Abstracts of title.

Copies and drafts of deeds, bonds, wills, settlements, &c.

Papers relating to the church, tithes, and glebe-lands of Great Ryburgh. Among these are—Depositions in a tithe suit in 1525; accounts between Thomas Buttes and successive parsons of Ryburgh; proceedings in a dispute between Mr. Buttes and the vicar there in the reign of Elizabeth, which ended in a suit in Chancery (Thomas Waterman *v.* Thomas Buttes); sundry accusations being made by Buttes against the vicar of neglecting the services, stirring up strife in the parish, &c.

The principal charges were the following: "There have been no catechising at G. Ryburgh for the space of theise iiij yeres last past and more, nor teaching the Articles of the Fayth, the Commaundementes, and the Lordes Prayer, as is prescribed in the Catechisme. No repayering the Chauncell, or personage, but letting to fearme his benefise there, and that vnto verie vnmeete persons. No hospytalitie kept, nor releeving the poore there by hym, but yerelie selling of dykerowes. No prayer for her Maiestie the xvij. daye of November last past, although the Inhabitauntes were redy at the Churche doores for that godly purpose: for he was then gadded to the spirituall Courte to followe his suyte ageinst Robert Harvy of G. Ryburgh for tythes oniustlie requyered. . . . . . . I [Thomas Buttes] have also glased at myne owne proper cost and chardge all the windowes in the Chauncell, which ar in nomber v, and those verie large & greate, which did cost mee with the scripture written within the said Chauncelles wales more then xx *li.*"

Letter from Thomas Touneshend to Mr. Myngaye, "from my poore howse," 18 July 1554, touching the advowson of Great Ryburgh. Sir Henry Maner, priest, under some title derived from the late Prior of Walsingham, had given it to one Deneye, late parson of Lynge, "a very busy man, and too stout for a priest," but it was claimed by Mr. Buttes, the true patron.

Papers relating to the advowson of Little Ryburgh. John Heath was accused of obtaining it by simony (in 1562?). He was presented by Edward Fitzgarret, Esq., who had married the widow of Sir Thomas Paston. The right of presentation was claimed by Thomas Buttes, as also a yearly pension out of the vicarage.

"Articles and Agreements," . . . Sept. 3 Eliz., (1561,) between Sir Nicholas Bacon, Lord Keeper, and Thomas Buttes of Great Ryburgh, Norfolk, Esq., concerning the marriage of Nicholas Bacon, son and heir apparent of the said Sir Nicholas Bacon and Anne Buttes, niece and heir apparent of Thomas Buttes. Signed by the parties.

Articles of Agreement (undated) for the sale by Thomas Buttes, Esquire, to Sir Nicholas Bacon and Dame Anne his wife of the manors of Great Rieborough and Woodhall, and the manor of Thornham, in consideration of annuities of 149*l.* 6*s.* 4¼*d.* and 29*l.* 14*s.* 10*d.*, payable at Redgrave. Not signed.

Draft letter from T. B. [Thomas Buttes] to Lord Cromwell at North Elmham, relative to a right of fishing claimed by the latter in waters belonging to the former, 1579; with another letter thereon from——.

Papers relating to the succession of Thomas Buttes to the estates of Sir William Buttes, as brother and heir, in 1584; the manner of taking the Inquisition and suing out the livery, payments to the Exchequer, &c.

Copy of the will of Thomas Geyton of Great Riburgh, 1503; proved in the same year.

Copy of the will of John Hervye of the same, 1547; proved 1547–8.

A paper relating to "a right of Shackage" at Little Ryburgh, being an agreement between Roger Towneshend, Esquire, Lord of the Manor of Pauleys, and William Salman, tenant of the foldcourse there of the Prior of Walsingham, 22 Aug. 9 Hen. VIII. (1517.)

The deposition of an old witness touching the graving of flaggs and the use of the foldcourse at Studdy. 1575.

A paper showing the abuttals of divers heaths in Stody and Hunworth. 17th cent.

Receipts by Edward Grey, feodary, for moneys due to the King for castle-ward from Sir Edmond Bacon, Bart., for the manor of Melton. 1618–1634.

Grant by Lord Townshend of liberty to kill rabbits on Stibbard Heath.

Copy of case with counsel's opinion as to Botesdale School [in Redgrave], founded by Sir Nicholas Bacon. 1740.

A document by Maurice Shelton, Esq., authorising Sir Edmond Bacon, Bart., and others to appoint an attorney to sue John Powell for 50*l.* 13*s.* 9*d.* for half a year's interest due on the joint stock of South Sea Annuities, standing in their names in the books of the South Sea Company. 1744.

Extracts from the Accounts of the Collectors of the Aids granted in 20 Edw. III., 3 Henry IV., &c., and from Rentals and Court Rolls; relating to tenements in Snoryng, held of Great Ryburgh.

Papers relating to the collection of the Taske (Tax) in Great Ryburgh, in 1564, 1568, 1571, 1576, 1581, &c. by Thomas Buttes, Esquire, high collector. The names of the persons assessed are given. Also, a Privy Seal, 31 October, 4 & 5 Philip and Mary, to Thomas Buttes, Esquire, asking for payment of 10*l.* "by way of loan;" with receipt at foot.

Rates made at Thornage, 1648–1653.

Letters from Edward Symondes, dated at Stody, Norf., in 1608 and 1609, to Sir Nicholas Bacon at Cullford, Suff.; the writer being apparently steward of some of the latter's manors.

Letters from Sir Allen Broderick and other papers relating to "Mr. Stewart's marriage with Lucy Hatton." 1647, &c. These are in a large bundle of documents relating to the estates of Sir Thomas Wendy, the rectory of Haslingfield, a yearly payment of 30*l.* due to the poor of Haslingfield, &c. (In Bundle 16.)

Letters from Mr. P. Jodrell and Sir Anthony Thomas Abdy, both of Lincoln's Inn, to Sir Edmond Bacon, Bart., at Garboldisham, Norf., with drafts of his replies, about law matters. 1749–1753.

Particulars of the estate of William, Earl of Yarmouth. 18th cent.

Petition of maltsters, merchants, and other persons interested in the Malt trade in the borough of King's Lynn, to the House of Commons, against a Bill for an additional duty on malt. 81 signatures. (About 1800? On parchment.)

A printed statement of church accounts, Yarmouth, 1803 *seq.*, with manuscript additions.

A printed list of the Corporation of Great Yarmouth, 1 Jan. 1816, with a list of mayors since the last charter, *i.e.*, from 1702 to 1815.

Three long letters from J. Nixon to Miss Bacon give minute accounts of his travels in England and France, being dated (1) Towcester, 14 Sept. 1745, (2) Towcester, 12 Nov. 1746, (3) Higham, 23 Nov. 1750. The first two, referring to England, have no address, but the third letter is addressed "To Miss Bacon, at Sir Edmund Bacon's Bart. at Garboldisham near Market Harling in Norfolk." The second and third letters however have no signatures, being incomplete. The last relates entirely to France; it bears a portion of a seal, and has this note on the back—"Coudn't you send me a frank?" (In bundle 15.) They are printed in Appendix E.

There is little internal evidence to show who the writer of these letters was, but what there is sufficiently identifies him with the Rev. John Nixon, M.A., rector of Cold Higham near Towcester. An ode, a sermon, and sundry essays of his are to be found in the British Museum Library, dated between 1728 and 1759; and in the Sloane MS. 4315 there are many letters from him to the Rev. Dr. Birch between 1740 and 1764, mostly very brief, on archæological matters, and showing that he was a Fellow of the Royal Society. In one of them he asks to be addressed at the school in Towcester. It is more difficult to identify the companion with whom he made these tours; but in 1755 he proposed making a tour in Italy in company with a Mr. Charlton, who may have been the person referred to in the letters. The lady addressed was doubtless Miss Mary Bacon, before mentioned.

Bills, receipts, &c.

Miscellaneous papers.

Most of the papers which are here more particularly described are in bundle 13.

Royal Letters Patent.

Bundle 17.

This bundle consists entirely of letters patent, mostly with Great Seals (some broken), viz.:—

30 Hen. VIII., 10 March.—Grant to William Butte, Esquire, and Margaret his wife, for 1000 marks, of the Manor of Great Riburgh, a watermill called the South Mille, a pasture called Sennowe, and the advowson; also the Manor called Woodhall in Little Riburgh, and liberty of faldage within those manors, with appurtenances in various towns, lately belonging to the Priory of Walsingham; also a messuage and lands in Great Riburgh lately belonging to the Priory of Hempton. Remainder to Thomas Butte, son of the said William, in tail male, then to William and Edmund, other sons, &c. Seal gone. Portrait of the King in the initial letter.

3 Elizabeth, 9 October.—Licence to Thomas Buttes, Esquire, to alienate the manors of Great Rybrough and Woodhall to Sir Nicholas Bacon Lord Keeper, and others.

4 Elizabeth, 21 November.—Inspeximus of a Recovery by Sir Nicholas Bacon and others against Thomas Buttes, Esquire, of the manors of Great Rybroughe and Woodhall, &c.

4 Elizabeth, 23 January.—Inspeximus of a Fine between Sir Nicholas Bacon and others, and Thomas Buttes and Bridget his wife, of the same manors.

Same date.—Inspeximus of a Fine between Sir Nicholas Bacon and others, and Sir William Buttes and Jane his wife, of the manors of Thornage, Melton, Cockefeld, and Egefeld, &c.

7 Elizabeth, 22 June.—Inspeximus, at the request of Thomas Buttes, Esquire, of charters of early Kings to the church of Holy Trinity of Norwich and to Sir Robert de Walkefare (lord of Ryburgh), granting them numerous liberties.

16 Elizabeth, 8 May.—Inspeximus of Charter of 28 March, 4 Ric. II., inspecting Charter of 12 October, 51 Henry III., granting to Roger le Poucre free warren in Stodeye, Huneworth, &c., and confirming the same to Master Simon de Sudbury and others. Queen Elizabeth confirms to Sir Nicholas Bacon and Nicholas Bacon, Esquire, his son and heir apparent. Portrait of the Queen in the initial letter.

21 Elizabeth, 20 December.—Licence to Thomas Buttes, Esquire, to alienate the manors of Great Ryburgh and Woodhall to Sir Nicholas Bacon, Junior, and Anne his wife.

35 Elizabeth, 6 September.—Commission to Richard Pryce and others in the bankruptcy of Robert Gunnell of St. Ives, chapman, with [a copy of] the Bill filed in Chancery by his creditors, Thomas Sandell and Henry Violett of King's Lynn, merchants.

40 Elizabeth, 29 May.—Inspeximus of a Recovery by William Downinge against Simon Grene and Edward Grene of the manor of Fytton, &c.

41 Elizabeth, 12 February.—Inspeximus of a Recovery by Sir John Heigham and Edward Bacon, Esquire, against Sir Nicholas Bacon and Anne his wife of the Manors of Woodhall, Ryborowe Magna and Parva, &c.

1 Charles I., 10 February.—"A general Pardon of grace" to Robert Bacon of Righborough, Norfolk, Esquire.

1651, 18 June.—Inspeximus of a Recovery by Sir John Tracy, Knight, and another, against Butts Bacon, Esquire, of the manor of Egmere, &c.

7 George III., 12 February.—Inspeximus of a Recovery by Robert Layman against William Burrell, Gentleman, of one messuage and lands in North Elmham. Portrait of the King in the initial letter.

[*Note.*—A few other letters patent of the reigns of Edward II., Henry VI., and Elizabeth will be found among the early Deeds—Nos. 228, 324, 424, 431, 627. An Inspeximus of 29 George II., being too large to go with these bundles, has been placed at the end in a bundle by itself—No. 30.]

Wills, Plans, &c.

Bundle 18.

This bundle contains several modern wills of members of the Bacon and Wodehouse families, and others, which need not be specified here. A few earlier wills are to be found in the boxes of early deeds. An early seal of the Consistory Court of Norwich is loose in this bundle, and may belong to one of the early wills.

In the same bundle have been placed, for convenience, the two immense counterparts of the Indenture of 3 October, 3 Elizabeth, 1561, between Sir Nicholas Bacon, Lord Keeper, and Thomas Buttes, Esquire, and Brygitt his wife, one of the daughters and heirs of Henry Bures, Esquire; being a settlement on the marriage of Nicholas Bacon, Esquire, son and heir apparent of Sir Nicholas and Anne Buttes, the younger, niece and heir apparent of Thomas Buttes, viz., daughter and heir of Edmund Buttes, Esquire, brother of Thomas Buttes, and daughter and heir apparent of Anne Buttes, widow of Edmund Buttes. It deals with the estates of Thomas Buttes as well as with those of his wife. Each counterpart consists of two large skins of vellum, and they are signed and sealed by the parties. They are splendidly engrossed on red lines, after the fashion of letters patent of that period. Bonds of Sir Nicholas Bacon and Thomas Buttes in 2000 marks each are attached.

There are also in this bundle a few plans or maps of some importance. The principal one is on two sheets of vellum, originally joined together, and was drawn about 1680, its title being as follows:—

"The Description of the Town and Fields of Little Riburgh in the county of Norfolk. All those lands coloured with yellow were of the Rectory; the pricked lines signify the meeres, and the black lines ditches and enclosures; nat. for copyhold and lb. for free; h. for Hempton; f. St. Faith's; w. Woodhall; c. Creak; ca. Castleacre; and p. Pavelyes."

Besides these abbreviations there occur "Dns." and "R. B.," both written in red ink on many of the divisions, but not explained. The names of the tenants are also given. They were few in number, and most of them held both freeholds and copyholds, the latter being more numerous than the former. Their houses are shown all together near the centre of the map, at some little distance from the church. There were several highways through the fields. One of the acres was called Dovehouse acre.

This plan shows all the numerous divisions and sub-divisions of the "common fields" very minutely, with the extent of each separate parcel of land. It is clear that the greater part of the arable land was originally divided into strips of about an acre each, but that some of them had been consolidated. The south side of the fields, however, towards "the Heath," is divided into much larger sections than the north side; in fact there are few traces of the single-acre system in that portion, which comprised the site of the manor of Woodhall (belonging to Sir Edmond Bacon), the site of the Rectory, Pavelyes manor, and some of the demesnes. The inquiry at once suggests itself whether the lords of the respective manors had managed to obliterate the original land-marks, if there were such, by exchange and consolidation, or whether this portion consisted of lands "approved" from the waste subsequently to the construction of the common fields, either on the introduction of the manorial system, or under the Statute of Merton.

With regard to the northern or larger portion of the fields, an important feature of this plan is that it gives the names of the manors included in or extending into the township, and states to which of them each acre or larger parcel of land respectively belonged, and whether it was freehold or copyhold. From these particulars it is evident that the demesnes and tenements of the different manors were inextricably inter-mixed, so that there were no manorial boundaries; an interesting fact which is not illustrated by the maps published in Mr. Seebohm's "English Village Community."

On the back of this plan is a reference to "the Field Book." A book with this title, without covers, has been found, and placed with the plan, with which it may be instructively compared. It gives a description of thirty-one furlongs, and of the holdings in each, with numbers corresponding to those given in the map, but the names of the tenants are different, and it does not refer to the demesnes. Indeed it appears to be of somewhat earlier date than the map, though of the same century, and to have been copied from a still earlier terrier, as the "Prior of Binham" is spoken of as a tenant in several places.

There are also two small plans of Stody and Harthill, on paper, showing the pasture close, the marsh, the sheepcourse, &c. (17th cent.)

MSS. OF E. R. WODEHOUSE, ESQ., M.P.

Also, a plan of "Stibbard, Little Ryburgh, and Great Ryburgh, as allotted in 1810," with lands in adjoining parishes. This shows every parcel of land distinctly, its acreage, the nature of its tenure, and the name of its owner.

Modern Deeds.

Bundles 19–28.

In these bundles are placed all the modern deeds, consisting of settlements, conveyances, leases, &c. from the 17th to the 19th century, and relating to the families of Bacon and Wodehouse, and their estates in the following places in Norfolk, Suffolk, and other counties:

Great Ryburgh (manor and church), Little Ryburgh, Ryburgh Paveless, Senhow, Testerton, Guist, North Elmham (Norf.), North Elmham Nowers, Stibbard, Stibbard Rectory, North Creake, Stody, Briningham, Hunworth, Harthill in Hunworth, Chosells, Brinton, Holt, Melton, Edgefield, Thornage, Sharington, Letheringsett, Bodham, Egmere (manor and church), Waterden, North Bassam, Wighton, Great and Little Walsingham, Horsham St. Faith's, Burnham Overy, Sudborne, Little Snoring (manor and church), Wesenham, Swanton Morley with Worthinge, Wyverston and Mettingham, Bungay, Ilketshall, South Elmham (Suffolk). Sheepmeadowe, Barsham, Beccles, Ellow, Westhorpe, Redgrave, Bodisdale, Gislingham, Burgate, Wortham, Mellis St. John's, Rushes and Mellis, Jennys, Walsham, Wattsfeild, Rickinghall alias Westhall, Rickinghall alias St. John's, Rickinghall alias Facon's Hall, Over Rickinghall, Nether Rickinghall, Hindercley, Wendy and Haslingfield (Cambridge), and lands in the counties of Montgomery, Cardigan, and Pembroke. Bundle 22 contains deeds relating to Egmere, and bundle 24 deeds relating to North Elmham and Swanton Morley.

Bundle 29.

Indenture of seven parts, 16 September 1752, between John Campbell the elder, of Stackpole Court in the county of Pembroke, Esquire, Sir Edmund Bacon, of Garboldisham, Norfolk, Bart., Armine Wodehouse, of Kimberley, Norfolk, Esquire, and others; being a settlement on the marriage of Pryse Campbell, eldest son and heir apparent of the said John Campbell, and Sarah Bacon, one of the daughters of Sir Edmund Bacon. 34 skins of parchment, rolled.

Bundle 30.

Letters Patent of 13 March 29 George II., being an Inspeximus of proceedings in Chancery in a suit by Mary Bacon, one of the daughters and coheirs of Sir Edmund Bacon, of Garboldisham, Bart., against Sir Armine Wodehouse, Bart., and Letitia his wife. Sir Edmund's Will is recited. Ten skins of vellum, rolled. Portrait of the King in the initial letter.

MS. Books.

A manuscript entitled "Policronicon," in double columns, on paper, folio, about 290 pages; c. 1500. This is a complete copy of Ranulph Higden's Polychronicon, and of the Continuation thereof, as printed in the "Chronicles and Memorials," where Mr. Churchill Babington makes some remarks (Introduction, p. xxi.) on the different readings of "the bombastic and not very intelligible prologue," which in this copy begins thus:—

"Cm. pm.—Post preclaros arcium scriptores quibus contra rerum noticiam ut morum modestiam dulce q° aduiuerent insudar', illi merito velut vtile dulci commiscentes grandisonis sunt preconijs attollendi, qui magnifica priscorum gesta beneficio scriptur' posteris diriuarunt."

It gives a description of the world, histories of the Jews, Greeks, Romans, &c., and the history of England from the earliest times to the reign of Edward III. The last paragraph relates to Master John Wyclyf's teaching in the university of Oxford. The chronicle is followed by a list of the Popes, a pedigree showing the relationship of Jhesus, John the Baptist, John the Evangelist, Judas, &c., an alphabetical Index to the volume, and a pedigree of the Kings of France from St. Louis.

As this MS. is evidently written by a learned man and not by an ordinary scribe, it may be worth consulting on questions of various and doubtful readings.

"Statutes of the Garter"; a manuscript of the 15th century so labelled, on vellum; small folio. It has a few illuminated initial letters, and the contents of the chapters are rubricated in the margin. Note at the top of the first page: "Extract. per Franc. Blomefield cleric. a° 1732." This volume contains transcripts of the foundation charter of St. George's Chapel, Windsor, 22 Edw. III.; the Papal bull of confirmation; the ordinances made by Edward III. for the rule of St. George's College, &c.; the injunctions of John, Archbishop of York, 1431; and other documents relating to the College, including two Charters touching the last of red herrings due from the town of Great Yarmouth to the warden and canons of the free chapel of St. George, Windsor; with the form of the oath of a Knight of the Garter.

An heraldic MS., showing the arms of the principal noble families of England, and giving a short account of each. (Folio, bound in vellum; 89 leaves, one loose; 17th cent.)

"A true Report of sundry memorable accidents befalling Mr. Daniel Archdeacon before and after the combat appointed between him and Francis Mowbray," &c.; signed, A. D. G. (Small 4to, bound in vellum. No date; temp. James I. There is another copy of this MS. among the Domestic State Papers, James I., vol. 59, No. 51; which is assigned to the year 1610.)

"The Calidonian Forest"; a poem in a hand of the 17th century. It begins—

Whilome devided from the mayne land stood
A Forrest in the circle of a flood.

The letters E. B. (Edmond Bacon?) are written at the top of the first page, but merely signify ownership. (Several other copies are described in the first Report of this Commission.)

"A Book of such things as have come to my hands concerning the business of the country." There is nothing to show who was the compiler of this volume, but he was probably one of the Bacon family. It is a letter-book of the Deputy Lieutenants and Justices of the Peace of the county of Suffolk, and contains copies of numerous letters and warrants from the King and the Privy Council, and from the successive Earls of Suffolk, Lords Lieutenant of the county, relative to public and local affairs from 1608 to 1640; with letters and orders from the Deputy Lieutenants and Justices to the chief constables of the several hundreds, accounts, memoranda, &c. Many of the Royal and Council letters are not to be found in the State Papers or in Rushworth's Historical Collections, and appear to have been unknown to the historians of the period. The replies of the Deputy Lieutenants to those letters are not, as a rule, contained in this volume, but some of them will be found among the State Papers. There are many blank leaves at the end of the volume, which would doubtless have been filled up if the then usual method of conducting public business had not been interrupted by the civil war. The Earls of Suffolk were also Lord Lieutenants of Dorset and Cambridge, so that many of the entries refer to those counties as well as to Suffolk. Earl Theophilus was moreover Lord Warden of the Cinque Ports. It was thought desirable to make ample extracts from this correspondence, which will be found in Appendix B. (Folio, bound in vellum.)

Another similar but smaller letter-book of the Deputy Lieutenants and Justices of the Peace of the county of Suffolk, 1664–1676; Sir Edmund Bacon being one of the Deputy Lieutenants. Extracts from this volume will be found in Appendix C. (Folio, bound in vellum, but one cover wanting.)

Reports of proceedings in Parliament, with copies of a few royal letters &c., 1625–8. This MS. gives summaries of speeches by the King, the Lord Keeper, Dr. Turner, Mr. Pym, Mr. John Selden, Sir John Elliot, the Earl of Bristol, &c.; proceedings against the Duke of Buckingham &c. It seems to contain nothing but what may be found either in Rushworth's Collections, or in Additional MS. 22,474; but as this MS. occasionally differs from the other versions, a list of the pieces contained in it is given in Appendix D. (Small 4to, bound in vellum, 75 leaves.)

The remainder of the books is made up chiefly of court books, account books, surveys, rentals, and valuations, with some old catalogues of deeds and rolls, viz.:—

Court Book of Burnham Priors, Swanton Newers, Walsingham, Ryburgh Magna, &c.; temp. Hen. VIII.

Court Book of Hartehille in Hunworth, 34 Henry VIII. to 3 Edw. VI. (A few leaves, in vellum covers.)

A similar book, 27–37 Elizabeth, without covers.

Court Book of Thornage, 1590–1593. The name of Bacon occurs in several places. (A paper book, without covers.)

Court Books of Stibbard, 17th and 18th century. (Several paper books, in vellum covers.)

Court Books of Horsham St. Faith's, Pavelees, and Ryburgh Parva, 17th cent. (Several books.)

Numerous Rentals of the Manors of Ryburgh Magna and Woodehall in Parva Ryburgh; 16th century. One of them contains a note of all lands purchased by Thomas Buttes, with a few verses probably by him. The covers of these Rentals consist in most cases of vellum leaves from an ancient antiphonal.

Several "Extents" or Surveys of the same Manors.

Survey of Gateley Manor, 1577; very minute. (Paper; no covers.)

Book of Receipts of money for Tithes due from the Manors of Redgrave, Wortham, &c. belonging to Sir Nicholas Bacon, and afterwards to Sir Edmund Bacon, 1592–1632.

Views of the Accounts of the Bailiffs of Robert Bacon of Redgrave Esq. in Suffolk and Essex, 1652–3, and 1653–4. (Paper; no covers.)

Valuation of Estates in Guist, Stibbard, and Little Ryburgh, 1814.

"The View of the Accounts" of all Bailiffs &c. of Sir Edmund Bacon, Bart., late of Robert Bacon Esq. his father, 1655–1656. (A paper book, without covers.)

Note-book of "Daniel Bedingfield, Steward, 1690."

Account Book, 1704–1745. Receipts from rents; disbursements, &c. Egmore is mentioned.

Account of "Rents due from Tenants," 1745–1762. (Place not stated.)

"Mary Bacon's Book of Record (?), begun May the 15th, 1755." It contains rentals, &c. (of Ryburgh Magna ?).

A Schedule of Deeds, Court Rolls, and Rentals relating to the Manors of Great Ryburgh and Woodhall. (51 pages.)

"An Extract of all such Deeds, Evidences, Court Books, Court Rolls, Accounts of Bailiffs, and all other writings whatsoever, as Sir Edmond Bacon, of Redgrave, in the County of Suffolk, Baronet, has remaining in his Evidence-Chamber at Redgrave Hall," &c. 1657. It contains several thousands of entries. (Large folio, 47 pages; parchment.)

Pedigrees, &c.

Pedigree of the Family of Bacon, beginning with William Bacon, temp. Edw. II., and ending with Edmond Bacon, son and heir of Nicholas Bacon of Redgrave Esq. and Anne his wife, daughter and heir of Edmond Buttes, &c.; with numerous coats of arms, in blazon. (A vellum roll.)

Pedigrees, with numerous coats of arms, in blazon: (1) beginning with Robert, Duke of Normandy, and tracing down through the Earls of Chester and Arundel, &c. to Sir Raufe Crumwell, Lord of Tattershall Castle; (2) beginning with William the Conqueror and ending with William Earl Warren; (3) the family of Fitzwilliam of Sprotborough, Lords of Emley, &c.; (4) the families of Sudeley, Butler, Belknopp, Cooke of Giddehalle in Essex, &c., ending with Anne (daughter of Cooke and Fitzwilliam), wife of Sir Nicholas Bacon, Lord Keeper, but giving the names of Anthony and Francis as sons of Sir Nicholas. (A long narrow roll of vellum.)

A very large roll, headed: "Baconorum Parentalia: The Genealogicall Tract or Pedigree of the Auncient Illustrious Family and Syr-Name of *Bacon*, resident chiefly in the Counties of Norfolk and Suffolk," &c. It professes to be extracted from records, wills, monastic registers, deeds, monumental inscriptions, &c., and is dedicated to Sir Edmund Bacon, Bart., by John Whyting. The writer's name is noted thus: "Westminster, John Raymond scripsit, 1655." The pedigree begins with Grimbaldus, founder of the church of Letherinset in Norfolk, who "came in with the Conqueror." Sundry references to chronicles and records are given. There are nearly 200 coats of arms, in blazon. (Vellum, about 12 ft. by 4½ ft., on rollers.)

Grant of arms to Sir Nicholas Bacon, Lord Keeper 1569, tracing his descent from William Bacon, Esquire, who lived in the time of Edward II. This is on vellum, beautifully illuminated, lined with silk, and rolled. It bears the signatures and seals of three Kings of Arms—G. Dethick, Rob. Cooke, and William Flower.

APPENDIX A.

Selections from the early Deeds.

[1243–57.]—Walter, Bishop of Norwich, enfeoffs Reginald de Meauton of three acres of land in Brinningham, which were the Bishop's escheat by the death of Nicholas son of Aylmer de Estker; to hold by the free service of 12*d.* yearly "ad quatuor terminos censuales manerii nostri de Thorndis." Witnesses.—No. 480.

[Temp. Hen. III.]—Amabilia wife of William de Claye gives to the church of St. Mary of Walsingham and the Canons there the homage of Cristiana who was the wife of Hugh de Riburg and William Fitz Hugh, with all their sequel, and with all the tenement which they held of the donor in Riburg, to wit, of her frank marriage, in frank almoign; saving the King's service, to wit, at 20*s.* for the shield (*scutum*), 3½*d.*, more or less; for the souls of herself, William de Claye, and Ralph de Munpinchun, her brother. Witnesses. Seal.—No. 44.

[Temp. Hen. III.]—Ralph son of Fulk de Munpincun releases to Sir Giles de Monte Pincun (*sic*) all right in the vill of Riburg for six acres of land given him. Witnesses: Sir Ralph de Gatelle, Sir Reg. de St. Martin, Sir Ralph de Paveli, Nicholas de Lenn, John, vicar of Little Riburg, Ralph de Tornekin. Seal.—No. 89.

[Temp. Edw. I.]—Ralph de Gatele enfeoffs Edmund de Munpyncun, for 100*s.*, of all his fishery which he has in the pond of Inlaunde, with the fishery of the sluices of the same pond. He will warrant against "all men, as well Christians as Jews." Witnesses. Endorsed: (1) Carta de piscaria in Gatelle; (2) Carta de Piscar̃; (3) Ryburgh.—No. 640.

[Temp. Edw. I.]—Thomas son of Gilbert de Hyndringham enfeoffs William son of Adam Palmer of Brinigham, his free man, of all the land and tenement which the donor or any of his ancestors held of Robert Mirker of Richemund or his ancestors; rendering 4*s.* 6½*d.* yearly, and "foreign services (to wit): for 20*s.* of scutage when it shall happen, 15*d.*, and for more more and for less less; for the ward of the castle of Richemund yearly 6½*d.* and half a farthing at St. Peter ad Vincula; at the feast of St. Andrew, for hundredesscoth, one penny; at Pentecost, for wardepund, three farthings; and at the sheriff's tourn once a year, three farthings." Seal.—No. 290.

1290.—Covenant between Giles son of John de Mumpincon, Lord of Great Riburg, and Thomas son of John de Ryseby. Whereas the latter's father had by grant of the former's father common with him, "as in feeding animals, digging turf, and mowing hay in a certain marsh in Great Riburg," between certain limits (stated), except fishing, and afterwards had a grant of the whole marsh, also except fishing, and a further grant of a fishpond (*vivarium*) called Musewellemere and twelve feet of dry land round it, to be enclosed, at the yearly rent of 20*s.* in all; the said Giles and Thomas confirm the covenants on both sides. Giles grants to Thomas and his heirs the said marsh and fishpond for ever, to hold by the service of 10*s.* yearly. Thomas subjects certain of his lands at Foxhilbotme and Bevereswelle to distress for non-payment. Thomas may have a free boat in all waters touching the marsh for a certain period in each year to carry hay, turf, and grass. Witnesses.—No. 667.

1304.—Roger de Estker of Briningham enfeoffs John del Grene of half an acre of land in Briningham abutting on "the common pasture of Brinton," &c. Rent to the chief lord, 3*d.* yearly. Witnesses.—No. 561.

1311.—William son of Giles de Monpinzon enfeoffs Robert son of John de Walkefare of Iselham of his manor of Great Riburgh, with the advowson of the church of the same vill, and the reversion of the dower which Cristiana who was the wife of Giles de Monpinzon holds of him in the same vill, of 100*s.* of rent which Fulk de Monpinzon holds of him for life in the same vill, of 15 acres of land which John de Lampet holds of him for life in the same vill, and of 15 acres which Stephen le Keu likewise holds. Witnesses. Dated at Plesses. Seal.—No. 9.

MSS. OF E. R. WODEHOUSE, ESQ., M.P.

1318.—Indenture between Robert de Walkefare, Knight, and Margery widow of Henry ate Milne of Great Roburgh (*sic*), whereby the former sells to the latter the wardship and marriage of Henry son and heir of the said Henry and the custody of his lands during his minority; and if he die within that period, Margery shall have the wardship of William and Alice, children of the said Henry deceased. She covenants not to make waste, nor to fell trees save for support of the houses. Witnesses.—No. 458.

1318.—Robert de Dunham enfeoffs Robert de Walkefare, Knight, of a certain river and fishery (*riparie et piscarie*) with appurtenances, from a place called Spykkeslode to Haywardeshowe, as it lies between the Marsh of Great Ryburgh and the marsh of North Elmham. Also of another river and fishery, which he held in parcenary with the commoners (*communicantibus*) of Gyldene Geyst, extending from Haywardeshowe to the sluices and mill of Geyst, and lying between the marsh of Geyst and the marsh of North Elmham. Also of a certain several fishery called Woderove Lode, extending from the said river (*ripa*) called Haywardeshowe to the arable land of North Elmham. Rent, 6*d*. yearly to the chief lords. Dated at Great Ryburgh. Witnesses. Seal.—No. 197.

1319.—Sir Oliver de Ingham, Knight, releases to Ralph de Roudham and Cecily his wife all right in the manor of Brinyngham which he had of the gift of Robert de Berford, son and heir of John de Berford. Witnesses. Seal.—No. 238.

1322.—John Jake of Great Ryburgh enfeoffs Agnes and Joan his daughters of two pieces of his arable land (bounds set out, including "the common pasture of Ryburgh"). Witnesses.—No. 500.

1338.—Sir John de Cokefield, Knight, grants to Robert de Cokefe[ld] and Joan his wife and the heirs of their bodies his manor of Melton Constable, except a third part which Lady Cecily his (Sir John's) mother holds in dower, and except the parcel of land which he acquired from Thomas de Milham: to hold by the service of one rose at Midsummer yearly. Witnesses. Seals of grantees (to one of "due carte cyrographate").—No. 414.

1350.—John de Wesenham, citizen of London, enfeoffs Sir Robert de Causton, Knight, and John Auntrous of his manor of Brynnyngham. Witnesses: Sirs Ralph de Estlee and Ead[mund ?] de Baconnesthorp, Knights, Thomas Bacun, and others. Seal.—No. 124.

1351.—Sir Robert de Causton, Knight, and John Auntrous enfeoff John de Stodeye, citizen of London, of their manor of Brynyngham, with all lands which they had of the gift of John de Wesenham in the vills of Brynyngham and Thornegge. Witnesses. Two seals.—No. 31.

1353.—Thomas Trendel of Geyste, chaplain, enfeoffs Sir Richard Walkefare, Knight, of the wardship and marriage of Christiana daughter and heir of John Calbot, viz. of all lands, foldages, &c. of the said John in Great Riburgh, Gatele, and Little Geyst, and the custody of all lands which descended to her from Alan Calbot, her uncle.—No. 569.

1362.—"This Indenture witnesseth that the Will of John Haliday is such:" William, rector of Great Riburgh, and others to hold all [his] tenements till Easter, and if he die before then, to make an estate to Agnes his wife for her life, remainder to Roger his son, &c. Some of the lands were at Midlestefurlong, Dedlond, &c. Dated at Great Riburgh.—No. 551.

1363.—Sir Robert de Erpingham, Knight, John de Berneye, and Robert Bulour of South Wutton enfeoff Sir Robert de Causton, Knight,

Sir Thomas de Felton, Knight, and others of the manor of Little Riburgh called "le Wodehall," except Reginald de Bergh, "breuster," dwelling in South Creyk, their bondman, with all his sequel; which manor they had of the gift of Sir John de Ratlisden, Knight. Witnesses. Three seals.—No. 270.

1384.—Indenture between Dame Joan, widow of Sir Thomas de Felton, Knight, and John de Snoryng, Prior of Walsyngham, and the Convent there, witnessing that Dame Joan shall enfeoff certain persons named by the Prior of the manors of Great Rybourg and Little Rybourgh, with the advowson of the church of Great Rybourgh, in order that they may enfeoff the Prior, for finding four chaplains to chant perpetually for the souls of the said Sir Thomas and Dame Joan and others in a chapel to be made over (*outre*) the tomb of Sir Thomas at Walsyngham; saving to Dame Joan the "value" of the said manors for term of her life. She will make the manor of Great Rybourgh sure against (*devers*) Sir John Straunge and Eleanor his wife and the heirs of Eleanor, and all others, &c. The feoffees shall grant an annuity of £40 to certain persons to be named, during the lives of Sibil and Mary, nuns, daughters of Sir Thomas and Dame Joan. Dame Mary is a minoress and recluse in the abbey of the Minoresses without Aldgate, London, and the other (Sibil) is a nun in the abbey of Berkynge. Dated at London. The Prior and Convent shall yearly keep the anniversar[ies] of the obit[s] of the said Sir Thomas and Dame Joan and Thomas their son. (In French.) Seal (of Dame Joan?).—No. 195.

1384.—Indenture between the Prior and Convent of Walsyngham of the one part, and Robert Braybrok, Bishop of London, Sir Thomas de Morlee, Marshal of Ireland, Sir Thomas de Erpyngham, Knight, and others, of the other part; whereby the Prior and Convent grant to the said Bishop and others a yearly rent of eighty marks during the lives of Joan who was the wife of Sir Thomas de Felton, Knight, John Sturmy of Incheton, Dame Sibille de Morlee, nun in the abbey of Berkyngg, and Dame Mary de Felton, nun in the abbey of Seynt Clare without Aldgate, London. Moreover, whereas the said Joan had granted to the said Bishop and others a yearly rent of £20 out of her manors of Great and Little Ryburgh from the date of her death, during the life of the said Dame Sibille, and another yearly rent of £20 during the life of the said Dame Mary; and whereas she had granted to John Sturmy of Incheton another yearly rent of 100*s*. out of the said manors; and whereas she had granted and leased the said manors to Sir Stephen de Halys, Knight, and others, their heirs and assigns, rendering yearly to her for life 80 marks; nevertheless the said Bishop and others grant that if the said Halys and others pay in the abbey of Seynt Clare the said three yearly rents of £20, £20, & 100*s*., &c., this present Indenture shall be held for naught. (In French.) Five seals remain. This deed is decayed.—No. 192.

1384.—Joan widow of Sir Thomas de Feltone, Knight, grants in fee-farm to Stephen de Halys, Oliver de Calthorp, Ralph de Shelton, Knights, William de Walsham, clerk, canon of Salisbury, and others, her manor of Great Ryburgh, formerly of Richard Walkefare, Knight, with the advowson, and the Manor of Little Ryburgh, formerly of John de Rattlesden, Knight, with the services, courts, moors, turbaries, fisheries, warrens, &c., which were formerly of Sir Thomas de Felton in the said vills, and in the vills of Little Snoryngg, Stybirde, Bentre, Gateleo, Geyst, Brysele, Penesthorp, Puddyngnorton, and Colkyrke, to hold on condition of rendering to the said Joan for term of her life in the church of St. Clare next Aldgate, London, eighty marks yearly;

power being reserved to distrain and reenter... Witnesses. Seal, large and good.—No. 12.

1390.—Sir John le Straunge, Knight, releases to Sir Stephen de Halys, Knight, Sir Oliver de Calthorp, Knight, Sir Ralph de Shelton, Knight, William Wynter, Geoffrey de Derham, parson of Tytleshale, William de Ellerton, parson of Thyrsforde, Richard Athewald, William de Norwich, John de Burgham, and John de Dyng all right which he had in right of Eleanor his wife, daughter and heir of the blood of Sir Richard de Walkfare, Knight, in the knights' fees in the manors late of Sir William Bole, Knight, and Sir Walter de Walcote, Knight, in Little Snoryngge, which manors are held of the manor of Great Rybour by knight service. Dated at Little Walsyngham. Large seal.—No. 11.

1390.—Andrew de Cavendish, Knight, son and heir of Sir John de Cavendish, Knight, grants licence (notwithstanding the Statute of Mortmain) to Stephen de Halys, Knight, Oliver de Calthorp, Knight, Ralph de Shelton, Knight, William Wynter, Geoffrey de Derham, parson of Tytleshale. William Ellerton, parson of Thirsforde, and others, to give to the Prior and Canons of Walsyngham all their lands in Little Ryburgh and Great Ryburgh, Norf., which are of his (Cavendish's) fee, appertaining to his manor of Fakenham Espes, Suff., and which they had of the gift of Joan who was the wife of Sir Thomas de Felton, Knight. Seal, large and good.—No. 50.

⁂ This kind of deed is somewhat rare. It is made out in the same form as a Royal licence in mortmain, beginning "Andreas de Cavendish," and reciting that the Statute provided that religious persons should not acquire lands "without the licence of the King *and of the chief lords*" of whom such lands were held.

1391.—Precisely to the same effect as No. 50, but dated fifteen months later. Seal.—No. 51.

1392.—Indenture between Richard Earl of Arundel and Surrey and the Prior and Convent of Walsyngham. The Earl grants licence to Stephen de Hales, Knight, and others to give the manor of Great Riburgh with the advowson to the said Prior and Convent, notwithstanding the Statute of Mortmain, to hold of the Earl by homage, fealty, and other knight's services, and paying to the Earl a heriot on every voidance of the priory, as former tenants of the Manor had done, and 100*s.* in name of relief; and also paying for the suit which they owe to the Earl's court at Castelacre for the said manor 3*s.* 4*d.* a year, during the Earl's life, and 6*s.* 8*d.* after his death. The Prior and Convent grant that they will keep the anniversary of Richard, late Earl of Arundel, and Lady Eleanor his wife, father and mother of the present Earl, and of Elizabeth, late wife of the present Earl, on 24th January, and will pray for the Earl and Lady "Phelipp," his present wife, who, after their deaths, shall be included in the said anniversary. Each prior to take oath before the chief officers of the Earl and his heirs to perform these divine services. The Earl has power to distrain for non-performance. (In French.) Endorsed: "Composition between the Earl of Arundel and the Prior of Walsyngham for the manor of Ryburgh."—No. 505.

1392.—Indenture between the Priors and Convents of Bynham and Walsyngham, whereby the former grant licence to Stephen de Halys, Knight, and others to give and assign to the latter 40 acres of arable land in Little Ryburgh, which are held of the former, notwithstanding the Statute of Mortmain. The latter covenant on every vacancy of their Prior's office to pay 6*s.* by name of a relief, or double the rent of the said lands. Fragments of the seal (of Bynham priory ?).—No. 410.

1395.—Inquisition at Walsyngham before the King's Escheator, finding that it is not to the damage of the King or of others if the King grant to Stephen de Hales, Knight, and others that they may give and assign the manor of Great Riburgh, the manor of Little Riburgh called Wodehalle, and the reversion of the advowson of Great Riburgh, and to Roger de Chester and others, chaplains, that they may give and assign one messuage and 7½ acres of land in Great and Little Walsyngham, to the Prior and Convent of Walsyngham, for finding four chaplains in a chapel of St. Anne to be built by them in their priory, and a lamp daily burning in the priory church at high mass. One parcel of the manor of Great Riburgh and the advowson are held of the Earl of Arundel by knight service and suit to the Earl's Court of Castelacre every three weeks, and the Earl holds of the King. The other parcel of the said manor is held of John Spoo as of his manor of Pensthorp by knight service and the yearly rent of 13*s.* 4*d.*, and the same John holds of the Earl of March, who holds of the King. The said manor of Great Ryburgh is charged with 26*s.* 8*d.* of yearly rent payable to the Prior and Convent of Bynham. The manor of Little Riburgh is held of Andrew de Cavendyssh, Knight, by knight service, and he holds of the King; it is charged with 6*s.* yearly to the Prior and Convent of Bynham. The said messuage is held of the Prior of Walsyngham by the rent of 12*d.* yearly, and the said land is held of the heirs of Robert Galon by the rent of 4½*d.*; and the Prior and Galon hold of the Earl of March by knight service, &c. The said manors and advowson are worth yearly 40 marks. The said Stephen and others have lands remaining to them in other places (described), &c.—No. 631.

1398.—Thomas Bewfort, son of the Duke of Guienne and Lancaster, testifies that he has received the homage of the Prior of Walsyngham for the manor of Great Ryb[urgh], which the Prior and Convent hold of him as appertaining to his lordship of Castela[cre]. (In French. Mutilated.)—No. 547.

1400.—The Rector of Ryburgh leases to John Attelathe 6½ acres of his land at Bereswelle and at Foxhil. Term, 5 years. Rent, 1 quarter of barley, "boni et bene mundati cum metilabro et cribro, per modium dicti rectoris," at Christmas.—No. 484.

1408.—Hugh the Prior and the Convent of Walsyngham lease to Roger Skynnere of Lycham their warren in Great and Little Ryburgh, "cum uno garyte apud Senhawe et uno cuniculario ibidem," containing 3 acres, with all beasts and fowl, except pheasants. Lessee not to hurt the beasts of the lessors entering into the "cunicularium," but to drive them away. Term, 15 years. Rent, 13*s.* 4*d.* yearly. Lessors covenant to maintain the said "garyte" (garret) and to make a small chimney therein. Fragment of seal (of lessee).—No. 353.

1408.—Deed by Ralph de Shelton, Knight, Richard Athewald, William de Norwich, and John Lyng, reciting that Sir Stephen de Hales, Sir Oliver de Calthorp, Sir Ralph de Shelton, Knights, and others, some deceased, had granted the manor of Great Ryburgh and the manor of Little Ryburgh called Wodehalle to the Prior and Convent of Walsyngham, and also the reversion of the advowson of the church of the manor of Great Ryburgh, which Joan widow of Sir Thomas de Felton, Knight, holds for life; to hold for the finding of four chaplains canonical or secular for the healthy estate of the said Joan while she shall live, and for her soul when she shall die, and also for the souls of the King's father, Richard late Prince of Wales, and the said Sir Thomas de Felton and Thomas his son, in a certain chapel of St. Anne within the said priory. Now, considering that the said Prior and Convent have sustained great charges "for the salvation of the estate of the said church," and for other causes, at the request of the said Joan, the said Sir Ralph de Shelton and others grant that the said Prior and Convent shall be quit and discharged from the finding of one of the said four chaplains of the chantry aforesaid. (Mutilated.) 2 seals. —No. 6. (Contemporary copies, Nos. 446, 579. There is also a deed by Lady Joan de Felton relating to the same matter, No. 506.)

1434.—Return by the Official of the Archdeacon of Norwich to a mandate of William, Bishop of Norwich, ordering an inquisition to be made touching the right of presentation to the church of Great Riburgh, claimed by the Prior and Convent of Walsyngham, who had presented Sir Richard Grunnok of Great Walsyngham, priest, and also by John Curson of Belhagh, Knight, who had presented Richard Fyssher, priest. The Inquisition was made by sundry rectors and laymen (named), who found that the Prior and Convent were patrons, and that Dame Joan, relict of Sir Thomas Felton, presented the last Rector, Sir John Lenot, deceased. "Dicta ecclesia non est litig̃, set porcionat̃ Priori et Conventui de Bynham, ut asseritur, estimac̃ vero xxiiij^or marc̃." The presentee is of good life and conversation, &c. Portions of the Official's seal, and five other seals.—No. 374.

1458.—Robert Smyth *alias* Bocher and Barth. Payn enfeoff John Lyncolne and others of "one messuage built containing one half-acre of land" in Great Ryburgh, with one acre in the field of that vill (bounds set out). Witnesses: William Butt, &c. Portions of two seals.—No. 384.

1480.—John Ayscogh and Richard his son, Esquires, sell to John Wymdham, Esquire, their manor in Melton Constable, called Cokefeldes, with all their lands in the Hundred of Holt, for 350 marks, payable by instalments. They "shall come to Burgh beside Briston or to London . . . to make a state of the premises." Other covenants. (In English.)—No. 545.

1481.—John, Prior, and the Convent of Walsyngham lease to Thomas Geyton and John Mylle their cornmill in Mykyll Ryburgh. Term, 5 years. Rent, 8*l.* 6*s.* 8*d.* yearly. Lessors to *bear* all repairs "except cogges, staves, keeping open the dam fro the said mill unto the great bridge in the same town, and reparation of the caucy (causeway) there." Lessees give a bond in 10*l.* (In English.)—No. 531.

1482. William Ayscogh, Gent., releases to John Wyndham, Esquire, all right in the manor of Melton Constable and lands, &c. there and in Brymyngham, Brystun, Burgh, Stodehay, and Gunthorp. Seal.—No. 425.

1503.—Will of Richard Harneyse, of Great Ryburgh. Bequests to the high altar in the church of St. Andrew there, and to St. Thomas's light, St. John's light, and Our Lady's light [in the same church]. Also to St. Erasmus' Gild in Fulmerston, to the Freers in Walsyngham, to poor householders in Ryburgh, Gild brethren and sisters, to priests &c. for dirges, "to every child that can say *De profundis* 1*d.*," for a light before Our Lady in Ryburgh church, &c. To Emma his wife, his place in Ryburgh, &c. To Robert his son, 40*s.* Other children mentioned. Sir Geffrey Howes, vicar of Little Ryburgh, and others to be executors. Moneys for repair of the leading of the church and bells. (In English.) . Probate endorsed 1503. Fragments of seal.—No. 395.

1517.—Exemplification by Thomas Hare, LL.D., principal Official of the Consistory Court of Norwich, of proceedings in a cause relating to the withdrawal of tithes between Sir Richard Ferror, perpetual vicar of Geyst, Plaintiff, and Sir Robert Newman, rector of Great Riburgh, Defendant; the sentence being in favour of the latter. Portion of seal. —No. 392.

1517–18.—Exemplification by Thomas Hare, LL.D., Official of Richard, Bishop of Norwich, of a recovery of tithes by Robert Newman, rector of Great Riburgh, against Nicholas Hunt of Hyldolveston, in the Consistory Court. Portion of seal.—No. 311.

1521.—Monition by the Official of the Court of Canterbury to Sir Richard Ferrar, vicar of Geyst, appellant, to pay to Sir Robert Newman, rector of Great Ryburgh, Defendant in an appeal heard before the Official, 4*l.* for the latter's costs, under pain of excommunication.—No. 661.

1528.—Ten bonds by William Buttes, M.D., Sir Thomas Tyrell of Gippyng, Suff., Knight, Philip Parys of Lynton, Cambr., Esquire, and John Crystmas of Colchester, Essex, Gent., to Brian Tuke, Treasurer of the King's Chamber, Thomas Englefild, Justice of the Common Pleas, and Sir William Paulet, Knight, to pay so many sums of 40 marks to the said Treasurer, at certain dates, for the wardship and marriage of the daughters and heirs of Henry Bures. Signatures and seals.—No. 700.

1529.—Two Bonds by William Buttes, M.D., Roger More, "ser-"vientem Domini Regis a panibus,"* and Simon Englisshe of London, skinner, to Brian Tuke, Esq., Treasurer of the King's Chamber, and William Paulett, Knight, each in £40, for the payment of two sums of £33 6*s.* 8*d.*, as instalments of £100 due to the King in part recompense of the King's gift of Robert† [Henry] Buer's lands to the said William Buttes during the minority of the daughters and heirs of the said Robert [Henry]. Signed and sealed. [These are the first and third of three bonds.]—No. 335.

1538.—Richard Vowell, Prior, and the Convent of Little Walsyngham, lease to Robert Towneshend, Esq., of Twyford, a pasture or ground called Senhaugh, in Grett Ryborough, and another pasture or moor adjoining called Aplemore, in Grett and Lytle Ryborough, with the warren called Senhaugh Warren, and the river called Senhaugh River, with all other several waters, fishings, &c. Term, 80 years. Rent, £4 4*s.* Lessee to repair the lodge of the warren, hedges, dyke-rowes, and fences, and cleanse and scour the river, waters, drains, and dykes. Lessors to provide wood for fences, &c. They reserve the right, when resorting to the manor for recreation, to fish the said river with nets and other engines, and to hunt conies in the warren to the number of 20 couple, yearly. Lessee to leave 300 conies. Signed by the Prior, Subprior, and 12 others (monks, including Richard Garnett). Large seal of the Priory, showing the church on one side, and the Virgin and Child on the other.—No. 671.

[*Note.*—Roger Tonneshend, Esquire, had a previous lease of Senhaugh in 1517.]

1543.—Commission by the Official of the Archdeacon of Norwich to the Dean of Bresele cum Toftes and Sir Thomas Bulman, to induct Master Roger Overey into the parish church of Great Ryburgh, to

* He signs "per me Rogerum More sergeaunt."

† In one bond "Robert" is erased, and "Henry" substituted.

which he has been admitted and instituted Rector by the Bishop of Norwich. (Paper.) Fragments of seal.—No. 679.

1549.—Thomas Woodhous of Waxham in co. Norfolk, Esquire, for a sum of money enfeoffs William Cockys, yeoman, of a rood of land in the vill and fields of Great Riburghe, granted to him (Woodhous) by Letters Patent, 29 September 2 Edw. VI., and he appoints Nicholas Jagges of Corpestie (?) as his attorney to deliver seisin. Signed: Thomas Wodehous (?). Seal, a stag (?).—No. 176.

1550.—Will of Edmonde Buttes of Barrowe, Suff., Esquire. Bequeaths his goods to Anne his wife, for life, then to Anne their daughter; except his best horse, which he has given to his uncle Robert Bures; his picture, which he gives to his brother Thomas Buttes; two pair of velvet hose to his cousin Edmonde Buttes; and his "frysade nyghtgowne" to the Vicar of Gaysle. His wife to be executrix. Dated 1549. Official copy. Probate endorsed, Norwich, 1550. Portion of seal.—No. 366.

1551.—Six bonds by Thomas Buttes of Great Ryburgh, Esq., Edmund Buttes, gent., and William Cokkes, yeoman, for the payment to Alex. Frankling, barber, Agnes his wife, and James Lynne, worsted weaver, of five marks at Michaelmas in 1551, 1552, 1553, 1554, 1555, and 1556, "upon the marble table in the common hall of the city of Norwich." Signed and sealed. Cancelled.—No. 286.

1553.—Roger Overey, parson of Great Righburgh, leases to William Moreton of Estderham, yeoman, the parsonage or rectory of Great Righburgh, with tithes, glebes, rents, offerings, duties, houses, &c.; except wood and "a house called the Stoarehowsse under the greyn chamber," and also the parlour and chambers over it for one month in each year, for lessor's occupation. Term, 3 years. Total payment, £20. Lessee to have the barn, bakehouse, and chambers of the parsonage, and to pay a priest to serve the cure. Other covenants. Sealed in the presence of Thomas Buttes, Esquire, and others.—No. 443.

1558.—Bond by Lady Katherine Fermour late of East Barsham, widow, and Henry Spelman of Beston, Norf., Esquire, to Thomas Buttes, Esquire, in £200, to save him harmless in respect of certain bonds to Sir James Boleyn, Knight. Signed. Two seals.—No. 291.

1559.—Admission and institition by the Royal Commissaries General of William Seton, clerk, to the rectory of the parish church of Great Riburgh, void by the death of the last incumbent, on the presentation of Thomas Buttes, Esq. Large seal (broken).—No. 240.

1559.—Sir William Buttes, Knight, grants to Frances widow of John Asteley, Esq., for £40, the wardship and marriage of Isaacke Asteley, son and heir of the said John, who held of Buttes the manor of Melton Constable as of his manor of Thornage, by the service of 1¼ knight's fee. Dated at Thornage. Counterpart, signed by grantee. Seal.—No. 649.

1560.—Sir James Boleyn, Knight, bargains and sells to Sir Thomas Gressham, Knight, the manor of Egmere, Norf., and all lands, fold-courses, &c. thereto belonging in Egmere, Waterden, Northbasham, Wighton, and Little and Great Walsingham. Gresham covenants to pay to Boleyn a yearly rent of 46*l*. 1*s*. 9*d*., and before Midsummer next to deliver to Boleyn at Clay, Norf., one tun of Gascoyne wine. And whereas by Indenture in 1556 Gresham covenanted to deliver to Boleyn one tun of Gascoyne wine yearly at London, he now agrees to deliver the same at Clay. Signed and sealed by Boleyn.—No. 664.

1560.—Robert Empson and Robert Manfeilde otherwise Peers, churchwardens of Great Ryburgh, and others, inhabitants of the said town, lease to Thomas Buttes, Esquire, two pieces of land called the Towne Lande in the field of Great Ryburgh (described). Term, 20 years. Rent, 13*s*. 4*d*. Nine seals and two signatures.—No. 189.

1561.—Sir Nicholas Bacon, Keeper of the Great Seal, for the good education of the children of the tenants of his manors of Redgrave, Wortham, Melles, Hyndercley, Rekynghall, Walsham, Wyverston, Ashefelde, Ingham, and Tymworth, and of the Hundred of Blackborne in co. Suffolk, and of Eccles in co. Norfolk, and those of his neighbours, grants to George Dedham and James Vale, Wardens and Governors of his free Grammar School in Redgrave, an annuity or annual rent of 13*l*. 6*s*. 8*d*. out of his manor of Ashefelde, to cease in case Sir Nicholas should grant them lands of that value. This grant is made pursuant to the Queen's letters patent of foundation, dated at Redgrave, 28 July 1561. (Beautifully written on vellum.) Signed by Sir Nicholas. Large seal of arms.—No. 652.

1566.—Will of Robert Harvye, of Great Ryburgh, yeoman. Mentions the churchyard there—"the poor men's box"—Helen or Elyn his wife—his freehold and copyhold lands in Great Ryburgh—his father John Harvye, deceased—his daughters, viz. Johan, Grysell, Alys, Margaret, Rose—a copyhold tenement in Northcreke—his "grete sprewse chest"—Johan Dyamon—Robert Dyamon—Robert Powle of Tostres, his brother-in-law. His wife to be executrix, and "Mr. Thomas Buttes, Esquire," to be "a counsellor of this my last will." Witnesses. Dated 1560. (In English.) Proved 1566. Seal (broken).—No. 451.

1567.—Robert Bozome of Stodye, Esq., son and heir of John Bozome, Esq., enfeoffs Gregory Warne of one inclose in Hunworth (3 acres) lying "between the common pasture of Hunworth called Richmon Common in part, and the land of William Seckell lying within the said common pasture at the south-east, and the common watercourse in part, and the close of the said Gregory Warne," &c. Rent, 2*s*. yearly, and suit of court to grantor's manor of Stodye, at Michaelmas, or 3*d*. for default, &c. Seal of lessee.—No. 373.

1568.—Institution by John Bishop of Norwich of Richard Harris, priest, to the parish church of Great Riboroughe, to which he had been presented by Queen Elizabeth. Portions of the episcopal seal remain.—No. 309.

1575.—William Fyncham of Fincham, Esqure, bargains and sells to Richard Stubbe of Edgefeylde, Gent., the manor of Harthill and lands &c. in Hunworth, Briston, Studdie, and Holte, Norf., latd of John Fyncham, his grandfather, and Thomas Fincham, his father, and late in the occupation of Robert Bozom, Esquire, or Richard Stubbe. Signed and sealed. Enrolled on the Close Rolls.—No. 49.

1578.—Richard Stubbe of Edgefeild, Gent., bargains and sells to Sir Nicholas Bacon of Redgrave, Knight, the manor called Harthill late [of] William Fyncham, Esquire, in Hunworthe, Briston, and Studdye, with lands, foldcourses, &c., and also one messuage newly built in Edgefeilde, and the close adjoining lying in Hunworth and Edgefeilde, lately purchased of George Brigges, Gent., &c.; except one piece of ground now enclosed called Froskewell *alias* Little Stodey (60 acres) in Stodey, and Sheppardes Close in Briston, &c. (bounds set out). If Stubbes acquire one close of William Baker's, Sir Nicholas is not to demand any right of shack or common feed therein, &c. Other covenants. The manor of Edgefeilde Buttes or Edgefeilde Prior is mentioned. Signed and sealed.—No. 686.

1579.—Indenture between Thomas Buttes of Great Ryburgh, Esquire, and Sir Nicholas Bacon of Redgrave, Suff., son and heir apparent of Sir Nicholas Bacon, Lord Keeper, and Dame Anne wife of Sir Nicholas the son. By Indenture in 1561 Thomas Buttes and Briget his wife conveyed to Sir Nicholas Bacon the father and others in fee simple the manors of Great Riebroughe and Woodhall. For 48*l.* Buttes covenants that he and all persons claiming interest in the said manors, or in the advowsons of Great and Little Riebroughe (except yearly pensions or portions of 40*s.* yearly issuing out of the former rectory, and 13*s.* 4*d.* out of the latter, a close called Skytes yard or Scottes yard of 1½ acre, and one free messuage lately bought of Thomas Browne and Hellen Browne), shall convey and release the said manors to Sir Nicholas and Dame Anne, who covenant to allow Buttes to take the revenues thereof till 1st April next, and from that date a yearly rentcharge of 130*l.* 6*s.* 2*d.* out of the premises for his life, payable at Redgrave. Signed by Buttes. Seal (of arms: on a chevron between three estoiles as many lozenges).—No. 658.

1579. Thomas Buttes, Esquire, leases to Simon Mussett, miller, his watermill with the millhouse in Great Ryburgh called Southemylle, "with all the going gear," and one messuage called Milles near the said mill, late of Thomas Browne, tanner, and one yard adjoining called Newesteade Yarde, and also one parcel of morishe (or marishe) ground (1 acre) on the east of the mill. Term, 7 years. Rent, 13*l.* 6*s.* 8*d.* The lessor is bound to grind at the mill. The lessee to leave one overstone and one netherstone of certain sizes, and shall not fish in any part of the dam, river, or stream that cometh to the mill, except that he may take eels and other fish at the "owteloades" of the mill or millwheel with shakenetts, a moiety of which eels and fish is to be delivered to the lessor.—No. 633.

1584.—Sir Nicholas Bacon of Redgrave, Knight, in performance of Indentures dated 1579, grants to Thomas Buttes of Great Riburgh, Esquire, an annuity of 160*l.* for life out of the manor of Egmere, Norf., payable at the church porch of Redgrave cum Bowsdale. Buttes shall have the mansion-house in Riburgh and certain closes there till All Saints next (1584); and he and Margaret M . . . . shall hold in survivorship all lands which he lately purchased of Helen Harvie and others. Bacon shall depasture four geldings of Buttes, &c. Signed and sealed by Buttes.—No. 234.

1592.—Thomas Buttes of Catton, Norf., Esquire, bargains and sells to Sir Nicholas Bacon of Redgrave, Suff., Knight, and Nathaniel Bacon of Styfkey, Norf., Esquire, the manor of Thornham in Thornham, Norf., with the demesne lands, pastures, marshes, foldcourses, courts, seawrecks, groundages, fishings, royalties, &c. in Thornham, Holme, Tychwell, Somer, and Stanhowe, Norf., and also the manor of Pannington Hall otherwise Paddington Hall, with demesne lands &c. in Whersteade, Suff. Signed: Nycholas Bacō, Natha: Bacon. Two seals (of arms).—No. 83.

1604.—Henry Seafoule, Edmond Seafoule, and John Gibson, of Waterden, Norf., Gent., enfeoff Sir Nicholas Bacon of Redgrave, Knight, of "all the common of pasture, commonage, and liberty of common shack" which they have in two pastures or closes of his in Waterden in the West field there (bounds set out); and they release all right in the same and other lands there. Signed: John Gibson. Seals lost.—No. 315.

1620.—Jerome Alexander enfeoffs John Howsigoe of one piece of land and pasture called Moyses Yarde, with bakehouse thereupon, at the east end of donor's capital messuage in North Elmeham, next "the common pasture of North Elmeham," called the Broome. Signed and sealed.—No. 695. I.

The following names of persons occur in the deeds relating to Great and Little Ryburgh and the neighbouring hamlets of Gateley, Testerton, &c., either as parties or as witnesses:—

Aunger, Aleyn, Atte Mille, Attewelle, Althorp, Atte Cros or Atte Cruche, Amy, Attelathe, Athewald, Alfred, Andrew, Andrewes Awncell, Ate Hill, Butt (Nos. 384, 440), Buttes, Bacon, Bowman Brese, Bole or Bule, Bulour, Bernard, Berneye, Baggard, Buurd, Botild, Bonde, Banyard, Bozoun, Baxstere, Berdewell, Billingford, Bussel or Buscel, Boylond, Browne, Browning, Binham, Boucher or Bocher, Benet, Bernham, Brect, Baxtere or Baxster, Bintre, Bulman, Boleyn, Bagby, Bedingfeld, Brandon, Claye, Clerk, Chaunceys, Chaunt, Coole, Cubald, Candelere, Capel, Childerhus or Childrus (of Gateley), Cromnyng, Calbot, Cok or Koc, Cokkes, Cook or le Cook, Cookes, Calthorp, Cursoun, Constantyng, Child, Cary, Crome, Downing, Dyrre or Dereye, Den, le Deu, Dele, Drury, Doyly, De la More, Del Heyse, Del Hil (of Testerton), Elvy, Elvive or Elvyne, Erpingham or Herpingham, Eyre, Empson, Everard or Evered, Felton, Fitz Simon, Fen, Fitz Hubert, Fitz John, Fitz Ralph, Fleyt, Frank, Fulfordhaghe, Frenge, Farewell or Farwell, Flight, Faucon, Fisher, Fuller, Fermour alias Cooper, Gode or Goode, Gayton or Geyton, Gottes or Gottys, Gateley, Gardener, Gerthere, Gostling, Huberd, Hoxlee, Heyward, Harvey, Harneys, Homelton, Hoo, Howe, Horn, Hetune or Ettune, Horewic, Hyndryngham, Haliday, Hagheman or Haweman, Hamund, Hales, Howard, Harman, Hows, Hoseȝere or Hoseyer, Huxter, Heydon. Inland or Inlaunde, Jake, Jagge, Kyrkeby, Keche, Kynges, Kinge, le Keu, Kempe, Ketyl or Ketell, Knatteshale or Gnateshale, Keythorp, Ladde, Lampet, Litelsmyt, Lyng, Lincolne, Lange. Lamberd, Lawrence, Lawes, Lovel, Lof or Loof, Lekesham or Lechesham, Loveday, Leek, Monpinzun, Mabbe or Mabbes, Manfyld, Milham, Malemusc, Malmhert, Mille, Morlee, Merlond, Nowers, Norton, Naringes, Neuman or le Neuman, Neel, Overmore (of Gateley), Oldhall, Owthwett, Perys, Perse, Peers or Peares, Poer, Palmere, Playforde, Payn, Pavely or le Pavely, Paulee or Paweli, Parson or Person, Preston, Pattesle, Pesenhale, Priour, Prat, Pytewyn, Porter, Powle, Roper, Risby, le Rede, the Reeve, Reyner, Ruheved or Roughhed, Rust, Robbis, Rawlyn, Rawlyns, Rycald, Reppes, Ratlisdene, Reynham, Riburg, Snetesham, Smyth, Sparhauk, Sylvester, Shelton, Spic or Spyck, Southgate, Scharneburn, Sprot, Straunge or le Straunge, Styberde, Scarlet, Stede, Sparke, Scothowe, Sander, Shovell, St. Martin, le Sutor, Skraggar, le Straggere, Symmes, Schepherd, Sherman or Scharman, Salman, Shirwyn, Trendel, Tomson or Tompson, le Taylour, Tornekyn or Thornekin, Testretun, Tytyng, Walkefare, Withy or Wethy, Wright, Wyllys, Wodedallyng, Warner, Welington, Whight or Whyte, Wutton, Wursly, Waterman, Yryng.

The following names of persons occur in the deeds relating to the manors and freeholds in Briningham, Hunsworth, Melton Constable, Stody, Little Burgh, Briston, Brinton, Thornage, Holt, and the neighbourhood, either as parties or as witnesses:—

Avenel, Astlee or Estlee, Atte Parke, Atte Whynnes or Attequinnes, Atte Dam, Atte Church, Attekyrke, Atte Grene, Atteheyth, Attehog, Atte Poo, Attewade, Annesley, Auntrous, Ayscogh, Brisele, Braunche, Bacoun (Nos. 27, 124, 142, 409), Bonde, Berford or Bereford, Berneye,

Burnavile, Bacunesthorp, Bernard, Bone or le Bone, Birston or Briston, Blakene (of London), Briningham, le Bulchere, Brice, Burgh, Burgeys, Buske, Blaxtere, Browne, Butt or Butte (Nos. 175, 210), Buttes, Bonjour, Bintre, Bozome or Bozom, Bussell, Bercator, Breton, Brightive or Britiffe, Brigges, Birny, Barbour, Bucher, Boleyn, Benyngfeld, Chaumberleyn, Calabre, Costwyck, Clerk, Cosyn, Curzoun, Chapman, Crepping, Carpenter, Clement, Colyne, Cloyte, Coksfeld, Causton, Colby, Corby, Cleare, Dandonay, Dalling, Daubeney, Dysselyng, Drury, Denham, Deye, Dynys, Estlee or Astlee, Eggefeld, Estker, Edrich, Edmund, Elvys, Fraunces, Flour, FitzAdam, Freman, Frogenhole or Frokenhole, Fichet, Fildallingg, Fuller, Fincham, Fox, Felbrygge, Grys, de la Grene (same as Atte Grene above), Geyste, Godfrey, Grygge, Godwyn, Goodes, Gloos, Holwell, Hindringham, Hallez, Hane, Hammond, Hanggebuk, Hert, Heydon, Hestinges, Huneworth, Horstede, Higham, Herdewyk, Hereward, Harald, Hunte, Ingham, Ingement, Jeckes or Jeckys, Jordan, Karmankyn, del Ker or in the Kar, Leggard, Lampet, Lawes, Leckys or Leccus, Lystere, Linnelee or Linley, Manneby, Melton, le May, Mercator, Matelaske, Manning, Medewe, Marix, Might, Murdeu or Murdieu, le Milieres, Morle, Milham, Noers or le Nouers, Norton, Neve, Newman, Ormesby, Overthewater, Pilemere or Pilmere, Playforde or Playforthe, Peronnel, Persone, Prat, Perers or Pereres, le Pevere or le Pouere, Piers, Pelles, Pineeware, Prentys, Pitelyn, le Paumer or Palmer, Plesaunce, Plowwryght, Pyle, Qwyte or Qwyth, Rolves, Ruddham or Rudam, Repon, Reynold, Reade, Roper, Smith, Soterlee, Stubbard, Shyttele, le Sutere, Sagge, Swyft, Staunford, Scharenton, Stodey (of London), Sterre, Sendall, Salmon, Skunfyt or Skumphyt, Seckell, Stubbe, Strelley, Shelton, Seaman, Scrope, Scolfeild, Thurkild, le Talyur or Letaliur, Thursford, Trusbut or Trussebut, Tussy, Tudenham, Urry, la Velye or la Veille, Wilkenes, Wither, Walsingham, Wesenham (of London), Wylles or Wyllys, Worstede, Wright, Wyndham, West, Weston, Warne, le Ward, Whit (same as Qwyth above), Watte, Walour, Woollsey.

APPENDIX B.

LETTER-BOOK of the DEPUTY LIEUTENANTS and JUSTICES of the PEACE of SUFFOLK, 1608–1640.

P. 1. The Division of the County of Suffolk, and how those rates and proportions have been always rated and taxed as to levy an 100*l*.

The franchise of Bury - - - - -		50*l*
The franchise of St. Etheldred - - - -		
Bury fr: - - - -	33*l*. 6*s*. 8*d*.	
Fr: of St. Etheldred - -	16*l*. 13*s*. 4*d*.	
The Guildable - - - - - - -		50*l*.

The Guildable's proportion for 50*l*. is thus (viz.):—

20	Blithing Hundred - - - -	10*l*.
16	Haxon Hundred - - - -	8*l*.
16	Hartsmere Hundred - - - -	8*l*.
14	Wangford Hundred - - - -	7*l*.
12	Bosmere cum Claydon - - - -	6*l*.
10	Sampford Hundred - - - -	5*l*.
6	Mutford cum Lothingford - - -	3*l*.
6	Stow Hundred - - - - -	3*l*.
	Sum - - - - -	50*l*.

P. 3. In a Rate of 1500*l.* for the whole County the franchise of Bury is 500*l.*; in which division Babergh Hundred is 100*l.*, which is levied upon every town within the said Hundred as followeth. Thirty-two places are then named, with the sum due from each.

P. 5. Court at Newmarket, 17 Nov. 1616.—A letter from the King's Majesty to the Justices of the Assizes, whereby it is recommended to their discretions for the holding of the same at Ipswich. *The letter is copied in full.*

P. 11. *No date.*—Articles of Instructions given by the Lords and others of the Queen's Majesty's Privy Council in her Highness' name to the Commissioners appointed for the general Musters to be taken in the County of Suffolk. * * *

Item, that no man be exempted from the said musters, of what estate or degree soever he be, not being let with sickness or other reasonable cause to be allowed by the Commissioners; but that as well they themselves, the gentlemen and others, appear there at the said musters both on horseback and on foot with their household servants, and that all others, being of the age of 16 and under 60, be also present at the same musters, according to the ancient custom of the realm.

Item, that they together in their divisions, at the several assemblies within every hundred, take there the musters without favour, malice, or partiality to every [any ?] man, or one of them to another, but choosing out all such as be able to bear armour [or] use weapon; and those that be men likely and sufficient for the purpose, they shall put the names of all such in a book.

Particulars are also to be taken as to horsemen, armour, &c.

P. 19. Ipswich, 12 October 1608.—Warrant from [Sir] Anthony Felton and Thomas Winckfeild to the chief Constables of the Hundred[s] within the Liberty of St. Etheldred.

Upon the perusing of the account of Mr. Thomas Lane of Causey Ashe, chosen compounder for the provisions of the King's Majesty's Household, for one year now last past, it doth appear unto us, that by reason that the prices of all things that are committed to his charge and purveyance are exceedingly increased, so as the money allotted for those provisions, amounting to the sum of 592*l.* 2*s.* 10*d.*, doth fall short the sum of 120*l.*; the which sum of 120*l.* we do think it very fit and do order that it shall be presently levied and gathered upon the country. The constables are to collect 20*l.* thereof in the parishes and towns within their limits.

The proportions due from the respective divisions of the whole county are stated.

Ib. 28 Feb. 1612(-13).—Appointment by T. Earl of Suffolk of Sir Edmond Wittipole to be one of his Deputy Lieutenants in the county of Suffolk, to act jointly with the Earl's cousin Felton.

P. 20. Whitehall, 31 Jan. 1612(-13).—Council letter to the Earl of Suffolk, concerning the taking of musters. Rec. 3° Julij 1612 (*sic*).

The happy times of peace we have enjoyed sithence his Majesty's coming to the Crown hath bred that security and neglect of necessary provisions for war as we cannot but very much doubt of a great decay of [such] arms and furniture as are requisite in a well ordered State for a continuance and support of that peace we do enjoy. And although the ease and convenience of provision in this kind, in respect of the less expence and trouble which it causeth, may induce every man to furnish himself as is meet for the service of the State and preventing such inconveniences as usually follow omission and neglect, yet the condition of these times withall is such, both in respect of the boldness and assurance which the Recusants have taken of late, as otherwise, as may require a ready and sufficient reply in this behalf.

His Majesty has therefore commanded us to give order for a general muster and survey to be made and certified of the armed forces of this realm. This will tend to the ease of every man's charge and trouble, which would be much more if it should be left to a sudden and unexpected necessity.

As Lieutenant in Suffolk, Cambridge, Dorset, and the town of Poole, you are to cause a general view to be taken accordingly of all forces therein, both horse & foot, and the trained bands to be made complete in regard to officers, men, armour, &c.

No persons shall be exempted from providing horse, arms, or furniture on pretence of being servants to his Majesty or to any nobleman, except his Majesty's ordinary servants and the household servants of noblemen. It shall be likewise expedient that such of the clergy as have been heretofore appointed to find arms, and others of them that are meet in like sort to be charged, may be ordered to cause the same to be shown at these musters.

A store of powder, with match, bullet, and other provisions for carriage, is to be kept in the shire towns or elsewhere. The beacons, having been long neglected and grown to decay, are to be speedily repaired. A certificate is to be returned by you before the 1st of April next of the view and musters, supplies, &c.

Pp. 22 *seq.* Letters of the Lord Lieutenant, Deputy-Lieutenants, &c. concerning the execution of the foregoing order, 1613, 1614. The Deputy-Lieutenants were Sir Anthony Felton, Sir William Waldegrave, Sir Robert Jermyn, Sir John Heigham, Sir Henry Glemham, and Sir Edmund Wittipoole. All men chargeable with horses and arms were to appear "at the market cross in Ipswich, at Rushemore Heath."

P. 25. Whitehall, 28 Feb. 1612(-13).—Council letter to [the Justices of the Peace].

Whereas you have formerly received directions from this Board for taking out of the hands and custody of all Recusants, as well such as be convicted as others known to be Recusants and ill affected in religion, in that county, all such armour, weapons, and other furniture of war as shall be found in their houses, or otherwise belonging unto them; the words "ill affected in religion" having been differently construed in divers shires, the King, with our advice, and according to the opinion of some of the chief Judges, has explained his meaning to be, all such persons as give any covert suspicion by not usually repairing to church and by not receiving the communion once a year at least, and those whose wives, children, or servants are Recusants or non-communicants, or Popishly affected, and especially those who have any extraordinary number of retainers or tenants of that kind; this sort of people being persons whom his Majesty has reason to hold in jealousy.

Pp. 26, 27. 1613.—Letters respecting the privileges claimed by the town of Ipswich in respect of the holding of musters.

Pp. 27 *seq.* 1613.—Orders respecting the provision of powder, allowances to the muster master, captains of horse, the maintenance of beacons, the arms of the clergy, &c.

P. 32. Whitehall, 13 Sept. 1614.—Council letter to [the Lord Lieutenant].

Whereas there is a great army now on foot, commanded by Marquis Spinola, in Cleveland and the parts thereabouts, that hath proceeded very far in taking in (*sic*) and possessing themselves of divers towns, to the great danger of the Protestant party and the religion that began so happily to flourish in those parts, together with the eminent perils of the States of the United Provinces; which although [it] be a sufficient motive in reason of State to move his Majesty to cast a vigilant and provident eye to the safety of his dominions, yet being withall advertised of a great fleet lately discovered upon the coast, full of soldiers and munitions, which are to take their descent either in the Low Countries or in some place more prejudicial to this realm, his Majesty in his high wisdom hath commanded at this time that order be given by us for a general muster and survey to be made of such armed forces of this realm as shall be thought meet to be prepared and had in readiness upon all occasions for the defence and safety of the Kingdom.

The Lord Lieutenant is to act accordingly, and especially to see that the trained bands be made complete by filling up vacancies occurring since the last muster with sufficient & apt men, as well of those of the better quality as of such other freeholders, farmers, owners of land, or householders as may be fit for the same; and to supply all defects of armour, &c. The country is not to be charged with coats and conduct-money till further directions are given. Instructions as to horsemen, the King's servants, the clergy, &c., as before.

Pp. 34 *seq*. Letters of the Earl of Suffolk to the Deputy Lieutenants (including Sir Lionel Talmache), and from them to one another and to the Chief Constables of the Hundreds and the Bailiffs of Ipswich, touching the execution of the foregoing warrant.

P. 36. A note of the Hundreds where every several Captain hath his Band, and their places of muster.

Sir Nicholas Bacon, the Hundred of Hartsmere and the half-Hundred of Haxon.—Mellis Green.

(*And six other similar entries.*)

P. 40. Whitehall, 14 Sept. 1614.– Council letter to ——.

Ordering a further search for arms to be made in the houses of Recusants, and the seizure of the same, excepting such weapons as shall seem necessary and expedient for the defence of their houses. Bills indented to be made of the arms so taken, and a certificate to be returned to us.

P. 41. Whitehall, 17 Dec. 1614.—Council letter to [the Deputy Lieutenants of Suffolk ?].

We lately addressed our letters unto you wherein we did exhort you, after the example of the Lords spiritual and other the nobility then residing about this town, out of your own free and voluntary contribution, to concur for the present relief of his Majesty's urgent necessities for the supply of Ireland, for the provision of the Cautionary Towns in Holland and Zealand, and for the furnishing of the Navy. Since then serious troubles (described) have happened in the neighbouring countries to the prejudice of the King's friends and allies, and the persons & states of the Elector Palatine & the Princess his lady, the King's only and dearest daughter, are environed on all sides by divers armies, to the imminent danger of these Kingdoms. His Majesty has therefore commanded a general muster to be made, his Navy to be put in order, and all Recusants to be disarmed, as not being well affectioned to his service. Having heard nothing from you, we write again, praying and requiring you, as you tender the preservation of your country and of yourselves, your wives, and children, to use your best endeavours for the return of this contribution.

P. 42. Court at Whitehall, 3 Jan. 1614(–15). Letter from E. [Lord] Wotton, Ro. Vernon, and three others to the Justices of the Peace [of co. Suffolk].

Whereas divers of you were before us in his Majesty's Counting-house the last term touching the difference between yourselves of service and carriage of wood and coals for His Highness' expence at Newmarkett, at which time you promised to make a general meeting amongst you all, when notice should be given unto his Majesty's Purveyors for those kind (*sic*) of provisions of the time and place where you would meet; at which meeting it was intended there should be a settled course not only how the defaults for the last year should be supplied, but also how his Majesty might be better served hereafter for those and the like provisions: now, forasmuch as by reason of his Majesty's living at that house the most part of these two last months, whereby the provisions of fuel formerly laid for store there is (*sic*) already spent, and besides his Majesty intendeth to come thither very shortly, and is like to be unfurnished of such necessary provision[s] as those, if speedy care be not forthwith taken therein: we have therefore thought good hereby to put you in remembrance thereof, and do also pray you to take some present order how his Majesty may be served with most ease to the country in general; otherwise we do propose to send his Majesty's Commission down thither, and also to call the default[er]s of the last summer's service before us, and cause them to perform that they were charged withall, which we know will be much more burdensome to the country than this which we do now desire. And so not doubting your respective cares herein, we commit you to God.

The justices specially named in the address are Sir Lionel Talmache, Bart., Sir Thomas Jermy[n], Sir Henry Glemham.

P. 43. 19 Nov. 1614.—Order [by the Deputy Lieutenants] to the chief Constables of the Hundred of Bosmere and Claydon, to levy a rate in the several towns therein to defray the cost (4*l.* 5*s.*) of certain armour provided by the chief constables for the said Hundred.

Ib. No date.—A warrant touching the repair of the Bridges called Snape and Wilford Bridges, lately fallen to ruin and decayed, so that the King's subjects cannot travel that way. *See also pp.* 45, 60, 64.

P. 44. Articles agreed upon, 28 May 1615, by the Justices of the Peace in co. Suffolk, touching the manner of levying charges on the country for the King's service, viz. for provision and carriages, for the Navy, for beacons, bridges, &c. 17 *names at foot, including* Ed. Bacon.

P. 45. 20 March 1615(–16). A warrant concerning a watch to be kept the 6th, 7th and 8th of April 1615, and for the arrest of all idle, vagrant, and wandering persons, who are to be brought before [the Justices] at the Crown in Woodbridge on the 12th April. *Addressed:* To the chief constables of—&c.

P. 46. Whitehall, 22 Feb. 1614(–15).—Council letter to the Deputy Lieutenants of Suffolk.

We send you herewithall a true declaration of the present estate of the English Colony planted in Virginia, together with a project to the help of a Lottery to bring at length that work to the success desired. We pray you to employ your good endeavours amongst the gentlemen and other persons of ability within that county to adventure in the said Lottery, destined to so good a purpose, such reasonable sums of money as each of them may conveniently and can willingly spare.

Received, 3rd April 1615.

P. 47. *No date.*—The Earl of Suffolk to Sir John Heigham and Sir Thomas Jermyn.

Touching an idle, foolish letter from the townsmen of Bury to Lord Chief Justice Cooke about the price of victuals, and reprimanding Sir John for not giving the Earl notice of it. A vacancy has been caused by the untimely death of Sir Robert Drury, Deputy Lieutenant. Also touching the holding of musters.

Other letters refer to the same matters. *See also pp.* 66, 78, 79.

P. 49. Articles agreed upon at Stowe Markett, the 3rd of June 1615, respecting musters to be taken in the several divisions of the county; viz. in Hoxon and Hartesmere under the conduction of Sir Nicholas Bacon, Bart., &c. Philip Colby, Esq., was muster-master.

Warrants to the chief constables and captains relative to the same.

Pp. 51 *seq.* Sundry other letters relating to musters, and the appointments of captains of companies.

Pp. 58, 59.—Letters between the Deputy Lieutenants and the Bailiffs of Ipswich, as to an exemption claimed by the latter.

P. 60. Articles agreed upon by the Justices of Peace of the county of Suffolk at the Assizes holden the 21st of July 1615, respecting accounts to be rendered by the Treasurers for Charitable Uses and Maimed Soldiers, the election of high constables, moneys levied by the Justices for the King's service, the licensing of ale-houses, innkeepers, tippling, rogues, presentments of the names of freeholders and others fit to be returned in juries, &c. 22 *names at the end.*

Pp. 62 *seq.* Letters and extracts from Statutes respecting the prices of ale and beer, and superfluous malting.

P. 69. Order by the Justices of the Peace for all churchwardens and overseers of the Poor to appear before them and render their accounts, and to bring bills of all the poor who are entitled to relief, and of all children bound apprentices.

P. 78. Bury St. Edmund's, 31 July 1617.—Letter from 23 [Justices of the Peace], including [Sir] Edw. Bacon, to the Duke of Lenox and residue of the honorable Officers of his Majesty's Greencloth, touching the carriages and provisions for his Majesty's Household.

P. 82. 1618.—Captain Henry Woodhowse is appointed muster-master. *See also pp.* 90, 101, 149, 302.

P. 83. Norwich, 11 May 1618.—The Chancellor of Norwich to the Deputy Lieutenants of Suffolk.

Touching certificates of the names of such ecclesiastical persons as had been formerly rated for the provisions of horse, arms, and other furniture for his Majesty's service.

Pp. 93 *seq.* 1618, 1619.—Correspondence between the Knights of the Guildable and the Knights of Bury, and the Deputy Lieutenants of the same divisions, touching the rates to be levied on each for providing powder and match, &c.

Also, letters to and from the Bailiffs of Eye and Ipswich on the same subject.

P. 102. Westminster, 31 May 1620.—Baron de Dona, Ambassador for the King of Bohemia, to the Lord Lieutenant and others of the County of Suffolk.

Requests them to join with the Lord Mayor and Aldermen of London in furnishing a loan to the King his master and the Queen of Bohemia, the most glorious mother and fruitful nursery of the Royal plants.

Other letters on the same subject.

P. 107. Form of the Oath of a Chief Constable: to execute warrants; to keep the peace; to suppress unlawful plays and games, drunkenness, and idleness; to levy rates and taxes; to keep the petty sessions, &c.

P. 108. 16 June 1621.—The Commission for the second Subsidy. (*Latin.*)

Council letter relating to the assessment of the same.

Schedule of the persons appointed assessors.

P. 112. Whitehall, 9 Feb. 1621 (-2).—Council letter to the Justices of the Peace in Suffolk.

We have taken notice, by letters written to this Board, of the decay of Clothing, and the great distress thereby fallen upon the weavers, spinners, and fullers in divers counties for want of work, and consequently of the means of relief of themselves & families which formerly they have earned by their labour; and although complaints of this kind are conceived to proceed in part out of the clamorous disposition of some idle persons, in repressing of whom we require and expect your best care and vigilancy, we have made this address unto you to let you know that as upon calling the merchants here before us, and due examination of the state of their trade at this present, we have taken order in the behalf of the clothier for the taking off (as far as may be) of such cloths as now lieth upon his hands, and will, as occasion shall give us leave, make further way for the vent of cloth in foreign parts and at home, so do hereby require you to call before you such clothiers as you shall think fitting, and to deal effectually with them for the employment of such weavers, spinners, & other persons as are now out of work; where we may not omit to let you know that as we have employed our best endeavours in favour of the clothier[s], both for the vent of their cloth and for moderation of the price of wools (of which we hope they shall speedily find the effects), so may we not endure that the clothiers in that or any other county should, at their pleasure, and without giving knowledge thereof to the Board, dismiss their workfolks, who, being many in number, and most of them of the poorest sort, are in such cases likely by their clamours to disturb the quiet and government of those places wherein they live. Public stocks are to be raised for the employment in that trade of poor people who want work. Wool growers shall not engross their wools and keep them in their hands two, three, or more years, to enhance the price thereof, in expectation of high prices arising from the death of sheep or other accidents. In the present decay of trade, all parties must bear a share of the public loss.

P. 114. Chilton, 19 Feb. 1621-2.—Warrant [by the Justices] to the high constables of the Hundred of Babergh to summon all persons who heretofore used the trade of clothing, and who now forbear to continue the same, before [the Justices] at the Crown in Sudbury on the 23rd instant; and to inquire what cloths remain unsold in the hands of all clothiers.

P. 115. Same date.—Warrant [by the Justices] to the churchwardens and overseers of the Poor of Boxford, Groton, and Edwardston, on a complaint that the aged and impotent poor are not relieved in such comfortable and sufficient manner as their necessity requireth, and that the other sort of poor which are of able bodies to work are in great distress and many of them likely to perish. The former are to be relieved, and the latter to be provided with work, by raising a stock, if need be.

P. 116. Bury, 13 March 1621 (–2).—Sir John Heigham and three others, [Justices, to the Privy Council].

We have dealt with the clothiers according to your letter of 9 Feb. They are much decayed in their estates by reason of the great losses they have received within these few years by merchants that have bankrupted, the sale of their cloths at under-prices, and the great quantity of cloth that doth lie dead upon their hands; and they live themselves in great want and misery, and cannot set the poor people on work, being many thousands. In twenty towns only there are 4,453 broadcloths in hand, valued at 39,282*l*. In twelve towns the clothiers have lost by the said bankrupts, within five years, 30,415*l*. Like losses would be found in other parts of the country. The clothiers think the deadness of their trade is caused by the merchants being incorporated and settled into companies, which limit the times, persons, numbers, and prices to be observed in buying cloths, contrary to the ancient custom of the trade; and by the transportation of English wool, fuller's earth, and woodashes to foreign parts, which increases the making of cloth in foreign parts, where English cloth was wont to be vented. The imposition lately laid on their cloths is none of the least hindrances to them. We make known these particulars to your Lordships, that you may take further order to remedy those inconveniences. We will use all diligence to cause the poor to be employed in labour.

P. 117. *No date.*—The opinion of the Lord Graye, Sir Francis Knowles, Sir John Norris, Sir Richard Bingham, Sir Roger Williams, and others, what places were most likely the enemy would land at, and what were most meet to be done to make head against him; with their answer to certain other propositions and heads set down by my Lords of the Council. 5 *pages.*

P. 123. *No date.*—Petition of the makers of Bayes and Sayes Stuffs and Fustians, commonly called the New Draperies, within the counties of Essex, Suffolk, and Norfolk, to the Privy Council, for redress against intruders into the said trade. With a Council letter thereon, dated 8 March 1621(–2). *See also p.* 139.

P. 125. ——, 23 Feb. 1621(–2).—Council letter to [the Justices of Assize].

Whereas many undertakers for the service of Compositions for his Majesty's House have lately failed and become bankrupt, by means whereof the inhabitants of the counties have been doubly charged; and whereas some Purveyors have likewise been employed for the bringing in of his Majesty's Composition, who, receiving money from his Majesty, have detained the same long after the said Compositions have been delivered; at the request of the Justices of the Peace, the King will accept a composition in money, calling to mind the general complaints in Parliament against the abuse in purveyance and cart-taking. You are to desire the gentlemen within your circuits to set down a valuation in money of their compositions in kind. Commissioners will be appointed to settle the same.

See also p. 260, *below.*

P. 126. Whitehall, 4 March 1621(–2).—Council letter to [the Deputy Lieutenants of Suffolk ?].

The unseasonableness of the last summer, together with the sudden rising of the price of corn, and the scarcity in many counties, have been taken into consideration by his Majesty. You are to take a perfect survey of the stores in that county, and return a certificate thereof to us, and what quantity may be spared for furnishing other parts of the

Kingdom, and also what hopes and expectation you have of the next harvest.

Pp. 127 *seq*. 1622–1624.—Letters from the Privy Council and the Lord Lieutenant, warrants, &c., relating to the decay of the cloth trade, the war of the Palatinate, a voluntary contribution in aid of his Majesty, the mustering and viewing of the trained forces, the excessive quantity of barley used by maltsters, the relief of the poor (especially in the Hundred of Babergh), providing work for the able-bodied, the licensing of ale-houses or tippling-houses, the price of corn and its scarcity, the suppression of tumultuous assemblies, compositions for the King's household, outrages committed in Essex by inhabitants of Sudbury and adjacent parts of Suffolk, the exercise of the trained bands, stores of powder and munition, the assessment of subsidies, fees of the muster-master and the officers of each band, &c.

P. 150. 29 Aug. 1623.—Letters Patent appointing Thomas Earl of Suffolk, K.G., to be Lord Lieutenant of the counties of Suffolk and Cambridge. His powers are fully specified. Also appointing Sir Lionel Talmache, Bart., Sir Henry Felton, Bart., Sir John Heigham, Sir Henry Glemham, Sir William Poley, Sir Thomas Jermyn, Sir John Wentworth, Sir Robert Crane, Sir John Rouse, Sir William Withipole, Sir Roger Northe, Sir Nathaniel Barnidiston, and Thomas Clenche, Esquire, to be the Earl's Deputies in co. Suffolk; and Sir Edward Peyton, Bart., [Sir] John Peyton the elder, Sir John Cuttes, Sir Symeon Steward, Sir Edward Hynd, and Sir William Wendie, to be his Deputies in co. Cambridge.

Correspondence thereupon.

P. 177. The Account taken between the Guildable and the Franchise for charges and carriages for the King's coming to Newmarket, for 1619, 20, 21, 22.

P. 178. Whitehall, 3 June 1624.—Council letter to [the Lord Lieutenant].

The States General of the United Provinces have by their embassadors humbly solicited his Majesty as well to renew the ancient defensive league between his Kingdom and their provinces, as also to permit them for the better confirmation thereof to raise some good number of voluntary soldiers within his dominions, to be employed in their service in these hazardous times, when the Emperor and the Romish Catholique League are preparing and drawing down towards their countries divers great and threatening troops to join with those armies that already lie upon their frontiers. His Majesty hath given way & permission for the raising of 6,000 voluntary soldiers for their service and assistance; his son-in-law, his only daughter, and his grand children being refugees in the United Provinces. The Earls of Oxford, Southampton, & Essex, and the Lord Willoughby have been appointed Colonels of such forces. You shall afford them & their officers your best assistance in levying the same, both in respect of the general cause and for the ease and benefit the country will find in being disburdened of many unnecessary persons that now want employment.

P. 180. 10 July 1624.—Bond given by the assessor and collector of a subsidy.

P. 181. Roystone, 19 Oct. 1624.—Royal warrant to the Earl of Suffolk for impressing 900 soldiers in Suffolk, Cambridge, and Dorset, to serve under Count Mansfeild for the recovery of the Palatinate.

Council letter on the same subject, and for the conducting of the soldiers to Dover, at the rate of ½*d.* a mile each, besides their ordinary pay of 8*d.* a day.

Also, a letter of the Council of War.

A warrant by ——— to the chief constables to issue precepts to the petty constables of every parish to warn all able men (not being of any trained band) within the franchise of Bury St. Edmunds, to appear "before us" at Sudbury, that we may impress 166 men for the King's service. *At the foot are these words, apparently to be uttered upon impressment*:—Here is press money to serve his Majesty, and we charge you thereby to be ready upon one hour's warning, when so ever you are called for, upon pain of death.

P. 188. Westminster, 30 Nov. 1624.—Royal warrant [to the Earl of Suffolk] for the levy of 100 men over and above the number previously required, viz., 50 in Cambridgeshire and 50 in Suffolk.

Council letters thereon, mentioning the names of the captains of the whole number of 1,000 men, who are to be at Dover on 24th December.

P. 194. Names of the persons impressed in the several Hundreds.

P. 196. Whitehall, 31 Jan. 1624(-5).—The Council of War to [the Deputy Lieutenants?].

Forasmuch as his Majesty upon some special occasions hath determined to set forth some part of his Navy Royal unto the Seas, and whereas although of late years he have had divers great services, yet in those employments his royal and tender care to avoid any trouble of his subjects hath been such, that there hath not been any corn, grain, or other provisions of victuals taken up by commission, as formerly upon less occasions hath been used; but now his Majesty's present service requiring an extraordinary proportion, we do therefore hereby will and require you to assemble yourselves, and to apportion upon each several division in that county such quantity of wheat as in your discretions shall be thought meet, so as his Majesty may be forthwith provided and furnished at reasonable prices of five hundred quarters of good and well-conditioned wheat; the same to be with all speed delivered unto Sir Allen Apsten (Apsley), one of the surveyors for the victualling of his Majesty's Navy, or his deputies, they paying ready money for the same; requiring you to take care that his Majesty may not be exacted upon in the price.

Warrant to the chief constables thereupon.

P. 199. Woodstock, 13 Aug. 1625.—Charles I. to the Earl of Suffolk.

The present doubtful and dangerous conditions of these times require more than ordinary care for the preservation of that happy peace that hath been so long continued within these our kingdoms; to effect which there can be no means more royal and useful than by putting the Trained Bands into such a readiness, and establishing such a Militia at home, as may give life and courage to our good subjects, and terror to those that may intend any disturbance or invasion; to which purpose there hath been certain rules set down and appointed by our late dear Father of most glorious memory, and sent to you in printed books to be put in execution. Yet we have upon inquiry found so much remissness and neglect as that in most counties those orders are scarce heard of, and in none put in real execution, nor anything done beyond the form of ordinary Musters, which works little reformation. Our express will and pleasure is to have those orders duly observed, and more especially for their horse; so that you may either give us an account of the exact accomplishment thereof, or of the defaults and causes of not performance, by 30th November next. New books are sent with these letters.

Council letter on the same subject, mentioning that the coasts of Suffolk and Dorset are in much danger and subject to be surprised, and giving particular directions touching the trained bands, beacons, powder magazines, watches, &c. Two regiments of a thousand a piece for each county are to be kept in readiness to march forward on the first alarm.

Also, a letter from the Earl of Suffolk, enclosing the two preceding letters, and appointing Sir Edmond Bacon and Sir Thomas Jermyn to be colonels for leading the troops to a place of rendezvous to be appointed by the Council.

P. 202. *No date.*—A Certificate from the Deputy Lieutenants to the Earl of Suffolk.

We have taken order for a speedy and exact mustering of all the Trained Bands, both horse and foot; we have also caused the beacons to be put in good reparation, and appointed persons carefully to watch them. Upon conference with understanding men inhabiting near the ports and coasts, we find the state thereof, with very little alteration, agrees with the Certificate in [15]88, which we send your Lordship with some additions. We directed our letters to so many captains as shall make (*sic*) two regiments of a thousand apiece, both of horse and foot, nearest to those places where an enemy might land. As to fortifications, we have not yet done anything. We have a magazine of powder of three lasts, but by long lying it is grown unserviceable, and therefore we desire a supply from above, as our neighbours of Essex have.

An Addition to the former Certificate [of 1588].

Langer Pointe.—We find all things to agree according to the former Certificate, but for the better securing of that dangerous harboroughe it is thought fit to have a fort built upon the same, where formerly there hath been one, for if the enemy should land there and build a sconce, he would command all the harboroughe, so that no ships can go in and out, the depth of the channel being very narrow and running near unto the point.

Albroughe.—We find the enemy may freely land at any time from Orford Nesse, all along by the said town of Albroughe unto Thorpe Nesse, which lieth a mile on the North side from the same; and for present defence we find but eight old iron pieces, whereof two are sacres and the rest minions, all defective, being honeycombed within, and three good brass bases.

Dunwich.—We find to be as it was in 88, differing in this, that the enemy may land at any time; and we find but two pieces of ordnance where ten are needful.

Southole [Southwold].—We find there two iron demiculverins being honeycombed, and do find it fit to have four more at the least.

P. 203. Ipswich, 11 Sept. 1625.—The Deputy Lieutenants to the Captains, in pursuance of the Council letter last mentioned.

P. 204. *No date.*—The Deputy Lieutenants to the Justices of the Peace.

We, having several complaints made to us of great resort to many Recusants' houses in this county, and great provision of powder and arms of all sorts, have certified my Lord of Suffolk, Lord Lieutenant, from whom we have received direction to use his authority to search for all such arms within their houses, and to take them into our custody, or else to take inventory. We therefore desire you, Sir G. W. and Mr. Wint: tomorrow morning, being the 11th of this month, to search Mr. D., and there to take into your custody such provision of arms or powder as you shall find in their (*sic*) houses, and them keep, and also to take the names of such persons as you shall there find, and the place of their abode. *No signatures.*

At foot.—Bedingfeild of Redlingsfeild, Mr. Jucksley of Jucksley, Mr. Evered of Linstead, Mr. Norton of Cheston, Mr. Rowse of Badinham.

P. 205. Palace of Westminster, 31 May 1627.—Royal warrant to [the Earl of Suffolk].

Whereas we did lately command certain companies to be levied in sundry countries within this our realm for our expedition now in hand, which falling out to be short in number and not proportionable for the execution of our design, for the more speedy supply thereof in respect of (*sic*) the season now draweth on so fast, our pleasure is, and we do hereby command and authorise you to cause presently to be levied within our county of Suffolk (being under your Lieutenancy) one hundred and fifty able men, to be conducted with all convenient speed to Portsmouth, so as they may arrive there at or before the 8th day of June next, following herein such further directions as you shall receive from our Privy Council in this behalf. And for so doing these our letters shall be your sufficient warrant and discharge. Given under our signet, &c.

Council letter on the same subject.

P. 213. 1625.—Form of a privy seal, asking the person addressed for a sum of money by way of loan, according to the custom of the former Kings and Queens upon extraordinary occasions, the sum being such as few men would deny a friend; with a promise of repayment within 18 months.

P. 214. Court at Plymouth, 17 Sept. 1625.—The King to Thomas Earl of Suffolk, Lord Lieutenant of Suffolk, Dorset, Cambridge, Isle of Ely, Poole, and Ipswich.

We have occasion to borrow, from some private gentlemen and others, competent sums of money for the public service. You are to return the names of as many persons as may be of ability to furnish us, that we may thereupon direct our privy seals unto them according to the form enclosed (see p. 213). We do not intend to deal with any noblemen, neither are you to deal with any of the clergy. *Printed in Rushworth's Historical Collections*, I. 192, *but without the date.*

P. 215. Audly-end, 27 Sept. 1625.—T. Earl of Suffolk to the Deputy Lieutenants of Suffolk.

Asking them to attend to the preceding letter. For the thousand foot which we are to send to Langer Pointe, I pray you let them be ready upon an hour's warning. For the horse company, they shall not move, for I find it not directed by my Lord Coneway, but only a motion out of my Lord Warwick's own humour.

P. 216. Court at Whitehall, 7 Jan. 1624–5.—Letter signed Hamilton, T. Edmondes, Jo. Sucklinge, the King's Commissioners to compound with Justices of the Peace for money in lieu of the composition-provisions, [to the Justices of the Peace in Suffolk]; giving notice for the discontinuance of the agreement heretofore made, as from Michaelmas next, after which they are to return to the former course of serving all provisions in kind, because some counties decline to contract for money.

P. 227. *No date.*—Council letter to [the Earl of Suffolk].

His Majesty and we of his Council having received information from so many several parts of the bold and impudent speeches used by many Romish Catholiques of this Realm, declaring how much they are offended with the gracious satisfaction given by his Majesty to the Lords and Commons in Parliament in the points concerning the conservation of true and pure religion, as it is at this day by authority practised in the Church of England, and having just cause to doubt [that] many violent misled Papists, through the instigation of Jesuited priests, may be inclined to take part with such as we well understand at this time practise with the King's subjects to raise stirs and tumults, which they [do?] not only by persuasions and instigations but with promise of assistance and seconding them by arms, their pretext being religion but their ends conquest, pushed thereunto by an unlimited ambition to a general Monarchy, of which we have too large and too clear proof; although we do not misjudge or condemn all his Majesty's subjects, Romish Catholiques, but believe that many of them will employ their arms and lives in his service: . . . These are therefore to pray and require your Lordship to repair to the houses of all Romish Recusants convicted or justly suspected, and to take their arms, warlike munition, and weapons into your possession, and to dispose of them as heretofore, certifying their names.

P. 228. Hampton Court, 31st Dec. 1625.—Council letter to the Earl of Suffolk.

Upon certificate of musters returned from sundry Lords Lieutenants of several shires of the realm, we find it generally complained of that divers principal mansion-houses and lands of value, which have heretofore found horse and foot, and shewed the same at the musters, towards the furnishing of the troops and bands of the county, are lately possessed either by new tenants, or by the owners themselves being new purchasers thereof, and do not now find those arms which these two (*sic*) houses and lands in former times did, to the disfurnishing of the bands. You shall take care that the trained bands both horse & foot be kept up to the full number they have formerly been at, &c. We send two printed books for exercise of the trained bands after the modern form.

Letter from the Earl to the Deputy Lieutenants thereupon.

Pp. 230, 231. Letters of the Council and Lord Lieutenant touching a fort to be erected by the Earl of Warwick upon Languer Point.

P. 232. Palace at Westminster, 14th Jan. 1625–6.—[The King] to his right trusty and right well beloved Cousin and Councillors and trusty and well beloved Councillors [*i.e.* the Privy Council].

We have caused a certain number of experienced soldiers [officers] to be sent from the Low Countries hither, to be distributed into the several counties, there to teach the captains, lieutenants, ensigns, and other officers and leaders of files in each company the true modern use of arms and order of soldiers. Accordingly we do hereby require you to make an equal distribution of the same soldiers into the several counties, and by our letters to the Lieutenants require them strictly in our name to give order that such as you address to them be presently put to employment in teaching the captains. Those officers, in regard of their employment in the Low Countries, cannot be spared to stay here above three months at the farthest. The times appointed in the printed books for these exercises are to be duly kept; and the words [of command] therein specified are to be used in training. The gentlemen

of the country will entertain the same officers, who are to be allowed 6*s.* a week each, besides their diet and lodging.
Council letter thereupon.

P. 234. Whitehall, 22 Jan. 1625(-6).—[Council letter to the Earl of Suffolk.]
By the relation of the Earl Marshal and a certificate made by his order, and by a petition of the Bailiffs and Commonalty of Yarmouth, we understand in what peril that town is in these dangerous times through want of being well furnished and fortified for defence. Use your best endeavours in procuring contributions from the counties of Norfolk and Suffolk for strengthening and securing that place, as was done heretofore in 1588 upon letters from the Council to the deputy lieutenants.

P. 235. Whitehall, 14 Jan. 1625 (-6).—Council letter to [the Earl of Suffolk].
We send you herewith a list of the companies of Sir Charles Riche's regiments [regiment ?], which are to be lodged in the maritime towns of that county, there to be ready upon all occasions for present defence, as also for such other employment abroad as his Majesty shall be pleased to resolve on. Take order for the billeting of them in fit manner; and as they are to keep a military watch, they are to have sufficient provision of fire whilst they are upon their guards during the sharpness of this winter season, the charges whereof will be repaid.
Note as to the numbers of the regiment of Sir C. Riche.

Pp. 235 *seq.* Letters from the Lord Lieutenant to the Deputy Lieutenants, and from the latter to the chief constables, touching the execution of several of the foregoing orders. Serjeant Hambdin and Serjeant Baker were sent down by the King to instruct the trained bands. Also, other documents relative thereto.

Pp. 239 *seq.* 1626.—Letters from the King, the Privy Council, Theophilus Earl of Suffolk, Lord Lieutenant, &c. relative to the trained bands.

P. 244. Whitehall, 30 June 1626.—Council letter to [the Deputy Lieutenants of Suffolk].
His Majesty, for the defence of the Kingdom against invasion, hath given order to all the ports to prepare a number of ships in warlike manner. We have appointed three ships to be made ready in your neighbour towns of Harwich, Ipswich, and Woodbridge. In regard of the readiness of the enemy and our late interruptions in Parliament, we are straightened in time; and as the the charge will fall heavy on those parts, which are much disabled by the late stand of their trade and other losses at sea, we require your friendly assistance therein. If the magistrates of those towns want men, you shall supply them from the country, and contribute corn, beeves, & such like; so that all men may approve your heartiness and zeal for the defence of your religious prince and country against that overgrowing Tyrant of Spain.

P. 245. Ipswich, 14 July 1626.—[The Deputy Lieutenants of Suffolk to the Privy Council.]
We have conferred with the Mayor of Harwich, the Bailiffs of Ipswich, and the chief inhabitants of Woodbridge and other towns, but cannot come to an agreement as to the proportions of the charge to be borne by them and by the country. They have never borne any part of the county charge for the public service, yet refuse the large offer made to them that the county should bear a third part of the present charge.

Pp. 246 *seq.* 1626.—Letters from the Council and Lord Lieutenant as to preparations to be made for defence against an expected invasion from Spain and Flanders; with other papers relating thereto.

P. 254. Palace of Westminster, 7 July 1626.—The King to the Justices of the Peace [in Suffolk].

Touching the agreement made in the late Parliament to give the King a supply of four entire subsidies and three fifteens, and not performed owing to the disordered passion of some members. We desire all our loving subjects freely & voluntarily to perform that which by law, if it had passed formally by an Act, as was intended, they had been compelled unto. You are to take order according to the instructions sent herewith. *See State Papers, Domestic.*

P. 255. Instructions to the Justices of the Peace within the county of Suffolk, how they are to propound a supply for the King, and collect the same. *See State Papers, Domestic.*

P. 256. Bury, 28 July 1626.—The Deputy Lieutenants to the Earl of Suffolk.

In pursuance of the letters from the King and the Council, we have made out warrants for the performance of most of the services required. As to drawing all the forces of the county to one place, in regard of the season of the year, the great charge, and the plague, we have deferred it till we shall receive further order. As to the clause requiring a proportion of victuals for ten days, we can always be furnished of the same for money, and therefore pray directions that upon any sudden alarum we may know how our soldiers, captains, & officers shall be paid. As to powder, lead, & match, we desire to be furnished out of his Majesty's storehouse, at his price. As for posthorses, finding the great benefit of the stages laid between London and Harwich, we desire the like favour from Yarmouth to Ipswich. It is necessary that eight field-pieces, two to each regiment, be laid at Ipswich, Wickham, Blibrough, and Beckles; and for defence of these coast towns, Albrough, Soale (Southwold), and Dunwich, we conceive it fit that certain fortifications, &c. (specified) should be undertaken. The chief inhabitants are willing to continue the three serjeants mentioned in the Council's letters, so as they may be freed from the charge of the muster-master.

P. 257. Whitehall, 26 July 1626.—Council letter to the Justices of the Peace in Suffolk.

It hath come to our knowledge that amongst other instructions lately sent unto you by his Majesty for the obtaining of a competent sum for the defence of the realm by way of free gift from the country, that instruction wherein mention is made of the subsidies & fifteens which the Parliament resolved to have given, is understood by some of you as if you were directed to demand expressly of the country as due to his Majesty the aforesaid subsidies & fifteens because they were intended to have been given by the Parliament.... We have thought good, for the clearing of all doubts, to let you know that the supply now demanded by his Majesty is in no ways meant to be by way of subsidy, but merely as a free gift from the subject to the sovereign; ... and in this sense & not otherwise you are to represent it unto the country. Upon some good effect thereof hereabouts it is conceived to be a more effectual way (than that formerly directed you) that you in your several divisions should send for such persons as are of ability to give, and deal with them particularly, by using such motives and persuasions as you are best acquainted withall.... We are given to understand by the Justices of the Peace who have the managing of this service in Middlesex and other counties hereabouts, that divers persons, having been demanded what they would give, have made answer that they have received privy seals for Loans to his Majesty, and that they conceived it was not his Majesty's pleasure that they should both lend & give, offering (or at least seeming willing) to give so they might be discharged of their privy seals.... We therefore authorise you to assure every such person that in case he shall freely give, you will make certificate to us of his forwardness & good example therein for his Majesty's service, not doubting but thereupon he shall be discharged of his privy seal. *See State Papers, Domestic, under* 25 *July* 1626. *In another MS. in this collection the date is* 27 *July*.

P. 258. Audliend (Audley End), 4 Aug. 1626.—Theo. Earl of Suffolk to [the Deputy Lieutenants].

Referring to the preceding letters from the King and the Council. I am resolved to come to Bury on Tuesday the 15th, when I desire that my Deputies & the Justices of Peace of the county will be there present; as also that two at the least of the chief inhabitants of every town in the county may be assembled at the sign of the Angel in Bury on the same day by 9 o'clock.

P. 260. 8 July 20 James I. (1622.)—Articles of Agreement between Sir Ralph Freeman and others, the King's Commissioners, and the Sheriff and Justices of the Peace of co. Suffolk, touching a composition in money instead of provisions towards the provision of his Majesty's Household. 2 *pages*.

P. 262. Whitehall, 29 July 1626.—Council letter to [the Earl of Suffolk].

Whereas we wrote to the Justices of the Peace of Suffolk for three ships to be set out & furnished from Ipswich, Harwich, and Woodbridge, the inhabitants of those towns have been suitors to this Board to be eased in the number of ships, &c. Knowing well the decay of trade & their losses at sea of late years, we have thought fit that they be charged to set out only two ships, and be eased by a contribution from the county of a moiety of the charge. Mariners are to be impressed.

Letter from the Earl thereupon.

P. 264. Bury, 28 July 1626.—Directions given [by the Deputy Lieutenants to the chief constables] respecting musters, beacons, &c. *See also p.* 267.

P. 265. Whitehall, 19 Aug. 1626. A letter from T. Edmondes and others touching 1050*l.* due from the county [of Suffolk] in lieu of compositions for the expense of his Majesty's house.

Letter from the Deputy Lieutenants to the chief constables of the Hundred of Babergh thereupon.

P. 268. Whitehall, 21 Dec. 1626.—Council letter to the Earl of Suffolk and the rest of the Commissioners for the Loan in Suffolk.

It hath been reported to his Majesty that there is great forwardness found in his loving subjects within the county for the Loan required from them by virtue of his Majesty's late commission. There is like forwardness in other counties. His Majesty's great affairs do daily and hourly press and call for the paying in of these moneys. Care is to be taken that the money lent be without delay collected. Where you find any persons that have absented themselves and not appeared before you, fail not to send for them, and require either assent or an absolute answer, wherein you shall provide accordingly to the instructions formerly sent you.

Letter from the Earl of Suffolk, [the Earl of ?] Salisbury, and R. Nanton to Sir Thomas Jermyn & others, commissioners for the Loan in Suffolk, on the same matter.

P. 271. The Account of John Scrivener, Esq., touching such moneys as he was to receive out of the divisions of Beckles and Woodbridge, payable thence to the franchise of Bury, 6th March 1625(-6). *2 pages.*

P. 274. An Agreement made at Stowmarkett, this 15th of March 1626. It relates to musters, training, wages, powder and match, &c. *Signed*: John Barker, Will. Poley, Hen. Glemham, Robt. Crane, Roger North, Will. Harvie.

P. 275. Whitehall, 14 March 1626(-7).—Council letter to [the Earl of Suffolk].

Give order to your deputy lieutenants to cause the next musters of that county for this year to be in or about Whitsun week next, being a time conceived to be most seasonable, & of least interruption to the business & occasions of the country. We marvel at your neglect in not sending the certificate & muster-rolls, which ought to have been returned by 10th August last.

Letter from the Earl thereupon. *See also p*. 205, *above*.

P. 277. *No date.*—Articles to be enquired of by the high constables of every hundred and the petty constables of every parish, and presentments thereof to be made to the Justices at their monthly meetings.

1. The names of Popish Recusants (with other particulars), and the names of such as resort to private conventicles.

2. The names of all such as do not resort to Divine service every Sunday, and whether 12*d*., every Sunday forfeited, be required and received, and duly employed for the poor.

3. What felonies have been committed, and what robberies. *Incomplete.*

P. 279. *No date.*—Orders by the Deputy Lieutenants touching the exercise and drilling of the trained bands; with a table of the wages payable to the officers (including the Low Country serjeant) and soldiers.

P. 281. Whitehall, 24 March 1626(-7).—Council letter to the Deputy Lieutenants and Justices of the Peace of co. Suffolk.

Touching assistance to be given to the port of Harwich, Ipswich, and Woodbridge in the setting forth of two ships. The Kingdom is daily threatened with preparations & approach of an enemy. For the strength of his Kingdom, and for the support of his allies & confederates, his Majesty hath at this present on foot some important design & expedition by sea, whereby, after the departure of the fleet prepared on that behalf, there will be great need of the said ships for the defence of the coasts and securing the Narrow Seas. Notwithstanding any former allegations & pretences by you made, you are to cause such sums of money to be assessed upon that county as may supply a full moiety of the charge of setting out the said two ships, which are to be at the rendezvous at Portsmouth by the 20th May next, victualled for four months from that date; requiring you not to fail hereof as you tender his Majesty's high displeasure. *Signed:* Buckenham, Theo. Suffolke, &c.

P. 282. Whitehall, 31 March 1627.—Council letter to [the same ?].

Concerning idle and dissolute persons running up and down the country, as also touching land-soldiers and mariners in his Majesty's pay that daily run away.

P. 283. Whitehall, 10 April 1627.—Council letter to [the Earl of Suffolk].

Concerning soldiers impressed for his Majesty's service that daily run away from their conductors. They were to have been sent to the King of Denmark. Thank Sir John Barker for his good service in assisting the conductors or commanders.

Letter from the Earl to [the Deputy Lieutenants] on the same subject, asking them to take pattern from Sir John Barker.

P. 286. *No date.*—An humble Remonstrance of those Reasons which the Inhabitants of the County of Suffolk do under favour conceive to be satisfactory to the Lords of the Council why they should not be enforced to contribute towards the setting forth of the two ships impressed upon the town of Ipswich.

It sets forth the charges borne by the county, and the exemptions and privileges enjoyed by the corporate towns.

P. 288. Chilton, 12 July 1627.—Warrant [by the Justices of the Peace?] to the [chief] Constables of the Hundred of Babergh for payment to the Bailiffs of Ipswich, for his Majesty's service, of their proportion of 525*l.* due from this county to the Cofferer of his Majesty's Household for provisions, as requested by the Lord Steward and other officers of the Household. Some persons in the Hundred having refused or neglected to pay, order is to be taken to effect their conformity.

P. 290. 14 Oct. 1626.—Warrant [by the Justices of the Peace] to the same, for levying money for relief of the town of Sudbury during the infection of the plague; except from such towns as were lately contributory to the town of Newmarket upon the like occasion, and such other towns as are now infected.

P. 291. Whitehall, 30 June 1627.—Council letter to the Justices of the Peace, &c.

We lately wrote letters unto you by his Majesty's command to quicken & call upon all those that are yet behind in their Loans or any portion thereof, and to cause the collectors speedily to return all their collections some time the last Term, as also to certify the names [of such] as remain refusers to lend, or to pay in that they promised to lend; of which letters we have no account, and but little of the towns paid in the last Term, which being past, we must let you know his Majesty imputes the fault rather to you who are entrusted as Commissioners than to those that are to lend, who have showed good affections in paying & promising, but there hath been much slackness in the calling for & collecting of the moneys. And these things are particularly observed: [first,] that many of the Commissioners absented themselves from the sitting that others made about this business, and have not as yet paid in their Loans; secondly, that many of the lenders who promised have not yet paid; thirdly, those to whom day was given for a second payment are neither called upon nor have paid in that second payment; fourthly, that many shift themselves from one county to another, and escape lending anywhere; lastly, that the refusers whom you are to bind over to appear before this Board, are neither bound nor their answers certified; [in] all which causes you are to use diligence, and straightly to give us accompt of your proceedings before the 15th of July next. And as his Majesty will interpret well where he finds diligence to be used, so the neglect herein will be as offensive to him, the public occasions so pressing as they do, and all the moneys collected upon the Loans, with much more of his own treasure, being wholly employed in those public occasions for the defence of the realm, succours of his Majesty's allies, [and] maintenance of the cause of religion, which were the motives that forced his Majesty to this course. And this farther we must let you know, that we are not ignorant of that you are ear-witnesses, that such as have shewed good affections & been forward in yielding to these Loans, find themselves aggrieved that others who stand in contempt & refuse to lend fare better than those that are the lenders, who have deserved thanks of his Majesty and are not so to be discouraged, nor these refusers & contemners to go free & unpunished, which causes the quicker calling upon you and straighter accompt from you than otherwise we should have needed.

P. 292. Audliend, 12 July 1627.—The Earl of Suffolk to the Deputy Lieutenants.

Touching a supply for the county of munition from his Majesty's store.

Council letter to the Earl of Totnes [Master of the Ordnance] for supply of field-pieces and powder, &c.

Letter of Sir Henry Glemham on the same matter, and the likelihood of another press coming shortly. Before we can send out our warrants (to impress men), every man runs away and hides himself, whereby we are enforced to take such as we can get.

P. 295. Honor of Hampton Court, 29 Sept. 1627.—Royal warrant to the Earl of Suffolk.

Being engaged in a war whereunto we have been provoked by just occasions, there is now a necessity for some speedy re-inforcement and supply. We authorise and require you to cause 100 able men to be levied in the county of Suffolk.

Council letter touching the same. None of the men are to be taken out of the trained bands. The King will not at this time put the county to the charge of arming them. They are to march 15 miles a day to the rendezvous at Plimouth, by 1st Nov. Coats & conduct money are to be paid for by the county. There is to be no selling or changing of able men by the constables or the conductors, as in former levies.

Letter from the Earl of Suffolk thereupon.

Warrant to the chief constables for the same (p. 303).

P. 299. Whitehall, 17 Dec. 1627.—Council letter to the Deputy Lieutenants of Suffolk.

All the forces remaining near Portsmouth are to be removed into other counties. Some of them are to be billeted in Suffolk, with the weekly allowance of 3*s.* 6*d.* a man, which is to be repaid by the Lord Treasurer and Mr. Chancellor of the Exchequer.

Other letters from the Council and the Earl of Suffolk touching the supply of ordnance and munition for the coast towns of Albroughe, Dunwich, & Southwold; a review of defects having been made by Sir John Poley and Mr. Gosnold. Also touching Sir William Withipoll's foot company, and the billeting of four companies of the regiment of the late Colonel Ratcliffe.

P. 306. Whitehall, 10 Jan. 1627(-8).—Council letter to [the Earl of Suffolk].

The trained bands are ill provided and furnished for service. Not only the defects are great in those that do show their horses and arms, but many for the saving of charges do borrow horses and arms to show as their own. His Majesty therefore thinks fit to take a view and muster the horse of very many of the shires in his own person, because the frequent directions and admonitions of this Table have not hitherto prevailed. Give directions to all the horse-companies within your Lieutenancy, as well in Suffolk as in Cambridge, to repair to his Majesty's presence on Hounslye Heath by nine of the clock in the morning on the 21st day of April next, together with the captains & officers, to be mustered before him. Directions as to exercise in the mean time. Recusants are to find such horses & arms as they are charged with, and the men appointed to serve for them are to be trained. Defaulters are to be sent before the Board. For security against foreign invasion, your Lordship & one or two of your deputy lieutenants are to repair to London on 7th May, to receive directions for the perfecting of musters and other warlike preparations.

Letter from the Earl, urging the diligent performance of the foregoing commands, and asking some of the deputy lieutenants to attend him at Suffolk House.

P. 309. *No date.*—[The Deputy Lieutenants] to the Lords of the Council.

Giving reasons for not levying arrears due to Captain [Henry] Woodhouse, muster-master of Suffolk, as directed. *See also pp.* 331, 332, 345.

P. 310.—A note of the powder, match, bullets, and lead bought for a magazine for the county of Suffolk, the 6th of March 1627(–8).

Pp. 311 *seq.* 1627–1638.—Other letters, warrants, &c. relating to munitions, the billeting of soldiers and the disputes thence arising, the enrolment of volunteers in the King's regiments billeted in Suffolk and Dorset, the exemption of the town of Ipswich from finding & furnishing light horse, Sir Richard Brooke and Captain North's cornets of horse, the appointment of four colonels by the Lord Lieutenant (Sir Edmund Bacon, Sir Thomas Jermyn, Sir Thomas Glemham, and Sir William Withipole), the musters & exercise of the trained bands both horse and foot, the decay of the cloth and woollen trade, tumults owing thereto, the relief of the poor and setting them on work, the watching of beacons, the spread of the plague, a petition by the poor spinsters weavers & combers of wool in Sudbury and other places, &c. The Earl of Suffolk is sometimes addressed as Lord Lieutenant of Cambridge, Suffolk, and Dorset, and Lord Warden of the Cinque Ports. The following entries require more particular notice :—

P. 314. Whitehall, 13 Feb. 1627–8.—Council letter respecting the billeting of soldiers, mentioning that the soldier complains on the one side for being billeted in the houses of such poor and indigent persons as are not able to provide for him according to the entertainment allowed by his Majesty; and the billeter on the other side complains on the soldier for disorder in not being content with the provision made for him according to his Majesty's said pay, but he will be his own carver of whatsoever he like best and can lay his hands on, to the great damage and impoverishment of the county.

P. 320. Whitehall, 12 June 1628.—Council letter touching the continuance of the soldiers billeted within the counties of Suffolk and Dorset.

Of late, [in] some parts of the said counties where soldiers are billeted, the inhabitants either out of some diffidence of his Majesty's royal promise [to hasten their removal], or by the example and encouragement of some persons ill affected to his Majesty's service, or out of sinister and false apprehensions of some misunderstanding between his Majesty and his Parliament, have, in disobedience to his Majesty's former commands, refused to billet the said soldiers any longer. His Majesty, having been made acquainted therewithall, however he is (as you cannot but conceive) highly offended with their refractory & undutiful carriage therein, yet is graciously pleased for the present to pass by their contempt without censure or punishment, willing them to know that he & his Parliament being now well & happily accorded & agreed, it is well known to all men that he shall be instantly supplied with means to take them off their hands, and to make repayment of the arrear due to them on that behalf.

P. 365. Court at Whitehall, 20 March 1633(-4).—Order in Council. His Majesty having been lately pleased to rectify and reform the March of this our English nation (corrupted by time and negligence of drummers), and for the honour of this Kingdom to restore it to the ancient gravity thereof, by ordaining an establishment of one certain & constant measure to be observed and beaten by all English drummers, as well in these his Majesty's dominions as abroad in the service of foreign princes, his Majesty's friends & allies; which said establishment signed by his Majesty & in his presence subscribed by our very good Lord the Earl Marshal of England remaineth upon record for a precedent for future times; we have thereupon thought fit & ordered that a duplicate or true copy of this establishment be fairly engrossed & delivered to your Lordship [the Earl of Suffolk] by Edward Norgate, Esq., Clerk of the Signet to his Majesty extraordinary, who is commanded to attend this service and the delivery of them at the Signet Chamber at Whitehall, to the end it being imparted by your Lordship to the deputy lieutenants, and by them to the captains & officers of [the] several regiments & divisions of those counties under your command, the same may be duly observed in all musters and military exercises of the trained bands.
Letter from the Earl thereupon, 1 May 1635 (p. 364).

P. 367. Whitehall, 15 June 1635.—Council letter to [the Earl of Suffolk].
Give speedy and effectual order to your deputy lieutenants to keep a watchful eye upon all the ports & places apt for landing within those counties, and especially the Cinque Ports; and that upon the first notice of the appearing or approach of any foreign fleet upon those coasts, they cause all the trained bands of those counties, or so many of them as you shall find needful, to be immediately drawn down thither, to repulse the landing of any enemy. Land-men are to be impressed for the supply of his Majesty's fleet.

P. 370. At Whitehall, the 26th of October 1635.
It was this day ordered, according to his Majesty's pleasure signified by Mr. Secretary Windebank, that the letter following from his Majesty to the Council Board should be entered into the Register of the Council Causes, and a copy thereof delivered to the Earl Marshal and to Lord Matrevers, Lord Lieutenant for the county of Norfolk and city of Norwich, and the original to remain in the Council chest, signed.

CHARLES R.

Right trusty and well beloved Cousins and Councillors, and right trusty and well beloved Councillors, we greet you well. Whereas we have understood lately how careful you have been, upon the occasion of a Petition exhibited by Atkins & Lane, Aldermen of Norwich, unto the Board, not only to approve well of and encourage the proceeding of the Lord Matrevors with those refractory persons, and of his father, our Earl Marshal, in their careful maintaining our authority of Lieftenancy given unto them, for which we heartily thank you; we have thought good to let you know that we do take the maintaining of this our power so much to heart, being of such consequence to the government & safety of our people, as that we hold any endeavour to resist or dispute our power in that kind to be tending to faction and sedition; and therefore do command that if hereafter any City, being a County, or any other Corporation, or any particular person therein whatsoever, shall presume to resist or dispute our said power of Lieftenancy given by us, from which no Corporation [may] have exemption, that our Attorney General for the time being shall not only proceed against them by *Quo warranto* or otherwise to call in their Charter, but by Information to our Court of Star Chamber, or otherwise, bring the Corporation or party or parties so offending to such exemplary punishment as shall be fit. Given at our Court of Oatland[s], the 24th of August in the eleventh year of our reign.

P. 377. At the Inner Star Chamber, 10 May 1637.

Council Order touching the maintenance and execution of an Act of Sewers made at King's Lynn, 13 Jan. 6 Chas. I. *See State Papers, Domestic.*

P. 380. —— 20 Dec. 1636.—Council letter to the High Sheriff of Kent, concerning the manner of assessing the Clergy to Ship-money.

An humble petition hath been presented to his Majesty in the name of sundry of the Clergy in that county, complaining of the great inequality that is used by their parishioners in assessing the moneys charged upon that county by his Majesty's late Writ for setting forth of Shipping for the defence of the Kingdom & his Majesty's just Royalties in the Narrow Seas; the said parishioners charging them not only with the tenth part of the land assessed, but also with the tenth part of the assessments taken by the abilities, which many times is (*sic*) charged upon men who live in their said parishes without occupying of land, being either sojourners, or usurers, or men of gainful trades, or otherwise able in respect of their stocks, from whom in regard of such stocks the said Clergy receive no profit of tithes, by which means it comes to pass that they are rated for that which they have not. Directions are given for remedying this grievance.

P. 381. 19 Sept. 1637.—The Sheriff's warrant for assessing the Ship-money on the Clergy in accordance with the preceding letter. It appears to have been addressed to the officers of a particular town, and refers to the parsonage of Cotteshrooke, and Dr. Morgan, parson there.

P. 386. Palace at Westminster, 18 Feb. 1638–9. The King to Theophilus Earl of Suffolk, L.L. of Cambridge, Suffolk, and Dorset.

The great and considerable forces lately raised in Scotland, without order or warrant from us, by the instigation of some factious persons ill affected to monarch[ich]al government, who seek to cloak their too apparent rebellious designs under pretence of religion, albeit we have often given them good assurance of our resolution constantly to maintain the religion established by the laws of that Kingdom, have moved us to take into our royal care to provide for the preservation & safety of this our Kingdom of England, which is by the tumultuous proceedings of those factious spirits in apparent danger to be annoyed & invaded; wherefore, upon serious debate and mature advice with our Privy Council we have resolved to repair in person to the Northern parts of this our kingdom with a Royal Army. And this being for the defence & safety of this our Kingdom, unto which all our good subjects are obliged, we have appointed that a select number of foot shall be presently taken out of our trained bands, and brought to our city of York, or such other rendezvous as the General of our Army shall appoint, there to attend our person & standard; of which number we require & command that you cause to be forthwith selected out of the trained bands in our county of Cambridge 400, in our county of Suffolk 1500, & in our county of Dorset 700, of the most able men, which, together with their arms complete, you are to cause to be presently put in readiness, & to be weekly exercised. (Directions as to the admission of substitutes, the charges of the journey, &c.) And our will & command is that you cause to be forthwith selected out of the troop of horse in Cambridge 40 horse, in Suffolk 150 horse, and in Dorset 50 horse, to be armed, & exercised weekly, so as to be ready to march to the rendezvous.

P. 388. Whitehall, 20 March 1638(-9).—Council letter to [the Earl of Suffolk].

Giving directions touching the selection of some of the foot of the trained bands, viz. 300 out of Cambridge and 1200 out of Suffolk, as required by his Majesty's letters (see p. 393). They are to be embarked & transported to such place of the Northern parts as shall be directed by the Earl Marshal, Lord General of his Majesty's Army. Two parts are to be muskets, and a third part pikes. The charge of performing these directions is to be levied upon the country, which is to be repaid out of the Exchequer.

P. 390. Stowmarket, 8 March 1638(-9).—[The Deputy Lieutenants] to the Captains.

Orders touching the selection of horse & foot, to attend his Majesty's person & standard at the city of York or elsewhere, and touching their exercise and arms. If any trained soldier, desirous to stay at home, being unable in body or unfit by reason of their (*sic*) charge for this employment, shall offer unto you some other sufficient man of the same county to be impressed & armed at his charge, you may excuse the trained soldier and list the person so offered unto you, if you think him every way able & sufficient, in his room. And we further order you, that every soldier in your company be ready with a snapsack.

P. 391. Whitehall, 30 March 1639.—Council letter to [the Earl of Suffolk].

Take order that all the muskets sent with the trained soldiers be of a bore [and] the pikes of a length, and that the arms be of the lightest & most serviceable. Two deputy lieutenants from each county (Suff. and Camb.), with the muster-masters, are to be at the ports to see them all mustered at their embarking, and that the lists or rolls be certified to the Lord General.

P.S.—Give order that there be allowed for the charge of transporting the 1200 trained soldiers of Suffolk from Harwich to the rendezvous after the rate of 8*d*. a man per diem for 17 days; and that the 400 men which we required to be raised in Suffolk be levied by an imprest, for which money is in Mr. Moore your secretary's hands.

Letter from the Earl thereupon. Mentions Mr. John Waldegrave, deputy muster-master to Captain Wodehouse, the deputy lieutenants of Ipswich, and the trained bands of that town.

P. 393. Palace at Westminster, 19 March 1638-9.—The King to Theophilus Earl of Suffolk, Lord Warden of the Cinque Ports and Lieutenant General of Cambridge and Suffolk.

Whereas we required you to cause men to be selected from the trained bands in Cambridge and Suffolk . . . .; forasmuch [as] those factious and rebellious spirits in Scotland continue still their warlike preparations, and proceed with as much disobedience as ever, we have therefore with the advice of our Privy Council resolved to provide in the best manner we may for defence & preservation of this our Kingdom. Cause 300 of the 400 in Cambridge and 1200 of the 1500 in Suffolk to be brought to Yarmouth on 12th April and to Harwich on 10th April respectively; two parts to be muskets, and the third part pikes, and to be transported to such place of the northern parts as shall be appointed by the General of our army.

Letter from [the Deputy Lieutenants of Suffolk] to the Captains and warrant to the chief Constables on the same subject. The latter recites as follows: Whereas we have received two several letters from his Majesty under his privy signet together with the commands of the Privy Council, importing that under pretence of religion divers disorders & tumults have been raised in Scotland & fomented by factious spirits there, whose chief aim is not only to shake off monarchical government & what is justly descended upon his most excellent Majesty, but in all likelihood to invade this Kingdom, as by their hostile preparations is apparent, with other important considerations, whereby his Majesty is enforced to arm himself for his own & his loyal subjects' safety, together with their wives & children and goods, & therefore hath required us to make several levies both of men & money, whereof 400 men are to be levied, coated, and conducted to Selby upon Owse, near York, and 1200 more, to be drawn out of the trained bands, to be conducted, coated, & embarked at Harwich to such place of rendezvous as the Lord General shall appoint; all which charge we have, as near as we can, cast up, and find it will amount unto 1500*l*. These are therefore by virtue of the said letters to require you to bring into Bury, the 8th day of April next, by eight of the clock in the morning, at the Angel, your proportionable part of 600 able men, that out of them may be selected such & so many for his Majesty's service as we are commanded, and also your proportion of 1500*l*., according to former & usual levies, with your proportion of coats, to be either blue lined with yellow, or grey lined with red, or red lined with white; the price not to exceed the sum of 10 or 11 shillings; all which charge shall be repaid you out of the general levy. You are to pay out of the moneys you collect to the captains in your Hundred or their officers deputed, when the soldiers march to Harwich, 8*d*. a day for every soldier and 6*s*. 8*d*. a day to every such officer deputed; and to charge so many carts as will suffice to carry their arms. These levies will be repaid out of his Majesty's Exchequer, as in former times.

P. 396.—The names of such as sent arms, and of the soldiers which were taken out of the trained band of Sir Robert Crane, Kt. and Bart., and were to be embarked at Harwich the 10th of April 1639.

Many names of persons and places.

P. 397.—The names of those soldiers which were imprest, listed, & to be sent away out of the Franchise of Bury, being their proportion of the 400 sent out of the county.

Many names of persons and places.

P. 398.—A note of what arms were sent back to Sir Robert Crane for his company, being part of the arms sent for the service in the North.

33 muskets, 14 bandaliers, 3 rests, 8 gorgets, 13 corslets and a bad one, 22 swords, 32 headpieces, & 15 pikes.

P. 401. Whitehall, 30 April 1639.—Council letter to [the Earl of Suffolk].

However we cannot conceive that your Lordship would omit a service so much importing the safety and defence of the realm, especially in these times of action, yet we have thought good by these our letters, according to our usual manner yearly, to pray & require your Lordship to cause a General Muster and view to be taken this summer, at such times as your Lordship shall think fittest, of all the arms & trained bands, both horse & foot, within those counties under your Lordship's Lieutenancy; returning a perfect muster roll & certificate thereof. In former years we required that the muster-rolls should be returned to Mr. Meautis, Clerk of the Council and muster-master general, but henceforth they are to be sent & directed immediately unto the Board.

Letter from the Earl thereupon. Besides, I may not omit to give you thanks from the Lords of the Council for your great care and well performance of his Majesty's service in sending your men of the trained bands by Marquis Hambleton; which was so well liked of, as their Lordships have written unto me, they will recommend your good service therein unto his Majesty. Dated at Suffolk House.

P. 403. Whitehall, 25 Aug. 1639.—Council letter to [the Deputy Lieutenants of Suffolk].

Whereas upon the discharging and disbanding of his Majesty's Army in the Northern parts there was by his Majesty's gracious command a liberal & large sum of money delivered to every conductor, to be distributed & paid unto the soldiers in their return home: forasmuch as great complaints have been made that the conductors have not paid the same, but converted a great part of it to their own use, thereby exposing the soldiers to much misery: we require you to call the conductors for that county and some of the soldiers before you, and inquire what abuses of that kind have been committed, and to certify the names of the offenders, taking security for their appearance here.

P. 404.—Names of three serjeants, with the numbers of men they conducted into Suffolk, and the amounts they received.

P. 405. Whitehall, 20th (or 10th?) June 1639.—Council letter to [the Earl of Suffolk].

Whereas you were commanded in February last to cause a certain number of foot & horse to be selected out of the trained bands; forasmuch as his Majesty's army is for the present dismissed, you are to give order to the deputy lieutenants to forbear training that selected number otherwise than as the other trained bands. The moneys levied for coating & conduct, or providing with horse or arms, are to be restored to those from whom they were collected.

P.S.—Give order for discharge of the watching of beacons.

Letter from the Earl thereupon.

P. 407. Whitehall, 1 Nov. 1639.—Council letter to the Earl of Suffolk.

Whereas upon the occasion of the arrival of a great navy together with a great proportion of land soldiers in the Downs, we did lately write on 12th Sept. for having in readiness the trained bands and for watching the beacons in the Cinque Ports, Suffolk, and Dorset: in regard the occasion is now past, we have thought fit to discharge any further execution of the said directions.

P. 409. From my house in Queen Street, 19 March 1639[-40].—A. Earl of Northumberland, Lord Admiral, to Sir Roger North, Sir Robert Crane, and Edmund Pooley, Esq., Deputy Lieutenants of Suffolk.

I am informed that Mr. John Harvy according to his commission hath raised a troop of horse for his Majesty's service, to be employed in this present expedition, and that the said troop is drawn together at Bury. As it would be inconvenient to send a commissary to muster them, I am to pray you to repair to Bury and carefully muster & enroll the said troop, sending one certificate to myself, and another to Sir William Uvedall, Treasurer at Wars.

P. 411. Palace of Westminster, 17 March 15 Chas. I.—Royal warrant to [the Earl of Suffolk].

The great care we have had of the safety of this our Kingdom and the peace of our subjects hath been of late manifested unto them by the chargeable & warlike preparations we made to withstand the disloyal designs of such ill affected persons who, as much as in them lay, endeavoured the disturbance of both; nor is it at present unknown to our subjects how just reasons we have to continue the same preparations and to be in like readiness as formerly; and therefore have with the advice of our Privy Council thought fit and do by these presents authorise & require you to cause three hundred able and serviceable men for the wars to be levied in that our county of Cambridge, three hundred men in our Cinque Ports, six hundred men in our county of Dorset, and six hundred like able men in that our county of Suffolk, under your Lieutenancy, and to observe in the choice of the men and the ordering & disposing of them such directions as you shall herewith receive by letters from the Lords & others of our Privy Council.

P. 413. Whitehall, 26 March 1640.—Council letter to [the Earl of Suffolk].

Giving instructions for the execution of the preceding warrant. 3 *pages*. *See Rushworth*, III. 1090.

P. 416. Same date.—The same to the same.

Touching the provision of horses and carters for the artillery and ammunition. *See Rushworth*, III. 1093.

P 417. Suffolk House, 1 April 1640.—Theo. Earl of Suffolk to [the Deputy Lieutenants of Suffolk].

Praying them, as they tender his Majesty's service, to attend to the execution of the foregoing letters.

Ib.—[Memorandum.]

Lieutenant Little and Serjeant Godbould, conductors of the 87 soldiers which were taken out of Sir Robert Crane's band, Sir Philip Parker's and Captain Waldgrave's bands, and went from Hadleigh the 29th of May 1640 to Beckels as their general rendezvous, for which they were allowed - - - - - - - - 3*l*. 0*s*. 0*d*.

The pay for the soldiers for four days in the march at 8*d*. per diem for 87 soldiers - - - - - - - 11*l*. 12*s*. 0*d*.

For 87 soldiers for 10 days - - - - - 29*l*. 0*s*. 0*d*.

P. 418.—The proportion for every Hundred within the county of Suffolk for the levying of 1500*l*. in the whole county.

The names of the Hundreds are given under the heads of—The Franchise of Bury St. Edmunds, The Liberty of St. Etheldred, The Guildable; with the sums due from each.

P. 419. Bury St. Edmund's, 10 April 1640.—[The Deputy Lieutenants of Suffolk] to the chief Constables of the Hundred of ——.

600 men are to be selected out of the trained bands in this county, and to be exercised by officers to be sent by the Earl of Northumberland, Lord General, which number will amount to 29 men out of every trained band, besides the town of Ipswich, their number being 18. We are required to levy money for coating them, and you are to provide coats

at 10*s.* or 11*s.* each, better than they were last year; and for the colour, we would have them red lined with white. Each soldier is to be allowed 8*d.* for every day of exercise. All are to meet at Beckles on 27th May, where they are to remain till 6th June, to be exercised. 60 horses & 20 able carters are to be provided for the artillery, and to be at Newcastle-upon-Tyne the 15th June. 10*l.* is a reasonable price for drawing-horses. All these charges will amount to 1500*l.* at least, and these are to require you (as much as in us lieth) to levy your proportion thereof.

P. 420. Whitehall, 27 May 1640.—Council letter to [the Earl of Suffolk].

Deferring the date fixed for the horses & carters to be at Newcastle from 15th June to 15th July. *See State Papers, Domestic.*

P. 421. Suffolk House, 29 May 1640.—Theo. Earl of Suffolk to [the Deputy Lieutenants of Suffolk].

I received a letter from you, Sir Robert Crane and Mr. Waldegrave, with returns of some towns and hamlets that refuse to pay the levies made by you for this service, but you return no particular men whereby course may be taken against them. These are therefore to pray and require you with all possible speed in your several divisions to return the names & surnames and places of abode of such persons as refuse to pay or to give obedience to your warrants sent forth for this weighty service, or some of the best in each township, whereupon you shall receive such farther directions as his Majesty with the advice of the Privy Council shall think meetest in a cause of this high consequence.

P.S.—You are also to return the names of such as refuse to receive press money, and that run away after they have received it, that some of them may be made examples.

Ib. Chilton, 30 May 1640.—[The Deputy Lieutenants of Suffolk] to the chief Constables of the Hundred of ——.

These are by virtue of letters received (as much as in us lieth) to require you, according to the contents of the said letters, that you do with all speed return us, or one of us, under the hands of every petty constable in their several towns, the names, surnames, & titles, with the places of abode, of all those persons that do refuse to pay such moneys as are assessed upon them by your warrant, for the coat and conduct money; which several notes we are to return up to our Lord Lieutenant (an act very unpleasing to us); of the due execution whereof fail not.

P. 422.—The names of Soldiers impressed for his Majesty's service, 27th May 1640.

28 names, with the names of the persons in whose stead they served, and of the places to which they belonged. In one case a soldier served for two persons.

P. 423. Chilton, 26 May 1640.—[Sir Robert Crane ?] to the Earl of Suffolk.

I have this day sent toward the general rendezvous for this county at Beckles those soldiers that were taken out of Sir Philip Parker's company, Captain Waldegrave's, and my own, who have been exercised once a week according to direction, and the rest of the week we were forced to pay them at their going away, or else they would not have stirred a foot. Of this company that have been pressed & exercised there is (*sic*) run away twenty one, which I have made out hue & cry after; and I fear a great many of the rest will follow, for that the last year there were some that ran away, which we committed to prison and had no punishment. There are many that doth absolutely refuse to take impress money, which we have committed to gaol, for want of sureties for their good behaviour, until we may receive your Honor's direction what to do with them.

P. 423. *No date.*—[The Deputy Lieutenants of Suffolk to the Earl of Suffolk.]

We made out warrants to the chief constables of the Hundreds of Babergh, Cosford, and Sampford to return the names of those who refused to contribute to the charge of coat & conduct money, but their returns are not so full as we required by reason of the petty constables' unperfect return; besides, the chief constables of the rest of the hundreds acquaint us with many that refuse in all parts of the country, but we had not time to send our warrants to them. We know not what to do for pay of the soldiers at the general rendezvous, who are so mutinous as we fear that when they come together there will be no ruling of them. We return a list of the names of persons refusing press money in the said three Hundreds, as also of such who being impressed are since run away. [*The list is not given.*]

P. 424. Whitehall, 12 June 1640.—Council letter to the Deputy Lieutenants of Suffolk.

We have been made acquainted with a letter from some of you to the Board of the 8th of this present, and find that the levies of soldiers and the raising of coat & conduct money formerly committed to your care by the Earl of Suffolk, deceased, late Lord Lieutenant, is like to be retarded, in regard you conceive your power is determined by his Lordship's death. These are to authorise you to proceed therein. We have granted our warrants and sent messengers for the apprehending & bringing before the Board of some of the delinquents who refuse to pay the rates assessed on them for this service.

P. 425. At Court, 8 June 1640.—[Sir] Tho. Jermyn to Sir William Playter, Sir Ro. Crane, and William Waldegrave, Esq.

The letter you were pleased to send to me, not knowing what haste the contents might import, coming to my hands in the forenoon this present Sunday, I shewed presently to his Majesty, who commanded me to cause the Clerk of the Council to read it in the afternoon at the Board, his Majesty being there; since which time I understand by his Majesty that he is resolved presently to appoint a Lord Lieftenant for that County, and to send him immediately down, by whom you shall fully know his Majesty's pleasure. In the mean time he doubts not but you will be ready with all care & diligence to advance his service in this present occasion, his Majesty having ever had a very good opinion of the love and duty of that County, in which I take myself to have such interest as it must very much grieve me to see it in the least degree diminisht. I shall, I think, wait upon my Lord Lieutenant myself down, whose coming I will hasten all I can.

P. 426.—The allowance that was made to Edmond Willis, conductor of 40 horses to Newcastle-upon-Tyne, 6 July 1640. Total, 47*l.* 14*s.* 8*d.*; including 2*l.* 13*s.* 4*d.* for ferrying over four ferries.

Ib.—The names of the Hundreds and high Constables of the same by whom this charge was paid.

Ib.—A note of such moneys as were paid to John Spaldin for necessaries for certain soldiers. Total, 9*l.* 10*s.*

P. 427. Court at Oatelands, 5 Aug. at night, 1640.—[Sir] Tho. Jermyn to [the Deputy Lieutenants of Suffolk].

It coming to my knowledge that his Majesty had a purpose to contract his Army, I apprehended that it would not be ungrateful to the country if those 160 men for the supplies of the 600 might be stayed at home, & as much of the charge as possible may be, to be spared; and to that end I presently moved his Majesty, whose pleasure therein is that if they be not yet sent away, they be stayed and discharged of this service. Captain Bosom shall give them some competent sum to bring them back again. If the 20 draught-horses be not gone, they also may be stayed. Both the King and the Lords of the Council take in very good part your care & industry for his Majesty's service. The scattering of the plague about most of the King's houses has severed their Lordships.

P. 429. Audly End, 1 Sept. 1640.—James Earl of Suffolk to [the Deputy Lieutenants].

You shall receive here inclosed letters from the Lord General his excellence. Put them in execution with all speed.

Ib. Arundel House, 27 Aug. 1640.—The Earl of Arundel and Surrey to [the Earl of Suffolk].

Whereas you have received an order from his Majesty dated 19th Aug. to put in readiness the trained bands in that county of your Lieuftenancy, with such further forces of horse & foot as you could possibly raise, to march upon certain days' warning, for repelling & suppressing the rebellious invasion of the Scots, to which end his Majesty hath adventured his own royal person, since whose departure I and others of the Privy Council have been informed that a great army of the Scots are now upon their march towards Newcastle-upon-Tyne; therefore, according to his Majesty's commission to me as Captain General of all his forces on this side of the River Trent, as well for the safeguard of the Queen, Prince Charles, & the rest of the Royal children, as for the safety of this realm, I require your Lordship to put the said trained bands in readiness to march upon 24 hours' warning when you shall receive order from me or my Lieuftenant. All other persons able in body or estate to do service are also to be in readiness.

P. 431. Stowe Markett, 7 Sept. 1640.—[Sir] R. Crane, Will. Hervy, and Roger North to the Deputy Lieutenants (*sic*; qu. Constables?).

To have all the trained bands in readiness upon 24 hours' warning, pursuant to the foregoing letters. The writers speak of the Earl of Suffolk as one of the Lord Lieutenants of this county.

P. 432. Hampton Court, 22 Sept. 1640.—Sir Tho. Jermyn to [the Deputy Lieutenants].

My long silence is due to the manifold business that have (*sic*) not a little perplext us here. I conceived that after the end of the harvest had been the fittest time to have warned the troops & arms of the country, and according to that calculation had demanded my leave of her Majesty to have gone down in the end of this week, but it pleased God to stay me with a violent fit of sickness. I hope soon to wait upon you at Bury. Touching your commis[sions] of deputation, I have them all lying by me, but have stayed for my Lord of Suffolk's hand.

P. 433. Same date.—The same to the same.

I send two letters from the Council. Touching the letter that speaks of the reason of people's serving at their proper charge in times of imminent danger, such as is our case now, the Scots having actually invaded the realm, and hold[ing] no inconsiderable part thereof by their garrisons, I rest assured that County will not be behind in his Majesty's service and their own preservation; but, formy part, if I had been at the

Board when this letter were (*sic*) ordered, I should rather have advised to have taken it for granted that the country would have done it than stir any question, or give them any imagination that it would be otherwise.

Pp. 434–435. Whitehall, 16 Sept. 1640.—Two Council letters to [the Earl of Suffolk].

Ordering the trained bands to be put in readiness against the Scotch rebels, &c. *See Rushworth*, III. 1268, 1269.

On a loose leaf. No date.—Arthur Goodwin, Thom. Turrell, and Richard Greenvill to ——.

Gentlemen,—We shall acquaint you that the Lord General hath afforded us about 2000 or 1500 (*sic*) horse and dragoneers to be aiding to your and our neighbour county, to preserve us all from plundering; but if the county will not rise & be helpful herein, his Lordship will withdraw his forces again, for it will not be safe for them to be so far from his Lordship & so near the enemy, & he can not spare us more. Our countrymen are all rising, and we hope you will do the like, as well for your own security as ours. We are promised the help of Hartfordshire, and presume that Northamptonshire & their associates will join with us. We desire you that in raising your country (*sic*) they may be directed to come on horseback as many as can, & the rest on foot, & to bring with them the best arms they have, and one month's pay, which if they cannot provide themselves, that the towns may furnish them and send it after them. We shall expect the assistance of the country with all possible speed at Windover by Wednesday at the farthest. We intend, God willing, to be at Windover with those Parliament forces to morrow. If your country will appear zealous a short time, [it] will put an end to those troubles, and therefore let us now acquit our selves like men or never; it concerns us all alike; therefore we hope your well affected gentry and your selves will come along with your countrymen, for their better encouragement. Thus, with our prayers to God for His blessing herein, we take our leaves, and rest

Your very loving friends to serve you,

ARTHUR GOODWIN,
THOM. TURRELL,
RICH. GREENVILL.

On the back of the same leaf: The Writ that his Majesty sent down for the Ship Money, Anno Dom. 1639.

Under this head are given the names of the counties, with the amount charged on each. Total, 212,400*l*.

Here follow many blank pages.

At the other end of the book are a few more copies, as follow:

P. 1. *No date.* [1616–20.] The Lord Chief Justice of the King's Bench to ——.

At the last assizes holden for the county of Suffolk there were divers presentments made by the chief constables of the several Hundreds concerning cottages erected since 31 Eliz., but in many of them there wanteth the names of the parties that erected the cottages and of those who continue the same, and many new-erected cottages were not presented at all. Call the constables before you to perfect those presentments, that so the cottages erected by licence according to the Statute for the relief of the poor may continue, and the rest may be presented in better form at the next assizes. *Signed:* Your loving friend, Henry Mountigue.

Ib.—Statutes to be put in execution by the Justices of the Peace, by the direction of the Lord Chief Justice.

These directions refer to the wages of servants & manual labourers, the raising of stocks for putting out poor folks' children as apprentices, the relief of the old, lame, blind, & impotent poor, begging, absence from church, unlicensed alehouses, tippling, drunkenness, rogues or vagrants, negligent constables, inmates, the erection of cottages, and the repair of highways.

P. 4. *No date.*—[Sir] H. Mountigue and [Sir] John Doddridge to [the Justices of the Peace for Suffolk].

At the last summer assizes for Suffolk we gave directions for putting forth poor children as apprentices, expecting that at these assizes we should have been by you informed what you had done therein. The like directions we left with the Justices of the Peace for Norfolk, who now have made to appear that some of them have already placed 500 poor children apprentices. At the next assizes we will expect the like performance of your parts. If any freeholder or other person sufficient to take an apprentice be disobedient to our order, bind them (*sic*) over to appear before us.

P. 5. At the Assizes holden at Bury St. Edmund's, 11 March 8 Chas. I.—[Order by the Justices of Assize.]

We having taken serious considerations of the great increase of cottagers & inmates contrary to the law, and finding that the cottages ought to be pulled down, yet being informed by the Justices of the Peace that if the extremity of the law should be used against them, these poor people would be exposed to misery & become a burthen to the parishes where they are settled; which cottages & inmates may peradventure be fit to be allowed by the Justices of Assize in open assizes, or by the Justices of the Peace in open sessions, according to the Statute of 31 Eliz.; wherefore the Justices of the Peace are required by the Court to set down in writing what cottages & inmates there are in every parish, who are the inhabitants and who the reputed owners, how long the cottages have been erected, &c., and to return the same before the end of the next term, that such course may be taken as shall be agreeable to the country. It is ordered that when any new cottage shall be attempted to be erected which hath not a legal warrant, the high constables & petty constables & the Justices of the Peace, upon complaint thereof to them, do disturb & hinder the building & finishing thereof, and destroy the same before any inhabitants be placed therein.—Walker. [Sir John Walter, Lord Chief Baron ?]

P. 6. Same date.—A similar order to inquire as to the number of inns, alehouses, & victualling houses, the continual increase of which pesters the country; by what authority they have been allowed or licensed; and what number is fit to be continued by the advice of the minister & principal inhabitants of every parish.—Walker.

APPENDIX C.

LETTER-BOOK of the DEPUTY LIEUTENANTS and JUSTICES of the PEACE of SUFFOLK, 1664–1676.

P. 1. Whitehall, 31 Dec. 1664.—Royal warrant to the Lord Lieutenant of Suffolk.

In the Act for ordering the forces in the several counties it is provided that in case of danger to the Government it shall be lawful to us to levy for three years from 25 June 1662 the sum of 70,000 a year for defraying [the charges of] the Militia. By the advice of our Privy Council we did the last two years send letters to the Lieutenants and their Deputies to cause the said sums to be paid, being thereunto moved by the apparent danger in which the Government was by the plots and conspiracies of some unquiet spirits, who had designed the subversion thereof; and several sums remain in the hands of the Sheriffs or of the Collectors for that county. Our will is, that you call them to account, and they are hereby required to make speedy payment. You shall put the moneys in a trunk or chest with three locks, and deliver the same to the governor of the castle or garrison next adjacent to your Lieutenancy, to remain in safe custody till we signify our further order for the disbursement thereof, which shall be to the end appointed by the said Act, and no otherwise. You are also to certify us how any part of the collected sums has been disbursed. Further it is our will that the officers & soldiers do 14 days' duty this next year, allowing pay to the commission officers of horse & foot, viz. to a captain of horse 10*s*. a day, to a lieutenant of horse 6*s*., to a cornet 5*s*., and to a quarter-master of horse 4*s*.; to a captain of foot 8*s*., to a lieutenant 4*s*., and to an ensign 3*s*. The serjeants, corporals, & drummers are to be paid (out of the week's pay ordered by the Act for providing of trophies and paying non-commissioned officers) 2*s*. 6*d*. a day to a serjeant, & 2*s*. a day to a corporal and drummer, for 14 days' duty in the year. Some of the Lord Lieutenants have neglected to put their forces upon duty according to the Act. You are to give order that the forces do enter upon duty, and continue constantly from time to time to do so.

Letter from [James] Earl of Suffolk to the Deputy Lieutenants thereupon.

Also a letter from the Deputy Lieutenants as to the execution thereof, stating that 6,000*l*. are due to the King's use, but they hesitate to lodge it in Langer Fort. Signed: [Sir] Edm. Poley, [Sir] E. Bacon, [Sir] Rob. Broke, [Sir] Nich. Bacon, Tho. Waldegrave.

Pp. 5 *seq*.—Accounts and assessments relative to the tax for the Militia, with the names of officers of companies and the places of muster.

P. 12.—Order made at the Lent Assizes at Bury St. Edmund's, 1663, for the alteration and repairing of the Shire-house in Bury.

Also a Report of what was done therein (very minute), with a further order and an account, 1665.

P. 16. 30 March 1665.—Lord Chancellor Clarendon to the Justices of the Peace in co. Suffolk.

His Majesty being well assured as well by the confession of some desperate persons lately apprehended as by other credible informations that, notwithstanding all his unparalelled lenity and mercy towards all his subjects for their past offences, how great soever, there are still amongst them many seditious persons who, instead of being sorry for the ill they have done, are still contriving by all the means they can to involve the Kingdom in a new civil war, and in order thereunto have made choice of a small number who under the title of a Council hold correspondence with the foreign enemies to this Kingdom, and distribute their orders to some signal men of their party in the several counties, who have provided arms and listed men to be ready upon any short warning to draw together in a body, by which, with the help they promise themselves from abroad, they presume to be able to do much mischief, which his Majesty hopes (with the blessing of God upon his great care and vigilance) to prevent, and to that purpose hath writ to his Lords Lieutenants of the several counties that they and their Deputy Lieutenants may do what belongs to them. But his Majesty, taking notice of great negligence and remissness in too many Justices of the Peace in the exercise of the trust committed to them, hath commanded me to write to the Justices of all counties what his Majesty expects at their hands. I choose this time, that this letter may find you at your quarter sessions. Take care that it be communicated to those who are absent at your next monthly meeting, which it is most necessary you keep constantly. Many who are in the commission of the peace neglect to be sworn. Cause the clerk of the peace to return me their names; the King hath already given order to the Attorney General to proceed against them. Others fail to attend the assizes & sessions. The King frequently saith he takes himself to be particularly beholding to every good justice of the peace who is cheerful & active in his place. The justices should be most solicitous to free the country from seditious persons and unlawful meetings & conventicles; the principal end of which meetings is, as appears now by several examinations & confessions, to confirm each other in their malice against the Government, and in making collections for the support of those of their party who are listed to appear in any desperate undertaking, the very time whereof they have designed. Use your uttermost diligence to discover the machinations of those men whom you know to be ill affected, and to secure the persons of those whom you find forward to disturb, or dangerous to the public peace.

P. 18. Hampton Court, 4 July 1665.—The King to the Deputy Lieutenants and Justices of the Peace of Suffolk.

Our commissioners for the sick and wounded men in those parts and the Dutch prisoners are reduced to much extremity for money, the assignments we intend for them being not yet regulated in such manner as to make these payments, through the pressing necessities of the war, which have surprised us with great expense. Contrive some means to prevail in our name with our good subjects in those parts to advance such sums of money upon the security of the Royal Aid as shall be requisite to support that charge. We shall remember it always to their advantage. Pay the same to Sir William Doyly or any other of our said commissioners. The trade and prosperity as well as the honour and reputation of this Kingdom are concerned.

P. 19. 25 July 1665.—Resolved, that the sum of 5000*l*. be endeavoured to be advanced for his Majesty's service by the Deputy Lieutenants, Justices of the Peace, and other persons of interest in the county of Suffolk, in obedience to his Majesty's letter of the 4th, upon the security of the three months' assessment, part of the Royal Aid, which shall be due on 1 Feb. 1666[–7], upon condition that the said sum be repaid with interest to the lenders; with other conditions.

P. 20. Oxford, 23 Oct. 1665.—The King to James Earl of Suffolk, Lord Lieutenant.

The Dutch fleet hath appeared a second time upon our coasts. Take order to have the militia of that county in readiness to prevent any descent. *See State Papers, Domestic.*

Letter from the Earl of Suffolk to Sir Henry North and other Deputy Lieutenants thereupon.

Also a letter from Sir Henry North, Ger. Elwes, Hen. Crofts, and Tho. Waldegrave to ———, touching the same.

P. 22. Treasury Chambers, Westminster, 24 Nov. 1665.—[Sir] H. Vernon and Robert Savery to Walter Devereux, Esq., Sir Edm. Bacon, and others, commissioners for the Royal Aid in Suffolk.

Touching the dilatory manner in which the Royal Aid is collected. The late Parliament at Oxford, in the Act granting an additional Aid, has made provision for its more speedy collection, and the Lord Treasurer & Lord Ashley have desired us to acquaint you therewith. Sundry directions are given.

P. 23. Oxford, 23 Nov. 1665.—T. [Earl of] Southampton and [Lord] Ashley to [the Deputy Lieutenants ?].

His Majesty's honour and the concerns of this nation are deeply involved in this present engagement in the Dutch war, which led the two Houses of Parliament the last Session to present unto his Majesty a further supply of 1,250,000*l.*; and because the present charge of that war required the advance of these moneys, there was by another part of that Act an invitation to all well affected to make loans of money and serve (send ?) in commodities necessary for that service, with provision for repayment with interest, &c. Use your utmost diligence for the speedy raising of these different moneys, keeping the sums so distinct that they may be entered apart in the Receipt of the Exchequer, but the same warrants will serve for assessing the several rates under both Acts, &c.

P. 24.—Form of the High Sheriff's oath. 48 *lines*.

P. 25. Oxford, 25 Jan. 1665(–6).—The King to the Lord Lieutenant or Deputy Lieutenants of Suffolk.

An invasion is intended by foreign enemies. Draw together into a body all the militia of that county, both horse & foot, near the ports or sea-coasts. The beacons to be repaired and watched. *See State Papers, Domestic.*

P. 26. Whitehall, 3 Feb. 1665(–6).—The King to [the Earl of Suffolk].

Revoking the foregoing order, but the beacons are to be kept in readiness to be fired, &c. *See State Papers, Domestic, under* 4 *Feb.*

P. 27.—Orders made by the Deputy Lieutenants at Snape, 12 Feb. 1665(–6).

Touching the firing of beacons. Forces on the sea-coast to do duty for 14 days, under command of Sir John Rous and Sir Philip Parker, two of the colonels of foot regiments in this county. Also touching ammunition.

Ib. Snape, 7 Feb. 1665(–6).—The Deputy Lieutenants to Lord Arlington, principal Secretary of State.

Touching the execution of the King's letters of 25 Jan. and [3 Feb.].

P. 28. Saxmundham, 3 Feb. 1665(–6).—Letters from the same to Secretary Morice and the Earl of Suffolk, on the same subject.

P. 29. Whitehall, 25 June 1666.—The King to the Lord Lieutenant and the Deputy Lieutenants.

Upon several intelligences from abroad we have reason to doubt that there are preparations made by our enemies towards an invasion of this our kingdom. We have concluded it requisite to put the Militia in a good posture of defence. Repair to some convenient place within your Lieutenancy, thereby to unite the gentry and to quicken all under your command to the discharge of their respective duties, that so the Militia may be in a readiness. Directions are given as to filling up vacancies in the companies, their arms, ammunition, &c. To avoid expense &

trouble to the country in this time of barvest, musters need not be held for the present. The beacons are to be watched, and fired as there shall be occasion. The assessment ordained by the Act shall be raised and levied.

P. 31. —— 29 June 1666.—The Earl of Suffolk to Sir Edmond Bacon; to be communicated to the rest of the Deputy Lieutenants.

Urging the execution of the preceding letter. Many complaints may arise upon the charging of arms where two or three have been joined together in one charge, and the alterations which have since such charge happened by the change of estates either by death or otherwise; all the particulars of which kind must be best known to the respective captains of companies.

P. 32. At a general meeting at Sir Henry Felton's at Playford upon Wednesday the 4th of July, James Earl of Suffolk, Lord Lieutenant of Suffolk, Sir Edmond Bacon, Sir Henry Felton, Sir Charles Gawdy, Sir Nicholas Bacon, Sir George Reve, and Thomas Waldegrave, Esq., being present:

His Lordship had his Majesty's letter read, and then gave certain orders (set out) for its execution. Sir Nicholas Bacon is to render his account to Sir Edmond Bacon and others of moneys received by him, and what ammunition he hath in magazine, &c. The regiments of Sir Edmond Bacon, Sir John Rous, Sir Henry North, and Sir Philip Parker are to be at a certain places, in case of invasion.

P. 33. Whitehall, 13 July 1666.—Royal warrant to [the Earl of Suffolk].

We have already upon different occasions signified to you the reasons we had to suspect an invasion intended of these our Kingdoms by our enemies from abroad, and how much it's the duty of our good subjects to join with us in our care and provision for the timely preventing these designs, the greatest ground of which we found to have been a relief and expectation they were led into by some malicious fugitives of our own subjects of public distractions and insurrections that would break out amongst us here at home. We have thought fit again to warn you of the same, that you have a particular eye to those you shall have reason to suspect, and secure the most dangerous among them, more especially those that keep horses or arms above their rank, which you are to seize; and find out what may be contriving or carrying on prejudicial to the peace of our Kingdoms and government. If any enemies attempt to land or make a descent to rob and spoil our subjects, you are to give strict order that immediately they be fallen upon, and no quarter be given to such of them as shall be so taken. By our letters of the 2nd inst., we directed that the remaining part of the three years' Militia money should be paid to Sir Stephen Fox or his order, but you shall first pay out the 14 days' pay of this year to the common officers.

P. 34. Whitehall, 24 Nov. 1666.—Royal warrant to James Earl of Suffolk, Lord Lieutenant of Suffolk.

In accordance with the Address made to us by Parliament, you are to give order that all Popish Recusants refusing to take the oaths of supremacy and allegiance shall be disarmed, &c. *See State Papers, Domestic.*

Letter from the Earl thereupon.

P. 36. Whitehall, 6 April 1667.—The Earl of Suffolk to [the Deputy Lieutenants].

I am commanded by His Majesty to put the Militia into such a posture as may best secure the quiet & peace of the country. Order the officers to see that all the soldiers have their arms ready fixed, to be ready at an hour's warning, and the beacons well watched.

Ib. Ipswich, 7 April 1668.—Ed. Keene to George Gipps, Esq., at Mr. Joseph Hornbey's in Broad Street, London.

Ever since I was last with you at Bury to make out the account, I have been so extremely perplexed and confounded for the great arrear upon me, that I could not take the journey to London, &c.

P. 37. Treasury Chambers, Whitehall, 10 April 1668.—[The Duke of] Albemarle, [Sir] T. Clifford, and [Sir] W. Coventry, [Lords of the Treasury,] to Sir Edm. Bacon and others, commissioners for the Aids in the divisions of Ipswich and Woodbridge.

We have taken notice from Mr. Gipps, receiver general of the Royal Aid and additional supply in Suffolk, that Mr. Edward Keene, the high collector of those divisions, is in arrear above 5000*l*. There must be no diminution or abatement, &c.

Letter in reply to the preceding. The offender had withdrawn, and his property had been seized. The late visitation has rendered our public meetings both unfrequent and unsafe.

Also, a resolution passed at a meeting of the commissioners at the Greyhound in Ipswich, touching the same matter.

P. 41. Whitehall, 5 June 1671.—The Earl of Suffolk to [the Deputy Lieutenants].

Not knowing how soon his Majesty may order a muster of the trained forces in your country, and having some reason to fear that the long discontinuance of musters may have occasioned great alterations in your Militia, I direct you to inspect the muster-rolls and supply the arms that you shall find changed or wanting, &c.

Other letters, resolutions, and orders relative to the same matter, and to musters, 1671–1672. The names of officers (some newly commissioned) are given.

P. 48. Whitehall, 26 March 1672.—The Privy Council to the Earl of Suffolk.

His Majesty hath been informed that at this time, when the good of his service and safety of this Kingdom do require the impresting of men for furnishing his Majesty's Fleets now setting forth to sea, many seamen and watermen fit for that service have withdrawn themselves from their usual habitations into the land countries, where they lie concealed to avoid his service, in hopes that when his Majesty's Fleet shall be out at sea, they may find more profitable employment by sailing in colliers' and merchants' ships. Search is to be made in Suffolk and Cambridge for all such loose & unknown persons as have not been inhabiting there for two months at the least, &c.

P. 49. [1673.]—Letter from —— to the Lord Treasurer, with a certificate touching the payment of the eighteen months' assessment in the several Hundreds of Suffolk.

P. 50. Ipswich, 1 July 1673.—Sir Charles Gaudy, Sir Robert Brooke, and Sir Nicholas Bacon to Sir Edmund Bacon.

We have not now time to acquaint you with the trouble we have had since the attendance of this regiment at the Fort. Having received his Majesty's commands for supplying the Fort with two companies at a time, we have so long obeyed them that this whole regiment hath performed the duty. Yesterday we sent to Sir John Pettus to relieve our two last companies. Take care that two of your companies which lie most convenient may be at Landguard Fort upon Sunday next, to relieve Sir John Pettus's two, &c.

Letter from Pettus on the same matter, mentioning his mother's death and funeral.

P. 52. —— 11 April 1674.—The Earl of Suffolk to [the Deputy Lieutenants].

By the long discontinuance of the musters of the several troops of horse and companies of foot of the trained forces in co. Suffolk, the Militia of the same is in a very unsettled condition. I therefore appoint a muster, &c.

P. 53. Bury, 25 April 1674.—Tho. Hervy and James Reynolds to ——.

Touching a muster of the late Sir Henry North's regiment. Sir Nicholas Bacon signified to the Deputy Lieutenants who met at Ipswich that the late loss of his Lady made him unfit to appear there. Particulars are given as to certain regiments and officers.

P. 54. Whitehall, 15 Nov. 1674.—The King to the Lord Lieutenant of Suffolk.

By our proclamation of 25 April last we prohibited our subjects to transport themselves out of this Kingdom into the service of any foreign prince or state without our leave; yet we receive daily information of several persons who still presume in divers places of this realm to list men and transport them into foreign parts. You are to seize and secure such persons. The commissioners of our Customs at London have sent orders to their under officers in our several ports to be vigilant herein, and you are to give them all aid.

P. 55. Whitehall, 10 Aug. 1675.—The Earl of Suffolk to [the Deputy Lieutenants].

The accounts of the moneys raised by virtue of the Act for ordering the Militia forces have not been certified at the quarter sessions as the Act directs.

Ib. Newmarkett, 13 April 1676.—The Deputy Lieutenants to the Lord Lieutenant.

Offering certain proposals touching the musters of companies and regiments, the appointment of officers, &c. The last proposal is, that where the deputy lieutenants see cause to make charges, they do not charge above two or three owners at most to the finding of a horse or foot arms; and that all estates of 100*l.* per annum be turned into foot arms, and estates of 20*l.* per annum be turned into town arms, to be provided by the constables of each town; no estate under 5*l.* per annum to be charged.

P. 57. Same date.—Orders touching musters at Bury, Sudbury, &c.

Here many pages were originally left blank, but some few have been used for farming accounts of about 1800. At the other end of the book there are a few pages of accounts of receipts and payments in respect of musters, in 1665, 1666, and 1667.

APPENDIX D.

PROCEEDINGS in PARLIAMENT, Royal letters, &c., 1625-1628, as follow:

The Duke of Buckingham's titles.

Dr. Turner's speech in Parliament, 11 March 1625(-6).

[The Speaker's address to the King], Banqueting-house, 14 March 1625(-6).

His Majesty's answer to the Commons, 14 March 1625(-6).

His Majesty's letter to [the Speaker of] the Commons, 20 March 1625(-6).

[Notes of agenda,] 27, 28, and 29 March 1626.

The King's speech to both Houses, 29 March.

The Lord Keeper's speech to the same.

A further speech by the King.

An abstract of the Account from the Council of War, delivered to the Commons, showing how the three subsidies and the three fifteens had been expended in 1625, viz., the amounts paid under warrants for the four regiments in the Low Countries, for the Navy, for the office of the Ordnance and the Forts in England, for Ireland, for the service under Count Mansfeild, &c.

The humble Remonstrance of the Commons to the King (no date).

A Remonstrance and Petition by the Commons to the King, 5 May 1626.

[Proposition by Sir William Walter,] Monday afternoon, 20 March 1625(-6).

The humble Remonstrances and Petition of the Peers (no date).

The Bishop of Lincoln's submissive letter to his Majesty (no date).

Lord Conway's letter to the Earl of Bristol, 24 March 1625(-6).

The Earl of Bristol's Answer, 30 March 1626.

The King's letter to Bristol, 20 Jan. 1625(-6).

Petition of John Earl of Bristol to the Lords.

The Lord Keeper's letter to the Earl of Bristol, 21 March 1625(-6).

The Earl of Bristol's answer to my Lord Keeper, 12 April 1626.

The Lord Keeper's speech in the higher House, 21 April 1626.

Petition of the Countess of Bristol.

Orders dated 25 April and 1 May.

Articles of the Earl of Bristol whereby he chargeth the Duke of Buckingham, 1 May 1626.

Motions, 3 & 4 May 1626.

The Earl of Bristol's speech at the Bar by way of narration, 6 May 1626.

His speech in Parliament, Friday, 19 May 1626.

Reasons why the Lords should not give way to the proceedings against the Earl of Bristol, &c.

Heads of the grievances against the Duke, 10 May 1626.

The King's speech in the Upper House, 11 May 1626; with notes of what took place afterwards, 11 and 12 May.

The message from the House of Commons to the Lords, delivered after his Majesty was departed.

Protestation to be made by every member of the House touching the words spoken by Sir Dudley Digges, 13 May 1626.

Questions touching the last complaint against the Duke, 28 April 1626.

[Speech by ?] Sir John Elliott.

The Commons' Declaration and Impeachment against the Duke of Buckingham.

Sir Dudley Diggs's prologue to the Articles of grievances against the Duke.

[Speech by] Mr. Harbert.

Mr. John Seldon's speech.

Mr. Sherland's inlardgment.

Mr. Pym's speech on the 11th & 12th Articles.

Mr. Wainsford's exposition on the 13th Article.

Sir John Elliot's Epilogue.

Letter from the King to [Justices of the Peace], with Instructions touching the raising of a supply, 7 July 1626. *See State Papers, Domestic, and Appendix B., ante.*

Letter from the Privy Council to the same, explaining the foregoing, 27 July 1626. *See as above.*

Instructions to be followed and observed by his Majesty's commissioners for the loan of money to his Majesty. 17 paragraphs.

The names of the Lords Itinerant appointed to work the Loan in several counties.

A declaration of his Majesty's clear intention in requiring a loan, 7 Oct. 1626.

His Majesty's speech in Parliament, 17 March 1627(-8).

Then follow many blank leaves, some of which have been used for a list of books (or catalogue of a library?), 18th cent.

APPENDIX E.

LETTERS from the REV. JOHN NIXON to MISS [MARY] BACON.

Towcester, 14th Septr. 1745.

Madam,—The honour of your last, which I beg leave to acknowledge with all due respect, arrived at my house while I was engaged in a tour into the north, the pleasures of which can be exceeded only by that which I should receive could I be persuaded that a recital of my adventures would agreeably amuse you. My companion was the same gentleman who travelled with me last summer, and our first sally was to *Warwick*, a place which (tho' often seen) always affords me new pleasure; especially the Castle, whose bold fortifications and martial air of defence, attempered with all the agreemens of nature and art, remind us of the character of its once famous Lord (*Guy*), who, after having signalized himself by all the heroic exploits of war, submitted to languish at the feet of fair Phyllis. Its present possessor, *Lord Brook*, has lately fitted up a new apartment in it in a very elegant taste, which shows us among other things the prodigious improvement of our paper-tapestry; several of the rooms (particularly Lady Brook's dressing room) being hung with that furniture with most surprising neatness and beauty. From hence (after a day's stay) we proceeded to visit *Kenilworth Castle*, the majestic ruins of which, while the spectator at the same time resolves in his thoughts the pomp and magnificence with which its once noble proprietor (*Lord Leicester*) entertained his Royal Mistress (Queen Elizabeth) there, strike the mind with a melancholy reflexion on the transitory state of all earthly grandeur. Our route led us next to *Coventry*, where, if we had arrived a day later, we had seen at a fair the anniversary representation of the memorable achievement of that truly patriot-Lady *Godwina* (*sic*), the wife of Leofric, a Mercian Earl, who, to recover the franchises of her favourite city, condescended to ride naked thro' the principal streets of it at noon-day. The magistrates (you may imagine) took all possible care to secure the Lady's modesty from insults by publishing a severe edict against any one that should presume to look out of their houses during this extraordinary parade; which one caitiff disregarding, Heaven (if ancient legends may be credited) prevented the punishment threatened by the civil powers by striking him blind upon the spot. His effigy ever since looks out from the place where he committed the crime, but being then taken down to be new dressed against the approaching solemnity, I could not gratify my friend with a sight of it.

A very pleasant road led us from this place to *Coleshill*, a small neat market town on an eminence; from the churchyard of which the eye is entertained with a wonderful large and beautiful prospect of the adjacent country; where in a valley just below you see the remains of the Castle and monastery of Maxstock, and at a greater distance the large Castle and town of Tamworth, on the confines of the counties of Warwick and Stafford. The other side of the town gives you a near view of the Park, and part of the old seat of the good *Lord Digby*, over which at a distance we could discover the smoke of *Birmingham*. The former of these objects brings to your mind a noble specimen of ancient uncorrupted English virtue; the latter an instance of modern industry and improvement in the iron manufacture, whose forges daily furnish out those arms, which, if managed with courage directed by prudence, would retrieve the old English glory, and give law to Europe.

Full of these agreeable reflexions we reached *Litchfield*, the situation of which (tho' in a bog) the inhabitants fancy to be as healthy as that of Montpellier. Next day, after viewing a seat of Lord Uxbridge's placed on the side of a beautiful hill among woods, we passed thro' the finest part of Staffordshire, and dined at *Utuxater*, from whence we saw *Sudbury* and *Tedbury* Castle. The former of these, belonging to Mr. Vernon, we visited, and found there a very good house cased with flint work in the old manner, to which you are no strangers in Norfolk. On the garden side was a large area sloping down to a serpentine river, and encompassed with an amphitheatre of greens; which scene, being at that time enriched by a set of haymakers actually at work, afforded what the French call *une beau païsage* [sic]. On the other side of the house, cross the road, lay a large and very beautiful Park, which our time would not permit us to survey at our leisure, the decline of the day calling upon us to make the best of our way to *Ashborn in the Peak*.

And here it will be proper once for all to obviate a mistake, which (I am sensible) the very mentioning of the *Peak* raises in the minds of those who know nothing of this country, but what they have [heard] from some travellers, who are pleased greatly to misrepresent it. I dare say, Madam, you have already formed a thousand hideous ideas of a wild uncomfortable barren desert, full of naked rocks, or covered only with russet heath or furze, and inhabited by wild creatures, which have nothing human but their outward appearance. But how agreeably surprised would you be, were you upon the spot, to find yourself travelling in exceeding good roads, breathing a pure air, and looking down (when on an eminence) upon rich valleys, either meadows plentifully watered with rivers affording the best of fish, as trout, grailing, &c., or farms in tillage laid out in the neatest and most husband-like manner? And then, for the politeness and humanity of its inhabitants, our next day's journey afforded us such repeated instances of it, as might put some gentlemen of the southern parts of the Island out of countenance.

As we were upon the great road from Ashborn to Buxton, perceiving a gentleman's seat in a valley below us, we agreed to strike down to it. It was a large house belonging to one *Mr. Okeover*, from whose family I presume the place takes its name, and who is now building new wings to it in a very handsome manner. We found him in the courtyard with one Sir Phil. Warburton of Cheshire; upon seeing us ride in he came up to us himself, and, finding us strangers travelling only for curiosity, asked us to alight, and to permit him to show us the civilities of his house: which he did in the most friendly and polite manner imaginable, by leading us through all parts of his new building, and acquainting us with his plans, designs, and conveniences of all sorts, &c. After this he conducted us into the main body of the old house, in the apartments of which were some of the finest pictures I ever saw, which had been collected by his father in Italy. Two particularly struck me and my friend: the first, that of the Holy Family in the most exquisite taste (I think) I ever met with. The solemn characters of the divine personages here represented, softened with all the graces it was possible for the pencil to bestow, raise at once in the mind of the beholder the most awful veneration and most exstatic love, the genuine ingredients of all true devotion. The other was the Unjust Steward appearing before his incensed Lord to account with him before he was discarded from his employment. He is attended by his distressed wife and several children in a group behind him, in whose faces appear such lively expressions of grief suitable to their respective ages and capacities of apprehension, that the very idea of it, still warm upon my heart, raises there those sympathizing emotions, which (next to a sense of duty to the Author of our being) 'tis in my opinion the noblest prerogative of our nature to be capable of being affected with them. But to return to the gentleman to whom we were obliged for this entertainment. Upon our taking leave of him he told us, that we should meet with something very well worth our seeing at a gentleman's house about 2 miles from him; and pressed us to let him send his servant along with us thither, who should have orders to stay for us and bring us into the high road from which we had deviated in the morning.

Conducted by this guide, we came to one Mr. *Porte's* of *Ilam*, whose place indeed exceeded everything that could be said or conceived of it. His house was no way remarkable in itself, but the situation of it was the most romantic one I every saw. It lay in a deep valley between 2 high mountains. Just in the front of it, at about a mile's distance, arose up a third in the form of an Egyptian pyramid, whose four sides were so regularly sloped, that (did not its enormous bulk contradict any such supposition) you would have judged it to have been the work of art. Descending from hence into his gardens, you see at the bottom a river rolling along with a brisk torrent over large stones, which oblige it to make several natural cascades within your view: then, turning towards the west, you enter upon a walk fenced on the right hand with a very high rock of marble, whose sides and top are covered with shrubs and trees nodding over your head and forming agreeable arbours; while from the bottom of it gush out two streams within a yard of each other, which unite to compose the river mentioned above. That they were really distinct rivulets before their conjunction appeared from a particular circumstance at the time of our viewing them, viz., that the one was discoloured by the rains that had lately fallen, and the other was clear. One of them is known by the name of the *Manyfold*, and emerges here, after a subterraneous passage for 3 miles together. Beyond this walk is a round meadow of about 6 or 7 acres, encompassed all round with very high hills covered with trees, appearing one above another almost as far as the eye can with pleasure follow them.

While we were viewing this wonderful scene, Mr. Porte, being informed that some strangers were come to see his place, sent his servant to invite us into the house, where we were entertained with a glass of wine and very agreeable conversation, and pressed to stay dinner with him; but that not suiting with our scheme, he insisted upon our accepting of his servant to show us to another extraordinary curiosity, viz. *Dove-Dale*. We passed over a very high hill, which yet (like most others in these parts) was covered with grass fit to feed an ox, till we arrived at a steep descent covered with bushes, among which lay several mazy tracks for the cattle to go up and down to water. Down one of these we led our horses for about a mile, when we came to the river *Dove*, a clear trout-stream rolling along over rocks in a deep vale at the bottom, which we crossing, left our horses upon its bank, and climbed by our hands and knees up a steep precipice on the other side to a considerable height, till passing under a natural portal of stone, like a triumphal arch, we entered into a vast cavern in the solid rock, which they call *Reynold's Hall*. From this aerial apartment we were entertained with a view of 2 chains of rocks of various figures and projections facing each other, and the Dove at several openings falling from one cascade to another, till she comes to the level below your eye. This is partly represented in one of the prints of some prospects in the counties of Derby &c. lately published.

After this pleasant excursion we regained the high road, which led us to *Buxton*. This village, I must confess, is situated in the most dreary spot imagination can well form an idea of, being almost all a bare rock, scarcely producing a tree or pot-herb for the use of its inhabitants, excepting the house where the wells are, which, lying low, has some walks and plantations about it. But the melancholy face of the country here was greatly exhilarated by the agreeable company we found in it, which consisted of about 40 or 50 ladies and gentlemen lodging in one house, eating at one common table, and conversing together promiscuously with the greatest freedom and affability imaginable

From this place we made an excursion of a morning's ride over a ridge of hills, from which we saw fruitful winding valleys on every side to a vast extent, to visit a gentleman of a great estate, who has long honoured me with his friendship, viz. *Mr. Legh* of *Lyme* in Cheshire. His house, which stands in a Park of 8 or 10 miles compass, is very magnificently built with stone round a court, with piazzas on two of its sides in a very elegant taste. But the chief curiosity of the place is a custom used here for the Keeper upon notice to collect all the stags in the Park, and to make them take and swim through a lake near the house as tamely as so many water-spaniels: and it really affords a very odd appearance to see 80 or 100 of those large animals, with only their branching antlets (*sic*) or the tips of their noses above water, voluntarily forcing a passage through an element to which they have naturally an aversion, till reaching the opposite shore they shake their ears, and disperse at pleasure as before.

Near Buxton are some of those stupendous works of nature commonly known by the name of the *Wonders of the Peak*, viz. *Pole's Hole*, within half a mile of the town, a subterraneous vault of 700 or 800 yards in length. The passage into it is so contracted, that you are obliged to stoop so low as almost to crawl on your hands and knees for several yards together. Then you enter into a capacious room, the vault rising over your head to a very great height. Here you soon begin to mount a range of rocks first on the right hand, but after some time you pass to the left; on both sides the way is extremely rugged and uncouth, perpetually obstructed by large shelves of rock, over which you are partly led, partly hauled up and down by the assistance of certain nymphs, who you would guess were some of the original race of females produced by the stones which Pyrrha cast over her head after the Deluge, their form so strongly sympathizing with the place where they reside. However, the traveller thankfully accepts of their guidance, when he finds himself led by the road so near to precipices, that he has scarce room to set both his feet between them and the rock, and where the consequence of making a false step would be bruising his body sufficiently, if not breaking his limbs, or his neck. I am surprised to think how the ladies should venture to make this subterraneous tour, which yet they daily do, partly I presume, out of curiosity, partly perhaps to follow the example of Mary Queen of Scots, whose *Pillar* is here shown to strangers by the female ciceronis above mentioned. This obelisc, which is nothing but a lump of congealed matter, suffers perpetual injuries from the ill-meant zeal of the votaries of that unfortunate Princess, who, while they profess a high regard for her memory, at the same time by their continual depredations contribute to destroy that which would otherwise be the most lasting monument of it. In returning, you pass along the lower way, which lies at the foot of the precipices mentioned before; where the road in some places is greatly straitened, and in others entirely closed up, by the rocks, which are daily increasing by water dripping from the vault and sides, and petrifying as soon as it falls; so that here you are obliged to creep under broad stones till you find the passage wide enough to admit you between the rocks, which form a natural wall or fence of each side.

About 6 miles from Buxton, at a village called *Castleton*, which (though in the *High Peak*) stands in a most fertile, beautiful valley, we were conducted to another grotto, partly of the same extent with the former, but different from it in other circumstances, as you will find by the following description of it. As you advance towards it from the village, the first scene that presents itself to the sight is a rock of an immense perpendicular height, partly bare, and partly adorned with hanging shrubs and trees of various kinds, and having its summit crowned with the ruins of an old Castle or fort, which, nodding o'er the brink of the precipice, threatens every minute to crush the adventurous head that dares approach the tremendous passage it seems designed to defend. This is a wide cavern, called by the politer part of the country *Peak-Hole*, though its unseemly appearance has induced the vulgar to stigmatize it with an appellation not decent to be mentioned to a lady. Its mouth is large enough to contain within it several cottages, the smoke of whose chimneys besmearing the vault above has greatly added to the native horrors of the place, and wrought it up to a lively resemblance with that through which the ancient Poets have imagined an entrance into their fabled hell. I must confess, that Virgil's description of his hero's descent into those invisible regions below never struck so strongly upon my imagination as at this time; only that instead of *one* Sibyl who conducted him, we were attended by a *troup* of antique *wayward sisters*, three of whose number you have seen upon the stage opening a *celebrated Tragedy*. These, joined with a mixed multitude of all ages, to the number of 30 or 40, march partly before, partly behind you, with each a glimmering make-weight candle in their hands, in a procession like that at a popish funeral, till they bring you to the side of a river. By this time you find the vault has gradually sunk so low as but just to leave room enough between it and the water for a boat, like a beer-cooler, to pass, in which the passenger, holding a candle in his hand, must lie flat on his back, while a descendant of old Charon, who for a minute or two is arbiter of his fate, pushes him for some yards to the other side. Then the vault by degrees resumes its former height and dimensions, while its ceiling, bespangled with native crystals of all sizes and figures, reflects a feeble light through the dusky gloom below.

Here the traveller, with solemn pace and slow, proceeds sometimes on plain ground, sometimes over heaps of rocks, which at various times have tumbled down from the top or sides to the spaces below. In the mean time, his ear is entertained with *liquid lapse of murmuring streams*, proceeding from some springs having been intercepted in their subterraneous passage by this gulph, and obliged to fall down abruptly through the chinks of the ceiling or sides of the vault. After some time your course is stopped by a second river, which (though it is much deeper) you ferry over with less inconvenience than over the first. At last you reach the brink of a third, where the vault closes and absolutely denies all further passage to the inquisitive traveller; nature seeming hereby to teach him to set bounds to his searches after (*sic*), as she has done to his capacity of attaining to a perfect knowledge of all her works. However, our guide convinced us that they were hollow spaces which extended themselves further on within the rock; for, upon his putting the water into agitation with his feet and stick, we perceived an echo or hollow groan reverberated from several parts, which could be occasioned only by the waves dashing in eddies against the caverns wherein they were imprisoned, and they resembled the music made by some of the deepest notes of a bass-viol or organ.

I have hardly room or inclination to mention *Elden Hole*, a frightful chasm of an immeasureable depth, about 2 or 3 miles from the place above mentioned, being in haste to divert your imagination from these scenes of horror to a spot of all others I have ever seen the most paradisiacal, I mean *Matlock*. But when I attempt to give you a sketch of this place, your fancy must assist in the draught; nor need you fear, that when you have indulged it in its utmost luxuriancy, the ideal picture will exceed the life. Imagine then you see a very handsome house of a pretty large extent in front, built of white stone, and situated on a plain area gained by considerable labour and expense from the shelving rock on the side of which it lies, and of a compass just wide enough to admit (besides the house) a parterre and bowling green, laid out before it. From this area you descend by steps into an irregular piece of ground full of rocks, among which several fine springs, having formed their wanton meanders, thro' (throw ?) themselves down a steep bank by natural cascades into the river *Derwent*, who returns the music made by their fall by his murmuring and chiding of the broken heaps of rocks that impede his course. From his bank on the opposite side arises a wall of solid rock, having a slope towards the bottom covered with wood, but soon springing up afterwards perpendicularly to an immense height; on the very brink of which, notwithstanding, you often see from below the peasants tending their cattle in very fruitful pastures, and looking down upon you, and sometimes entertaining you with a wild kind of music, both vocal and instrumental, to your no small surprise and terror.

From the area you pass eastwards into a grove or copse with natural walks, where you have the river on one side and cascades rolling down through the bushes on the other; but the most beautiful cascade, which terminated the principal walk, has lately been destroyed, the water being diverted from its usual course to supply a bath at a new-erected house not far from that which I have above described. From both the other sides you ascend up high mountains, which frequently, during our abode there, might literally challenge the epithet of *cloud-capt*, which Shakespear bestows upon towers. One of these arises directly from the south side of the house, and diffuses a very agreeable morning-shade over the whole area during the rage of Sirius in the summer months; but I fancy those who are stationed here in winter have too just reason to complain of this impenetrable umbrello, which quite deprives them of the cheering rays of the sun for the greatest part of the day during that gloomy season.

The other hill stands on the west side, and abounds with great plenty of lead mines in the upper part of it, while the lower, sloping down towards the river, is laid out in several inclosed meadow-grounds, intermingled with spots of shrubs and trees. In one of these I used from my window to see my favourite mare grazing on her hanging pasture, like a wild goat; a circumstance which afforded me no small pleasure, as it had an appearance of being at home in this charming place: as the critics observe, that Sappho, by reminding Venus that when she honoured her with her company she used to dismiss her equipage (with orders I presume to her charioteer to unharness her Doves), implied that her visits were of a considerable length.

Adjoining to this is a place called *Love-walk*, from which there is a prospect of the house and its environs above described, and likewise a new rural scene of corn-fields, pastures, &c., for which we are obliged to the turning of the rock, which here makes an abrupt angle. I must not omit to tell you, that from this point the printed view of Matlock was taken; to which I must beg leave to refer you for a supplement to this imperfect account, and proceed to acquaint you with what that cannot inform you of, viz. that I came hither by appointment to meet a gentleman and 2 young ladies of our county, with whom (and the other accidental company, which varied every day) we had the perpetual pleasure of the most agreeable conversation imaginable. We lived in one long room fitted up in a very elegant manner, where we eat, drank, played, sung, danced, &c. in a way (I fancy) perfectly resembling that of the happy mortals in the Golden Age.

One morning our party made a visit to *Chattesworth*, which is undoubtedly a fine seat, built of a brownish stone with a yellow cast, round a court in a very grand and beautiful style, and highly finished both within and without, particularly the Chapel, which is wainscoted with cedar finely carved, and painted with some historical pieces of Scripture by Verrio. The gardens, I must confess, did not answer the idea I had formed of them: there were indeed 2 pieces of water, one square, at the first entrance at a corner of the house, the other of a length too great for its breadth, in the front; besides 2 good jet d'eaus, and a cascade, which exceeded everything of that kind I ever met with. But nothing of this nature hits my goût, which was more exquisitely gratified by the little natural rills at Matlock trilling down from every rising bank with a ceaseless flow of water, than it would be with the most pompous fountains, which are the work of art, and taught to flow at the turn of a cock; where you know you are grudged every drop of water they throw out for your amusement by the penurious reservoir that supplies them. It always reminds me of a miser's feast, where an extravagant profusion at one meal is to be made up by a succeeding fast for a month.

After a week's stay at Matlock we set out for our respective homes. Our first stage, being only a morning's ride, brought us to *Derby*, a very pretty agreeable town, where we spent the afternoon with one Mr. Gisborn, a gentleman with whom we had contracted an acquaintance at Buxton. He showed us the chief curiosities of the place; particularly the famous *Silk-mills*, the model of which was brought over from Italy by Sir Thomas Lomb. We passed the evening at the monthly Assembly there, and next morning, pursuing our journey on fine roads through a rich and pleasant country, we dined at *Leicester*, and afterwards reached *Market-Harboro'*. The next day brought us safe (by the kind favour of Providence) to *Towcester*, which place, as it afforded me an agreeable repose after so long a peregrination, so (I fancy) it will sufficiently recommend itself to your regards by putting a period to the tedious narration with which I have now troubled you.

My compliments to Sir Edmund Baccon [*sic*], Miss Sarah, and the good family at Kimberly (upon whose late increase I beg leave to congratulate yourself and them), conclude me,

Madam,

Your most obedient, humble servant,

J. NIXON.

Towcester, Nov. 12th, 1746.

Madam,—I am almost ashamed to acknowledge the receipt of your last favour, when I review the date of it, and at the same time consider the great honour you do me by your candid acceptance of my former journal, and your encouraging me to hope that a sequel containing an account of my last summer's expedition would not be disagreeable to you. This tour (I must own) was more extensive, but I am afraid it will not afford you so much amusement; as neither the scenes I visited, nor the occurrences I met with, were so romantic, as those of the other. However, as your commands must not be disputed, I beg leave to acquaint you, that my first stage (July 7th) brought me to *Sir Thomas Cave's* at *Stanford;* a gentleman, who as he has honoured me with his friendship from the earliest period of his youth, so every opportunity I have had of visiting or conversing with him has increased my respect for him; as it has given me fresh instances of his worth and goodness in the several most important points of action in life. His family (though the lowest of his recommendations) claims a rank among those of the first note in these parts, not only for its great antiquity, but also for the many useful persons it has produced for the service of their country, and the public good of mankind. Their mansion house was formerly in this county, till the present gentleman's grandfather, when he rebuilt it, removed it about ¼ of a mile higher up into the Park, whereby Leicestershire acquired an addition of another fine seat, and of a worthy patriot, whom (in conjunction with one Mr. Smith of Edmondthorp) she entrusts with her interests in Parliament.

Sir Thomas, as he is no sportsman, spends his time in the country for the most part in finishing and adorning his premises, which he does in a very handsome manner and with a good taste. His last improvements have been in his Hall, by removing entirely the upper row of windows (which I think have generally a disagreeable effect) and sinking the ceiling by a cove, which (as well as the compartments in the walls below) is finished with stucco in such an elegant and chaste style, as seems (in my opinion) to have hit the very line which when this kind of work exceeds, it ceases to be just, or proper. Imitations in general should be modest, and decline appearing in too glaring a light. That of plaster in particular, tho' in lofty ceilings, and other parts of the building more removed from the examination of the eye, it may be allowed to project out from the plane in circles or festoons of fruits and flowers, yet in those more immediately under view it should never (in my judgment) exceed a relievo, nor in human representations venture beyond the profile of a face in a medaillon. An instance of excess in this point I remember to have met with some years ago at Ditchly, the fine seat of Lord Lichfield, and another last summer at Mr. Duncomb's in Yorkshire, of which more in its proper place. In the former the Hall, being extremely lightsome, regular, and beautifully ornamented, strikes the stranger at his first entrance with uncommon pleasure; but when he recovers his discerning faculty and exercises it upon the several groups of figures, as large as the life, reclined on pediments over each of the door-cases, besides a series of busts, which seem to have been all brethren of one birth, or cast in the same mold, and are stuck up all round above the cornish; the connoisseur (I say) reflecting upon the unmeaning flatness, and the many inaccuracies and disproportions generally attending this work, and likewise upon the coarseness of the materials which had imposed upon him in such profusion, he finds his taste palled, and his admiration succeeded by a satiety and disgust.

But now, Madam, be pleased to return with me to the Hall at Stanford, where, having taken notice of the fine organ at the bottom of it, be so good as to step into an apartment now finishing, and designed to be hung with a rich green damask, with a bed, chairs, &c. of the same; a circumstance I should not have troubled you with had it not been for its giving me an opportunity of informing you, that the whole furniture is a present from the Lady Dowager Cave (Sir Thomas's mother), and as such will suggest to you some inferences, which may not be disadvantageous to the moral character of my worthy friend her son.

As Stanford lies in a rich vale, the chief beauty of its environs are the numerous herds of beasts, and flocks of sheep, which cover its wide-extended pastures on every side: the only distant view is a scene that must afflict every loyal eye, viz. *Naseby Field;* out of which arises the Avon. This river, after running about 3 or 4 miles, shapes its infant course through Sir Thomas's Park, where it receives great favours from his generosity, which it gratefully repays by the plenty it diffuses through his large demains. As Sir Thomas has a very mechanical turn, and a particular taste for marine affairs, he has by a lock swelled this rivulet to such an height, as to afford at once a fine prospect from his house, and also room for him to navigate a sloop or two of his own building upon it. This yields a most agreeable entertainment in a summer's evening; especially as in our voyage we generally touched at a small fort in an island near one end of the lake to take in some liquors more suitable to gentlemen-sailors than fresh water.

But I should be highly unjust to the religious character of my much honoured friend, as well as guilty of an improper omission with regard to my own, should I dismiss the present subject without mentioning with all due commendation his singular care and munificence in repairing and beautifying his parish church, which he has effected in a good taste, and not without a considerable expense. The entrance at the west end (which would remind you of that at Redgrave in Suffolk) presents you with a handsome white marble font supported by branches of iron work. The nave of the church is uniformly paved, and accommodated with good oak-wainscot pews; and the reading-desk and pulpit newly erected, of neat workmanship, and inlaid in an elegant manner. The roof is painted, and the walls adorned with stucco-work,

Then you proceed to the chancel, the windows of which (particularly that of the east) are enriched with very good old painted glass, exhibiting the arms of the family, and those of their most considerable alliances. Below, on the floor, which is laid with black and white marble, and on the side walls, are several monuments; particularly one erected for the late Sir Verney Cave (the present gentleman's brother) in the middle of the south side of the fabric, which t'other day occasioned a little incident, that will make you smile. A tenant's wife belonging to a neighbouring village having dined with Lady Cave in Sir Thomas's absence, after tea her Ladyship (with that great good nature, which so highly recommends her other many virtues) proposed a little walk in the Park, which was to terminate at the church adjoining to it. The païsanne was wonderfully charmed with the decorations and improvements already made, but with great simplicity asked Lady Cave, whether she did not think, that another monument of the same fashion with that of Sir Verney's, and erected just over against it for Sir Thomas, would not make the chancel *quite pretty?*

Leaving Stanford in company with Mr. Smith (mentioned above), whom with his wife and her sister (I should have told you) we found at our arrival there, we passed over a rich (but deep and unentertaining) country for about 12 miles to *Leicester*, and from thence to a seat of *Mr. Philips'* about a long mile beyond *Loughborough*. This gentleman's brother was representative for the county in the last Parliament, and (as I am informed) had a very good taste for drawing, paintings, architecture, &c., which he cultivated by a considerable stay abroad, particularly at Rome; and indeed the improvements he began to make in his place are a sufficient specimen of his genius that way. His house is a large old stone building, of which he only lived to new-case the garden front; which he completed in a very elegant style, with a portico in the middle supported by six columns of the Ionic order, and of beautiful proportion. An ascent of about half a mile brings you to an étoile in his Park of six points, whereof the 1st looks down to the house, lake, wood, &c., the 2nd is terminated by a prospect of woods, the 3rd by a hill covered with heath, the 4th by a temple, the 5th by a woody country, and the 6th by a stately guglio at the entrance of the Park from Loughborough. After another shorter ascent we reached a second étoile of 8 points, one of which (not to mention the others which had for the most part the same terminations as those of the lower one) leads the eye to a noble portail quite in the grand antique taste. In the centre of this étoile stands a beautiful temple or rotundo of stone, surrounded by 16 Ionic columns, upon which rests an entablature charged with festoons tied to ox-sculls, or supported by Genii alternately. Over this rises a dome, whose cupolo lets down light into the inside of the building, which is extremely elegant, adorned with fine carvings, and a good model of the Medicean Venus.

Our curiosity had thrown us so far into the evening, that we were obliged to take up our lodgings at a small town named *Kegworth*, which we did with some reluctance, though our landlady gave us the strongest demonstration possible of the high reputation of her house by assuring us, that their worships the neighbouring Justices had once dined, and Sir Robert Burdett and his Honor Grevile had frequently lain there. Next morning's ride brought us to *Derby*, where we were chiefly entertained with memoirs relating to their last winter's visitants, the Scotch Rebels, male and female, particularly her Grace of P——, who (as our barber informed us) during her stay there affected to be seen (even by those of our sex) in as high a dishabille, as was that of our original Mother before the Fall.

In order to diversify our route from this place to Matlock, we this year agreed to direct our course by *Kidleston*, a seat of *Sir Nathaniel Curson's*. As we had then no intimation of there being anything remarkably curious in the house, we contented ourselves with a view of its environs without. And here your eye first falls upon a spacious and beautiful lawn, or meadow, in his Park, through which runs a river forming several cascades in a long succession within view; beyond this is a gentle ascent covered with fine woods, excepting a large area, or vista, opposite to the front of the house. At one corner of the Park, at a place called *Ireton*, about a mile from Kidleston, is a pleasure-house with a spot of ground adjoining thereunto, the oddness of which a good deal puzzles the imagination to describe it. The compass of it indeed is not large, yet such as affords sufficient scope for Lady Curson to display her fine genius in gardening, and architecture; the whole (as we were informed) being planned, and executed by her Ladyship's sole direction. One peculiar happiness of its situation (and that to which it owes its chiefest beauty) is its lying pretty high, and yet affording a plentiful spring of water sufficient to supply several canals, and particularly a serpentine river, which is so contrived, that its dimensions still lessening the further it is removed from its source tempt the eye to conclude that it runs upwards: a circumstance (by the by) which, if verified, would release many a hampered swain from the obligation of certain vows generally made under the guaranty of every star auspicious to love, and ratified by the solemn ceremony of breaking a crooked sixpence. As the inequality of the ground cannot fail of leading an enterprising genius to strike out many bold (tho' beautiful) extravaganza's, so particularly her Ladyship is now building an hermitage, or tea-room, in a kind of stone-quarry, in the front of which a cascade is destined to fall down over the rude shelves of the rock.

In the bowling-green, from whence you are entertained with a prodigious fine and extensive prospect of Derby, and the country round it for several miles, stands a summer-house, which has the panels of its doors withoutside, as well as the floor, seats, and windows within, all inlaid with wood of divers sorts and colours in a pretty manner; but the most surprising thing in this building is the frames which contain the wainscot and looking-glasses, whereof there are several: they seem to be of the richest high-raised carving imaginable, but upon closer examination it proves nothing but a tissu or continued cluster of little odd knots of wood which once grew in a thousand various and distorted figures, and are now polished or lacquered, and artificially joined together.

Beyond the bowling-green lies a spot divided into a kind of wilderness-walks, lined with fruit trees on each side; one of these leads to the most whimsical fabric I ever saw. The materials that compose it would tempt one to call it the Temple or triumphal arch of Death, while its colour and appearance challenge the name of the Ivory-Gate described by Virgil towards the end of the 6th Æneid, thro' which I hope those dreams will always pass, which seem to forbode ill to Miss Bacon, or any that are dear to her. In short, it is a kind of little Gothic fort or lodge, of three arches in front, made altogether of bones in their proper colour. The walls within are all wainscoted with the round ends of sheep's trotters, as those without exhibit nothing but the smooth protuberances of marrow-bones of large cattle. The other members of the building are finished with [a] variety of bones in a very natural and beautiful manner: particularly I observed her Ladyship had been greatly obliged to the vertebræ or joints of the back-bone of a cow or horse for a principal part of the Gothic ornaments, which enriched the arches, windows, and battlements of this romantic structure.

After surveying these curiosities, our evening's ride landed us at *Matlock*, a place, whose name (I fancy) gives you some terrible apprehensions, and that not without reason, considering the satiety you must have received from my prolix account of it in my last year's journal. But, Madam, if I had an inclination to tease you afresh, yet the subject would not bear me out in it; for, as for the scene itself, which is invariably the same, I have given you a tolerable idea of it already; and the company, tho' different, yet being all (except your friend Major Geddes) unknown to you, I cannot with any propriety introduce them to your acquaintance at this distance. The chief novelty we struck out was (a pleasure which the weather would not permit us to enjoy last season) the boating up the *Derwent* in the afternoons, and in our return drinking tea under some natural arbour formed by trees hanging down from the wild rocks on each side the river. On these occasions we were attended by music, which, if not quite equal to Mr. Handel's *Water-music*, yet was so entirely suited to the romantic genius and whole turn of the place, that it had an effect which defies the power of description. You will smile after this, when I tell you, that it was our boat-man playing upon his fiddle, and his little boy accompanying him with his drum. This concert of instrumental music was intermixed with some of the vocal kind, several ladies of our company obliging us with singing in a very agreeable manner. In short, the whole entertainment, taken together, was in so high a goût, that it would be unjust to compare it to anything less than Cleopatra's tour upon the river Cydnus to meet her Lord M. Anthony, of which Dryden (I think) gives so pompous a description in his *All for Love*, &c.

You'll pardon me, if upon this occasion I subjoin a little incident only to show you how strong a passion for music and dancing prevails in this obscure corner of the world, which the southern gentry of our Island are apt to treat upon the same footing of barbarism as they do Lapland, or Tartary.

One evening, after our water-entertainment, calling in at a cottage on the bank of the river, almost covered by a prodigious rock hanging over it, we found a collection of the young fry of both sexes, the sons and daughters of farmers and miners, met together in their holiday-clothes to learn to dance minuets, hornpipes, and country dances. The first were over before we came, but the two last they executed in a manner that would have pleased and surprised you. They were directed by a maître de danse, a tight young fellow of a neighbouring village, to whose taber and pipe they were exercised 3 times a week at the expence of one penny each time of performing.

My dwelling upon Matlock so long (contrary to the intimation dropped at the beginning of this article) is pardonable upon no other principle, than that which is natural to mankind, viz. the persuasion that what affects themselves cannot be unentertaining to others. This will plead my excuse for relating the following particular. You may recollect, that in my last journal I mentioned the great civilities we received from *Mr. Okeover*. I remember, that upon parting with that gentleman my friend and I agreed in our reflexions, that the satisfaction one feels in receiving obligations from strangers is alloyed by a secret regret from the thoughts that (in all human probability) we shall never have an opportunity of returning them. You may conceive (in consequence of such sentiments as these) how great was our pleasure to find fortune more favourable to us in this respect, than we could ever flatter ourselves she would be. The circumstance was this. One evening, when our house was as full as a beehive, and scarce a corner left to hold a mouse, we saw a large company of ladies and gentlemen arrive just before supper-time; and among the rest, whom should we discover but our friend mentioned above, and his lady. The gentlemen with much ado got lodging for the ladies, despairing of any for themselves, which (considering they were to set out again the next morning upon a journey) it would have been greatly inconvenient for them to have gone without; whereupon my companion and I agreed to join quarters, and compliment Mr. Okeover with one of our beds; which convenience was readily accepted of by him with much greater acknowledgment than it deserved.

July 19th. We mounted very early in the morning for Nottingham. Nothing worthy of notice occurred in the road thither, till we came within two miles of the town to *Lord Middleton's*. His house stands in a pretty Park, and is a large fabric in the Gothic style, but lightsome and beautiful enough, had it not been encumbered with an enormous square pile of building in the middle, the lower part of which is the Hall. This rises up to a considerable height above the other parts of the house, and its heaviness is greatly increased by four watch towers, or sentry-boxes, projecting out one at each corner with the most disagreeable effect imaginable.

But if the eye has received any disgust here, it is soon recompensed by the beautiful prospect, which next entertains it; I mean the Castle and Town of *Nottingham*. The former is a magnificent building erected on the plane of a steep rock. It consists of one story, and an attic, and has in its principal front towards the town eastwards 9 windows in length, each of them crowned with a broken pediment above to admit a bust, and adorned with a balustrade below. Its pilasters are of the Corinthian order, except two in the centre, which are of the Ionic, and support a pediment charged with an equestrian statue in a large niche. In the south-east front are only three windows, and a spacious corridor under the first floor. The west or back front projects with two wings, each of three windows, to the west. The body has two, and a glass door. You mount from the town to the area on which the Castle stands by two or three flights of large stone steps. The area itself is all paved with square stones, and enclosed with a balustrade. It serves as a Mall for the Nottingham belles, where they may breathe a pure air themselves, and hear their lovers breathe something similar to it, viz. vows of love, and what not. The prospect you enjoy from this spot is very extensive and delicious, to a degree little inferior to the environs of Windsor. To the west you have a view of Lord Middleton's seat, described above, venerably rising above the woods in his Park. South-west your eye falls immediately upon wide meadows, through which runs the *Trent;* and from thence catches *Sir Robert Clifton's* seat. To the left more eastwardly you have variety of country, partly in grazing, and partly in tillage, till your view is terminated by the cloud-capt towers of *Beauvoir Castle.*

I shall omit the agreeable situation and neat buildings of the town, particularly those around the market-place (of which you must have had frequent accounts from other travellers), and (if you will not think the transition too Pindaric) from these aërial heights shall beg leave to conduct you immediately to some subterraneous wonders more remote from common observation; I mean the Cellars in the town, which (next to the Castle) are in my opinion some of the greatest curiosities belonging to the place. Those of the Inn, where we lodged, were of a surprising depth, and seemed to consist of more stories than one, each branching itself into several vaults, whose ceiling, sides, and floor were all of the same materials, viz. the natural sand-stone. The disposition of these uncouth apartments put me greatly in mind of the description which travellers give of the Catacombs abroad, though the appearance here was much more joyous, as each of these cells, instead of mouldering bones, and dried mummies, were well stored with large butts of racy beer, of which some contained 20 hogsheads apiece. But whatever difference there might be in the air of the two sorts of repositories above mentioned, perhaps there will be found in fact a nearer relation between them than you would at first imagine, as the vaults at the inns are in some measure nurseries to people those in consecrated ground; the natives of towns famous for good ale generally having their bodies well pickled or embalmed in it before they are conveyed to the dark mansions of the dead.

From Nottingham a gentle airing thro' a plain country by the side of the Trent brought us on Sunday morning to *Newark*, where after breakfast we went in a Christian-like manner to the parish church, which is a very handsome edifice, adorned with a gallery, and the solemnity of the service is improved by an organ and choir. From the tower of the church (where at all places we came to (I should have told you) we generally took our stand of observation, and the apparent usefulness of such a practice must recommend it to all travellers) we discovered the bearings and connexion of the several parts of the country we were now in with those we left behind us, and those we were soon to enter upon. To S.E. appears *Beauvoir Castle*. More E. a fresh object strikes your eye very well worthy of notice, viz. *Lincoln Minster*. N.E. *Lord Robert Sutton's* seat at *Kelham*, with a summer pavillion at a considerable distance amongst woods. In the plain N. you have the branching of the Great Northern Road, one part leading to York, the other to Mansfield; nearer under you, the remaining walls of the old Castle washed by the Trent, and whose area is now a bowling-green. To N.W. is *Southwell Abbey*. The rest of the country is beautified with the mæanders formed by the Trent catching the eye at several openings E. and W.

Our afternoon and evening were spent in passing on through a flat country (chiefly a fine heath) for many miles to *Lincoln*, during which time we had its stately Cathedral in full view all the way; a circumstance of great use to a stranger steering his course cross a wild and unknown country, but at the same time apt to give the eye a satiety, and to add an imaginary length to the real distance. The great eminence of Lincoln (I mean the upper part of it) makes the traveller for several hours together fancy himself under her walls, and that the next stretch will bring him to her gates, when to his great disappointment he still finds fresh and unexpected tracts of land open themselves before him in a disagreeable succession, to exercise his patience and renew his toil; like a coquetting nymph continually throwing herself into the full view of her lover, and continually withdrawing at his nearer approach.

Imagine us now actually arrived at and entering Lincoln, a place greatly different from any I ever saw either at home or abroad. Its first entrance is a wide street at least a mile long, indifferently built, having several parish churches at proper intervals, and remains of religious houses, guilds, hospitals, &c., the whole interspersed with orchards, gardens, and trees. This brings you to a very steep hill pitched with stones, up which you climb with difficulty on horseback to an higher ground, where stands the Cathedral, Bishop's Palace, Prebendal mansions, &c. The first of these is a most spacious and venerable piece of Gothic architecture, especially the W. front, which has the greatest air of magnificence imaginable, and is inferior to nothing I ever saw, but that of York; and the difference lies in this, that in this of Lincoln the greatest part of the wall is void of ornaments, except a course or 2 of little arches without any meaning; whereas that of York is diversified by pillars, compartments, &c. of a more sensible style and proportion. From the top of its towers your view extends to a prodigious tract of country every way, so as to take in Beauvoir Castle, Newark, Boston, Tattershall, &c. Below in the town you have great remains of antiquity, as the vallum or entrenchment which surrounded the old city *Lindum*, and some gates of Roman work, one of which is so entire as to be a thoroughfare to Burton. But perhaps it may be more agreeable to a young lady to hear, that there is a modern structure of a more entertaining taste just finished here, containing a Ball-room 27 yards long, and 12 wide, accompanied with offices of all kinds suitable to the design of its foundation.

Monday, July 21. After dinner we pursued our journey for the most part over a fine heath, like that which brought us to Lincoln, for many miles having a row of villages at some distance in a vale on our right hand, and a wild country, of which we could discover but little, on our left. Nothing worthy of notice occurred in this period of our tour, till the *Humber* opening to our view greatly distinguished the scene. We lay at the Ferry-house near *Barton* on the bank of the river, and next day about 7 in the morning embarked for *Hull*. Tho' from the time of the year we might have expected great serenity in the elements, yet the Humber, the monarch of the Northern Rivers, had taken it into his head that morning to be extremely turbulent. His rage was occasioned partly by his own natural rapidity, and the swell of the tide, and partly by a concurrence of a strong N.E. wind blowing directly down the channel. My fellow traveller, recalling to mind the many tragical accounts he had heard of accidents which had happened in this passage, which is at least 6 miles in length, seemed sufficiently affrighted. I (for my own part), if I had any fears, thought it expedient to conceal them in order to calm his; but we had not got 200 yards from shore before a sad catastrophe had like to have fully justified our apprehensions how great soever they were; for our vessel, thoroughly loaded, and in full sail with wind and tide, all on a sudden (thro' the fault of the steersman) was fixed upon land. Babel could convey *

[*The rest is wanting.*]

Higham, Nov. 23rd, 1750.

Madam,—I shall be the more sparing in apologizing for my silence, because I shall have occasion to draw sufficiently upon your good nature to excuse my imperfections, when I actually do myself the honour to write to you. The subject of my present letter will be an account of my tour last summer, which began on June 10th. On the 11th I arrived at London, and set out after dinner with my old fellow-traveller in a post-chaise for Dover, which place we reached about 7 next morning, and (after a very rough passage, which made me inexpressibly sick) got to *Boulogne* by midnight. When we arrived next day at *Abbeville*, I remonstrated to my friend, that the direct road from that place to Paris through Picardy was what I had passed before, and that it would afford no entertainment even to a stranger: therefore I desired we might diversify the route by striking out on the right hand, and so passing through Normandy.

To this he readily consented, and accordingly next morning (June 14th) we bent our course S.W., and travelled through an open country, the soil of which seemed to be generally light, and produced corn of all sorts, besides flax; and at proper distances appeared several villages inclosed without, and also lined within, with rows of trees, chiefly elms.

Seven leagues brought us to the confines of Normandy, which province we entered near a pleasant little town called *ville d'Eu*, where there is a château, park, and gardens by the side of a clear river, belonging to the Duke de Dombes. After six leagues more we approached *Dieppe*, which, with its harbour and environs viewed from an eminence, afforded us a very agreeable prospect. It is a sea-port, and lies low: the principal streets are long and well built, particularly the quay, where is the *cours* or mall. The most remarkable commodity here is ivory, wrought and carved in all manner of curious forms, from the *solemn object* of superstitious worship down to the lowest toy suited to please the taste of a lady, or a beau.

After dining at Dieppe we entered upon the fine new road, which is now making from this place to Rouen; a thing greatly wanted in this country, the natural roads being exceedingly bad. It is very large and magnificent, consisting of a broad stone *pavée* in the middle, and spaces of the natural ground on each side. The expenses of this, as well as of all other works for the public utility here, are defrayed out of the King's Exchequer. It begins with an ascent from the town in the manner of a regular hanging slope for about half a mile, for the effecting of which the hill is in some places cut down several yards deep, and, as you advance further, the valleys are filled up to the same height; subterraneous surfs or bridges being left in the lowest places to drain off the waters. The extremities of these bridges appear on each side adorned with white wrought stone in an elegant manner. The direction of this road runs in a straight line, sometimes to so great a length, that the rows of trees which bound it on each side, close upon the eye, before it can reach a turning. The country hereabouts is much the same as that between Abbeville and Dieppe, viz., open, full of corn, woods, villages, &c.

We lay that night at a village called *Tôstes*, six leagues from Dieppe. Here we saw a little country house of Mons. Ronquier, and his farm of about 2,000 livres per annum, which gave us a specimen of the manner of disposing the conveniences requisite for a farmer in this part of the world. Within a large square orchard, planted in a regular form, was situated the dwelling-house in the principal point of view, like the general's tent in an army, the several buildings of an inferior order, viz., barn, stable, granary, carthouse, &c., being all separate, and placed at due distances in a line within the same area. This spot was fenced round with a deep ditch, and a raised bank next to the orchard planted thick with elm-trees. Around the whole on the outer side ran two or three walks of beech trees, which lead to little groves or plantations on the waste ground near the open field. In our next day's journey we saw several other gentlemen's seats, with their farms in this disposition, which (with the long vistos of apple trees growing naturally with round heads, and running in several directions through the open corn fields) have a most agreeable effect, and give this country the air of one continued garden or orchard.*

After six leagues from Tôstes we approached *Rouen* by a descent extremely fine. On the left was a regular row of little hills, with gentlemen's seats, villages, &c. spread along them. Below appeared the town in an oval form, its greatest extent being from east to west; beyond it to S.W. lay the Seine, skirted by a long series of hills, each sloping down towards the river in the figure of dove-tails or triangles, as if made by art. Rouen for many ages was reckoned the second city

* Here several lines are struck out.

in France, and is now the capital of Upper Normandy. It is in compass about 1¾ league, and inclosed on three sides with hills, two little rivulets running through its streets. It contains 37 parish churches, 17 chapels, 48 monasteries, 35 public fountains, 5 gates on the land side, and 13 towards the river. In one of its seven principal market places, viz., *marché de veaux*, stands a fountain, having on its top the effigy of poor Joan of Arc, who was cruelly used and at last burnt on this spot by our countrymen. Charles the 7th of France reversed her sentence and declared her innocence, erecting at the same time this monument to her memory, and ennobling her three brothers.

This city is a place of great commerce, being the repository of all the commodities imported from the Ocean into France, which are first landed here, and from hence transmitted to Paris, &c., for which purpose it is furnished with several warehouses, reckoned the largest and most convenient in the world. Its streets (though narrow) and its public buildings are very good; especially the Cathedral, a most magnificent Gothic structure 408 feet long, 83 feet wide, and 84 high. On the *croisée* rises a tower 152 feet high, and which supports a steeple 380 feet high. The choir is sustained by 14 columns, and enclosed by a screen of copper. The grand altar is separated from the choir by a balustrade of the same metal, and 4 pillars, with an angel on the top of each pillar. In the middle of the choir is the tomb of Charles 5th, whose figure of white marble holds his heart, which was deposited here, in his hand. On the right side of the altar is the monument of our Richard 1st, and on the left that of his nephew [*sic*] John, son of Henry 2nd. The famous Duke of Bedford, formerly Regent of France, was buried near the altar. In the chapel of the Blessed Virgin, behind the choir, you see the magnificent mausoleum of the two Cardinals d'Amboise, uncle and nephew, whose figures are kneeling upon their tomb in a posture of devotion. The base is adorned with six figures of good workmanship representing six virtues, each in its separate niche or shrine. One of these gentlemen (among other very considerable benefactions) gave the great bell, which hangs in one of the towers, and still bears the name of George d'Amboise. It weighs 36,000 *lb*., is 30 feet round, and 10 high. They tell you that the founder of it was so well pleased with the success of his art, that he died for joy the nineteenth day after it was hung.

Another thing, which deserves our admiration here, is the fine quay, very large and spacious, running along the N.E. side of the river; at the end of which are the venerable remains of a castle, begun to be built by Henry 5th of England, and finished by Henry 6th, 1443. From the quay there is a passage over the river by a bridge of boats, 270 paces long, and so contrived, that in case of any imminent danger from floods, flakes of ice upon a thaw, &c., it may be taken to pieces in six hours' time, and restored again without any damage. A passage is opened in the night in the middle of it for vessels to go through, and it rises and sinks with the tide, which at Rouen is remarkably high and violent. On the other side, facing the city, is a row of buildings, chiefly belonging to the public; one of them, viz. *grenier à sel*, is a very magnificent structure. Further on to the left hand lies the mall, esteemed the best of its kind in France. It consists of one grand alley and two smaller ones, reaching near a mile in length, on the borders of a meadow by the bank of the Seine, commanding a most delicious view of the city, river, and the chain of hills mentioned above, at the foot of which runs the great road to Paris.

But I must not forget one thing, which (I own) affected me more than all the curiosities I saw in this place, viz., the scholars of the

Jesuits' College, which is very grand and beautiful, in their chapel at mass. They seemed to be 150 or 200, many of them of the best families in this, and the adjacent provinces; all upon their knees on the pavement before the high altar. The solemnity of the office, however eclipsed by ridiculous ceremonies, and the serious attention of the young audience, gave me an internal sensation, which no words can express. But I remember I then vented the fulness of my heart by sending up a fervent prayer to heaven, that the Supreme Being would accept graciously the offerings *of*, and pour down a blessing *upon*, those his tender votaries; and that if there was any blemish in their sacrifice, occasioned by the superstitious errors of their education, *He* would pardon it in *them*, and rather visit it upon their spiritual guides, who had mingled the poison of human inventions with the sincere milk of God's word, when they instilled it into the minds of those young disciples of Christ.

July 16th.—Our road from Rouen to Paris gave us frequent and most delightsome views of the Seine, sometimes on one hand of us, and sometimes on the other. For as this river serpentizes through the whole length of our way in a very remarkable manner, as if unwilling to quit so charming a country, we had occasion to cross it in several places.

The first thing we saw worthy of notice was *Vaudreuil*, about five leagues from Rouen, the seat of Monsr. ———, a President of the Parliament of Paris. It consisted of two corps or wings, separated from each other by a large space, which gave entrance into a fine parterre of flowers, with bousquets or arbours of trilliage-work on each hand. Beyond this was a large wilderness laid out in walks, and a visto extending near half a league, which was the length of the gardens. In pursuing this walk we crossed the river Urz, which, dividing itself into two branches, incloses the whole spot. In one part we came to an *étoile* of several points, from which we saw the boundaries all around, which were hills of several forms and sizes. On the brow of one of them stood a large venerable convent called *De deux Amans;* the reason of which name our guide was not able to explain to us.

After four leagues we came to *Gaillon*, a bourg belonging to the archbishops of Rouen, who have here a country seat of residence. This is a noble castle, boldly situated, and built in a very magnificent (though Gothic) style by George d'Amboise, formerly archbishop of the See, above mentioned, and since greatly embellished by the Cardinal de Bourbon, and would be little inferior to any palace in France had it an entrance proportionable to its grandeur in other respects. It consists of two courts, the first of which has a large fountain in the middle of it; the buildings which compose its sides being very richly ornamented with the busts of Roman Emperors, and triumphs, &c. in relievo. In the upper part of the second court is a fine orangery in the form of an amphitheatre: the lower side has a corridor of several arches built of white stone, through which you have surprisingly pleasant views of the adjacent country for some miles. On the right hand gentle hills in vineyards with tufts of woods present themselves to your view; on the left you have the same; while the Seine, serpentizing through the plain below, appears in one part of it like a grand canal formed by nature as on purpose to adorn the prospect from the castle. The building within consists of two grand apartments, one below, the other above, each containing a good suite of rooms, unfurnished, and terminating in a gallery. From each of these state apartments (as the castle stands on the side of an hill) you enter into a parterre in the gardens, of which there are two or three, rising above each other, being supported by very high walls, and laid out in grass-plots, walks, and a little grove of limes under the wall of the next parterre above. Adjoining to these is a park of about 800 acres.

At about ¾ of a mile from the castle, in the plain, is a large well-built convent of Carthusian monks, founded by the above-mentioned Cardinal de Bourbon, Count de Soissons, who, with his wife, son, and daughter lie buried in one of the chapels belonging to the church. On the top of the tomb, which is a stately mausoleum of black and white marble, are the effigies of the Cardinal and his Lady lying along; on the sides are those of their children. The figures of the four cardinal virtues support the four corners of the stone. The church is large, but devoid of all decorations. The cloisters inclose the burying-place (as is the manner in all the monasteries of this order that I have seen) and are very spacious, having cells for 21 Fathers and 19 Brothers. The solemnity of this appearance, increased by the profound silence, which for ever reigns within these walls, naturally inspires the stranger with a sort of religious horror, suspending for a while every sentiment, which has any of the joys of this life for its object. Accordingly I found it strongly affected my young fellow-traveller, who never had been in any convent before, nor had any notion of the nature of such establishments, especially of this order, whose rules are extremely rigid. He seemed to listen with great attention and a melancholy air of pity to our ciceroni [*sic*], while he recounted the many painful austerities these recluses undergo; as their feeding only on vegetables, observing perpetual silence, praying three or four hours in the middle of the night, &c.; but he never seemed to think these messieurs completely miserable, till he understood, that (to crown their affliction) they were entirely excluded from the converse of the softer part of our species; they being never permitted to go out, nor any female allowed to enter within the walls of the convent. And indeed, when I reflect on the exceeding great pleasure I always find in the conversation of *one particular lady, who honours me with her acquaintance and correspondence*, I am strongly induced to enter into the sentiments of my friend upon this article.

I must not omit to tell you, that in returning to our inn we met an hermit, who (we were told) had made himself a room and an oratory in the rock on a neighbouring hill, where he lived by himself; only at certain times he came down to the convent for victuals. What a strange passion must a man have for solitude, who thinks there is too much society in a Carthusian monastery!

After having breakfasted for the first time in the true French taste, viz., on bread and butter and raw young artichokes cut in slices and seasoned with salt and red Burgundy vinegar, we proceeded on our journey, and after three leagues travelling reached *Vernon*, a bourg on the Seine. A little before we came to this place, we turned up on the right about a mile out of the great road to see *Belle-Isle*, a seat belonging to the Duke of that name. The house itself is but indifferent, but as you go up to it, you have on your right hand a magnificent range of building of white stone for offices, servants' lodging, stables, &c., with 18 or 20 large windows in front. In the center of this building you enter by an arch into a square court, in the middle of which is a watering place for horses, with a fountain always playing. Above this, in the same line of direction, one perceives through an opposite arch, in the back part of the court, another cascade on rising ground at some distance in the garden, which seems to compose one piece of water with this, and has a very agreeable effect.

The garden-front of the house opens upon a large parterre of flowers, bounded on the right with a covered walk of trees on a terras above the parterre. The gardens are large, partly on plain ground, but chiefly on the side of an hill, consisting of grass walks, and alleys cut through woods, or wilderness work. From the several openings you have delightful views of the country below, viz., the Seine, villages, and the town of Vernon. The disposition of the whole was in a taste somewhat superior to what one commonly meets with in France, as the genius of that country seems not to lie either for good gardening or architecture; though the defect with regard to the former of these articles must be partly charged upon their want of proper materials, as you will readily allow, when you are informed that there is scarcely any gravel in this country.

Somewhat more than two leagues from hence brought us into the Isle of France; and after about four more, we arrived at *Mante*, where we lodged, being Saturday night. Next morning, after crossing the Seine over a fine stone bridge of 39 arches, we passed through a spot of land, the beauties of which for three leagues together defy all description. However, to help you to form some tolerable idea of this part of the world, and of our joyous situation, while we were passing through it, imagine you see two of the happiest fellows in life, having left every care behind them in their native land, in high spirits, breathing the most delicious air in the world, in a fine summer morning, rolling along on a broad smooth causey considerably elevated above the plain, as it were on purpose to shew us the adjacent country to the greatest advantage. On the right hand see the ground covered interchangeably with plots of vines, corn, garden-stuff, cherry and other fruit-trees. Beyond the Seine, which forms a large bend all the way from Mante to Meulan, the country opens at several distances in gently rising hills planted with vineyards, and adorned with towns, gentlemen's seats, and convents. Nor is it less beautiful on the left; only as it rises (though by an easy ascent) immediately from the road, the prospect on that side is necessarily more contracted.

At *Meulan*, which terminated our first stage, having breakfasted and dressed, we went to see a little island near the town, which truly answers its name, viz., *L'Isle-Belle*. It is wholly occupied with the pleasant house and gardens of Mons. Bignon, nephew to the late Abbé Bignon, a man of the first rank among the literati of France. This spot lies in the middle of the Seine from N.E. to S.W., as near as I could guess about ¾ of a mile in length, and about ⅛ of that space in breadth. The house stands on the north branch of the river, and consists of three pavilions, the whole being about 200 feet in front. The apartments are very lightsome and elegant, entirely in the French way where everything strikes you with a fluttering superficial air of gaiety, and but few things will bear a critical examination. Upon this account on country can be better calculated than this is for the amusement of travellers, whoso time will generally permit them to take only a transient view of what they meet with in foreign parts.

On the back-front is a large parterre reaching from the house to a grand walk, which bounds the island, and runs the whole length of it along the S. branch of the river. Upon entering upon this parterre, on the left your eye is soon attracted by a long walk, which leads it to a very pleasant summer-house opening full upon the Seine, town, and country beyond it. Returning from this building by another walk to the parterre above mentioned, you enter that part of the garden, which lies on the right hand, and is of much greater extent than the other. Here first a little grove brought us to a meadow planted with *abeilles*

[sic], and to a menagerie on the right; while the left presented us with a little field in this form ( ), bearing a crop of wheat, inclosed with a neat-cut hedge, and bordered by a walk, which in this quarter divides the garden into two parts; and somewhat further the island is traversed again by a threefold walk; and after that you come to another corn-field, and meadow as before. Beyond this is a little wilderness, and an oval grass-plot encompassed with Dutch elms. Then you soon find yourself in an *étoile* of five points, crossed by the covered walk extending itself from the S.W. corner of the garden to the summer-house on the N.E. point, and which we judged to be near ¾ mile long. Advancing further we gained the extremity of the island, and from thence winding round towards the N. branch of the Seine, found the landskip very agreeably diversified. On a bank on the opposite side of the river runs the high road from Rouen to Paris: higher above that appeared slopes with vineyards, villas, &c., and further to E. the town of Meulan, spreading itself on the side of an hill. The most distinguished objects in it were a good monastery, and an infirmary, a new building of white stone situated near the church, and overlooking the whole bourg.

Our next stage was to Poissi, by a place called *Treil*, three leagues. The last league, viz., the space between the two towns above mentioned, lay in a straight line along a fine paved causey, from which we had a view of the Forest of St. Germain on rising ground before us.

Poissi is a pretty little bourg on the Seine, where the old kings of France had formerly a noble castle, in which St. Louis was born, whose grandfather Philip le Bel began to build here a magnificent abbey for Dominican nuns, and endowed it very liberally; but it was not finished till the time of Philip de Valois, 1330. It was designed for 40 young ladies, who were to be of the best families in France, and its present revenues amount to 6,000*l.* per annum; but the ministry sometimes draw considerable sums from these rich foundations, by way of loans, or free-gifts, which we call in England *quartering*. The church has some peculiarities, viz., 1st. The choir is boarded, and separated from the church by a grille, and a curtain: in the middle of it is interred the heart of Philip le Bel, and over the place stands his bier, covered with a black velvet pall. 2nd. The church is not duly situated with regard to the points of the compass: the reason they give for it is this, that the church being built on the site of the old castle, the high altar was placed on the very spot, where the bed stood, in which Queen Blanche was delivered of St. Louis. Here we enter the Forest of St. Germain, which leads us quite to the town, and is reckoned a league. The road passes only through the skirts of the forest, the main extent of which runs on two leagues to the left hand, being divided into ridings and alleys, within a large bend formed by the Seine between Poissi and the place above mentioned.

St. Germain is situated partly on low ground, partly on a rocky hill, at the foot of which runs the Seine. It enjoys a pure and healthy air, and is adorned with several good houses, built by the nobility, while the Court resided here. At our arrival here a little incident happened, which will give you a strong idea of the French politeness. It was almost ten years ago since I was at this town before, with Lord and Lady Pomfret, when we lodged at the same inn, at which we now purposed to dine. But notwithstanding the great length of time, and the many thousands of faces my landlady must have seen since the time above mentioned, she immediately challenged your humble servant, declaring, that she knew even my voice, when I called to the hostler out of the chaise, before she saw my person. To confirm the truth of her assertion, she inquired particularly after every branch of our noble family, that she had known, and repeated with great accuracy several little incidents, that happened during our abode at her house; even to the very rooms where each of us lay. Upon my expressing some surprise at the punctuality of her memory, she replied with a very genteel curtsey, that she could never forget those whom she loved.

The most remarkable thing here is the Castle, the first foundation of which was laid by Charles 5th as long ago as 1370. The English made themselves masters of it under Charles 6th. Charles 7th bought it of an English officer, who was the governor of it. At length Francis 1st, whose device, viz., a salamander in flames, appears in several parts of it, rebuilt it for a royal palace, and gave it the form of a Gothic D (D) in honour of his mistress, Diana of Poitiers. It has since received considerable improvements from his successors Henry 4th and Louis 14th. It stands on the highest parts of the town, and is surrounded by a wall and a deep fosse. The three lowermost stories are of white square stone, well wrought. Then it is encompassed with a balcony of iron-work. Above this are two stories more on the sides, and three in the pavilions jutting out at each corner, built of small stone plaistered over with mortar; the window cases, mouldings, &c., being of brick, appear in their proper colour.

I need not inform you, that this was the residence of the late King James and his Queen, after that Prince had abdicated the English throne. I am told that Louis 14th allowed him a yearly pension of 50,000*l.* sterling for the support of his royal dignity, to be paid monthly; as [*sic*] the present King has continued to show great marks of his liberality to several of the Chevalier's adherents, who have enjoyed lodgings in the castle ever since. And surely, if the place of abode could contribute anything towards human happiness, the unfortunate pair above mentioned might have found it in some measure in this delightsome retreat, after they were eased of the troublesome load of a crown. But, by the accounts I have met with abroad, they seem to have carried the seeds of their own misery in their own bosoms, being very uneasy in their domestic establishment during the remainder of their days, which they passed here. So true is Milton's observation,

> 'The mind is its own place, and in itself
> Can make a heav'n of hell, a hell of heav'n.

Within this castle there is a very handsome chapel with galleries. Above the altar is a good piece by Poussin, and before it hangs a rich lamp of silver gilt, being the gift of Louis 13th. The priests' vestments, &c. are also very magnificent, having been the presents of several princes for the ornament of this chapel.

Some years ago Louis 15th came to see this place, and was so highly pleased with the situation, that he expressed a great inclination and purpose to have it fitted up for his residence. This (you may imagine) struck the inhabitants with a great consternation, but a slight accident quickly dissipated the occasion of their fears. The King, as he made this visit in his return from the chace, being in boots, in descending from the apartments, one of his spurs hit against a step of the stairs, which caused him to fall down. This put him into a passion, and made him alter his resolution entirely.

At a small distance from the castle stands a châtelet built by Henry 4th and rendered famous for being the birth-place of Louis 14th. It is a low building consisting of three courts, the first of which is of a circular form, and built of white stone, and at present is let out in lodgings. The house is situated on the very brow of the hill, and the gardens descend quite to the Seine, being supported by terras's at a great expence.

The gardens belonging to the castle, being parterres of grass, and some walks of trees meeting in an arch at top, are open to all persons. From the end of them towards the north on the edge of an high slope runs a noble large terras, supported by a strong stone wall to the length of 2,700 yards. The descent on the right hand is covered with vines, corn, fruit trees, &c. At the bottom is a large meadow, through which the Seine serpentizing forms a kind of peninsula inclosing the Forest of La Pecque, cut out in alleys and ridings, and lying full under the command of the eye, just before you. As you extend your prospect, on the right hand beyond the town of St. Germain you have a view of the forest, part of the town, palace, gardens, aqueduct, and machine of Masli, a fine seat of the Countess of Clermont's, &c., all on a range of hills covered with woods, and forming an amphitheatre, as on purpose to humour the course of the river. More towards the east you see Mount Calvare, the town of Nanteuil, the dome of the church of the Hôtel des Invalides at Paris, Mount Martyr, St. Denys, &c.; till the prospect closes with the Forest of St. Germain, where this terras ends at a little lodge called La Val.

Our stage after dinner brought us through a prodigiously beautiful country full of towns, villas, &c. to *Paris*. Upon my advancing towards this capital, I could not but observe an effect, which is contrary to experience in most other cases, viz., that every object appeared to me with a more agreeable air now, than at the first view I had of it formerly; though I had then the same organs of perception, enjoyed the same good state of health, and was some years younger. I could account for this upon no other principle than the natural alliance that subsists between the several faculties of the human soul; whereby it comes to pass, that the pleasure, which any one sense receives from its own proper object is improved in proportion as the other senses are more or less gratified with the enjoyment of theirs. Thus the sight of the company, the hearing of the music, &c. give an additional relish to the wine and eatables at Ranelagh or Vauxhall. So the impression made upon all the senses in general affects the mind in a degree suitable to its present disposition, whether of complacency or disquietude, from whatever adventitious circumstances that disposition may arise. Upon this hypothesis I could easily give a reason why everything I saw in these parts might affect me with a more lively sensation in my present independent and agreeable situation, than when I viewed it in connexion with a *family*, who, being greatly miserable in themselves, were not apt to communicate happiness to those who belonged to them.

After this little philosophical digression, you may imagine you see us lodged *en grands Seigneurs* at our Hôtel in Rue Columbier, Fauxbourg St. Germain. Our apartment, consisting of four rooms, stood us in two louis per week. A *traiteur* provided our dinner at three livres a head, for which he gave us a soup and *bouillé*, an *entré*, *quelque chose rôtie*, and a dessert of fruit. As for our breakfast, every article of it was supplied by a different hand at the following rates, viz. coffee, four dishes, at 16 sous; bread, 1 sou; butter, 5 sous. Our supper was generally [a] roll and butter, or two broad biscuits, at 8 sous, with some fruit, and a bottle of Burgundy at 35 sous. We hired a valet at 30 sous, and a coach at 12 livres a day, while in town, and 18 livres when we made excursions into the country.

You will perhaps, Madam, be surprised, that I should enter so little into the description of this great city, upon which my predecessors in tour-writing have enlarged so copiously, but that very reason induces me to contract my account; especially as I have little to add to that which they have already given. Leaving it therefore to the next *well-travelled* gentleman you shall meet with to entertain you with the amusements of the opera, comedy, gardens of the Tuilleries, &c., I shall beg leave to touch upon some other articles more in my way, and which I flatter myself will not be entirely disagreeable to you. The chief of these are the two curious collections of paintings, the one in the Luxembourg Gallery, the other in the Palais Royal. The former of these is the property of the Crown, and contains a series of the most important events, which happened during the regency of Marie de' Medici, mother of Louis 14th. It is sufficient to say, that they are done in the highest style of that great master, Rubens. But the pleasure with which we view these paintings is greatly alloyed by the melancholy reflection that they are on the bare wall, and consequently liable to the injuries which time and weather may produce in it; and indeed they had suffered in some parts, when I saw them; but a friend of mine just returned from Paris tells me, they have lately been cleaned, and restored in some measure to their original beauty. The Palais Royal belongs to the Duke of Orleans, and may be called an epitome of all that's most valuable in painting, at least on this side the Alps. It is an immense warehouse or magazine rather than a collection; for it fills most of the apartments of a large palace with some of the best performances of all the best masters in Europe. This treasure was partly purchased by, partly presented to, the late Duke of Orleans, who was Regent of France. As that Prince (among his other polite accomplishments) was known to have a high taste for painting, it was natural for those, who either in a public or private capacity stood in need of his favour, to court it by such presents as would be most acceptable to him in that way; which (considering the extent and continuance of his power) may well account for the largeness and value of this collection.

During my stay here I paid my compliments to Mons. l'Abbé Sallier, the King's Librarian, to whom I was recommended by Mr. Folkes, (late) President of the Royal Society in London. He received me with great politeness, and (besides the Library) showed us the *sales* where the members of the Academy of Inscriptions and Belles Lettres, as also of that of Science, held their assemblies, being two fine rooms in the old Louvre. In the former of these *sales* were two grand paintings by Coypel, one of which represented the founding of the Academy by Louis 14th. The latter was adorned with the portraits of persons of the highest note for learning and genius, who had belonged to that institution. We were afterwards conducted to the Academies of Sculpture and Painting, which were likewise embellished with the works of such French masters, as were allowed to excel in those arts. But our attention was particularly engaged by a fine marble statue done by Bouchardin. It was a Cupid gently bending to form a bow out of Hercules's * * * * * *

[*The rest is wanting.*]

Although the last two letters have no signatures, owing to their incompleteness, there can be no doubt as to the name of their writer, the handwriting of both being precisely similar to that of the first letter, which is signed as above. There is a duplicate of a few pages of the last letter, with some slight variations.

R. E. G. KIRK.

THE MANUSCRIPTS OF THE EARL OF DARTMOUTH. (SUPPLEMENTARY REPORT.)

The documents here described were found by Lord Dartmouth after the publication of the Calendar of his Manuscripts in 1887 (Eleventh Report, Appendix V.). The letters of George III. to his Colonial Secretary at the time of the struggle of America for independence are of some interest and importance; and those of the eminent thief catcher, Jonathan Wild, are rare enough also to be quoted at full length. There are two or three papers relating to dramatic affairs in 1807 and 1809; the remainder require no special mention.

Bundle marked "Privy Council Minutes" by the first Earl of Dartmouth, 1710–1711.

N.D. (1711, after May 17th).—Unsigned and unaddressed letter in Lord Dartmouth's hand to Lord Peterborough, commencing "My Lord." Acknowledging receipt of a letter "from the Venerie" which was immediately laid before the Queen. Her Majesty was pleased to hear of the Duke of Savoy's intention to take the field in person, of which he had already assured her in a letter brought by the Marquis Du Bourg express from Holland. Her Majesty disapproves of the proposal for taking up money at Milan to enable the King of Spain to come from Barcelona, unless it is approved by the Lords Commissioners of the Treasury. But orders have been given to the Queen's Admirals in the Mediterranean to assist the King of Spain in case he desires it. [This is the draft of a letter ordered at a Council held at Kensington on May 17th, 1711.]

1710, Aug. 24th. Kensington.—Lord President, Lord Chancellor, Duke of Somerset, Duke of Queensberry, Lord Anglesey, Lord Orford, Lord Poulet, Mr. Harley, Mr. Secretary Boyle, Lord Dartmouth. "The woman at Salisbury to be examined at the Cockpit before the Committee, and that she be not suffered to speak to anybody."

1710, Aug. 26th. "Cockpit, ten at night." — Examination of the woman, a Mrs. Crisp, referred to in the preceding paragraph. Relates to an alleged threat made by Lord Carmarthen to kill the Queen and Lord Sunderland. One Mr. Rusher said before Lord Carmarthen "that the Queen was a silly woman led by the nose." Mrs. Crisp in her further examination on the 30th of August denied that she had heard Lord Carmarthen threaten the Queen's life, or that he had said "he could or would at the head of the mob seize the guards; that he only said he could . . . . that he did not say he would kill my Lord Sunderland, but seize him. She does not remember there was any mention of the Pretender when my Lord spoke to her about the Lords, &c., in her information."

1710, Oct. 27th. Cockpit.—Lord Steward, Duke of Queensberry, Lord Poulet, Mr. Secretary St. John, Lord Dartmouth, Lord President, Duke of Ormond.

The Duke of Queensberry read a report from the Attorney and Solicitor about the information against my Lord Carmarthen. Ordered that it should be laid before the Queen next Monday, and that the Lords are of opinion that my Lord Carmarthen should be informed of it and heard to it.

1710, Nov. 8th. Cockpit.—Lord President, Lord Steward, Duke of Queensberry, Mr. Secretary St. John, Lord Dartmouth, Lord Poulet, Lord Keeper, Lord Chancellor, Mr. Harley.

My Lord Carmarthen called in.

Was asked if he had ever heard of articles from the Pretender; he said he had formerly, some years ago, and that he has often said so to several people; and that he had said he believed the Whigs would bring him in about the time of Dr. Sacheverell's trial.

That he never heard of any designs against the Queen's person.

That he said at the time of Dr. Sacheverell that he hated the mob upon any account, and that when he heard they had pulled down Mr. Burgess' meeting house he said he wondered they did not rather fall upon the Bank.

That he had received a letter from Mr. Wood that gave him an account of the information given in against him by Mrs. Hill (*sic*). My Lord was desired to fetch the letter dated Sept. 19th, 1710, which was read.

1711, May 11th. Cockpit.—Duke of Queensberry, Mr. St. John, Lord Dartmouth.

Examination of Mr. Dabriel, a Scotchman born, two years and a half in the French service, as to the movements and designs of the Pretender on the north of Scotland.

1711[-2], Feb. 25th. St. James'.—Lord President, Lord Steward, Lord Lieutenant, Duke of Queensberry, Lord Poulet, Mr. Secretary St. John, Lord Chamberlain, Mr. Harley, Lord Dartmouth.

That I should acquaint the Morocco Ambassador that spotted deer are so scarce the Treasury cannot get above ten brace, and that the Queen has ordered the Lords of the Treasury to get them as soon as possible.

Papers of Uncertain Date.

N.D. (1660–65.) Sir W. Dunville to Col. William Legge of H.M. Bedchamber.—Hopes to obtain the office of Lord Chancellor of Ireland, which is likely soon to be vacant by the retirement of Sir Maurice Eustace.

N.D. [*Temp*. Charles II.] — Paper endorsed "Earl of Arran's cipher."

An envelope of Miscellaneous letters.

1723[-4], Jan. 9. Thomas Ward, to whom is not stated, possibly to Mr. Heneage Legge.—"Mr. Burnet and his brethren have been teazed so much about the publication of the first volume of the Bishop's history that I believe it will be a long time before they will let the second volume see the light."

1724, March 23rd. Jonathan Wild to the Earl of Dartmouth.—"I doe not doubt but that your Lordship will be surprized at my presumeing to write to you, but I cannot but hope your Lordship will pardon me for soe doeing, because I am Compelled to seek Protection, by the Violent Prosecution of some Magistrates, (whom I never offended) who have encouraged Severall Notorious Thieves to swear against me, and to qualify them to be Legall Evidences, have procured his Majesties most Gracious Pardon for them, for Crimes for which they have been condemned, tho' when this done, all they can or dare pretend to swear, amounts to no more then that they have paid back Goods to me, which they had stollen, and which I got restored to the right owners, and for this my service, the mistaken Zeale of those Gentlemen hurries them on to seek my ruine. But if your Lordship would be pleased to give me a letter to such person as you shall judge proper to hear and redress me, I am confident that the Designes of my Enemyes will be frustrated and I thereby at Liberty to discover apprehend and convict Numbers of Notorious Criminalls, which will be great service to the Publick; and for which your Lordship will merit thanks and also the hearty Prayers for your Lordship's long life and Prosperity."

1724, June 15. Jonathan Wild to the Earl of Dartmouth.—"I am informed by Mr. Woolley's man that your Lordship has lost some things on the road. I humbly beg your Lordship will please to order me a particular of them per next post, and I will use all the Diligence I can to serve your Lordship to the uttmost of my power."

1724, Aug. 11th. Jonathan Wild to the Earl of Dartmouth.—"Some time agoe your Lordship signifyed that you had lost some writings, which I endeavoured to discover and after the Reward of 10 Guineas was published, they demanded 20 for themselves, which your Stewart proposed to pay in part, if he could see all the writings, which were considerably more than your Lordship at first seemed to mention, and had your Stewart paid all the money down your Lordship undoubtedly would have had them before now, I was upwards of six pounds out of pockett, and I would still endeavour to procure them for your Lordship would you please to order any one else to me than your Stewart, he allways making so many triffling and needless excuses and put off's in paying the money and Expenses I have been at. Mr. Woolley's man James Bridgen was with me last Sunday and told me that your Lordship wanted to hear further from me, which is the Occasion of troubling your Lordship with this, and shou'd your Lordship please to order your Commands to be signifyed they shall be faithfully obeyed."

Bundle marked "1700 to 1793."

Letters from Lord Halifax (1767); King George III (1779), not autograph; Henry Dundas (1786), a long letter commencing "Dear Sir" in holograph, and endorsed "Letter from Mr. Dundas: Observations on the treaty or convention of Governor General and the French Governor General at Mauritius."

1799–1800–1801.—Letters from Sir Robert Abercrombie, Mr. Henry Addington and others. A letter from Colonel Wood, dated Dec. 21, 1800, to Mr. Dundas, declares at some length the designs of Russia and France upon India by means of the Shah of Persia, and the necessity for English influence to be brought to bear on the Shah; letter from Charles Greville, June 10, 1801, asking for promotion for a Mr. Palton, an East India Company's servant; and from Lord Essex from Cashiobury, May 20, 1801, recommending Major Cocks.

MSS. OF EARL OF DARTMOUTH.

1801, Oct. 1st. Castle Hill Lodge, Middlesex.—Edward Duke of Kent to Lord Dartmouth, asking an appointment for a Mr. Rose.

1801, Nov. 30th. Eden Farm. Lord Auckland to Lord Dartmouth. Enclosing letters from a Mr. Coxe who wishes to be recommended to Lord Clive's successor in India. The letter ends, "You probably know that Dr. Heath will succeed in his pursuit of the Eton fellowship, and will of course be succeeded by Dr. Goodall."

1801, Dec. 5th. Lissausure, Ballymoney, Ireland.—Lord Macartney to Lord Dartmouth, recommending Mr. Sydenham.

1801, Dec. 11. Plas Newydd, Anglesey.—Lady Uxbridge to Lord Dartmouth, asking for a post in India for her nephew Mr. Stepney.

1801, Dec. 15th.—Lord Guilford to Lord Dartmouth, recommending Lord Henry Stuart to be Governor of Bombay.

Bundle marked "1802."

1802, Feb. 20th. Horse Guards.—Frederick Duke of York to Lord Dartmouth, enclosing a letter from Lieut Col. MacGregor.

1802, Feb. 24th. Serjeants' Inn.—Serjeant Remmington to Lord Dartmouth for the post of Advocate General at Madras.

1802, March 12th. Benares. Private.—Lord Wellesley to Lord Dartmouth, as to the promotions given to various persons recommended by Lord Dartmouth.
A duplicate of this letter in holograph.

1802, March 13th. Benares.—Lord Wellesley to Lord Dartmouth, announcing his intended resignation of his office unless he can secure the full confidence of the Board of Directors of the East India Company. Several duplicates of this letter: one in holograph.

1802, March 13th. Palace Yard. Lord Redesdale to Lord Dartmouth recommending Mr. Edward Hargraves.

1802, March 25th. Fort St. George. (*Copy.*)—Lord Clive to the Chairman of the Board of Directors of the East India Company, as to the state of the Company's territories and finances at the conclusion of the war.

1802, March 25th. Fort St. George.—Lord Clive to Lord Dartmouth, enclosing a copy of the above letter.
"I cannot however conceal from your Lordship that the successful administration of British India is in my judgment absolutely dependent on an early revision of the principles on which the Court of Directors appears to be desirous of degrading the Government abroad."

1802, April 14th. Clarges Street.—Henry Dundas to Lord Dartmouth, in favour of a Mr. Jones.

1802.—Several private letters from Sir John Macpherson to Lord Dartmouth on Indian affairs.

1802, May.—Charles Greville to Lord Dartmouth; endorsed "Charles Greville's answer to my letter by order of His Majesty for the resignation of the key of the Vice-Chamberlain."
"Many thanks for the obliging expressions in your letter just received on my return from visiting Gardens. I am not surprised that

an office so distinguished in the King's Household should be wanted, and whatever the precedent you mention may produce I shall consider it a substantial comfort from believing that it would not have been extended to me if my gratitude, and affectionate remembrance of repeated favors, were not known to be deeply impressed in my heart, with respectful duty to His Majesty. I will deposit the key to-morrow about one in Berkeley Square, and if you are from home I will leave it sealed up."

1802, Sept. 4th. Fort St. George.—Lord Clive to Lord Dartmouth on Indian affairs.

1802, Sept. (?) 14th.—Lord Castlereagh to Lord Dartmouth on Indian affairs.

Letters of George III.

1773, Nov. 19th. Kew. The King to Lord Dartmouth.—"The candid and frank manner with which Mr. Hutchinson has laid before you the state of his Province, claims that circumspection in mentioning any of the contents which may preserve him from fresh attacks; the letter wrote by Dr. Franklin though too characteristick of his sentiments I chuse to avoid making any remarks upon, as they must naturally occur to you."

1774, Jan. 19th. Queen's House. The same to the same.—"I am much hurt that the instigation of bad men hath again drawn the people of Boston to take such unjustifiable steps; but I trust by degrees tea will find its way there; for when Quebec is stocked with that commodity it will spread southward."

1774, Feb. 26th, 40 m. past 7 a.m. Queen's House. The same to the same.—"Though I fully unburdened my mind to you yesterday, yet on receiving a short note this instant from Lord North with an account that Sir Edward Astley's motion was carried by 250 against 122, I cannot refrain just to mention a few of the many arguments that crowd in upon me as proper to be used with Lord North, most of which I certainly mentioned to you in that interesting conversation, but when much interested prolixity is but too common.

"The eagerness of the House appears plain by the great appearance for the motion, and the fair arguments Lord North certainly used against confirming the bill without its having had the trial the framer of it himself recommended; consequently the House have acted by passion not cool reason, therefore not from a desire of dressing (*sic*) Lord North; therefore though I think the plea of his resolution never to remain in office if again in a minority has no weight when opposed to his duty not to throw this country into confusion whilst the colonies are in a state of insanity; yet the present occasion does not appear agreable to what he has laid down, for that cannot be understood to exist but when the House coolly takes up a matter to distress him, which I am certain no one can on this occasion admit.

"So many of his best friends having gone in the Majority must also shew that no malice was intended; and his not having called gentlemen together to open himself to them may have let many inadvertently be drawn in to promise support to the proposition, who if properly talked to might have avoided giving him uneasiness.

"Though I think these reflections must have arose in your mind when discoursing with him, I have too much the interest of this country at heart not to wish every one that can be suggested should be used to prevent his taking a step destructive to his country, his King who loves him, and his own honour. When you have seen him I beg just to hear how matters stand, for by the want of connection in this letter you may easily guess how agitated my mind is."

1774, March 1st. Queen's House. The same to the same.—"The opinion come to at the meeting last night meets with my fullest approbation; considering the time the Attorney and Sollicitor General took previous to their opinion of the disturbance of Boston, I should have hoped they had so thoroughly examined the questions put to them as not to have now retracted that opinion; but as they have, nothing can be more proper than what is now proposed, but the seeming delay since Lord Buckinghamshire's motion arises from the Gentlemen of Long Robe."

1774, March 5th. Queen's House. The same to the same.—"Lord North's not insisting upon his friends opposing the bill for regulating the mode of deciding controverted elections gives me satisfaction as the attempting to do it effectually at so short notice would probably prove fruitless, and I trust he will continue in that way of thinking; Lord Dartmouth has given me no less pleasure by his opinion that Lord North has no particular cause of uneasiness upon his mind, and as to the depression he labours under, that seems constitutional and will at times occur."

1774, March 7th. Queen's House. The same to the same.—"The address having been ordered without debate gives a proper impression of the House of Lords unanimously seeing the necessity of some measures being taken to bring the town of Boston to a due obedience to the laws of this Realm. I have the satisfaction to assure you that Lord North was this day in as good spirits as I could wish to see him, which I trust is owing to his good sense having conquered his feelings on the bill depending in the House of Lords, and being probably convinced that your supporting the bill is the kindest part towards him."

1774, May 16th. Kew. The same to the same.—"The last letters from Governor Hutchinson seem very proper at the present crisis to be layed before the two Houses. I am sorry to find your predecessor shewed so little temper on Friday, but think he met with a very proper rebuke from you."

1774, Oct. 5th. Queen's House. The same to the same.—"I have just received Lord North's letter with the notification of Lord Abercorn's desire not to be of the Sixteen; I have therefore acquainted him how things stand this day, and desire you will send it enclosed by a messenger, and shall write to Lord Suffolk to take no step until he hears from Lord North. I desire you will send to Mr. Robinson to send me the account of the poll at Guildhull of this day. I shall remain this night in town."

1775, Jan. 28. Queen's House. The King to Lord Dartmouth.—"I should not have till now deferred opening myself to you on the following subject, had not Lord North promised to mention it to you when I saw him on Wednesday, and not reported that he had done so till yesterday.

"It regards the opinion of the troops in America and of the General Officers in this Kingdom, that should matters become serious in that part of the globe, more activity and decision would be requisite than they esteem the present Commander possessed of. I know the worth of Lieut. Gen. Gage, and therefore should wish the affair treated with all imaginable tenderness; he ought undoubtedly to keep his pay as Commander-in-Chief; and the reason of appointing Sir Jeffrey Amherst to command the troops in America to be stated thus; that as the ports of all North America are to be shut up the Commander-in-Chief must be in a situation to go wherever the exigency of the times may call him; that Gage as Governor of Massachusets Bay cannot leave that Province where he conducts himself so well. I am [of opinion] not only from the consideration that troops never conduct themselves so well as under the command of a General they have an opinion of, but also from the political one of the necessity of having some one in America, unattached to any particular Province, ready to transmit the sentiments of those who wish well to English Government; the giving this command to Sir Jeffrey Amherst would answer both these objects, and be a good succedanium to your original idea of a Commission; for as he is respected by the Colonies they will give more credit to his assertions than those of any other person.

"When I see you to-morrow I shall wish to hear your ideas on this subject, and then to authorize you to acquaint him when I mean to see him and press him to accept; I have no doubt but he will wish to be excused, therefore shall only desire you to acquaint him with the cause of my wishing to see him, and take myself the task of obtaining his submission to what I think so essential to perhaps preventing the effusion of blood in that deluded part of my dominions."

1775, Jan. 31st. Queen's House. The King to Lord Dartmouth.—"Thinking you will be anxious to hear what success I have had this day, I can in few words state it. My negociation proved fruitless. I stated very fully the intending to send him with an olive branch in one hand, whilst the other should be prepared to obtain submission, but the ground first taken was never quitted, that nothing but retreat would bring him to go again to America. I am much hurt at not succeeding, as I think it bore a prosperous aspect of bringing those deluded people to due obedience without putting the dagger to their throats. I see he cannot be persuaded, we must do what is next best, leave the command to Gage, send the best Generals that can be thought of to his assistance, and give him private instructions to insinuate to New York and such other provinces as are not guided by the madness of the times what the other would have been entrusted to negotiate."

1775, June 10th. Kew. The King to Lord Dartmouth.—"Lord Dartmouth, by the account just received I see the troops have done their duty, and doubt not but the 20,000 provincials are a magnified force occasioned by the fears of the correspondent. Should the numbers prove true it would be highly fortunate as so large a corps must soon retire to their respective homes for want of subsistence. I am not apt to be over sanguine, but I cannot help being of opinion that with firmness and perseverance America will be brought to submission; if not, old England will though perhaps not appear so formidable in the eyes of Europe as at other periods, but yet will be able to make her rebellious children rue the hour that they cast off obedience: America must be a colony of England or treated as an enemy. Distant possessions standing upon an equality with the superior State is more ruinous than being deprived of such connections."

1775, July 2nd. Kew. The King to Lord Dartmouth.—With a suggested alteration in a draft prepared by Lord Dartmouth for the Lords of the Admiralty.

1775, July 31st. Kew. The King to Lord Dartmouth.—As to the despatches to Major-General Howe in America, and the preparations for reinforcing him.

Further short letters from the King to Lord Dartmouth dated Aug. 1, 1775, July 27th, 1776.

1780, April 17th. Bushy Park. Lord North to Lord Dartmouth.—Unsigned but addressed and franked on the back. "I am sending a messenger to London and cannot help writing a few words to you to tell you that upon maturely weighing the circumstance you mentioned to me on Saturday, I think I cannot in honour extend my communication of the business you mentioned further than I have already. I know I may be sure of your discretion."

1780, April 18th. Queen's House. The King to Lord Dartmouth returning the above letter from Lord North.—"I thank Lord Dartmouth for the communication of the letter he received last night from Lord North, which certainly ought to have been delivered sooner to Lord Dartmouth as it appears to have been sent to town by the same messenger that brought the enclosed, which I received about two; I transmit it as it seems more fully to explain Lord North's disinclination to acquaint the Cabinet with the imprudent step he has taken, and I confess I attribute it more to his being ashamed of the transaction than to his feeling it would be dishonourable for him to relate what has passed in this transaction."

1782, March 27th. Queen's House. The King to Lord Dartmouth.—"Lord Dartmouth the manner I parted with you was the only one I can ever have towards you as it must even be founded on the regard I have for your virtues. I shall ever gladly seize when in *my power* the opportunity of testifying my sentiments by the honorable decoration you hint at; but at the present hour you must yourself see the impossibility of doing that which is the more mortifying as I fear those vacant must be otherwise disposed of. A politician would have been less explicit, but as I pretend to nothing but honesty, I thought it best to express what I know I cannot do, and what I shall eagerly embrace the opportunity of performing when in my power."

[Compare letter of same date on p. 442 of Eleventh Report, App. 5.]

1804, May 10th. Queen's Palace.—The King to Lord Dartmouth, entrusting to him the task of calling on the Marquess of Salisbury to inform him of the necessity the King is under of forming a new Administration, and "that the Marquess having held his situation above twenty years and received in consequence of it a marquessate and a

Garter, the King trusts the attachment and duty the Marquess of Salisbury has ever avowed for His Majesty will make him willingly resign his employment of Chamberlain when the King's sentiments on that subject have been explained to him. Audiences on these occasions are very unpleasant; Lord Dartmouth is therefore to bring the keys with him, the Staff is of course under the care of the Porter at this and every other Palace.

1804, May 14th. Queen's Palace.—The King to Lord Dartmouth, to prepare warrant appointing Dr. Samuel Simmons Physician Extraordinary.

1780, Feb. 12th. Princess Amelia to Lord Dartmouth. — Unimportant.

1780, March 5th.—Princess Amelia to Lord Dartmouth.—"I am most sincerely obliged to you, my good Lord Dartmouth, for your constant attention to me. I wish you joy again at your repeated successes at sea, and am rejoyced that our Island is again formidable to our enemies. I only wish now, that all ill humour may be banished amongst us at home, and then we may be a happy country and people."

1802, June 21. Brompton. "Very private." Sir J. Macpherson to Lord Dartmouth.—A long letter on Indian affairs, marked on the back "Private and for immediate perusal." It does not appear of much historical importance or interest.

1804, May 15th. Packington.—Lord Aylesford to Lord Dartmouth, expressing his gratification at the offer of the office of Lord Steward of the Household. See Eleventh Report, Appendix 5, p. 443, letter from the King to Lord Dartmouth, dated 14th May 1804.

1805, June 12th. Kensington Palace.—Edward, Duke of Kent to Lord Dartmouth, as to the payment of an account for furniture supplied to the Duke's apartments in the Palace.

1806, June 26. Downing Street. Private. Lord Grenville to Lord Dartmouth.—As to the great expenditure over the estimates incurred in the Lord Chamberlain's office (Lord Dartmouth was at this time Lord Chamberlain), and the necessity for an investigation into the matter with a view to reducing the annual charges. Draft reply to this letter in Lord Dartmouth's handwriting enclosing a short account (imperfect) to show that the excess is almost wholly due to the Board of Works department which is out of Lord Dartmouth's control, and to various extraordinary and unexpected charges.

N.D.—Petition to the King from the Lord Mayor and several gentlemen (Members for the City and others, including Richard Cumberland, the dramatist) praying letters patent for the erection of a new theatre in London.

N.D. [1807.]—"Comments on an humble Petition presented to the Right Honourable the Lord Chamberlain on Feb. 2nd 1807 in behalf of James Grant Raymond, Robert Palmer, and others.

"The majority of the persons, whose signatures, either real or forged, are subscribed to the above mentioned petition are of minor ability as performers; some of them the mere refuse of the London Theatres;—and the names of these last seem affixed merely to swell the list, and make a shew in numbers—'Fortemque Gyan, fortemque Cloanthum!'" . . . . "The grievances under which the petitions appear to labour (if they ever did exist) exist no longer: but the fact is that the winter London Performers *never* were aggrieved by the Summer Theatre, while the Summer Theatre has been long struggling to prevent itself from sinking under the power of its winter neighbours."

As to the licence given to the Haymarket Theatre (since the death of Foote who held it by patent) to perform plays from 15th May to the 15th September, the three Theatres licensed by the Crown "risk their fortunes on the faith of a monopoly" and in the event of the Royal protection being withdrawn "the property must inevitably be ruined." The proprietor of the Haymarket "found the actors, whose assistance he most endeavoured to obtain for the prosperity of his plan, engaged in the Winter Theatres. Their articles which have been drawn in the same manner for years, do not allow them to perform out of the Theatres of Drury Lane and Covent Garden within ten miles of London in any part of the year whatsoever." Last summer the names of Messrs. Fawcett, Mathews, Liston, &c. Mesdames Glover, Gibbs, Tyler, &c., were to be found among the company of performers at the Haymarket. "Here is a decided refutation of the falsehood advanced by the Petitioners who state that the Haymarket engages but one considerable performer from the Winter Theatres." The Haymarket proprietor "depended on the courtesy of the Winter Theatres to permit their performers to come to him *when they* (the Proprietors) *chose*:—that is, when they had finished their season:—in consequence of which the Haymarket Theatre was curtailed sometimes one quarter, sometimes one third, of the benefit of its licence. To obviate this evil, George Colman (then the sole proprietor) attempted, by a fair effort, to establish a company independent of his superior rivals. The success of that effort, after a few summers' trial, even during which many winter performers have been gradually returning to the Haymarket, has not been found commensurate to the hopes on which it was founded; and the plan is now so decidedly abandoned that the Theatre has reverted to its old system of dependence on the Winter houses, and he is arranging a company to be formed from the members whom they think most eligible of Drury Lane and Covent Garden."

"Many of the signatures," to the Petition, "have the appearance of forgery from the circumstance of several Christian names not being those of the performers they pretended to designate."

1809, Aug. 17th. St. James'. T. B. Nash to Lord Dartmouth, Lord Chamberlain.—Enclosing documents—not now with the letter—relative to the Lord Chamberlain's authority over all theatres and places of public entertainment. "The other papers all clearly make it appear that the Lord Chamberlain has hitherto had the entire disposal of the arrangement of the Theatres with regard to the settlement of the salaries of the comedians and all differences that may have arisen between them and the proprietors in which his Lordship's decision was final, and in no instance can I trace that his Lordship's authority has ever been doubted except in the case of Sir Richard Steele, who opposed the interference of the Lord Chamberlain with his theatre upon the ground that, as his Patent was granted by the King, his Majesty only was the person whose commands he was bound to obey. The consequences of such conduct appear in the papers I have transmitted your Lordship the heads of.

"It has been intimated to me that a very curious proposal has been made by Mr. Sheridan to Mr. Greville, viz., that he should relinquish such a paltry protection as that of the Lord Chamberlain's licence, which according to Mr. Sheridan's pretensions will avail him nothing when opposed by the Patentees, as they shall certainly crush all those places of entertainment acting under such authority, and that therefore for Mr. Greville's better security they should, with Taylor and his son Tom, jointly open the Opera House four nights a week for English operas under the dormant patent. I have not seen Col. Greville since, but on the morning (last Thursday) he received the invitation from Mr. Sheridan to meet him at Kelly's the comedian, who keeps a music shop in Pall Mall, to dine with him there, he told me that if anything particular transpired he would call upon me the following morning, and not having seen him, ... looks I think a little like as though Mr. Greville was nibbling at the bait Mr. Sheridan has thrown out. I am also further informed that Mr. Sheridan slept at Kelly's that night, as he said, for the purpose of being near Carlton House, to be ready the next morning to accompany the Prince to Windsor in order that His Royal Highness might introduce him with his memorial to the King, and desired when he went to bed that he might be called at eight o'clock, but unfortunately having made too free with Kelly's wine, he could not rise till near two, and thereby lost a fine opportunity of carrying his threats into execution."

N.D. [circa 1809.]—Memorial to the Lord Chamberlain signed "R. Dundas" (either Robert Dundas of Armiston, Lord Chief Baron of the Exchequer in Scotland, or Robert Dundas, Keeper of the Signet), on behalf of the Duke of Buccleugh, Lord Melville, and others (including "Walter Scott, Esq., Advocate,") on behalf of the Theatre Royal, Edinburgh, granted to the memorialists by Royal Letters Patent and conveyed by them to Mr. Henry Siddons, the proprietors of the old theatre claiming under a former patent the exclusive right to theatrical performances in Edinburgh.

With a copy reply of the Lord Chamberlain recommending the reference of the dispute to arbitration.

1809, Aug. 29th. St. James'. T. B. Nash to Lord Dartmouth, as to the Edinburgh Theatre dispute, and other matters.—"Mr. Scott, the proprietor of the small Theatre situate in Bullen Court in the Strand has just called to solicit a renewal of his licence, and humbly hopes that your Lordship will see no objection to the introduction of the word 'Burlettas,' which are strictly musical pieces without dialogue, and which have hitherto been performed under his present licence for music, dancing, song recitative, recitation, and pantomine with optical and mechanical exhibition, but which he is now, like Mr. Astley, apprehensive is not sufficient to authorise him to continue such representation, and is therefore only desirous that the word 'Burletta' should be inserted, merely for the sake of security, without the smallest intention of extending his performances in the least."

1810, Jan. 25th. Kensington Palace.—The Duke of Sussex to Lord Dartmouth as to the rooms in Kensington Palace for which he has asked the King, and the means whereby they could be accorded him.

1810, Jan. 27th. Windsor.—Col. C. H. Taylor informs Lord Dartmouth, as to the application from the Duke of Sussex for rooms in Kensington Palace, that the King has no objection provided a compensation be made to the housekeeper for the advantages she is called upon to relinquish.

N.D. (about 1805).—Paper in Lord Dartmouth's hand for the King's consideration, headed "Establishment proposed for Her Royal Highness the Princess Charlotte."

1801.—Petition of Charles Grant Vicomte de Vaux, a sufferer by the Revolution, to the East India Company for employment in their service. With letters in this and the following year from him to Lord Dartmouth on the same subject, and for assistance towards publishing a geographical work relating to the Island of Mauritius.

Various Indian papers, extracts from letters of residents, drafts in Lord Dartmouth's handwriting; extracts from a letter from Capt. Malcolm (the Envoy to Persia), dated Teheran, 22nd Jan. 1801, to Mr. Strachey, stating the success of his Embassy and the conclusion of commercial and political engagements with the Court of Persia. At the foot of the extract is:—"It is remarkable that this despatch has been only 46 days from Bagdad. It left that city on the 12th of last month." The despatch appears to have been received the 28th April 1801; "Abstract of statements relative to the affairs of the East India Company, 1801"; List of officers and clerks belonging to the India Board, with their salaries, 1801; Minutes of the Court of Directors of the East India Company from 26th May 1802 to 8th July same year; "Extract from the Fort St. George military consultation the 24th Oct. 1795"; copy letter from Lord Mornington, dated 3rd Aug. 1799, and other miscellaneous papers and copies.

W. O. Hewlett.

The Manuscripts of Rev. William Dunn Macray, M.A., F.S.A., Ducklington Rectory, Witney.

Macray MSS.

1. In an octavo vellum volume, in date of about 1380–1400, containing various scientific and astronomical tracts, there is an alphabetical table (headed "Sinonima herbarum") of the Latin names of herbs with their English equivalents, which fills 13 pages. It is mentioned at p. lxxxvii of the preface to vol. I. of Mr. Cockayne's *Leechdoms*, &c. (Rolls' Series, 1864), and occasionally referred to in the notes upon the text of that work.

2. A small folio, towards the end of the 15th cent., containing, on eleven paper leaves, a short French Chronicle of the wars of the English in France in 1414–1429. Beg. "En lan mil cccc. et xiiii. au mois daoust "au commencement arriva le Roy dangleterre a toute sa puissance "en Normandie, et prist port empres Harrefleu et assiegea Harrefleu "et les bones villes dentour." Formerly in Archbishop Tenison's Library in Westmnister, which library was sold by auction under the authority of the Charity Commissioners in 1861. It has marginal notes made by some French scholar at a recent date, who has noted at the beginning that it is a "Cronique tres interessante." It belonged in the 16th cent. to one "George Neudigate." Its original vellum cover is the will of Marguerite d'Aubigné, widow of Jehan Royrand, sieur de la Claye et de Bretignolles, dated 20 Jan. 1512.

3. 8vo on paper. "Ritus jejunii Judaici, cum præcipuis cir"cumstantiis, ex Mishneh Torah desumpti," by Richard Brett, of Lincoln College, Oxford. A beautifully written little book, in Hebrew and Latin, which is specially interesting from its dedication, under date of Sept. 2, 1605, to the Lady Arabella ("Angabellæ") Stuart; from which it appears that the book was sent to her at Windsor as a memento of her visit to Oxford with James I. in that year.

4. A 4to volume of sermons for several saints' days, in the handwriting (very closely written) of George Wishart, chaplain to the Marq. of Montrose, and afterwards bishop of Edinburgh. The authorship is ascertained from internal evidence. The sermons were preached in a town during its siege ~~(which had lasted for~~ some months) by Parliamentary forces, by one who had been recently appointed to a lectureship. The town is shown by several allusions to be Newcastle, which was besieged by the Scottish army, in league with the English, from Feb. to Oct. 1644; and we learn from Brand's *History of Newcastle* that Wishart was appointed lecturer at St. Nicholas, 12 May, 1643. Several incidents which occurred during the siege are mentioned; *e.g.*, a narrow escape of having the powder-magazine blown up, the passing of a shot between the Mayor (elected for the third time, Sir John Marley) and his sword-bearer, and the slaying of "a whole crew of enemies" by a shot fired from Westgate. In a sermon on St. Matthew's day the writer says that he had written some treatise on the question of the original language of St. Matthew's Gospel. This is not known to be extant, but may possibly exist, like these sermons, in some anonymous manuscript. This volume was formerly in the library of George Chalmers, and was described in his Sale Catalogue as containing "sermons of the latter "part of the sixteenth century."

5. A curious volume (in quarto, pp. 136) of poems written by a lady who had gone into exile in France as one of the attendants on the Queen of James II. They have no poetical merit, but are interesting as

relating chiefly to the Revolution, and to the events of the years following, up to the death of James II. in 1701. The authoress had published a small volume in 1688, from which some of the pieces are taken; but this has not been traced. She was of a Leicestershire family; her father and uncle fought for Charles I., and their gardener, "a tippling swain," fought at Edgehill, Naseby, &c.; she had a brother a physician who was dead; another brother and an uncle appear to have been killed in fighting against Monmouth; two Colonels *Connock* are mentioned, who were respectively her uncle and cousin by her mother's side. She describes the miseries suffered by the people at St. Germain's, and especially by the English exiles, from pestilence and famine in 1694 and 1695. When she wrote this volume she was becoming blind. She was a convert from the Church of England to that of Rome, and writes with the coarsest bitterness against the Church she had forsaken. The volume is dedicated to the Prince of Wales, and has many verses relating to persons in the exiled Court, with pieces on the relief of Londonderry, the battle of the Boyne, &c.

INDEX.

A.

C.

D.

F.

G.

H.

I.

J.

K.

L.

M.

N.

O.

P.

Q.

R.

S.

T.

U.

V.

W.

Y.

Z.

LONDON: Printed by EYRE and SPOTTISWOODE,
Printers to the Queen's most Excellent Majesty.
For Her Majesty's Stationery Office.

HISTORICAL MANUSCRIPTS COMMISSION.

Date.	—	Size.	Sessional Paper.	Price.
				s. d.
1870 (Reprinted 1874.)	FIRST REPORT, WITH APPENDIX - Contents :— ENGLAND. House of Lords; Cambridge Colleges; Abingdon, and other Corporations, &c. SCOTLAND. Advocates' Library, Glasgow Corporation, &c. IRELAND. Dublin, Cork, and other Corporations, &c.	f'cap	[C. 55]	1 6
1871	SECOND REPORT, WITH APPENDIX, AND INDEX TO THE FIRST AND SECOND REPORTS - - - - - - Contents :— ENGLAND. House of Lords; Cambridge Colleges; Oxford Colleges; Monastery of Dominican Friars at Woodchester, Duke of Bedford, Earl Spencer, &c. SCOTLAND. Aberdeen and St. Andrew's Universities, &c. IRELAND. Marquis of Ormonde; Dr. Lyons, &c.	„	[C. 441]	3 10
1872	THIRD REPORT, WITH APPENDIX AND INDEX - - - - - - Contents :— ENGLAND. House of Lords; Cambridge Colleges; Stonyhurst College; Bridgewater and other Corporations; Duke of Northumberland, Marquis of Lansdowne, Marquis of Bath, &c. SCOTLAND. University of Glasgow; Duke of Montrose, &c. IRELAND. Marquis of Ormonde; Black Book of Limerick, &c.	„	[C. 673]	[*Out of print.*]
1873	FOURTH REPORT, WITH APPENDIX. PART I. - - - - - - Contents :— ENGLAND. House of Lords; Westminster Abbey; Cambridge and Oxford Colleges; Cinque Ports, Hythe, and other Corporations, Marquis of Bath, Earl of Denbigh, &c. SCOTLAND. Duke of Argyll, &c. IRELAND. Trinity College, Dublin; Marquis of Ormonde.	„	[C. 857]	6 8
1873	DITTO. PART II. INDEX - - -	„	[C.857i.]	2 6
1876	FIFTH REPORT, WITH APPENDIX. PART I. - Contents :— ENGLAND. House of Lords; Oxford and Cambridge Colleges; Dean and Chapter of Canterbury; Rye, Lydd, and other Corporations, Duke of Sutherland, Marquis of Lansdowne, Reginald Cholmondeley, Esq., &c. SCOTLAND. Earl of Aberdeen, &c.	„	[C.1432]	7 0
„	DITTO. PART II. INDEX - - -	„	[C.1432 i.]	3 6

Date.		Size.	Sessional Paper.	Price.
				s. d.
1877	SIXTH REPORT, WITH APPENDIX. PART I. - Contents :— ENGLAND. House of Lords; Oxford and Cambridge Colleges; Lambeth Palace; Black Book of the Archdeacon of Canterbury; Bridport, Wallingford, and other Corporations; Lord Leconfield, Sir Reginald Graham, Sir Henry Ingilby, &c. SCOTLAND. Duke of Argyll, Earl of Moray, &c. IRELAND. Marquis of Ormonde.	f'cap	[C.1745]	8 6
	DITTO. PART II. INDEX - - -	,,	[C.2102]	[*Out of print.*]
1879	SEVENTH REPORT, WITH APPENDIX. PART I. - - - - - - Contents :— House of Lords; County of Somerset; Earl of Egmont, Sir Frederick Graham, Sir Harry Verney, &c.	,,	[C.2340]	[*Out of print.*]
	DITTO. PART II. APPENDIX AND INDEX - Contents :— Duke of Athole, Marquis of Ormonde, S. F. Livingstone, Esq., &c.	,,	[C. 2340 i.]	[*Out of print.*]
1881	EIGHTH REPORT, WITH APPENDIX AND INDEX. PART I. - - - - Contents :— List of collections examined, 1869–1880. ENGLAND. House of Lords; Duke of Marlborough; Magdalen College, Oxford; Royal College of Physicians; Queen Anne's Bounty Office; Corporations of Chester, Leicester, &c. IRELAND. Marquis of Ormonde, Lord Emly, The O'Conor Don, Trinity College, Dublin, &c.	,,	[C.3040]	8 6
1881	DITTO. PART II. APPENDIX AND INDEX - Contents :— Duke of Manchester.	,,	[C. 3040 i.]	1 9
1881	EIGHTH REPORT. PART III. APPENDIX AND INDEX - - - - - - - Contents :— Earl of Ashburnham.	,,	[C.3040 ii.]	1 4
1883	NINTH REPORT, WITH APPENDIX AND INDEX. PART I. - - - - - Contents :— St. Paul's and Canterbury Cathedrals; Eton College; Carlisle, Yarmouth, Canterbury, and Barnstaple Corporations, &c.	,,	[C.3773]	[*Out of print.*]
1884	DITTO. PART II. APPENDIX AND INDEX - Contents :— ENGLAND. House of Lords, Earl of Leicester; C. Pole Gell, Alfred Morrison, Esqs., &c. SCOTLAND. Lord Elphinstone, H. C. Maxwell Stuart, Esq., &c. IRELAND. Duke of Leinster, Marquis of Drogheda, &c.	,,	[C.3773 i.]	6 3
1884	DITTO. PART III. APPENDIX AND INDEX - - - - - - - Contents :— Mrs. Stopford Sackville.	,,	[C.3773 ii.]	1 7

Date.	——	Size.	Sessional Paper.	Price.
				s. d.
1883	CALENDAR OF THE MANUSCRIPTS OF THE MARQUIS OF SALISBURY, K.G. (or CECIL MSS.). PART I.	8vo.	[C.3777]	[*Out of print.*]
1888	DITTO. PART II.	"	[C.5463]	3 5
1889	DITTO. PART III.	"	[C. 5889 v.]	2 1
	DITTO. PART IV.	*In the Press.*		
1885	TENTH REPORT This is introductory to the following :—	"	[C.4548]	0 $3\frac{1}{2}$
1885	(1.) APPENDIX AND INDEX Earl of Eglinton, Sir J. S. Maxwell, Bart., and C. S. H. D. Moray, C. F. Weston Underwood, G. W. Digby, Esqs.	"	[C.4575]	[*Out of print.*]
1885	(2.) APPENDIX AND INDEX The Family of Gawdy.	"	[C.4576 iii.]	1 4
1885	(3.) APPENDIX AND INDEX Wells Cathedral.	"	[C.4576 ii.]	2 0
1885	(4.) APPENDIX AND INDEX Earl of Westmorland; Capt. Stewart; Lord Stafford; Sir N. W. Throckmorton, Stonyhurst College; Sir P. T. Mainwaring, Misses Boycott, Lord Muncaster, M.P., Capt. J. F. Bagot, Earl of Kilmorey, Earl of Powis, Rev. T. S. Hill and others, the Corporations of Kendal, Wenlock, Bridgnorth, Eye, Plymouth, and the County of Essex.	"	[C.4576]	3 6
1885	(5.) APPENDIX AND INDEX The Marquis of Ormonde, Earl of Fingall, Corporations of Galway, Waterford, the Sees of Dublin and Ossory, the Jesuits in Ireland.	"	[4576 i.]	[*Out of print.*]
1887	(6.) APPENDIX AND INDEX Marquis of Abergavenny, Lord Braye, G. F. Luttrell, P. P. Bouverie, W. B. Davenport, M.P., R. T. Balfour, Esquires.	"	[C.5242]	1 7
1887	ELEVENTH REPORT This is introductory to the following :—	"	[C. 5060 vi.]	0 3
1887	(1.) APPENDIX AND INDEX H. D. Skrine, Esq., Salvetti Correspondence.	"	[C.5060]	1 1
1887	(2.) APPENDIX AND INDEX House of Lords. 1678-1688.	"	[C. 5060 i.]	2 0
1887	(3.) APPENDIX AND INDEX Corporations of Southampton and Lynn.	"	[C. 5060 ii.]	1 8
1887	(4.) APPENDIX AND INDEX Marquess Townshend.	"	[C. 5060 iii.]	2 6
1887	(5.) APPENDIX AND INDEX Earl of Dartmouth.	"	[C. 5060 iv.]	2 8

Date.	——	Size.	Sessional Paper.	Price.
				s. d.
1887	(6.) APPENDIX AND INDEX - - - Duke of Hamilton.	8vo.	[C. 5060 v.]	1 6
1888	(7.) APPENDIX AND INDEX - - - Duke of Leeds, Marchioness of Waterford, Lord Hothfield, &c.; Bridgwater Trust Office, Reading Corporation, Inner Temple Library.	,,	[C.5612]	2 0
1890	TWELFTH REPORT - - - - This is introductory to the following:—	,,	[C.5889]	0 3
1888	(1.) APPENDIX - - - - - Earl Cowper, K.G. (Coke MSS., at Melbourne Hall, Derby) Vol. I.	,,	[C.5472]	2 7
1888	(2.) APPENDIX - - - - - Ditto. Vol. II.	,,	[C.5613]	2 5
1889	(3.) APPENDIX AND INDEX - - - Ditto. Vol. III.	,,	[C. 5889 i.]	1 4
1888	(4.) APPENDIX - - - - - The Duke of Rutland, G.C.B. Vol. I.	,,	[C.5614]	3 2
1891	(5.) APPENDIX AND INDEX - - - Ditto. Vol. II.	,,	[C. 5889 ii.]	2 0
1889	(6.) APPENDIX AND INDEX - - - House of Lords, 1689–1690.	,,	[C. 5889 iii.]	2 1½
1890	(7.) APPENDIX AND INDEX - - - S. H. le Fleming, Esq., of Rydal.	,,	[C. 5889 iv.]	1 11
1891	(8.) APPENDIX AND INDEX - - - The Duke of Athole, K.T., and the Earl of Home.	,,	[C.6338]	1 0
1891	(9.) APPENDIX AND INDEX - - - The Duke of Beaufort, K.G., the Earl of Donoughmore, J. H. Gurney, W. W. B. Hulton, R. W. Ketton, G. A. Aitken, P. V. Smith, Esqs.; Bishop of Ely; Cathedrals of Ely, Gloucester, Lincoln, and Peterborough; Corporations of Gloucester, Higham Ferrers, and Newark; Southwell Minster; Lincoln District Registry.	,,	[C. 6338 i.]	2 6
1891	(10.) APPENDIX - - - - - The First Earl of Charlemont. 1745–1783. Vol. I.	,,	[C. 6338 ii.]	1 11
	THIRTEENTH REPORT. This is introductory to the following:—			
1891	(1.) APPENDIX - - - - - The Duke of Portland. Vol. I.	,,	[C.6474]	3 0
	(2.) APPENDIX AND INDEX. Ditto. Vol. II. - -	*In the Press.*		
1892	(3.) APPENDIX. J. B. Fortescue, Esq. Vol. I. -	,,	[C.6660]	2 7
	(4.) APPENDIX AND INDEX. Corporations of Rye and Hereford, &c.	*In the Press.*		
	(5.) APPENDIX AND INDEX. House of Lords, 1691 - - -	*In the Press.*		

Lightning Source UK Ltd.
Milton Keynes UK
UKHW050816250322
400611UK00007B/427

9 781141 869558